D1200496

NEW WAYS TO
PERFECT
COOKING

NEW WAYS TO PERFECT COOKING

MARGUERITE PATTEN

OCTOPUS BOOKS

CONTENTS

First published 1984 by Octopus Books Limited
59 Grosvenor Street, London W1

© 1984 Octopus Books Limited
ISBN 0 7064 2050 0

Produced by Mandarin Publishers Ltd
22a Westlands Rd, Quarry Bay, Hong Kong

Printed in Hong Kong

INTRODUCTION

It has given me great pleasure to compile New Ways to Perfect Cooking. I have tried to reflect in it the way most of us live today and the kind of food we enjoy now and will be cooking in the future.

In every decade there are developments and differences in the way we serve food. Certainly within the last years these changes have been very apparent.

Our tastes have become more varied because we travel more and have the opportunity to experience and enjoy dishes from other countries. Many foods that were previously unknown, are now imported and are freely available giving us the opportunity to try them in our own homes. We also have an almost unequalled selection of home-produced foods of very high quality. Make the best use of this wonderfully varied range of produce to create nutritious, imaginative, and economical meals.

Not only have there been changes in the foods we cook but there is now a great deal of sensible interest in healthy living, keeping fit, and keeping slim. The aspects of healthy eating are dealt with in this book and I think you will find the family will enjoy the dishes made with what could be called 'health' or vegetarian foods as well as dishes based on good protein foods such as meat, poultry and fish. The interest in the 'Nouvelle Cuisine' from France is also reflected in some of the recipes.

In the last few years kitchen appliances have shown great advances in design. You will see I have included advice on using a freezer, a microwave cooker, a pressure cooker and an electric slow cooker (a crock-pot). Food processors, mixers and blenders or liquidizers enable a busy cook to deal with quite complex recipes in a matter of seconds.

I have been delighted with the many kind comments I have received over the years about Perfect Cooking. You tell me you found the recipes helpful and practical and that you liked the fact that so much of the information was simplified by being based on Blue Print Recipes.

In New Ways to Perfect Cooking I have used Master Recipes and Special Techniques to outline basic principles, so that even a new cook will find the recipes easy to follow and the many colour photographs illustrate how dishes should look when cooked.

New Ways to Perfect Cooking is an entirely new book. I hope it will give you great pleasure and help you when cooking for your family and friends.

Marguerite Patten

To Ensure Perfect Cooking

Recipes give metric, imperial and American weights and measures. In order to achieve complete success it is important to follow one set of measures only.

Sometimes the metric amount given is slightly different from usual.

When using some recipes for cakes, pastry, etc., you will find I have given less standard metric weights, e.g. in a Victoria sandwich I state 110g butter or margarine, 110g caster sugar and 110g flour with the 2 large eggs. This is to produce the same sized cake that will fit into the same sized tins as when following the imperial weights.

Spoon Measures All spoons are a level measurement. Standard spoon measures are used in all recipes; 1 tablespoon equals 15ml spoon, 1 teaspoon equals 5ml spoon.

American Measures Follow one set of measures only, because they are not interchangeable. American tablespoons are smaller than imperial spoons, so make certain American spoon measures are *well* filled but not piled high with the ingredient.

An imperial tablespoon equals 1½ American tablespoons.

An American pint is 16 fl oz not 20 fl oz as an imperial pint.

Choice of Ingredients In some recipes I give a choice of ingredients — butter or margarine; 2 or 3 onions. The first is my personal choice but the recipe can be made with the second ingredient if you prefer. Sometimes I specify the size of onions or other foods, this is because I feel it important; in other recipes I do not mention the size because it will not affect the success of the dish.

Oven Settings I use a variety of cookers when I travel and give demonstrations. This has made me appreciate just how individual ovens vary. All recipes are carefully tested in both electric and gas ovens, but please check the recommended temperatures and adjust if necessary depending upon your particular cooker.

Microwave Cooking When using a microwave cooker follow the settings recommended in the manufacturer's manual.

Freezing A question I am invariably asked when cooking a particular dish is "Will it freeze?" You will find ⁂ by dishes that I consider freeze well. Please read the Freezing Notes in each section though, for although this symbol generally means the cooked dish will freeze, there are exceptions. In the case of fish dishes, I prefer to freeze the prepared, but uncooked dish to avoid over-cooking the fish.

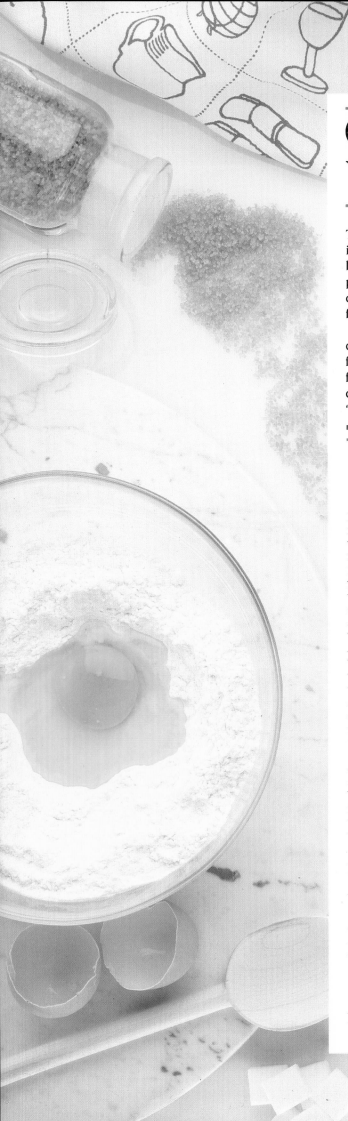

CHOOSING WISELY

The wise choice of ingredients plays an important part in cooking. If food is slightly stale, or of poor quality, the flavour of the finished dish cannot be as perfect as one would wish. This does not mean that you must purchase the most expensive ingredients, but rather that you develop a critical eye when shopping, so that you select perishable foods, such as fish, meat, poultry and vegetables when they are in prime condition.

It is also important to select the best ingredient for a particular dish; obviously it would be a waste of money to buy costly fillet steak to make a family stew, but it would be equally unwise to purchase economical steak for speedy frying or grilling (broiling). You will find advice on the selection of perishable foods at the beginning of the relevant chapters under 'Buying Points'.

Storecupboard Foods

Items like flour, pasta, rice and sugar are needed for a variety of dishes; it saves valuable shopping time if you keep a reasonable supply of these ingredients in the storecupboard. You may find yourself a little bewildered as to just what kind of flour or rice to buy for a specific dish so advice is given on this, and the following pages.

Flour

These are the various kinds of flour from which you can choose. The recipes in this book use plain white flour unless stated to the contrary. If you decide to substitute wholewheat or wheatmeal flour for white flour in baking you will need extra liquid, see pages 144 and 154.

Keep flour in an airtight container in a cool place; do not buy too large a supply.

White Flour is preferred by most people for general purposes for it is lighter in texture as well as in colour. In this flour the bran and most of the wheatgerm have been extracted, leaving between 72 and 74% of the whole wheat grain. White flour may be plain, self-raising or strong.

Plain Flour (All-Purpose Flour) has no raising agent, so is ideal for use in sauces, thickening liquids, making various kinds of pastry, biscuits (cookies) and certain rich fruit cakes. This flour can be used for other cakes if baking powder (raising agent) is added. Always sift the recommended quantity of baking powder with the flour before using.

Self-Raising Flour contains the correct amount of baking powder for a wide range of cakes and other recipes.

Strong Flour (Bread Flour) This type of white flour is milled from wheats that have a higher gluten content than ordinary plain flour. Strong flour is ideal for many yeast recipes, for it produces a well-risen dough. It is also excellent for puff or similar pastry.

Soft Wheat Sponge Flour (Cake Flour) is new to the British market. It is a particularly light flour which is ideal for sponges and delicate cakes, especially American-type cakes. The British product is self-raising; the American cake flour is not.

Non-White Flours

There is a wide variety of 'brown' flours available that may contain as much as 100% of the grain so that the wheatgerm and the bran are retained.

Wholewheat Flour is produced from 100% whole wheat; it makes excellent bread.

Wheatmeal Flour is milled from 80 to 90% of the whole wheat grain; it is therefore lighter than wholewheat flour and is suitable for cakes, pastry and general purposes, see page 144.

Granary Flour is a wheatmeal flour with added grains of malted wheat which gives a nutty taste. It can be used in baking cakes, scones or breads. It is a plain flour.

Brown Flour is a mixture of white and wholewheat flours.

'Stoneground' refers to the milling process used in producing the flour.

Cornflour and Arrowroot

Cornflour (Cornstarch) A flour which is produced from maize and is used in a variety of dishes, such as biscuits (cookies) and some pastry, see pages 102, 172 and 173, and to thicken liquids. If substituting cornflour (cornstarch) for flour in a sauce or stew use only 15 g/½ oz (2 tablespoons) cornflour (cornstarch) in place of 25 g/1 oz (¼ cup) flour.

<u>Arrowroot</u> This is especially successful in thickening clear liquids in sauces and fruit juices, see page 186.

Pasta

The various shapes of pasta are detailed more fully on page 139. Keep good stocks of pasta for making economical and speedy meals.

Commercially made white pasta is produced from durum (a very hard) wheat. It is possible to make pasta at home (see page 139), and also to buy wholewheat or spinach-flavoured pasta.

Rice

In order to achieve the best results choose rice critically and cook it with loving care, see pages 136 to 138. The following types are available:

<u>Long-Grain Rice</u> Originally this came from Patna in India but nowadays it is widely grown in the U.S.A. Use in savoury dishes but not in milk puddings.

<u>Short-Grain Rice</u> Often called pudding or round rice, this rice is not suitable for savoury dishes as the grains become too soft and sticky in cooking. It does, however, make a creamy milk pudding.

<u>Medium-Grain Rice</u> This is often called Italian rice for it generally comes from that country and it is the ideal rice for a risotto since it gives a slight thickening to the liquid (see page 137). Unfortunately not as easily obtainable as one would wish.

<u>Par-Boiled Rice</u> The name is slightly misleading, for it does not mean you can shorten the cooking time; it refers to the fact that the long-grain rice was heated when the husk was removed. This rice does give very good results in cooking, the grains are exceptionally white and keep well separated.

<u>Brown Rice</u> A light brown rice which has a delicious and more definite flavour, plus a higher vitamin content, than ordinary white rice because more of the husk is retained. It is a long-grain rice which is good for savoury dishes although it does takes longer to cook than white rice.

<u>Basmati Rice</u> A more expensive long-grain pale brown rice from India with a particularly fine flavour.

<u>Ground Rice and Rice Flour</u> These are made from powdered rice; the flour being the finer. Ground rice is added to some biscuits (cookies), see page 173, and the flour is used in cakes and puddings.

<u>Wild Rice</u> A luxury ingredient, which is not rice but the seed of a wild grass. It can be used in savoury dishes.

Sugar

In most recipes the kind of sugar is stated, but it is important to appreciate just how the various kinds differ.

White Sugars

Granulated Sugar is household sugar used for general flavouring and cooking. Unrefined granulated sugar is pale golden in colour.

Caster Sugar is a fine sugar and is better for baking as the grains dissolve readily.

Preserving Sugar is for making jam and other preserves and loaf (lump) sugar for table use.

Icing Sugar (Confectioners' Sugar) is the sugar for making most icings, but it is suggested as an ingredient in some biscuits or meringues, see pages 170 and 173. It generally needs sifting before use. Choose a hair or nylon sieve; a metal sieve can make the sugar slightly grey in colour.

Brown Sugars

There is a wide choice of refined and unrefined brown sugars.

Demerara Sugar is a coarse, light brown sugar which adds a pleasing flavour and texture in cooking and baking.

Light and Dark Brown Sugars are fine sugars which dissolve easily and are suitable for baking.

Barbados, Muscovado and Molasses Sugars are best for making rich fruit cakes and gingerbread. You can buy both light and dark Barbados sugar. Molasses sugar has a strong taste of black treacle, so use sparingly.

STORING SUGAR

Keep sugar in the packet or sealed container. If the dark moist sugars become over-hard in the packet, stand over a pan of very hot water until softened, or break up the lumps in a food processor or blender.

Flour, sugar, fats and storecupboard ingredients are used to create a whole host of cakes and biscuits.

Fats

Although listed here as foods to be kept in the storecupboard, most fats, in fact, should be kept well covered (so they do not absorb the flavour of stronger foods) and stored in the refrigerator. Your first choice will probably be between butter and margarine.

Butter

Butter gives a good flavour to all kinds of dishes. It is excellent for pastry-making and many kinds of cakes and biscuits. Butter can be used for shallow frying, but in many recipes it is advisable to use equal quantities of butter and oil. This mixture allows the food to absorb the good flavour of butter but the oil helps to prevent the butter from becoming overheated and over-brown in colour.

Use unsalted butter for butter icings or puff pastry or where specifically recommended.

Margarine

Margarine is cheaper so is frequently used instead of butter. You can choose between hard or soft margarine.

Hard Margarine like butter, should be removed from the refrigerator some time before using for creaming, rubbing-in etc.

Soft, or Luxury, Margarines tend to be 'polyunsaturated' ie their chemical composition makes them suitable for people following a low cholesterol diet. They should be used straight from the refrigerator and should *not* be left at room temperature. Use them for pastry and cake-making.

Low Fat Spreads have fewer calories than butter or margarine. Use them for spreading and for cake making but do not use for pastry.

Cooking Fats, Lard and Dripping

Light-Textured White Cooking Fats are made from edible oils. These soft fats can be used to make shortcrust pastry (basic pie dough), or some cakes or in frying. They should not be chosen if you are following a low cholesterol diet.

Lard is a hard pork fat. It is excellent used with butter or margarine in shortcrust (basic pie dough) or flaky pastries or by itself in hot water pastry. Lard is good for frying.

Dripping is the fat drawn from meat during cooking. If you have dripping from roasting meat, put this into a saucepan and add cold water to cover. Heat slowly until the dripping melts then allow to cool. Lift the hardened dripping from the water, scrape away any residue of food if necessary. This process clarifies (clears) the dripping and it can then be used for frying or roasting.

Oils

There are many kinds of oil. Pure, high-quality olive oil is excellent for salad dressings, but too heavy, as well as too expensive, for frying.

Corn oil is a good light oil for salad dressings (either by itself or mixed with richer olive oil); it is good for frying and it can be used in making some cakes and a form of shortcrust pastry (basic pie dough), see page 144. Corn oil is a polyunsaturated oil so a wise choice for those on a low cholesterol diet.

Flavourings

Good flavour is an essential part of good cooking; it is achieved by the wise choice of ingredients in a dish and by careful cooking. The flavour is often enhanced by those extra touches – a pinch of spice, a teaspoon of herbs, a few drops of special sauce. Taste the food carefully and critically as it cooks and, if there is not as much flavour or colour in the dish as you wish, add that extra ingredient, as suggested on this and the following pages.

Colourings, Essences and Sauces

Edible Colourings These do not give flavour but eye-appeal. Add sparingly to the food. Insert a fine skewer into the bottle and use the drops adhering to it. Use only a pinch of powdered colouring.

Essences (Extracts) These range from fruit flavours, such as banana, raspberry, to spirit flavours, such as rum. The most useful are almond and vanilla, see also Vanilla and Anchovy Essence below.

Anchovy Essence or Sauce The essence is stronger than the sauce, but both impart an excellent pale pinkish-brown colour and fish flavour to sauces.

Mushroom Ketchup Not as common as other flavourings, but a few drops of this very dark brown sauce give an excellent flavour to gravies or sauces.

Soy Sauce A valuable ingredient in Chinese cooking or to serve with oriental dishes; a deep brown sauce with a pungent taste.

Tabasco Sauce (Hot Pepper Sauce) A very hot sauce, red in colour. Add just a few drops to savoury dishes.

Tomato Ketchup This is a favourite accompaniment to various foods, and a little can add a piquant sweet flavour to stews and sauces.

Tomato Purée (Paste) This concentrated tomato pulp, sold in small cans or tubes, is an invaluable ingredient in savoury dishes. Store opened tubes in the refrigerator. Sometimes known as tomato paste.

Vinegar Choose good quality white or brown malt vinegar for pickles and chutneys; use white or red wine vinegar in salad dressings.

Worcestershire Sauce A widely used ingredient in savoury dishes. Use sparingly as this brown sauce has a strong and pungent flavour.

Spices

Unless otherwise stated spices are ground and are available as a powder. Here are some of the most useful.

Allspice This tastes like a mixture of several spices. Use in sweet dishes and a few savoury ones.

Cardamom A slightly hot, bitter-sweet flavour. Sold as seeds as well as powder.

Use in some cakes and in curries.

Cayenne A pungent, red or reddish brown pepper from a type of chilli or capsicum. It is very hot, so use with caution.

Chilli From dried chilli peppers, use sparingly. Also available as a sauce or as dried whole chilli peppers.

Cinnamon A pleasant sweet taste. Use in cakes and puddings. Cinnamon sticks are used in drinks.

Clove Use ground in baking, the dried flower buds are used with apples, baked ham etc. Use sparingly because cloves are strong in flavour.

Coriander The seeds are available whole or ground. See also page 12.

Cumin Sold ground or as seeds. Used in some Scandinavian cheeses and in savoury dishes, including curry.

Curry Powder A combination of spices, see page 71.

Garam Masala A combination of spices, used in Indian cooking.

Ginger Produced from the root of a plant. Green (fresh) ginger is obtainable and you can buy crystallized and preserved ginger as well as the ground spice. This is used in a variety of sweet and savoury dishes.

Juniper Buy dried berries; used in pâtés and savoury dishes.

Mace The outer skin of nutmeg seed; mild and slightly bitter, use as blades or ground in pickles and savoury dishes.

Mustard The powdered seed gives the familiar hot condiment. If mixed with milk, rather than water, the mustard keeps more moist. Allow to stand for 10 to 15 minutes after mixing. French, German and American types of mustard are more piquant in taste than the hotter English type.

Nutmeg Sold ground or as the whole dried seed which you grate. Use in and on milk puddings and in baking.

Paprika Dried powder from a special variety of peppers. Usually associated with Hungarian cooking. Generally mild and sweet but there are hotter varieties. Paprika should be red in colour and deteriorates rapidly so only buy small quantities at at time.

Pepper You can buy green (unripe) peppercorns from specialist shops or dried black and white peppercorns, which you grind as required through a pepper-mill. Black pepper has more flavour than white pepper, although considered slightly more crude by some cooks. Use white pepper for white sauces. The fresher the pepper the better the taste.

Pickling Spices A mixture of spices designed for use in pickles, generally sold as whole spices rather than ground so tie in muslin or boil first in the vinegar. The spices are more potent when crushed so the quantity used in a recipe should be reduced.

Tandoori Spice A mixture of spices used in Indian cooking, see page 71.

Turmeric An ingredient in curry powder; also a spice used to give colour as well as a slight flavour to various dishes, but particularly mustard pickles. Use as directed – too much gives a musty flavour to the dish.

Vanilla The dried pod (bean) is generally distilled into an essence. You can buy vanilla-flavoured sugar but the best flavour is obtained by using the dried vanilla pod. Infuse in liquids, rinse in cold water, dry and use again or store the halved pod in sugar to make your own vanilla-flavoured sugar to use in baking (see page 120).

A touch of spice enhances the flavour of both sweet and savoury dishes

11

Ensure a constant supply of fresh herbs by growing your own

Herbs

For centuries herbs have been cultivated for use in cooking as well as for medicinal purposes. The list below does not cover every edible herb, but it includes those that are the most valuable in cooking.

You will find the letters (P) and (A) after the name of the herbs. (P) means it is a perennial plant and it should come up every year, even though it may die back in winter. (A) means it is an annual and seeds of the plant should be planted each year.

It is possible to have access to many fresh herbs throughout the year by planting them in pots and keeping them in a heated greenhouse or warm room.

Herbs can be dried or frozen (see opposite). You can obtain supplies of commercially dried herbs in attractive containers.

Angelica (P) Not regarded as a herb, as it is bought in crystallized form. A little fresh angelica stem can be chopped and added to rhubarb jam. The fleshy stem can be blanched in boiling water, chopped and added to salads or it can be cooked and served as a vegetable.

Balm (P) This has a lemon aroma and taste. It is excellent in drinks of all kinds.

Basil (A) An invaluable herb. Add to tomato dishes especially tomato salad.

Bay (P) An edible laurel. Use in stews, sauces and milk puddings. Only use 1 or 2 leaves and remove these before serving the dish.

Borage (A) This herb has a faint cucumber taste. Use in sauces, fish dishes and soups. It is also used in drinks, particularly in Pimms. Borage often seeds itself and the blue flowers are very decorative.

Burnet (P) A lesser known herb with a slight cucumber smell. A small amount of the finely chopped leaves can be added to sauces to serve with fish or be added to cold drinks.

Chervil (A) A herb with a mild celery flavour. Use as parsley or in salads.

Chives (P) This herb has a mild onion taste. Use in salads, egg and fish dishes or for garnishing soups and stews.

Coriander (A) The seeds of coriander can be harvested in August or September, when they are just ripe, to use in curries or pickles. The leaves are used in many Indian and Middle Eastern dishes.

Dill (A) A mild aniseed flavour. Use in fish or vegetable dishes and pickles.

Fennel (P) This plant has a strong anise flavour. Use the leaves in fish or vegetable dishes and the fleshy white base raw in salads or cooked as a vegetable.

Garlic (A) A very pungent onion flavour. Use 1 or 2 cloves only from the garlic head unless the recipe states otherwise. You can use a garlic press to extract the juice or finely chop the garlic cloves, this is easier if you put a little salt on the chopping board.

Horseradish (P) The pungent root is used to make the famous sauce to serve with beef. Gardeners advocate digging up the mature root in winter, storing it in damp sand and planting small pieces of the root for a fresh crop in the spring.

Marjoram (P) A slightly sweet herb. Use in soups, sauces and stuffings.

Mint (P) Use with lamb, in drinks and salads (sweet or savoury). There are several kinds of mint, the most attractive being apple mint.

Oregano (P) This is a wild form of marjoram, similar to the ordinary herb but with a stronger flavour. It is very suitable for Italian dishes, such as pizza, (see page 135).

Parsley (A) This is actually a biennial since the plants form seeds in the second year. Use in savoury dishes, or as a garnish. The curly leaf parsley has a mild flavour, the flat leaf a stronger flavour. Do not confuse this with the leaves of coriander (often called oriental parsley). Parsley stalks impart more flavour than the leaves, add to stews and soups but remove before serving.

Rosemary (P) Use small sprigs with lamb, chicken or rabbit or add to a savoury salad.

Sage (P) This is a very pungent herb. Use the leaves sparingly in stuffings, sauces and stews.

Savory (A and P) Summer savory is an annual, Winter savory a perennial. This herb is rather like strong thyme. Use in stuffings or add a few leaves when cooking all types of beans, especially haricot (navy) and red beans.

Sorrel (P) This herb makes a delicious soup, or can be added to sauces and stuffings. It looks rather like spinach but has a more bitter taste.

Tarragon (P) French Tarragon is milder than the Russian type and more likely to die in winter. Use in fish dishes, salad dressings and vinegars.

Thyme (P) There are various kinds of thyme, try lemon thyme and the attractive golden thyme. Thyme has a mild flavour and is good in soups, stuffings and stews.

Drying Herbs
Choose a dry day on which to pick the herbs. Wash and dry the sprigs or leaves on absorbent paper. Cover baking trays with a padding of thick brown paper and then a layer of muslin (cheesecloth). Place the herbs in one flat layer on the prepared trays. Dry slowly in a heated airing cupboard, in the sun, or in the oven, which should be set to a very low temperature (90°C/200°F, Gas Mark ¼) – keep the door ajar during the process.

Parsley can be dried like this but it keeps a better colour if it is dried for about 3 minutes in a very hot oven (230 to 240°C/450 to 475°F, Gas Mark 8 to 9).

When the herbs feel brittle, crumble them finely, or chop them in a blender or food processor, and store in an airtight container.

Using Dried Herbs
Dried herbs have a very concentrated flavour, so use them sparingly. They tend to give a slightly musty taste to food if you use too generous an amount. If a recipe says '1 teaspoon chopped fresh herbs', use no more than ½ teaspoon of dried herbs.

Freezing Herbs
Frozen herbs can be stored for up to 1 year. They can be frozen in three ways:
a) Put a small amount of chopped herbs into ice cube trays, cover with cold water and freeze. Simply add one or more of the herb ice cubes to a soup or stew.
b) Pack small amounts of the chopped herb into small containers or polythene bags and freeze. This method is particularly satisfactory for mint.
c) Freeze sprigs of herbs on a baking sheet. When quite frozen pack into polythene bags. When the herb is required, remove from the bag and crumble the dried leaves or add whole leaves or sprigs to the food.

Healthy Eating

Good health is a priceless possession and well-chosen food can certainly contribute to a feeling of well-being. Well-balanced meals should provide the essential nutrients required by children and adults.

Convenience and processed foods fulfil a useful purpose – they save time and energy and enable us to enjoy vegetables when they are not in season. Do, however, use them wisely and make sure that you and your family also have generous amounts of fresh fruits and vegetables throughout the year.

Do not serve an excess of sugary foods; these are pleasant, but not as important as foods that provide protein and vitamins. The main sources of protein are meat, fish, poultry, eggs, milk and cheese together with nuts and pulses (dried peas, beans and lentils). Other foods provide some protein, these include wheat (used in bread), brown rice and some seeds, such as sesame.

Vitamins can be described as protective elements in food; if we eat a variety of nutritious foods we should obtain an adequate amount of the essential vitamins.

Nowadays there is much discussion about lack of fibre in our diet. In prosperous countries, we tend to eat a great deal of highly refined food and this lack of fibre can contribute to a variety of gastric disorders.

It is easy to provide our bodies with dietary fibre; eat plenty of raw or lightly cooked vegetables; add a little bran to breakfast cereals, choose wholewheat rather than white bread.

Health Foods
This term is used to describe the natural foods sold by health food shops. Wheatgerm, brewer's yeast, yeast extract, nuts and seeds are not cranks' food, but natural ingredients that add goodness and flavour to many dishes.

The *Nouvelle Cuisine* style of cooking from France approaches healthy eating in a different way. The recipes based upon this concept avoid the use of fat, cream and flour and rely upon the natural flavour and texture of the fruits, vegetables and other ingredients to give the dish both eye and taste appeal. *Nouvelle Cuisine* type meals should help you to lose weight and still enable you to enjoy cooking and eating delicious foods. In several sections of this book you will find recipes that follow this style of cooking. See also the slimming menus on pages 180 to 181.

The Food For Health section (page 176) contains recipes using health foods. Try these ideas, they make a pleasant change in the family menus.

Dried and fresh fruit, cereals, and nuts are valuable components of a healthy diet

Small Kitchen Equipment

Good cooking equipment helps ensure good results.

The equipment used in preparing and cooking food could be termed 'the tools of the trade'. As any good workman would agree, first-class tools are an important and wise investment.

Whisks

A balloon whisk is invaluable for whisking cream and egg whites. If you whisk a sauce as it thickens instead of stirring it, the sauce keeps beautifully smooth. Wash the whisk thoroughly after use and dry it near the warmth of the cooker.

Colanders and Sieves

A colander is needed to strain vegetables but the holes are too large for straining rice and fine pasta, for this you need to use a sieve. A sieve is also needed when making purées and for sifting flour and icing sugar.

The mesh of a sieve can be made from metal-wire, nylon or hair. A metal sieve should not be used with acid fruits.

Wooden Spoons

Buy several spoons with different handle lengths. A shorter handle is easier to hold but it is safer to have long handles when stirring boiling preserves.

Chopping Board

Most kitchen working surfaces are harmed by chopping or cutting ingredients on them so buy a good strong chopping board.

Good Knives

Before buying knives, handle them to make sure they feel comfortable in your hand. The weight and shape of the handle is important. You can gradually build up an impressive range of specialist knives but here are the essential knives that will enable you to tackle most kitchen chores.
a) One or more small knives for preparing vegetables.
b) One or two kitchen knives – often called cook's knives – for slicing and cutting, excellent for chopping too.
c) A bread knife – with a serrated edge.
d) A carving knife, plus carving fork.
e) A wide bladed palette knife (spatula) – use for mixing ingredients and lifting food. This does not take the place of a fish slice – which you will also find useful.

A flexible knife for filleting fish is another good investment and so is a long, slim-bladed sharp knife for slicing cooked ham etc. A proper freezing knife is a good investment if you buy large packs of frozen foods.
Note Remember that you should not chop or cut foods on laminated surfaces, so always use a good solid chopping board.

Pots and Pans

Frying pans (skillets) and saucepans can be made of the following metals:
a) Aluminium – relatively inexpensive and practical.
b) Stainless steel – expensive but an excellent hard-wearing and easy to clean material.
c) Enamel coated iron, aluminium or stainless steel – the enamel looks beautiful and is easy to clean but store with care because it is inclined to chip.
d) Cast iron – heavy but durable, the bases of the pans always stay flat. The pans should be dried thoroughly or they will rust.
e) Pans with a silicone (non-stick) finish – these are easy to clean, but take care not to scratch the finish with metal cooking utensils.
f) Ceramic ware – this is often both ovenproof and flameproof, i.e. suitable for use in the oven and on the hotplate.
g) Copper ware – usually tin lined. Expensive but they conduct the heat extremely well.

You will need at least one frying pan (skillet). If possible buy a special omelette pan, which can also be used for making pancakes, and a frying pan (skillet) with a lid (which doubles up as a shallow saucepan).

You will require several saucepans of varying sizes – some of the saucepans with short ovenproof handles can also be used as casseroles.

Baking Trays and Cake Tins

The shape and number of trays and tins (pans) required depends upon the amount of baking you do. The size and shape of tin (pan) required is usually stated in the recipe.

You will need some flat baking trays (with very shallow rims) on which to bake scones and biscuits (cookies). These are also known as baking sheets. It is possible to buy silicone (non-stick) bakeware.

A Food Mixer

The larger machines consist of a mixer attached to a stand plus a whisk and beater. These machines can be left to operate with the minimum of attention. Smaller mixers with a bowl and stand can also be obtained. With these, the mixer, which is generally equipped with double whisks, can be removed and used as a hand held machine.

You can also buy mixers without a stand which have to be held in the hand. These can be used over any suitably sized bowl or saucepan.

Buying Points
The Functions of a Basic Mixer
a) To beat cooked vegetables, such as potatoes, into a smooth purée, or to beat mixtures like Royal Icing, (see page 168).
b) To cream fat and sugar, incorporate the eggs and, in some cases, the flour too, in cake and pudding mixtures.
c) To knead biscuit (cookie) and yeast doughs.
d) To rub fat into flour for pastry or similar mixtures.
e) To whisk together eggs and sugar for

sponges and other light mixtures; to beat egg yolks for a mayonnaise (adding the oil gradually); to whisk egg whites for meringues and soufflés; to whip cream.

Most large mixers and some smaller mixers on a stand have a range of optional attachments which can include those for shredding and slicing, mincing, grinding coffee beans, cream making. These extras are not available for small independent hand held mixers.

Advantages The whisk(s) or beater can be used to simulate hand mixing and give excellent results without the hard work.

Disadvantages It is possible to overbeat foods, so care must be taken to time the process carefully, (see also pages 144, and 164), and to use the correct speed – mixers have a choice of speeds.

Limitations The basic mixer is of greatest value if you do a lot of baking; the additional attachments are often expensive and may then sit idle in the cupboard.

Many people find that a small hand held mixer, plus a liquidizer (blender) or food processor is the most useful combination.

A Blender or Liquidizer

A blender is sometimes an integral part of a large mixer, with some models it is an optional extra, or a blender can be purchased as an entirely separate appliance.

Buying Points
The Functions of a Blender
a) To purée raw or cooked vegetables and fruits, the cooked ingredients for a soup or a baby's meal. To turn the cooked ingredients of a pâté into a smooth mixture. If a cooked sauce is liquidized it becomes ultra-smooth.

b) To chop herbs, bread, nuts or a mixture of dry ingredients.

c) To emulsify eggs (not just the yolks) with oil for a mayonnaise or with melted butter for a Hollandaise or similar sauce.

d) To mix drinks of all kinds; a blender produces beautifully fluffy milk shakes or elegant cocktails.

Advantages A blender is incredibly fast and in most instances eliminates the need to purée foods through a sieve.

Disadvantages It cannot cream fat and sugar for cakes or puddings, whisk egg whites or cream or knead a dough.

Limitations The main limitation is that a blender can only deal with relatively small amounts of food at one time. When blending liquids take care not to overfill the goblet, as the mixture rises dramatically in the goblet.

Although you can purée most ingredients very efficiently you will find that tough tomato skins or seeds and raspberry pips have to be sieved out of the mixture afterwards.

A Food Processor

A basic food processor consists of a bowl in which the blade or cutting knife

sits, a lid and the motor. You are supplied with a double bladed cutting attachment, a plastic beating blade and various discs for shredding, grating or slicing. Other attachments are available for making potato chips (French fries), extracting fruit juices etc.

A metal sieve is a vital piece of kitchen equipment

Buying Points
The Functions of a Food Processor
A processor can purée, blend and chop like a blender. It can also:

a) Cream fat and sugar and mix the ingredients for a cake or pudding.

b) Blend fat into flour for rubbed-in mixtures.

c) Mince (grind) cooked or uncooked meats, fish or poultry.

Advantages It is possible to deal with larger quantities of food at one time than when using a blender and the processes are carried out in a matter of seconds.

Disadvantages If used correctly there are few disadvantages, and the machine can save a great deal of time. Handle the cutting blades carefully, they are ultra-sharp.

Limitations It is very easy to overprocess foods so follow the manufacturer's instructions.

Although suitable for making sponges and cakes, the texture of creamed mixtures is not as light as when using a food mixer since there is little aeration of the fat, sugar and eggs. A food processor cannot handle as much mixture as a large mixer either.

While adaptations are constantly being made to the design of the blades, many food processors do not have blades suitable for whisking together eggs and sugar, whisking egg whites or whipping cream.

A food processor can be used to prepare a wide range of baked food

15

Large Kitchen Equipment

The choice of cooking equipment is obviously important as incorrect cooking can spoil good ingredients.

Your first consideration is to select the type of cooker (range) which is efficient and adequate for your family's needs. You may then feel it necessary to buy additional cooking equipment. Some of the other appliances listed below may sound unnecessary and extravagant but most of them can save you an appreciable amount on your fuel bill.

The Choice of Cooker

The choice is between gas, electricity and solid fuel, although some solid fuel stoves can be converted to gas or oil so eliminating the work involved with solid fuel. A solid fuel stove generally provides constant heat, heats water and provides two ovens, one can be used for quicker cooking and the second for slow cooking.

An electric slow cooker can double up as a fondue pot, see pages 27 and 182

Gas cookers now have the many design features found on electric cookers – some even have a setting that allows the food to be cooked very slowly.

Ceramic hobs found on some electric cookers look elegant and are easy to control but you must make certain that any saucepan used on such a hob has a flat base that makes good contact with the ceramic surface. Many modern electric cookers have two ovens which give a greater choice of cooking space.

Automatic timing is an accepted feature of modern gas and electric cookers; this means that the food can be placed in the unheated oven and the controls set to switch the heat on and off at the required time. It is a very convenient feature for busy people, but it must be used with common sense. Do not leave food in the oven for too long a period before cooking commences, for the food could develop harmful bacteria.

The position in which most food is placed in the oven is important and is clearly stated in the recipes. Different shelf positions in most ovens give slightly different heats. If, however, you have a fan-assisted electric oven, all positions give the same heat; when using this type of oven it is advisable to reduce the cooking temperatures slightly, i.e. by 10°C/25°F, Gas Mark 1.

An Electric Deep-Fat Fryer

Frying is undoubtedly one of the more difficult methods of cooking. You have to be selective in the kind of foods you are frying, choose the correct fat or oil for the recipe and make sure it is heated to the right temperature (see page 90).

Buying Points
An electric deep-fat fryer eliminates all the guess-work. The heat of the fat or oil is thermostatically controlled. The models are attractive in appearance and most have filters in the lid that reduce the smell and fumes of frying.

Advantages The chief advantage is safety; deep frying in an ordinary pan can be dangerous. If the fat or oil is overheated it ignites and could cause a fire. The thermostatic control means the oil cannot overheat. The second advantage is that you pre-set the thermostat so that you know the oil is always at the correct temperature.

Disadvantages You have to use a large amount of oil (most manufacturers do not advocate the use of fat).

Limitations It is not worth buying if you only deep fry occasionally.

An Electric Slow-Cooker

The electric slow-cooker or crock-pot consists of a ceramic dish surrounded by an element which cooks the food at a very low temperature.

Buying Points
Most models have two temperature settings (follow the manufacturer's instructions) and some models will automatically switch from one to the other.

A slow cooker can be used for many purposes:
a) To make stock and soups (see pages 28 and 51).
b) To cook stews made from the less tender cuts of meat (see the recipes on page 54). Evaporation is minimal so the amount of liquid used should be reduced. (Fish can be cooked in an electric slow-cooker, but as this is such a quickly cooked food it seems rather pointless.)
c) To cook root vegetables (see page 88).
d) To cook milk puddings, steamed puddings and a few cakes (see pages 110, 119, 124 and 142).
e) It can take the place of a fondue pot for a Cheese Fondue (see pages 27 and 182).

Advantages The food cooks so slowly that careful timing is less important than when using other appliances. It is safe and uses little electricity.

Disadvantages For best results, the ingredients for stews need browning, before they are transferred to the slow cooker (another pan to wash up).

Limitations Obviously this appliance is of no value for speedy cooking.

Choosing Wisely

A Pressure Cooker

A modern pressure cooker looks like, and can be used as, a large saucepan until the lid is fixed and the pressure weight used. When under pressure the steam inside the pan cannot escape and so the temperature of the liquid is raised well above normal boiling point i.e., 100°C/212°F. This means that food is cooked within a very short time.

Buying Points
Consider the types of food you will be cooking in your pressure cooker and choose a model of adequate size. Most modern models have three or four variable pressures. Consult the manufacturer's instructions as to the correct procedure for using each pressure.

Functions of a Pressure Cooker
a) To tenderize meats of all kinds quickly. A stew, such as the recipe on page 54, takes only 15 to 20 minutes pressure cooking time.
b) To make stocks and soups (see pages 28 and 51).
c) To cook vegetables in minutes (see page 88).
d) To steam puddings (see page 124).
e) To tenderize the fruit or vegetables for jams and preserves, and to bottle fruit and vegetables. (It is unsafe to bottle vegetables unless you use medium/10 lb pressure.)

Advantages You save on fuel since you can produce meals within minutes and it is possible to cook a variety of foods, in separate containers in the pressure cooker without the various flavours intermingling.

Disadvantages You must time the cooking processes with great care. One minute's over-cooking, especially of green vegetables, could spoil the food.

Limitations As liquid must be used in the cooker to create steam and pressure, you cannot cook anything that needs to be crisp, as when baked in an oven.

A Microwave Cooker

These are becoming increasingly popular. The microwaves generated cause the moisture molecules in the food to vibrate rapidly, this causes friction which creates the heat that cooks the food in a matter of seconds.

Buying Points
The versatile microwave cooker can be used to:
a) Quickly thaw frozen food (see your microwave instruction manual for the correct setting to use).
b) Reheat cooked dishes.
c) Cook eggs, fish, tender meats and tender poultry. If your model has variable power control you can also use it to cook stews that usually require long slow cooking (see page 48).
d) Cook fruit and vegetables (see pages 88 and 181).
e) Cook a variety of desserts, including steamed puddings, and certain cakes and biscuits (cookies) (see pages 110, 124, 142 and 148).

Advantages The great advantage is the speed with which it thaws frozen food and reheats cooked foods. In many instances you cook the food in the serving container so you have less washing up. Less fat is needed in some recipes so it is an ideal method of cooking for slimmers.

Disadvantages Careful timing is essential since cooking time is measured in seconds. Set the timer for the shortest time you feel may be necessary and then check the food constantly. It is very easy to overcook food in a microwave cooker.

Limitations There are some foods that can be very successfully cooked in a microwave cooker, with others the texture and flavour do not compare with foods cooked by conventional methods. Always use the type of cooking utensil recommended by the manufacturer of your cooker – glass, china, pottery and

some plastics. Metal containers cannot be used, nor those with a metal trim. Food tends to look pale when cooked in a microwave cooker and does not have the golden crispness achieved by frying, grilling (broiling) or baking.

See the individual sections in this book for more details on how to cook various foods in a microwave cooker.

Microwave cooking is fast cooking

A Freezer

A freezer is an invaluable appliance if it is used wisely. In each section of this book you will be given general advice on freezing various foods and finished dishes.

Save time by making two or three times the quantity of cooked dishes, cakes, bread and certain desserts. Enjoy the freshly cooked dish, freeze the remainder. The maximum time for freezing each kind of food is given in the various sections. If stored after this time the food tends to lose taste and texture but will still be safe to eat.

Save money by buying vegetables and fruit when in season and therefore at their best and cheapest. If you grow fruit and vegetables, then freeze some when it is freshly picked.

Save last-minute shopping by having a carefully chosen selection of foods in the freezer, so that you can cope with unexpected guests or family requirements.

Save the problems and expense of freezer maintenance by defrosting regularly as recommended by the manufacturer and freezing the food at the right setting.

All the recipes in this book that are marked with our freezer symbol **, freeze extremely well.

A stew takes only 15 to 20 minutes to cook in a pressure cooker, see page 54

17

HORS D'OEUVRE

A good hors d'oeuvre sets the tone of the meal and sharpens the appetite for the courses that are to follow.

Choose starters with care; they should not be over-filling, nor too highly flavoured, for if they are, they spoil the appetite for the next course.

There are no rules about what should, or should not, be served as an hors d'oeuvre; you can use fruits, vegetables, salad greens, fish, meat, pasta or rice dishes. A selection of my favourite ideas follow.

The first recipes are 'made in minutes', so are ideal for making an interesting meal for unexpected guests, the following recipes range from economical ideas to those that are deliciously extravagant for special occasions.

Buying Points

Shopping for the ingredients for an hors d'oeuvre should not be too difficult, except perhaps when you are buying fruit like avocados or melon which are very unappetizing if underripe. Often though it is a good idea to buy avocados or melon when they are available and of good quality, but not necessarily fully ripe, and keep them in a warm place so they ripen gradually. You then can serve them at the peak of perfection. The airing cupboard is frequently suggested as the ideal place for ripening avocados; but be careful it is not too warm or they will become slightly brown in colour before they ripen; slower ripening is better.

To judge whether an avocado is ripe, cradle it gently in your hand, it should feel slightly soft all over. A melon yields to gentle pressure at the stalk end when it is ripe.

Freezing Note

While many hors d'oeuvre are not suitable for freezing, it is extremely useful to keep supplies of ingredients like peeled prawns (shrimp) and smoked fish in the freezer; also ready-prepared fish, rice and pasta dishes that could be served either as a main dish or start to the meal.

Microwave Cooking

You will find that a microwave cooker is excellent for thawing and/or heating frozen dishes.

Freeze prepared foods in individual portions so that they can be reheated in a very short time.

Made in Minutes

Fruit

Orange and Tomato Cocktail Mix equal amounts of fresh or canned orange juice and tomato juice. Chill well and serve in small glasses with a sprig of mint in each and a slice of fresh orange balanced on each rim.

Grapefruit and Orange Baskets Combine equal amounts of fresh grapefruit and orange segments; moisten with a little sweet sherry. Add sugar if required. Serve in small glasses or the hollowed out grapefruit skins and top with chopped nuts.

Melon, Avocado and Grapefruit Cocktail Combine diced melon, sliced avocado (dipped in lemon juice immediately after slicing) and fresh grapefruit segments. Spoon over shredded lettuce and top with a little well-seasoned yogurt or mayonnaise.

Vegetables

Artichokes Vinaigrette Drain canned globe artichoke hearts, place on lettuce, top with Vinaigrette Dressing (see page 105) and garnish with chopped hard-boiled (hard-cooked) egg.

See page 21 for ways to cook and serve fresh artichokes.

Asparagus au Gratin Drain canned asparagus, arrange in an ovenproof serving dish. Top with a thick layer of soft breadcrumbs, then with grated cheese and a little melted butter. Heat towards the top of a moderately hot oven (200°C/400°F, Gas Mark 6) for 10 to 15 minutes.

Palm Hearts Vinaigrette Palm Hearts are available only in canned form. Drain well and serve as the artichokes above.

Salads

Small portions of many of the salads in this book can be served at the start of the meal; they do not have to be complicated; a simple tomato salad, when tomatoes are at their best, takes a lot of beating. See also page 22.

Eggs

Fish Omelette Make an omelette and fill with canned, fresh or thawed, frozen peeled prawns (shrimp) tossed in a little cream or top of the milk (half and half).

Bacon Omelette Grill (broil) or fry bacon,

chop and add to the beaten eggs. Cook in the usual way.

Scrambled Egg and Salmon Add finely chopped dill or parsley to the beaten eggs and scramble in a generous amount of butter. Arrange slices of smoked salmon on individual plates and top with the creamy scrambled egg.

Stuffed Eggs Hard-boiled (hard-cooked) eggs can be shelled, halved and topped with pâté, prawns (shrimp) in mayonnaise, sardines or anchovy fillets. Alternatively remove the yolks of the halved eggs, and mash with butter or mayonnaise and one of the following flavourings – chopped prawns (shrimp); chopped anchovy fillets or anchovy essence; mashed sardines; curry powder or curry paste; chopped or minced chicken, ham, tongue or pâté. Pile or pipe the smooth mixture back into the whites of the eggs and serve on a bed of salad.

The stuffed eggs can be topped with finely grated cheese and heated under the grill (broiler) for a few minutes.

Fish

Many fish dishes make a good hors d'oeuvre. Large prawns (jumbo shrimp) can be coated with seasoned flour, beaten egg and breadcrumbs and deep fried. You can of course buy ready-coated frozen scampi (jumbo shrimp) that can be fried in minutes.

Fish Cocktails Undoubtedly one of the most popular starters to a meal. Purchase a selection of fresh fish, prawns (shrimp), mussels and crabmeat or use canned fish. Drain canned prawns (shrimp) and leave in milk for a few minutes, then drain again to get rid of the rather over-salt taste.

Mary Rose Dressing The most important feature in a fish cocktail is the dressing. Blend mayonnaise with a little fresh tomato purée or tomato ketchup and a little cream, sherry, brandy or lemon juice. You may like to add a few drops of soy or chilli or Worcestershire sauce. Blend with the fish and serve in glasses on a bed of finely shredded lettuce.

Spiced Goujons Using monkfish, cod, coley, or haddock fillets, cut the fish into small ribbons and coat with flour seasoned with salt, pepper, mustard powder and pinch of dry ginger. Brush with beaten egg mixed with a little Worcestershire or soy sauce then coat with breadcrumbs. Heat oil in a frying pan (skillet) and fry the fish strips for about 4 minutes, turning once or twice. Drain on absorbent kitchen paper and serve garnished with lemon wedges.

Meat

There are many kinds of smoked meats, salamis and flavoured sausages available, serve just one kind or a selection.

Top left: Avocado and Seafood Salad, page 22
Bottom left: Duchy of Cornwall Pâté, page 24
Top right: Parmesan Smokies, page 23
Bottom right: Walnut Pears, page 20

Fruit Hors d'oeuvre

If you cannot decide what to offer as a start to the meal, you would be wise to select fruit. The most usual fruits are avocado, grapefruit and melon, but many other fruits are delicious.

LEFTOVERS
Leftover fruit can be combined to make a Melon Basket. When a melon is not available, halve grapefruit, remove the pulp and mix with leftover fruit, put back into the grapefruit skin.
Jamaican Grapefruit Moisten the grapefruit segments with a little rum and sweeten with brown sugar.

Made in Minutes

Apples Dessert fruit can be cored, cut into rings, marinated in a lemon-flavoured mayonnaise then topped with cottage or curd cheese, chopped nuts and finely diced ham.

Avocados These have become universally available and their unusual flavour, plus their versatility, makes them a splendid choice.

The most usual method of serving this fruit is in a Vinaigrette Dressing (see page 105), or filled with a prawn (shrimp) or fish mixture tossed in a Mary Rose Dressing (see page 19).

Piquant Fruit Salad Combine apple, grapefruit segments, deseeded grapes and melon. Moisten with a little lemon juice and dry sherry. Serve in grapefruit shells or glasses topped with yogurt or a refreshing sorbet (see page 117).

Figs Fresh or well-drained canned figs blend well with salami, which is much more economical than prosciutto (the expensive Italian smoked ham).

Melon Really perfect melons need few extra flavourings; simply remove the seeds from thick slices of melon or halve small fruit (such as the Ogen melon)

Minted Melon Basket

and remove the seeds. Serve with a little sugar and ground ginger.

Melon and Ginger Cocktail Cut the pulp of melon into neat dice or small balls (use a vegetable scoop). Marinate in the syrup from preserved ginger, plus a little sweet sherry then dice preserved ginger and mix with the fruit.

Minted Melon Basket Halve several small melons. Remove and discard the seeds and remove the pulp with a vegetable scoop. Mix with seasonal fruit like strawberries or raspberries and add sliced cucumber and a little chopped fresh mint. Moisten with a little orange juice or white wine and spoon back into the melon cases. Top with mint leaves and a scattering of grated orange peel, pistachio nuts or toasted almonds. See the picture below.

Never over-sweeten fruit that is to be served as the first course; it should be pleasantly refreshing in flavour.

There are other suggestions based on fruit on page 18 and in the menu section.

Grapefruit and Mushroom Cocktail

2 medium grapefruit
100 g/4 oz (1 cup) small button mushrooms
1 small lettuce heart
FOR THE DRESSING:
2 tablespoons thick mayonnaise
4 tablespoons yogurt
1 teaspoon lemon juice
pinch cayenne pepper
1 teaspoon sugar (optional)

Cut away the peel and pith from the grapefruit, then cut the fruit into neat segments, free from skin and pips; do this over a bowl so no juice is wasted. Wipe the mushrooms or wash in cold water and dry. Shred the lettuce very finely and put into individual dishes or glasses. Blend the ingredients for the dressing with any grapefruit juice in the bowl. Add the mushrooms, mix with the dressing, then add the grapefruit segments. Spoon over the shredded lettuce. Serves 4 to 6.

VARIATIONS
Grapefruit, Avocado and Mushroom Cocktail Dice or slice the flesh of 1 or 2 avocados; add to the ingredients in the recipe above. Increase the lemon juice to 1 tablespoon. By adding the avocado this cocktail would serve up to 8 people.

Melon and Ginger Lemon Sorbet

This makes a delicious dessert as well as an hors d'oeuvre.

2 small melons
Ginger Lemon Sorbet, see page 117
TO GARNISH
mint leaves

Halve the melons, scoop out the seeds. Chill for a short time. Fill the centres with scoops of the sorbet just before serving and garnish with the mint leaves. Serves 4.

VARIATIONS
Other sorbets can be used, the most refreshing and suitable for the start of a meal are lemon, orange and raspberry.

Walnut Pears

2 large or 4 small ripe dessert pears
2 tablespoons olive oil
2 tablespoons lemon juice
salt and pepper
½ teaspoon sugar
1 small lettuce heart
175 g/6 oz (¾ cup) curd cheese
3 tablespoons soured cream or yogurt
50 g/2 oz (½ cup) walnuts

Peel, halve and core the pears. Blend the oil, lemon juice, salt, pepper and sugar together. Pour into a dish, add the pear halves and turn in the dressing; this keeps the pears a good colour.

Arrange the lettuce on 4 plates. Mix the cheese, and cream or yogurt. Chop the walnuts, add half to the cheese mixture. Put the pears and dressing on the lettuce. Top with the cheese mixture and remaining walnuts. Serves 4.

Vegetable Hors d'oeuvre

You can appreciate the flavour of fresh young vegetables more if they are served by themselves as a starter rather than as an accompaniment to a main dish.

Made in Minutes

Globe artichokes and asparagus (see page 92), are ideal to serve at the start of a meal but other vegetable dishes are equally delicious.

Ratatouille is one of the easiest starters, whether served hot or cold. The recipe is on page 203, but here is a simpler dish, using fewer vegetables.

Courgettes (Zucchini) Provençales Peel and chop 1 to 2 garlic cloves and 1 medium onion. Heat 1 tablespoon oil in a saucepan; fry the garlic and onion for several minutes. Add a 425 g/15 oz can of plum tomatoes with the liquid from the can. Cover, and simmer for 10 minutes. Cut the tough ends from 450 g/1 lb courgettes (zucchini); slice the unpeeled vegetables thinly. Add to the tomato mixture and stir to blend. Season well and cook steadily for a further 10 minutes until the slices are soft, but unbroken. Garnish with plenty of chopped parsley; serve hot or cold. Serves 4.

Corn on the Cob Extremely popular, particularly with the young. Strip away the outer green leaves, put the corn cobs into boiling water. Cook steadily for about 15 minutes. Add the salt towards the end of the cooking time, if added too early it tends to toughen the corn. Do not overcook the corn, test early. Serve with a generous amount of melted butter, or butter blended with chopped fresh herbs.

Champignons en Cocotte

100 g/4 oz (1 cup) button mushrooms	
25 g/1 oz (2 tablespoons) butter	
300 ml/½ pint (1¼ cups) double (heavy) cream	
salt and pepper	
4 tablespoons grated Parmesan cheese	

∗∗Wipe the mushrooms, trim the ends of the stalks. Spread all the butter on the base and sides of four cocotte dishes. Add a little cream, then the mushrooms and season to taste. Top with the remainder of the cream and the cheese.

Bake just above the centre of a preheated moderately hot oven (190 to 200°C/375 to 400°F, Gas Mark 5 to 6) for 15 minutes or until the cheese is brown. Serve with Melba toast (see page 28). Serves 4.

Special Technique
TO COOK GLOBE ARTICHOKES

Globe artichokes can be served hot or cold and in many different ways (see right). You generally allow 1 artichoke per person; if very small and young allow 2 artichokes.

First pull away the tough outer leaves and cut away the stalk; the artichokes should stand upright when cooked. You can trim the tops of the leaves with a pair of kitchen scissors but this is not necessary; in fact artichokes look more attractive with shaped leaves.

Wash the artichokes in cold water, put into a large pan of boiling salted water to cover and cook until tender. The cooking time varies a great deal; small young artichokes are ready within 25 minutes, large mature vegetables can take up to 35 or 40 minutes. The way to test if they are ready is to lift one artichoke out of the water and pull away an outer leaf; it should come away easily and if the base of the leaf is tender the artichoke is ready.

Remove from the water and drain, then cut away and discard the 'choke'; this consists of the central leaves with a hairy growth at the base.

When serving artichokes you need finger bowls (as the leaves are eaten with the fingers) and a small knife and fork to eat the base of the vegetable, often called the artichoke heart.

Ways to Serve

Artichokes Served Hot

With Butter Heat a generous amount of butter, at least 25 g/1 oz (2 tablespoons) per person, season lightly and serve with the artichokes. The end of the leaves are dipped into the hot butter and eaten, then the heart of the artichoke is topped with butter and eaten with a knife and fork.

With Cheese Make a Cheese Sauce (see page 102) or Fonduta, (see page 27). Allow 3 to 4 tablespoons per person. Put the sauce into individual dishes and serve with the hot artichokes.

Fricassée of Artichokes Take the hearts from 4 artichokes, slice these neatly. Remove the fleshy part from the base of the leaves and put this purée on one side. Melt 50 g/2 oz (4 tablespoons) butter in a saucepan, add the sliced artichokes, heat for 2 to 3 minutes. Beat 4 eggs with 2 tablespoons single (light) cream, 2 tablespoons chopped parsley. Pour into the pan and scramble lightly. Serve topped with the artichoke purée and grated Parmesan. Serves 4.

Artichokes Served Cold

With Vinaigrette Dressing Allow the artichokes to become quite cold. Serve with Vinaigrette Dressing (see page 105), allowing about 3 tablespoons dressing per person.

Artichokes with Pâté Marinate the warm artichokes in a little well-seasoned oil and lemon juice. Cool, lift out of the marinade, put on to serving plates.

Make a fish pâté (see page 25) but add more cream or liquid to make the pâté softer. Spoon a little in the centre of each artichoke, and serve a little extra in a separate container.

USING CANNED CORN

If fresh or frozen corn is not available make an hors d'oeuvre from canned corn (whole kernels). Drain the corn and heat in a little butter or margarine.

Corn au Gratin
Arrange the corn on a bed of cooked tomatoes, in a flameproof dish or dishes; top with a thick layer of grated cheese and put under a preheated grill (broiler). Heat until the cheese melts.

A beautifully cooked Globe Artichoke

21

Salad Hors d'oeuvre

Avocado Salad

A crisp and colourful salad makes a perfect start to a meal. Remember though that most salads are fairly satisfying so do not serve portions that are too large. Here are a few simple suggestions.

Simple Salads

Carrot Salad Cook whole baby carrots, drain and toss in a little Vinaigrette Dressing. Allow to cool. Arrange on a bed of lettuce and top with grated cheese and chopped parsley.

Cucumber and Herb Salad Slice cucumber very thinly, sprinkle with finely chopped chives, dill and parsley. Season well and moisten with a little white wine vinegar. Serve with sliced tomatoes and shredded lettuce.

Egg and Potato Salad Hard-boil (hard-cook) 2 eggs and cut into quarters. Cook 175 g/6 oz small new potatoes and quarter while hot. Blend the potatoes with a little mayonnaise, 2 tablespoons chopped spring onions (scallions) or chives, 2 tablespoons diced gherkins or cucumber. Place on a bed of watercress and lettuce. Arrange the eggs around the edge of the dish. Serves 4.

Celeriac Rémoulade Visitors to France know the popularity of this simple blend of sauce and raw vegetable. Make Rémoulade Sauce (see page 104). Peel raw celeriac and cut into matchstick pieces or shred it with an electric mixer or food processor. Blend the pieces immediately with the sauce for celeriac discolours with exposure to the air. Alternatively, dip the celeriac in lemon juice before adding it to the sauce. Top with chopped parsley.

Tomato Salad Slice tomatoes thinly, sprinkle with finely chopped basil, parsley and tarragon. Season well and serve in a border of watercress and shredded lettuce.

The tomatoes can be moistened with Vinaigrette Dressing if desired.

Avocado and Seafood Salad

2 cooked scallops, see page 44
12 prepared, cooked mussels, see page 44
50 g/2 oz (⅓ cup) peeled prawns (shelled shrimp)
2 tablespoons mayonnaise
1½ tablespoons lemon juice
½ tablespoon dry sherry
1 teaspoon tomato purée (paste)
Tabasco (hot pepper) sauce
2 avocados
TO GARNISH: 1 small lettuce
1 lemon

Cut the scallops into thin slices, mix with the mussels, prawns (shrimp), may-onnaise, ½ tablespoon of the lemon juice, the sherry, tomato purée (paste) and 2 or 3 drops of Tabasco sauce. Chill until ready to serve.

Peel and halve the avocados just before serving; place on lettuce leaves on individual plates and sprinkle with the remaining lemon juice. Spoon the salad over the avocados. Cut the lemon into wedges and arrange on the plates. Serves 4.

Avocado Salad

4 large lettuce leaves
4 tomatoes
175 to 200 g/6 to 7 oz Mozzarella cheese
4 tablespoons oil
2 tablespoons white wine vinegar or lemon juice
salt and pepper
2 avocados
½ to 1 teaspoon dried oregano

Place the lettuce on 4 individual serving plates. Skin and slice the tomatoes; slice the cheese. Blend the oil, vinegar or lemon juice and a little seasoning to-gether.

Halve the avocados, skin and remove the stones, place on the lettuce leaves with the cut side down; slice carefully. Arrange the tomato and cheese slices on the lettuce. Top with the dressing and the oregano. Serves 4.

VARIATION
Use finely chopped fresh marjoram in place of the oregano.

Eggs in Watercress Sauce

8 eggs
100 g/4 oz (½ cup) cottage cheese
3 tablespoons mayonnaise
salt and pepper
1 bunch watercress
150 ml/¼ pint (⅔ cup) yogurt
4 tomatoes
1 small lettuce

Hard-boil (hard-cook) the eggs, cool and shell; halve lengthways and remove the yolks. Blend the yolks with the cottage cheese, 1 tablespoon mayonnaise and a very little seasoning.

Remove all the watercress leaves, wash in cold water, dry well, either chop finely and mix with the yogurt and remaining mayonnaise or put into a blender with the yogurt and mayonnaise and switch on for a few seconds; do not leave for too long a period. Season well.

Slice the tomatoes; arrange the lettuce on individual plates, add the eggs and tomato slices. Top with the sauce. Serves 4.

Fish Hors d'oeuvre

Fish is one of the most suitable and popular foods to serve as a starter. It is light in texture and not too filling. Some speedy suggestions using fish are on page 19 and there are more elaborate dishes in the chapter that starts on page 36.

Smoked Fish

Smoked fish makes one of the simplest and most popular hors d'oeuvre.

For luxury choose smoked salmon or smoked eel. Smoked salmon can be served very simply with cayenne pepper, lemon and brown bread and butter. It can be made into a more elaborate dish by rolling the slices around prawns (shrimp) in mayonnaise, one of the fish pâtés on pages 25 and 26, or with lightly scrambled egg flavoured with chopped fennel leaves.

Smoked eel is generally served with lemon, horseradish sauce or horseradish cream but scrambled egg makes an interesting contrast to the rich fish.

The more economical mackerel is served as for eel and is also excellent with Waldorf Salad (see page 95).

Smoked trout can also be served like smoked eel but if you would like it to be slightly more original, slit and bone the fish and fill with equal quantities of peeled prawns (shrimp), finely chopped celery and finely diced dessert apple in a horseradish-flavoured mayonnaise (see page 104).

Lightly cooked kipper fillet can be tossed in Vinaigrette Dressing and topped with chopped spring onions.

Herring Roes in Garlic Butter

450 g/1 lb soft herring roes
25 g/1 oz (¼ cup) flour
salt and pepper
1 to 2 garlic cloves
75 to 100 g/3 to 4 oz (⅓ to ½ cup) butter
1 to 2 tablespoons finely chopped parsley

Separate the herring roes and pat dry on absorbent paper. If using frozen roes allow these to thaw out and dry very thoroughly.

Blend the flour with a little salt and pepper, coat the roes in the seasoned flour. Peel and crush the garlic. Heat the butter in a large frying pan (skillet), add the garlic and the roes and fry for 4 to 5 minutes. Turn the roes halfway through the cooking period. Add the parsley just before serving. Serves 4 to 6.

Parmesan Smokies

50 g/2 oz (½ cup) grated Parmesan cheese
50 g/2 oz (½ cup) grated Cheddar cheese
450 g/1 lb Arbroath Smokies or smoked haddock, weight without bones and skin
300 ml/½ pint (1¼ cups) water
1 small sprig tarragon
50 g/2 oz (¼ cup) butter or margarine
50 g/2 oz (½ cup) flour
300 ml/½ pint (1¼ cups) milk
150 ml/¼ pint (⅔ cup) single (light) cream
4 tablespoons white wine
salt and pepper
25 g/1 oz (½ cup) soft fine breadcrumbs

∗∗Put 25 g/1 oz (¼ cup) Parmesan cheese on one side for the topping.

Place the fish in the cold water in a saucepan, add the tarragon and bring the water to the boil. Poach the fish until just tender; Smokies take about 5 minutes, the thicker haddock about 10 minutes. Lift the fish from the liquid and finely flake it. Strain the liquid and retain a generous 150 ml/¼ pint (⅔ cup).

Heat the butter or margarine in a saucepan, stir in the flour and gently cook for 2 to 3 minutes. Gradually blend in the milk, reserved fish stock and the cream. Stir as the sauce comes to the boil and thickens. Remove from the heat. Stir in the fish, all the Cheddar cheese, 25 g/1 oz (¼ cup) Parmesan cheese and the white wine together with any seasoning required. Spoon into 4 to 6 individual ovenproof dishes. Top with the breadcrumbs and remaining Parmesan cheese.

Heat for 10 to 15 minutes towards the top of a preheated moderately hot oven (200°C/400°F, Gas Mark 6). Serve with hot toast and butter. Serves 4 to 6.

VARIATION

Use any cooked white fish instead of the smoked fish.

Prawn Ramekins

2 eggs
1 × 200 g/7 oz can sweetcorn (whole kernels)
100 g/4 oz (1 cup) grated Gouda cheese
25 g/1 oz (2 tablespoons) butter
20 g/¾ oz (3 tablespoons) flour
150 ml/¼ pint (⅔ cup) milk
100 g/4 oz (⅔ cup) cooked peeled prawns (shelled shrimp)
1 tablespoon chopped parsley
salt and pepper
TO GARNISH
1 lime or lemon

Hard-boil (hard-cook), shell and chop the eggs. Heat the butter in a pan, stir in the flour, then blend in the milk. Stir or whisk as the mixture thickens to become a thick coating sauce. Add the eggs, sweetcorn, all the prawns (shrimp), except 4 that should be put on one side for garnish, 75 g/3 oz (¾ cup) of the cheese, the parsley and seasoning.

Divide the mixture between four individual flameproof dishes. Top with the remaining cheese and heat under a preheated grill (broiler) until the top of the mixture is golden brown.

Cut the lime or lemon into thin slices, cut each slice into small portions, arrange on top of the prawn (shrimp) mixture. Garnish with the remaining prawns (shrimp). Serves 4.

LEFTOVERS
Use a little cooked fish or shellfish as a filling for pancakes or omelettes. **Potted Fish** Flake or chop leftover fish then pound with melted butter, seasoning and a little grated nutmeg. Put into a small container, top with more melted butter and shrimps or small prawns.

FOR ECONOMY
Cut monkfish (sometimes called angler) into neat pieces. Cook (see page 44), cool and use in place of more expensive shellfish. It has a similar texture to shellfish, but is far cheaper.

Smoked Salmon served with Prawns tossed in Mayonnaise

Pâtés

A pâté can be based upon fish, meat, game or vegetables. They are amazingly easy to prepare using a food processor or blender. The pâtés opposite are prepared without cooking the ingredients, or by cooking them for a short time only, whereas the pâtés and terrines on this page are cooked after the ingredients have been minced (ground) or blended.

Making Meat Pâtés

Traditionally a mixture without pastry should be called a terrine and a mixture cooked in pastry a pâté. Nowadays, though, we have adopted the word pâté to cover most of these mixtures.

Mince (grind) the meat carefully or use the food processor to chop it; the finer the meat is cut, the smoother the pâté will be.

Pigs' liver gives a stronger taste to the mixture than either calves' or lambs' liver; some of the best pâtés are made by mixing two or three types of liver together. It is usual to add a little fat pork to keep the lean meat moist. If your family dislikes cooked liver the chances are they will enjoy a pâté and this is an excellent way of introducing a highly nutritious food into the menu.

When cooking the pâté, stand the pan or dish in another containing cold water, a *bain-marie*.

Blender Pâtés

Do not try to blend too large a quantity of food at one time. A food processor will accommodate larger amounts than a blender but be careful not to over-process the ingredients or you will produce a rather sticky mixture.

Many pâté recipes contain single (light) cream which gives a light and delicate mixture. You can substitute yogurt if preferred.

Freezing Note

Never freeze pâté for too long a period. Use within 4 to 6 weeks. A pâté that is left in the freezer longer than this loses its pleasantly moist texture and some of the flavour too. You can restore it to a degree if you tip the pâté into a bowl, allow it to thaw out completely then blend it with a generous amount of melted or creamed butter and/or cream. Taste the mixture and add extra seasoning and suitable herbs. Use as soon as possible.

LEFTOVERS
Use leftover pâté as a sandwich filling, as a topping for hard-boiled (hard-cooked) eggs or as a stuffing for fish, meat or chicken.

Bacon Pâté, a variation of Creamy Liver Pâté

Master Recipe
CREAMY LIVER PÂTÉ

350 g/12 oz calves' liver
225 g/8 oz pigs' liver
100 g/4 oz fat belly of pork
1 small onion
1 garlic clove
50 g/2 oz (¼ cup) butter
150 ml/¼ pint (⅔ cup) double (heavy) cream
2 eggs
salt and pepper
2 tablespoons brandy or dry sherry
¼ teaspoon allspice

Mince (grind) or finely chop the liver and pork. Peel and finely chop the onion and garlic. Heat the butter in a frying pan (skillet) and toss the onion and garlic in this; do not allow to colour. Blend all the ingredients together.

Put into a well greased 1.25 kg/2½ lb pan or ovenproof dish, cover with buttered foil, stand in a *bain-marie* and bake in the centre of a preheated moderate oven (160°C/325°F, Gas Mark 3) for 1¼ hours. Allow to cool in the cooking container, then turn out and serve with hot toast and butter. This pâté is extremely good if served slightly warm instead of cold. Serves up to 8.

Variations

Chicken Pâté Either use all chicken livers, mince (grind) these then follow the recipe above, or use 225 g/8 oz (1 cup) chicken livers and 350 g/12 oz (1½ cups) minced (ground) raw chicken flesh. Flavour the mixture with 1 teaspoon finely grated lemon rind and 1 teaspoon thyme.

Country Pâté Use all pigs' liver and a good brown stock instead of cream. Add 2 tablespoons chopped parsley to the ingredients. Serve with Cranberry Sauce.

Duck Pâté Cut the flesh from a duck; you need 550 g/1¼ lb duck flesh (to include the duck liver). Simmer the bones in water to cover with strips of orange rind to flavour. Use 150 ml/¼ pint (⅔ cup) of this stock instead of double (heavy) cream in the Master Recipe and add ½ teaspoon sage.

Game Pâté Use the flesh plus livers from game birds and follow the Master Recipe. Add ½ to 1 tablespoon juniper berries to the mixture.

Bacon Pâté Use streaky bacon instead of pork and top the pâté with a few additional slices. Serve from the dish.

Duchy of Cornwall Pâté

FOR THE PÂTÉ
1 garlic clove
175 g/6 oz smoked cod's roe, weight when skinned
black pepper
2 tablespoons chopped parsley
150 ml/¼ pint (⅔ cup) oil
2 tablespoons lemon juice
2 tablespoons boiling water
225 g/8 oz smoked mackerel
FOR THE BASE:
8 large flat mushrooms
50 g/2 oz (¼ cup) butter
1 tablespoon oil
8 small slices bread
TO GARNISH
parsley sprigs

⁂Peel and crush the garlic. Place the roe, pepper, parsley and garlic in a bowl, blender or food processor, mix until smooth. Gradually beat in half the oil to form a smooth creamy mixture (like mayonnaise) and then slowly add the lemon juice and boiling water. Continue to slowly beat in the rest of the oil or blend in the blender or processor. Remove the skin and any bones from the mackerel and flake the fish, then blend with the roe mixture. Chill well.

Carefully remove the stalks from the mushrooms. Set aside. Heat the butter and oil in a frying pan (skillet). Lightly fry the cups and stalks. Drain and cool. Cut circles out of the bread a little larger than the mushrooms. Fry in the remaining butter and oil until golden. Drain on absorbent paper.

Spoon a little pâté into each mushroom cup, top with the mushroom stalks. Place on the bread croûtes. Top with parsley. Serves 8.

Master Recipe
Smoked Trout Pâté

75 g/3 oz (6 tablespoons) butter or margarine
2 medium smoked trout
1 teaspoon finely grated lemon rind
150 ml/¼ pint (⅔ cup) single (light) cream
1 tablespoon horseradish cream
1 teaspoon chopped dill
1 teaspoon chopped parsley
1 to 2 tablespoons lemon juice
cayenne or white pepper

⁂Smoked trout has such a delicate texture and flavour that additional ingredients should not be too heavy; that is why less butter or margarine is used in this pâté than in several with similar fish. Cream the butter or margarine until soft and light; remove all the flesh from the fish, add to the creamed fat, then gradually add all the other ingredients, beating hard to make a light mixture. Serves 4 to 6.

Variations

⁂Fresh and Smoked Trout Pâtés Either make the pâté as above, or grill (broil) 2 or 3 fresh trout, cool and proceed as above, then add 2 tablespoons finely chopped spring onions (scallion) or chives and 2 teaspoons capers, plus salt to taste.

⁂Smoked Salmon Pâté Omit the horseradish cream, increase the butter or margarine to at least 100 g/4 oz (½ cup). This should be melted rather than creamed. Use 225 g/8 oz smoked salmon. Dice about 50 g/2 oz of the smoked fish, put on one side. Chop the rest. Make the pâté as above – a blender or food processor is ideal. When prepared add the chopped salmon.

⁂Taramasalata Smoked cod's roe can be made in exactly the same way as the Smoked Trout Pâté, but omit the horseradish cream and melt 100 g/4 oz (½ cup) butter or margarine; use 225 g/8 oz roe, (weight when skinned). Add 2 skinned and finely chopped garlic cloves to the other ingredients. This is a strongly flavoured pâté, quite different from the other recipes on this page.

Ham and Liver Pâté

2 small onions
8 chicken livers
225 g/8 oz (1 cup) diced cooked ham
50 g/2 oz (¼ cup) butter
3 tablespoons single (light) cream
2 tablespoons dry sherry
½ teaspoon chopped thyme or ¼ teaspoon dried thyme
salt and pepper

⁂Peel and chop the onions, skin and dice the livers. Heat the butter in a frying pan (skillet) and cook the onions and livers until tender; do not allow the onions to brown. Put into a blender or food processor. Pour the cream and sherry into the pan, stir well to absorb the meat juices, add to the livers and onions together with the ham, thyme and a little seasoning. Switch on until a smooth pâté. Spoon into 4 to 6 small ramekin dishes or one large dish and allow to become cold. Serve with hot toast and butter. Serves 4 to 6.

Note The ingredients can be put through the fine plate of a mincer if preferred.

Brazil Pâté

25 g/1 oz (2 tablespoons) margarine
25 g/1 oz (¼ cup) flour, preferably wheatmeal
150 ml/¼ pint (⅔ cup) milk
¼ teaspoon yeast extract
50 g/2 oz (1 cup) wholewheat breadcrumbs
1 egg
225 g/8 oz (2 cups) Brazil nuts
pinch ground nutmeg
1 tablespoon chopped parsley
1 tablespoon chopped chives
salt and pepper
TO GARNISH
2 or 3 tomatoes
few lettuce leaves

⁂Heat the margarine in a pan, stir in the flour and cook for several minutes over a low heat, then gradually blend in the milk. Return to the heat and continue stirring until the mixture becomes a thick binding sauce. Add the yeast extract and the breadcrumbs. Allow to cool slightly then beat in the egg.

Chop the nuts finely in a mincer, blender or food processor. Add these together with the nutmeg, herbs and seasoning to the sauce. Put the mixture into a well greased 450 g/1 lb loaf pan or container. Stand in a dish of cold water and cover with a piece of greased foil. Bake in the centre of a preheated moderate oven (180°C/350°F, Gas Mark 4) for 35 to 40 minutes. Allow to cool then turn out of the container.

Slice the tomatoes and arrange around the pâté with the lettuce leaves. Serves 4 to 6.

Mushroom Terrine

350 g/12 oz open mushrooms
75 g/3 oz onion
175 g/6 oz (¾ cup) cooked ham
40 g/1½ oz (¾ cup) bread, weight without crusts
350 g/12 oz (1½ cups) pork sausagemeat
2 medium tomatoes
1 teaspoon chopped fresh mixed herbs or ½ teaspoon dried mixed herbs
1 tablespoon chopped parsley
2 small eggs
salt and pepper

⁂Wipe the mushrooms, trim the end of the stalks, chop neatly. Peel the onion, put through the coarse plate of a mincer (grinder) with the ham and bread; or chop in a food processor. Mix all the ingredients together and season well. Put into a 1.2 litre/2 pint (5 cup) greased bowl or container, cover with greased greaseproof (waxed) paper and foil. Steam over boiling water for 2 hours. Allow to cool. Serves 8 to 12.

Ham and Liver Pâté and Smoked Trout Pâté

LEFTOVERS

Leftover pâté must be stored with great care, for it is highly perishable.

Pâté-stuffed Eggs
Hard-boil (hard-cook) eggs, shell and halve, remove the yolks, blend these with a small amount of pâté, spoon or pipe into the egg whites. Serve on salad.

Tournedos Rossini
This is the name given to cooked tournedos (rounds of fillet steak) topped with pâté; this is a good way of using a small amount of meat pâté for a special occasion.

Pâté Fritters
Make thin sandwiches of bread, butter and pâté. Cut into fingers, dip for a few seconds into beaten egg and fry in hot butter until crisp and brown on either side.

Savoury Dips

Make two or three different dips, place in small bowls and arrange on a large tray or dish with the various foods to be used for dipping. You can serve a selection of the raw vegetables listed under Crudités (see opposite), popular with anyone who is slimming. You can also include small biscuits, crisps (chips) and cooked sausages.

A good dip should be the consistency of a thick cream.

Spicy Tomato Dip

255 g/8 oz (1 cup) cream cheese
2 tablespoons milk
2 tablespoons tomato chutney or relish
2 teaspoons lemon juice
Worcestershire sauce
Tabasco (hot pepper) sauce
salt and pepper
TO GARNISH: paprika

MELBA TOAST
Cut stale bread into wafer thin slices, remove the crusts. If the bread is not as thin as it should be, roll it out with a rolling pin, as though making pastry.

Crisp for at least 1 hour in a very cool oven (120 to 140°C/250 to 275°F, Gas Mark ½ to 1) until golden brown. Store in an airtight tin.

✲✲Blend the cheese and milk. If using a chutney or relish that contains large chunks, chop these finely. (This is not necessary if using a blender or food processor to make the dip.) Add the tomato chutney or relish to the cheese mixture, together with enough lemon juice, Worcestershire and Tabasco sauces and seasoning, to give a very definite taste.

Spoon into a bowl and top with paprika. Serves 4 to 6.

Smoked Mackerel Pâté

175 g/6 oz (¾ cup) margarine
225 g/8 oz smoked mackerel, weight without skin or bones
100 g/4 oz (½ cup) cottage cheese
150 ml/¼ pint (⅔ cup) single (light) cream or yogurt
1 to 1½ tablespoons lemon juice
a little cayenne pepper
a little grated nutmeg
TO GARNISH: 1 lemon slice

✲✲Melt the margarine, flake the fish, blend with the margarine. Sieve the cottage cheese for a very smooth texture, and add to the fish mixture together with the cream or yogurt. Add the lemon juice, pepper and nutmeg gradually and taste as you do so. Serve topped with the lemon slice. Serves 4. Note This pâté type mixture is ideal to

serve as a dip. The blender or food processor makes it beautifully smooth in seconds.

VARIATIONS
Add 1 to 2 peeled and crushed garlic cloves to the mixture; obviously there is no need to crush them if using a blender or food processor.

✲✲Mackerel and Horseradish Pâté Either grate a small piece of fresh horseradish and add to the other ingredients or use a little less cream or yogurt and add 1 to 2 tablespoons horseradish cream.

✲✲Kipper Pâté Use lightly cooked kippers in place of mackerel; the cottage cheese could be omitted.

Taramasalata Spread

150 g/5 oz white bread, weight without crusts
300 ml/½ pint (1¼ cups) milk
175 g/6 oz (¾ cup) smoked cod's roe, weight without skin
2 teaspoons finely chopped onion
3 to 4 tablespoons lemon juice
up to 300 ml/½ pint (1¼ cups) oil
pepper

✲✲Remove the crusts from the bread; use these to crisp for raspings. Put the bread into a bowl, add the milk and soak for about 10 minutes. Lift the bread from the milk and squeeze it firmly until as dry as possible. Put the bread into a bowl and beat it as hard as possible until very smooth, then gradually beat in the cod's roe, onion and lemon juice. Add the oil steadily, beating all the time, until the mixture becomes very light and smooth. Season with pepper.

Serve with hot toast or pitta bread. Serves 6.
Note This is one of the many recipes for Taramasalata (Cod's Roe Pâté). It is particularly delicate in flavour.

Onion and Cucumber Dip

3 tablespoons finely chopped spring onions (scallions)
5 tablespoons peeled and finely diced cucumber
225 g/8 oz (1 cup) cream cheese
2 tablespoons milk

Blend all the ingredients together. Serves 4 to 6.

VARIATION
Use 2 tablespoons dehydrated onion soup mix in place of chopped onions; allow the dip to stand for some time.

Crudités with Vinaigrette Dressing, Ravigote Dressing and Bagna Caôda

International Dishes

Master Recipe
LES CRUDITÉS

We have adopted the habit of serving raw vegetables as an hors d'oeuvre from the French, and it is an excellent idea, particularly if the main course is creamy and rich in flavour.

Many vegetables can be included, but they should be prepared in such a way that they are easy to eat with the fingers.

Each person should have a sharp knife to cut the vegetables into smaller portions, a bowl of dressing (or you can provide a choice of dressings) together with a finger bowl and a table napkin. The vegetables are dipped into the dressing before being eaten.

Include Brussels sprouts – choose small firm ones; red or green cabbage; cauliflower; young courgettes (zucchini); cucumber; fennel root; lettuce; green and red peppers; radishes; spring onions (scallions); tomatoes.

You may also include hard-boiled (hard-cooked) eggs but do not shell them; they keep better in their shells. You could add apples or pears.

Crudités Dressings

<u>Vinaigrette Dressing</u> Make up the recipe (see page 105) and serve in one large or several small containers.

<u>Anchovy Dressing</u> Flavour the Vinaigrette Dressing with a little anchovy essence. To make a thicker dressing, liquidize 1 to 2 tablespoons anchovy paste with each 150 ml/¼ pint (⅔ cup) of dressing.

<u>Ravigote Dressing</u> Blend 150 ml/¼ pint (⅔ cup) of Vinaigrette Dressing with 2 tablespoons finely chopped onion, ½ to 1 tablespoon chopped capers, 1 tablespoon chopped parsley, ½ teaspoon chopped chervil and ½ teaspoon chopped tarragon.

Bagna Caôda
[Anchovy Dip]

This dip is excellent with Crudités. Although it is an Italian recipe it is frequently served in France. The quantities may seem small, but it is a very rich and oily dip.

2 to 3 garlic cloves
1 × 50 g/2 oz can anchovies
150 ml/¼ pint (⅔ cup) olive oil
50 to 75 g/2 to 3 oz (¼ to ½ cup) unsalted butter

Peel and crush the garlic; drain the anchovies, pour the oil from the can into a frying pan (skillet), chop the salted fish very finely. Add the olive oil to the small amount of oil in the frying pan, heat gently then add the garlic and chopped anchovy fillets and fry slowly for 10 to 15 minutes, stirring frequently.

Add the butter and heat until melted. Pour into a strong heated bowl or a metal fondue pan and keep hot. Serve with a selection of raw vegetables and toast or bread. Serves 4 to 6.

Bignè di Sardine
[Sardine Fritters]

16 fresh sardines
8 small Mozzarella cheese slices
TO COAT: salt and pepper
2 tablespoons flour
1 egg
50 g/2 oz (½ cup) crisp breadcrumbs
FOR FRYING: 2 tablespoons oil

Cut the heads off the sardines, split the fish and remove the backbones. Place the cheese on 8 of the split sardines, top with the remaining sardines, secure with wooden cocktail sticks. Blend a little seasoning with the flour. Coat the fish in this and then the beaten egg and breadcrumbs. Heat the oil in a large frying pan (skillet) and fry the fish for 2 minutes, turn and fry on the second side for 2 minutes. Drain on absorbent paper and serve at once. Serves 4.

VARIATION
Use sprats (smelts) instead of sardines and Gouda cheese instead of Mozzarella.

Fonduta
[Italian Fondue]

This is the Piedmontese version of a fondue, it does not contain any alcohol and is deliciously light yet rich in flavour. The first method is the traditional recipe, but the variation below is quicker to prepare.

Fontina cheese is a well-known Italian semi-hard cheese, but Italian Mozzarella or any good cooking cheese could be substituted.

350 g/12 oz (1½ cups) Fontina cheese, see method
300 ml/½ pint (1¼ cups) milk
salt and pepper
50 g/2 oz (¼ cup) butter
4 egg yolks
TO GARNISH: 4 to 6 mushrooms

Slice the cheese very thinly or grate it. Put into the top of a double saucepan or bowl over a pan of water. You could use a ceramic fondue pot on a table heater. Add most of the milk and heat slowly until the cheese has melted. Add a very little seasoning. Meanwhile allow the butter to soften at room temperature. Blend the egg yolks with the remaining milk; whisk into the melted cheese mixture then add the butter gradually. Stir or whisk all the time until the mixture becomes slightly thickened and very smooth and creamy.

Keep warm over a low heat. Serve in individual bowls. Thinly slice the raw mushrooms, sprinkle on the cheese mixture.

Serve with toast or fresh bread. Serves 4 to 6.

VARIATION
For a creamier fondue: Blend 1 tablespoon cornflour (cornstarch) with the milk, pour into a saucepan; stir over a low heat until thickened and smooth. Add the sliced or grated cheese. Gradually add the softened butter and seasoning.

Transfer to a ceramic fondue pot or bowl over hot, but not boiling, water. Blend the egg yolks with 150 ml/¼ pint (⅔ cup) double (heavy) cream, whisk into the hot milk mixture and continue whisking for several minutes. Garnish with the mushrooms above or with diced red pepper before serving.

GARLIC BREAD
Make diagonal cuts along 1 French loaf, but do not cut through the base of the bread. Peel and crush 1 to 2 cloves of garlic, see page 155. Blend with 100 g/4 oz (½ cup) margarine. Spread the garlic mixture into each cut. Wrap the loaf in foil. Bake near the top of a preheated moderate oven (180°C/350°F, Gas Mark 4) for 25 to 30 minutes or use a slightly hotter oven for a shorter heating period.

The bread could be put into a long polythene bag or loosely wrapped in clingfilm and heated for several minutes in a microwave cooker. Serves 4.

LEFTOVERS
Always use up potted meats and fish pastes once the jar is opened; you could use anchovy paste or other fish pastes in the dressing on this page.

27

SOUPS

Soup is not only an excellent start to a meal, but a sustaining soup, such as one of those on page 30, can be served as a complete light meal. Quite frequently a soup can be prepared from leftover ingredients you have in the refrigerator.

In this chapter you will find recipes for soups that are made in minutes; economical family recipes; special occasion soups and some unusual ideas from other countries.

Over the years cold soups have become extremely popular, not only for serving in hot weather, but at all times of the year. A selection of these recipes begins on page 33.

Types of Soup

There are various kinds of soup:

Broths and Chowders These are satisfying soups made with a variety of ingredients. The mixture is not sieved or blended (see page 31).

Clear Soups A consommé is the classic example of this kind of soup (see page 32).

Cream Soups A purée of vegetables and other ingredients which is thickened and blended with cream or added to a sauce.

Purée Soups Generally these are made from a vegetable, or mixture of vegetables, which are cooked with herbs and flavouring in stock or water, then sieved, or put into a blender or food processor to form a purée. The thickness of the soup varies according to the vegetable used. Leftover poultry can also make a delicious purée soup (see page 31).

Buying Points

Do not waste money by buying top quality ingredients to make a soup; for example, less than perfectly shaped tomatoes or cucumbers will be just as satisfactory as the better looking variety, and probably cheaper. On the other hand, though, avoid overripe or blemished vegetables which could spoil the flavour of the soup.

Be adventurous in your choice of ingredients for a soup. Often there are inexpensive fish or vegetables available which would make an unusual and interesting soup.

Make clever use of herbs and other flavourings and serve interesting garnishes (see pages 32, 34 and 35).

Microwave Cooking

Many soups can be made in a microwave cooker, although the saving of time will not be as great as in many dishes because soups contain a high percentage of liquid and this does not heat particularly quickly.

If the soup contains onions that are to be sieved or blended later, they should be chopped more finely than when cooking in a saucepan. If left in larger pieces it is difficult to tenderize them.

A microwave cooker is splendid for heating ready prepared soups, but transfer canned soups to a ceramic dish before heating.

The joy of using the microwave cooker is that you can pour individual helpings into soup cups and heat each portion as required – a great benefit for latecomers!

Freezing Note

Most soups can be frozen; look for the freezer symbol (∗∗). Often a purée soup will separate on thawing; if this happens whisk or blend the mixture to its original texture.

Made in Minutes

Do not imagine that all soups require prolonged cooking. In many cases the flavour is better if the foods are cooked for a shorter time.

A blender or food processor produces smooth puréed mixtures in seconds. You can also save time by grating vegetables for speedy cooking.

Ten-minute Vegetable Soup Bring 900 ml/1½ pints (3¾ cups) bacon or chicken stock, or water and a stock cube (2 bouillon cubes) to the boil, add 350 g/12 oz (2 cups) grated root vegetables. Use carrots and/or celeriac and a grated onion. Cook for 10 minutes, blend until smooth and season well. Top the soup with grated cheese. Serves 4.

∗∗Asparagus Soup Blend or sieve a 425 g/15 oz can of asparagus with the liquid from the can; mix with 300 ml/½ pint (1¼ cups) milk, 2 tablespoons chopped chives and seasoning. Heat and serve.

To serve cold, blend or sieve the asparagus with 150 ml/¼ pint (⅔ cup) single (light) cream and 150 ml/¼ pint

(⅔ cup) yogurt. Season well and top with chopped chives. Serves 4.

✱✱Speedy Tomato Soup Chop 550 g/1¼ lb ripe tomatoes and peel 8 spring onions (scallions). Place in a blender or food processor with a few basil leaves and purée until smooth. Tip into a saucepan and add ½ chicken stock cube (1 bouillon cube), ½ tablespoon lemon juice, salt, pepper and ½ teaspoon brown sugar. Heat for a few minutes only then serve. Serves 4.

Tomato and Apple Soup Follow Speedy Tomato Soup recipe above but purée a small peeled and cored dessert apple with the tomatoes and onion and add 1 cooked and finely chopped bacon rasher (slice) just before serving.

Speedy Soups for Slimmers

Soup is so warming and satisfying that many dieters think of soup as a 'forbidden' food. Try these quick recipes, all of them low in calories.

Curry Chowder Bring 900 ml/1½ pints (3¾ cups) well-seasoned consommé or a mixture of consommé and tomato juice to the boil. Add 100 g/4 oz (1 cup) chopped celery, 100 g/4 oz (1 cup) chopped spring onions (scallions) and 50 g/2 oz (¾ cup) finely shredded cabbage heart to the liquid. Boil briskly for 1 to 2 minutes only. Season well and serve. Serves 4.

Egg in Consommé Bring 900 ml/1½ pints (3¾ cups) well-seasoned consommé to the boil in a deep frying pan (skillet). Carefully break 4 eggs into the liquid. Lower the heat and cook steadily for 3 to 4 minutes until just set. If the consommé is swirled gently around the eggs they set in a neat shape. Serve the soup and eggs in soup cups. Serves 4.

Tomato and Prawn Bisque Whisk 900 ml/1½ pints (3¾ cups) cold tomato juice into 225 g/8 oz (1 cup) sieved cottage cheese or mix these together in a blender or food processor. Add 175 g/6 oz (1 cup) peeled prawns (shrimp), 1 to 2 teaspoons chopped fennel leaves and a squeeze of lemon juice. Serves 4.

Yogurt and Cucumber Soup Blend together 300 ml/½ pint (1¼ cups) plain low calorie yogurt, 300 ml/½ pint (1¼ cups) chicken stock, 2 tablespoons chopped spring onions (scallions).

Peel and coarsely grate approximately ¼ of a large cucumber, mix with the other ingredients, then add salt and pepper to taste together with a few drops of lemon juice or white wine vinegar. Top each portion of the soup with matchstick pieces of unpeeled cucumber. Serves 4.

Top left: Cream of Spinach Soup, page 30
Bottom left: Soto Ajam, page 34
Right: Cucumber and Prawn Soup, page 33

Family Soups

Soups are perfect for the family, they are satisfying and can be made with inexpensive ingredients. When you are busy you may feel there is no time to make elaborate soups, but here are basic recipes that can be varied throughout the year depending upon ingredients available.

Purée of Celery Soup

Simple Skill

Take advantage of seasonal foods. There are occasions when vegetables like tomatoes and cucumbers are cheap, or when you have a glut in the garden.

Purée of Celery Soup is a Master Recipe for many other vegetable soups. In addition to the ideas suggested, use Jerusalem artichokes, carrots, parsnips, turnips, celeriac or peas instead of the celery and potatoes.

Cream of Spinach Soup typifies a soup made from vegetables that needs the addition of a sauce. Use Brussels sprouts, cauliflower or lettuce instead of spinach.

The soups opposite are sufficiently sustaining to provide the basis of a light meal. Remember a good stock makes a good soup. See the easy ways of preparing stock on page 51.

FOR EASE

When freezing soup, it saves last minute effort if the chopped herbs to be used for garnish are frozen in a small polythene bag or box and stored with the soup.

Master Recipe
PURÉE OF CELERY SOUP

450 g/1 lb celery
225 g/8 oz potatoes
50 g/2 oz (¼ cup) butter or margarine
1.2 litres/2 pints (5 cups) chicken stock or water and 1 chicken stock cube (2 bouillon cubes)
1 bouquet garni
salt and pepper
150 ml/¼ pint (⅔ cup) single (light) cream
TO GARNISH: chopped chervil or parsley

✽Cut the celery into 1.5 cm/½ inch pieces; peel the potatoes and cut into 2.5 cm/1 inch dice. Heat the butter or margarine in a large pan, toss the vegetables in this. Add the stock, or water and stock cube (bouillon cubes), the bouquet garni and seasoning. Simmer for 30 minutes.

Remove the herbs if desired, although these can be puréed with the other ingredients. Sieve, or purée the soup in a blender or food processor, return to the pan with the cream and heat. Top with the herbs. Serves 4 to 6.

Variations

✽Celery and Tomato Purée Use the recipe above but add 450 g/1 lb skinned and chopped tomatoes and use 900 ml/1½ pints (3¾ cups) stock only.

✽Potage Parmentier Peel and dice 550 g/1¼ lb (3⅓ cups) potatoes, slice 3 large leeks. Cook in 900 ml/1½ pints (3¾ cups) ham stock with a bouquet garni and pepper to taste. Simmer steadily for 30 to 40 minutes.

Sieve or purée the soup in a blender or food processor, return to the saucepan and heat then add 300 ml/½ pint (1¼ cups) milk and heat. Top with chopped watercress. No butter is used in this soup, but a small knob can be put into each portion. Serves 4 to 6.

Cream of Spinach Soup

450 g/1 lb spinach
1 medium onion
150 ml/¼ pint (⅔ cup) chicken stock or water
salt and pepper
FOR THE SAUCE: 40 g/1½ oz (3 tablespoons) butter or margarine
25 g/1 oz (¼ cup) flour
450 ml/¾ pint (2 cups) milk or milk and chicken stock, see method
2 teaspoons grated lemon rind
150 ml/¼ pint (⅔ cup) single (light) cream

✽Wash the spinach, remove any tough stalks; peel and finely chop the onion. Put into a saucepan with the stock or water, season lightly. Cook for 10 minutes or until tender. Meanwhile heat the butter or margarine in a second saucepan, stir in the flour, cook gently for 2 to 3 minutes, then blend in the milk or milk and stock. Stir as the sauce comes to the boil and thickens slightly, add the lemon rind.

Purée or sieve the vegetables in the liquid in which they were cooked. Add to the sauce with half the cream, stir well to blend, season to taste. Reheat and top with the rest of the cream. Serves 4. Note If too thick add extra milk.

Tomato and Cucumber Soup

1 medium onion
½ small cucumber
450 g/1 lb tomatoes
450 ml/¾ pint (2 cups) chicken stock
150 ml/¼ pint (⅔ cup) dry cider or white wine
1 bay leaf
2 to 3 basil or tarragon leaves
salt and pepper
TO GARNISH: 4 tablespoons soured cream
a little chopped parsley

✽Peel and chop the onion and cucumber. Skin and chop the tomatoes. Put all the ingredients into a saucepan, season to taste and cook for 15 to 20 minutes. Remove the herbs.

Sieve or purée the soup in a blender or food processor and serve hot or cold. Top with the cream and parsley just before serving. Serves 4 to 6.

Cheese and Potato Soup

3 medium potatoes
2 medium onions
50 g/2 oz (¼ cup) butter or margarine
900 ml/1½ pints (3¾ cups) chicken stock or water and 1 chicken stock cube (2 bouillon cubes)
1 teaspoon made mustard
150 ml/¼ pint (⅔ cup) single (light) cream or milk
100 g/4 oz (1 cup) grated Cheddar cheese
salt and pepper
TO GARNISH: 1 tablespoon chopped savory or parsley

✽Peel the potatoes and onions, cut into small neat dice. Heat the butter or margarine in a saucepan, add the vegetables and gently fry until pale golden in colour. Add the stock, or water and stock cube (bouillon cubes). Bring to boiling point, lower the heat and simmer for 10 to 15 minutes, or until the vegetables are softened, but unbroken. Add the mustard and cream or milk, heat for 2 to 3 minutes.

Stir the grated cheese into the hot soup, but do not cook after adding the cheese. Season to taste (it is always wise to season after adding cheese to a dish, for the amount of salt needed depends on the flavour of the cheese). Top with the savory or parsley. Serves 4.

VARIATIONS

✷✷Creamy Cheese and Potato Soup Proceed as above, but sieve or purée the soup in a blender or food processor before adding the cheese. Reheat and then add cheese and seasoning.

✷✷Speedy Cheese and Potato Soup Omit the fresh potatoes, proceed as above, using just the onions. When these are tender, blend in 3 tablespoons dehydrated potato powder. Continue as the recipe above.

Mussel and Basil Soup

1 small celery heart
4 medium onions
750 g/1½ lb tomatoes
4 tablespoons oil
1.8 litres/3 pints (7½ cups) water
50 g/2 oz (4 tablespoons) long-grain rice
salt and cayenne pepper
about 24 small fresh basil leaves
1.8 litres/3 pints (7½ cups) mussels

Cut the celery into small dice; use green parts of the stalks if possible but remove any tough pieces. Peel and dice the onions. Skin and halve the tomatoes, remove all seeds and dice the pulp. The vegetables should be cut into small and uniform-sized pieces.

Heat half the oil in a large saucepan, add half the onions and cook for 5 minutes or until the onions are pale golden in colour. Add half the celery and cook for a further minute, then pour in all the water, except about 150 ml/¼ pint (⅔ cup) and bring to the boil. Add the rice with a very little seasoning and cook for 5 minutes. Put in the tomatoes and basil. Cover the saucepan and continue to cook gently for 10 minutes or until the rice is tender. Turn the heat off until the next stage is completed.

Preparing the mussels While the rice is cooking, scrub the mussels and discard any that will not close when sharply tapped, (see page 00). Heat the remaining oil in a second saucepan and cook the rest of the onions and celery for 10 minutes. Add the rest of the liquid, the 150 ml/¼ pint (⅔ cup) water and the mussels. Heat briskly until the mussels open. Remove them from the saucepan with a perforated spoon and take them off the shells.

Add the mussels, onions, celery and the liquid from the second pan to the rice mixture. Heat the soup for a short time and add any seasoning required. Serves 4 to 8.

Note You can use canned mussels (discard the brine), or thawed frozen mussels in their shells instead of fresh.

Prawn Chowder

450 g/1 lb prawns (shrimp) weight in shells
900 ml/1½ pints (3¾ cups) water
1 bay leaf
1 sprig fennel or parsley
2 to 3 bacon rashers (slices)
1 small onion
2 large potatoes
50 g/2 oz (¼ cup) butter
150 ml/¼ pint (⅔ cup) single (light) cream or milk
salt and pepper
2 tablespoons chopped fennel leaves or parsley

✷✷Wash, then peel the prawns (shrimp). Put the shells into a pan with the water, bay leaf and fennel or parsley. Cover the pan and simmer for 10 minutes, then strain this fish stock.

De-rind and chop the bacon, peel and finely dice the onion. Peel and cut the potatoes into small dice, keep in cold water until ready to cook, so the flesh does not discolour. Heat the butter in a large saucepan, put in the bacon and onion and fry for 2 to 3 minutes.

Pour the fish stock into the pan, bring to the boil, drain the potatoes, add to the stock mixture and cook for 4 to 5 minutes or until the potatoes are soft, but unbroken. Add the prawns, cream or milk, seasoning to taste and the chopped herbs. Heat thoroughly but do not overcook. Serve with toast. Serves 4.

LEFTOVERS
Cream of Chicken Soup

✷✷*Remove all the meat from a chicken carcass. Simmer the bones with water to cover, 1 onion, 1 carrot and a bouquet garni.*

Either sieve or liquidize the small pieces of cooked chicken with the vegetables and stock or dice the chicken meat and add to the strained stock. Blend with a sauce, made as in the Cream of Spinach Soup, (see opposite).

The carcass of a turkey or carcasses of several game birds can be used in the same way.

Cheese and Potato Soup, Mussel and Basil Soup, and Prawn Chowder

Consommés and Cold Soups

Consommé Julienne

Comsommé is the name given to a clear soup based upon meat, poultry or game. It can also be made from fish or shellfish, but this is less usual.

A consommé is ideal to serve if the rest of the menu is very rich because it is full of flavour but lighter than most soups.

You need a good stock for consommé. Unfortunately stock made from bones alone rarely has enough flavour so you need to add uncooked meat of some kind (see suggestions below). A slow cooker or a pressure cooker is ideal to use when making stock (for cooking times see page 51).

Master Recipe
BEEF CONSOMMÉ

2.25 litres/4 pints (10 cups) beef stock, see page 51
1 kg/2¼ lb shin (fore shank) of beef
1 to 2 onions
1 to 2 carrots
1 to 2 bay leaves
dry sherry to taste

✳Dice the beef, place in a saucepan with the stock and remaining ingredients except the sherry and simmer uncovered for 1½ to 2 hours. Clarify (see below), season and add dry sherry to taste.

To clarify consommé A consommé must be well-clarified (cleared) before the flavouring and garnishes are added. The easiest method is to strain it through several thicknesses of muslin (cheesecloth) supported on a large sieve. If the soup is still not clear enough then return it to the saucepan. Add the crushed shells of several eggs plus 1 or 2 whisked egg whites. Simmer for 15 to 20 minutes then strain again. The shells and egg whites will have collected any tiny particles of food.

Variations

✳Veal Consommé is prepared as Beef Consommé but use a knuckle of veal plus 450 g/1 lb diced stewing veal and veal or chicken stock. Flavour with a little lemon juice and dry light sherry.

✳Poultry and Game Consommés Use the wings and backs of chicken, turkey or game birds (see there is plenty of uncooked flesh on these) plus 450 g/1 lb uncooked flesh. Proceed as Beef Consommé using chicken or game stock. Flavour with a dry Madeira wine or port wine.

✳Fish Consommé Simmer 675 g/1½ lb white fish with fish stock for 1 hour. Clarify and flavour with anchovy essence (extract), seasoning, lemon juice and dry white wine.

To Serve Consommé

Allow 200 to 300 ml/⅓ to ½ pint (1 cup) per person. Serve hot, topped with a garnish (see below).

✳Cold Consommé Chill the soup and serve topped with a little yogurt and lemon slices or with finely shredded cucumber and skinned and chopped tomato.

✳Iced Consommé Lightly freeze the consommé. Serve in chilled glasses. Garnish as for Cold Consommé.

Jellied Consommé Veal Consommé forms a natural jelly when chilled but other consommés require the addition of a little gelatine. Dissolve 2 teaspoons gelatine (unflavoured) in each 600 ml/1 pint (2½ cups) hot consommé. Allow to cool and set very lightly. Whisk and spoon into chilled soup cups. Top with chopped herbs and serve with wedges of lemon.

Simple Skill

Garnishes for Consommés Top the consommé with miniature profiteroles, (see page 152); with strips of cooked pancakes; thin slices of lemon or toasted flaked almonds.

✳Consommé de Gibier Top hot game consommé with finely diced cooked giblets.

✳Consommé Julienne Cut mixed vegetables into matchstick-sized pieces. Cook and add to the consommé.

✳Three-flavoured Consommé Mix equal amounts of beef, veal and chicken stocks. Top with chopped tarragon.

✳Consommé Madrilène Blend equal amounts of freshly made tomato juice or canned or bottled juice with the consommé. The classic recipe has a small amount of cooked noodles added. Top with chopped herbs. This can be served hot or cold.

✳Seafood Consommé Top fish consommé with tiny pieces of smoked salmon and chopped prawns (shrimp) or a little flaked crab.

Luxury Consommé

1 × 425 g/15 oz can consommé (bouillon)
150 ml/¼ pint (⅔ cup) double (heavy) cream
salt and pepper
2 tablespoons blanched chopped almonds
1 tablespoon chopped chives

Blend the consommé and cream, taste and add extra seasoning as required. Chill well. Spoon into soup cups and top with the almonds and chives just before serving. Serves 4.

VARIATIONS

Use about 600 ml/1 pint (2½ cups) home-made Consommé (see left).

Serve the soup hot instead of cold.

Special Technique
COLD SOUPS

Cold soups make a pleasing change. While they are particularly suitable for warm days, they are satisfying and full of flavour as well as being a refreshing start to a meal.

Always season the soup well, particularly if it contains a high percentage of cream, a chilled soup must not be bland.

Never make the soup too thick; creamy cold soups should pour like double (heavy) or whipping cream.

In recipes where the cream is added to a smooth cold purée you will find you produce an ultra smooth mixture if you do this in a blender or food processor.

Chill individual soup cups or bowls before serving the soup. Small soup cups look interesting if the rim is first dipped in a little whisked egg white or water, and then into finely chopped parsley.

Cucumber and Prawn Soup

| 1 large cucumber |
| 2 tablespoons finely chopped mint |
| 300 ml/½ pint (1¼ cups) chicken stock |
| 300 ml/½ pint (1¼ cups) single (light) cream |
| 300 ml/½ pint (1¼ cups) yogurt |
| 100 g/4 oz (⅔ cup) peeled prawns (shrimp) |
| squeeze lemon juice |
| salt and pepper |

Cut a few wafer thin slices of cucumber for topping the soup. Peel the remainder of the cucumber and finely dice or grate the cucumber pulp. Mix this with all the other ingredients. Chill well. Serve topped with cucumber slices. Serves 4 to 6.

Cucumber and Yogurt Soup

| 150 ml/¼ pint (⅔ cup) milk |
| 600 ml/1 pint (2½ cups) yogurt |
| ½ medium cucumber |
| 2 tablespoons chopped chives |
| 1 teaspoon chopped mint |
| 1 tablespoon chopped parsley |
| salt and pepper |

Combine the milk and yogurt in a blender or food processor. Or beat well to make a smooth liquid. Peel and finely dice the cucumber. Add the cucumber and herbs to the yogurt and milk. Season well and chill. Serve in well-chilled soup cups with crisp melba toast or water biscuits (crackers). Serves 4 to 6.

Avocado Soup

| 1 tablespoon lemon juice |
| 2 ripe avocados |
| 1 tablespoon finely chopped parsley |
| 1 tablespoon finely chopped chives |
| 450 ml/¾ pint (2 cups) chicken stock |
| 300 ml/½ pint (1¼ cups) single (light) cream |
| salt and pepper |
| a few drops Worcestershire sauce |
| **TO GARNISH:** chopped chives or spring onions (scallions) |
| 4 tablespoons double (heavy) cream |

Put the lemon juice into a bowl. Halve and peel the avocados, discard the stones. Put the avocado pulp into the bowl with the lemon juice, mash carefully until smooth, then blend in the herbs. Add the stock gradually, beating until well blended with the purée, then add the cream. Season to taste and flavour with the Worcestershire sauce. Cover the bowl to keep the soup a good colour and serve within 1 to 2 hours. Garnish with the chives or spring onions (scallions) and cream. Serves 4 to 6.

Note This soup can be made using a blender or food processor. Always put the lemon juice into the goblet or bowl before adding the avocado pulp so the fruit will not discolour.

VARIATION

Yogurt and Avocado Soup Blend the lemon juice, avocado pulp, herbs and only 300 ml/½ pint (1¼ cups) chicken stock, then add 450 ml/¾ pint (2 cups) yogurt and seasoning to taste. Garnish with finely diced red pepper.

Courgette Cream Soup

| 1 medium onion |
| 350 g/12 oz courgettes (zucchini) |
| 450 ml/¾ pint (2 cups) chicken stock |
| 1 sprig parsley |
| salt and pepper |
| 300 ml/½ pint (1¼ cups) double (heavy) cream |
| **TO GARNISH:** 4 tablespoons chopped chives |
| paprika |

Peel and chop or slice the onion and courgettes (zucchini). Put into a saucepan with the stock and parsley. Bring to the boil, season to taste. Lower the heat and cook steadily for 10 minutes only. Remove parsley if desired, and then sieve or purée the soup in a blender or food processor.

Allow to cool then blend in most of the cream, together with any extra seasoning required. This can be done in the blender or food processor (see Special Technique). Chill well. Whip the remaining cream. Spoon the soup into bowls. Top with whipped cream, the chopped chives and a sprinkling of paprika. Serves 4 to 6.

LEFTOVERS
Reduce leftover soup by simmering it until it thickens, or blend 1 teaspoon cornflour (cornstarch) with each 300 ml/½ pint (1¼ cups) soup and stir over a low heat until thickened.
Use as a sauce to serve over pancakes or omelettes.

Cucumber and Yogurt Soup

International Soups

Vichyssoise

8 medium leeks
2 medium old potatoes
50 g/2 oz (¼ cup) butter
750 ml/1¼ pints (3 cups) chicken stock
salt and pepper
150 ml/¼ pint (⅔ cup) white wine
150 ml/¼ pint (⅔ cup) double (heavy) or whipping cream
TO GARNISH: 2 tablespoons chopped chives

SIMPLE SKILL
Garnishing Soups
Yogurt, soured cream
and ordinary cream are
ideal garnishes for most
soups, particularly dark
soups where they add a
contrasting colour.

Sprinkle a little
paprika or chopped
parsley over the yogurt or
cream if liked.

Grated cheese adds
food value to vegetable
soups or you can make
tiny balls of cream cheese
and float these on the
soup just before serving.

Chopped nuts,
especially almonds, are
another interesting
garnish.

Avgolemono

⁘Wash and chop the leeks, including some of the green tops. Peel and dice the potatoes. Heat the butter in a large saucepan. Add the leeks and potatoes and turn in the butter for several minutes; do not allow to brown. Pour in the chicken stock and add a little salt and pepper to taste. Simmer the mixture gently for 20 to 25 minutes until the vegetables are tender; do not overcook as this will darken the soup. Allow to cool.

Sieve or purée the ingredients in a blender or food processor with the wine and cream to give a velvet-like soup. Chill the soup well and top with the chives. Serves 4 to 6.

VARIATIONS

⁘Crab Vichyssoise Use fish stock rather than chicken stock if possible. Proceed as in the recipe above. When the mixture is cold, sieve or purée in a blender with 100 to 175 g/4 to 6 oz (½ to ⅔ cup) white crabmeat. Add a few drops anchovy essence to give a good flavour and colour, but be sparing with the salt.

⁘Green Pea Vichyssoise Use only 6 leeks and 1 potato in the recipe above; add 100 g/4 oz (¾ cup) shelled peas half way through the cooking period, together with a small sprig of mint. Remove the mint before sieving or blending the soup.

Avgolemono

1.2 litres/2 pints (5 cups) chicken stock
2 teaspoons finely grated lemon rind
1 sprig each parsley and thyme
50 g/2 oz (¼ cup) long-grain rice
salt and pepper
2 eggs
2 tablespoons lemon juice
TO GARNISH: lemon slices

Pour the stock into a saucepan, add the lemon rind and herbs. Bring to the boil, add the rice and a little seasoning. Reduce heat and simmer for 20 minutes, or until the rice is tender.

Beat the eggs and lemon juice together in a bowl, whisk on a little hot, but not boiling, stock from the saucepan. Pour the egg mixture into the hot soup; simmer gently until the soup thickens, do not allow to boil as the eggs may curdle. Add any extra seasoning required, remove the sprigs of herbs and serve at once topped with lemon slices. Serves 4.

Biersuppe
[Beer Soup]

50 g/2 oz (¼ cup) butter
40 g/1½ oz (5 tablespoons) flour
1.2 litres/2 pints (5 cups) lager (light beer)
1 teaspoon grated lemon rind
1 tablespoon lemon juice
salt and pepper
2 eggs
½ to 1 teaspoon ground cinnamon
sugar to taste
TO GARNISH: chopped parsley

Heat the butter in a saucepan, stir in the flour. Cook gently for several minutes, stirring all the time, until the flour

becomes golden-brown in colour. Do not allow it to become too dark.

Gradually blend in nearly all the lager; bring the liquid to the boil and stir until thickened. Add the lemon rind and juice then allow the soup to simmer very gently for 10 minutes. Season lightly. Beat the eggs with the remaining cold lager then gradually whisk a little of the hot soup into the egg mixture.

Take the saucepan off the heat so the soup is no longer boiling. Whisk the egg mixture into the soup. Return the pan to a very low heat and whisk as the soup simmers for 3 to 4 minutes.

Add the cinnamon, a little sugar and any extra seasoning required. Top with parsley. Serves 4 to 6.

Soto Ajam
[Indonesian Chicken Soup]

1.5 litres/2½ pints (6 cups) Chicken Consommé, see page 32
2 medium onions
2 garlic cloves
2 tablespoons oil
1 teaspoon ground ginger
2 eggs
2 small cooked potatoes
2 small cooked carrots
2 small cooked leeks
salt and pepper
1 tablespoon lemon juice

The Chicken Consommé should be strained, (see the recipe on page 32), but it is not essential to clarify it with egg whites.

Peel and neatly dice the onions. Peel and finely chop the garlic. Heat 1 tablespoon oil in a saucepan, fry the onions and garlic until nearly soft. Add the consommé with the ground ginger and simmer for 30 minutes. Meanwhile hard-boil, shell and slice the eggs.

Dice the cooked vegetables very neatly. Heat the remaining oil and fry the vegetables for several minutes. Divide between the heated soup cups or plates. Add seasoning and lemon juice to the consommé. Spoon over the vegetables. Finally add the slices of hard-boiled egg. Serves 6.

Brøtsuppe
[Bread Soup]

2 onions
2 carrots
1 small leek
1.8 litres/3 pints (7½ cups) canned or home-made Veal or Chicken Consommé, see page 32
salt and pepper
2 teaspoons chopped mixed herbs or 1 teaspoon dried mixed herbs

1 tablespoon chopped parsley
150 ml/¼ pint (⅔ cup) white wine
2 to 3 soft rolls
40 g/1½ oz (3 tablespoons) butter
50 to 75 g/2 to 3 oz (½ to ¾ cup) grated Cheddar or other hard cheese
1 teaspoon paprika

Peel and roughly chop the onions and carrots; slice the leek. Put the consommé and the vegetables into a saucepan. Simmer for 30 minutes. Lift the lid towards the end of this time so the liquid is reduced to 1.2 litres/2 pints (5 cups). Strain the soup, discard the vegetables.

Return the soup to the saucepan add the seasoning, herbs and wine. Bring just to boiling point, do not boil for any length of time.

Split the rolls and spread with the butter. Press the grated cheese on top of the buttered rolls, then cut into neat strips. Pour the soup into a large flameproof soup tureen or into 4 to 6 individual dishes. Place the rolls, with the cheese side uppermost in the soup.

Heat for 2 to 3 minutes under a preheated grill (broiler), set to a moderate heat. Top with paprika. Serves 4 to 6.

Yugoslavian Spinach Soup

450 g/1 lb spinach
1 medium onion
1 tablespoon oil
2 tablespoons ground almonds
100 g/4 oz (½ cup) long-grain rice
1 litre/1¾ pints (4¼ cups) chicken stock
salt and pepper
1 to 2 tablespoons chopped dill
300 ml/½ pint (1¼ cups) yogurt
2 to 3 slices of bread
75 g/3 oz (3 tablespoons) Feta or cottage cheese

Wash the spinach and discard any tough stalks; coarsely shred the leaves. Peel and finely chop the onion. Heat the oil in a large saucepan, fry the onion until nearly tender, then add the ground almonds and heat until a delicate brown colour. Stir in the rice and blend with the onion and almonds. Pour in the stock, bring to the boil then add the spinach. Simmer steadily for 15 to 20 minutes, or until the rice is tender. Add seasoning, the dill and half the yogurt. Heat gently.

Meanwhile, toast the bread, cut into triangles and top with the cheese. Spoon the soup into individual soup cups and top with the remaining yogurt; serve with the cheese-topped toast. Serves 4 to 6.

Note You can vary the cheese. In Yugoslavia you would be served sheep's

cheese. If using frozen leaf or chopped spinach, allow 350 g/12 oz only. This does not need as much cooking as fresh spinach so add after cooking the rice for about 10 minutes.

Chinese Watermelon Soup

This is a colourful and unusual soup. The chicken mixture is prepared and put into the melon which is then steamed.

25 g/1 oz dried mushrooms
150 ml/¼ pint (⅔ cup) boiling water
175 g/6 oz chicken
175 g/6 oz lean pork
600 ml/1 pint (2½ cups) chicken stock (broth)
salt and pepper
100 g/4 oz canned bamboo shoots
100 g/4 oz lean ham
100 g/4 oz (¾ cup) shelled or frozen peas
1.75 kg/4 lb watermelon

Cut the mushrooms into small pieces, cover with the boiling water and leave for 1 hour. Mince or finely chop the chicken and pork. Put the stock into a saucepan; add the chicken and pork with a very little seasoning. Simmer for just 10 minutes.

Cut the bamboo shoots into thin shreds, mince or finely chop the ham, drain the mushrooms, add to the chicken mixture with the peas.

Cut a slice from the top of the melon; scoop out the seeds and sufficient pulp to accommodate the chicken mixture. Pour this into the melon, replace the slice. Stand the filled melon in a basin, put into a steamer over a saucepan of boiling water. Steam for 1½ hours.

To serve the soup put the melon on a flat dish on the table, scoop out the soup plus the melon pulp. Serves 6.

VARIATION

Cold Watermelon Soup In this case prepare the chicken mixture, then allow it to become very cold.

Remove the seeds and pulp from the watermelon as above then add the cold soup. Do not cook the melon.

CROÛTONS

These are the ideal garnish for soups.

Fried Croûtons

✳✳ *Cut the bread into small dice and fry in hot oil or butter. Drain on absorbent kitchen paper. The fried bread can be frozen on flat trays then packed into containers. Reheat from frozen on a flat tray in the oven.*

Garlic Croûtons

✳✳ *Toss the hot croûtons in a little garlic salt or add crushed garlic to the butter in which the bread is fried.*

Baked Croûtons

✳✳ *Brush the diced bread with melted butter, put on baking trays and bake for about 1 hour in a cool oven (140°C/ 275°F, Gas Mark 1).*

Cheese Croûtons

✳✳ *Brush the diced bread with melted butter, roll in grated Parmesan cheese and bake as above.*

Yugoslavian Spinach Soup

FISH DISHES

Fish is one of the most delicious and easily digested foods. There is such a wide range available that you can create an almost endless variety of dishes.

Most fish can be cooked by the basic methods outlined in this chapter. Whichever method of cooking you choose take care not to overcook the fish or both the texture and the flavour will be spoilt. Serve fish as soon as possible after cooking.

Buying Points

Fish is a very perishable food, so take great care when buying, and store it with equal care. Cook as soon as possible after purchase.

Be adventurous in your choice of fish; sometimes a less popular variety is more suitable and cheaper than your first choice. If you live near the coast look for 'locally caught fish', nothing can equal the taste of really fresh caught fish.

When shopping look for fish that is firm, has clear bright skin or scales and bright eyes. Shellfish should have firm shells and if you handle lobster or prawns (shrimp), pull the tails gently; they should spring back if the fish is really fresh. Always avoid fish which smells of ammonia; this indicates that the fish is stale.

Allow 175 g/6 oz fish (without bones); 2 small or 1 large fillet; or 1 medium fish per person.

Here is a list of fish that is readily available:

White Fish
Less expensive coley, huss, monkfish, whiting.
Medium priced bass, brill, cod, dab, haddock, hake, skate, sea bream.
Luxury fish halibut, turbot.

Oily Fish
Less expensive herring, mackerel, sprats.
Medium priced mullet, fresh sardines, whitebait, farmed salmon.
Luxury fish wild salmon.

Shellfish
Less expensive cockles, mussels, whelks, winkles.
Medium priced clams, crab, medium-sized prawns (shrimp), scallops, shrimps.
Luxury fish crawfish (langouste), fresh-water crayfish, langoustines – like baby lobster or giant prawns (jumbo shrimp), lobster, oysters.

Freshwater Fish
Inexpensive eel.
Medium priced bream, carp (use just for slow baking), perch, trout (farmed trout has become reasonable).
Luxury fish smelt.

Preparation

Cut off the heads, if desired. Slit the fish along the stomach and remove and discard the intestines. The roes can be saved (see pages 23 and 187). Wash and dry the fish.

To bone and fillet round fish Slit the fish along the stomach. Turn over, so the cut side is on a board and run your thumb firmly down the back, so loosening the back bone. Turn the fish over again and you will find the back bone comes away. Any tiny bones can be pulled away with the fingers or a pair of eyebrow tweezers. Cut into two fillets.

To bone and fillet flat fish Make a slit down the centre of the fish, then around the edge of the fish. Insert the tip of the knife at the tail and gently cut the fish away from the bone. Lift the fish with your free hand as you cut. Do this on the upper side, making two fillets. Turn the fish over and repeat on the under side. A little salt on the blade of the knife helps.

To skin fish Use a very sharp knife, as for filleting. Make a little slit at the tip of one fillet, then work carefully to loosen the flesh away from the skin; a little salt on the knife and on your hands helps you to get better grip on the fish.

Basic Cooking Methods

Baking Put the fish into a well-greased dish, top with a little butter of margarine, a small amount of milk plus butter or margarine, or a sauce, and bake in a moderately hot oven (190°C/375°F, Gas Mark 5) or as given in the recipe. The time depends upon the thickness of the fish and the other ingredients used.

Frying This can be done in shallow or deep fat. The fish can be coated or uncoated.

Grilling (Broiling) This preserves a lot of the natural flavour of the fish. Keep it well basted with oil or fat and always preheat the grill (broiler) before cooking (see page 41).

Poaching Often the term used is 'boiling' and this is a mistake as the liquid in which the fish is cooked should just simmer gently (see the Sole recipes on page 40 and Smoked Haddock Cream page 43).

Steaming The fish is cooked over boiling liquid or it is wrapped in foil and cooked in its own juice (see page 42).

To test if fish is cooked White fish should lose its transparent look and become opaque. The flesh should just come away from the bones, but should not break into pieces.

Cooking Times for Fish

Cooking times are given in individual recipes. As a general guide however these are the approximate timings for various cuts of fish, although these will vary slightly according to the type of fish, as well as the thickness of the portions.

Fillets Allow 4 to 6 minutes if frying in shallow fat, 3 to 4 minutes in deep fat and 7 to 10 minutes under the grill (broiler).

If poaching or steaming, allow 7 to 10 minutes.

Steaks (thick slices) or whole fish Allow 10 minutes if frying in shallow fat or 6 to 7 minutes in deep fat and 10 to 12 minutes to grill (broil).

If poaching or steaming, allow 10 to 12 minutes or 7 to 10 minutes (depending on the type of fish) per 450 g/1 lb.

Microwave Cooking

Fish tends to keep more of its flavour when cooked in a microwave cooker.

Never deep or shallow fry fish, or indeed any other foods in a microwave cooker. However Fish in Black Butter (see page 39) can be cooked in the microwave cooker but take care not to overbrown the butter and use the correct cooking utensil.

Fish varies in thickness and you must take this into account when using a microwave cooker. Either fold the thin tail portion of the fish fillet underneath the middle part to give even thickness throughout the fillet, or cover the thinner portion with a little foil when cooking begins; remove this after 1 to 2 minutes. The foil prevents the heat reaching the thin portions; you must, however, check that foil can be used in your model of microwave cooker.

Frozen fish rarely needs to be thawed before cooking in a microwave cooker.

Freezing note

Uncooked fish freezes very successfully.

The cooked dishes marked with the freezing symbol (✳) can be frozen without any fear of losing either flavour or texture. You may be surprised to find there are relatively few marked; this is because so many fish dishes are spoiled by being reheated after freezing. Fish, on the whole, is better served as soon as possible after cooking.

Top right: Salmon Walewska, page 41
Bottom right: Sweet and Sour Mackerel, page 41

White Fish

Although specific fish are mentioned in most of these recipes you can substitute another fish of the same type, i.e. choose whiting instead of plaice or cod instead of hake.

LEFTOVERS
Do not waste bacon rinds. Fry them until very crisp, break into small pieces and serve as a cocktail snack or a soup topping. Reserve the bacon fat for future use.

Often a recipe needs canned pineapple rings, but not the syrup from the can. Use the syrup as the liquid in a fresh fruit salad or as part of the liquid in a fruit jelly.

Fish in Black Butter

Made in Minutes

Baked Cod and Bacon Take 4 portions of frozen cod and 4 long rashers (slices) of streaky bacon. Wrap the bacon around the fish to cover it. Slice 4 large tomatoes and place in an oblong casserole with a little chopped parsley and chopped chives. Season lightly. Arrange the bacon-wrapped fish over the tomatoes. Melt 25 g/1 oz (2 tablespoons) butter or margarine, spoon over the top. Bake uncovered for 25 to 30 minutes in the centre of a preheated moderately hot oven (190°C/375°F, Gas Mark 5). Serves 4.

Whiting with Cheese Cream Split and bone 4 whiting (see page 36). Brush the cut surface with melted butter or margarine. Do not fold the fish over again. Season lightly.

Place under a preheated grill (broiler) and cook for about 6 minutes then spread each fish with 2 tablespoons whipped cream and 1 tablespoon of finely grated cheese. Cook for a further 1 to 2 minutes. Garnish with parsley or fennel leaves. Serves 4.

Curried Plaice

4 large or 8 small plaice fillets
2 medium onions
2 garlic cloves
2 tablespoons oil
2 tablespoons tomato purée (paste)
1 to 2 teaspoons mild curry powder
300 ml/½ pint (1¼ cups) dry white wine
salt and pepper
TO GARNISH: 1 lemon
green olives

✱✱If using frozen fish, allow it to thaw. Dry well. Peel the onions and garlic and chop very finely. Heat the oil in a large frying pan (skillet), add the onions and garlic and fry gently for 4 to 5 minutes; do not allow to colour. Blend in the tomato purée (paste), curry powder, wine and a very little seasoning.

Put the fish into the wine mixture and cook for 8 minutes. Spoon the mixture over the fish during cooking, so it becomes coated with the colourful mixture. Spoon on to a hot serving dish. Cut the lemon into 4 thick wedges, place on the dish and top the fish with the olives.

Serve with cooked rice, pasta or tiny new potatoes and a tossed green salad. Serves 4.

VARIATION
Devilled Plaice Use only ½ teaspoon curry powder and add 2 teaspoons Worcestershire sauce and a few drops Tabasco (hot pepper) sauce to the tomato mixture.

Roquefort Plaice

50 g/2 oz (¼ cup) butter
4 small plaice
salt and pepper
150 ml/¼ pint (⅔ cup) soured cream
75 g/3 oz (½ cup) diced Roquefort cheese
TO GARNISH 4 lemon slices
parsley

Melt the butter. Cut 4 squares of foil sufficiently large to envelop the fish. Use half the butter to coat the middle of each square of foil. Put the plaice on the foil and season lightly.

Blend the cream and cheese, spread on top of the fish and spoon the remaining melted butter over the cheese top-

ping. Fold the foil to cover the fish lightly (do not press down on the topping). Lift the foil parcels on to a flat baking tray. Bake for 30 to 35 minutes just above the centre of a preheated moderately hot oven (200°C/400°F, Gas Mark 6). Unwrap the foil carefully (steam builds up inside the package). Lift the fish on to heated serving plates, pour any butter in the foil over the fish. Garnish with lemon and sprigs of parsley. Serves 4.

Fish in Black Butter

4 portions of white fish (skate, plaice, flounder or sole are ideal) or 4 trout
salt and pepper
100 g/4 oz (½ cup) butter
1 to 2 tablespoons lemon juice or white wine vinegar
2 teaspoons capers
1 to 2 tablespoons chopped parsley

In this particular dish it is essential that frozen fish be completely thawed out and well dried. Leave the heads on trout, but split and remove the intestines. Season the fish. Heat half the butter in a large frying pan (skillet) and cook the fish until just tender, see Cooking Times for Fish (page 37). Lift the fish on to a heated dish and keep hot. Put the remaining butter into the pan, heat until it turns a pleasant dark brown (the title of this dish is not accurate – the butter should never become black). Add the lemon juice or vinegar, capers and parsley. Heat for 1 to 2 minutes then spoon over the fish. Serves 4.

Special Technique
HEATING BUTTER TO FLAVOUR FOOD

The recipe above is a classic one. Brains and sweetbreads can be served in the same way (see pages 72 and 189).

The butter develops a deliciously nutty taste. Take care it does not burn; see the recipe above.

Quite often a mixture of oil and butter is used for frying food. The oil helps to prevent the butter overheating, but the food still absorbs the good flavour of butter.

Pineapple Plaice

4 large plaice fillets
8 back bacon rashers (Canadian bacon slices)
2 canned pineapple rings (slices)
50 g/2 oz (¼ cup) butter
salt and pepper
TO GARNISH: 2 to 3 pineapple rings (slices)
1 lemon

Wash and dry the fillets. Remove the bacon rinds and stretch each bacon rasher (slice) with a knife, then cut in half. Cut the 2 pineapple rings into quarters. Roll two bits of bacon around each piece of pineapple to make 8 rolls. Secure with wooden cocktail sticks.

Arrange the fillets on the grid of the grill (broiler) pan and top each fillet with a knob of butter – use 25 g/1 oz (2 tablespoons). Lightly season. Place the bacon rolls beside the fish fillets. Cook under a preheated grill (broiler) for 3 to 4 minutes.

Turn the fish, top with the remaining butter and turn the bacon rolls. Continue cooking for a further 4 to 5 minutes, or until the fish is tender and the bacon crisp.

Chop the remaining pineapple rings into small pieces and cut the lemon into 4 rings. Top each fillet with a lemon ring, chopped pineapple and 2 bacon rolls. This is excellent served with the Bacon and Pepper Râgout (see page 188). Serves 4.

Skate with Courgettes

½ tablespoon oil
4 skate wings
1 to 2 tablespoons lemon juice
salt and pepper
FOR THE TOPPING: 4 courgettes (zucchini)
1 onion
1 × 50 g/2 oz can anchovy fillets
75 g/3 oz (6 tablespoons) butter
1 tablespoon capers
TO GARNISH: lemon slices

Put a large sheet of foil on a flat baking sheet or in a roasting pan. Brush with half the oil. Wash the skate wings and lay them side by side on the foil. Sprinkle the fish with the lemon juice and season to taste. Brush a second sheet of foil with the remaining oil and place over the fish. Press the edges of the two sheets of foil together to seal in the fish. Bake in the centre of a preheated moderately hot oven (200°C/400°F, Gas Mark 6) for 20 to 25 minutes.

Topping Meanwhile wash the courgettes (zucchini) and remove the tough ends, but do not peel. Cut into thick matchstick pieces. Peel and thinly slice the onion, drain and chop the anchovies. Heat the butter in a frying pan (skillet), cook the onions until soft then add the courgettes (zucchini) and continue cooking for 5 minutes. Turn the courgettes (zucchini) once or twice; they should retain a fairly firm texture when cooked. Add the chopped anchovies, the capers and a shake of pepper and heat for 1 to 2 minutes.

Arrange the skate on a heated dish, pour any juices left from baking over the fish then spoon the courgette (zucchini) mixture on top. Garnish with lemon. Serves 4.

Skate with Courgettes

LEFTOVERS
Leftover white fish makes delicious fish balls, based on a Chinese recipe.
Crispy Fish Balls
Blend about 225 g/8 oz (2 cups) cooked and finely flaked fish with 15 g/½ oz (2 tablespoons) flour and salt and pepper to taste. Form into balls, each about the size of a large hazelnut.

Blend 75 g/3 oz (¾ cup) self-raising or plain (all-purpose) flour with ¾ teaspoon baking powder, a pinch of salt, 1 egg, 2 teaspoons oil with 150 ml/¼ pint (⅔ cup) water.

Dip the small fish balls into the batter. Fry in hot oil for 3 to 4 minutes. Drain and serve with the sauce on page 47.

39

Sole Normandie

Sole Normandie

2 medium sole
600 ml/1 pint (2½ cup) mussels
150 ml/¼ pint (⅔ cup) water
150 ml/¼ pint (⅔ cup) white wine
1 bouquet garni
salt and pepper
225 g/8 oz (1⅓ cups) prawns (shrimp), weight in shells
4 oysters (optional)
1 small onion or shallot
100 g/4 oz (1 cup) button mushrooms
75 g/3 oz (6 tablespoons) butter
40 g/1½ oz (6 tablespoons) flour
150 ml/¼ pint (⅔ cup) milk
150 ml/¼ pint (⅔ cup) double (heavy) cream
TO GARNISH: 1 tablespoon chopped parsley

Fillet the sole and skin each fillet (see page 36); retain the skins. Prepare the mussels carefully (see page 44).

Put the mussels into a large saucepan with the water, wine, bouquet garni and a little seasoning. Heat for 5 to 6 minutes or until the shells open. Do not attempt to open any shells that have remained closed during the heating process. These mussels must be discarded. Remove the mussels from the pan, but retain the liquid.

Peel the prawns (shrimp) and reserve. Add the prawn (shrimp) shells, the skins of the sole and any liquid from the oyster shells to the mussel liquid. Chop the onion or shallot and put this into the mussel liquid. Cover the pan and simmer the liquid gently for 15 minutes then strain and return to the saucepan.

Fold the fillets of sole in half so they fit into the pan; add to the liquid. Cover the pan and simmer gently for 8 to 10 minutes or until the sole is tender. Lift the fillets from the pan with a fish slice or perforated spoon so they drain well. Arrange on one heated dish or in individual heated containers.

Sauce While the fish is cooking, fry the mushrooms and make the sauce. Wipe the mushrooms and slice if rather large. Heat half the butter in a pan and fry the mushrooms until tender. Heat the remaining butter in a saucepan, stir in the flour, cook over a low heat for a few minutes, then gradually blend in the milk and cream and strain the wine liquid from the saucepan – by this time it will have been reduced to just over 150 ml/¼ pint (⅔ cup). Stir as the sauce comes to the boil and thickens, taste and add more seasoning if required. Add the mussels, oysters (if used) and prawns (shrimp) and heat for 2 to 3 minutes only. Finally add the cooked mushrooms. Spoon over the sole and serve sprinkled with parsley. Serves 4.

For Special Occasions

Here are two fish dishes with a touch of luxury. Sole is given as the fish in each case, but turbot, halibut or fresh salmon would make an excellent alternative.

Sole with Prawn Sauce

2 sole
150 ml/¼ pint (⅔ cup) dry white wine
600 ml/1 pint (2½ cups) water
1 leek
2 carrots, peeled
1 small onion, peeled
a sprig of thyme
1 bay leaf
salt and pepper
FOR THE CUCUMBER RICE: 225 g/8 oz (1 cup) long-grain rice
450 ml/¾ pint (generous measure) (2 cups) water
1 small or ½ large cucumber
1 onion
50 g/2 oz (¼ cup) butter
2 tablespoons chopped parsley
FOR THE HOLLANDAISE SAUCE: 3 egg yolks
1 tablespoon white wine vinegar
1 tablespoon lemon juice
100 to 175 g/4 to 6 oz (½ to ¾ cup) butter
100 g/4 oz (⅔ cup) large peeled prawns (shelled shrimp)

FOR EASE
Prepare Ahead
Try not to leave preparations to the last minute when entertaining.

When making Sole Normandie the mussels can be prepared in advance, the sauce and stock made and the mushrooms fried so the dish is ready to be assembled once the fish is cooked.

For Sole with Prawn Sauce make the Court Bouillon and prepare the herbs and the cucumber in advance but keep well covered.

The Hollandaise Sauce can be made in advance and frozen (see page 105).

Cut the sole into 8 skinned fillets, or ask the fishmonger to do this. Set the fillets aside.

Court Bouillon Place the sole skin and bones into a pan with the wine and water. Slice the leek and the carrots but leave the onion whole. Add the vegetables and herbs to the liquid in the saucepan, season well and simmer for 20 to 30 minutes. Strain the liquid and return it to a pan. Keep it warm.

Cucumber Rice Put the rice, water and seasoning into a saucepan, bring the water to the boil, stir briskly with a fork; lower the heat, cover and simmer for 15 minutes. Peel the cucumber, cut in balls with a vegetable scoop. Peel and finely chop the onion. Heat the 50 g/2 oz (¼ cup) butter in a saucepan, add the onion and cook gently until tender; add the cucumber balls, turn in the onion and butter mixture and heat for 1 to 2 minutes. Mix the hot rice, cucumber balls and onion together; arrange on a heated serving dish. Top with the parsley. Cover the rice with foil and keep hot while cooking the fish and making the sauce.

Sauce Put the egg yolks, vinegar and lemon juice with a little seasoning into a basin. Stand over a pan of hot, but not boiling water. Whisk briskly until the egg mixture is thick and creamy. Gradually add the butter. Add the prawns to the hot sauce.

Roll the sole fillets and place in the Court Bouillon. Simmer for 6 to 7 minutes. Lift the cooked fish fillets from the Court Bouillon on to the rice. Coat with the sauce and prawns. Serves 4.

Oily Fish

The fish in this group are full of good flavour and important vitamins too. They range from the 'humble', but delicious herring to luxurious salmon. You may be offered two kinds of salmon, farmed and wild. Salmon farms enable us to buy salmon all the year round at a moderate price.

Lemon Sardines

about 20 fresh sardines
75 g/3 oz (6 tablespoons) butter
salt and pepper
1 large lemon
1 tablespoon chopped parsley or fennel leaves

Cut the heads off the fish, clean and dry well. Melt the butter and add seasoning. Brush 25 g/1 oz (2 tablespoons) of the butter over the fish then cook them under a preheated grill (broiler) for about 6 minutes. Meanwhile halve the lemon, take out all the pulp, chop this finely and mix with the remaining hot butter and chopped parsley or fennel leaves. Spoon over the fish just before serving. Serves 4.

Sweet and Sour Mackerel

4 mackerel
FOR THE MARINADE: 1 small onion
1 medium carrot
2 tablespoons white wine vinegar or lemon juice
2 tablespoons brown sugar
1 tablespoon soy sauce
1 tablespoon oil
salt and pepper
TO GARNISH: 25 g/1 oz (¼ cup) blanched almonds
1 lemon

Remove the heads and intestines from the mackerel and clean them well. Peel the onion and carrot and grate coarsely. Mix the vegetables with the other ingredients for the marinade and pour into a large dish. Place the mackerel in the mixture and leave for 1 hour, turning once or twice.

Lift the fish from the marinade; save this. Put the mackerel into an ovenproof dish and bake, uncovered, in the centre of a moderately hot oven (190°C/375°F, Gas Mark 5) for 10 minutes. Pour the marinade over the fish, cover the dish and bake for a further 20 minutes. The vegetables should retain a slightly firm texture. Cut the almonds into shreds and sprinkle over the fish just before serving. Slice the lemon and arrange round the fish. Serves 4.

Salmon Walewska

25 g/1 oz (2 tablespoons) butter
4 salmon cutlets
½ tablespoon lemon juice
salt and pepper
1 small lobster
FOR THE HOLLANDAISE SAUCE: 3 egg yolks
1 tablespoon lemon juice
75 g/3 oz (6 tablespoons) butter
TO GARNISH: 1 lemon
cucumber

Melt the 25 g/1 oz (2 tablespoons) butter, spread the salmon with this and sprinkle with the ½ tablespoon lemon juice; season lightly. Put into a shallow casserole, cover with foil and bake in the centre of a moderate to moderately hot oven (180 to 190°C/350 to 375°F, Gas Mark 4 to 5) for 20 to 25 minutes or until just tender; do *not* overcook.

Meanwhile split the lobster and crack the large claws (see page 47). Dice the flesh neatly. Put the small claws on one side for garnish.

Sauce Put the egg yolks, a little seasoning and the tablespoon of lemon juice into a bowl over a pan of hot, but not boiling water and whisk until thick. Gradually whisk in the butter and then add the diced pieces of lobster. Keep warm but do not overheat otherwise the sauce will curdle. Slice the lemon and cucumber and arrange round the edge of a hot serving dish. Lift the portions of salmon from the casserole and put into the middle of the serving dish, top with the sauce and garnish with the small lobster claws. Serves 4.

Spiced Herrings

2 medium onions
4 large herrings with soft roes
salt and pepper
1 to 2 tablespoons mixed pickling spice
450 ml/¾ pint (2 cups) dry cider

Peel and finely chop the onions. Split the herrings open and clean; put the roes into a basin and mix with a quarter of the onions and a little seasoning. Wash and dry the herrings, fill with the mashed roes. Place into a baking dish.

Top with the remaining onion, the pickling spice, cider and seasoning. Cover and bake in the centre of a preheated moderate oven (160°C/325°F, Gas Mark 3) for 1¼ hours. Allow the fish to cool in the cooking liquid. Serve cold with a salad. Serves 4.

Note Makes of pickling spice vary in strength. The finer the pieces the stronger the taste.

SOURED CREAM
Commercially soured cream gives a piquant flavour to sweet and savoury dishes. When you have no soured cream use 150 ml/¼ pint (⅔ cup) fresh cream, preferably whipping cream plus ½ to 1 tablespoon of fresh lemon juice.

Spiced Herrings and prawns (shrimp) tossed in a Vinaigrette Dressing, page 105

Freshwater Fish

Trout, the best known freshwater fish, was once comparatively rare and enjoyed by few people except fishermen. Nowadays, due to the success of trout farms, it is readily available at a reasonable price.

The other freshwater fish listed on page 36 are less plentiful.

Be generous with the amount of fat used when cooking trout to help keep the flesh moist.

LEFTOVERS
The following recipe uses a moderate amount of cooked salmon to make a sustaining dish for 4 to 6 people.

Salmon Cream
✳✳Dissolve 15 g/½ oz (1 envelope) gelatine (unflavored) in 150 ml/¼ pint (⅔ cup) heated white wine or fish stock, flavoured with a little white wine vinegar; allow to cool. Hard-boil (hard-cook) and chop 2 eggs; flake 350 g/12 oz (1½ cups) cooked salmon. Blend the salmon and eggs with the gelatine liquid, add 3 tablespoons mayonnaise and 2 teaspoons chopped dill or fennel leaves. Whip 150 ml/¼ pint (⅔ cup) double (heavy) cream until it just holds its shape. Fold into the mixture and season well. Spoon into an oiled mould and allow to set. Turn out and serve with salad. Serves 4 to 6.

Baked Trout with Herbs

4 medium trout
FOR THE HERB SPREAD:
100 g/4 oz (½ cup) margarine
2 tablespoons chopped mixed herbs, see Note
salt and pepper
TO GARNISH:
4 lemon wedges
parsley

Slit the trout and remove the intestines. Although it is not usual to bone trout before cooking, this can be done if desired. Make 3 or 4 diagonal cuts on each side of the fish and place the fish on a large piece of foil.

Herb Spread Cream the margarine until soft, add the herbs and seasoning. Top the trout with the herb spread and wrap loosely in the foil. Bake in the centre of a moderate oven (180°C/350°F, Gas Mark 4) for 25 to 30 minutes. Unwrap the foil carefully and place the fish, still on the foil, on a heated dish.

Garnish with lemon and large sprigs of parsley. Serve with Mushroom and Cucumber Salad (see page 96) and Garlic Bread. Serves 4.

Note The mixed herbs ideally should be chervil, chives, dill, fennel, a very little lemon thyme, parsley, very little rosemary and tarragon.

Trout Caprice

4 trout
25 g/1 oz (2 tablespoons) flour
salt and pepper
75 g/3 oz (6 tablespoons) butter
1 tablespoon lemon juice
4 bananas
TO GARNISH:
parsley

Clean the fish, but do not remove the heads. Blend the flour with a little seasoning and coat the fish. Heat 50 g/2 oz (¼ cup) of the butter in a large frying pan (skillet), add the fish and cook for 10 to 12 minutes. Sprinkle with the lemon juice towards the end of the cooking time. Lift on to a heated dish.

Heat the remaining butter in the frying pan (skillet) and cook the peeled bananas for 3 to 4 minutes only. Serve with the fish. Garnish with sprigs of parsley. Serves 4.

VARIATION
Scottish Trout Trout, like herrings, are excellent if coated with well-seasoned fine or medium oatmeal and fried in butter as above.

Prawn Stuffed Trout

4 trout
FOR THE STUFFING:
1 onion
65 to 75 g/2½ to 3 oz watercress
50 g/2 oz (¼ cup) butter
50 g/2 oz (½ cup) ground almonds
150 to 175 g/5 to 6 oz (1 cup) peeled prawns (shelled shrimp)
50 g/2 oz (1 cup) soft breadcrumbs
1 egg
3 teaspoons soy sauce
salt and pepper
TO GARNISH unpeeled prawns (shrimp)
lemon slices

Cut the heads off the fish, slit, remove the intestines then divide each fish into 2 fillets (see page 36).

Peel and chop the onion, chop the watercress. To make the stuffing, heat 25 g/1 oz (2 tablespoons) of the butter in a pan, fry the onion until soft, blend with the watercress, ground almonds, peeled prawns (shrimp), breadcrumbs, egg and 1 teaspoon of the soy sauce. Season lightly.

Melt the remaining butter. Grease the bottom and sides of an ovenproof dish with half the butter. Put 4 fillets into the dish and top with the stuffing. Cover with the remaining fillets; the skin side should be outside. Secure with wooden cocktail sticks.

Blend the last of the melted butter with the remaining 2 teaspoons of soy sauce. Brush over the fish and bake in the centre of a moderately hot oven (190°C/375°F, Gas Mark 5) for 30 to 40 minutes. Remove the cocktail sticks and garnish with the prawns (shrimp) and lemon. Serves 4.

VARIATION
Normandy Trout Omit the prawns, ground almonds and soy sauce in the recipe above. Use 100 g/4 oz (2 cups) soft breadcrumbs and 24 cooked mussels. Bind with the egg and 1 tablespoon sherry.

Smoked Fish

Smoked fish is often served as an hors d'oeuvre (see page 23), but smoked haddock, kippers and smoked cod lend themselves to many more excellent dishes.

Haddock and Egg Crumble

350 g/¾ lb cooked smoked haddock
225 g/½ lb cooked carrots
5 eggs
25 g/1 oz (2 tablespoons) butter
25 g/1 oz (¼ cup) flour
300 ml/½ pint (1¼ cups) milk
1 tablespoon lemon juice
salt and pepper
FOR THE TOPPING:
75 g/3 oz (¾ cup) grated Cheddar cheese
100 g/4 oz (2 cups) soft brown breadcrumbs
TO GARNISH:
2 lemon slices

Flake the haddock and neatly slice the carrots. Hard-boil (hard-cook), shell and chop four of the eggs, but save the fifth egg for garnishing the dish.

Heat the butter in a saucepan, stir in the flour and cook gently for 2 to 3

Smoked Haddock Cream

450 g/1 lb smoked haddock, weight without bones
300 ml/½ pint (1¼ cups) milk, see method
shake of pepper
25 g/1 oz (2 tablespoons) butter
25 g/1 oz (¼ cup) flour
150 ml/¼ pint (⅔ cup) single (light) cream
2 tablespoons chopped parsley
3 tablespoons white wine
15 g/½ oz (1 envelope) gelatine (unflavored)
1 tablespoon lemon juice
few drops anchovy essence
TO GARNISH: lettuce
small piece of cucumber
1 lemon

✻Cut the haddock into 3 or 4 portions. Pour the milk into a frying pan (skillet) or large saucepan, add the pepper, but no salt, and the haddock. Bring the milk to simmering point and allow it to simmer steadily for 6 to 8 minutes or until the haddock is soft; do not overcook.

Remove the haddock from the milk, discard the skin and finely flake the fish. Strain the milk into a measuring jug; you should now have 150 ml/¼ pint (⅔ cup). If necessary, make up the quantity by adding a little extra.

Heat the butter in a saucepan, stir in the flour, and cook over a low heat for 1 to 2 minutes. Blend in the milk and cream, then stir as the sauce comes to the boil and thickens. Add the parsley and the flaked fish.

Meanwhile pour the wine into a heatproof bowl, sprinkle the gelatine on top, place over a saucepan of boiling water and leave until the gelatine has dissolved. Add the lemon juice and blend with the fish mixture. Stir in the anchovy essence and any more pepper if required.

Rub the inside of a 1.2 litre/2 pint (5 cup) mould with a few drops of oil or rinse out in cold water. Spoon in the fish mixture and allow to set. Turn out on to a bed of lettuce, slice the cucumber and lemon and arrange around the mould. Serves 4.

VARIATION

Haddock and Tuna Cream Poach 350 g/ 2 oz (¾ lb) haddock fillet in 300 ml/½ pint (1¼ cups) milk with ¼ teaspoon anchovy essence and pepper to taste. When tender drain, discard the skin. Flake the fish, mix with 225 g/8 oz (1 cup) drained flaked canned tuna. Continue as Smoked Haddock Cream, but add 2 teaspoons capers.

Smoked Haddock Cream

---

minutes, then blend in the milk. Stir as the liquid comes to the boil, and thickens. Remove the pan from the heat then whisk in the lemon juice. Add the haddock, carrots and eggs and season to taste.

Put the mixture into a 1.2 litre/2 pint (5 cup) ovenproof dish. Grate the cheese, mix with the breadcrumbs and sprinkle evenly over the haddock mixture. Bake in the centre of a moderately hot oven (200°C/400°F, Gas Mark 6) for 30 minutes. Quarter the remaining egg and place on top of the dish together with the lemon slices. Serves 4 to 6.

Haddock and Egg Slice

shortcrust pastry made with 225 g/8 oz (2 cups) flour etc., see page 144
FOR THE FILLING: 450 g/1 lb smoked haddock fillet
300 ml/½ pint (1¼ cups) milk see method
2 eggs
2 sticks of celery
40 g/1½ oz (3 tablespoons) butter
25 g/1 oz (¼ cup) flour
2 tablespoons chopped parsley
shake of cayenne pepper
TO GLAZE: 1 egg
TO GARNISH: parsley

✻First make the filling. Cut the haddock into 3 or 4 portions. Put the cold milk into a large saucepan or frying pan (skillet), add the haddock and poach for 10 minutes. Remove the fish and flake it, discarding the skin. Measure the milk that is left. It should be at least 150 ml/ ¼ pint (⅔ cup); if necessary add a little more. Hard-boil (hard-cook), shell and chop the eggs. Finely chop the celery.

Heat the butter in a saucepan, add the celery and cook very gently for 5 minutes. Gradually blend in the flour, stir over a low heat for 1 to 2 minutes then blend in the milk. Return the pan to the heat, bring the sauce to the boil and allow to thicken to form a panada (binding sauce). Remove from the heat and add the fish, eggs, parsley and cayenne pepper. Allow to cool, but keep covered.

Roll out the pastry and cut into two rectangles; the first, for the base, should be approximately 30 × 15 cm/ 12 × 6 inches; the second rectangle, to cover the filling, should be slightly larger. Save the pastry trimmings. Place the pastry for the base on to a baking tray. Spread the filling over the pastry to within 1 cm/½ inch of the edges. Dampen these with a little water and place the second piece of pastry over the top. Seal the edges then trim them with a knife. Beat the egg and brush over the pastry. Roll out pastry trimmings, cut into narrow strips, twist and place over the top of the pastry. Brush the strips with beaten egg.

Bake in the centre of a preheated moderately hot oven (190°C/375°F, Gas Mark 5) for 25 to 30 minutes. Serve hot or cold, garnished with parsley. Serves 6.

Shellfish

Scampi (jumbo shrimp) have become a popular dish. Frozen ready coated scampi can be shallow fried without being thawed (see Goujons on page 19) or deep fried as Camarones Fritos (see page 47). Uncoated scampi can be cooked in a sauce in the same way as Moules à la Provençale below.

(see Goujons on page 19) ... Camarones Fritos (see page 47)

Special Technique
PREPARING MUSSELS

Mussels have an interesting flavour and are an excellent ingredient in a variety of dishes, but they must be prepared with great care.

Wash the mussels in plenty of cold water, take off any odd weeds that may be attached to the shells. Check each mussel carefully. The shells should be tightly closed. If any are open, tap them sharply and they should close. Discard any that do not close immediately.

Mussels are opened over heat. Place in a large saucepan with 300 ml/½ pint (1¼ cups) water, cover and cook over high heat for 5 to 6 minutes. Always remove from the heat as soon as the shells are fully opened. Over-cooking toughens them.

In some recipes the mussels are served on one shell; in other recipes both shells are removed. When lifting away one or both shells, remove any stringy pieces from the shellfish or any tiny weeds that may be on the inside of the shells. Never try to force open the shells and only use mussels that have opened naturally during the cooking process.

Moules à la Provençale

2.25 litres/4 pints (10 cups) mussels
2 medium onions
2 garlic cloves
450 g/1 lb tomatoes
2 tablespoons oil
25 g/1 oz (2 tablespoons) butter
150 ml/¼ pint (⅔ cup) white wine
2 tablespoons chopped parsley
2 tablespoons black olives
salt and pepper

FOR ECONOMY
Monkfish can be used as an economical substitute for scampi (jumbo shrimp). Cut the fish into narrow ribbons (goujons) by making diagonal cuts in the fish 2 cm (¾ inch) apart. These will have very much the same texture and flavour as scampi and can be cooked in the same way.

Prepare and cook the mussels as above and remove from shells. Strain the cooking liquid and save 150 ml/¼ pint (⅔ cup). Peel and finely chop the onions and garlic. Skin and chop the tomatoes. Heat the oil and butter in a large frying pan (skillet), cook the onions and garlic until nearly soft, then add the tomatoes with the mussel stock and cook for a further 5 to 10 minutes.

Add the wine, parsley and olives, bring just to boiling point, then put in the mussels. Stir well to blend with the hot mixture, add a little seasoning and heat for 2 to 3 minutes only. Serves 4.

VARIATION
Moules à la Crème Omit the tomatoes and olives. Add 150 ml/¼ pint (⅔ cup) double (heavy) cream to the pan with the mussels.

Scallops Venetian Style

4 large or 8 small scallops
TO COAT: salt and pepper
1 tablespoon flour
1 egg
40 g/1½ oz (⅓ cup) crisp breadcrumbs
1 garlic clove
50 g/2 oz (¼ cup) butter
2 tablespoons oil
2 tablespoons sherry
2 tablespoons lemon juice
TO GARNISH: chopped parsley

Detach the orange roes from the white flesh of the scallops. Mix a little seasoning with the flour. Dust both the roes and white parts of the scallops in the seasoned flour. Beat the egg, then coat the fish in the egg and breadcrumbs.

Peel and chop the garlic. Heat the butter and oil in a frying pan (skillet), add the garlic and fry gently for 1 minute. Remove the garlic from the pan with a small spoon; fry the scallops and corals (roes) for 2 to 3 minutes until tender. Just before serving add the sherry and lemon juice and heat for another minute.

Serve the fish piled up in the scallop shells, garnished with chopped parsley. Serves 2 as a main course, 4 as an hors d'oeuvre.

Prawns Indienne

1 small onion
1 large dessert apple
½ small celery heart
50 g/2 oz (¼ cup) butter
2 to 3 teaspoons curry powder
1 teaspoon cornflour (cornstarch)
300 ml/½ pint (1¼ cups) single (light) cream
1 teaspoon tomato purée (paste)
1 tablespoon desiccated (shredded) coconut
salt and pepper
350 to 450 g/12 oz to 1 lb (2 cups) peeled prawns (shelled shrimp)

Peel the onion and chop very finely. Peel and core the apple and cut it into small neat dice. Chop the celery heart into small pieces. Heat the butter in a large frying pan (skillet) and cook the onion for 4 to 5 minutes until nearly soft then add the apple and celery and cook for 3 to 4 minutes. Do not overcook, for these foods should retain their pleasant firmness. Stir the curry powder into the fried ingredients.

Blend the cornflour (cornstarch) with the cream and pour into the frying pan (skillet). Stir as the mixture thickens slightly. Cook for 1 to 2 minutes, then add the remaining ingredients and heat thoroughly, but do not overcook. Serve with cooked rice and chutney. Serves 4 as a main course, 6 to 8 as an hors d'oeuvre.

Note It is important to thaw out and drain frozen prawns (shrimp) well.

Lobster Thermidor

2 medium lobsters
few drops olive oil
1 small onion or shallot
50 g/2 oz (¼ cup) butter
25 g/1 oz (¼ cup) flour
300 ml/½ pint (1¼ cups) milk
1 teaspoon chopped chervil
½ teaspoon chopped tarragon
1 teaspoon chopped parsley
salt and pepper
1 to 2 teaspoons French or made English mustard
6 tablespoons white wine
3 tablespoons double (heavy) cream
2 to 3 tablespoons grated Parmesan cheese
TO GARNISH: 2 lemons
sprig of parsley

Split the lobster. Remove the intestinal vein and discard. Take the flesh from the shells carefully and put on one side. Polish the shells with 2 or 3 drops of olive oil. Crack the claws and remove the flesh from them. These stages are shown in the picture on this page.

Chop the onion or shallot very finely then heat the butter and fry the onion or shallot until tender; do not allow to brown. Stir in the flour and cook for several minutes, stirring all the time. Gradually blend in the milk, bring to the boil, stir well to keep the sauce smooth and cook until a coating consistency. Lower the heat, add the herbs and seasoning, including the mustard. This dish *should* have a definite flavour of mustard, but add this gradually to the sauce, tasting as you do so. Remove the pan from the heat, so the sauce is no longer boiling and whisk in the wine and then the cream. Return the pan to a low heat. Simmer very gently until the sauce becomes a coating consistency again. Add the lobster flesh to the sauce and heat for a few minutes only. Do *not* overcook for this toughens shellfish. Spoon the mixture into the lobster shells. Top with the cheese and brown under the preheated grill (broiler). Slice the lemons and arrange round the edge of the serving dish. Add the filled lobster shells and garnish with the parsley. Serves 4.

Scallop Ramekins

| 1 small onion |
| 1 to 2 garlic clove(s) |
| 2 tablespoons oil |
| 50 g/2 oz (¼ cup) butter |
| 225 g/8 oz (2 cups) button mushrooms |
| 8 to 10 large scallops |
| 1 tablespoon plain (all-purpose) flour |
| salt and pepper |
| 1 tablespoon lemon juice |
| 4 to 5 tablespoons fine white breadcrumbs |
| 3 tablespoons chopped parsley |
| 4 lemon wedges |

Peel the onion and garlic. Finely chop the onion; crush the garlic. Heat half the oil and half the butter in a large frying pan (skillet). Gently fry the onion for 5 minutes, add the garlic and cook for a further minute. Quarter the mushrooms.

Wash the scallops, separate the roes and cut each white part (cushion) horizontally in half, sprinkle with the flour and a little seasoning. Add the scallops (but not the roes) to the onion mixture. Cook gently for 5 to 6 minutes or until nearly tender then add the roes, mushrooms and lemon juice. Cook for a further 3 to 4 minutes; stir from time to time.

Meanwhile heat the remaining oil and butter in a small frying pan (skillet) and fry the breadcrumbs until crisp and brown. Add the parsley. Spoon the scallop mixture into 4 heated scallop shells or individual ramekin dishes, top with the breadcrumbs, and serve with lemon wedges. Serves 4.

Crab Cakes

| 25 g/1 oz (2 tablespoons) butter or margarine |
| 25 g/1 oz (¼ cup) flour |
| 150 ml/¼ pint (⅔ cup) milk |
| salt and pepper |
| 1 teaspoon Worcestershire sauce |
| 2 tablespoons chopped parsley |
| 225 g/½ lb fresh, canned or frozen crabmeat |
| 225 g/8 oz (1 cup) cooked old potatoes |

| **TO COAT:** |
| 25 g/1 oz (¼ cup) flour |
| 1 egg |
| 40 g/1½ oz (6 tablespoons) crisp breadcrumbs |
| **FOR FRYING:** |
| 50 g/2 oz (¼ cup) butter or 2 tablespoons oil |

Heat the 25 g/1 oz (2 tablespoons) butter or margarine in a saucepan, add the flour and stir over a low heat for 2 to 3 minutes. Blend in the milk and stir as the liquid comes to the boil and thickens. Season lightly and add the Worcestershire sauce, parsley and crabmeat. Mash the potatoes, but do not add any liquid to them. Blend the potato with the crabmeat mixture. Divide into 8 portions, chill until firm enough to handle, then form into round cakes. Blend the flour with a little seasoning and coat the fish cakes in this. Beat the egg, brush over the cakes, then roll in the breadcrumbs.

Heat the butter or oil in a large frying pan (skillet) and fry the cakes until crisp and brown on both sides. Serve with Tomato Sauce (see page 103). Serves 4.

VARIATIONS

Use 50 g/2 oz (¼ cup) butter or margarine in the sauce and fry 1 finely chopped onion and 50 g/2 oz (½ cup) chopped mushrooms before adding the flour.

Flavour the sauce with a little curry powder and omit the Worcestershire sauce.

LEFTOVERS
Cooked mussels are excellent in a Seafood Cocktail. Blend prawns (shrimp), mussels, diced cooked scallops and other shellfish in the Mary Rose Dressing (see page 19). Serve on a bed of shredded lettuce. Never store shellfish for a long period.

Scallop Ramekins, and Moules à la Crème, page 44

Jansson's Temptation

Canned Fish

Canned salmon and tuna form the basis for salads, sandwich fillings and hot dishes. The Salmon Cream on page 42 can be made with well-drained canned salmon or tuna. Canned sardines are not really an alternative to fresh sardines in the recipe on page 27 – the canned fish is too delicate and inclined to break – but these nutritious little fish make an excellent salad or quick savoury when served on toast.

Jansson's Temptation

8 medium potatoes
3 medium onions
2 × 50 g/2 oz cans anchovy fillets
150 ml/¼ pint (⅔ cup) whipping or single (light) cream
pepper
25 g/1 oz (2 tablespoons) butter
50 g/2 oz (1 cup) soft fine breadcrumbs

Peel the potatoes, cut into thin slices, then cut each slice into strips about 5 mm/¼ inch wide. Peel and finely chop the onions. Arrange the potatoes, onions and anchovy fillets in a greased ovenproof dish, with a layer of potatoes as the topping. Mix the cream with some pepper. Pour over the potatoes. Melt the butter, mix with the breadcrumbs and sprinkle over the top of the potatoes.

Bake in the centre of a preheated moderate to moderately hot oven (180 to 190°C/350 to 375°F, Gas Mark 4 to 5) for about 1 hour until the potatoes are soft. Serves 4 to 6.

Avocado and Tuna au Gratin

675 g/1½ lb (3 cups) Duchesse Potatoes, see page 92
4 eggs
40 g/1½ oz (3 tablespoons) butter or margarine
40 g/1½ oz (6 tablespoons) flour
450 ml/¾ pint (2 cups) milk
salt and pepper
1 teaspoon French mustard
1 tablespoon white wine vinegar or lemon juice
1 × 196 g/7 oz can tuna
1 avocado
FOR THE TOPPING: 50 g/2 oz (½ cup) Cheddar cheese
50 g/2 oz (1 cup) breadcrumbs
TO GARNISH: watercress

Pipe the potatoes around the edge of a shallow ovenproof dish. Place just above the centre of a moderately hot oven (200°C/400°F, Gas Mark 6) for 15 minutes, or until the potatoes begin to change colour. Do not overcook.

Meanwhile hard-boil (hard-cook), shell and coarsely chop the eggs. Heat the butter or margarine in a saucepan. Add the flour, and stir over a low heat for 2 to 3 minutes. Blend in the milk and stir as the sauce comes to the boil and thickens, then add the salt, pepper and mustard. Take the saucepan off the heat, add the vinegar or lemon juice to the hot but not boiling sauce. Drain the canned tuna; flake the fish.

Peel and dice the avocado and mix with the tuna and the chopped eggs.

Remove the dish from the oven. Put the tuna mixture in the centre and immediately coat with the sauce. Grate the cheese, sprinkle over the sauce; add the breadcrumbs. Return to the oven for a further 15 to 20 minutes. Garnish with watercress. Serves 4.

VARIATION

Use creamed potatoes instead of Duchesse potatoes. If there is no time to pipe the potatoes just spoon in a neat pattern round the sides of the dish.

Salad Niçoise

There are many recipes for this salad; even in the South of France you are likely to find variations.

2 eggs
100 to 175 g/4 to 6 oz new potatoes
salt and pepper
1 small green pepper
3 to 4 tomatoes
1 × 227 g/8 oz can tuna
1 × 50 g/2 oz can anchovy fillets
1 lettuce
FOR THE DRESSING: 3 tablespoons oil
1 teaspoon French mustard
1 teaspoon sugar
1 tablespoon white wine vinegar
1 tablespoon lemon juice
1 teaspoon chopped tarragon
½ teaspoon chopped basil
TO GARNISH: black olives

Hard-boil (hard-cook), shell and quarter the eggs. Cook the potatoes in salted water until just soft, cut into halves or quarters or leave whole if small. Dice the green pepper, discard the core and seeds and quarter the tomatoes.

Pour off the oil from the two cans of fish; this can be added to the dressing.

Line the salad bowl with the lettuce. Add the potatoes, eggs, tomatoes, pepper and the fish. Blend the ingredients for the dressing and add to the salad. Toss before serving then garnish with the olives. Serves 4 to 6.

International Fish Dishes

Every country has its favourite ways of serving fish. Varieties of fish vary from country to country. The recipes on this page are adapted to suit the types of fish that are readily available but each dish retains an individual flavour that reminders us of its origin.

Camarones Fritos
[Prawn Fritters]

450 g/1 lb (2½ cups) peeled prawns (shelled shrimp)
2 tablespoons lemon juice
2 tablespoons olive oil
salt and pepper
oil for frying
FOR THE BATTER:
100 g/4 oz (1 cup) plain (all-purpose) flour
pinch salt
2 eggs
150 ml/¼ pint (⅔ cup) water

If the prawns (shrimp) are very large it is advisable to chop them. Put the shellfish into a bowl with the lemon juice, oil and a little seasoning. Leave for 1 hour.

Blend together all the ingredients for the batter. Drain the shellfish well and mix with the batter.

Heat the oil until it reaches 170°C/340° (see page 90 for method of testing oil). Drop spoonfuls of the fish mixture into the hot oil and fry steadily for 4 to 5 minutes until golden brown. Drain on absorbent paper. Serve with a Tomato Sauce (see page 103). Serves 4 to 6.

Otak-Otak

This Indonesian dish is ideal for whole small fish like trout, mackerel, codling (baby cod) or small fresh haddock.

4 small fish, see above
¼ teaspoon coriander seeds
salt and pepper
1 egg
3 tablespoons milk
1 small onion
1 garlic clove
50 g/2 oz (4 tablespoons) melted butter or margarine
cabbage leaves for steaming
TO GARNISH
sliced tomatoes
sliced red peppers

Cut the heads from the fish, remove the intestines and back bones, wash and dry.

Place the fish with the skin side uppermost on a work surface and beat gently with a wooden spoon. This loosens the skin. Turn the fish over and very carefully cut away the raw flesh, leaving the skin intact. Finely chop the fish. Mix the flesh with the coriander, seasoning, egg and milk. Peel and grate the onion and crush the garlic. Add to the fish with half of the melted butter. Spoon the mixture back over the fish skins, then fold to look like the whole fish again.

Wrap each fish in large cabbage leaves and place in a steamer or on a large dish over a pan of boiling water. Cover the steamer or dish very tightly and steam for 25 to 30 minutes until tender. Unwrap and top with remaining melted butter. Garnish with sliced tomatoes and rings of red pepper. Serves 4.

Crescented Prawn Curry

1 large onion
2 garlic cloves
25 g/1 oz (2 tablespoons) butter
1 tablespoon oil
2 teaspoons coriander powder
1 teaspoon turmeric
1 teaspoon chilli powder
salt and pepper
2 tablespoons lemon juice
200 ml/⅓ pint (⅞ cup) coconut milk, see below
2 tablespoons tomato purée (paste)
50 g/2 oz (⅓ cup) sultanas (golden raisins)
450 g/1 lb (2½ cups) peeled prawns (shelled shrimp)
225 g/8 oz (1 cup) long-grain rice, cooked, see page 136
TO GARNISH:
lime or lemon slices

∴Peel the onion and cut into thin slices. Peel and crush the garlic. Heat the butter and oil in a large frying pan (skillet) and fry the onion and garlic until soft. Mix all the spices and seasonings with the lemon juice to form a smooth paste. Add this to the pan and fry for 2 minutes, stirring all the time. Blend in the coconut milk (see below) and tomato purée (paste). Simmer for 5 minutes. Add the sultanas (golden raisins) and prawns (shrimp) and gently fry for a further 2 minutes.

Serve with cooked long-grain rice shaped into a crescent and garnish with slices of lime or lemon. Serves 4.

To Make Coconut Milk Infuse 25 g/1 oz (⅓ cup) dessicated (shredded) coconut in 200 ml/⅓ pint (⅞ cup) boiling water for 10 minutes. Strain and use the liquid.

Pescado con Guindilla
[Chilli-Flavoured Fish]

2 medium onions
2 garlic cloves
2 tablespoons oil
300 ml/½ pint (1½ cups) white wine
a few drops Tabasco (hot pepper) sauce
2 tablespoons tomato purée (paste)
salt and pepper
4 portions fresh or frozen cod
TO GARNISH:
2 to 3 tablespoons green olives

This chilli-flavoured fish is an excellent way of serving fresh or frozen cod. Peel the onions and cut into thin rings; peel and chop the garlic. Heat the oil in a large frying pan (skillet) and fry the onions and garlic until soft. Add the wine, Tabasco (hot pepper) sauce, tomato purée (paste) and a little salt and pepper. Put the fish portions in the sauce; turn over several times so they become moistened and coloured with the mixture. Cook for 15 minutes. Transfer to a serving dish and top with the olives. Serves 4.

VARIATION

Paprika Fish Omit the Tabasco sauce (hot pepper sauce) in the recipe above. Blend 2 teaspoons sweet paprika with the wine; cook as the recipe above. Top with yogurt and more paprika.

LEFTOVERS
Leftover whole fish may be served with the following sauce.
Pineapple Sweet and Sour Sauce
Chop about 4 canned pineapple rings, and 1 small green pepper discarding the core and seeds.

Blend 2 teaspoons cornflour (cornstarch) with about 150 ml/¼ pint (⅔ cup) syrup from the can of pineapple. Put into a saucepan and add 1 tablespoon clear honey, 1 tablespoon soy sauce and 2 to 3 tablespoons of brown or red wine vinegar. Stir until thickened then add a little salt and pepper and the chopped pineapple and pepper. Heat for 2 to 3 minutes only.

Crescented Prawn Curry

47

MEAT DISHES

Meat is considered by most people to be one of the most important protein foods. It is expensive and should be bought and cooked carefully, so that it retains the maximum flavour.

Although it is quite wrong to undercook meat, except prime beef or young lamb, many people make the mistake of overcooking the meat, so it loses flavour and becomes dry and hard. Check the meat as it cooks for, while cooking times in this book are based upon careful testing of the recipes, the quality and age of meat varies and this determines the exact cooking time.

Buying Points

If you are new to cooking, you may find it more helpful to buy meat from a butcher rather than from a supermarket. You can then seek advice and learn about the various cuts of meat. Once you can recognize these, shopping at a supermarket is less puzzling. Individual cuts and suitable cooking methods are described under each particular type.

Beef The lean meat should be reddish although the colour will vary according to the length of time the meat has been hung. Beef should never be dull and brown. The fat should be firm and cream in colour. Some people dislike eating fat, but good beef should always have some fat otherwise the meat will be dry.

Lamb The lean meat should be a pink-brown in colour with firm white fat.

Mutton This is rarely seen but can be ordered from some butchers.

Pork The lean meat should be a delicate pale pink and the fat white and dry.

Veal The lean meat must be very pale pink in colour and the fat firm and white.

Bacon The lean part should be pleasantly reddish in colour with a reasonable distribution of white fat. Cooked ham must be moist and pale pink and the fat white and firm.

Do not ignore cheaper cuts of meat and offal (variety meats). These meats make interesting and economical meals.

Some of the meat we buy today is sold frozen, making it difficult to assess its quality. The only solution is to shop where you know the quality is good.

Chops and steaks can be cooked from frozen; there is no need to thaw them before cooking unless the meat has to be coated or put into a marinade.

While joints of meat can be cooked from frozen, it will be difficult to judge whether the meat is completely cooked unless you have a special meat thermometer (see page 50). It is therefore wiser, in most cases, to thaw the meat (and dry it well) before cooking.

Microwave Cooking

Tender meat cooks well in a microwave cooker, although it does not brown as it would if cooked in a conventional frying pan (skillet), under a grill (broiler) or in an oven.

Meat stews and casseroles are only successful if your microwave cooker has variable control and you are able to cook them at a low setting. Consult the manufacturer's handbook for settings.

Pressure Cooking

As you will see from the various recipes in this book a pressure cooker can be used, with great success, for making stews and for pot-roasting meat that usually require long slow cooking.

Slow Cooking

A slow cooker is invaluable if you lead a busy life for it enables you to leave a stew, casserole, or even a pot-roast, cooking unattended for many hours. The exceptionally low temperature inside the slow cooker means that the food cannot burn, but it is still possible to overcook meat. In order to give an attractive appearance to the meat it is important to brown it in a frying pan (skillet) or saucepan before adding it to the slow cooker.

∴Freezing Note

The recommended freezing times for meats are up to 1 year for beef, up to 9 months for lamb and veal and 6 months for pork. I prefer to use the meat before these times as I feel it has a better flavour. Salted meat should be used within 2 months, minced (ground) beef or sausages (pork sausage links) within 3 months. Smoked bacon can be frozen for up to 1 month; vacuum packed bacon joints keep well for up to 4 months and rashers (slices) up to 5 months, or as indicated on the pack.

Cooked meat dishes are best used within 3 months of freezing.

Cooking Methods

There are various ways of cooking meat and it is vital that you select the method that will enhance both the flavour and texture of the meat available.

Stewing or Casseroling

Use these long slow cooking methods to tenderize cheaper cuts of meat. The meat is cooked in liquid with vegetables, herbs and other ingredients to add interest. Cook in a cool oven; over a very low heat; in a microwave cooker on the low setting recommended in the manufacturers instruction manual; in a slow cooker or in a pressure cooker which tenderizes stewing meat in minutes.

Boiling

This word is in fact incorrect, since the meat (generally salted) is cooked in liquid that simmers gently but does not boil (see page 62). A microwave cooker is not particularly successful for this type of cooking, but a slow cooker or pressure cooker is excellent.

Braising

Although this method of cooking can be used for cheaper cuts, it is equally suitable for prime quality meat. When braising the meat is cooked above the liquid (see page 54).

Frying and Grilling (Broiling)

Only prime quality meat should be used; generally one chooses small portions such as chops and steaks.

Put the meat into hot fat when frying, or preheat the grill (broiler) so that the outside of the meat is sealed quickly.

Pot Roasting

This is not unlike braising (see the recipe on page 70). A pressure cooker or slow cooker can be used.

Roasting

This is the method of cooking associated with really good quality joints of meat. When roasting thawed frozen meat, or chilled meat, use the Slower Roasting method (see page 50).

The timings given for the various kinds of meat assume that it is being cooked uncovered in a roasting pan.

You can use a covered roasting pan. This allows meat to brown well but keeps it moist and saves fat splashing in the oven. Increase the cooking time by 15 minutes if Fast Roasting, or 25 minutes if Slow Roasting.

You can wrap the meat in foil; this keeps the meat moist but does not allow it to brown, unless you open the foil for the last 20 to 30 minutes of the cooking time. Allow extra time as above or increase the oven setting by 10°C or 25°F or 1 Gas Mark.

Modern roasting bags keep the meat moist and allow it to brown. It is not necessary to increase the cooking time.

Top right: Lamb with Cucumber Sauce, page 58
Bottom right: Roast Loin of Pork, page 64

BEEF DISHES

Beef is excellent for all forms of cooking. When you buy beef on the bone for roasting remember to allow for the weight of the bone when you assess the cooking time.

Stewing beef is boneless and so are the various prime steaks for frying or grilling (broiling).

Quantities

The amount of meat needed for each person varies according to the way it is cooked and the accompaniments, but an average allowance would be:
For Frying or Grilling (broiling) A minimum of 100 to 175 g/4 to 6 oz per person.
For Roasting About 350 g/12 oz meat on the bone, per person.
For Stews From 100 to 175 g/4 to 6 oz per person.

Beef Cuts

Always select the correct cut of meat for the cooking method.
For Stock Flank.
For Stewing, Casseroling or Braising Blade, brisket, flank, skirt or chuck (round steak).
For Boiling Aitch-bone, brisket, flank, shin (shank), silverside (bottom round) also oxtail and tongue.
For Frying or Grilling (broiling) Entre-côte, fillet, rump, sirloin, T-bone steaks.
For Roasting Aitch-bone, brisket (both must be good quality), fillet, rib, rump, sirloin, topside (top round).

Roast Beef

Roasting Times for Beef

Fast Roasting Preheat the oven to moderately hot to hot (200 to 220°C/400 to 425°F, Gas Mark 6 to 7).
Allow 15 to 20 minutes per 450 g/1 lb plus 15 to 20 minutes over for rare to medium cooked beef.
Slower Roasting Preheat the oven (moderate 160 to 180°C/325 to 350°F, Gas Mark 3 to 4).
Allow 25 to 30 minutes per 450 g/1 lb plus 25 to 30 minutes over for rare to medium cooked beef.
Very well cooked beef can take up to 35 minutes per 450 g/1 lb and 35 minutes over at this setting.

Freezing Note

It is possible to freeze leftover cooked joints although it does tend to lose some of its flavour. Slice the meat and separate each slice with waxed or greaseproof paper rather then freeze the whole joint.

Special Technique
PERFECT ROAST BEEF

You may find there are sharp differences of opinion within your family as to what constitutes perfect roast beef. If you like meat well-cooked, the appearance of rare (underdone) beef will fill you with horror, whereas to many people well-cooked beef is spoiled beef.

It is not easy to please both groups of people at one time but it is not impossible. Follow the timing for rare beef left, adding about 10 minutes for a joint of about 1.5 kg/3 lb in weight. For this last 10 minutes, raise the temperature of the oven to hot (230°C/450°F, Gas Mark 8) so the outside of the meat is very well done. Carve well-done slices from both ends of the joint.

Choose the cuts of beef given opposite and roast according to the timings on this page. If the beef is very lean add about 25 g/1 oz (2 tablespoons) fat, but no more. If the beef has sufficient natural fat on the joint, do not add extra fat, for this only hardens the meat.

Serve with Yorkshire Pudding (see below), mustard and/or Horseradish Sauce (see page 102) or horseradish cream (bought in jars) and a thin gravy, see opposite; or follow the suggestions on this page.

If you are roasting potatoes or other vegetables round the meat you will need an extra 50 g/2 oz (¼ cup) fat which must be well heated before you add the vegetables.

Using a Meat Thermometer

Insert the thermometer into the very centre of the joint; avoid any bones.
Cook the meat until the thermometer registers the required temperature:

BEEF	well done	76°C/170°F
	medium	71°C/160°F
	rare	66°C/150°F
	very rare	60°C/140°F
LAMB	well done	82°C/180°F
	underdone	76°C/170°F
PORK		88°C/190°F
VEAL		88°C/190°F

Never use an ordinary meat thermometer in a microwave cooker; microwave meat thermometers are available.

Microwave Roasting

It is important to remember that individual microwave cookers vary in output and the setting that is recommended for roasting meat, so always check with your manufacturer's handbook. The following information is based upon using a cooker of 700 watt output, the maximum setting, and a 1.75 kg/4 lb joint.

Stand the beef, fat side downwards, on a microwave roasting rack or an upturned saucer in a suitable dish, or put the meat into a roasting bag. Pierce the bag to allow steam to escape.

Allow 5 to 9 minutes per 450 g/1 lb depending upon how well done you like the meat. Turn the joint over once. Wrap the meat in foil the moment it comes from the oven and allow it to stand for a minimum of 15 minutes. The meat does not cool but continues to cook during this period.

If using a special microwave meat thermometer insert this and check the reading. To compensate for the fact that the temperature rises during the standing time and remove the meat from the microwave cooker when the thermometer readings are as follows: 71°C/160°F for well-done beef; 66°C/150°F for medium cooked beef; and 55°C/130°F for rare beef. These are lower temperatures than those given below left, but remember the temperature will rise during the standing period.

A New Look for Roast Beef

The flavourings below do not detract in any way from the good flavour of the beef, but they do give a slightly unusual touch. The quantities are for a joint weighing about 1.75 kg/4 lb.
Mustard Beef Spread each side of the joint with 1 tablespoon French mustard, sprinkle with garlic salt, roast as usual.
New Zealand Coffee Roast Blend 25 g/1 oz (¼ cup) flour with 2 teaspoons instant coffee powder and 2 teaspoons brown sugar, add 1 to 2 teaspoons dry mustard powder, a little salt and a good pinch of cayenne pepper. Sprinkle on one side of the meat, press hard into the flesh with the back of a wooden spoon then gently pierce holes in the beef with a skewer so the coffee mixture penetrates the meat. Roast as usual.
Stuffed Beef Ideal for topside (top round) or brisket. Cut the joint vertically to make two sections; sandwich together with a suitable stuffing. Tie the meat securely to make a neat joint again, weigh and roast as usual.
Sweet and Sour Beef Mix together 150 ml/¼ pint (⅔ cup) pineapple juice, 2 teaspoons made mustard and 2 tablespoons red wine vinegar. When the beef is nearly cooked, spoon out the fat from the roasting pan and pour the sweet and sour mixture over the beef. Turn the beef once or twice in the mixture then continue cooking.

Gravy and Sauces

A good gravy is essential to complement a perfect roast. The proportions for gravy are given below. Make full use of all the delicious little morsels of meat and stuffing that may have dropped into the roasting pan by incorporating them into the gravy. Strain it before serving.
Thin gravy Heat 1½ to 2 tablespoons

Perfect Roast Beef

meat dripping, stir in a scant 25 g/1 oz (¼ cup) flour, allow to turn golden brown. Blend in 600 ml/1 pint (2½ cups) meat stock or liquid from cooking vegetables, stir as the gravy comes to the boil and thickens slightly. Add flavouring; strain before serving. Serves 6.

Thick Gravy Use 2 tablespoons meat dripping and 40 g/1½ oz (6 tablespoons) flour to 600 ml/1 pint (2½ cups) stock. Make as above. Serves 6.

Flavouring Gravy Add a little red wine, sherry or mushroom ketchup.

If using a gravy browning powder, use rather less flour.

Yorkshire Pudding

Beat together 100 g/4 oz (1 cup) plain (all-purpose) flour, a pinch of salt, 1 egg and 250 ml/8 fl oz (1 cup) milk until a smooth batter forms. Heat 25 g/1 oz (2 tablespoons) fat in a Yorkshire Pudding pan. Pour in the batter and cook towards the top of a hot to very hot oven (220 to 230°C/425 to 450°F, Gas Mark 7 to 8), for 25 to 35 minutes depending on the depth of the pan. Lower the heat slightly after the first 10 minutes or when the pudding starts to rise. Serves 4.

Special Technique
MAKING STOCK

Although modern stock (bouillon) cubes give an acceptable flavour to stews, soups and sauces, it is still sensible to make stock if you have bones or a carcass of poultry available.

A pressure cooker is a speedy way of preparing stock. Normally you would simmer the stock for 2 to 3 hours in a saucepan. When using a pressure cooker, cooking for 40 minutes to 1 hour at HIGH/15 lb pressure will produce an excellent stock. Since little evaporation takes place reduce the amount of liquid used by at least one-third.

A microwave cooker can also be used; put the bones in a large bowl and cover with a plate or plastic wrap (pierce the wrap to make a small hole). The cooking time in a microwave cooker will be a little longer than in a pressure cooker, but there is little evaporation of liquid and no fear of boiling dry.

A slow cooker also makes excellent stock; allow 8 to 10 hours on the LOW.

White Stock is made by simmering the carcass of a chicken or veal bones, with water to cover, for several hours. Chicken stock can also be made by simmering the giblets of the bird.

Brown Stock is made by simmering beef or game bones or the giblets of game.

Gravy Stock is made by simmering the bones from the meat, or giblets from poultry or game.

Fish stock is made by simmering the bones and skin of the fish in water for a *maximum* of 30 to 40 minutes, or 10 to 15 minutes at HIGH/15 lb pressure.

You can add seasoning and herbs or vegetables to all stocks, but take care these flavourings do not conflict with the ingredients in the recipe. If you use vegetables to give flavour to the stock it is less likely to keep well.

Always store stock in the refrigerator, where it will keep for several days, or freezer (see below).

⁂ To Freeze Stock It saves valuable freezer space if you boil the stock until it is very concentrated. Cool the stock, refrigerate for several hours and remove all surplus fat before freezing.

LEFTOVERS
Slices of cooked beef are delicious if sandwiched together with horseradish cream or mustard pickle, then dipped in a very thin coating of batter and fried. The batter is similar to Yorkshire Pudding batter, but use only 200 ml/⅓ pint (⅞ cup) liquid.

Minced Beef

Minced (ground) beef is economical and extremely versatile. On this page are two basic recipes – Beef Loaf and Beef Cakes – plus numerous flavour variations.

Master Recipe
BEEF LOAF

1 medium onion
1 medium carrot
100 g/4 oz mushrooms
25 g/1 oz (2 tablespoons) butter or margarine
450 g/1 lb (2 cups) minced (ground) beef
225 g/8 oz (4 cups) soft breadcrumbs
75 g/3 oz (½ cup) shredded suet
2 tablespoons chopped parsley
salt and pepper
2 teaspoons chopped fresh mixed herbs or a good pinch mixed dried herbs
1 egg
3 to 4 rashers (slices) streaky bacon
TO GARNISH: 1 small onion
1 small piece of cucumber
little parsley

✶✶Peel and chop the onion, peel and dice or coarsely grate the carrot, wipe and thinly slice the mushrooms. Heat the butter or margarine in a pan and fry the vegetables gently for 2 to 3 minutes. Blend with the rest of the ingredients except the bacon.

Cut the rinds from the bacon, stretch with the back of a knife and halve. Use the bacon to line the bottom of a lightly greased 1 kg/2 lb loaf tin (9 × 5 inch loaf pan). Spoon the meat mixture on top, taking care not to dislodge the bacon. Cover the top of the loaf tin with greased foil.

If you prefer a very moist meat loaf half fill a large container with cold water and stand the loaf tin in this. If you like a firm outside do not stand the tin in a *bain-marie* of cold water.

Bake in the centre of a moderate to moderately hot oven (180 to 190°C/350 to 375°F, Gas Mark 4 to 5) for 1 hour.

If serving hot, turn out carefully, but if serving cold put a plate on top of the loaf and top with a light weight. This makes a firmer texture that is easier to slice. If serving the loaf cold, garnish it with the onion, peeled and cut into thin rings, thin slices of cucumber and parsley. Serves 6.

Variations

✶✶Beef and Ham Loaf Use 350 g/12 oz (1½ cups) minced (ground) raw beef and 175 g/6 oz (¾ cup) finely chopped ham in the recipe above but use only 50 g/2 oz (¼ cup) shredded suet.

✶✶Cheese and Beef Loaf Prepare the basic recipe but add 175 g/6 oz (1 cup) diced cheese. Omit the bacon used to line the pan; simply grease it well, add the mixture, cover and bake as above.

✶✶Liver Loaf Use 450 g/1 lb finely minced (ground) raw lambs' liver. Reduce the breadcrumbs to 100 g/4 oz (2 cups) only; use 1 teaspoon chopped fresh sage or ½ teaspoon dried sage instead of mixed herbs.

✶✶Tomato and Beef Loaf Omit the carrot and mushrooms in the recipe above but fry 4 skinned and chopped tomatoes with the onion.

Swedish Beef Cakes

Meat cakes and meat balls are popular in many parts of the world (see Variations). The basic ingredients used are usually similar to those used in this versatile recipe.

450 g/1 lb topside (top round) of beef
1 small onion
1 medium cooked potato
1 small cooked beetroot
1 egg
2 teaspoons capers
salt and pepper
FOR FRYING: 50 g/2 oz (¼ cup) fat
FOR GARNISH: 8 small rounds of rye bread
25 g/1 oz (2 tablespoons) butter
1 small lettuce
1 small cooked beetroot
a few capers
1 tablespoon chopped parsley

Put the beef and onion through a mincer (grinder). Mash the potato. Peel and finely dice the beetroot. Blend the potato, beetroot, egg and capers with the beef and onion. Season well. Form into about 8 flat cakes. Heat the fat in a frying pan (skillet) and fry the beef cakes for 2 minutes. Turn and cook for the same time on the second side. The meat should not be over-cooked. Drain on absorbent paper.

Spread the slices of bread with butter. Top with lettuce leaves. Place the hot meat cakes on top of the lettuce. Peel and dice the second beetroot, spoon on top of the beef cakes and add the capers and parsley. Serves 4.

VARIATIONS

✶✶Creamed Beef Cakes Omit the beetroot from the recipe above and add 1 tablespoon double (heavy) cream to the meat mixture. Form into flat cakes, as in the recipe, or into small balls. Fry for 2 to 3 minutes only in 50 g/2 oz (¼ cup) hot butter (instead of fat). When cooked,

pour 150 ml/¼ pint (⅔ cup) beef stock and 150 ml/¼ pint (⅔ cup) single (light) cream into the pan; simmer gently for 5 minutes. Lift the cakes out of the liquid with a perforated spoon, put on to a dish and keep hot. Blend 2 teaspoons cornflour (cornstarch) with 2 tablespoons milk or stock, stir into the liquid in the frying pan (skillet) and cook gently until thickened. Season well. Spoon over the beef cakes, top with chopped parsley and chopped hard-boiled (hard-cooked) egg. Serve with boiled rice or creamed potatoes.

✶✶Dutch Meat Balls Omit the potato and beetroot in the recipe above; add 75 g/3 oz (1½ cups) soft fine breadcrumbs. Form into balls and fry as above.

✶✶Fruit and Nut Meat Balls Omit the beetroot, capers and onion in the basic recipe, but retain the potato and mix with the beef, egg and seasoning together with 2 tablespoons currants or sultanas (golden raisins) and 50 g/2 oz (½ cup) pine nuts or chopped blanched almonds. Form into balls. Fry as above.

✶✶Köttbuller Soak 50 g/2 oz (1 cup) soft breadcrumbs in 150 ml/¼ pint (⅔ cup) double (heavy) cream for 15 minutes. Peel and chop 1 onion, and fry in 25 g/1 oz (2 tablespoons) butter until soft. Mince (grind) 350 g/12 oz beef and 100 g/4 oz pork together. Blend all these ingredients together, season well and form into miniature meat balls with 2 teaspoons. Fry in about 40 g/1½ oz (3 tablespoons) hot butter until golden. Serve with well seasoned Béchamel Sauce (see page 102).

Swedish Beef Cakes

LEFTOVERS
Slice any leftover meat loaf and fry in a little fat. Top each slice with a fried egg and serve as a light meal.
Store both cooked and uncooked minced (ground) beef with great care, so it does not spoil. Use a small quantity of good quality raw minced (ground) beef to make:
Potted Beef
✶✶Put 225 g/8 oz minced (ground) beef into a heatproof bowl with 2 tablespoons water, salt, pepper, 1 to 2 teaspoons chopped mixed herbs and 1 to 2 tablespoons sherry. Cover the bowl and cook over boiling water for 1 to 1¼ hours or until tender. Pound the meat until smooth with 50 g/2 oz (¼ cup) melted butter and a little grated nutmeg or blend in a food processor.
Serve as a pâté or sandwich filling.

To Grill or Fry Beef

The steaks that are suitable for frying or grilling (broiling) are not only very tender, but lean as well. This means they should be kept well-moistened with fat during frying or grilling (broiling) or they will dry out.

Butter gives flavour but always add a little oil when frying steaks as this prevents the butter from over-heating.

People have very definite ideas as to how they like steaks cooked so always ask before you begin cooking.

To Grill (Broil) Steaks

Allow 15 to 25 g/½ to 1 oz (1 to 2 tablespoons) butter for each steak and thoroughly preheat the grill (broiler). Place the steak(s) on the rack of the grill (broiler) pan. Melt the butter and brush half of it over the meat.

The timing below refers to steaks of between 1.5 and 2 cm/½ and ¾ inch in thickness.

Rare Steaks Grill (broil) rapidly for 2 to 3 minutes, turn, brush with the remaining butter and cook for the same time on the second side.

Medium-cooked Steaks Cook for 2 to 3 minutes quickly on either side, lower the heat and cook for a further 5 to 6 minutes.

Well-cooked Steaks Cook for 2 to 3 minutes quickly on either side, lower the heat and cook for a further 8 to 10 minutes.

To Fry Steaks

For 4 steaks, heat 75 g/3 oz (6 tablespoons) butter with 1 tablespoon oil in a large frying pan (skillet). If you are using a non-stick (silicone coated) pan you can halve the amount of butter and oil.

Follow the timings given for grilled steaks.

Accompaniments

Cooked mushrooms and tomatoes are the usual accompaniments to grilled (broiled) and fried meats, particularly steaks. Fried onions are another pleasant accompaniment (see page 90).

If the steaks are to be grilled (broiled), you can cook the mushrooms and/or tomatoes in the grill (broiler) pan at the same time. Heat a little butter or margarine in the pan, add the whole mushrooms and halved tomatoes and season lightly. Cook for a few minutes under the preheated grill (broiler), then add the steaks on the rack of the grill (broiler) pan and all the food will be ready at the same time.

If the steaks are to be fried heat a little butter or margarine and then add the mushrooms and/or halved tomatoes, cook for a few minutes. Sprinkle with a little lemon juice, chopped chives and parsley before serving.

Do not cook the meat first and keep it waiting. It should be served as soon as possible after cooking. This is why no grilled (broiled) or fried meat recipes have a freezing symbol. Suitable meats can be grilled (broiled) from their frozen state, or after thawing but it is not a good idea to freeze the cooked meat.

Carpet Bag Steak

| 4 thick pieces of fillet or rump steak |
| 4 to 8 oysters or 16 to 20 mussels (for preparation see page 46) |
| 75 g/3 oz (6 tablespoons) butter |
| 2 to 3 teaspoons chopped parsley |
| a squeeze of lemon juice |
| salt and pepper |
| TO GARNISH: |
| halved and cooked tomatoes |
| cooked mushrooms |
| sprig of parsley |

Slit each steak horizontally to make pockets. Slice the oysters, if using. Melt 25 g/1 oz (2 tablespoons) of the butter and blend with the oysters or mussels, the chopped parsley, the lemon juice and seasoning. Put into the pockets in the steaks. Skewer the steaks firmly or close with fine string or cotton. Melt the remaining butter and brush the steaks with it. Cook under a preheated grill (broiler) to personal taste. Remove the skewers, string or cotton. Serve the steaks garnished with grilled (broiled) tomatoes, mushrooms and parsley. Serves 4.

Steak Diane

This recipe uses Minute steaks which are very thin slices of steak. Use sirloin so you have a good distribution of fat and lean, or very thin slices of rump steak.

| 4 minute steaks |
| 1 medium onion or 2 shallots |
| 75 g/3 oz (6 tablespoons) butter |
| a few drops of Worcestershire sauce |
| 1 to 2 tablespoons chopped parsley |
| 2 tablespoons brandy |

Peel the onion or shallots and chop very finely. Heat the butter in a large frying pan (skillet), fry the onion or shallots until nearly tender, add the meat and cook for 1 minute on each side. Add the sauce and parsley during this time.

Warm the brandy, ignite if desired, pour over the steaks and stir to blend with the other ingredients. Serve at once. Serves 4.

TOURNEDOS

Tie fillet steaks into neat rounds and fry or grill (broil) as above. The garnish which is served on the cooked steak gives its name to the completed dish, see below.

It is usual to fry rounds of bread in hot butter or fat and serve the tournedos on these.

Tournedos Africaine
Top the steaks with fried bananas and serve with horseradish sauce.

Tournedos Batonne
Top the steaks with cooked mushrooms and a thick cooked tomato purée. Serve with Béarnaise Sauce (see page 195).

Tournedos Dumas
Top the steaks with Onion Sauce (see page 102), and cover with slices of cooked ham then grated cheese. Brown under the grill (broiler).

Tournedos Othello
Top the steaks with fried or poached eggs.

Tournedos Rossini
Top the steaks with neat rounds of pâté. You can also add small fried mushrooms.

Fried Steaks with mushroom accompaniment and Steak Diane

Beef Stews and Casseroles

Beef could be termed a robust meat, so flavourings and additional ingredients can be fairly strong in taste. Beef used for stewing needs long slow cooking.

Master Recipe
Braised Beef

Portions of veal, lamb, kidney, game or poultry can also be braised by this method. Adjust the liquids to suit.

1 kg/2 lb topside (top round) or fresh brisket of beef
50 g/2 oz fat pork (fresh pork sides), cut in 1 slice
FOR THE MIREPOIX:
25 g/1 oz streaky bacon (2 bacon slices)
2 large carrots
1 large onion
1 small turnip
1 or 2 sticks of celery
25 g/1 oz (2 tablespoons) butter
150 ml/¼ pint (⅔ cup) red wine
150 ml/¼ pint (⅔ cup) beef stock
1 bouquet garni
salt and pepper

✱Cut the beef into 4 to 6 portions, and dice the pork. Heat the pork in a strong saucepan, add the beef and fry until golden brown. Remove from the pan. De-rind and dice the bacon, peel and chop the root vegetables and dice the celery. Heat the butter and fry the bacon and vegetables for a few minutes. Add the wine and stock, the bouquet garni and a little seasoning. Place the beef and diced pork on top of the mirepoix and cover the pan tightly.

Cook over a low heat for 1¼ to 1½ hours, or until the beef is tender, then lift it on to a hot dish. Remove the bouquet garni and sieve or blend the mirepoix to make a thick smooth sauce. Serve over the meat. Serves 4 to 6.

Variations

Cook the beef for the same time in a tightly covered casserole in a moderate oven (160°C/325°F, Gas Mark 3).
Hungarian Style Braised Beef Flavour the beef with a little paprika before frying. Add 100 g/4 oz button mushrooms and 225 g/8 oz diced tomatoes to the mirepoix and omit the turnip.
Irish Style Braised Beef Add 100 to 175 g/4 to 6 oz (1 cup) soaked, but not cooked, prunes to the vegetables for the mirepoix. Use stout (dark beer) instead of wine and stock. Omit the turnip and celery. Serve the prunes with the beef and blend the other ingredients as in the Master Recipe.

Beef and Tomato Casserole

550 g/1¼ lb stewing steak
225 g/8 oz onions
450 g/1 lb tomatoes
25 g/1 oz (¼ cup) flour
salt and pepper
50 g/2 oz (¼ cup) cooking fat or dripping
300 ml/½ pint (1¼ cups) beef stock or water and ½ beef stock cube (1 bouillon)
1 wineglass dry sherry
1 teaspoon chopped marjoram
2 tablespoons chopped parsley

✱Cut the steak into neat fingers. Peel the onions and cut into thin rings. Skin and thickly slice the tomatoes. Blend the flour with a little salt and pepper and use to coat the beef.

Heat the fat or dripping in a frying pan (skillet), add the beef and onions and fry for several minutes. Spoon into a casserole; add the tomatoes. Pour the stock and the sherry into the frying pan (skillet). Stir well to absorb the meat juices. Pour over the ingredients in the casserole. Add the herbs.

Cover the casserole and cook in the centre of a cool oven (150°C/300°F, Gas Mark 2) for 2 hours. Serves 4 to 6.

VARIATIONS
Omit the sherry and use extra stock.
✱Beef and Apricot Casserole Use only 2 tomatoes in the recipe above. Cut 175 g/6 oz (1 cup) dried apricots into narrow strips, soak for 2 hours in the beef stock. Pour the stock and apricots into the frying pan (skillet) used for frying the meat and heat for 2 to 3 minutes with 150 ml/¼ pint (⅔ cup) sweet brown sherry before adding to the casserole. Season lightly but omit the herbs.
✱Steak, Kidney and Mushroom Casserole Use 450 g/1 lb stewing steak with 100 to 175 g/4 to 6 oz ox (beef) kidney. Omit the tomatoes. Dice the meats, coat with seasoned flour, and fry with the onions as above together with 100 g/4 oz button mushrooms. Proceed as above.

Beef Cobbler

Beef and tomato casserole or one of the variations
FOR THE COBBLER:
175 g/6 oz (1½ cups) self-raising flour or plain (all-purpose) flour with 1½ teaspoons baking powder
pinch of salt
25 g/1 oz (2 tablespoons) butter or margarine
milk to bind

✱Prepare the ingredients for the casserole and cook as above. Raise the oven temperature to moderately hot (200°C/400°F, Gas Mark 6).

Sift the flour, or flour and baking powder, and salt together. Rub in (cut in) the butter or margarine and add enough milk to make a soft consistency.

Roll out the dough until 1.5 cm/½ inch in thickness. Cut into small rounds.

Remove the lid from the casserole and arrange rounds of the cobbler mixture over the meat. Bake uncovered in the centre of the moderately hot oven for 15 minutes. Serves 4 to 6.

Beef and Orange Stew

2 oranges
550 g/1¼ lb stewing beef
350 g/12 oz very small shallots or onions
25 g/1 oz (¼ cup) flour
salt and pepper
50 g/2 oz (¼ cup) butter or margarine
water, see method

⁂Grate the rind from the oranges, halve and squeeze out the juice. Cut the beef into neat fingers. Peel the shallots or onions; keep them whole. Mix the orange rind, flour and a little seasoning and coat the meat. Heat the butter or margarine and fry the coated meat and onions for 5 minutes.

Measure the orange juice and add sufficient water to make 600 ml/1 pint (2½ cups). Pour into the saucepan and stir over a low heat until the sauce thickens slightly.

Cover the saucepan and simmer gently for 2 hours until the meat is tender. Lift the lid towards the end of the cooking time to allow the sauce to become a little thicker. Serve with cooked rice. Serves 4 to 6.

International Dishes

Chilli con Carne

225 g/8 oz (¾ cup) red kidney beans or 225 g/8 oz (1 cup) haricot (navy) beans or 1 × 425 g/15 oz can red kidney beans
salt and pepper
2 to 3 medium onions
2 garlic cloves
1 green pepper
4 large tomatoes
50 g/2 oz (¼ cup) cooking fat
550 g/1¼ lb (2½ cups) minced (ground) beef
pinch of dried cumin
450 ml/¾ pint (2 cups) beef stock
1 teaspoon to 2 tablespoons chilli powder, see method

⁂If using dried beans, cover with cold water and leave soaking overnight. Next day, place in a pan with the water in which they were soaked and boil hard for 10 minutes; this is essential to make sure the beans are not to be harmful to health. This must be done even if you are cooking them for a long time in a slow cooker. The canned variety are quite safe, as they have been subjected to considerable heat.

Reduce the heat and simmer for about 1½ hours until just tender. Season lightly.

Peel and chop the onions and garlic. Dice and pepper, discard the core and seeds. Skin and chop the tomatoes. Heat the cooking fat in a large saucepan, and fry the meat, onions and garlic for several minutes, then add the tomatoes and the rest of the ingredients, including the well-drained beans. The amount of chilli powder needed varies a great deal. Add it gradually, for it is very hot and different makes vary considerably in strength. You may not want the full amount, but 2 tablespoons is quite usual in this dish, if you are used to, and like, hot flavours.

Cook steadily for 1 hour, stirring from time to time as the mixture thickens. Serve with cooked rice. Serves 4 to 6.

Boeuf à la Mode

Boeuf à la Mode is a rather grand kind of pot-roast. For luxury occasions, thick rump would be ideal, but it is a very good way of using topside (top round) of beef too. The flavour of the meat when cold is delicious. That is why it is worthwhile cooking a large joint. The trotter or calf's foot gives the unthickened liquid its rich flavour. It could be omitted and the liquid could be thickened with flour or cornflour (cornstarch) to make a gravy.

Chilli Con Carne

1.75 kg/4 lb joint of beef, see above
175 g/6 oz fat belly of pork (fresh pork sides) or streaky bacon cut in 1 piece
1 wineglass of brandy or red wine
12 shallots or small onions
12 medium carrots
50 g/2 oz (¼ cup) butter or beef dripping
1 pig's trotter or calf's foot (optional)
600 ml/1 pint (2½ cups) water
salt and pepper
1 bouquet garni

⁂Tie the meat into a round that fits into a large heavy saucepan. Cut the pork or bacon into long, very narrow strips; derind the bacon but keep the rind.

Thread the fat pork or bacon through the meat, see 'SIMPLE SKILL', right. Pour the brandy or red wine into a dish. Marinate the beef in this for 2 hours, turning once. Peel the shallots or onions and the carrots, and leave whole.

Heat the butter or dripping in the saucepan, put in the meat and cook slowly for 5 minutes. Turn the joint and cook for the same time on the second side. Add all the other ingredients. Cover the pan very tightly (put a piece of foil under the lid to ensure a perfect fit). Simmer gently for 2 to 2¼ hours. Serve with the shallots or onions and carrots and freshly cooked vegetables of your own choice together with a little stock from the pan. Serves 8.

VARIATIONS

The vegetables tend to be very well cooked. If you would prefer them less well cooked, add them 45 minutes before the end of the cooking time.

You can cook the meal in a covered casserole in the centre of a cool oven (150°C/300°F, Gas Mark 2) for 2½ hours.

SIMPLE SKILL
Larding Meat
Larding is the name given to the process by which fat in some form is added to lean meat, such as veal, or the joint of beef on this page.

You can buy a special larding needle which is rather like a carpet needle.

Thread the fat meat or bacon through the eye of the needle and then through the meat.

LEFTOVERS
Serve leftover Chilli con Carne as an hors d'oeuvre. Heat in individual dishes and serve with hot toast.

55

Carbonnade de Boeuf à la Flamande and Stifatho

Note If you like a thicker gravy use only 150 ml/¼ pint (⅔ cup) stock or water.

Grill (broil) to personal taste (see page 53).

VARIATIONS

Slow Cooking First brown the onions and garlic and then the meat in olive oil in a saucepan then transfer to the slow cooker. Add the blended tomatoes, potatoes and remaining ingredients as above. Cook on HIGH for 5 hours or on LOW for 8 to 10 hours.

Pressure Cooking This thick stew is not entirely suitable for cooking in a pressure cooker as you need to add more water. Fry the shallots or onions and garlic, then the meat in the bottom of the pressure cooker as in the recipe. Add the blended tomatoes, 300 ml/½ pint (1¼ cups) water and the remaining ingredients. Allow 15 minutes on HIGH 15 lb pressure, reduce pressure and serve.

Boeuf Bourguignonne
[Beef in Burgundy]

This dish is similar to Stifatho above. Omit the tomatoes, water and red wine vinegar; add 4 medium carrots and 175 to 225 g/6 to 8 oz (1½ to 2 cups) button mushrooms. Use 300 ml/½ pint (1¼ cups) red Burgundy wine plus 150 ml/¼ pint (⅔ cup) beef stock.

Fry the onions, mushrooms and meat as in Stifatho, blend in the wine and stock, peel and slice the carrots, add to the stew and cook as the Stifatho. Top with chopped parsley. Serves 4 to 6.

Cariucho
[Steak with Peanut Sauce]

2 medium onions
1 small green pepper
4 medium tomatoes
100 g/4 oz (⅔ cup) peanuts
2 tablespoons olive oil
½ teaspoon paprika
¼ teaspoon chilli powder, see method
150 ml/¼ pint (⅔ cup) beef stock
4 tablespoons double (heavy) cream
salt and pepper
a little butter
4 fillet or rump steaks

Peel and finely chop the onions. Dice the pepper, discard the core and seeds. Skin and chop the tomatoes. Chop or grind the peanuts in a food processor or blender. Heat the oil in a frying pan (skillet) and cook the onions until nearly soft then add the pepper and tomatoes. Continue cooking for 5 minutes and blend in the spices (add the chilli powder gradually, it is very hot), the peanuts and the stock. Simmer for 5 minutes, then stir in the cream and season to taste.

Meanwhile melt the butter and brush over the steaks. Grill (broil) to personal taste (see page 53). Serve topped with the sauce. Serves 4.

Carbonnade de Boeuf à la Flamande
[Beef Stew with Beer]

4 large onions
550 to 675 g/1¼ to 1½ lb stewing beef
50 g/2 oz streaky bacon cut in 1 piece if possible
salt and pepper
25 g/1 oz (¼ cup) flour
50 g/2 oz (¼ cup) dripping or fat
300 ml/½ pint (1¼ cups) beer
300 ml/½ pint (1¼ cups) beef stock or water and ½ beef stock (1 bouillon) cube
1 teaspoon French mustard
2 teaspoons brown sugar
1 bouquet garni

✷✷Peel the onions, cut into rings. Cut the beef into narrow strips or cubes. De-rind the bacon and cut into fingers but do not discard the rind. Add a little salt and pepper to the flour and coat the meat. Heat the dripping or fat and bacon rind in a saucepan, add the onions, coated beef and bacon and cook for 5 minutes, then transfer to a casserole. Pour the beer and stock into the saucepan. Bring to the boil and stir well to absorb any flour or meat juices. Add the mustard, sugar, bouquet garni and seasoning.

Pour over the meat in the casserole, cover and cook for 2¼ to 2½ hours in the centre of a preheated cool oven (150°C/300°F, Gas Mark 2). Serves 4 to 6.

FOR FLAVOUR
Many beef stews benefit from the use of beer in the liquid. The Carbonnade on this page is one example. The beer mellows in flavour as it cooks and helps to tenderize the meat.

Stifatho
[Greek Beef Stew]

750 g/1½ lb stewing beef
450 g/1 lb shallots or small onions
1 to 2 garlic cloves
450 g/1 lb tomatoes
150 ml/¼ pint (⅔ cup) water
450 g/1 lb potatoes
2 tablespoons olive oil
1 bay leaf
sprig of rosemary
2 tablespoons red wine vinegar
salt and pepper

✷✷Cut the meat into neat small pieces. Peel the shallots or onions and keep them whole. Skin and crush the garlic. Skin the tomatoes and sieve or blend, mix with the water. Peel and quarter the potatoes.

Heat the oil in a heavy saucepan and fry the shallots or onions with the garlic until just golden. Remove the shallots or onions from the pan. Add the meat and gently fry this for 5 to 10 minutes. Pour the tomato mixture into the saucepan, return the shallots or onions then add all the other ingredients. Cover the saucepan very tightly and cook for 2 hours or until the meat is tender. Add the potatoes after 1½ hours. This is a stew with very little liquid. Remove the herbs, then serve. Serves 4 to 6.

LAMB DISHES

Lamb is readily available and a relatively inexpensive meat which can be cooked in various ways.

When buying lamb remember there is a comparatively large weight of bone, so allow for this when calculating the cooking time.

Lamb or Mutton Cuts

Always select the correct cuts of meat for the cooking method.

For Stock and Brawn Head, scrag end of neck (neck slices), trotters.

For Stewing, Casseroling, Braising or Boiling Breast, leg (shank), neck (blade chops), shoulder.

For Frying or Grilling (Broiling) Best end of neck chops (rib chops), cutlets, slices from leg, loin chops.

For Roasting Best end of neck (rack), breast, leg, loin, saddle, shoulder.

Quantities

For Frying or Grilling (Broiling) Allow 1 large or 2 small chops per portion.

For Roasting Allow about 350 g/12 oz meat on the bone per person.

For Stewing Allow about 350 g/12 oz meat on the bone or 175 to 225 g/6 to 8 oz off the bone.

Lamb Stews and Casseroles

Lamb is a meat with great scope as it blends equally well with sweet or savoury ingredients. Even stewing lamb is relatively tender so do not overcook it.

Mutton can be substituted for lamb in these recipes but it will need about 50% longer cooking time.

Navarin of Lamb

This is a French method of 'boiling' lamb. The word 'boiling' is a little misleading for the liquid should only simmer very gently.

1 kg/2 lb leg or shoulder of lamb, weight without bone
salt and pepper
½ tablespoon caster sugar
25 g/1 oz (¼ cup) flour
50 g/2 oz (¼ cup) butter or margarine
600 ml/1 pint (2½ cups) water
750 g/1½ lb mixed vegetables, see method
1 bouquet garni
1 or 2 garlic cloves
1 tablespoon chopped parsley

✳Dice the meat neatly. Blend a little salt and pepper, the sugar and the flour and coat the meat.

Heat the butter or margarine in a large saucepan and gently fry the meat until golden brown; the small amount of sugar gives a very faint caramel flavour to the meat and encourages the meat to brown. Blend in the water. Stir as the liquid comes to the boil.

Prepare the vegetables and add to the saucepan; use a mixture of peeled diced celeriac, sliced carrots, whole onions and diced potatoes. Prepare the bouquet garni. Peel the garlic and tie it in muslin with the other herbs. Add to the saucepan, cover the pan and simmer gently for 1 to 1¼ hours. Remove the bouquet garni before serving sprinkled with parsley. Serves 6.

Harvest Casserole

675 g/1½ lb lean lamb, cut from the leg
1 large onion
4 large carrots
1 medium aubergine (eggplant)
salt and pepper
2 tablespoons oil
25 g/1 oz (2 tablespoons) butter or margarine, see method
50 g/2 oz (½ cup) flour
600 ml/1 pint (2½ cups) cider
1 bay leaf
175 g/6 oz (1 cup) pumpkin or marrow (squash), weight without peel and seeds

✳Dice the lamb neatly. Peel the onion and carrots. Chop the onion and slice the carrots. Score the skin of the aubergine (eggplant), sprinkle with a little salt and leave for about 30 minutes. Drain, rinse in cold water, then dry and slice. Cut each slice into halves or quarters.

Heat the oil in a large frying pan (skillet), fry the lamb until golden in colour and put into a casserole. Fry the onion and carrots for several minutes; add to the lamb. If there is no fat left in the pan, use some or all of the butter or margarine. Heat the fat in the frying pan (skillet), stir well to absorb any meat juices, blend in the flour and then the cider. Stir briskly as the sauce comes to the boil and season to taste. Pour the sauce over the meat and vegetables and add the aubergine (eggplant) slices and the bay leaf. Cover the casserole and cook in the centre of a moderate oven (160°C/325°F, Gas Mark 3) for an hour, or until the lamb is nearly tender.

Peel and de-seed the pumpkin or marrow (squash), cut the flesh into small cubes, add to the casserole, cover and continue to cook for a further 30 minutes. Remove the bay leaf and serve with cooked pasta or jacket potatoes. Serves 4 to 6.

VARIATION

Omit the pumpkin or marrow (squash). Add a few firm small tomatoes 10 minutes before serving.

FOR ECONOMY
✳When pears are plentiful use 2 firm ripe pears in place of the aubergine (eggplant) in the Harvest Casserole.

Peel the pears and cut them into thick slices; add with the pumpkin or marrow (squash).

Navarin of Lamb

To Grill or Fry

Lamb chops or cutlets can be grilled (broiled) or fried with equal success. Even young lamb has a certain amount of fat, so additional fat should not be required when grilling (broiling) the meat and relatively little when frying.

Cooking Times

Medium-sized chops, about 2 cm/¾ inch in thickness, should be cooked quickly under a preheated hot grill (broiler) for 2 to 3 minutes on either side, then for 6 to 8 minutes on a lower heat.

Frying times are similar; heat about 25 g/1 oz (2 tablespoons) fat in a large frying pan (skillet), add the meat and cook as above.

Cutlets of lamb, i.e. chops from which the meat is removed from the base of the bones, leaving just the very tender lean meat, are cooked in a slightly shorter time. (These are sometimes called Frenched rib lamb chops).

Freezing Note

There are no freezing symbols against the fried and grilled (broiled) dishes on this page, nor the roasts on page 59 as they should be served as soon as possible after cooking. Uncooked lamb freezes well. While cuts of lamb can be used frozen in some recipes, allow the lamb to thaw before using in Caribbean Lamb and Lamb and Cucumber Sauce, and before making the special roasts opposite.

FOR ECONOMY

When cucumbers are plentiful and inexpensive, use them as a hot vegetable. Peel and thinly slice the cucumber and fry for 10 minutes in a little hot butter or margarine.

The sauce given on this page is a well-known and popular one to serve with a curry.

Noisettes Niçoise

Special Technique
PERFECT NOISETTES

A noisette is a round of lamb, similar in shape to a tournedos of steak. Any butcher will prepare noisettes, given sufficient notice, but it is not difficult to do it yourself.

Choose loin or best end of neck chops (rib chops). Very carefully cut the meat from the bone. (Use the bones for stock). Roll the meat into a neat round with the lean part in the centre. Tie into shape with fine string. Grill (broil) or fry following the timing given under Cooking Times.

Sometimes veal or pork chops are made into rounds. Purists say these should not be called noisettes; that word belongs to lamb.

Noisettes Niçoise

8 noisettes of lamb, made as above
2 medium onions
2 garlic cloves
4 large tomatoes
1 tablespoon oil
salt and pepper
8 black (ripe) olives

Grill (broil) or fry the lamb, following the timing on this page. Meanwhile peel and finely chop the onions and garlic. Skin and chop the tomatoes. Heat the oil in a saucepan; fry the onions and garlic until nearly tender. Add the tomatoes with a little seasoning and cook gently for several minutes. Spoon over the cooked lamb and top with olives. Serves 4.

VARIATION

Noisettes with Herbs Grill (broil) or fry the noisettes. Meanwhile blend 75 g/3 oz (6 tablespoons) soft cream or curd cheese with 2 tablespoons chopped parsley, 1 teaspoon chopped rosemary and 1 tablespoon chopped chives. Spread on the noisettes and serve at once.

Caribbean Lamb

8 lamb chops
FOR THE MARINADE:
1 to 2 garlic cloves
1 small onion
3 tablespoons lime or lemon juice
2 tablespoons corn oil
½ teaspoon curry powder
1 teaspoon ground ginger
a few drops Tabasco sauce (hot pepper sauce)

Trim any excess fat from the chops. Peel the garlic and onion and chop very finely. Mix with the other ingredients for the marinade. Place the chops on a flat dish, prick on both sides with a fork then cover with the marinade. Leave for 1 hour, turn over and leave for another hour.

Drain the meat then grill (broil) or fry in the usual way. If grilling (broiling) the meat, it is a good idea to lay the moistened meat on a sheet of foil in the grill (broiler) pan. Serves 4.

Lamb with Cucumber Sauce

8 lamb chops
8 small slices of bread
25 to 50 g/1 to 2 oz (2 to 4 tablespoons) butter
FOR THE SAUCE:
½ small cucumber
150 ml/¼ pint (⅔ cup) yogurt
½ tablespoon chopped mint
salt and pepper

Ask the butcher to bone the lamb and turn the chops into noisettes or follow the instructions on this page. Grill (broil) or fry until tender.

Meanwhile, cut the bread into rounds. Heat the butter in a frying pan (skillet) fry the bread until golden on both sides. Lift the chops on to the croûtes.

Peel and grate or neatly dice the cucumber and stir into the yogurt with the mint and seasoning. Serve cold with the hot lamb. Serves 4.

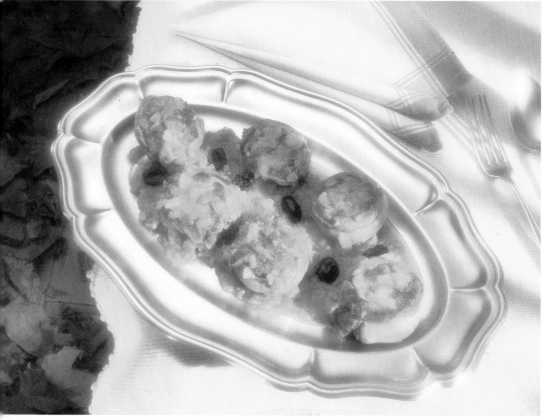

Roast Lamb

Roasting Times for Lamb

<u>Fast Roasting</u> Set the oven to moderately hot to hot (200 to 220°C/400 to 425°F, Gas Mark 6 to 7).

Allow 20 minutes per 450 g/1 lb and 20 minutes over for medium cooked meat; slightly less time if you prefer it 'pink' as French style.

<u>Slower Roasting</u> Set the oven to moderate (160 to 180°C/325 to 350°F, Gas Mark 3 to 4).

Allow 35 minutes per 450 g/1 lb and 35 minutes over for medium cooked meat.

Mutton needs a little longer cooking and is better Slow Roasted.

Microwave Roasting

First read the general comments given on page 48. Allow 8 to 10 minutes per 450 g/1 lb then wrap the cooked meat in foil and allow to stand for a minimum of 15 minutes.

The meat should be removed from the microwave cooker when a microwave meat thermometer registers slightly lower settings than given on page 50, i.e. from 74°C/165°F to 80°C/176°F as the internal temperature of the meat will rise during standing time.

Lamb with Grapefruit Stuffing

Breast of lamb is a joint that has a fairly high percentage of fat so choose stuffings that counteract this, like the one used here. The breasts should be boned before making this dish.

2 breasts of lamb, each weighing about 750 g/1½ lb when boned
FOR THE STUFFING: 1 large onion
2 grapefruit
75 g/3 oz (6 tablespoons) butter
225 g/8 oz (4 cups) soft breadcrumbs
2 tablespoons chopped mint
2 tablespoons chopped parsley
1 egg
salt and pepper
TO GARNISH: 1 grapefruit
watercress

Peel and chop the onion. Grate the rind from the grapefruit, then cut away the pith and cut out the segments of fruit (see page 96). Heat 50 g/2 oz (¼ cup) of the butter in a saucepan, add the onion and fry for several minutes. Add the breadcrumbs, herbs, grapefruit rind and segments and mix with the onion. Blend in the egg and seasoning to taste.

Lay one lamb breast flat and cover with the stuffing. Place the second breast on top of the stuffing and shape the meat to form a long roll. Secure with string or several skewers. Put into the meat tin and brush with the remaining butter; do not cover the tin.

Roast in a preheated moderate oven (180°C/350°F, Gas Mark 4) for 1 hour and 10 minutes, then raise the heat to moderately hot (200°C/400°F, Gas Mark 6) and cook for a further 15 to 20 minutes until the meat is very brown.

Shred a little peel from the grapefruit for the garnish and sprinkle over the meat. Cut away the rind and then cut out neat segments of fruit. Arrange around the joint with the watercress. Serves 6.

Herb Crusted Lamb

1 leg of lamb
FOR THE STUFFING: 1 large onion
100 g/4 oz (1 cup) mushrooms
1 orange
50 g/2 oz (¼ cup) butter
1 teaspoon chopped rosemary
1 teaspoon chopped thyme
1 tablespoon chopped parsley
50 g/2 oz (1 cup) soft breadcrumbs
1 tablespoon sherry
salt and pepper
FOR THE CRUST: ½ tablespoon oil or lamb fat
100 g/4 oz (2 cups) soft breadcrumbs
2 tablespoons chopped parsley
1 teaspoon chopped rosemary
1 teaspoon chopped thyme
1 teaspoon grated orange rind

Bone the meat and use the bone to make good stock. Peel and finely chop

the onion. Wipe and slice the mushrooms. Finely grate the rind from the orange (use only the orange zest), then remove the rest of the peel and pith and dice the fruit.

Heat the butter in a pan, cook the onion and mushrooms for 5 minutes, remove from the heat and mix with the remainder of the stuffing ingredients. Allow to cool, then spread over the meat. Form the meat into a neat shape, tie or skewer securely, weigh and roast in a preheated moderate oven (180°C/350°F, Gas Mark 4) as the timing on this page suggests, but remove from the oven 20 minutes before the end of the cooking time.

<u>Crust</u> Blend the ingredients together and season the mixture. Press evenly and firmly over the top of the lamb and return to the oven for the final 20 minutes. Serve with gravy or Sweet Orange Sauce (see page 102). Serves 6.

Lamb with Grapefruit Stuffing

FOR FLAVOUR

Peel 1 to 2 garlic cloves, cut into thin slivers and insert under the skin of the lamb. Alternatively shake garlic salt over the meat before roasting.

Place a spray of rosemary over the lamb before cooking.

Brush the fat with a mixture of 1 tablespoon honey and 1 tablespoon lemon juice 15 minutes before the end of the cooking time.

Special Technique
PERFECT ROAST LAMB

Choose the cuts of lamb given on page 57 and roast for the times given on this page. Many people prefer lamb well-cooked, but it can also be served under-done so that it is still slightly pink inside. This is how the French serve their lamb.

Even young lamb has a little natural fat on the outside so the addition of extra fat should be unnecessary unless potatoes or other vegetables are being roasted round the meat. If doing this, check the amount of fat in the tin and if necessary add an extra 50 g/2 oz (¼ cup) fat, which must be well heated before the vegetables are added.

Lamb is also excellent if cooked in a covered roasting tin, in foil or in a roasting bag.

59

Moussaka

International Dishes

Carré d'Agneau Boulangère

2 best end of neck joints (racks of lamb), each consisting of 6 chops
450 g/1 lb onions
1 kg/2 lb potatoes
salt and pepper
150 ml/¼ pint (⅔ cup) stock from simmering lamb bones or water and ¼ chicken stock cube (½ bouillon cube)
25 g/1 oz (2 tablespoons) margarine
TO GARNISH: chopped parsley

Trim any surplus fat from the meat. Peel the onions and potatoes, cut the onions into wafer thin slices and the potatoes into 5 mm/¼ inch slices. Mix all the onions with three-quarters of the potatoes, season well and put into a small roasting tin or large casserole. Add the stock. Arrange the remaining potato slices in a neat design over the mixed vegetables, melt the margarine and brush over the potatoes.

Place the two small joints on top of the potatoes. Roast in the centre of a preheated moderately hot oven (190°C/375°F, Gas Mark 5) for 1¼ hours or until the meat is tender. Remove the meat from the top of the potatoes and keep hot. Move the tin or casserole to the top shelf of the oven and leave for about 10 minutes to allow the potatoes to brown more.

Carve the meat, arrange on the potato and onion base and top with chopped parsley. Serve with gravy. Serves 6.

VARIATION

Roast a leg of lamb this way but since cooking time is longer the vegetables should be cut more thickly.

Moussaka

2 medium aubergines (eggplants)
salt and pepper
4 medium potatoes
2 to 3 medium onions
4 medium tomatoes
450 g/1 lb lean lamb or mutton
50 g/2 oz (¼ cup) butter
2 tablespoons oil
FOR THE SAUCE: Cheese Sauce made with 40 g/1½ oz (3 tablespoons) butter or margarine, see page 102
pinch of grated nutmeg
1 or 2 eggs
2 tablespoons grated cheese
TO GARNISH: chopped parsley

⁎⁎Slice the aubergines (eggplants). Peel and slice the potatoes and onions. Skin and slice the tomatoes.

Mince (grind) the lamb or mutton or chop in a food processor.

Heat half the butter and oil in a large pan and fry the aubergines (eggplants) and potatoes for 5 to 10 minutes; stir well. Remove from the pan. Heat the remaining butter and oil. Fry the onions until nearly soft, add the tomatoes and meat and continue cooking for a further 2 to 3 minutes.

Add the nutmeg and then whisk in the egg or eggs. It is worthwhile using a second egg for it makes the sauce puff up in cooking.

Arrange layers of aubergine (eggplant) and potatoes and the meat mixture in a casserole; end with a vegetable layer. Moisten each layer with a little sauce but reserve sufficient for a good layer on top of the vegetables. Top with the 2 tablespoons of grated cheese.

Bake in the centre of a preheated moderate oven (160°C/325°F, Gas Mark 3) for 1½ hours. The casserole can be left uncovered if you like a firm golden brown topping. Cover for a softer mixture. Top with parsley before serving. Serves 4.

Bobotie

300 ml/½ pint (1¼ cups) milk
75 g/3 oz (1½ cups) white bread, weight without crusts
2 medium onions
40 g/1½ oz (3 tablespoons) butter or margarine
450 to 550 g/1 to 1¼ lb (2–2½ cups) minced (ground) lamb
1 to 2 tablespoons curry powder
1 tablespoon brown malt vinegar
salt and pepper
1 teaspoon brown sugar
2 eggs
2 tablespoons chopped blanched almonds
2 bay leaves

⁎⁎Pour half the milk into a bowl. Crumble the bread into the milk and allow to stand for 30 minutes. Peel and finely chop the onions. Heat the butter or margarine in a saucepan and fry the onions for 5 minutes. Add the lamb and continue cooking for a further 5 minutes; stir well to blend the meat with the onions. Add the curry powder, vinegar, the soaked bread and any milk left in the bowl. Season lightly and add the sugar.

Spoon the mixture into a 1.5 litre/2½ pint (2 quart) pie dish or casserole and smooth the top until quite flat. Beat the eggs and remaining milk together, pour over the meat and top with the nuts and bay leaves.

Bake in the centre of a moderate oven (160°C/325°F, Gas Mark 3) for 45 minutes to 1 hour. Serve with cooked rice and chutney. Serves 4.

LEFTOVERS

⁎⁎*Leftover cooked lamb makes an excellent Moussaka. Prepare and fry the vegetables as right, but cut them a little thinner, as the cooking time will be shorter.*

Dice, rather than mince (grind), the cooked meat. Cook for only 45 minutes to 1 hour.

PORK AND BACON DISHES

Pork has a great deal of flavour which most people enjoy. The modern methods of rearing pigs for pork or bacon mean there is a relatively small amount of fat on the cuts of meat.

Quantities

For Frying or Grilling (Broiling) Allow 1 good-sized chop or 175 g/6 oz or the same amount of bacon per portion.
For Roasting Allow about 350 g/12 oz meat on the bone or 175 g/6 oz boneless meat or bacon per person.
For Stewing Allow about 175 g/6 oz boneless meat per person.

Cuts of Pork

Always select the correct cut for the cooking method.
For Stock and Brawn Head, trotters.
For Stewing, Casseroling, Boiling (pork is not a braising meat) Belly (fresh pork sides), hand and spring (arm and blade roast), head; also cuts given for roasting.
For Frying and Grilling (Broiling) Chump chops (rib chops), loin chops, spare rib chops (country-style ribs).
For Roasting Blade, leg (fresh ham), loin, spare ribs (country-style ribs).

Cuts of Bacon

For Stewing, Casseroling or Boiling: Collar (smoked shoulder butt), forehock or gammon (smoked arm picnic, shoulder roll or smoked ham).
For Frying or Grilling Back rashers (Canadian bacon) bacon chops (thick back rashers), rashers or slices of gammon (smoked ham), streaky bacon (bacon slices).
For Roasting Collar (smoked shoulder butt), forehock or gammon (smoked arm picnic, shoulder roll or smoked ham).

Buying Points

Good quality bacon should look pleasantly moist with a good colour. Bacon which looks dull and dry is inclined to be stale. Packed bacon rashers (slices) are dated; check this date carefully.

You have a choice between smoked and unsmoked (green) bacon; rashers (slices) of bacon cut from economical short and long streaky bacon, (in which there is an appreciable amount of fat; leaner short and long back bacon (Canadian bacon) and prime gammon (smoked ham) which is very lean.

Thick rashers (slices) of back bacon are known as bacon chops; these are excellent for main meals. Thick slices of gammon (smoked ham) are generally called gammon (ham) steaks.

Bacon rashers (bacon slices and Canadian bacon), chops and steaks can all be fried or grilled (broiled).

You can buy unsmoked, smoked bacon or special mild sweet cure bacon joints. For economical joints choose collar (smoked shoulder butt) or forehock; for special occasions buy gammon (smoked ham).

Ham is cured in a different manner from bacon and is generally sold ready cooked. Check that the ham is pleasantly pink and the fat is firm and white.

Pork Stews and Casseroles

Pork is less suitable than other meats for standard casserole recipes unless the surplus fat is removed.

Sweet-Sour Pork with Chive Rice

450 g/1 lb shoulder of pork (shoulder butt or blade roast)
1 large onion
2 tablespoons oil
2 tablespoons red wine vinegar
1 tablespoon brown sugar
3 tablespoons tomato ketchup
150 ml/¼ pint (⅔ cup) chicken stock
½ to 1 teaspoon ground ginger
salt and pepper
2 teaspoons cornflour (cornstarch)
3 tablespoons water
225 g/8 oz (1 cup) long-grain rice, cooked (see page 136)
3 tablespoons chopped chives

⁎⁎Cut the meat into neat dice; peel and chop the onion. Heat the oil in a large pan and fry the meat for 5 to 6 minutes, turning several times. Lift the meat from the pan and pour out all excess fat, leaving just 1 tablespoon in the pan.

Cook the onion in this fat until tender. Add the vinegar, sugar, ketchup, stock and ginger. Stir as the mixture comes to the boil. Return the pork and season lightly. Cover the pan tightly. Simmer for 15 minutes. Blend the cornflour (cornstarch) with the water, stir into the pork mixture and continue stirring as the mixture thickens. Blend the hot rice and half the chives. Top with the remaining chives and serve alongside the pork mixture. Serves 4.

Country Pork Casserole

450 g/1 lb pork fillet (tenderloin)
25 g/1 oz (¼ cup) flour
salt and pepper
2 medium onions
1 to 2 leeks
2 to 3 celery stalks (sticks)
1 small green pepper
225 g/8 oz tomatoes
50 g/2 oz (¼ cup) butter or margarine
1 tablespoon lemon juice or white wine vinegar
150 ml/¼ pint (⅔ cup) chicken stock
1 to 2 tablespoons tomato purée (paste)

Cut the pork into neat slices. Blend the flour, salt and pepper and use to coat the meat. Peel and slice the onions, slice the leek(s), dice the celery then de-seed and dice the pepper. Concass the tomatoes. Heat the butter or margarine in a large frying pan (skillet), fry the pork slices on either side until golden brown then transfer to a casserole. Add the onions, leeks and celery to the pan and fry gently for 10 minutes, do not allow to brown. Spoon these vegetables over the pork, then add the pepper and tomatoes.

Pour the lemon juice or vinegar, chicken stock and tomato purée (paste) into the pan; stir well to absorb any meat juices, season to taste, then spoon over the pork and vegetables. Cover the casserole and cook in the centre of a moderate oven (180°C/350°F, Gas Mark 4) for 40 to 50 minutes or until the meat is tender. Serves 4.

Country Pork Casserole

DUMPLINGS

Sift 100 g/4 oz (1 cup) self-raising flour into a bowl and add a pinch of salt and 50 g/2 oz (½ cup) shredded suet. Alternatively rub in 50 g/2 oz (½ cup) margarine until the mixture resembles breadcrumbs. Add sufficient water to make a sticky dough, then roll into 8 to 12 small balls with floured hands. Check there is plenty of liquid in the saucepan and bring it to a brisk boil before adding the dumplings. Drop into the boiling liquid and cook briskly for 8 minutes. After this the liquid can simmer gently again for 12 to 17 minutes.

Flavour the dumplings with finely chopped fresh herbs or up to 50 g/2 oz (¼ cup) chopped cooked bacon if liked.

Note Plain (all-purpose) flour can be used but add 1 teaspoon baking powder.

Part boiled bacon with Peach and Barbecue Glaze, page 64

Sweet and Sour Pork Hotpot

550 g/1¼ lb boneless pork, cut from the leg
salt and pepper
25 g/1 oz (¼ cup) flour
2 tablespoons oil
2 medium onions
1 small green pepper
100 g/4 oz (1 cup) small button mushrooms
1 × 227 g/8 oz can pineapple chunks
150 ml/¼ pint (⅔ cup) sweet cider
2 tablespoons redcurrant jelly
750 g/1½ lb potatoes, weight when peeled
25 g/1 oz (2 tablespoons) butter or margarine

✲✲Cut the pork into 2.5 cm/1 inch cubes. Blend a little seasoning with the flour and coat the meat. Heat the oil in a saucepan and fry the pork for several minutes until pale golden in colour. Remove the meat from the pan and put into a deep 1.8 litre/3 pint (2 quart) casserole. Peel and neatly dice the onions, dice the green pepper, discarding the core and seeds, and wipe the mushrooms. Add the vegetables to any oil remaining in the saucepan, cook for 4 to 5 minutes then add to the pork.

Open the can of pineapple, pour the syrup into the saucepan and add the fruit to the ingredients in the casserole. Add the cider and redcurrant jelly to the pineapple syrup. Heat for 2 to 3 minutes, stirring to absorb any fat or juices left in the saucepan. Season well and pour over the pork, vegetables and fruit.

Cut the potatoes into very thin slices and arrange on top of the ingredients in the casserole. Melt the butter or margarine and brush over the potatoes. Cook in the centre of a preheated moderately hot oven (190°C/375°F, Gas Mark 5) for 20 minutes, then cover the casserole with a lid and lower the heat slightly to moderate (180°C/350°F, Gas Mark 4). Cook for a further 1 hour. Remove the lid once more, so the potatoes will brown, and continue cooking for 20 minutes. Serves 4 to 6.

Bacon Hotpot

1 kg/2 lb unsmoked collar (smoked shoulder butt) or forehock of bacon
225 g/8 oz onions
225 g/8 oz carrots
450 g/1 lb potatoes
1 tablespoon flour
25 g/1 oz (2 tablespoons) butter
1 × 425 g/15 oz can tomatoes
pinch of black pepper

✲✲Remove the rind and fat from the meat but do not discard the fat. Peel and slice the onions, carrots and potatoes.

Dice the meat and dust with the flour. Heat the bacon fat and half the butter and fry the meat for 5 minutes. Add the onions and carrots and cook for a further 5 minutes. Add the tomatoes with the liquid from the can, mix with the meat and season with pepper.

Spoon half the meat mixture into a casserole. Dry half the potato slices and arrange over the meat and vegetables. Add the remainder of the meat mixture then a final layer of potatoes arranged neatly to form a pattern. Cover the casserole and bake in the centre of a preheated moderate oven (180°C/350°F, Gas Mark 4) for 1¼ hours. Remove the lid and dot the potatoes with the remaining butter. Cook uncovered, for a further 45 minutes. Serves 4 to 6.

Pork in Ginger Sauce

2 medium onions
4 pork chops
1 tablespoon oil
2 dessert apples
1 tablespoon flour
300 ml/½ pint (1¼ cups) ginger beer
1 teaspoon Worcestershire sauce
1 teaspoon brown sugar
salt and pepper
TO GARNISH: 4 slices preserved ginger
watercress

✲✲Peel the onions and cut into wafer-thin rings. Fry the pork chops steadily in a frying pan (skillet) until tender, turning once or twice. Remove from the pan to a heated dish and keep hot.

Add the oil to the pan and fry the onions for 2 minutes. Core but do not peel the apples, cut into 5 mm/¼ inch rings, add to the onions and fry steadily for 5 minutes. Blend the flour with the ginger beer and pour over the onions and apples. Simmer for 5 minutes, then add the Worcestershire sauce, sugar and seasoning to taste.

Arrange the onion and apple rings around the pork chops. Spoon the sauce over the meat. Top with preserved ginger and watercress. Serves 4.

Special Technique
PERFECT BOILED BACON

Green (unsmoked) bacon is very mild and so is Danish bacon and these joints do not require soaking before cooking. If you have bought smoked bacon, soak for up to 12 hours in cold water to cover, then drain well.

Choose collar (smoked shoulder butt) forehock or gammon (smoked arm picnic, or smoked ham) for boiling and soak if necessary (see above). Weigh the joint and calculate the cooking time.

A prime piece of gammon (smoked ham) needs 20 to 25 minutes per 450 g/1 lb plus 20 to 25 minutes over. The difference in time depends upon the quality and the shape of the joint. Wide joints of middle gammon (smoked ham) cook more quickly than thick ones.

A more economical joint of collar (smoked shoulder butt) or forehock (smoked arm picnic) needs 30 to 35 minutes per 450 g/1 lb and 30 to 35 minutes over.

Place the joint in a saucepan and completely cover with fresh cold water or another liquid such as cider or ginger ale. Cover, bring to the boil then turn down heat and simmer gently until meat is tender.

Variations

To make a more substantial meal you can add dumplings to the cooking liquid 20 to 25 minutes before the end of the cooking time (see recipe left).

To serve hot Remove the rind and fat. Use some of the stock to make a Parsley Sauce (see page 102).

To serve cold Cool the joint in the liquid, then lift out and remove the skin. Coat the fat with crisp breadcrumbs and serve with salad or chutney. Alternatively coat the fat with a Chaudfroid Sauce or glaze (see pages 194 and 195).

Part Boiling and Part Roasting Many people prefer the flavour of bacon if it is boiled (see page 64) for two-thirds of the total cooking time, then drained well and roasted in the oven for the remainder of the period.

Grilled Gammon with Orange Butter

To Grill or Fry

To encourage the fat of pork chops to become pleasantly crisp in cooking, snip it at 1.5 cm/½ inch intervals. The cooking times I recommend refer to chops of about 2 cm/¾ inch in thickness.

To grill (broil) pork chops, preheat the grill (broiler) and cook the chops rapidly for 4 to 5 minutes on each side. Lower the heat and cook for approximately 8 to 10 minutes.

If frying pork chops with a reasonable amount of fat, simply grease the frying pan (skillet) and put in the meat. Cook steadily, rather than rapidly, so the fat begins to run from the chops, then time the cooking as above.

Fillets of Pork, i.e. thin slices cut from the leg, are very lean. They should be cooked in fat in the same way as escalopes (cutlets) of veal (see page 67).

Thick Back Rashers of bacon known as bacon chops, or slices of gammon (ham steaks) are excellent grilled (broiled) or fried. No extra fat is required when grilling (broiling) bacon chops and very little when frying the bacon. Gammon (smoked ham) however is lean bacon and needs fat for frying or grilling (broiling). Melt butter and brush over the lean meat before grilling (broiling) or heat a little butter or other fat in the frying pan (skillet), then cook the gammon (smoked ham).

Do not preheat the grill (broiler) or have the frying pan (skillet) too hot when grilling (broiling) or frying bacon chops or gammon (smoked ham). Too great a heat causes the fat to curl and burn before the lean is cooked.

Thin Bacon Rashers (slices) take only 2 to 3 minutes to cook under the grill (broiler) or in the frying pan (skillet).

Accompaniments

Whether you are frying or grilling (broiling) bacon, fruit is an excellent accompaniment. Add rings of cooking or dessert apples to the frying pan (skillet) when cooking pork or bacon, and cook steadily until tender. Heat cooked prunes, fresh or canned peaches, pineapple rings or canned apricots with grilled (broiled) or fried pork or bacon rashers (slices). If using the grill (broiler), brush the fruit with a little melted butter before heating.

Grilled Gammon with Orange Butter

1 small orange
65 g/2½ oz (5 tablespoons) butter
2 teaspoons finely chopped parsley
2 gammon steaks (smoked ham steaks)
TO GARNISH: parsley

Grate the rind (zest) from the orange. Add this to 50 g/2 oz (¼ cup) of the butter. Mix well, form into a neat roll and coat the outer rim in the parsley. Chill well.

Melt the remaining butter. Snip the rind of the steaks at 1 cm/½ inch intervals, and place under the grill (broiler). Only heat the grill (broiler) at the last minute. If it is preheated the edges of the meat curl and burn before the rest is cooked. Cook for approximately 5 minutes on each side, brushing with the melted butter.

Meanwhile peel and slice the orange. Cut the Orange Butter into two portions. Arrange the meat on a dish with the orange slices and parsley. Top with the flavoured butter just before serving. Serves 2.

Dijon Pork

4 pork chops
100 g/4 oz (1 cup) Gruyère cheese
4 teaspoons Dijon mustard
½ teaspoon finely chopped sage
black pepper
2 tablespoons soured cream
TO GARNISH: watercress

Snip the fat of the pork at regular intervals. Cook under a preheated grill (broiler) for 8 to 10 minutes on each side until tender.

Grate the cheese and mix with the rest of the ingredients. Spread over one side only of the chops and grill (broil) for a further 3 to 4 minutes, until the cheese melts. Garnish with watercress. Serves 4.

Bacon with Pineapple Sauce

4 thick back bacon chops (smoked ham slices)
FOR THE SAUCE: 4 canned pineapple rings (slices)
150 ml/¼ pint (⅔ cup) pineapple syrup
1 teaspoon arrowroot
1 tablespoon honey
1 tablespoon lemon juice
TO GARNISH: watercress

Grill (broil) or fry the meat. Meanwhile chop the pineapple rings. Blend the syrup with the arrowroot, put into a saucepan with the honey and lemon juice, stir over a low heat until thickened then add the chopped pineapple.

Spoon on the cooked meat just before serving. Garnish with watercress. Serves 4.

FOR FLAVOUR
When cooking bacon always place the fat of the second rasher (slice) over the lean of the first.

Continue like this so that the fat is basting the lean part as the bacon cooks.

Perfect Roast Pork

LEFTOVERS
Bacon Rissoles
⁘ *Mince (grind) or finely chop 225 to 350 g/8 to 12 oz cooked bacon. Peel and chop 1 medium onion. Heat 50 g/2 oz (¼ cup) butter or margarine in a saucepan, add the onion and cook gently until soft; then blend in 25 g/ 1 oz (¼ cup) flour. Add either 150 ml/¼ pint (⅔ cup) of milk or tomato juice. Bring to the boil, stir over a low heat until it forms a thick panada (binding sauce). Add 50 g/2 oz (1 cup) soft breadcrumbs and the minced (ground) meat.*

Flavour with 1 to 2 tablespoons chopped parsley, a shake of pepper (salt may not be necessary) and a few drops of Worcestershire sauce.

Form into 8 flat cakes, coat in seasoned flour, beaten egg and crisp breadcrumbs.

Heat a little fat and fry the rissoles until crisp and brown on both sides. Drain on absorbent kitchen paper.

Roast Pork and Bacon

Roasting Times for Pork

Fast Roasting Set the oven at moderately hot or hot (200 to 220°C/400 to 425°F, Gas Mark 6 to 7).

Allow 25 minutes per 450 g/1 lb and 25 minutes over. Never undercook pork.

Slower Roasting Set the oven at moderate (160 to 180°C/325 to 350°F, Gas Mark 3 to 4).

Allow 40 minutes per 450 g/1 lb and 40 minutes over.

Microwave Roasting of Pork

Since crisp crackling is so important, conventional roasting is better for pork. If you do decide to roast it in a microwave cooker then first read the comments on page 50.

Allow 10 minutes per 450 g/1 lb and cook uncovered. Remove from the oven, wrap it in foil and allow 15 minutes standing time.

The microwave meat thermometer should register 85°C/185°F and this must rise to 88°C/190°F when the meat stands, for pork must always be adequately cooked.

Accompaniments

The richness of pork demands well-flavoured accompaniments. It is traditional to serve Sage and Onion Stuffing and Apple Sauce but both of these recipes can be varied and made more interesting. The amounts below

are sufficient to serve up to 6 people.

⁘Sage and Onion Stuffing Peel and chop 2 large onions and simmer in 150 ml/¼ pint (⅔ cup) lightly salted water for about 10 minutes. Do not overcook for the flavour is easily lost. Drain the onions, mix with 100 g/4 oz (2 cups) soft breadcrumbs, 25 to 50 g/1 to 2 oz (3 to 6 tablespoons) shredded suet or melted margarine, 1 to 2 teaspoons chopped fresh sage or ½ to 1 teaspoon dried sage. Season well, bind with 1 egg or the onion stock. Bake the stuffing in a dish alongside the roast until golden.

Celery and Onion Stuffing Use only 50 g/2 oz (1 cup) soft breadcrumbs and 100 g/4 oz (1 cup) very finely chopped celery (1 cup minced celery).

Sage and Chestnut Stuffing Omit the breadcrumbs and use 175 g/6 oz (¾ cup) canned chestnut purée instead.

⁘Apple Sauce Peel and slice 450 g/1 lb cooking (tart) apples. Simmer in 4 to 5 tablespoons water until a thick pulp. If using a good cooking apple there is no need to sieve or blend the mixture. Stir 1 to 2 tablespoons caster or light brown sugar and 15 to 25 g/½ to 1 oz (1 to 2 tablespoons) butter into the sauce.

⁘Apple and Orange Sauce Cook the apples in orange juice instead of water with ½ to 1 tablespoon very finely grated orange rind. Sweeten to taste.

⁘Apple and Prune Sauce: Blend the cooked apples with 175 g/6 oz (¾ cups) diced cooked prunes.

Microwave Roasting of Bacon

Even mildly cured bacon has a definite flavour, which is emphasized when roasted in a microwave cooker. Bacon

also tends to become drier when roasted in a microwave oven so it is best to roast bacon conventionally.

Roasting Times for Bacon

The salt flavour is more apparent when bacon is cooked without liquid in the oven so soaking may be necessary (see page 62). If roasting prime cuts such as gammon (smoked ham) you can choose either the Fast or Slower method (see left). Allow 30 minutes per 450 g/1 lb and 30 minutes over.

If roasting cheaper joints such as collar (smoked shoulder butt) and forehock then you are well advised to choose the Slower method. Allow 40 minutes per 450 g/1 lb and 40 minutes over.

If cooking the bacon in foil or in a covered roasting pan allow extra cooking time (see page 49).

To Glaze Bacon

Remove the rind, score (cut) the fat in a definite design. Cover with a glaze – brown sugar, honey, golden (light corn) syrup or black treacle with mustard powder and ground cinnamon to taste or with grated orange rind and juice or with pineapple syrup. Return the joint to the oven for about 20 minutes.

Peach and Barbecue Glaze Stud the scored bacon with whole cloves. Mix 2 tablespoons brown sugar with 1 teaspoon each of mustard powder, Worcestershire sauce, tomato purée and vinegar. Add 3 tablespoons of the juice from a 410 g can peach halves and brush over the bacon. Return to the oven with the peaches, for a further 20 minutes.

Pork must be well-cooked – it is highly dangerous to health to serve it underdone. I prefer using the slower roasting method for all pork joints, since it gives deliciously tender meat with good crisp crackling.

To achieve good crackling score (cut) the rind (if not already done by the butcher) then brush it with a little melted lard or oil and sprinkle it with salt. The salt draws out the moisture from the skin and aids crisping but some people dislike its flavour so it could be omitted.

It can be difficult to achieve good crackling on thawed or even well-chilled, pork because the outside becomes so moist. The best solution is to dry the skin well with absorbent kitchen paper towels, roast the meat for 30 to 40 minutes to dry out the skin and then brush it with the melted lard or oil and a sprinkling of salt.

Pork is better if cooked on a trivet in an open roasting pan so the excess fat drains away in cooking.

International Dishes

Barbecued Spare Ribs

1.5 kg/3 lb pork spare ribs
1 litre/1¾ pints (4 cups) water
2 tablespoons white wine vinegar or white malt vinegar
FOR THE SAUCE: 1 tablespoon oil
1 onion
1 carrot
2 tablespoons white wine vinegar or white malt vinegar
2 tablespoons soy sauce
2 tablespoons brown sugar
2 tablespoons plum jam
2 teaspoons Worcestershire sauce
2 teaspoons tomato purée (paste)
salt and pepper
TO GARNISH: spring onions (scallions), see page 000

Ask for the spare ribs to be cut into neat pieces, then remove any excess fat. Put the water and 2 tablespoons of vinegar into a saucepan and bring to the boil. Add the spare ribs and simmer for 15 minutes. Drain the meat and dry on absorbent paper. Discard the liquid.

Place the spare ribs in a good-sized roasting pan, allowing space between the pieces of meat.

Sauce Peel and chop the onion. Peel and cut the carrot into thin strips. Heat the oil in a saucepan and fry the onion and carrot for 5 minutes. Add the remaining ingredients for the sauce and pour over the meat. Put into a preheated moderate oven (180°C/350°F, Gas Mark 4) and cook for 20 minutes in the uncovered pan. Turn the meat and baste with the sauce. Continue cooking for a further 25 minutes. Serve hot garnished with spring onions (scallions). Serves 4 as a main dish or 6 as an hors d'oeuvre to a Chinese meal.

Maiale allo Spiedo
[Kebabs of Pork]

450 g/1 lb lean pork fillet (tenderloin)
225 g/8 oz bread, cut in 2 thick slices
225 g/8 oz gammon (smoked ham) cut in 2 thick slices
2 to 3 tablespoons olive oil
salt and pepper
6 bay leaves

Cut the pork, bread and gammon (ham) into 2.5 cm/1 inch cubes. Brush the bread with the oil and sprinkle with seasoning; lightly brush both the meats with oil. Thread the meat and bread on to 6 long metal skewers, adding a bay leaf to each skewer. Make quite sure the bread is placed between portions of meat.

Cook under a preheated grill (broiler) for 10 to 12 minutes turning several times, or place in a roasting pan and cook just above the centre of a preheated hot oven (220°C/425°F, Gas Mark 7) for 25 minutes or until the meat is tender and the bread crisp. Turn once during the baking period and brush with a little more oil. Serves 6.

Schweinebraten mit Bier
[Roast Pork in Beer]

If cooking a joint of 1.5 to 1.75 kg/3 to 4 lb in weight, put approximately 600 ml/1 pint (2½ cups) beer into the roasting pan before adding the joint of pork. Add a number of small peeled onions and soaked, but not cooked, prunes.

Prepare the pork joint for roasting; blend 2 teaspoons of dry mustard powder with 2 tablespoons of flour and press this into the fat. Cook in the covered roasting pan following the timing given on page 64. The lid of the pan can be lifted for the final 30 to 40 minutes cooking time. Serve the pork with the onions and prunes. Thicken the cooking liquid and serve as a sauce.

Pork à l'orange

2 large oranges
150 ml/¼ pint (⅔ cup) water
4 pork fillets (slices from the leg)
4 medium carrots
50 g/2 oz (4 tablespoons butter)
½ tablespoon oil
150 ml/¼ pint (⅔ cup) white wine
sprig of tarragon
sprig of sage
salt and pepper

Peel the oranges, remove any white pith, cut the orange zest into matchstick pieces. Put the water into a saucepan, add the peel, simmer gently for 10 minutes. Strain and discard the water. Squeeze the oranges.

Flatten the pork fillets with a rolling pin. Peel and slice the carrots. Heat the butter and oil in a large frying pan (skillet). Fry the pork fillets for 2 minutes on each side; remove from the pan, then fry the carrots for several minutes.

Return the pork to the pan, add the orange juice, wine, herbs, orange peel and a little seasoning. Cook gently for 10 minutes. Remove the herbs and serve with cooked rice. Serves 4.

SIMPLE SKILL
Cut the stems of spring onions (scallions) downwards, put into cold water and they will open out into flower shapes.
Lengths of celery can be cut in the same way.

Barbecued Spare Ribs

VEAL DISHES

Veal is a delicately flavoured meat with very little fat. It is important to cook it adequately so that the meat is tender, yet care must be taken to keep the flesh moist.

Quantities

Since veal has no excess fat there is little wastage.

For Frying or Grilling (Broiling) Allow 1 good-sized chop or 175 g/6 oz fillet of veal, cut from the leg or escalope, per person.

For Roasting About 175 to 225 g/6 to 8 oz boneless meat per person.

For Stewing About 175 g/6 oz boneless meat per person.

Cuts of Veal

Always select the correct cut for the cooking method.

For Stock and Brawn Feet, head, knuckle (shank).

For Stewing, Casseroling, Braising or Boiling Breast, feet, fillet (cut from leg), head, knuckle (shank), middle or scrag end of neck (arm roast, blade roast, boneless rolled shoulder).

For Frying or Grilling (Broiling) Best end of neck (rib chops), fillets, escalopes (cutlets and round steaks), loin chops.

For Roasting Best end of neck (rib roast), breast, fillet (round roast), loin, shoulder.

Paprika Veal Chops

Veal Stews and Casseroles

Veal is excellent in a stew or casserole dish. The recipes here include subtle flavourings and plenty of fat, which helps to keep the meat moist.

Veal Turbigo

450 g/1 lb stewing veal
4 streaky bacon rashers (slices)
225 g/8 oz chipolata sausages (pork link sausages)
2 medium onions
100 g/4 oz (1 cup) button mushrooms
50 g/2 oz (¼ cup) butter or margarine
25 g/1 oz (¼ cup) flour
450 ml/¾ pint (2 cups) veal or chicken stock or water with ½ chicken stock (1 bouillon) cube
salt and pepper
1 teaspoon French mustard
1 teaspoon Worcestershire sauce
2 tablespoons port wine
2 tablespoons chopped parsley
TO GARNISH:
croûtons of fried bread, see page 35

⁂Dice the veal, de-rind and chop the bacon and halve the sausages. Peel the onions and cut into rings; wipe the mushrooms and leave whole if small, but cut into thick slices if large.

Heat half the butter or margarine in a large frying pan (skillet), add the bacon and fry gently for 2 to 3 minutes then spoon the bacon into a casserole, leaving as much fat as possible in the pan.

Put the veal, sausages, onions and mushrooms into the pan. Cook over a low heat for nearly 10 minutes, until the meat and sausages are pale golden in colour, turning several times. Add all these ingredients to the bacon in the casserole.

Heat the remaining butter or margarine in the pan, add the flour and stir well to incorporate any meat juices remaining in the pan. Blend in the stock, then bring the sauce to the boil and stir over the heat until slightly thickened. Add all the remaining ingredients and pour over the veal. Cover the casserole and cook in the centre of a moderate oven (160°C/325°F, Gas Mark 3) for 1¾ hours.

Arrange the croûtons on top of the sauce immediately before serving with rice and a tossed salad or selection of seasonal vegetables. Serves 4 to 6.

Paprika Veal Chops

2 to 3 medium onions
1 garlic clove
100 g/4 oz (1 cup) mushrooms
25 g/1 oz (¼ cup) flour
salt and pepper
2 teaspoons paprika
4 medium veal chops
50 g/2 oz (¼ cup) butter or margarine
450 ml/¾ pint (2 cups) veal or chicken stock or water with ½ chicken stock (1 bouillon) cube
3 tablespoons tomato purée (paste)
150 ml/¼ pint (⅔ cup) soured cream or yogurt
TO GARNISH:
2 tablespoons chopped parsley

⁂Peel the onions and garlic. Cut the onions into rings and crush the garlic. Wipe the mushrooms and cut into thick slices. Blend the flour with a little salt and pepper and add the paprika. Coat the chops with the mixture of flour and paprika.

Heat the butter or margarine in a saucepan and add the onions, garlic and mushrooms. Fry steadily for 2 to 3 minutes then spoon into a shallow casserole. Put the chops into the saucepan, fry on both sides until delicately browned and add to the casserole. Pour the stock into the saucepan. Stir well to absorb any fat and flour left in the bottom of the saucepan, then blend in the tomato purée (paste). Simmer the liquid for 5 minutes then spoon over the meat and vegetables. Cover the casserole and cook in the centre of a moderate oven (160°C/325°F, Gas Mark 3) for 1¼ hours. Lift the lid at the end of this period, lightly blend the soured cream or yogurt into the sauce, return to the oven for 3 to 4 minutes and then garnish with the parsley. Serves 4.

VARIATION

Use diced stewing veal in place of the chops. Follow the method given above, but allow 1¾ hours cooking time.

Veal Mock Birds

4 thin fillets (escalopes) of veal
4 streaky bacon rashers (slices)
FOR THE STUFFING:
1 medium onion
25 g/1 oz (2 tablespoons) butter or margarine
75 g/3 oz (1½ cups) soft breadcrumbs
1 teaspoon grated lemon rind
1 tablespoon lemon juice
2 tablespoons chopped parsley
salt and pepper
FOR THE SAUCE:
1 large onion

100 g/4 oz (1 cup) small button mushrooms

50 g/2 oz (¼ cup) butter or margarine

25 g/1 oz (¼ cup) flour

450 ml/¾ pint (2 cups) chicken stock or water with 1 chicken stock cube (2 bouillon cubes)

1 tablespoon tomato purée (paste)

1 bouquet garni

✳ Flatten the pieces of veal. Cut the rind from the bacon and place the bacon on the pieces of veal.

Stuffing Peel and chop the onion. Heat the 25 g/1 oz (2 tablespoons) butter or margarine and fry the onion until soft. Mix with the remainder of the stuffing ingredients.

Divide the mixture into 4 portions and place them on the bacon and veal. Roll the meat very firmly around the stuffing to make meat rolls and secure with string.

Sauce Peel and finely chop the onion and wipe the mushrooms. Heat the butter or margarine and fry the onion and mushrooms for 5 minutes.

Blend the flour with the stock. Pour over the onions and mushrooms. Stir briskly as the liquid comes to the boil and thickens slightly. Add the tomato purée (paste), seasoning to taste and the bouquet garni.

Arrange the veal birds in a casserole and pour over the sauce. Cover the casserole and cook in the centre of a preheated moderate oven (160°C/325°F, Gas Mark 3) for 1¼ hours. Remove the bouquet garni. Serve with mixed vegetables. Serves 4.

VARIATION

Use thin slices of topside (top round) of beef instead of veal and cook for 1½ hours.

To Grill or Fry

Care must be taken when grilling (broiling) veal otherwise the meat will dry out. Brush the flesh with plenty of melted butter or oil before and during cooking.

Veal chops are the most suitable portions to grill (broil). As veal has a very delicate flavour, the melted butter could be blended with lemon juice or a crushed clove of garlic or a pinch of grated nutmeg.

The cooking time for chops of about 2 cm/¾ inch in thickness would be 12 to 15 minutes.

If frying chops, allow at least 25 g/1 oz (2 tablespoons) butter or fat per chop and cook the meat for the timing given for grilling (broiling).

The most popular portions of veal for frying are thin slices cut from the leg; these are known as fillets or escalopes. The slices can be cooked with or without a coating as in the recipes that follow.

Veal Mornay

4 thin fillets (escalopes) of veal

4 small slices cooked ham

salt and pepper

1 tablespoon flour

1 egg

40 g/1½ oz (⅓ cup) crisp breadcrumbs

50 g/2 oz (¼ cup) butter

1 tablespoon olive oil

FOR THE SAUCE:
100 g/4 oz Cheddar or Gruyère cheese

25 g/1 oz (2 tablespoons) butter

25 g/1 oz (¼ cup) flour

150 ml/¼ pint (⅔ cup) milk

150 ml/¼ pint (⅔ cup) white wine

1 teaspoon French mustard

2 tablespoons double (heavy) cream

TO GARNISH:
cooked small new potatoes

1 to 2 tablespoons chopped parsley

1 lemon

a few cooked or canned asparagus tips

Flatten the veal with a rolling pin, as described on this page. (They should be very thin and twice the size of the pieces of ham). Place the slices of ham on the veal, covering half of each slice, then fold the veal to enclose the ham.

Season the flour and dust the veal with this, then coat with beaten egg and breadcrumbs. Heat the butter and oil in a large pan and fry the veal quickly on both sides until crisp and golden brown. Lower the heat and continue cooking for 10 minutes or until the meat is tender. Lift out of the pan and drain on absorbent paper. This is necessary as the veal is served with a rather rich cheese sauce. Put the meat on a heated dish.

Make the sauce while the meat is cooking. Grate the cheese. Heat the butter in a saucepan, stir in the flour and cook for several minutes. Gradually blend in the milk and stir over the heat until thickened. Lower the heat; make sure the sauce is no longer boiling, then add the wine, mustard and seasoning. Stir the cream and cheese into the sauce just before serving. Do not allow the sauce to boil.

To serve, arrange a border of cooked small new potatoes round the meat, top with chopped parsley and slices of lemon. Put a spoonful of sauce in the centre of each piece of meat, top with a twist of lemon and an asparagus tip. Serve the rest of the sauce separately. Serves 4.

Veal Mornay

Veal with Mushroom Sauce

25 g/1 oz (2 tablespoons) butter

4 to 6 veal chops

FOR THE SAUCE:
25 g/1 oz (2 tablespoons) butter

100 g/4 oz (1 cup) small button mushrooms

150 ml/¼ pint (⅔ cup) yogurt

100 g/4 oz (½ cup) cream cheese

few drops of Tabasco sauce (hot pepper sauce)

salt and pepper

Melt the butter, brush over the chops and grill (broil) until tender.

Sauce Heat the butter and fry the mushrooms for a few minutes. Mix the yogurt, cheese, sauce and a little seasoning in a basin. Stand over a pan of hot water and heat gently. Add the mushrooms. Serve the sauce with the chops. Serves 4 to 6.

Perfect Roast Veal

Roast Veal

Special Technique
PERFECT ROAST VEAL

Choose one of the cuts of veal given on page 66 and roast as the timing below.

Veal is exceptionally lean and yet it is a meat that must be thoroughly cooked. It is not served underdone. This means that every effort must be made to keep the meat well moistened during cooking. The ideal way is to lard the meat, see page 52; failing that, cover the joint with a generous amount of butter or fat bacon rashers (slices).

Serve veal with bacon rolls, a parsley and thyme or other stuffing and sausages, all of which add flavour to the meat. There are, however, many other interesting ways to serve the meat.

Veal is best cooked in a covered roasting pan, wrapped in foil or in a roasting bag.

Roasting Times for Veal

Fast Roasting Set the oven at moderately hot to hot (200 to 220°C/400 to 425°F, Gas Mark 6 to 7).

Allow 25 minutes per 450 g/1 lb and 25 minutes over.

Slower Roasting Set the oven to moderate (160 to 180°C/325 to 350°F, Gas Mark 3 to 4).

Allow 40 minutes per 450 g/1 lb and 40 minutes over.

STUFFING VEAL
If stuffing breast or fillet (escalopes) of veal, lay the meat as flat as possible, cover with the stuffing and roll firmly. Tie or skewer into a neat round. Weigh and roast accordingly.

If baking the stuffing in a separate dish, allow 35 to 45 minutes, depending upon the oven setting.

Microwave Roasting

To prevent the veal from drying, lard the meat with fat (see page 52). It is best to put the veal into a roasting bag. Allow 10 minutes per 450 g/1 lb, then wrap the meat in foil and allow it to stand for at least 15 minutes.

The microwave meat thermometer should register 85°C/185°F and rise to 88°C/190°F as the meat stands.

Accompaniments

The usual accompaniments to roast veal are bacon rolls, sausages and/or some kind of savoury stuffing.

✳Forcemeat Balls Mix 350 g/12 oz (1½ cups) pork sausagemeat (sausage mince) with 1 tablespoon chopped parsley, 1 teaspoon chopped fresh mixed herbs or ½ teaspoon dried mixed herbs and 1 egg. Either use to stuff the veal or form into small balls and bake for 20 minutes if fast roasting or 30 minutes if roasting by the slower method.

✳Parsley and Thyme Stuffing Blend together 100 g/4 oz (2 cups) soft breadcrumbs, 1 to 2 tablespoons chopped parsley, 1 teaspoon chopped fresh thyme or ½ teaspoon dried thyme, 50 g/2 oz (6 tablespoons) shredded suet or melted butter or margarine, 1 teaspoon grated lemon rind, 1 tablespoon lemon juice and a little seasoning.

Bind with 1 egg if using the stuffing in the meat or baking in a dish, or use just the egg yolk to give a stiffer consistency if forming the mixture into balls. Cook as above.

Kidney-stuffed Veal

1.25 to 1.5 kg/2½ to 3 lb boned breast of veal or boned loin (in one piece)
450 g/1 lb veal kidney
25 g/1 oz (2 tablespoons) butter
150 ml/¼ pint (⅔ cup) dry white wine
150 ml/¼ pint (⅔ cup) double (heavy) cream
salt and pepper

Flatten the meat to give a large oblong shape. Check there is no gristle or skin on the kidney then stuff the veal with the kidney. Roll firmly and tie into a neat roll. Melt the butter, brush over the meat. Roast using timing on this page.

When the joint is cooked, remove from the meat pan and keep it warm. Pour away any fat in excess of 2 tablespoons; blend the wine and cream with the fat remaining in the pan. Heat, without boiling, over a low heat, season and serve in a sauceboat.

Serve the meat with cooked rice, flavoured with fried onion, and with broccoli. Serves 6 to 8.

Stuffed Breast of Veal

1 kg/2 lb breast of veal
3 bacon rashers (slices)
2 medium onions
100 g/4 oz (¼ lb) mushrooms
50 g/2 oz (¼ cup) butter
100 g/4 oz (2 cups) soft breadcrumbs
225 g/8 oz (½ lb) sausagemeat (sausage mince)
salt and pepper
TO COAT: 4 to 5 bacon rashers (slices)

Flatten the breast of veal. De-rind and chop the bacon rashers (slices); peel and chop the onions, slice the mushrooms. Heat the bacon rinds and butter in a frying pan (skillet) then toss the onions and mushrooms in this for 5 minutes. Discard the bacon rinds. Blend the breadcrumbs with the onions and mushrooms in the pan, this makes certain all the fat is absorbed. Add the uncooked bacon and sausagemeat. Mix well, season lightly.

Spread the stuffing over the veal, roll and tie or skewer. Wrap remaining bacon around the veal. Roast for 40 minutes per 450 g/1 lb and 40 minutes over in a moderate oven (160 to 180°C/325 to 350°F, Gas Mark 3 to 4).

When making gravy to serve with this joint add 2 to 3 tablespoons port wine. Serves 6 to 8.

VARIATION

Omit the mushrooms in the stuffing, use concassed (skinned, deseeded and chopped) tomatoes instead, together with 2 tablespoons chopped parsley and 1 teaspoon chopped lemon thyme.

International Dishes

Pieczén Cieleca ze Smietana
[Roast Veal with Soured Cream]

1 joint of veal, prepared (see left)
150 ml/¼ pint (⅔ cup) soured cream
1 tablespoon flour

Prepare the veal by larding it and roast for the time stated on page 70 less 30 to 35 minutes.

Blend the soured cream with the flour. Remove the veal from the oven and spread with the soured cream and flour. Return the meat to the roasting pan. Do not cover it with foil or put into a roasting bag; a covered roasting pan can be used. Continue cooking for the final 30 to 35 minutes.

Blanquette de Veau
[Creamy Veal Stew]

750 g/1½ lb lean shoulder or breast of veal
2 onions
2 medium carrots
1 lemon
600 ml/1 pint (2½ cups) chicken stock
1 bouquet garni
salt and pepper
75 g/3 oz (6 tablespoons) butter
175 to 225 g/6 to 8 oz (1½ to 2 cups) small button mushrooms
40 g/1½ oz (6 tablespoons) flour
150 ml/¼ pint ⅔ cup single (light) cream
2 egg yolks
TO GARNISH:
triangles of fried bread

⁂Cut the veal into neat pieces. Peel the onions and carrots and leave whole. Pare the rind from the lemon, taking care not to use any of the white pith. Put the veal and lemon rind into a saucepan with water to cover, bring to the boil, strain and discard the liquid. Return the veal to the saucepan. Add the onions, carrots, chicken stock, herbs and a little seasoning. Simmer gently for 1 to 1¼ hours. Strain off the stock and keep 450 ml/¾ pint (2 cups). Heat 25 g/1 oz (2 tablespoons) butter in a pan and cook the mushrooms. Heat the remaining butter in a saucepan, stir in the flour and cook over a low heat for 2 to 3 minutes. Blend in the stock and stir as the sauce thickens. Add the veal and mushrooms. Blend the cream and egg yolks, whisk on 2 to 3 tablespoons of the hot sauce then pour into the pan containing the veal mixture. Squeeze out 1 tablespoon lemon juice and add to the sauce. Stir over a low heat for several minutes but do not allow to boil. Garnish with fried bread. Serves 4 to 6.

Freezing Note It is better to freeze this dish before adding the cream and egg yolks. Reheat then add the above ingredients.

Vitello Tonnato
[Veal with Tuna]

1.75 kg/4 lb fillet of veal joint (round roast)
1 × 50 g/2 oz can anchovy fillets
1 medium onion
4 to 5 cloves, optional
2 carrots
1 stick of celery
salt and pepper
FOR THE SAUCE:
1 × 200 g/7 oz can tuna in oil
1 lemon
1 to 2 tablespoons capers
TO GARNISH:
1 lemon

Trim the veal and cut away any gristle. Drain the anchovies and use half the small fish to lard the veal (see page 52). Peel the onion and press in the cloves, if used. Peel and slice the carrots. Chop the celery.

Put the veal into a large saucepan, add the vegetables and just enough water to cover the meat. Add a little seasoning, but remember that anchovies are very salty. Cover the saucepan and simmer very gently for 1½ hours.

While the meat is cooking prepare the sauce. Chop the remaining anchovies. Drain the tuna, reserving the oil. Flake the tuna and mix with the anchovies; pound or blend to a smooth mixture. The oil from the canned tuna can be used if desired; this should be added slowly. Halve the lemon, squeeze out the juice and add as desired. Lastly add the capers.

Remove the meat from the liquid, carve into thin slices, top with the sauce. Slice the lemon and arrange over the sauce. Serve with boiled potatoes and a green salad. Serves 6 to 8.

Note The sauce is often made ahead and allowed to stand for 24 hours, so the flavours blend more readily.

Do not throw away the cooking liquid and vegetables. Add extra vegetables, rice or pasta and serve as a soup at a separate meal.

SIMPLE SKILL
⁂ Fried bread is best made from stale bread; you will find it absorbs less fat than fresher bread. If not required at once, freeze on flat trays and reheat in the oven as required.

Blanquette de Veau and Vitello Tonnato

Pot-roast of Beef

Suitable for Most Meats

On this page are two contrasting recipes that can be adapted for any type of meat. In the Gulyas you can use a mixture of meats – the flavour of the dish is better if you do so.

The Pot-roast is the kind of recipe which can be adapted for most meats and for poultry too.

Master Recipe
Pot-roast of Beef

1 kg/2 lb vegetables, see Variations
50 g/2 oz (¼ cup) fat
about 1.75 kg/4 lb topside, rolled rib or fresh brisket of beef (top round, or boneless chuck eye)
water, see method
salt and pepper

Heat the fat in a very large strong saucepan. Dry the meat well with absorbent paper then cook in the hot fat until well browned. Remove the meat from the saucepan and pour out any surplus fat.

Peel the vegetables and leave them whole. Put in the vegetables, add just enough water to cover them, season lightly then place the joint of meat on top of the vegetables. Cover the pan very tightly and cook over a low heat.

The cooking time for a pot-roast is fairly long – 30 minutes per 450 g/1 lb for prime joints like rolled rib of beef (chuck eye roast) or 35 minutes per 450 g/1 lb for less tender joints.

Serve the joint with the vegetables. The liquid in the saucepan makes an excellent gravy. Serves 6 to 8.

FOR EASE
If the lid of the saucepan or casserole in which you are pot-roasting is not a good fit, put a piece of foil under it; it is important that the small amount of liquid used does not evaporate during cooking.

LEFTOVERS
Leftover Gulyas can be made into a wonderful soup. In fact this dish was a soup originally and then became a stew.

Add extra stock or tomato juice, blend the ingredients and then reheat.

Variations

It is essential that the vegetables are large so they keep their shape during cooking. Choose onions, carrots, potatoes or any other root vegetables.

Seasonal vegetables, such as peas and beans can be added towards the end of the cooking time.

Cook the pot-roast in a tightly covered casserole dish in the oven. Alternatively use a Slow Cooker or Pressure Cooker.

In a Slow Cooker Brown the meat and vegetables in an ordinary saucepan, put into the slow cooker with 300 ml/½ pint (1¼ cups) boiling beef stock or water, season lightly. Cook on HIGH for 6 to 7 hours or HIGH for 1 hour then LOW for 10 hours.

Adjust the amount of meat according to the size of the slow cooker.

In a Pressure Cooker The joint should not exceed 1.5 kg/3 lb in weight. Brown the meat in a little fat in the base of the pressure cooker, remove from the pan and pour out the excess fat. Add 600 ml/1 pint (2½ cups) boiling beef stock or water and 1 beef stock cube (2 bouillon cubes). Stir well to absorb any residue in the base of the pan. Add the trivet (rack) of the cooker. Place the meat on the rack, put on the lid; bring up to HIGH 15 lb pressure and allow 9 to 10 minutes per 450 g/1 lb cooking time for prime beef and 12 to 15 minutes cooking time for less tender cuts, such as fresh brisket. Vegetables can be added during the cooking process.

Pot-roast of Chicken Brown a whole chicken in fat, (see the recipe for beef above). Add the vegetables, flavouring them with a little chopped fresh rosemary and thyme. You can use white wine in place of water in the pan.

Allow 25 to 30 minutes per 450 g/1 lb over a gentle heat for a young chicken.

The timing in a slow cooker is similar to that suggested for beef. If pressure cooking allow 5 minutes per 450 g/1 lb at HIGH pressure.

Pot-roast of Lamb Follow the directions for beef; you may have to bone and roll the joint to fit the container. Brown the meat well to extract surplus fat, pour off the excess, then continue as for beef; allow 35 minutes per 450 g/1 lb. A little red wine can be added. Pot-roasting is a good way of cooking less tender mutton. Allow 40 to 45 minutes per 450 g/1 lb.

Increase the cooking time in a slow cooker to 11 hours on LOW. In a pressure cooker allow 10 minutes at HIGH per 450 g/1 lb for prime cuts, but 12 to 14 minutes per 450 g/1 lb for mutton.

Pot-roast of Veal Allow 40 minutes per 450 g/1 lb in an ordinary pan or 10 to 12 minutes at HIGH pressure per 450 g/1 lb in a pressure cooker. The cooking time in a slow cooker is the same as lamb.

Pork and duck, are less successful for pot-roasting.

Gulyas

I have included this dish here, since traditional recipes often use a mixture of meats. You can, of course, select just one meat if you would rather.

The following mixture of beef and veal is excellent, you could also use lean pork or 225 g/8 oz of each meat.

350 g/12 oz lean good quality stewing beef
350 g/12 oz stewing veal
225 to 350 g/8 to 12 oz onions
450 g/1 lb tomatoes
50 g/2 oz (¼ cup) beef dripping or fat
1 to 2 tablespoons sweet paprika
approximately 300 ml/½ pint (1¼ cups) veal or beef stock or water
salt and pepper
450 g/1 lb potatoes, weight when peeled
TO GARNISH:
150 ml/¼ pint (⅔ cup) yogurt or soured cream
chopped parsley

⁂Dice the meat. Peel and chop the onions; skin and chop the tomatoes. Heat the dripping or fat in a large saucepan and fry the meat and onions gently for about 6 minutes. Add the paprika and blend with the meat; make sure the heat is very low as paprika burns readily. Add the tomatoes, stock or water and a little seasoning. Stir well to mix the ingredients. Cover the saucepan and simmer for 1 to 1¼ hours.

Peel and thickly slice the potatoes; before adding them to the stew check there is sufficient liquid. Add the potatoes and cook for a further 1 hour. Add the garnish. Serves 4 to 6.

Curries

Master Technique
MAKING A PERFECT CURRY

There is a belief that the hotter a curry the more authentically Indian and better it will be. Nothing can be further from the truth. There is a great variety of curries, not only those made in India, but in other parts of the world too, where well spiced food is appreciated. It is therefore a good idea to treat each curried dish you make as a speciality and add different flavourings to blend with the food. Fish curries on the whole are better with a relatively small amount of hot flavour. The more robust meats, such as beef and lamb, can be very well spiced.

Modern curry powders are good and you can buy various strength, but the following mixture produces a particularly good medium strength homemade curry powder.

Homemade curry powder Put 2 teaspoons mustard seed, 2 teaspoons black peppercorns, 2 tablespoons coriander seeds, 2 teaspoons poppy seeds, 1 teaspoon cumin seed and 2 teaspoons fenugreek on to a flat baking tray. Roast towards the top of a preheated moderate oven (180°C/350°F, Gas Mark 4) for about 10 to 15 minutes or until you can smell the spices. Do not allow them to burn. Grind to a fine powder in a food processor then sieve and mix with 50 g/2 oz (½ cup) turmeric, 2 teaspoons ground ginger, 1 teaspoon chilli powder, 1 teaspoon ground cinnamon, ½ to 1 teaspoon ground cloves.

Put into a well-sealed container and use as required. The flavour tends to improve with keeping.

Accompaniments

There are numerous side dishes that help to make a curry more interesting.

Serve the curry with chutney; sliced tomatoes, red and green peppers (remove the cores and seeds); thinly sliced raw onions or tiny cocktail onions; cucumber in yogurt mixed with a little chopped fresh mint; sliced bananas (dipped in lemon juice to keep them a good colour), diced canned or fresh pineapple; salted peanuts and raisins.

The Puris on this page are another good accompaniment to curried dishes; they make a change from the more familiar Chapatis.

Tandoori Cooking

The word 'tandoor' means a clay cooking pot which is placed over the heat. It has a tightly fitting lid, so the food is pot-roasted and retains the maximum amount of flavouring. One of the characteristics of tandoori food is the bright red colour. This is achieved by adding a few drops of red liquid or a pinch of powdered food colouring to the other ingredients. The spiced mixture needs to soak into the food, so leave it for about 12 hours before cooking. Chicken can be treated in the same way as meat.

1.5 to 1.75 kg/3½ to 4 lb meat or chicken
FOR THE TANDOORI COATING: 2 medium onions
1 to 2 garlic cloves
½ teaspoon chilli powder
½ teaspoon ground cinnamon
½ teaspoon ground cardamon
½ teaspoon ground coriander
3 tablespoons lemon juice
1 to 2 teaspoons salt
red colouring

Remove the skin from the chicken and make fairly deep cuts over all the meat or chicken flesh. Peel and very finely chop the onions and garlic – this could be done in the food processor. Combine with the spices, lemon juice, salt and enough colouring to give a distinctly red tint. Press this mixture very thoroughly into the meat or chicken flesh, then leave to stand for 12 hours.

Roast according to the directions on page 78. Serve with cooked rice. Serves 4 to 6.

Beef Curry

750 g/1½ lb chuck or other stewing steak
1 to 2 onions
3 tablespoons oil or beef dripping
½ to 1 teaspoon chilli powder
2 teaspoons ground coriander
2 teaspoons ground cumin
1 teaspoon ground fenugreek
1 to 2 teaspoons ground ginger
1 teaspoon ground turmeric
25 g/1 oz (¼ cup) flour
750 ml/1¼ pints (3 cups) beef stock or water and ½ beef stock cube (1 bouillon cube)
4 tablespoons coconut milk
1 tablespoon tomato purée (paste)
50 g/2 oz (⅓ cup) sultanas (golden raisins)
salt and pepper
a squeeze of lemon juice
sugar to taste

Cut the beef into neat dice. Peel and chop the onion(s). Heat the oil or dripping in a large saucepan and lightly fry the meat and onions. Mix the curry spices with the flour, stir into the meat and onions and cook over a low heat for 2 to 3 minutes. Add beef stock, or water and stock cube, and the coconut milk. Stir over a low heat as the mixture comes to the boil and slightly thickens, then add the tomato purée (paste), sultanas (golden raisins), a very little seasoning and lemon juice.

Cover the pan and simmer gently for 1½ hours, then taste the curry. Add more seasoning and a little sugar if required, continue cooking very slowly for a further ½ to 1 hour.

Cook rice as directed on page 136 but add a pinch of saffron to the water. Serve the curry in a border of the rice with the accompaniments suggested on this page. Serves 4 to 6.

VARIATION
Use 1 tablespoon curry powder in place of the 6 spices suggested.

PURIS
Sift 225 g/8 oz (2 cups) self-raising wholewheat flour with a little salt and pepper. Rub (cut) in 40 g/1½ oz (3 tablespoons) margarine, then add enough water to make a rolling consistency. Knead, firmly; put the dough back in the bowl, cover and leave for 30 minutes.

Knead the dough again, roll out to 5 mm/ ¼ inch in thickness and cut into small rounds or squares. Heat 2 to 3 tablespoons oil in a large frying pan (skillet) and fry the bread for 1½ to 2 minutes or until golden brown on the under side. Turn and fry on the second side for the same time.

Drain on absorbent kitchen paper and serve hot or cold as bread. Makes 8 to 12.

Beef Curry with accompaniments

Offal (Variety Meats)

Offal (Variety meats) provides an excellent selection of foods, all of which are highly nutritious.

Stuffed Lambs' Hearts

Calf's Head Brawn

1 calf's head
350 g/12 oz stewing veal
1 lemon
2 onions
2 bay leaves
1 bouquet garni
salt and pepper
225 g/8 oz cooked ham or boiled bacon cut in 1 thick slice
2 teaspoons gelatine (unflavored gelatin)

✲✲Ask the butcher to split the head. Soak it in plenty of cold water for 1 to 2 hours. Change the water once or twice. Put the head into a very large pan. Dice the veal and add to the pan. Pare the rind from the lemon; do not use any of the bitter white pith. Peel the onions but keep whole. Cover the head and veal with cold water, add the lemon rind, onions, herbs and a little seasoning.

Cover the pan and simmer gently for 2 hours. Lift the head and veal out of the saucepan and leave until cold enough to handle. Boil the stock in the uncovered pan until reduced to about 300 ml/½ pint (1¼ cups).

Dice all the meat from the calf's head; dice the ham or bacon. Put the meat from the calf's head, the diced veal and ham or bacon into a 1.5 to 1.8 litre/2½ to 3 pint (6 to 7½ cup) bowl.

Dissolve the gelatine in the very hot stock, strain over the meat and allow to set.

Turn out and serve with salad. Serves 8 to 10.

VARIATIONS
Use pig's or sheep's head instead of calf's head, omit the ham or bacon and use 225 g/8 oz cooked tongue instead.

Brains in Lemon Butter

4 sets of brains
300 ml/½ pint (1¼ cups) chicken stock, or water and ½ chicken stock (1 bouillon) cube
salt and pepper
2 tablespoons lemon juice
50 g/2 oz (¼ cup) butter
TO GARNISH:
2 tablespoons chopped parsley
paprika

Soak the brains in cold water for 1 to 1½ hours, drain well. Remove all traces of blood and the skin. Place in a saucepan with the stock, a little seasoning and ½ tablespoon lemon juice.

Simmer for 10 minutes then lift the brains from the liquid. Heat the butter in a large frying pan (skillet), add the brains and cook steadily for 10 minutes until golden in colour. Add the remaining lemon juice towards the end of the cooking period. Top with the parsley and paprika. Serves 4.

Kidney and Mushroom Râgout

225 to 350 g/8 to 12 oz lambs' kidneys
25 g/1 oz (¼ cup) flour
salt and pepper
50 g/2 oz (¼ cup) butter or margarine
300 ml/½ pint (1¼ cups) chicken stock or water and ½ chicken stock (1 bouillon) cube
100 g/4 oz (1 cup) small button mushrooms
3 tablespoons dry sherry
2 tablespoons chopped parsley
1 teaspoon French mustard

✲✲Halve the kidneys, remove all the skin and gristle. Blend the flour with a little seasoning and coat the kidneys. Heat the butter or margarine in a saucepan, add the kidneys and fry gently for 10 minutes or until golden brown.

Blend in the stock. Stir as the mixture comes to the boil and thickens. Add the mushrooms and sherry, then simmer for a further 10 minutes. Add half the parsley and the mustard towards the end of the cooking time together with any extra seasoning required.

Top with remaining parsley. Serves 4.

Stuffed Lambs' Hearts

Lambs' hearts make a delicious meal; they retain most of their flavour if they are wrapped in foil and roasted in the oven, but pressure cooking is another excellent way to tenderize the meat.

8 small or 4 large lambs' hearts
stuffing, see method
50 g/2 oz (¼ cup) butter or margarine
FOR THE STUFFING: a stuffing of your choice, see pages 108 and 109 or Sage and Onion, page 64
FOR THE SAUCE: 25 g/1 oz (¼ cup) cornflour (cornstarch)
450 ml/¾ pint (2 cups) beef stock, or water and 1 beef stock cube (2 bouillon cubes)
4 tablespoons dry sherry
salt and pepper

Wash the hearts in plenty of cold water; cut away the fat, gristle and the tubes. Split and fill with stuffing.

Divide foil into 8 or 4 squares. Spread the butter or margarine in the centre of each piece of foil and place a heart on top of each. Wrap tightly in the foil. Put into a roasting tin with the join of the foil uppermost. Cook in the centre of a moderate oven (160°C/325°F, Gas Mark 3) for 2 hours. Open the foil carefully, drain out the fat into a saucepan and use this as the basis for the sauce. Place the hearts on a heated serving dish. Keep warm while making the sauce.

For the sauce Blend the cornflour (cornstarch) with the stock and sherry, pour into the saucepan with the fat from cooking the hearts. Stir until thickened and season to taste. Serves 4.

VARIATION
If you use a pressure cooker, tie each stuffed heart securely with fine string. Heat 25 g/1 oz (2 tablespoons) cooking fat or margarine in the bottom of the pressure cooker and brown the hearts; remove from the cooker and pour out any surplus fat. Add 600 ml/1 pint (2½ cups) hot beef stock or water and 1 beef stock cube (2 bouillon cubes) to the pressure cooker, return the hearts to the cooker, bring up to HIGH 15 lb pressure and cook for 30 minutes. Reduce the pressure quickly. Lift out the hearts and keep hot. Blend 25 g/1 oz (¼ cup) cornflour (cornstarch) with the 4 tablespoons dry sherry, add to the liquid in the pressure cooker and stir over a low heat until thickened. Season to taste before serving.

Liver Râgout

450 g/1 lb lambs' or pigs' liver
2 small onions
2 tablespoons oil
1 × 397 g/14 oz (16 oz) can tomatoes
6 tablespoons dry sherry
salt and pepper
1 to 2 teaspoons chopped marjoram or ½ to 1 teaspoon dried marjoram
Cheese Rice Ring, see page 137
2 tablespoons chopped parsley

⁂Dice the liver or cut into neat strips. Peel and chop the onions. Heat the oil in a pan and fry the onions for 4 to 5 minutes, then add the liver and turn in the hot oil for 2 to 3 minutes only. Add the canned tomatoes with the liquid from the can, the sherry, seasoning, marjoram and simmer gently for 10 to 15 minutes or until the liver is just cooked but still slightly pink. Spoon into the centre of the Rice Ring and sprinkle with parsley. Serves 4 to 6.

Oxtail Casserole

2 medium oxtails
salt and pepper
1 teaspoon mustard powder
50 g/2 oz (½ cup) flour
50 g/2 oz (¼ cup) cooking fat or 2 tablespoons oil
4 medium onions
4 medium carrots
4 medium tomatoes
1 garlic clove
600 ml/1 pint (2½ cups) beef stock with 300 ml/½ pint (1¼ cups) red wine or 900 ml/1½ pints (3¾ cups) beef stock
1 tablespoon tomato purée (paste)
2 bay leaves
about 1 tablespoon lemon juice
1 tablespoon chopped parsley

⁂Cut the oxtails into neat joints, if not already done by the butcher. Mix a generous amount of seasoning, including mustard powder, with the flour and use to coat the oxtail.

Heat the fat or oil in a large saucepan and fry the meat until golden brown. Lift out of the pan and put into a casserole. Peel and thickly slice the onions and carrots. Skin and slice the tomatoes; peel and crush the garlic.

Add all the vegetables to the fat remaining in the saucepan and cook over a low heat for 5 minutes. Stir in the stock or stock and wine, bring slowly to the boil, stirring well to absorb the fat, and simmer for 5 minutes. Add the tomato purée (paste), bay leaves and any extra seasoning required.

Pour over the oxtail, cover the cas-serole and cook in the centre of a preheated cool oven (150°C/300°F, Gas Mark 2) for 3½ hours.

Lift the lid, remove the bay leaves. Add lemon juice to taste and the pars-ley. Serves 6.

Note If possible cook this one day, allow it to cool, remove the excess fat from the top of the casserole and reheat thoroughly.

VARIATIONS

Simmer gently in a saucepan for the time given above; check occasionally that there is plenty of liquid.

Soak 100 g/4 oz (⅔ cup) haricot (navy) beans overnight; drain and add to the casserole with the tomato paste and seasoning.

Liver and Tomato Casserole

6 streaky bacon rashers (slices)
2 large onions
450 g/1 lb tomatoes
450 g/1 lb lambs' liver
1 tablespoon flour
salt and pepper
½ teaspoon mustard powder
½ teaspoon chopped thyme or ¼ teaspoon dried thyme
50 g/2 oz (¼ cup) butter or margarine
150 ml/¼ pint (⅔ cup) chicken stock, or water and ½ chicken stock (1 bouillon) cube

⁂Cut the rinds from the bacon but do not discard them. Stretch and halve the bacon rashers (slices) and form into rolls. Peel the onions and cut into wafer thin rings; slice the tomatoes; cut the liver into thin fingers. Mix the flour with the salt, pepper, mustard and thyme and coat the liver.

Heat the butter or margarine and bacon rinds in a frying pan (skillet) and fry the liver for 2 minutes only. Put into a shallow casserole, discarding the bacon rinds.

Add the onions to the pan and cook until soft, pouring in the stock towards the end of the cooking time. Blend the stock with the onions and spoon over the liver. Top with the tomatoes.

Cover the casserole and bake in the centre of a preheated moderate oven (180°C/350°F, Gas Mark 4) for 20 min-utes. Remove the lid of the casserole, place the bacon rolls on top of the food and move the casserole to a shelf above the centre of the oven. Continue cook-ing, uncovered, for a further 20 minutes. Serves 4.

VARIATION

Avocados and Liver Peel and slice 2 ripe avocados. Add to the Liver and Tomato Casserole just 10 minutes before serving.

SIMPLE SKILL
Blanching certain meats whitens the flesh and gives it a better flavour.

⁂**FREEZER NOTE**
While oxtail can be frozen, use as soon as possible as it tends to lose the sticky texture which is so delicious.

Liver Râgout

73

Cooked Meats and Sausages

The cooked meat counters in shops and supermarkets provide a tempting display and the cooked meats can be used in a great variety of recipes. Most of them need little addition; they can be served cold with salad to make a light main meal.

These recipes give simple suggestions using boiled bacon or cooked ham and sausages for main dishes or quick snacks.

Danish Herder's Pie

| 1 large onion |
| 450 g/1 lb boiled bacon (smoked cooked ham) |
| 100 g/4 oz (1 cup) button mushrooms |
| 1 red pepper |
| 25 g/1 oz (2 tablespoons) butter |
| 1 tablespoon flour |
| 1 × 397 g/14 oz can tomatoes |
| 2 tablespoons tomato ketchup |
| ½ to 1 tablespoon Worcestershire sauce |
| 1 teaspoon finely chopped rosemary or ½ teaspoon dried rosemary |
| salt and pepper |
| 100 g/4 oz (¾ cup) frozen peas |
| **FOR THE TOPPING:** 750 g/1½ lb cooked potatoes |
| 1 large carrot |
| 50 g/2 oz Samsoe cheese |
| 25 g/1 oz (2 tablespoons) butter |

LEFTOVERS
Curried Ham
Mince (grind) leftover cooked ham or boiled bacon, or chop it in a food processor.

Blend a little curry powder or curry paste with mayonnaise and add the ham. The mixture should be the consistency of a soft pâté.

Use the mixture as a topping for halved hard-boiled (hard-cooked) eggs and serve in a salad; serve as a pâté, or as a sandwich filling.

Ham and Pineapple Kebabs

✶✶Peel and chop the onion. Dice the meat; wipe and quarter the mushrooms. Dice the red pepper and discard the core and seeds. Heat the butter in a large saucepan, add the onion and cook for 5 minutes or until soft; then add the meat, mushrooms and pepper. Cook for a further 3 to 4 minutes. Stir in the flour, blend with the ingredients in the pan, then drain the tomatoes and add to the saucepan with the ketchup, Worcestershire sauce, rosemary, a very little salt, pepper and the peas. Mix thoroughly and spoon into a large ovenproof dish. Topping Mash the potatoes, peel and grate the carrot and grate the cheese. Blend the butter, carrot and cheese with the potatoes. Spread over the meat mixture in the dish. Bake in the centre of a moderately hot oven (190°C/375°F, Gas Mark 5) for 45 minutes, until the topping is golden brown. Serves 4 to 6.

Sausage Kebabs

| 450 g/1 lb smoked or cooked sausages (sausage links) |
| 225 g/8 oz Edam cheese |
| 100 g/4 oz (1 cup) small button mushrooms |
| 1 Ogen (Cantaloupe) melon |
| **TO GARNISH:** 225 g/8 oz tomatoes |
| 1 to 2 green peppers |
| salt and pepper |

Cut the sausages into thick slices. Dice the cheese, wipe the mushrooms. Peel and dice the melon. Thread on to 4 or 6 long skewers.

Slice the tomatoes and put into a serving dish. Dice or slice the pepper, sprinkle over the tomatoes and add salt and pepper to taste.

Arrange the skewers over the tomato mixture. Serve with your favourite salad dressing or mayonnaise (see page 104). Serves 4 or 6.

Ham and Pineapple Kebabs

| **FOR THE COCONUT RICE:** 75 to 100 g/3 to 4 oz fresh coconut |
| 175 g/6 oz (1 cup) long-grain rice |
| 350 ml/12 fl oz (1½ cups) water |
| pinch of salt |
| **FOR THE KEBABS:** ½ large or 1 small pineapple |
| 450 g/1 lb cooked ham (smoked cooked ham), cut in one thick slice |
| 1 tablespoon oil |
| ¼ teaspoon ground ginger |
| **FOR THE SAUCE:** 300 ml/½ pint (1¼ cups) plain yogurt |
| 1 to 2 teaspoons curry paste or curry powder |
| 1 teaspoon sugar |

Coconut Rice Rub the coconut against the coarse side of a grater, put into a saucepan and heat very gently until lightly browned. Remove half of the coconut from the saucepan, put on one side. Add the rice, water and a pinch of salt to the coconut in the saucepan. Bring the water to the boil. Stir briskly with a fork, cover the pan, lower the heat and simmer for 15 minutes.

Kebabs Meanwhile, cut the pineapple into thick slices, then into neat cubes. Dice the ham. Thread the pineapple and ham on to metal skewers. Blend the oil and ginger; brush over the pineapple and ham. Cook under a preheated grill (broiler) for 2 to 3 minutes. Turn the skewers and grill (broil) on the second side for a further 2 to 3 minutes.

Sauce Blend the yogurt, curry paste or powder, sugar and salt. Spoon into a sauce-boat. Serve the coconut rice on a heated dish, and place the kebabs on top. Sprinkle with the remaining coconut. Serves 4.

Salami Cornets

Choose a salami about 5 cm/2 inches in diameter and ask for it to be very thinly sliced.

175 g/6 oz salami, see above
75 g/3 oz (6 tablespoons) cream cheese
2 to 3 sticks of celery
salt and cayenne pepper
dry sherry or dry cider

Put the cream cheese into a bowl. Finely chop the celery, add to the cheese with salt and pepper to taste and enough sherry or cider to make a soft mixture.

Spread the cheese mixture on the salami slices then fold to make cornet shapes. Put on to a flat dish and hold in position with cocktail sticks (toothpicks). Makes 36 to 40.

Real Toad-in-the-Hole

FOR THE BATTER:
100 g/4 oz (1 cup) plain (all purpose) flour
pinch of salt
1 or 2 eggs
300 ml/½ pint (1¼ cups) milk (less 2 tablespoons if using 2 eggs)
FOR THE BASE:
50 g/2 oz (¼ cup) cooking fat or see method
4 lambs' kidneys
4 sausages (sausage links)
made mustard
4 firm tomatoes
salt and pepper
4 lamb cutlets

Batter Sift the flour and salt into a bowl. Beat the egg(s) and milk gradually into the flour to produce a smooth, thin batter. Place the fat in a large shallow casserole and heat just above the centre of a preheated hot oven (220°C/425°F, Gas Mark 7) until melted. If there is a lot of fat on the cutlets you can use less than 50 g/2 oz (¼ cup).

Base meanwhile skin and halve the kidneys. Halve the sausages lengthways, spread with mustard and sandwich to-

gether again. Halve the tomatoes and season lightly. Arrange the cutlets, kidneys, sausages and tomatoes in the hot fat. Cook for 10 minutes above the centre of the oven. Remove the dish from the oven and pour the batter over the meats and tomatoes. Cook for 35 to 40 minutes until the batter is firm and golden and the cutlets and sausages are cooked through.

Reduce the heat slightly after 20 to 25 minutes to avoid the batter becoming too brown. Serves 4.

VARIATION

Omit the kidneys and use either loin or spare rib (country-style pork ribs) pork chops in place of lamb cutlets.

Sausages with Chilli Dip

1 to 2 garlic cloves
2 medium carrots
25 g/1 oz (¼ cup) cornflour (cornstarch)
300 ml/½ pint (1¼ cups) dry white wine or dry cider
2 tablespoons brown malt vinegar
1 tablespoon Worcestershire sauce
2 tablespoons tomato ketchup
1 tablespoon brown sugar
good pinch of chilli powder or a few drops of Tabasco sauce (hot pepper sauce)
salt and pepper
TO SERVE:
450 g/1 lb sausages (pork sausage links)

Skin and crush the garlic; peel and finely grate the carrots. Blend the cornflour (cornstarch) with the wine or cider, put into a saucepan and stir over a low heat until thickened and smooth. Add all the other ingredients. The chilli powder or sauce and seasoning should be added gradually to taste.

Grill (broil) or fry the sausages while the dip is heating. Pour the dip into a heated dish or bowl. Arrange the cooked sausages around the dip; press a cocktail stick (toothpick) into each sausage. Serves 6 to 8.

Sausages with Broccoli

25 g/1 oz dripping or lard
2 garlic cloves
1 piece canned red pepper
450 g/1 lb Italian Salamelle or pork sausages (sausage links)
salt and pepper
750 g/1½ lb broccoli

Melt the dripping or lard in a flameproof casserole, add the garlic and fry gently until browned. Chop the red pepper and add to the pan with the sausages and salt and pepper to taste. Cover and bake in a preheated moderately hot oven (190°C/375°F, Gas Mark 5) for about 45 minutes until the sausages are cooked. Meanwhile cook the broccoli in boiling salted water until tender. Drain and place in a warmed serving dish. Add the sausages and toss well. Serves 4.

Sausages with Broccoli

LEFTOVERS
Horseradish sausages
Slice leftover cold cooked sausages. Mix equal equal amounts of horseradish cream and mayonnaise (use enough to coat the sausages). Stir the sausages into the mixture, add a few small cocktail onions, salted peanuts and seedless raisins.

This dish is excellent as part of a mixed hors d'oeuvre. Children may prefer the mayonnaise flavoured with tomato ketchup rather than horseradish.

POULTRY AND GAME

Poultry was once a food for special occasions, but modern methods of rearing chickens, turkeys and ducks have produced good quality birds that are available throughout the year at comparatively reasonable prices. Goose and guinea fowl are less plentiful.

Another welcome development is that you can now buy portions of fresh or frozen chicken and turkey. This means that people living alone, or small families, can cook a suitable amount of poultry, see page 80.

If you live in the country game may be plentiful, but most poulterers will be able to offer game birds when they are in season. Look out for venison and try the dishes made with rabbit and hare on pages 85–86.

Types of Poultry

There are various terms used to describe the kind of poultry available today.

Oven-ready (Roasting) Chickens This generally applies to frozen poultry. It means the bird is trussed ready to be cooked after thawing.

Roasting Birds These are sufficiently tender to be roasted, but they can also be used for casseroles. The joints are rather big for frying or grilling (broiling).

Broilers or Frying Chickens Small birds, often sold jointed; suitable for quick cooking. Often sold frozen. You may be offered spring chicken or poussin (Rock Cornish game hen) which is especially tender.

Turkey (Fresh or Frozen) Whole birds and portions are now available all the year.

Types of Game

The season for shooting game birds and venison is limited but frozen game is available all the year.

Rabbit There are plentiful supplies of rabbit, which makes an economical meal. You can buy diced meat for casseroles or whole rabbits. Young rabbits can be roasted, older animals are best casseroled.

Hare Less easy to buy in shops today, but most game dealers will obtain one if given sufficient notice.

Game Birds Young grouse, partridge, pheasant, pigeon and quail can be roasted, (see page 78). Older birds should be cooked in a casserole or stew (see page 86). Guinea Fowl is also available and can be cooked like chicken or any of the game birds.

Venison is the name given to the flesh of deer; while it is not readily available, there are times when you may be able to obtain it. The flavour of venison is not unlike that of strongly flavoured veal.

Young tender venison can be roasted, (see page 85). Older meat can be diced and cooked in the various casserole recipes in this section.

Buying Points

You have the choice between purchasing fresh or frozen poultry. Frozen poultry tends to be cheaper than fresh, so if price is your first consideration, buy frozen chicken, turkey or duck.

When buying fresh poultry or game birds look for a plump breast; check that the breast bone is pliable – this denotes a young bird. The legs should be plump, too, and not over-sinewy.

Store poultry in a cool place and cook it soon after purchase. Game needs to be hung before cooking to develop its full flavour. The hanging time can range from 2 to 7 days according to how strong a flavour you enjoy.

The quantities of poultry and game to buy are given below and on page 80. The amount of meat on the bone to allow per person may seem high, but both poultry and game birds have a high percentage of bone compared to flesh. Remember this when buying a small turkey; it might be better to select a slightly larger bird which would give a greater amount of flesh and probably almost the same amount of bone.

Ducks and geese have relatively little breast meat compared to that on plump chickens and turkeys, so be prepared to buy a generous amount.

Quantities

If buying chicken or turkey portions to grill (broil) or fry, allow 175 g to 225 g/6 to 8 oz boneless flesh or 350 g/12 oz flesh on the bone per person.

If roasting whole chicken or turkey allow 350 g/12 oz flesh and bone per person. If the turkey has a very thick breast you can allow slightly less per portion.

If stewing the bird allow 175 g/6 oz boneless flesh or 350 g/12 oz meat on the bone per portion.

When buying small game birds, such as partridge, pigeon or quail you need to allow at least 1 bird per person, or 2 birds for larger portions.

A young grouse can be halved; a whole bird is a very generous portion. Older and larger birds cooked in a casserole will certainly provide good portions for 2 or 3 people.

Pheasants are surprisingly plump. A good bird can be carved like a small chicken and can give about 3 portions.

Allow 1 or 2 joints of rabbit or hare, depending on the size and the recipe.

Venison is like any meat, calculate 175 to 225 g/6 to 8 oz per portion of boneless meat or up to 350 g/12 oz if buying a joint with bone.

Freezing Note

Uncooked poultry and game freeze extremely well. Cover the ends of bones with foil before wrapping the bird.

Always remove the giblets and wrap them separately. Do not stuff the bird before freezing. If freezing portions of chicken or turkey, separate them with squares of waxed or greaseproof paper before wrapping, so you can remove the required number of portions.

While you can cook small portions of the poultry from the frozen state, provided this is suitable for the recipe, it is essential to allow whole birds to thaw out completely.

A chicken of about 1.5 kg/3 lb takes about 24 hours to defrost in a refrigerator, 10 hours at room temperature 5 to 6 hours if put into cold water or 6 to 8 minutes per 450 g/1 lb on the defrost setting of a microwave cooker.

A large turkey of about 9 kg/20 lb would need 3 or even 4 days in a refrigerator, 30 hours at room temperature, and 15 hours if put into cold water.

Duck, goose and game birds need the same thawing time. It is important to hang the game before freezing it.

Chickens and turkey can be stored in the freezer for up to 1 year, duck, goose, and game up to 6 months.

Microwave Cooking

The tender texture of young poultry and game makes it extremely suitable for microwave cooking. Stews and casseroles can be cooked in the microwave on a HIGH setting if really young flesh is used. Consult your manufacturer's instruction book for detailed information.

Top right: Roast Pigeons, page 78
Below right: Sate Ajam, page 87

Cooking Techniques

A perfect roast chicken

There are more unusual stuffings on pages 108 to 109, and ideas for flavouring duck and goose are on page 84. The following suggestions are both quick and delicious. The proportions in the suggestions below are a matter of personal taste.

☐ Stuff the bird with lightly fried mushrooms and chopped bacon; flavour with a little chopped rosemary.

☐ Add the chopped cooked giblets to cooked rice (brown rice is particularly good) with chopped almonds, raisins and a little chopped celery. Season well and bind with egg(s). Use as a stuffing.

☐ Fill the bird with peeled potatoes, onions and a little butter and seasoning.

☐ Baste the bird with a little red wine or cider during the roasting period.

☐ Brush the bird with Cranberry Sauce 15 minutes before the end of the cooking period.

Accompaniments
Stuff the bird with Parsley and Thyme Stuffing, (see Veal), and serve with bacon rolls and sausages or Forcemeat Balls, (see page 68).

Chestnut Stuffing is excellent in both chicken and turkey; there are two recipes on page 108. Serve with Bread Sauce and/or Cranberry Sauce, (see page 104).

New Flavours for Roast Game Birds

☐ Serve the game with one of the unusual stuffings suggested on page 108 to 109.

☐ Fill game birds with lemon-flavoured cream cheese or cream cheese and deseeded and skinned grapes.

☐ Blend finely chopped tarragon, chives and parsley with butter or cream cheese. Use 25 to 50 g/1 to 2 oz (2 to 4 tablespoons) inside each bird.

☐ Fill the birds with sweetened black (bing) cherries.

Accompaniments
Serve Game Chips – wafer thin slices of potato, fried until crisp (see page 90). You can of course buy potato crisps (chips) and heat them on a flat baking tray or sheet.

In addition serve fried breadcrumbs, and either Bread Sauce or redcurrant jelly with the game.

Bread Sauce This sauce only has a good flavour if the onion is infused in the milk. The more generous the amount of butter and cream used, the better the sauce will be.

Place 300 ml/½ pint (1¼ cups) milk in a saucepan, add 1 small peeled onion, 50 g/2 oz (1 cup) soft white breadcrumbs, 15 to 25 g/½ to 1 oz (1 to 2 tablespoons) butter and salt and pepper. Bring the milk to boiling point, remove from the heat, cover and leave to stand for at least 1 hour. Reheat, remove the onion just before serving.

SLOW COOKING
The long slow cooking process in a slow cooker will ensure tender chicken, turkey and game but it is less satisfactory for the richer duck and goose. These birds are better cooked in the dry heat of an oven so that excess fat runs from the bird.

PRESSURE COOKING
This appliance is excellent for tenderizing poultry and game, but take great care that the delicate textured flesh is not overcooked.

Special Technique
A PERFECT ROAST BIRD

It is important to appreciate the differences in the various types of poultry and game and how they should be roasted. Chicken, turkey and game birds tend to be very lean and they need fat of some kind to keep them moist during cooking. Stuffing inside the birds helps to give extra moisture. If you prefer to serve game birds without a stuffing put about 25 g/1 oz (2 tablespoonss) butter inside each bird.

Cover the outside of the birds with softened butter or with fat bacon rashers (slices). If you wish to reduce the amount of fat used, roast the birds in a well-greased roasting bag, a covered roasting pan or in a pan tightly covered with foil. The brown skin is part of the appeal of roasted birds so always remove the foil for the last part of the cooking time.

It is a good idea to roast turkey or large chickens with the breast turned downwards for the first half of the roasting time, then turn the bird uppermost to brown.

Slow Roast frozen birds that have been thawed. Fresh young birds can be roasted by the fast or slower method.

Duck or goose These should not be greasy if cooked correctly. Dry the flesh very well. This is particularly important if you are using thawed frozen birds. Place the stuffing inside the bird or cook it separately. Do not add fat to fresh birds, but lightly grease the outside of thawed birds to compensate for the extra moisture in the skin. Stand the bird(s) on a rack in the roasting pan, so excess fat runs out in cooking.

Choose the temperature for roasting as suggested below, but after 30 to 40 minutes *lightly* prick the skin to allow excess fat to run out. Do this at 30 to 40 minute intervals.

Roasting Times

Fast Roasting Set the oven to moderately hot to hot (200 to 220°C/400 to 425°F, Gas Mark 6 to 7). For poultry and game birds, allow 15 minutes per 450 g/1 lb and 15 minutes over for birds up to 5.5 kg/12 lb; after this weight allow 12 minutes per additional 450 g/1 lb.

Slower Roasting Set the oven to moderate (160 to 180°C/325 to 350°F, Gas Mark 3 to 4). For poultry and game birds, allow 22 to 25 minutes per 450 g/1 lb and 22 to 25 minutes over for birds up to 5.5 kg/12 lb; after this weight allow 20 minutes per additional 450 g/1 lb.

Special Technique
TO BONE POULTRY AND GAME BIRDS

Use a well sharpened, flexible knife, for this is essential if you are not to break the delicate flesh. Work slowly so that you ease the flesh away from the bones without wasting flesh. You should end with all the flesh intact and free from bones.

1. Position the bird with the neck towards you. Loosen the skin from the flesh at the neck end of the bird by inserting your finger under the skin. Gradually work your finger (better than a knife) under the skin over the breasts. Do not tear the skin – simply loosen it from the flesh, (see Fig 1).

2. Cut away the wishbone with the knife (Fig 2).

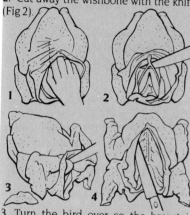

3. Turn the bird over so the breast is placed downwards on the chopping board. Cut the shoulder bones from the flesh of the bird and sever them from the body. Cut off the wing tips, ease the flesh from the wing bones.

4. Ease the skin away from the flesh of the thighs, then gradually cut the flesh from the thighbones and the drumsticks, (Fig 3). Some people retain the very end piece of the drumsticks (where it joins the foot) as this gives a more interesting shape to the bird.

5. Working slowly and carefully, cut away the breast bone, back bone and the parson's nose (Fig 4).

You will then end with a strangely flat amount of flesh, but it can be re-formed into a neat shape for various recipes. The skin helps to create a good shape which is why it is important to retain it unless the recipe states the contrary.

Boning Joints of poultry This is done in the same way, although it is not necessary to loosen the skin from the flesh.

Breast Joints – simply ease the bones away from the flesh; take great care not to tear the delicate flesh of the breast. The flattened breast meat is frequently cooked as an escalope, (see page 67).

Leg Joints – you need to make a firm cut in the flesh until the knife touches the bone, then turn the knife and ease the flesh away from the thigh bone and drumstick.

Chicken à la Kiev

This classic chicken dish is deliciously simple but the chicken must be cooked in deep fat or oil until crisp, which is troublesome if you are entertaining. I have experimented and discovered an alternative method. Fry the chickens for about 5 minutes until very crisp on the outside, drain, then put them on to a baking tray to cook for 25 to 30 minutes in a hot oven.

4 small young spring chickens (Rock Cornish game hens)
100 g/4 oz (½ cup) butter
2 tablespoons chopped parsley
TO COAT:
1 tablespoon flour
salt and pepper
2 eggs
75 g/3 oz (¾ cup) crisp breadcrumbs
TO FRY:
olive oil or well-clarified fat

Bone the chickens, (see Special Technique), or ask the butcher to do it for you. In this particular recipe you can remove the skin after boning but it is not essential. Spread the boned chickens out flat. Put a quarter of the butter on each chicken and sprinkle with parsley. Roll firmly so the butter is enclosed. This is very important.

Mix the flour with the seasoning; beat the eggs. Coat the chicken in the flour, then the egg and finally in the crumbs. Make certain the portions of chicken are well coated.

Heat the oil or fat to 190°C/375°F – the method of testing oil or fat is on page 92. Put in the chicken, fry for 2 to 3 minutes until the chicken starts to change colour. This makes certain that the coating is well set. Then reduce the heat and fry for a further 10 to 12 minutes until golden brown and tender. Serves 4.

VARIATIONS

Add chopped fried red and green pepper and onions to the butter. Chill well and use as above.

Use pâté instead of butter. Chill the pâté very well. If the pâté is not particularly rich use pâté and butter.

Special Technique
'BOILED' OR STEAMED CHICKEN

Now that older boiling fowls (stewing chicken) are not readily available this old-fashioned dish tends to be overlooked. You will find a tender roasting chicken is delicious if it is 'boiled' or steamed. The cooked bird can be served with a flavourful sauce.

First grease the breast of the chicken with butter. Put it into a large saucepan with water to come half-way up the bird. Add the giblets, a few vegetables and herbs to flavour the liquid and seasoning. Bring the liquid just to boiling point, cover the pan, lower the heat and cook gently. Do not boil the liquid in which the chicken is cooked but allow it to simmer gently. Allow just 20 minutes per 450 g/1 lb (the exact time depends on the tenderness of the bird) plus 20 minutes. Check the bird towards the end of the cooking time, for young birds are spoiled by being overcooked.

To steam the bird, grease the breast with butter and cook in a covered steamer over steadily boiling water for the time given above.

SIMPLE SKILL

To skin poultry, make a slit on one side of the bird or the poultry joint. Loosen the skin from the flesh, then gently and slowly pull the skin away from the flesh with the fingers of one hand while holding the flesh with the flat blade of the knife. This method makes certain the flesh is not torn.

Chicken à la Kiev

Herbed Chicken with Rice

Boiled Chicken

Lemon Chicken

1.75 kg/4 lb chicken, weight when trussed with giblets
1 large lemon
12 shallots or small onions
¼ small celery heart
1 bay leaf
salt and pepper
water, see method
25 g/1 oz (2 tablespoons) butter
FOR THE SAUCE: 100 g/4 oz (1 cup) mushrooms
50 g/2 oz (¼ cup) butter
3 egg yolks or 2 eggs
150 ml/¼ pint (⅔ cup) double (heavy) cream
150 ml/¼ pint (⅔ cup) chicken stock, see method
150 ml/¼ pint (⅔ cup) dry sherry

Wipe the chicken thoroughly. A frozen chicken must be allowed to thaw completely. This can be done very easily and quickly in a microwave oven. Wash the giblets. Halve the lemon, remove all pips and squeeze the lemon juice over the outside of the chicken, then put the lemon halves inside the bird. Place the bird in a deep casserole and add the giblets, except the liver, which would give too definite a flavour and would darken the liquid.

Peel the shallots or onions, and leave whole. Chop the celery. Arrange the vegetables around the chicken and add the bay leaf and a little seasoning. Pour enough water into the casserole to come halfway up the chicken. Finally spread the breast of the bird, which is above the liquid, with the butter. Cover the casserole and cook in the centre of a preheated moderately hot oven (190°C/375°F, Gas Mark 5) for 1½ hours or until the chicken and vegetables are tender.

Meanwhile make the sauce. Slice the mushrooms. Heat the butter in a saucepan and fry the mushrooms until soft. In a small bowl, beat the egg yolks or eggs with the cream; measure off 150 ml/¼ pint (⅔ cup) liquid from the casserole and strain into the egg and cream mixture.

Transfer the mushrooms to a bowl and stand this over a pan of hot, but not boiling water.

Pour the egg and cream mixture onto the mushrooms. Whisk over a low heat until the mixture begins to thicken, then whisk in the sherry and continue cooking until the egg sauce just coats the back of a spoon. Season to taste.

Carve the chicken; place on a heated dish and top with the mushrooms and egg sauce. Serve the shallots or onions round the chicken. Serves 6.

Chicken Portions

The recipes which follow are ideal for using portions of poultry. Although these recipes are based on 4 or 6 servings, it would be easy to adapt the quantities to give a single portion. The following suggestions for grilling (broiling) and frying are ideal for one portion of chicken.

To Grill (Broil) Chicken Allow about 25 g/1 oz (2 tablespoons) butter for a portion of chicken. Cook under a preheated grill (broiler) for 12 to 15 minutes. Turn once or twice and each time brush the chicken with more butter.

For a delicate flavour, add a little finely grated lemon or orange rind and juice to the butter or about 1 tablespoon chopped fresh herbs.

For a more definite flavour, add a peeled crushed clove of garlic or ½ teaspoon curry paste or ½ teaspoon Worcestershire sauce.

To Fry Chicken The chicken can be left uncoated or coated in a little flour or in egg and breadcrumbs.

Allow a generous 25 g/1 oz (2 tablespoons) butter or fat for frying the chicken. Cook for about 15 minutes in shallow fat or 10 to 12 minutes in deep fat. You can add flavour by frying bacon and/or chopped onions or mushrooms in the pan with the chicken.

Try mixing finely chopped chives or other fresh herbs or finely grated Parmesan cheese with the flour or breadcrumbs used to coat the chicken.

Chicken Breasts in Rum and Orange Sauce

4 chicken breasts
3 oranges
1 tablespoon flour
salt and pepper
40 g/1½ oz (3 tablespoons) butter
2 tablespoons dark rum
4 tablespoons double (heavy) cream
TO GARNISH: orange segments
watercress

Frozen chicken breasts should be thawed and well dried. Grate the rind from the oranges and put a little on one side for garnish; halve the fruit and

LEFTOVERS
Celery and Chicken Soup
The stock and celery left from cooking Lemon Chicken makes an excellent soup. Remove the bay leaf and blend the celery and enough stock to give a flowing consistency.

You could add the uncooked chicken liver to the stock and simmer for a short time before blending, to make a stock with more flavour.

Chicken Breasts in Rum and Orange Sauce

squeeze out the juice. Mix the flour with a generous amount of seasoning and sprinkle over the chicken breasts.

Heat the butter and fry the chicken breasts quickly for 2 minutes on each side, then lower the heat and cook slowly until tender. This will take 8 to 10 minutes. Lift on to a heated dish.

Add the grated orange rind, juice, rum and cream to the pan; stir well to blend with the chicken juices. Spoon a little sauce over the chicken breasts, and pour the remainder into a sauce-boat. Top with the grated orange rind.

Garnish with orange segments and watercress. Serves 4.

VARIATIONS

Slices of turkey meat or veal fillets (escalopes) can be cooked in the same way.

Herbed Chicken and Rice

| 100 g/4 oz (1 cup) mushrooms |
| 1 onion |
| 2 garlic cloves |
| 50 g/2 oz (¼ cup) butter |
| 4 chicken portions |
| 150 ml/¼ pint (⅔ cup) chicken stock |
| 150 ml/¼ pint (⅔ cup) dry cider |
| 2 teaspoons chopped fresh mixed herbs |
| salt and pepper |
| 100 g/4 oz (½ cup) long-grain rice |
| 2 tablespoons oil |
| pinch of powdered saffron |

Wipe and slice the mushrooms. Peel and chop the onion and garlic. Melt the butter in a saucepan, fry the onion and garlic with the chicken pieces until golden. Add the mushrooms, stock, cider, herbs and salt and pepper. Cover and simmer gently for 1 hour. Meanwhile cook the rice (see page 136), it should be free from liquid. Heat the oil in a pan, add the rice and saffron and sauté for 6 to 7 minutes, stirring frequently. To serve the dish, arrange the rice on a warmed serving dish, put the chicken pieces and vegetables on top. Serves 4.

<u>Note</u> If preferred, heat the stock with the herbs first, allow to stand for several hours, strain and use as above.

Vermouth Chicken

| 2 small onions |
| 100 g/4 oz (1 cup) small button mushrooms |
| 25 g/1 oz (¼ cup) flour |
| salt and pepper |
| 4 chicken portions |
| 75 g/3 oz (6 tablespoons) butter |

| 300 ml/½ pint (1¼ cups) chicken stock |
| 1 tablespoon mushroom ketchup |
| 5 tablespoons white vermouth |
| 1 bouquet garni |
| **TO SERVE:** |
| 450 g/1 lb (4 cups) hot cooked rice |
| 1 lemon |
| parsley |

Peel the onions and cut into rings. Wipe the mushrooms, leave whole. Mix the flour with a little seasoning and coat the chicken joints. Heat the butter in a large frying pan (skillet), preferably one with a lid, or a large shallow saucepan. Fry the chicken for 4 to 5 minutes, or until pale golden. Remove from the pan. Add the onion rings and fry these until pale golden, then blend in the stock, ketchup, vermouth and bouquet garni. Stir well so the liquid absorbs any fat and flour left in the pan.

Return the chicken joints to the pan, cover tightly and simmer for 10 minutes. Add the mushrooms, stir the sauce well, cover the pan again and continue cooking slowly for a further 10 minutes.

Spoon the chicken and sauce over the cooked rice. Cut the lemon into 4 wedges, place on the chicken, garnish with parsley. Serves 4.

Chicken Napoleon

| 450 g/1 lb potatoes |
| 225 g/8 oz onions |
| 100 g/4 oz (1 cup) mushrooms |
| 4 chicken portions |
| 2 tablespoons oil |
| 25 g/1 oz (¼ cup) flour |
| 1 × 425 g/15 oz can tomatoes |
| 300 ml/½ pint (1¼ cups) chicken stock, or water and ½ chicken stock (1 bouillon) cube |
| 2 tablespoons tomato purée (paste) |
| 1 teaspoon chopped fresh mixed herbs or ½ teaspoon dried herbs |
| salt and pepper |

Peel and slice the potatoes and onions, wipe the mushrooms and cut into thick slices. Dry the chicken portions well. (In this recipe, they can be cooked without thawing.)

Heat the oil in a frying pan (skillet) and fry the chicken portions until brown. Spoon into a casserole. Add the vegetables and fry gently until a pale golden brown, turning several times. Add to the chicken in the casserole. Stir the flour into the residue in the pan, add the tomatoes, plus the liquid from the can, the stock, the tomato purée (paste), herbs and seasoning. Stir over a low heat until thickened and pour over the chicken and vegetables.

Cover the casserole and cook in the centre of a moderate oven (180°C/350°F,

Chicken with Yogurt

Gas Mark 4) for 1¼ to 1½ hours until chicken is tender. Serves 4.

VARIATIONS

<u>Pigeon Casserole</u> Use 4 large or 8 small pigeons in place of the chicken portions. Use beef stock, or water and ½ beef stock (1 bouillon) cube instead of chicken stock or add half stock and half red wine. Cook for 1¾ to 2 hours.

Jointed grouse or pheasants can be cooked in the same way.

Chicken with Yogurt

| 1.5 kg/3 lb chicken |
| 1 onion |
| 1 garlic clove |
| ½ green pepper |
| 50 g/2 oz (¼ cup) butter |
| 65 g/2½ oz (½ cup plus 2 tablespoons) flour |
| 600 ml/1 pint (2½ cups) chicken stock |
| salt and pepper |
| 300 ml/½ pint (1¼ cups) natural yogurt |
| **TO GARNISH:** |
| chopped fresh chives or parsley |

Cut the chicken into portions. Peel the onion and garlic; chop the onion, crush the garlic. Deseed and chop the green pepper. Heat the butter in a flameproof casserole or saucepan, add the chicken pieces, onion, green pepper and garlic and fry the chicken until lightly browned on all sides.

Sprinkle over the flour and cook, stirring for 1 minute. Stir in the stock with salt and pepper to taste. Bring to the boil, lower the heat, cover the casserole or saucepan and simmer for 30 minutes. Stir in the yogurt and continue cooking gently for 30 minutes. Adjust the seasoning to taste before serving. Sprinkle with a little chopped chives or parsley. Serves 4.

Versatile Turkey

As already mentioned, turkey can be bought in portions and cooked in various ways but it makes economic sense to buy a whole turkey, cut it into portions and use them in a variety of different dishes.

Remember, you can roast portions of turkey just as you would roast a whole bird (see page 78).

Turkey Portions Creole

1 kg/2 lb turkey portions
2 tablespoons plain (all-purpose) flour
salt and pepper
1 tablespoon oil
25 g/1 oz butter (2 tablespoons)
2 onions
1 green pepper
1 garlic clove
1 × 400 g/14 oz can peeled tomatoes
1 bouquet garni
150 ml/¼ pint (⅔ cup) chicken stock
TO GARNISH: chopped parsley

Season the flour and use to coat the turkey portions. Heat the oil and butter in a large flameproof casserole and fry the turkey portions until golden on all sides. Peel and slice the onions. Core, seed and slice the green pepper. Peel and crush the garlic. Add to the turkey, lower the heat and cook gently for 5 minutes. Sprinkle with any remaining flour. Cook for a minute then add the tomatoes and juice, bouquet garni, and stock. Bring to the boil, stirring, cover tightly and simmer gently for 1¼ hours or until turkey portions are tender. When cooked lift the turkey pieces on to a hot serving dish and keep hot. Discard the bouquet garni and boil the sauce rapidly, uncovered, until reduced to a coating consistency. Adjust seasoning to taste and pour over the turkey. Serve sprinkled with parsley. Serves 6.

Turkey Stroganoff

450 to 550 g/1 to 1¼ lb turkey breast
2 onions
75 g/3 oz (6 tablespoons) butter
300 ml/½ pint (1¼ cups) soured cream or double (thick) cream with 1 to 2 tablespoons lemon juice
2 tablespoons dry sherry
salt and pepper
2 tablespoons tomato purée (paste)
3 to 4 tablespoons chopped gherkins or pickled cucumber
TO SERVE: cooked rice
tomato wedges
chopped parsley

Cut the turkey into thin strips, peel and chop the onions. Melt the butter in a large frying pan (skillet) and cook the onion and turkey meat together for about 15 minutes; do not allow to brown. Stir the soured cream into the turkey mixture together with the sherry and salt and pepper to taste. Heat gently then stir in the tomato purée (paste) and the chopped gherkins.

Serve on a bed of cooked rice, garnished with tomato wedges and chopped parsley. Serves 4.

VARIATIONS
Fry 100 g/4 oz (1 cup) small button mushrooms with the turkey and onion.

Use half soured cream and half double (heavy) cream for a milder flavour.

Devilled Drumsticks

2 turkey drumsticks
FOR THE TOPPING: 40 g/1½ oz (3 tablespoons) butter
2 teaspoons mustard powder
1 to 2 teaspoons curry powder
pinch of cayenne pepper
2 teaspoons Worcestershire sauce
few drops of soy sauce

Make several very shallow cuts in the drumsticks, this allows the topping to penetrate the meat.

Mix the topping ingredients thoroughly and spread over the drumsticks. Transfer to an ovenproof dish and bake, uncovered, in the centre of a moderately hot oven (190 to 200°C/375 to 400°F, Gas Mark 5 to 6) for 50 minutes to 1 hour, depending on the thickness of the legs. Serves 2.

Turkey Escalopes

4 large thin slices turkey breast
flour to coat
salt and pepper
1 egg, beaten
50 g/2 oz (¼ cup) crisp white breadcrumbs
50 g/2 oz (¼ cup) butter
2 tablespoons oil
lemon slices

Season the flour with salt and pepper to taste and use to coat the turkey slices. Coat the slices with the beaten egg and then cover with breadcrumbs.

Heat the butter and oil in a frying pan (skillet) and fry the escalopes for 1½ to 2 minutes until golden brown and crisp. Lower the heat and cook for a further 5 to 6 minutes until tender. Top with slices of lemon. Serves 4.

VARIATIONS
Escalopes with Cream Sauce Remove the cooked escalopes from the pan and then add 6 tablespoons dry white vermouth and 2 tablespoons chicken stock. Boil rapidly until reduced by half, then add 150 ml/¼ pint (⅔ cup) thick (heavy) cream and continue boiling uncovered, until sauce becomes a coating consistency. Strain the sauce and season to taste. Arrange cooked escalopes on a serving dish, pour over the strained sauce and serve garnished with lightly cooked button mushrooms if liked. Sprinkle with freshly chopped parsley or a little paprika.

Escalopes Rossini Simmer turkey giblets and make into a Rillette mixture (see page 84). Top each escalope with a generous mound of the soft pâté type mixture before serving.

For a richer pâté use just the turkey liver in the same recipe as given under Rillette on page 84.

Turkey Portions Creole

82

Using Leftovers

Leftover chicken or turkey can be used in a variety of interesting dishes. One way to make poultry go further is to use it in a mould or loaf.

Chicken Biryani

600 ml/1 pint (2½ cups) chicken stock, see page 51

pinch of saffron powder or a few saffron strands

450 g/1 lb cooked chicken

2 medium onions

1 garlic clove

50 g/2 oz (¼ cup) chicken fat or margarine

¼ teaspoon ground cumin

salt and pepper

225 g/8 oz (1 cup) long-grain rice

50 g/2 oz (⅓ cup) seedless raisins

50 g/2 oz (⅓ or ½ cup) salted peanuts or almonds

Strain the hot stock and add the saffron powder or strands. If using the latter, allow the stock to stand for 30 minutes then strain it if desired.

Dice the chicken. Peel and chop the onions and garlic. Heat the chicken fat or margarine in a large saucepan and fry the onions and garlic for 5 minutes. Add the stock, and ground cumin, a little seasoning and the rice. Stir as the mixture comes to the boil, lower the heat and cook for 15 minutes. Add the chicken, half the raisins and half the nuts. Continue cooking for a further 5 to 10 minutes, or until the rice is tender. Spoon into a heated dish and top with the remaining raisins and nuts. Serves 4.

Chicken Mould

1 chicken, about 1.75 kg/4 lb when trussed

2 medium onions

3 bay leaves

1 bouquet garni

600 ml/1 pint (2½ cups) water

25 g/1 oz (2 tablespoons) butter

25 g/1 oz (¼ cup) flour

150 ml/¼ pint (⅔ cup) single (light) cream or milk

100 g/4 oz lean bacon rashers (slices)

salt and pepper

1 tablespoon lemon juice

Cut all the flesh from the chicken; keep covered while making the stock. Put the chicken bones, giblets, whole onions, 1 bay leaf and bouquet garni into a saucepan. Cover with the water and simmer steadily for 1 hour.

Reserve 150 ml/¼ pint (⅔ cup) of stock for this mould; the remainder can be used to make a gravy or sauce. Heat the butter in a good-sized saucepan, stir in the flour and cook over a low heat for 2 to 3 minutes. Blend in the 150 ml/¼ pint (⅔ cup) of stock and the cream or milk. Bring the liquid to the boil and stir until it reaches a coating consistency.

De-rind the bacon. Mince (grind) the bacon with the leg, wing and back meat from the chicken and either put through a mincer (grinder) or chop finely in a food processor. Cut the breast meat into 5 mm/¼ inch dice. Blend all the chicken and bacon with the sauce, season the mixture and add the lemon juice.

Spoon into a greased 1.2 to 1.5 litre/2 to 2½ pint (1 to 1½ quart) heatproof terrine or loaf pan. Arrange the two remaining bay leaves on top, cover with greased foil and steam over steadily boiling water for 1¾ hours.

If serving hot, turn out and serve with a gravy made with chicken stock or make one of the sauces on pages 102 to 105.

If serving cold, pour off any fat, put a saucer and light weight on top of the mould and allow to cool. Serve with salad. Serves 4 to 6.

Turkey Nut Loaf

1 medium onion

100 g/4 oz (1 cup) walnuts

750 g/1½ lb raw turkey meat

175 g/6 oz (3 cups) soft breadcrumbs (wholewheat bread is excellent in this dish)

1 tablespoon Worcestershire sauce

½ teaspoon chopped fresh mixed herbs or ¼ teaspoon dried mixed herbs

1 tablespoon chopped parsley

1 egg

salt and pepper

FOR THE GLAZE AND GARNISH:
1 × 425 g/15 oz can apricot halves

2 teaspoons arrowroot or cornflour (cornstarch)

150 ml/¼ pint (⅔ cup) dry white wine

stuffed olives

a little lemon juice or vinegar, see method

lettuce

Peel and finely chop the onion, chop the walnuts and mince (grind) the turkey. Blend the onion, walnuts and turkey with the breadcrumbs, sauce, herbs, egg and plenty of seasoning. This gives the loaf a crumbly texture. Spoon the mixture into a well greased 1 kg/2 lb loaf tin (23 × 13 cm/9 × 5 inch loaf pan) and cover with greased foil.

Bake in the centre of a moderate oven (180°C/350°F, Gas Mark 4) for 1½ hours; a *bain-marie* is not necessary. Cool in the pan for 30 minutes then turn out and allow to become quite cold.

Drain the apricots, reserving the syrup. Arrange some of the halves over the top of the loaf. Any leftover can be added to a salad to serve with the loaf.

Blend the arrowroot or cornflour (cornstarch) with the syrup from the can of apricots and the white wine. Tip into a saucepan, heat and stir until thickened and clear.

Allow the sauce to cool slightly. Slice the olives and place on the top edges of the loaf. Brush the glaze over the top and sides of the loaf. Any glaze left over can be blended with a little lemon juice to make a sauce to serve with the loaf. Garnish with lettuce. Serves 8.

Chicken Mould

LEFTOVERS
Curried Turkey Salad
Dice leftover turkey while still warm if possible. Mix a little curry paste (smoother than curry powder) with mayonnaise, add the turkey and allow to cool.

Mix in chopped celery, chopped spring onions (scallions) and chopped dessert apple. Serve on shredded lettuce.

Duck and Goose

Both these birds have a smaller amount of flesh on the bone than you find on chicken or turkey, therefore the quantities given under chicken and turkey on page 76 should be increased slightly. Due to the higher fat content of these birds they are rarely used for frying or grilling (broiling). They are better roasted.

LEFTOVERS
Use the giblets of game or poultry to make pâté-type Rillettes.
Rillettes
Cook the giblets in seasoned water to make good stock. Drain the giblets. Chop the meat then put into a food processor with a generous amount of butter, chopped herbs, 1 tablespoon stock or brandy and seasoning to taste. Switch on until smooth. Serve as a pâté.

Duckling with Walnut Rice

Quantities

For Roasting Allow 1 large duck to give 4 small portions or 2 smaller duckling to give 4 slightly larger portions. It is usual to joint the duck and to halve duckling but you may like to carve the birds.

Allow at least 450 g/1 lb of meat on the bone when buying a goose. (This is trussed weight.)

Accompaniments

The accompaniments given for pork (see page 64) are equally good for duck or goose.

Goose can be filled with sliced apples and soaked, but not cooked, prunes.

The flavour of duck blends well with most fruit sauces especially Apple Sauce and Orange Sauce (see page 64). Try other fruits as they come into season, such as apricots, blackcurrants and black (bing) cherries. Simmer the fruit with a little clear stock made from the duck giblets to give a more savoury taste; add sugar to taste and a little brandy.

Duck also blends with less sweet ingredients, such as olives.

Cold or hot duck is delicious with fruit flavoured salads.

Duckling with Walnut Rice

2 ducklings
salt and pepper
2 medium onions
2 bay leaves
½ teaspoon ground cloves or allspice
FOR THE WALNUT RICE:
450 ml/¾ pint (2 cups) chicken stock
150 ml/¼ pint (⅔ cup) orange juice
300 g/10 oz (1½ cups) long-grain rice
75 to 100 g/3 to 4 oz (1 cup) walnuts
25 g/1 oz (2 tablespoons) butter
TO GARNISH:
orange slices
watercress

Dry the ducklings well, season inside and out. Peel the onions, put 1 onion and 1 bay leaf inside each bird. Rub the skins with cloves or allspice (check that everyone likes cloves, for it is a most definite flavour).

Roast the ducklings (see page 78). Put the stock and orange juice into a saucepan and add the rice. Bring the liquid to the boil, add a little seasoning, stir the rice briskly, cover the pan and simmer for 15 minutes.

Meanwhile chop the walnuts coarsely.

Heat the butter, add the walnuts and cook until brown. Blend the walnuts with the rice. Serve with the portions of duckling and garnish with orange slices and watercress. Serve with red cabbage. Serves 6.

VARIATION
If using parboiled rice, increase the chicken stock to 600 ml/1 pint (2½ cups) and simmer for 20 minutes.

Canard aux Navets
[Duck with Turnips]

1 large or 2 smaller ducklings
300 ml/½ pint (1¼ cups) duck stock, see method
750 g/1½ lb young turnips
50 g/2 oz (¼ cup) butter
salt and pepper

Roast the duckling(s) as described on this page and make stock from the neck(s) of the birds. Do not use the liver in the stock for this particular recipe as it would darken the liquid. Peel and thickly slice the turnips. Heat the butter in a large saucepan, add the turnips and turn in the butter until golden in colour. Pour in the stock, and seasoning to taste. Simmer steadily in a covered saucepan for 15 to 20 minutes until the turnips are nearly soft. Remove the saucepan lid to allow the excess liquid to evaporate. Serve with the duckling(s). Serves 4.

Duck with Chinese Salad

1 duck
¼ head of Chinese leaves (bok choy)
2 sticks of celery
1 small onion
1 garlic clove
½ teaspoon ground ginger
2 tablespoons oil
4 tablespoons duck or chicken stock or water with ½ stock (1 bouillon) cube
1 tablespoon sherry
1 teaspoon cornflour (cornstarch)

Roast the duck, allow it to become cold, and then slice it. Arrange the slices on a serving dish.

Shred the Chinese leaves (bok choy), chop the celery, peel and slice the onion, peel and crush the garlic and mix all the vegetables with the ginger. Heat the oil in a pan and toss the vegetable mixture in this for about 2 minutes. Blend together the duck or chicken stock, the sherry, the cornflour (cornstarch). Pour this over the vegetables in the pan and stir over a low heat until the mixture is thickened and clear. Serve the Chinese salad at once with the slices of cold duck. Serves 4.

Dishes with Game

Young and tender game birds are generally roasted and older birds used in a casserole, where the long slow cooking tenderizes the flesh. Follow the timing for roasting on page 78.

Most people prefer to use hare and rabbit in some kind of casserole or stew as the additional ingredients added to the sauce give interest to the dish and keep the lean flesh beautifully moist.

Roasting

A really young rabbit or hare (a leveret) can be roasted. Follow the method and timings given for poultry on page 78. Serve with the accompaniments suggested for duck or goose. Keep the flesh moist by covering it with plenty of fat or fat bacon.

Venison Râgout

| 675 g/1½ lb venison |
| 25 g/1 oz (¼ cup) flour |
| salt and pepper |
| 2 large onions |
| 2 tablespoons oil |
| 300 ml/½ pint (1¼ cups) chicken stock or water with ½ stock (1 bouillon) cube |
| 300 ml/½ pint (1¼ cups) red wine |
| pinch of ground cloves |
| ½ to 1 tablespoon juniper berries |
| 1 teaspoon honey |
| 4 tablespoons (¼ cup) soured cream |
| **FOR THE MUSHROOM RICE:** |
| 225 g/8 oz (2 cups) large flat mushrooms |
| 25 g/1 oz (2 tablespoons) butter |
| 500 ml/1 fl oz (2 cups) water |
| 225 g/8 oz (1 cup) long-grain rice |

Cut the venison into neat dice. Mix the flour and seasoning and use to coat the meat. Peel and chop the onions. Heat the oil in a large pan and fry the venison and onions until golden in colour. Pour in the stock and wine. Bring steadily to the boil and stir until thickened. Add the cloves, juniper berries, seasoning and the honey. Cover the pan very tightly, reduce the heat and simmer for 1½ hours or until the meat is tender. This is a very thick stew and the mixture should be stirred once or twice during cooking to prevent its sticking to the pan. Stir in the cream just before serving. Serve with the mushroom rice and a green salad. Mushroom Rice Cut the mushrooms into pieces. Heat the butter in a pan and toss the mushrooms in this, then add

the water, rice and a little seasoning and cook until tender, (see page 136). Serves 4 to 6.

<u>Note</u> This is an excellent stew to prepare in a pressure cooker. Cook for 20 minutes on HIGH/15 lb pressure and thicken the liquid before serving. Alternatively cook for 8 to 10 hours in a slow cooker set on LOW but fry the coated venison and onions in a separate saucepan before adding to the cooker.

Roast Venison

| 1.75 kg/4 lb joint of venison |
| 50 g/2 oz (¼ cup) butter |
| **FOR THE MARINADE:** |
| 2 medium onions |
| 300 ml/½ pint (1¼ cups) red wine |
| 2 tablespoons red wine vinegar |
| 4 tablespoons olive oil |
| 2 bay leaves |
| 1 teaspoon ground ginger |
| 1 tablespoon brown sugar |
| 2 teaspoons made mustard |
| salt and pepper |

Allow the venison to hang for 2 days if it is very fresh.

Marinade Peel and chop the onions and mix with the other ingredients. Pour into a casserole. Place the joint of venison in the marinade and leave for 24 hours. Turn the meat over several times during this period, so it absorbs the flavour of the mixture.

Lift the venison from the marinade and drain well, put into a roasting pan and spread with the butter. As venison is a dry meat it is a good idea to use a roasting bag, covered roasting pan or to wrap the meat in foil (see page 49).

Roast the venison in a preheated moderate oven (160 to 180°C/325 to 350°F, Gas Mark 3 to 4) allowing 40 minutes per 450 g/1 lb and 40 minutes over.

Serve with Sage and Onion Stuffing, (see page 64); Parsley and Thyme Stuffing, (see Veal, page 68), redcurrant jelly or Bread Sauce, (see page 78) or any of the stuffings and sauces in the section that begins on page 100. Serves 8.

VARIATION
The joint can be larded with fat bacon or pork (see page 55).

Fried Rabbit

| 1 young small rabbit |
| **FOR THE MARINADE:** |
| 1 shallot or small onion |
| 4 tablespoons oil |
| 2 tablespoons tarragon vinegar |

| 2 to 3 cloves, optional |
| 1 bay leaf |
| 1 blade of mace |
| salt and pepper |
| **TO COAT:** |
| 25 g/1 oz (¼ cup) flour |
| 1 egg |
| 50 g/2 oz (½ cup) crisp breadcrumbs |
| **TO FRY:** |
| 3 to 4 tablespoons oil |

Cut the rabbit into 8 pieces; divide each leg into 2 joints, make 2 joints of the back and then cut the flesh from the bones to give 4 more portions.

Marinade Peel and chop the shallot or onion, mix with the other marinade ingredients and pour into a casserole. Add the rabbit and leave for 12 hours.

Remove the rabbit from the marinade, allow to dry out on a flat plate. Coat rabbit pieces in the flour, then in the beaten egg and finally in the breadcrumbs.

Heat the oil in a large frying pan (skillet) and fry the rabbit steadily for about 15 minutes, or until tender. Drain on absorbent paper and serve with Tartare Sauce, (see page 105). Serves 4.

VARIATIONS
If you are not sure whether the rabbit is sufficiently tender to cook in this way, simmer the joints in a seasoned stock (made from the head and liver of the rabbit) for about 1 hour. Drain, then add to the marinade and proceed as above.

Chicken joints can be marinated in the same way before frying.

Venison Râgout with Mushroom Rice

LEFTOVERS
Crispy Duck Pieces
Cut cooked duckling into bite-sized pieces.
Marinate for a short time in orange juice. Drain well then coat in seasoned flour, beaten egg and crisp breadcrumbs or a batter made with 50 g/ 2 oz (½ cup) plain (all purpose) flour, pinch salt, 1 egg, 4 tablespoons water and 2 teaspoons oil.

Fry in hot fat for a few minutes. Serve as an hors d'oeuvre or snack.

FOR FLAVOUR
The term 'marinate' means to steep food in a liquid or a mixture of ingredients which gives flavour to food and helps keep it moist. Often the marinade includes wine or vinegar which tenderizes the meat.

Allow the food to stand in the marinade for some considerable time. The marinade is generally added to the gravy or sauce served with the meat.

Spezzatino di Pollo
[Italian Chicken Stew]

4 young chicken portions, preferably leg
3 medium onions
450 g/1 lb tomatoes
75 g/3 oz (6 tablespoons) butter
1 tablespoon tomato purée (paste)
1.2 litres/2 pints (5 cups) chicken stock or water with 1 chicken stock (2 bouillon cubes)
1 to 2 teaspoons chopped mixed herbs or ½ teaspoon dried mixed herbs
100 g/4 oz (½ cup) long-grain rice
salt and pepper
TO GARNISH: 1 tablespoon chopped parsley

Dry the chicken portions well. The chicken can be skinned, but it is not essential. Frozen chicken must be thawed thoroughly. Peel the onions, cut into wafer thin rings; concass the tomatoes, (see opposite).

Heat the butter in a pan and fry the chicken portions until golden in colour. Add the onions, tomatoes, tomato purée (paste) and stock or water and stock to the chicken. Bring the liquid to simmering point and simmer for 5 minutes. Add the herbs and rice, with seasoning to taste. Simmer for a further 5 minutes then transfer to a warmed 2 litre/3½ pint (2½ quart) casserole. Put in the centre of a preheated moderate oven (180°C/350°F, Gas Mark 4) and cook for 35 to 40 minutes, or until the rice and chicken are tender. Top with parsley. Serves 4.

Hasenpfeffer
[German Rabbit Casserole]

1 rabbit
1 large onion
600 ml/1 pint (2½ cups) red wine vinegar
40 g/1½ oz (6 tablespoons) flour
salt and pepper
50 g/2 oz (¼ cup) butter or fat or 2 tablespoons oil
pinch of ground cloves or 4 to 5 whole cloves
1 tablespoon French mustard
1 to 2 bay leaves
½ tablespoon brown sugar
150 ml/¼ pint (⅔ cup) stock, see method

Hare with Prunes and Normandy Pheasants

LEFTOVERS
Use leftover small pieces of hare and the stock from this dish as the basis for a Hare Soup. Blend or sieve the game meat and liquid together. Dilute with more stock and a little more red wine. Season well.

Hare with Prunes

175 g/6 oz (1 cup) dried prunes
600 ml/1 pint (2½ cups) water
1 hare with the liver and blood
150 ml/¼ pint (⅔ cup) red wine
3 medium onions
salt and pepper
40 g/1½ oz (6 tablespoons) flour
75 g/3 oz (6 tablespoons) cooking fat
900 ml/1½ pints (3¾ cups) brown stock, see page 51
1 tablespoon lemon juice
2 tablespoons redcurrant jelly
50 g/2 oz (⅓ cup) raisins
TO GARNISH: croûtons of fried bread, see page 35

Soak the prunes in the water for 12 hours. Ask your supplier to joint the hare. Wash it in plenty of cold water and dry well. Keep the liver and blood in two separate containers. Spoon the prunes out of the water, pour this liquid into a saucepan, add the liver of the hare and simmer for 30 minutes. Put the soaked prunes into a bowl and add the wine; soak for at least 30 minutes.

Peel and slice the onions. Add a little seasoning to the flour and coat the hare in this. Heat the fat in a very large pan and fry the onions and hare for 5 minutes. Lift out of the pan. Add the stock and blood to the fat remaining in the saucepan. Take the liver out of the liquid and sieve, mash or blend it to make a purée. Add the liver purée to the stock and blood in the pan, heat gently and stir well to absorb the fat and meat juices and thicken slightly. Lastly add the liquid left from cooking the liver. Replace the onions and hare in the saucepan, cover and simmer for 30 minutes.

Put the prunes, the wine in which they were soaked, lemon juice, jelly and raisins into the saucepan containing the hare. Cover the pan again and simmer gently for 1½ to 2 hours, or until the hare is tender. Spoon all the ingredients on to a heated dish and garnish with the croûtons.

Note Like many casseroles this can be cooked on one day, refrigerated overnight then reheated on the second day. The flavour seems to improve but always make certain that any meat, poultry or game casserole is boiled for several minutes when reheating.

Normandy Pheasants

2 small young pheasants
2 tablespoons flour
salt and pepper
100 g/4 oz (½ cup) butter
750 g/1½ lb cooking (tart) apples
300 ml/½ pint (1¼ cups) double (heavy) cream

Wipe the pheasants and dry well. Blend the flour with a little salt and pepper and dust the game birds with the seasoned flour. Melt half the butter in a large saucepan, add the pheasants and turn in the butter until golden brown in colour.

Peel, core and slice the apples. Put half the fruit into the bottom of a deep casserole. Put 15 g/½ oz (1 tablespoon) butter inside each pheasant. Place the birds on top of the apples and spread the breasts with the remaining butter.

Arrange the rest of the apple slices around the birds. Cover the casserole very tightly; cook for 1 hour in the centre of a preheated moderate oven (180°C/350°F, Gas Mark 4). Pour the cream over the birds and cook for a further 20 to 30 minutes, or until the birds are tender. Serves 6.

Cut the rabbit into joints – 2 legs and 2 back portions; wash well in cold water. Put the liver and head into a pan, cover with water and simmer for 1 hour to obtain stock, (see the Note below). If you are following this recipe exactly then allow the stock to boil until only 150 ml/¼ pint (⅔ cup) remains.

Peel and chop the onion. Put the rabbit joints and onion into the vinegar and leave for at least 12 hours. Remove the rabbit from the vinegar and dry the joints carefully. Blend the flour with a little seasoning and use just half to coat the rabbit. Heat the butter, fat or oil in a large saucepan and fry the rabbit until golden brown. Add the vinegar, onion, cloves, mustard, bay leaves and sugar. Cover the pan and simmer gently until tender; this takes approximately 1¼ to 1½ hours. Blend the reserved flour with the rabbit stock, add to the pan and stir over the heat until the sauce has thickened. Serve with dumplings (see page 62). Serves 4.

<u>Note</u> The sauce has a distinct bite. You can substitute an inexpensive red wine instead of vinegar or use just 150 ml/¼ pint (⅔ cup) vinegar plus 600 ml/1 pint (2½ cups) rabbit stock.

Sweet-sour Chinese Turkey

Tender turkey breast is ideal for this quick cooking dish.

450 g/1 lb turkey breast
2 tablespoons lemon juice
5 tablespoons orange juice
4 or 5 sticks of celery
2 sharon fruit or firm tomatoes
8 to 10 radishes
½ Chinese cabbage (bok choy)
1 large green pepper
3 tablespoons oil
150 ml/¼ pint (⅔ cup) chicken stock
1½ teaspoons cornflour (cornstarch)
1 tablespoon soy sauce
1 to 2 tablespoons brown sugar

Cut the turkey breast into thin strips. Marinate in the lemon and orange juice for 30 minutes only. Cut the celery, sharon fruit or tomatoes, radishes and Chinese cabbage (bok choy) into small neat pieces. Discard the core and seeds from the green pepper and cut this into neat pieces. Heat the oil in a wok or a large frying pan (skillet). Drain the turkey and save the fruit juice. Fry the turkey in the oil until nearly tender. Add the vegetables and sharon fruit or tomatoes and heat for 2 to 3 minutes only. Blend the chicken stock with the fruit juice marinade and the cornflour (cornstarch). Add the soy sauce and sugar. Pour over the ingredients in the pan and stir until thickened. Serves 4.

Saté Ajam
[Chicken Kebabs]

If you are buying portions of chicken, choose leg meat which is thicker than the breast. If taking the meat from a whole bird, cut away the breast in thick portions.

750 g/1½ lb chicken flesh
2 garlic cloves
1 tablespoon oil
½ tablespoon vinegar
4 tablespoons water
FOR THE SAUCE: 1 garlic clove
4 tablespoons peanut butter
6 tablespoons coconut milk, see page 47
¼ to ½ teaspoon chilli powder
1 to 2 teaspoons soy sauce
1 bay leaf
1 teaspoon brown sugar
salt and pepper

Cut the chicken into 1.5 cm/½ inch dice. Peel and crush the garlic, mix with the oil, vinegar and water. Pour into a flat dish. Put the chicken on to 4 to 6 long metal skewers or a greater number of shorter skewers. Lay in the garlic marinade for 5 to 10 minutes then cook under a preheated grill (broiler).
<u>Sauce</u> Peel and crush the garlic. Mix all the ingredients together in a saucepan and simmer for 10 minutes, season to taste. Remove the bay leaf before serving over Saté. Serve with Nasi Kuning (see page 138). Serves 4 to 6.

Piquant Goujons of Turkey

750 g/1½ lb turkey breasts
2 tablespoons oil
50 g/2 oz (¼ cup) butter
FOR THE APRICOT SAUCE 1 × 425 g/15 oz can apricot halves
150 ml/¼ pint (⅔ cup) turkey or chicken stock or water and ½ chicken stock (1 bouillon) cube
1 tablespoon vinegar
2 teaspoons cornflour (cornstarch)
1 teaspoon brown sugar
salt and pepper
3 tablespoons cocktail (pearl) onions

Prepare the sauce, but do not allow it to cook for any length of time, for the fruit and onions should keep firm. Drain the fruit, cut the apricots into thick slices. Mix the syrup from the can with the stock and the vinegar, and blend with the cornflour (cornstarch). Put into a saucepan and stir over moderate heat until thickened. Add the sugar and seasoning. Stir the apricots and onions into the sauce and heat for a few minutes only.

Cut the turkey breasts into 1.5 cm/½ inch slices, or flatten with a rolling pin. Cut the slices into narrow ribbons or goujons.

Heat the oil and butter in a large frying pan (skillet) and fry the turkey goujons for 10 to 15 minutes, until tender. Spoon on to a dish and top with the sauce. Serve with cooked rice or green salad. Serves 6.

SIMPLE SKILL
To concass tomatoes
First skin the tomatoes. There are two ways of doing this: Put into boiling water for about 30 seconds, then cool in cold water; or insert a fine skewer into a tomato and hold it over a heated gas ring or electric hotplate until the skin pops.

Pull away the skin, then halve the tomato. Remove all seeds, leave just the pulp behind. Discard the seeds and skin.

Sweet-sour Chinese Turkey

VEGETABLES AND SALADS

Britain has a relatively temperate climate which enables our farmers to provide us with a wide range of first-class fresh vegetables. A good cook will always make full use of such vegetables as they come into season.

The adventurous cook will also delight in the great variety of imported exotic vegetables that have become readily available in recent years.

When cooking vegetables, take care to retain their crisp texture, bright colour, flavour and nutritional value.

Serve them as soon as possible after cooking.

Experiment with imaginative ways of serving familiar vegetables to make them more exciting, and remember to consider their aesthetic value too. Raw salads, for example, should be a delight to the eye as well as to the palate. (A selection of light salads is on pages 95 to 97).

Buying Points

When shopping for vegetables, be very critical about the quality offered in shops and supermarkets.

Great emphasis is often given to the advantage of buying ready-washed potatoes, other root vegetables and celery. Certainly these look more appealing and are excellent if you plan to use the food within a relatively short time after purchase, but washed vegetables deteriorate more rapidly than those that are unwashed.

Vegetables should look firm and free from blemishes; green vegetables should be a good colour and crisp. Inspect wrapped vegetables very critically and assess the quality and price against those you buy by weight.

If possible, avoid buying vegetables on a Monday, for supplies are scarce and frequently stale. It is better to buy more on Friday and Saturday and prepare and store these in the salad container of the refrigerator or a cool place with good ventilation.

Microwave Cooking

Always time the cooking of vegetables with care as a few seconds over-cooking can spoil them.

Commercially frozen vegetables are ideal to use because they are young and tender and have been blanched before freezing. Check the bag (package) for recommended cooking times, also check whether the packaging can be used in a microwave cooker. Some plastics and colourings used in printing are not suitable. If so, you must then repack the vegetables in another plain container. Flatten the bag to give a single layer of vegetable, make a small split in the bag

(to allow steam to escape) and cook for the time recommended in the instruction book for your particular cooker or on the pack. It is not easy to add salt to the package of vegetables so season after cooking.

Home-frozen vegetables will probably be in a freezer bag. Replace the twist that seals the bag, in case it contains metal, and proceed as above.

Fresh vegetables are less satisfactory when cooked in a microwave cooker, mainly because their age and quality is rather inconsistent. Woody stems and older root vegetables do not soften readily; small vegetables like young peas are excellent and so of course, are potatoes and young beetroot – where you save a great deal of cooking time.

Most green vegetables are better cooked by conventional methods.

Slow-Cooking

While old root vegetables could be tenderized in a slow-cooker, they take several hours on LOW and most vegetables benefit from a short cooking time.

Pressure Cooking

A pressure cooker is excellent for cooking most vegetables. Green vegetables retain their fresh colour and flavour while older root vegetables become deliciously tender. You must, however, follow the manufacturer's timing instructions carefully because over-cooking by even a minute in a pressure cooker can spoil a green vegetable.

Storing Vegetables

Root vegetables should be taken out of their bags and stored in a vegetable rack. Green vegetables should be unwrapped and stored in either a vegetable rack

(kept in a cool place) or in the salad container of a refrigerator. Green salad vegetables should be refrigerated; they keep better if they are not washed.

Red and green peppers, tomatoes and other salad vegetables also keep well in a salad container. Asparagus or celery should be stored in a vegetable rack or a salad container or put into a large bowl or jug with a little water in the bottom, then kept in a cool place. Never leave vegetables unwrapped on the shelves of a refrigerator. They will dry and shrivel.

Less Usual Vegetables

The following are some of the more unusual vegetables available:

Aubergine (eggplant) Try baking them in a well-buttered and covered dish for 30 to 40 minutes in a preheated moderate oven (180°C/350°F, Gas Mark 4). They are delicious when fried (see page 90), or stuffed (see page 180).

Bean sprouts Usually grown from mung beans. These require very little cooking: they can be stir-fried in a little butter or cooked in boiling salted water for 1 minute. An ingredient in many Chinese recipes, they are also delicious raw.

Swiss chard This vegetable makes a change from cabbage and can be cooked like other green vegetables.

Chicory Called endive in some countries. The leaves can be separated and eaten raw in salads, or the whole vegetable can be cooked.

Chinese leaves (Bok choy) Readily available. Although the price may seem high, this vegetable keeps for an incredibly long time. Serve raw in salads or cook as for green vegetables or as on page 91.

Endive Called chicory in the United States. A salad vegetable with curly leaves, used instead of lettuce.

Fennel The white base can be chopped and served raw in salads, or sliced or kept whole and cooked in boiling salted water, or coated and fried. The leaves have a distinct aniseed flavour.

Mange-tout (snow peas) A type of pea which is eaten whole, not shelled. Cook in boiling salted water for about 8 minutes. Do not overcook; the pods should be crisp. Delicious cooked and served cold in salads.

Okra Often known as lady fingers or gumbo. The whole vegetable can be boiled for about 8 minutes and served with butter, or shallow fried in hot butter for the same time.

Salsify Often called oyster plant, because it does have a faint taste of oysters. Scrape well to remove blackish outside just before cooking, cut into convenient lengths, boil for about 10 to 15 minutes. Serve with melted butter.

Left: Peperonata, page 91
Top right: Spinach and Chicken Mould, page 98
Bottom right: Cooked Asparagus, page 92

VEGETABLES

Deep-fried onion rings

The following pages deal mainly with the techniques of cooking vegetables. You will find imaginative vegetable dishes in the Menu Section (page 184) and the Health Food Section (page 176).

Cooking Methods

<u>Baking</u> The unpeeled vegetables are cooked in the dry heat of the oven. Potatoes are the most usual vegetable to bake but see page 93 for other suggestions.

<u>Boiling</u> If vegetables are boiled correctly you can conserve precious vitamins, flavour and colour. (See page 92).

<u>Braising</u> Cooking whole or large portions of vegetables above a *mirepoix* (see page 94).

<u>Casseroling</u> Vegetables are not only added to casseroles but can be casseroled as a complete dish, (see page 93).

<u>Deep-Frying</u> A method that retains the full flavour of the vegetable. It is important to have fat or oil at the correct temperature, (see the Special Technique).

<u>Shallow Frying</u> Heat 50 to 75 g/2 to 3 oz (4 to 6 tablespoons) fat or 2 to 3 tablespoons oil in a frying pan (skillet). Test the temperature before frying (see Special Technique) and turn the food so that it browns evenly on all sides.

<u>Grilling (broiling)</u> A method that is used

to cook mushrooms and tomatoes, generally as an accompaniment to main dishes.

<u>Roasting</u> One of the most popular methods for cooking potatoes, but many other vegetables can be cooked by this method, (see page 94).

<u>Steaming</u> This is an excellent method of cooking vegetables as it keeps them firm in texture and retains their nutritional value. Cook over rapidly boiling water, (see page 94).

Frying

Deep-frying Uncoated Vegetables

Suitable vegetables to use are raw, sliced Jerusalem artichokes; sliced, or baby carrots and of course potatoes. The best result is obtained by frying twice: first to tenderize or 'blanch' the vegetables and then to crisp and brown them. Follow the example below.

Peel old potatoes and cut into slices, chips or potato balls. Dry well. Fry for 5 to 6 minutes or until tender at 170°C/340°F, remove from the pan. Heat oil or fat to 190°C/375°F and fry for 1 to 2 minutes or until crisp and brown. Drain and serve. Frozen potato chips (French fries) do not need double cooking; follow packet instructions.

Game chips, wafer thin slices of potato, need one frying only at 180 to 190°C/350 to 375°F.

Deep-frying Coated Vegetables

Suitable vegetables are raw sliced aubergines (eggplant), courgettes (zucchini) or cucumber; onion rings, whole mushrooms, lightly cooked cauliflower florets or the prepared potato dishes on page 92.

Dry the vegetables well. Coat in a little seasoned flour, beaten egg and fine crisp breadcrumbs or a light batter. The batter recipe for Celeriac Fritters opposite is ideal.

Fry pre-cooked or very thinly sliced vegetables at 190°C/375°F until crisp and brown, but choose a lower setting, 180°C/350°F, for more solid portions. Drain as described in the Special Technique.

<u>Note</u> If shallow frying the above vegetables it is best to fry them in small batches and turn them over when well-browned to cook the second side.

It is better to coat the vegetables in seasoned flour and then egg and breadcrumbs rather than in batter.

Drain well (see Special Technique).

Celeriac Fritters

1 celeriac root
1 tablespoon lemon juice
FOR THE BATTER: 50 g/2 oz (½ cup) plain (all-purpose) flour
salt and pepper
1 egg
6 tablespoons water
1 tablespoon corn oil
TO FRY: oil
TO COAT: 2 tablespoons plain (all-purpose) flour
TO GARNISH: lemon wedges
parsley

Peel the celeriac root, cut into 0.5 cm/¼ inch slices, then divide each slice in half or quarters. Keep in a bowl of water with the lemon juice until ready to fry. Meanwhile blend the ingredients together for the batter.

Heat the oil to 185°C/365°F. Dry the celeriac well, dust with the flour then thinly coat in batter. Fry for about 6 minutes; drain on absorbent kitchen paper and serve with the lemon and parsley.

VARIATION
Use the same batter for coating 2 sliced fennel bulbs.

Pâté Stuffed Mushrooms

32 medium button mushrooms
Liver Pâté, made using 225 g/8 oz liver etc., see page 24
TO COAT: salt and pepper
25 g/1 oz (¼ cup) plain (all-purpose) flour
2 eggs
50 to 75 g/2 to 3 oz (½ to ¾ cup) crisp breadcrumbs
TO FRY: oil

Remove the stalks from the mushroom caps; these stalks can be used in a stew or soup. Wipe or wash and dry the mushroom caps. Press the pâté on the dark side of half the mushrooms, then top with the remaining mushrooms, so making almost a round shape. Add seasoning to the flour, roll the mushrooms in this (use all the flour). Beat the eggs, brush over the mushrooms, then coat in the breadcrumbs. It is essential that you give a good coating, so that the soft pâté does not come out during frying.

Heat the oil to 185°C/365°F, fry the mushrooms for 3 to 4 minutes only then drain on absorbent paper. Serve hot as an hors d'oeuvre or light main dish.

The Devilled Sauce on page 103 is an excellent accompaniment.

VARIATIONS
Good quality commercial pâté can be used.

Cheese Filling Blend 225 g/8 oz (1 cup) curd or cream cheese with 2 tablespoons grated Parmesan cheese, 1 tablespoon finely chopped parsley and 1 to 2 teaspoons chopped capers. Use instead of the liver pâté.

Stir-fried Chinese Leaves

This is excellent with any meat, fish or poultry dish.

8 to 10 stems Chinese leaves (bok choy)
100 g/4 oz bamboo shoots
1 onion
1 stick of celery
2 tablespoons oil
a little lemon juice
salt and pepper

Cut the chinese leaves diagonally into 3 mm/⅛ inch strips and slice the bamboo shoots, onions and celery. Heat the oil, add the vegetables and fry gently for about 8 minutes, stirring frequently. Add lemon juice and seasoning to taste. Serves 4.

Peperonata

2 medium onions
2 garlic cloves
550 g/1¼ lb ripe tomatoes
4 large red peppers
3 tablespoons oil or 2 tablespoons oil and 25 g/1 oz (2 tablespoons) butter
1 teaspoon chopped fresh basil or ½ teaspoon dried basil
2 bay leaves
salt and pepper
2 tablespoons chopped parsley

❋Peel and finely chop the onions and garlic cloves. Skin, halve and de-seed the tomatoes, cut the pulp neatly. Cut the peppers into thin strips, discard the cores and seeds.

Heat the oil, or oil and butter, in a saucepan, add the chopped onions and garlic. Fry slowly for 10 minutes or until the onions are transparent, then add the peppers. Stir well so that they absorb some of the oil. Cover the saucepan, lower the heat and cook very gently for 10 minutes. Stir once or twice.

Add the tomatoes, basil, bay leaves and a little seasoning, cover the saucepan once again and continue cooking for a further 15 minutes, or until the vegetables are tender, but not overcooked.

Add the parsley and any extra seasoning required. Serve hot or cold as a salad. Serves 4 to 6.

Stir-fried Chinese Leaves

LEFTOVERS
Leftover cooked vegetables can be turned into delicious salads.
Brussels Sprouts *Toss in a cheese or curry-flavoured mayonnaise and top with toasted coconut.*
Cauliflower *Coat the florets with mayonnaise, grated cheese and chopped chives.*
Root Vegetables *Dice neatly, blend with mayonnaise, chopped hard-boiled (hard-cooked) egg; diced ham or tongue and chopped parsley to make an interesting Russian Salad.*
Beetroot *Mix diced cooked beetroot with diced eating apple and a little dressing. This is an excellent accompaniment to hot or cold pork or duck.*

Boiling and Steaming

Boiling

Use the minimum quantity of water, no more than 2.5 cm/1 inch water for green vegetables, rather more for root vegetables. Spinach, however, does not need any additional water. The amount adhering to the leaves after washing will be enough.

Bring the water to the boil, add a little salt (remember when using a restricted amount of water that less salt is required).

Prepare the vegetables just before cooking, then add them gradually to the boiling water so that the liquid continues to boil. Cover tightly and cook green vegetables as quickly as possible, root vegetables, beans and peas at a steady boil and potatoes quite slowly.

Drain and serve plain, with a sauce, or with melted butter and chopped parsley, if desired.

Steaming

Steaming differs from boiling in that the vegetables are cooked above, rather than in, boiling water so little flavour or nutritional value is lost.

Vegetables that tend to discolour easily, such as Jerusalem artichokes, potatoes and celeriac, should be kept in lemon-flavoured water until they are steamed.

Check that there is always plenty of steam rising from the saucepan so that the vegetables are immediately subjected to steam and heat.

The cooking time tends to be slightly longer than when boiling vegetables.

Cooked Asparagus

Ways with Boiled Potatoes

Boil 450 g/1 lb potatoes and drain. Sieve them to obtain a really smooth mixture; (not necessary if serving them simply mashed or creamed). If you use an electric mixer or food processor, take great care not to over-handle the mixture or it will become sticky and heavy. It should in fact be light and floury.

⁎⁎Byron Sieve the potatoes, add 25 g/ 1 oz (¼ cup) grated cheese, 25 g/1 oz (2 tablespoons) butter or margarine, 2 tablespoons single (light) cream or milk, seasoning and a little grated nutmeg. Form the mixture into neat thin cakes. Fry in a little hot fat until brown on both sides. Top with more grated cheese and brown under a preheated grill (broiler). These are excellent with cold meat.

Creamed Potatoes Return the boiled potatoes to the pan and dry for 2 to 3 minutes over a very low heat. Mash with a potato masher or fork. Beat in 25 to 50 g/1 to 2 oz (2 to 4 tablespoons) butter or margarine, then 3 to 4 tablespoons very hot milk (the amount depends on how soft you like the mixture). Season to taste.

You can add grated nutmeg, chopped herbs or grated cheese to taste if liked.

⁎⁎Duchesse Potatoes Sieve the potatoes, heat gently then add 50 g/2 oz (¼ cup) butter or margarine and the yolks of 1 or 2 eggs. Do not add milk. Season well. Pipe into small pyramids or any desired shape on a well-greased baking sheet or ovenproof serving dish. Brown under a preheated grill (broiler) or in a moderately hot oven (200°C/400°F, Gas Mark 6) until golden brown.

⁎⁎Almond Make Duchesse Potatoes (left), form into round cakes, coat with seasoned flour then beaten egg. Finely chop 40 to 50 g/1½ to 2 oz (½ cup) blanched almonds. Coat the cakes in the chopped nuts then press a whole blanched almond on top of each. Chill before frying.

⁎⁎Croquette Potatoes Form Duchesse Potatoes into finger shapes, coat very thoroughly in seasoned flour then beaten egg and crisp breadcrumbs. Deep fry in oil or fat heated to 190°C/ 375°F until golden brown and crisp. Drain on absorbent paper.

Special Technique
TO COOK ASPARAGUS

Allow about 225 g/8 oz per person, depending on the variety. Some varieties of asparagus have long green stems (known as spears) all of which is edible, while other kinds have a high proportion of firm white stem that cannot be eaten. Obviously you need rather less of the all-green type.

Trim the ends of the stems and gently scrape away any brown parts. Try to make sure all the stems are of an even length; then wash them in cold water.

Asparagus should be put into boiling salted water. Thin spears take about 20 minutes to cook; thick spears 25 to 30 minutes. Test by feeling the green part of a spear (not the tip).

If you have a very deep pan the asparagus can be cooked upright. It should be tied gently into bundles to support the long stems or put into a deep basket. The boiling water should come as high in the pan as possible. Cover the pan with a lid or with foil.

It is also possible to cook asparagus lying lengthways in a large pan; a flameproof roasting pan can be used.

When cooked, lift the asparagus from the boiling water, drain and serve. See suggestions below. Provide finger bowls and a knife and fork, for some people prefer to cut asparagus rather than eat it in their fingers.

To Serve Hot

Asparagus with Butter Melt the butter, season it well, adding a little lemon juice if liked, and serve with the asparagus. Allow 25 to 50 g/1 to 2 oz (2 to 4 tablespoons) butter per person.

Asparagus with Flavoured Butter Add a small amount of finely chopped anchovy fillets or anchovy essence to the heated butter, or add finely chopped chives, parsley and tarragon. Be careful not to over-flavour the butter.

Asparagus with Parmesan Butter Place the cooked asparagus in a flameproof dish. Top with a generous amount of butter, then a topping of grated Parmesan cheese and soft breadcrumbs. Brown under a preheated grill (broiler).

To Serve Cold

Asparagus with Cheese Cream Blend cream cheese with sufficient single (light) cream and a little mayonnaise to make a flowing consistency. Use to coat the asparagus.

Asparagus with Ham Spread thin slices of lean ham with a little mayonnaise flavoured with French (Dijon) mustard. Roll around cold asparagus spears.

Asparagus with Smoked Salmon Roll small, thin slices of smoked salmon around asparagus tips, serve with lemon wedges. The salmon can be spread with a very thin layer of Taramasalata (see page 26), then rolled around the asparagus if liked.

Baking and Casseroling

Baking

Most people would agree that a perfect baked potato has a unique flavour. By cooking the vegetable in its skin, without additional ingredients, you retain the best taste and texture. Try baking other vegetables in the same way, using a preheated moderate oven (180°C/350°F, Gas Mark 4) unless otherwise stated.

Aubergine (Eggplant) Wash and dry, brush the skin with a little oil. Bake for 30 to 40 minutes until just soft. (See also Swiss Aubergines (Eggplant) on page 180).

Beetroot Young beetroot should be washed and baked for 1½ to 2 hours. Skin when cooked.

Courgettes (Zucchini) Wash and dry, brush the skin with a little oil. Use a covered container and allow 35 minutes for small courgettes (zucchini).

Onions Wipe but do not skin. Bake in a covered container for 1½ to 1¾ hours, depending on size. Skin while hot. Serve with melted butter or cottage cheese.

Potatoes Most people bake old potatoes but new potatoes are equally delicious, although the skin is less crisp than that of old potatoes. Scrub the potatoes and bake for 1 to 1½ hours, depending upon the size. New potatoes need longer cooking than old. Top with butter, cream or cottage cheese, or soured cream, chopped chives or other herbs.

Vegetable Casseroles

Most root vegetables, peas and beans can be cooked in a covered casserole in the oven – an excellent method if you are planning to cook a complete meal in the oven.

Put the prepared vegetables into a deep casserole or ovenproof dish. Add sufficient boiling water to cover, plus a little salt and a knob of butter or margarine. Cover the casserole or dish very tightly.

Cook in the centre of a preheated moderate oven (180°C/350°F, Gas Mark 4). The cooking time will be about 50% longer than if boiling on top of the cooker. Strain the vegetables and serve in the usual way.

Courgette, Tomato and Onion Casserole

| 450 g/1 lb courgettes (zucchini) |
| 450 g/1 lb tomatoes |
| 450 g/1 lb onions |
| 2 tablespoons oil |
| 4 tablespoons chopped parsley |
| 1 teaspoon chopped fresh sage or ½ teaspoon dried sage |
| 3 tablespoons white wine or 2 tablespoons water and 1 tablespoon lemon juice |
| salt and pepper |

✳✳Wash and dry the courgettes (zucchini), but do not peel them. Cut into thin slices. Skin the tomatoes and cut into thick slices. Peel the onions and cut into thin rings. Heat the oil in a frying pan (skillet), add the onions and fry gently for 10 minutes until nearly, but not completely, tender. Add half the parsley, the sage, wine or water and lemon juice and seasoning.

Layer the onion mixture, tomatoes and courgettes (zucchini) in a casserole, beginning and ending with the onion mixture. Sprinkle the courgette (zucchini) layers with the remaining parsley and season well. Cover the casserole and bake in the centre of a preheated moderate oven (160°C/325°F, Gas Mark 3) for 1¼ hours. Serves 4 to 6.

Scalloped Apple and Potato Bake

Scalloped Apple and Potato Bake

| 225 g/8 oz onions |
| 450 g/1 lb potatoes |
| 675 g/1½ lb Bramley or other good cooking (tart) apples |
| 225 g/8 oz cooked ham |
| 100 g/4 oz Cheddar or other good cooking cheese |
| 40 g/1½ oz (3 tablespoons) butter |
| salt and pepper |
| 300 ml/½ pint (1¼ cups) milk |
| 1 egg |
| **TO GARNISH:** parsley |

✳✳Peel and thinly slice the onions and potatoes. Peel and core the apples and cut into fairly thick rings. Cut the ham into neat dice and grate the cheese.

Soften the butter to a spreading consistency, spread half over the bottom of a shallow ovenproof serving dish. Cover with half the onions and potatoes and season lightly. Top with half the apple rings and half the ham and grated cheese. Add the remaining onions and potatoes, season, then arrange the remaining apples, ham and cheese neatly over the top.

Beat the milk and egg together, pour over the other ingredients. Dot the rest of the butter over the top. Cover the dish with foil and bake in the centre of a preheated moderate oven, (180°C/350°F, Gas Mark 4) for 1½ hours. Remove the foil for the last 30 minutes so the top browns well. Garnish with parsley.

This dish is excellent served with grilled (broiled) pork chops or gammon (ham) steaks. Serves 4 to 6.

FOR FLAVOUR
Add a sprig, or a small amount of chopped fresh basil to any dish containing tomatoes.

Mint is the obvious herb to use when cooking new potatoes but try adding a sprig of tarragon instead.

A bay leaf or a sprig of savory is excellent when cooking green beans.

Add a verbena leaf or a sprig of rosemary when cooking carrots.

A selection of roast
vegetables

SIMPLE SKILL
Fantail Potatoes
*Make vertical slits but do
not cut right through the
potato.*

FOR FLAVOUR
*Use the dripping from
the joint to roast
vegetables. If there is
insufficient fat, add a
little lard, cooking fat or
oil. You do not need a
great amount of fat, just
enough to coat the
vegetables evenly.*

*It is important to turn
the vegetables at the
beginning of the cooking
period so that they are
well covered with fat.
Turn the vegetables
halfway through the
cooking time.*

*Roasted Fantail
Potatoes (see right) are
more delicate and cannot
be turned in the same
way.*

Roasting
and Braising

Roasting
To many people a roast joint without
roast potatoes is incomplete. Many
other vegetables can be roasted and are
just as appetizing.

There are three ways to roast potatoes, and all three methods can be
used for other vegetables:

☐ Peel old potatoes (new potatoes
should not be peeled), roll in the very
hot fat and cook for 45 minutes to 1 hour
in a preheated moderately hot to hot
oven (200 to 220°C/400 to 425°F, Gas
Mark 6 to 7), turning halfway through the
roasting time.

The other vegetables that can be
roasted this way are Jerusalem artichokes, *young* carrots, sliced celeriac,
fennel bulb (which remains rather hard),
young diced marrow (squash) or unpeeled courgettes (zucchini), leeks,
onions, sweet potatoes or yams (watch
carefully – these and onions brown very
easily).

☐ Put the peeled potatoes or other
vegetables into salted boiling water and
cook for 5 to 10 minutes, depending on
the size, drain and dry well. Roast as
above, but reduce the cooking time by
10 to 15 minutes. This method produces
a pleasantly floury old potato.

Other vegetables that can be roasted
in the same way are skinned cooked
beetroot – rolled in flour; halved par-

snips; whole small turnips and thick
slices or pieces of swede (rutabaga).

☐ This is not true roasting but an
excellent method to use when roasting
meat at a lower temperature such as
moderate (160 to 180°C/325 to 350°F,
Gas Mark 3 to 4). Roll the peeled
potatoes in a little very hot fat. Spoon
out any excess fat, add 150 ml/¼ pint
(⅔ cup) chicken stock to the roasting
pan or dish. Cook, uncovered, for 1 to
1¼ hours at the moderate heat. The
liquid evaporates and leaves soft potatoes that are pleasantly golden on top.
These are often called 'Fondant Potatoes'.

Other vegetables that can be cooked
this way are parsnips, sweet potatoes
and yams.

Note If using an automatic oven where
the food is to be left in the cold oven
before cooking, toss the vegetables in
hot fat for several minutes before transferring them to the roasting pan. Roast
by the first method.

Braising
Many people wrongly think that vegetables are braised when they are cooked
in a pleasantly flavoured liquid. The
principle of true braising applies to
vegetables, just as it does to meat and
other foods. The food is first sautéed in
fat and then cooked above a *mirepoix* or
bed of vegetables which is sieved at the
end of the cooking time to give a good
sauce (see Braised Celery).

A wide variety of vegetables can be
cooked in this way. They range from
green vegetables like lettuce and Chin-

ese leaves (bok choy), to onions, leeks
and celery.

Cut lettuce into halves or quarters
and Chinese leaves (bok choy) into neat
pieces, retain plenty of stalk so that the
pieces keep intact. Celery heads should
be trimmed, then halved or quartered
and onions and leeks kept whole. As
celery is one of the most popular vegetables, the recipe below applies to this.

Special Technique
FANTAIL POTATOES
Peel medium-sized old potatoes or
scrape new potatoes. Keep them in cold
water until ready to cook, then dry well
on absorbent paper. To make fantail
potatoes make vertical slits about 3 mm/
⅛ inch apart, but do not cut right
through the potatoes (see left).

Heat the fat in a roasting pan, allowing about 50 g/2 oz (¼ cup) to each
450 g/1 lb potatoes. Put the potatoes
into the pan with the cut side uppermost and baste with the hot fat. Do not
turn the potatoes. Place the pan towards
the top of the oven. Cook for about 1
hour in a preheated moderately hot
oven (190 to 200°C/375 to 400°F, Gas
Mark 5 to 6) or a slightly shorter time in
a hot oven (200 to 220°C/400 to 425°F,
Gas Mark 6 to 7).

Baste the potatoes with the fat once
or twice during the cooking process.

Braised Celery

1 large or 2 smaller heads of celery
50 g/2 oz (¼ cup) margarine
FOR THE MIREPOIX: 2 medium onions
2 medium carrots
1 leek
2 tomatoes
salt and pepper

∗∗Wash the celery and cut into 4 to 8
portions that will fit into a large saucepan. Chop any small pieces of leftover
celery. Heat the margarine in the saucepan, add the celery portions and turn in
the margarine. Heat gently until the
celery has browned a little; remove from
the pan. Peel the onions and carrots,
leave whole; wash and halve the leek,
put into the saucepan with the whole
tomatoes and celery trimmings. Add just
enough water to cover these vegetables,
season lightly. Place the celery portions
on top of the mirepoix. Cover the saucepan very tightly, lower the heat and cook
for approximately 45 minutes to 1 hour,
or until the celery is tender. Lift the
celery on to a heated dish. Sieve or
blend the mirepoix, adding a little extra
water to dilute the mixture if it is too
thick. Reheat, season to taste and pour
over the celery. Serves 4 to 8.

SALADS

Do not be too conservative when making a salad. Consider how you can vary the ingredients to give additional flavour, colour and interest.

Many different vegetables can be used in salads. Include leafy vegetables like young spinach leaves, shredded Brussels sprouts or red cabbage. Use young root vegetables, grating them in the same way as carrots.

Vegetable Salads

Mix different types of lettuce (there are several varieties available) or use Chinese leaves (bok choy), shredded cabbage or Brussels sprouts or very young spinach leaves.

In addition to the usual salad ingredients – cucumber, tomatoes, radishes, spring onions (scallions) and peppers – include chopped fennel (which gives a delicious aniseed taste), shredded celeriac (always toss in lemon juice) and other root vegetables.

Lightly cooked root vegetables, tossed in a dressing, make excellent salads. Include seasonal fresh fruit or canned fruits and nuts, and use herbs to add extra flavour.

Hungry families will appreciate salads based on pasta, rice, dried beans, red or brown lentils.

Rice Salads

Rice turns a light salad into a real meal. Use cooked long-grain, pre-cooked or brown rice (see page 136).

The rice can be rinsed after cooking, though this is not essential if it has been correctly cooked. It is best to mix the rice with a dressing, such as mayonnaise, while it is still warm, so that the rice absorbs the flavour better. Add any crisp ingredients to the rice when it is cold.

The salad on page 98, which uses cooked rice, is not typical of rice salads for the rice is allowed to become cold before being blended with a dressing; obviously this is a good way to use up leftover cooked rice.

Paella Salad Cook 100 g/4 oz (scant ½ cup) rice, strain and blend with Vinaigrette Dressing (see page 105). Dice about 100 g/4 oz (½ cup) cooked chicken, add to the rice together with 100 g/4 oz (⅔ cup) peeled prawns (shrimp), 100 g/4 oz (⅔ cup) prepared mussels (see page 44) and 100 g/4 oz (¾ cup) cooked peas. Serve on a bed of shredded lettuce and top with Herb-flavoured Mayonnaise (see page 105). Serves 4.

Pasta Salads

Pasta is an excellent ingredient for sustaining salads. Cook the pasta in boiling salted water (see page 139), drain and rince in cold water. Shake dry and immediately blend with the dressing. Allow to cool, then combine with the other ingredients.

Pasta Salad Niçoise The salad illustrated on page 99 is an interesting version of the famous Salad Niçoise. Cook 75 to 100 g/3 to 4 oz (1 cup) pasta spirals (tortiglioni) in boiling salted water until just al dente. Strain, rinse and combine with a little Vinaigrette Dressing, (see page 108. Allow to cool then mix with cooked vegetables, chopped spring onions (scallions), wedges of tomato and hard-boiled (hard-cooked) eggs, flaked canned tuna and black (ripe) olives. Serve on a bed of lettuce and watercress. Serves 4.

Fruit in Salads

Fruit helps to make a most refreshing salad which goes well with cheese, fish or meats.

Avocado and Iceberg Salad Wash an Iceberg lettuce, drain well and cut into sections. Place on a flat dish. Blend 2 tablespoons of lemon juice with 2 tablespoons mayonnaise and 1 tablespoon grated horseradish. Skin an avocado, mash the pulp and mix with the dressing above. Spoon on to the lettuce and top with more grated horseradish and/or chopped parsley. Serves 4.

Grapefruit and Grape Salad Mix the segments from 3 grapefruit with 75 g/3 oz (¾ cup) halved and deseeded grapes and a few hazelnuts. Combine with Vinaigrette Dressing (see page 105). Excellent with duck. Serves 4.

Waldorf Salad Combine 3 diced eating apples with a little lemon juice, 3 to 4 diced sticks of celery, 25 g/1 oz (¼ cup) chopped walnuts and 25 g/1 oz (¼ cup) hazelnuts. Mix with mayonnaise. Serve on lettuce. Serves 4.

Side Salads

Coconut and Pineapple Coleslaw

| ½ small white cabbage |
| 100 g/4 oz fresh coconut |
| 6 canned pineapple rings (slices) |
| **FOR THE DRESSING:** |
| 4 tablespoons pineapple syrup from the can |
| 1 tablespoon lemon juice |
| 1 tablespoon oil |
| salt and pepper |

Add a pinch of salt to cold water and wash the cabbage. Drain well and dry on absorbent kitchen paper. Shred very finely (the device on an electric mixer or the shredding attachment on a food processor does this perfectly).

Coarsely grate or shred the coconut. Chop the pineapple. Mix the pineapple and coconut with the cabbage. Mix the dressing ingredients together and add to the cabbage mixture. Serve this with cheese, fish or poultry. Serves 4 to 6.

Chicory and Apple Salad

| 2 eggs |
| 2 heads of chicory (endive) |
| 2 dessert apples |
| 1 small celery heart |
| 2 medium cooked beetroot |
| Vinaigrette Dressing, see page 105 |

Hard-boil (hard-cook) the eggs, slice and and set aside. Cut the chicory (endive) in slices. Cut the unpeeled apples, celery and peeled beetroot into neat dice. Toss in the dressing and top with the egg slices This salad is excellent as a light supper dish or with cold chicken. Serves 4 to 6.

SIMPLE SKILL
Keeping Salads Fresh
Cover the prepared, undressed salad with plastic wrap and keep in a cool place.

Add the dressing just before the salad is served; if dressed too early, green salad ingredients become limp.

A mixed vegetable salad lightly tossed in Vinaigrette Dressing, see page 105

Orange Potato Salad

| 900 g/2 lb very small new potatoes |
| sprig of mint |
| 4 oranges |
| 4 tablespoons mayonnaise |
| salt and pepper |
| 1 lettuce |
| 1 tablespoon chopped chives |

SIMPLE SKILL
To Segment Oranges
Cut away the peel either in downward strips or a spiral. Make sure you cut away the white pith too.

Now cut between the skin of the segments and the flesh of the fruit, leaving the skin behind.

This should be done over a bowl so no juice is wasted.

Remove any pips from the neat segments of fruit.

Grapefruit is prepared in the same way.

Scrub the potatoes very well, put into boiling salted water and add a sprig of mint. Cook for approximately 20 minutes until tender, then strain.

Meanwhile grate the rind from 2 oranges and mix with the mayonnaise. Add a little seasoning and mix with the warm potatoes. Peel and cut the 4 oranges into segments (do this over the container of potatoes and mayonnaise so that any juice that runs from the fruit flavours the potato mixture).

Mix the orange segments with the potatoes and mayonnaise. Shred the lettuce and put into a shallow dish. Top with the salad and garnish with the chives.

Serve with extra mayonnaise topped with shredded orange rind. This salad is excellent with cold poultry or meat. Serves 6 to 8.

Mushroom and Cucumber Salad

| 100 g/4 oz (1 cup) button mushrooms |
| ½ cucumber |
| 4 large tomatoes |
| 1 small lettuce |
| a little mustard and cress |
| **FOR THE DRESSING:**
1 bay leaf |
| 1 garlic clove |
| sprig of rosemary |
| sprig of tarragon |
| 2 tablespoons white wine vinegar |
| 2 tablespoons oil |
| salt and pepper |

Wipe the mushrooms and cut into thin slices. Cut the cucumber into thick chunks. Slice the tomatoes. Wash and drain the lettuce and the mustard and cress.

Crush the bay leaf; peel and chop the clove of garlic. Put all the herbs into a basin and add the vinegar, oil and seasoning. Marinate the mushrooms and cucumber in the dressing for 30 minutes.

Arrange the lettuce in a bowl. Lift the mushrooms and cucumber from the dressing and put over the lettuce; top with tomato slices and cress.

Strain the dressing and pour over the salad just before serving. This salad is excellent with fish. Serves 4.

Orange Beetroot Salad

| **FOR THE DRESSING:**
2 tablespoons orange juice |
| 1 tablespoon lemon juice |
| 2 tablespoons oil |
| salt and pepper |
| 2 teaspoons chopped chives |
| 1 teaspoon sugar |
| **FOR THE SALAD:**
a few Chinese leaves (bok choy) or 1 small lettuce |
| 8 cooked baby beetroot |
| 2 large oranges |
| **TO GARNISH:**
chopped chives |

Mix the ingredients together for the dressing.

Shred the Chinese leaves (bok choy) or lettuce, and arrange on a flat dish. Skin and halve the beetroot. Cut away the peel and pith from the oranges and cut the fruit into segments.

Arrange the beetroot and oranges on the dish. Sprinkle with chives. Top with the dressing. Serve this with cheese, veal or poultry. Serves 4 to 6.

VARIATION

Green Bean and Orange Salad Use cooked green beans in place of beetroot. Add a little chopped parsley and a crushed garlic clove to the dressing.

Peanut and Celery Salad

| 1 lettuce |
| ½ small celery heart |
| ¼ small cucumber |
| 1 small green pepper |
| 100 g/4 oz (⅔ cup) salted peanuts |
| 4 tomatoes |
| **FOR THE DRESSING:**
2 tablespoons mayonnaise |
| 2 tablespoons oil |
| 2 tablespoons lemon juice |
| salt and pepper |

Shred the lettuce and put into the salad bowl. Cut the celery, the unpeeled cucumber and the green pepper into small dice, discarding the core and seeds from the pepper. Mix the celery, cucumber, pepper and half the peanuts together. Put on top of the lettuce. Slice the tomatoes and cut each slice in half; arrange around the edge of the salad bowl. Sprinkle the remainder of the peanuts on top of the salad.

Mix the ingredients for the dressing together and spoon over the salad just before serving. Serves 4.

Note Use only tender celery heart in this salad, not the firmer outer sticks.

VARIATION

Almond Coleslaw Use half a small white cabbage in place of the lettuce and whole almonds instead of peanuts.

Hot Potato Salad

| 450 g/1 lb new potatoes |
| 1 or 2 large onions |
| 1 green pepper |
| 4 tablespoons olive or corn oil |
| 4 tablespoons white wine vinegar |
| 1 tablespoon tarragon vinegar |
| 2 tablespoons chopped spring onions (scallions) |
| 2 tablespoons diced gherkins |
| salt and pepper |
| **TO GARNISH:**
parsley |
| celery |

Cook the potatoes and slice when cool. Peel and chop the onion(s). Dice the green pepper, discarding the core and seeds. Heat the olive or corn oil in a pan and fry the onion(s) until soft. Pour in the vinegars and heat well. Add the potatoes to the onion mixture with the spring onions (scallions), the green pepper, the gherkins and seasoning to taste. Top with chopped parsley and diced celery just before serving.

Serve this salad hot with cold meat. Serves 4 to 6.

VARIATION

Fry a little diced bacon until crisp and sprinkle over the salad.

Gado-Gado
[Cooked Vegetable Salad]

| 3 medium carrots |
| 3 medium potatoes |
| 225 g/8 oz (1 cup) green beans |
| ½ small cabbage |
| salt and pepper |
| 2 eggs |
| 3 tomatoes |
| ¼ cucumber |
| a few lettuce leaves |

FOR THE SAUCE:

| 300 ml/½ pint (1¼ cups) coconut milk, see page 47 |
| 1 garlic clove |
| 1 small onion |
| 3 tablespoons peanut butter |
| ½ tablespoon oil |
| ¼ to ½ teaspoon chilli powder |
| 1 to 2 teaspoons brown sugar |
| 1 tablespoon lemon juice |
| 1 bay leaf |

Peel the carrots and potatoes, dice the beans and shred the cabbage. Cook the vegetables in boiling, well seasoned water until just tender; do not overcook. Allow to cool then neatly slice the potatoes and carrots. Hard-boil (hard-cook), shell and quarter the eggs. Slice the tomatoes and cucumber. Arrange the vegetables and egg in layers on the lettuce, saving some egg and tomatoes to arrange round the salad.

Strain the coconut milk. Peel the garlic and onion; crush the garlic, grate the onion. Heat the peanut butter with the oil in a pan, add the garlic and onion, fry for 2 to 3 minutes, then add all the other ingredients and stir briskly until well mixed. Simmer for 15 minutes or until thickened. Remove the bay leaf and serve with the salad. Serves 4.

Sweet and Sour Salad

| 2 tablespoons white wine vinegar |
| 1 tablespoon corn oil |
| 1 tablespoon honey |
| salt and pepper |
| 225 g/8 oz (2 cups) cooked long-grain rice |
| 100 g/4 oz (1 cup) button mushrooms |
| 100 g/4 oz (1 cup) cooked French beans |
| 4 medium tomatoes |
| 3 tablespoons chopped spring onions (scallions) |
| 3 tablespoons sliced radishes |
| 1 lettuce |

Mix together the vinegar, oil and honey. Season well and combine with the rice. Wipe, but do not peel, the mushrooms and slice thickly. Dice the beans and slice the tomatoes. Mix the prepared vegetables with the rice, onions and radishes.

Arrange the lettuce in a salad bowl and top with the rice mixture.

This is excellent with fish or meat. Serves 4 to 6.

Jellied Apple Salad

| 450 ml/¾ pint (2 cups) apple juice |
| 1 lemon-flavoured jelly tablet (1 package lemon-flavored gelatin) |
| 2 small, young carrots |
| 7.5 cm/3 inch length of cucumber |
| 2 sticks celery |
| 1 lettuce heart |

Heat the apple juice and dissolve the jelly (gelatin) in this. Allow to cool and stiffen very slightly. Peel and grate the carrots and cucumber. Chop the celery into very small pieces. Add to the partially-set jelly. Spoon into a lightly oiled 1 litre/1¾ pint (4 to 5 cup) mould and allow to set. Arrange the lettuce on a flat dish and top with the jellied salad. Serve with mayonnaise.

Delicious with cheese, meat or poultry. Serves 4 to 6.

Orange Beetroot Salad, Jellied Apple Salad and Gado-Gado

Main Meal Salads

These salads are sufficiently sustaining to serve as the mainstay of a light lunch or supper. You can make the salad more filling by increasing the amount of protein – fish, meat or cheese – in the dish.

Melon and Chicken Salad

I Ogen (Cantaloupe or Crenshaw) melon
450 g/1 lb cooked chicken
50 to 100 g/2 to 4 oz (½ to I cup) walnuts
I green pepper
6 tablespoons mayonnaise
I lettuce
TO GARNISH: watercress

Halve the melon and discard the seeds. Remove the melon pulp with a vegetable scoop or teaspoon and put into a bowl. Cut the chicken into bite-sized pieces. Chop the walnuts and green pepper, discarding the core and seeds. Mix the chicken, walnuts and pepper with the mayonnaise. Arrange the lettuce in a dish, top with the chicken mixture and melon. Garnish with watercress. Serves 4 to 6.

Stuffed Pepper Salad

2 small green peppers
2 small red peppers
FOR THE FILLING: 100 g/4 oz Cheddar cheese
100 g/4 oz (I cup) button mushrooms
225 g/8 oz (I cup) cream or curd cheese
2 tablespoons chopped spring onions (scallions) or chives
2 tablespoons chopped parsley
2 tablespoons mayonnaise
salt and pepper
TO GARNISH: lettuce
watercress

Wipe the peppers and cut a thin slice from the stalk end of each. Dice each slice very finely and put into a basin. Remove the cores and seeds from the peppers. Grate the Cheddar cheese. Wipe and chop the mushrooms. Add to the diced pepper flesh with all the other ingredients. Press a quarter of the mixture into each pepper. Chill for about 1 hour then cut each pepper into 4 thin rings. Shred the lettuce and remove the stems from the watercress. Arrange on a flat dish and top with the pepper rings. Serve this salad as a light main course. Serves 4 to 6.

Spinach and Chicken Mould

225 g/8 oz young spinach leaves
salt and pepper
600 ml/1 pint (2½ cups) water
FOR THE FILLING: I medium onion
100 g/4 oz (I cup) button mushrooms
25 g/1 oz (2 tablespoons) butter
2 teaspoons chopped fresh or I teaspoon dried oregano or marjoram
225 g/8 oz cooked chicken
3 medium tomatoes
¼ medium cucumber
175 g/6 oz Edam cheese
4 tablespoons mayonnaise

Wash the spinach leaves in plenty of cold water and drain. Pour the water into a saucepan, season very lightly and bring to the boil. Put in the spinach leaves and cook for 1 to 2 minutes only, until just softened. Drain very thoroughly then line a 23 cm/9 inch sandwich tin or flan dish (pie pan) with the leaves; leave sufficient hanging over the edges to cover the filling.

Peel and finely chop the onion; wipe and thinly slice the mushrooms. Heat the butter in a pan and fry the onion, mushrooms and herbs together until vegetables are soft. Season well and allow to cool.

Chop the chicken finely. Concass the tomatoes (see page 87). Peel and finely dice most of the cucumber but cut several slices for garnish. Grate the cheese. Combine all the ingredients, except the spinach leaves, with the mayonnaise. Spoon into the tin or dish and cover with the spinach leaves. Chill for several hours then turn out and garnish with the cucumber slices. Serve cut into slices like a cake. Serves 4 to 6.

Pineapple, Ham and Rice Salad

1 × 227 g/8 oz can pineapple rings (slices)
175 g/6 oz cooked ham, in two thick slices
I red pepper
75 g/3 oz (¾ cup) cooked rice
4 tablespoons Vinaigrette, or Cheese Dressing, see pages 99, 105 and 181
TO GARNISH: watercress

Drain the pineapple and cut each ring into quarters. Dice the ham. Halve the pepper, remove the core and seeds and dice the flesh. Mix the pineapple, ham and pepper with the rice and selected dressing. Spoon into a salad bowl. Garnish with watercress. Serves 4.

Lemon Sardine Salad

450 g/1 lb fresh sardines
1 tablespoon oil
salt and pepper
1 small onion
4 medium tomatoes
4 large firm lemons
2 teaspoons white wine vinegar
12 black (ripe) olives
TO GARNISH: parsley

Brush the sardines with a little oil. Season lightly and grill (broil) for 6 to 7 minutes until tender. Allow to cool, remove the heads and bones; mash the fish to a smooth consistency. Peel and chop the onion very finely. Skin and slice the tomatoes.

Cut a slice from each lemon and scoop out the pulp. Discard all the skin and pips but retain the lemon shells. Chop the lemon pulp into tiny pieces and blend with the rest of the oil, the sardines and the vinegar. Chop 8 of the olives, add to the sardine mixture and season to taste. Put tomato slices at the bottom of each lemon shell. Spoon the sardine mixture over the tomatoes, piling it high in the lemon shells. Top with the remaining olives and garnish with parsley. Serves 4.

VARIATIONS

Use cooked sprats (smelts) in place of sardines.

Use 2 cans of sardines; omit the oil in the recipe above and discard any surplus oil from the cans.

Mackerel Salad

4 medium mackerel
150 ml/¼ pint (⅔ cup) water
2 tablespoons white wine vinegar
salt and pepper
2 dessert apples
½ small cucumber
3 tablespoons chopped spring onions (scallions)
1 tablespoon oil
1 teaspoon lemon juice
lettuce
1 medium cooked beetroot

Clean the mackerel, split each fish and divide into 2 fillets. Pour the water into a large shallow pan, add 1 tablespoon vinegar and a little salt and pepper. Add the fish, bring the water to simmering point and gently cook the fish for about 8 minutes. Do not overcook, for the fillets should keep a good shape. Lift the fish from the liquid and allow to cool.

Peel and finely dice the apples; peel half the cucumber and dice the pulp. Mix the apples, diced cucumber and spring onions (scallions) with the re-

maining vinegar, the oil and the lemon juice.

Arrange the fish on a bed of lettuce and top with the apple mixture. Slice the remaining cucumber and arrange around the fish. Skin the beetroot, cut into small neat dice and arrange around the cucumber. Serve the salad with Vinaigrette Dressing (see page 105). Serves 4 as a main dish, 8 as an hors d'oeuvre.

Cauliflower and Salami Salad

1 lettuce
1 very small cauliflower
2 medium carrots
50 g/2 oz (½ cup) button mushrooms
50 g/2 oz (⅓ cup) sultanas (golden raisins)
6 to 8 slices of salami

Wash and dry the lettuce and arrange in a shallow salad bow. Remove all the green stalk and leaves from the cauliflower (these could be used in the soup on page 186). Divide the cauliflower into small even-sized florets. Peel and coarsely grate the carrots; wash, dry and slice the mushrooms.

Arrange the cauliflower, carrots and mushrooms on the lettuce and add the sultanas (golden raisins). Skin the slices of salami and roll into cornets; place round the edge of the dish.

Serve with the Blue Cheese Dressing (see right). Serves 4 to 6.

Mimosa Fish Salad

FOR THE DRESSING:
4 tablespoons mayonnaise
4 tablespoons yogurt
1 tablespoon lemon juice
2 teaspoons tomato ketchup
2 teaspoons horseradish cream or relish
freshly milled black pepper
FOR THE SALAD:
1 large smoked mackerel fillet
12 peeled prawns (shelled shrimp)
12 mussels, prepared as page 44
2 hard-boiled (hard-cooked) eggs
¼ small cucumber
1 lettuce
a few watercress sprigs
a few radishes

Mix all the ingredients for the dressing in a large bowl. Do not add salt as the fish provides this taste.

Cut the mackerel into neat portions, discard the skin; add to the dressing with the prawns (shrimp) and mussels. Shell and halve the eggs, chop the whites, mix with the fish. Peel and dice half the cucumber, add to the fish. Mix well.

Arrange the lettuce in a salad bowl. Top with the fish mixture. Cut the remaining cucumber into slices and place round the edge of the salad. Add the watercress and radishes. Finally sieve the egg yolks over the top of the salad. Serves 4 to 6.

FOR FLAVOUR
Blue Cheese Dressing
Place a pinch each of sugar and mustard powder in a bowl and blend in 1 tablespoon olive or salad oil, ½ tablespoon lemon juice and 150 ml/¼ pint (⅔ cup) soured cream. Add half a grated onion and 50 g/2 oz (½ cup) grated or crumbled blue cheese. Finally add 1 to 2 tablespoons chopped parsley and mix well. Serves 4 to 6.

Potato Salad Niçoise is sustaining enough to serve as a lunch or supper dish, see page 95

SAUCES AND STUFFINGS

A good sauce and an interesting stuffing can turn a well-cooked meal into a gourmet's delight. Sauces and stuffings add not only flavour, but food value to many dishes. Here are some traditional sauces, plus purée sauces of the type favoured by 'Nouvelle Cuisine'. These do not rely upon fat or flour for thickening, but upon the basic ingredients used.

A food processor or blender makes it easy to create smooth purées of fruits and vegetables or to correct any sauce that may not be as smooth as one would wish (see page 107).

Both a blender and a food processor are invaluable when making stuffings. Do not over-blend or over-process the ingredients – switch off immediately the ingredients are chopped as finely and evenly as desired.

Buying Points

Obviously you will shop for the sauce or stuffing ingredients when buying the food for the main course. Be flexible – if parsley is scarce and therefore expensive, choose an alternative ingredient or re-think all or part of your menu.

Buy seasonal foods such as cranberries, when available and freeze them or make Cranberry Sauce (see page 106), and refrigerate until required.

Freezing Note

Most sauces and stuffings freeze well. It is therefore a sensible idea to make larger quantities than required and freeze the surplus. Specific freezing advice is given for each type of sauce or stuffing on the following pages.

White and Brown sauces can be frozen, although they tend to separate before, or during, thawing. To thicken again, blend 1 teaspoon cornflour (cornstarch) or 2 teaspoons flour with 2 to 3 tablespoons liquid, as used in the sauce, for each 300 ml/½ pint (1¼ cups) sauce.

Put the sauce in the container for freezing, then top with the blended flour or cornflour (cornstarch). Stir this thickening agent into the sauce as it reheats.

Microwave Cooking

A sauce based upon a roux can be prepared in the microwave cooker by the classic method of melting the fat, then adding the flour and cooking this for a few seconds before incorporating the liquid, but you will find it easier to use the One-stage method (see Special Technique, page 102).

Make sure the flour is adequately blended with the liquid before placing it in the microwave cooker. Stir the sauce very briskly every minute to make sure it stays smooth. If the sauce contains wine or eggs it can curdle through overheating in the microwave cooker just as it can on an ordinary cooker.

A whisked sauce (see page 105), cooks perfectly in the microwave; whisk every 30 seconds once the sauce starts to thicken.

It is often convenient to make a sauce in advance. Place it in a sauce-boat and reheat it in the microwave cooker when required.

Stuffings will cook in minutes in a microwave cooker. Put the mixture into a ceramic dish and cover; stir the ingredients once or twice during the cooking process.

The flavour of the stuffing tends to be better when cooked in this way rather than in a conventional oven.

Blender Sauces

When making a sauce by the roux method you will not need the help of the food processor or blender unless the sauce is lumpy. Blend a lumpy sauce for a few seconds. The sauce will become very smooth, but slightly thinner in consistency, so simmer it in an uncovered saucepan for a short time.

Fruit and vegetable sauces can be blended until smooth. If there are any pips or particles of skin you may want to sieve the mixture. This is easier to do after blending.

Sauces made by the whisked method (see 105) can be speedily made with the help of a blender or food processor. Put the egg yolks, seasoning and lemon juice or vinegar into the blender goblet or food processor bowl. Switch on for a few seconds to blend.

Heat the butter until it reaches boiling

point; do not allow it to darken in colour. Have the machine running (use a medium speed if you have a choice). Pour the butter into the blender or food processor in a slow steady stream. The sauce will thicken as you do so, (see also Mayonnaise page 104).

Flavoured Butters

Some people like their food fairly dry, without a sauce; the butter toppings given below are excellent alternatives to liquid sauces.

Flavoured butters can be used to top savoury dishes, meat, fish or poultry.

They can also be spread or piped into small cocktail canapés. The amounts given below are sufficient for about 24.

Cream the butter well and then add the extra ingredients. If using a food processor, you can add whole herbs as these will be chopped as the butter is softened.

Flavoured butters may be frozen for several weeks. Do not freeze Garlic Butter, it develops a less than pleasant flavour.

In each of the recipes below, the suggested flavourings should be added to 100 g/4 oz (½ cup) butter, enough to top 4 to 6 portions of food.

⁂Anchovy Butter Blend in a few drops of anchovy essence, up to 1 teaspoon anchovy ketchup or 2 to 3 finely chopped anchovy fillets. Use with fish dishes.

<u>Garlic Butter</u> Peel and crush 1 or 2 garlic cloves, put them through a garlic press or use a little garlic salt. Add to the butter. This is not only good for bread but an excellent topping on grilled (broiled) meats.

⁂Herb Butter Use enough mixed fresh herbs to give 3 tablespoons when chopped. Add to the butter. This is excellent on fish dishes.

⁂Maître d'Hôtel Butter (Parsley Butter) Add 1 to 2 tablespoons chopped parsley, salt, pepper and a little lemon juice to the butter. Make into neat pats and chill. The easiest way to do this is to shape the butter into a roll between two pieces of greaseproof (waxed) paper. Chill or freeze until firm then cut into slices. This is the traditional topping for grilled (broiled) foods.

⁂Mustard Butter Blend ½ to 1 tablespoon Dijon mustard with the butter. Use on fish, meat or canapés.

Top right: Avocado Sauce, page 106
Centre right: Sweet Pineapple Dressing, page 108
Bottom right: Sorrel Stuffing, page 109

BASIC SAUCES

One-stage White Sauce

Sauces and sauce-making are very much part of *Haute Cuisine*. Sauces have been created by master chefs and the recipes handed down and used with little, if any, alteration. There has been no good reason to change the recipes for the ingredients used give a splendid balance of flavours.

Special Technique
ONE-STAGE WHITE SAUCE

⁂This method of cooking a sauce means you must whisk, rather than stir, the ingredients.

The proportions used for this easy method are exactly the same as when making the sauce by the roux method (see left), you require 50 g/2 oz (¼ cup) butter or margarine, 50 g/2 oz (½ cup) flour and 600 ml/1 pint (2½ cups) milk with salt and pepper to taste.

Put the butter or margarine, flour and milk into a saucepan over a moderate heat. Whisk as the fat melts and the liquid comes to the boil, then continue whisking as the sauce thickens. Add seasoning.

Remember that the secret of a good sauce is to allow the thickened liquid to cook for several minutes so there can be no flavour of uncooked flour.

If you prefer to substitute cornflour (cornstarch) for flour use only 25 g/1 oz (¼ cup) cornflour (cornstarch) instead of 50 g/2 oz (½ cup) flour.

TRADITIONAL WHITE SAUCE
⁂ Melt 50 g/2 oz (¼ cup) butter or margarine in a saucepan and stir in 50 g/2 oz (½ cup) flour. Using a wooden spoon, continue stirring over a low heat until a dry mixture or 'roux' forms. Remove the pan from the heat and gradually add 600 ml/1 pint (2½ cups) milk, stirring briskly. Return the pan to the heat and continue stirring until the sauce comes to the boil and thickens. Cook for a few minutes then add seasoning to taste.

Variations

⁂Béchamel Sauce Add a piece of celery, 1 or 2 whole peeled onions and whole peeled carrots, a sprig of parsley and a blade of mace to 600 ml/1 pint (2½ cups) milk. Bring to boiling point, remove from the heat, cover and allow to stand for an hour. Strain before using to make white sauce above.

⁂Anchovy Sauce Add a little anchovy essence or sieved anchovies. Serve with fish.

⁂Cheese Sauce Add 100 to 225 g/4 to 8 oz (1 to 2 cups) grated Cheddar, or other good cooking cheese, to the hot thickened sauce with a little made mustard. Do not over-heat.

⁂Doria Sauce Add a generous 150 ml/¼ pint (⅔ cup) sieved cooked cucumber pulp and a little double (heavy) cream. Serve with fish or lamb.

⁂Horseradish Sauce Add 3 tablespoons grated fresh horseradish with 1 to 2 teaspoons sugar, 4 tablespoons double (heavy) cream. Heat well then add 1 to 2 tablespoons lemon juice or vinegar just before serving. Serve with beef or fish dishes.

⁂Onion Sauce Cook 3 large onions in boiling salted water, strain and chop, sieve or blend. Add to the sauce with 3 tablespoons double (heavy) cream. Serve with lamb, mutton or savoury dishes.

⁂Parsley Sauce Add 3 to 4 tablespoons chopped parsley to the sauce.

Basic Brown Sauce

This is the simplest sauce to serve with meat dishes. It can be made either by the traditional roux method or by the One-stage method, (see left).

50 g/2 oz (¼ cup) well-clarified dripping, cooking fat or lard
50 g/2 oz (½ cup) flour
600 ml/1 pint (2½ cup) brown stock, see page 51
salt and pepper

⁂Heat the fat in a saucepan. Add the flour and stir over a low heat until the roux (fat and flour) becomes dry and a pleasant golden brown colour. Gradually add the stock and stir as the mixture comes to the boil and thickens. Season to taste.

VARIATIONS
A sauce with appreciably more flavour is made by frying 1 or 2 peeled, chopped onion(s) and carrots in 75 to 100 g/3 to 4 oz (½ cup) fat, then adding the flour etc. This sauce can be sieved or blended to incorporate the vegetables, or strained before using. Serve with savoury dishes.

Use a Brown Sauce or Espagnole Sauce as the basis for the following sauces.

⁂Brown Mustard Sauce Add 1 to 2 tablespoons French (Dijon) mustard to Brown or Espagnole Sauce. Serve with most meats, poultry or game.

⁂Red Wine Sauce Use half stock and half red wine. Excellent with most meats, poultry and game.

⁂Speedy Espagnole Sauce Make a Brown Sauce, sieve or blend then add 1 to 2 tablespoons tomato purée (paste) and 1 tablespoon mushroom ketchup and reheat.

This sauce is a coating consistency; for a thicker sauce return to the pan and simmer for 25 minutes instead of 15 minutes.

Bigarade Sauce

This famous sauce uses Espagnole Sauce as its base. As it is generally served with duck, the Espagnole Sauce should ideally be made from duck fat (if available) and duck stock.

1 quantity Espagnole Sauce, see right
1 large Seville orange
150 ml/¼ pint (⅔ cup) water
1 tablespoon lemon juice
2 tablespoons port wine
salt and pepper
sugar

⁂Sieve or blend the Espagnole Sauce and return to the saucepan.

Meanwhile cut the outer surface of the rind (known as the zest) from the orange; make sure any bitter white pith is discarded. Cut the zest into matchstick strips. Put into a saucepan with the water and simmer gently for 10 minutes; by this time most of the liquid should have evaporated, leaving only about 2 tablespoons.

Halve the orange, squeeze out the juice and add to the smooth Espagnole Sauce in the pan, together with the orange peel and the liquid used to soften it, the lemon juice and port wine. Simmer for about 10 minutes, or until the sauce resumes a coating consistency. Taste and add extra seasoning and sugar that may be required to give the sauce a piquant flavour. Serve with duck or goose. Serves 4 to 6.

VARIATIONS
⁂Sweet Orange Sauce Use 1 large or 2 small oranges, instead of the Seville orange. Omit the lemon juice. Add 2 to 3 tablespoons redcurrant jelly or orange jelly marmalade with the port wine.

⁂Piquant Orange Sauce Make the Bigarade Sauce and add 50 g/2 oz (2 squares) plain semi-sweet chocolate to the mixture about 5 minutes before serving. Stir well as the chocolate melts.

This unusual use of chocolate gives a dark rich colour and interesting flavour, but does not make the sauce over-sweet.

Master Recipe
ESPAGNOLE SAUCE

This sauce is the accepted basis for a number of other interesting classic savoury sauces.

1 medium onion
50 g/2 oz (½ cup) mushrooms or mushroom stalks
2 medium to large tomatoes
1 bacon rasher (slice)
50 g/2 oz (¼ cup) dripping or butter, see Note
25 g/1 oz (¼ cup) flour
300 ml/½ pint (1¼ cups) brown stock, see Note
1 bouquet garni
salt and pepper
2 tablespoons brown sherry

❖ Peel and chop the onion. Wipe and slice the mushrooms or chop the stalks. Skin and chop the tomatoes (if sieving the sauce, skinning the tomatoes is unnecessary). De-rind and chop the bacon and keep the rind. Heat the dripping or butter with the bacon rind in a saucepan, then add the bacon and vegetables and fry for 3 to 4 minutes.

Add the flour and stir over a low heat until the flour changes colour and becomes golden brown. Gradually blend in the stock and continue stirring as the sauce comes to the boil and thickens. Add the bouquet garni and a little seasoning. Cover the pan and simmer for 15 minutes, then remove the bacon rind and bouquet garni. Sieve or blend the mixture. Return to the saucepan, add the sherry and any extra seasoning required. Heat for a few minutes.

This sauce is a good accompaniment for most savoury meat, poultry and game dishes. Serves 4.

Note The flavour of the sauce is particularly good if you use dripping and stock from the meat, poultry or game with which the sauce is served.

Espagnole Sauce can be served without sieving or blending. In this case chop the ingredients evenly and finely. Serves 4 to 6.

Variations

❖ Poivrade Sauce The basic Espagnole Sauce can be flavoured with a generous amount of peppercorns. Sieve the Espagnole Sauce and then reheat it with white, black or green peppercorns to taste. Poivrade Sauce is excellent with steak or any grilled (broiled) meat.

❖ Madeira Sauce Make the sauce with half, or all, Madeira wine instead of stock to provide an excellent Madeira Sauce to serve with boiled ham or tongue.

Game Sauce Sieve the basic sauce and add 150 ml/¼ pint (⅔ cup) red wine, 1 tablespoon red wine vinegar, 1 to 2 tablespoons light brown sugar and 4 to 6 tablespoons redcurrant jelly.

Heat through gently and serve with venison or guinea fowl.

Creole Sauce Sieve the basic Espagnole Sauce and add 3 skinned and diced tomatoes, 1 small cored and diced green pepper and a whole peeled clove of garlic. Simmer the sauce for 10 to 15 minutes, remove the garlic, add salt, pepper and cayenne pepper to taste.

Serve with grilled (broiled) meat or chicken.

Devilled Sauce Sieve the basic sauce. Add 1 tablespoon Worcestershire sauce, 2 teaspoons made English mustard, salt, pepper and a pinch of cayenne pepper.

Heat through and serve with grilled (broiled) or barbecued meat and sausages or chicken.

Game Sauce

1 medium tomato
25 g/1 oz (¼ cup) mushrooms or mushroom stalks
1 small onion
1 small bacon rasher (slice)
50 g/2 oz (¼ cup) dripping or butter
25 g/1 oz (¼ cup) flour
250 ml/8 fl oz (1 cup) brown stock
150 ml/¼ pint (⅔ cup) port wine
1 tablespoon brown vinegar
6 tablespoons redcurrant jelly
salt and pepper
sugar to taste

❖ Skin and chop the tomato. Wipe and slice the mushrooms or chop the stalks. Peel and chop the onion; de-rind and dice the bacon and keep the rind. Heat the dripping or butter and bacon rind in a saucepan. Add the bacon and vegetables and fry for 3 to 4 minutes. Add the flour and stir over a low heat until it changes colour and becomes a golden brown. Gradually blend in the stock and continue stirring as the sauce comes to the boil and thickens.

Cover the pan very tightly and simmer very slowly for 15 minutes. Remove the bacon rind and either rub the sauce through a sieve or blend until smooth. Return to the pan, add the port wine and vinegar. Bring to the boil, reduce heat and simmer for 5 minutes. Add the redcurrant jelly, seasoning and a little sugar to taste and boil briskly for 5 minutes until the sauce reaches a smooth coating consistency.

Serve hot instead of gravy with roast game. This sauce is also good cold. Serves 4 to 6.

VARIATION

❖ Port Wine Sauce Follow the recipe for Game Sauce above but omit the vinegar and use 1 tablespoon only of redcurrant jelly.

Basic Brown Sauce

Tomato Sauce

1 small onion
1 small carrot
1 garlic clove
450 g/1 lb tomatoes
1 bacon rasher (slice)
25 g/1 oz (2 tablespoons) butter or margarine
2 teaspoons cornflour (cornstarch)
300 ml/½ pint (1¼ cups) chicken or white stock
1 bay leaf
salt and pepper
1 teaspoon brown sugar

❖ Peel and chop the onion, carrot and garlic. Skin and chop the tomatoes (if sieving the sauce it is not necessary to skin the tomatoes). De-rind and chop the bacon and keep the rind. Heat the butter or margarine and bacon rind, add the bacon and vegetables and cook for 5 minutes.

Combine the cornflour (cornstarch) and stock; add to the pan with the bay leaf and a little seasoning. Cover the pan and simmer for 20 minutes. Remove the bay leaf and bacon rind and then sieve or blend the sauce. Return to the saucepan, add the sugar and extra seasoning, if required and reheat. Serves 4.

LEFTOVERS
Use any leftover Espagnole or Tomato Sauce as a filling for an omelette.

FREEZING NOTE
The season for Seville oranges is a short one, so freeze whole oranges to use in Bigarade Sauce, or prepare the orange rind by simmering in water as in the recipe, then pack the rind and liquid in suitably sized quantities and freeze. Use within 1 year.

Both Espagnole and Tomato Sauce freeze well. Use within 3 months.

103

Cold Sauces

Many cold sauces are based upon homemade mayonnaise, which is not difficult to make, especially with the help of a blender or food processor.

Blender Mayonnaise

The ingredients are combined in the same order as when making mayonnaise by hand (see Variations).

Although you can add the lemon juice and/or vinegar to the egg yolks or eggs before the oil, you never achieve such a light sauce.

You can use whole eggs if you wish in blender mayonnaise. This makes a less rich and lighter dressing.

2 egg yolks
salt and pepper
½ to 1 teaspoon made English or French (Dijon) mustard
½ to 1 teaspoon caster sugar
300 ml/½ pint (1¼ cups) oil
1 to 2 tablespoons lemon juice or white wine vinegar
1 tablespoon boiling water

Put the eggs or yolks, seasonings and sugar into the goblet. Switch on for a few seconds to mix.

Add the oil very slowly. In order to do this with the machine in operation, use the feed tube of a food processor or remove the small cap in the lid of a blender. If the mixture splashes, fit a funnel into this hole. If your blender does not have a removable cap in the lid, then simply make a funnel that fits completely into the top. Or make a foil cover with a hole removed. Add the oil steadily, not rapidly, with the machine running. Use a moderate speed. When all the oil is added, add the lemon juice and/or vinegar and boiling water with the machine still in operation.

VARIATIONS

Curry Mayonnaise Mix in 1 to 2 teaspoons curry paste; although not essential the sauce is better if a little whipped cream is also added.

Fennel Mayonnaise Add 1 to 2 tablespoons finely chopped fennel leaves and a little extra lemon juice. This is excellent with fish dishes.

Garlic Mayonnaise (Aïoli Sauce) Peel and crush 2 or 3 garlic cloves and mix with the mayonnaise. For a milder sauce simmer the peeled garlic in salted water then crush and add to the 2 egg yolks with 2 tablespoons soft breadcrumbs. Beat with the seasonings and sugar, then add the other ingredients.

Handmade Mayonnaise Put the egg yolks in a bowl with a good pinch of salt and a shake of pepper plus the mustard and sugar. Beat with a wooden spoon or whisk. Gradually add the oil, initially drop by drop. When all the oil is incorporated, beat or whisk in the lemon juice or wine vinegar to taste, adding more salt and pepper if necessary. When satisfied with both the consistency and the flavour whisk in the boiling water which will both lighten and stabilize the sauce. You cannot use whole eggs when making mayonnaise by hand.

Special Technique
PERFECT MAYONNAISE

The secret of a perfect mayonnaise:
☐ Keep all ingredients at room temperature. The most common cause of curdling (separating) is that the oil and egg yolks are at different temperatures.
☐ Make sure all utensils are scrupulously clean and dry.
☐ If the mayonnaise shows signs of curdling put another egg yolk into a bowl, and very slowly whisk the curdled sauce on to this.
☐ Add the oil very slowly if making the mayonnaise by hand.
☐ You can use olive oil, corn oil or a mixture of olive and corn oil or best quality salad oil.

Rémoulade Sauce

2 eggs
1 egg yolk
salt and pepper
½ to 1 tablespoon French (Dijon) mustard
up to 300 ml/½ pint (1¼ cups) olive or salad oil
1 to 2 tablespoons lemon juice or white wine vinegar

Hard-boil (hard-cook) and shell the eggs. Remove the yolks – the egg whites can be chopped and used in a salad or sandwich filling (see page 190).

Put the hard-boiled (hard-cooked) egg yolks into a basin with the uncooked yolk and cream well until smooth. Add a little salt, pepper and the mustard, then

LEFTOVERS
Freeze any leftover egg-based sauces. Pack into small containers. When thawed the sauce may be slightly less fluffy than when first made, but it should still be extremely good. Whisk again for 2 to 3 minutes over hot water to freshen the sauce.

FREEZING NOTE
Homemade mayonnaise freezes better than commercial mayonnaise but it does tend to separate.

gradually blend in the oil, in the same way as when making mayonnaise, (see page 104). When all the oil is incorporated whisk in the lemon juice or vinegar. Serves 4 to 6.

VARIATION

The sauce can be made in the blender or food processor, see Blender Mayonnaise.

Mayonnaise Verte

I quantity Mayonnaise, see left
I to 2 tablespoons finely chopped parsley
I to 2 tablespoons finely chopped tarragon
I to 2 tablespoons finely chopped chives
I to 2 tablespoons finely chopped fresh spinach or watercress leaves
2 tablespoons water

Place the herbs and spinach or watercress in a bowl. Boil the water, add to the ingredients in the bowl and allow to stand for 5 minutes. Drain and discard the liquid. Blend the herbs and spinach or watercress with the mayonnaise. Serve with salad. Serves 4 to 6.

VARIATION

If making the Mayonnaise in a blender or food processor there is no need to chop the ingredients finely: chop coarsely and add to the mayonnaise in the blender goblet or processor bowl and switch on for a few seconds.

Vinaigrette Dressing

This dressing, sometimes called French Dressing, is ideal to serve with most salads. The basic proportions are as given below but these can be varied according to personal taste and the foods with which the salad is to be served.

Use the best quality olive oil or salad oil. Choose corn oil for a light dressing. It is a polyunsaturated oil and is an ideal choice for anyone following a low cholesterol diet. You can use all vinegar (preferably white or red wine vinegar) or half vinegar and half lemon juice.

I teaspoon French (Dijon) mustard
150 ml/¼ pint (⅔ cup) oil
4 tablespoons wine vinegar or vinegar and lemon juice
salt and pepper
sugar to taste

Combine the mustard, the oil, the vinegar, lemon juice if using, salt, pepper and sugar to taste. Serves 4 to 6.

VARIATIONS

Chopped fresh herbs can be added to the dressing or you can include a crushed garlic clove.

The ingredients can be mixed in a blender or food processor.

Egg Sauces

The sauces based upon eggs or egg yolks are often considered difficult to make because, in the past, they had to be whisked by hand. Nowadays this is not a problem. The whisking can be done with an electric mixer, or easier still, in a blender or a food processor.

Blender Hollandaise Sauce

3 egg yolks
I tablespoon vinegar
I tablespoon lemon juice
salt and pepper
up to 175 g/6 oz (¾ cup) butter

⁂Place the egg yolks in the goblet of a blender or the bowl of a food processor. Add the vinegar and lemon juice, salt and pepper and mix thoroughly by running the motor for a few seconds. Melt the butter in a small pan over low heat then with the motor running, very gradually pour the melted butter through the processor feeding tube or hole in the lid of the blender. When all the butter has been incorporated, stop the motor and adjust the seasoning to taste. Serves 4 to 6.

Note Whole eggs can be used. The resulting sauce is lighter and not as rich as when egg yolks only are used.

VARIATIONS

⁂Mousseline Sauce Make Hollandaise as left, then fold in 2 to 3 tablespoons whipped double (heavy) cream just before serving. Serve with cooked asparagus or fish.

Parloise Sauce Make Hollandaise as left, blending ½ tablespoon French (Dijon) mustard with the egg yolks. Add 2 tablespoons finely chopped mint to the thickened sauce and serve with lamb.

Tartare Sauce Blend in 1 to 2 tablespoons each of chopped parsley and chopped gherkins plus 1 to 2 teaspoons chopped capers to Hollandaise. The resulting sauce is more delicate than one based on mayonnaise. Serve with fish.

Avgolemono Sauce

4 egg yolks or 2 eggs
salt and pepper
4 tablespoons lemon juice

Put the yolks or whole eggs into the top of a double saucepan or heatproof bowl. Stand over a pan of hot, but not boiling, water and add a little salt and pepper. Whisk until thick and creamy, then gradually whisk in the lemon juice and continue whisking until thickened again. Serve with fish. Serves 4.

VARIATIONS

Chicken Avgolemono Sauce Proceed as above and when the lemon juice has been incorporated, gradually whisk in up to 150 ml/¼ pint (⅔ cup) very strongly flavoured chicken stock. Excellent with boiled chicken, (see page 80).

FOR EASE

If adding butter to an egg sauce by hand keep the butter at room temperature. Do not heat it, as you do when making these sauces in a blender or food processor.

Add the butter in small pieces; make sure each portion of butter is absorbed before adding the next amount of butter. If added too quickly, the sauce becomes oily instead of light and fluffy.

LEFTOVERS

Leftover Vinaigrette Dressing can be stored in a screw-topped jar. Keep refrigerated. If the dressing contains fresh herbs it should be used within 48 hours.

Shake the jar briskly before serving.

Avgolemono Sauce

Fruit Sauces

If you are anxious to reduce the calories in these fruit-based sauces you can sweeten them with a sugar substitute instead of sugar.

Apple Sauce with Sage

Sherry and Orange Sauce

Excellent with duck, goose, lamb or pork.

40 g/1½ oz (3 tablespoons) dripping or butter, see method
450 ml/¾ pint (2 cups) stock, see method
2 medium oranges
40 g/1½ oz (6 tablespoons) flour
2 tablespoons sweet sherry
salt and pepper

FOR FLAVOUR
Instead of apples in the Cider Apple Sauce use gooseberries, cooking plums or rhubarb. Use slightly less liquid with rhubarb which contains a high percentage of water.

Instead of oranges in the Sherry and Orange Sauce use 1 large grapefruit or 1 small grapefruit and 1 tangerine.

FREEZING NOTE
These sauces all freeze well, except the Avocado Sauce, which is better freshly made.

⁎⁎Try to use dripping and stock from the kind of poultry or meat with which this sauce is to be served. Cut the outer rind from the oranges and halve and squeeze out the juice. Heat the dripping or butter in a pan, stir in the flour and continue stirring over a low heat until the flour turns golden in colour. Remove the pan from the heat and gradually blend in the stock. Add the pieces of orange rind and return the pan to the heat. Stir as the sauce comes to the boil and thickens.

Remove from the heat, add the orange juice and sherry and allow the sauce to stand for at least 30 minutes. Return to the heat. Stir as the sauce comes to the boil; take out the pieces of orange rind and season the sauce to taste. Serves 4 to 6.

Avocado Sauce

This sauce is excellent with hot or cold fish dishes. It is equally good with fried or grilled liver.

1 egg
50 g/2 oz (½ cup) walnuts
2 teaspoons lemon juice
1½ tablespoons mayonnaise
1 large avocado
salt and cayenne pepper
TO GARNISH: a few walnuts

Hard-boil (hard-cook), shell and chop the egg; chop the walnuts. Allow the egg to cool, then blend with the lemon juice and mayonnaise. This can be done any time before the meal.

Peel the avocado just before serving the sauce. Mash the flesh, season well and stir into the egg mixture.

Chop the walnuts for the garnish and scatter over the very thick cold sauce. Serves 4.

Cranberry Sauce

There are many recipes for Cranberry Sauce which is traditionally served with turkey. The simplest is to cook the fruit with a little water and a generous amount of sugar (cranberries are very sour), until the berries are soft. This recipe gives another variation.

450 g/1 lb (4 cups) cranberries
2 large oranges
5 tablespoons water
150 g/5 oz (½ cup plus 2 tablespoons) caster sugar

⁎⁎Wash and drain the cranberries. Grate the rind from the oranges. Put the water, orange rind and sugar into a saucepan, stir until the sugar has dissolved, add the cranberries and simmer for 5 minutes. Cover the pan, for the cranberries explode as they cook. Cut away the pith from the oranges and dice the pulp. Add to the cranberries and cook for a further 4 to 5 minutes. Allow to cool. Serves 8.

Cider Apple Sauce

Serve with grilled (broiled) gammon (ham), pork, duck or goose.

350 g/12 oz cooking (tart) apples
150 ml/¼ pint (⅔ cup) sweet cider
1 to 2 tablespoons sugar, preferably demerara
15 to 25 g/½ to 1 oz (1 to 2 tablespoons) butter
1 to 2 tablespoons sultanas (golden raisins)

⁎⁎Peel, core and slice the apples. Put into a saucepan with the cider and

sugar. Stir until the sugar has dissolved then allow to simmer until it forms a thick pulp. Add the butter with the sultanas (golden raisins) towards the end of the cooking time.

Good cooking apples become a fluffy purée during cooking, but the sauce can be beaten with a wooden spoon or put into a blender or food processor to make the purée perfectly smooth. Do not add the sultanas (golden raisins) until this stage is completed. Serves 4 to 6.

VARIATION
Traditional Apple Sauce Simmer the apples in 3 to 4 tablespoons water with sugar to taste. The butter is not essential but it makes a richer sauce.

Apple Sauce with Sage

450 g/1 lb cooking (tart) apples
2 tablespoons water, or see method
sugar to taste
shake of black pepper
1 teaspoon finely chopped sage

Peel, quarter and slice the apples. Put into the saucepan with the water or use a little lemon or orange juice with the water. Do not add the sugar at this stage for a sugar syrup helps to keep fruit a good shape and in this particular case it is important for the apples to soften and become a smooth purée. Cook gently until nearly soft, remove from the heat, add the sugar, pepper and sage, cover the pan tightly. The apples continue to cook in the steam in the pan and there is no fear of their burning or over-cooking. Remove the lid, beat vigorously to make a smooth pulp. Serve hot or cold with duck, goose or pork.

Spiced Tomato Dressing

Although tomatoes are generally regarded as a vegetable, they are in fact a fruit and I have included this particular tomato-flavoured dressing under Fruit Sauces since it has the freshness of spiced fruit.

1 garlic clove
4 tablespoons corn oil
2 to 4 tablespoons Worcestershire or other spiced sauce
2 tablespoons white wine vinegar
salt and pepper
1 bay leaf
225 g/8 oz ripe tomatoes

⁎⁎Peel and crush the garlic clove. Put it into a saucepan with all the ingredients except the tomatoes. Boil briskly for 2 minutes, remove the bay leaf and cool.

Meanwhile skin the tomatoes, halve and remove the seeds. Cut the flesh into small neat pieces, add to the chilled dressing. Serves 4.

Purée Sauces

During the past few years there has been considerable interest in what is known as *Nouvelle Cuisine*, for many people want to lose weight and avoid eating too much fat. One way to do this is to avoid rich sauces which invariably contain fat and flour, and rely instead upon sauces which owe their taste and texture to fruit and vegetables.

The recipes on this page are not substitutes for classic sauces, they are appetizing alternatives. The sauces are easily made with the help of a blender or food processor.

Simple Sauces

Never over-cook purée sauces or you will destroy their fresh flavour.
Apple-Beetroot Sauce Skin and neatly dice a medium-sized, peeled, cooked beetroot. Blend with 300 ml/½ pint (1¼ cups) thick unsweetened apple purée (applesauce). The beetroot provides the sweet flavour. Serve with duck or pork.

To give variety, flavour the sauce with ½ to 1 teaspoon chopped dill or a little Dijon mustard.
Cottage Cheese Sauce Sieve 225 g/8 oz (1 cup) cottage cheese. Blend with 2 tablespoons chopped fresh herbs and 3 tablespoons chicken stock (if serving the sauce hot) or yogurt (if serving the sauce

cold). Season well. Heat for a short time only in a bowl over hot water. Serve with any savoury foods.

To give variety, add 1 or 2 neatly diced skinned tomatoes and a little diced cucumber.
⁂Cucumber Sauce Peel and purée 1 large cucumber. Blend with 150 ml/¼ pint (⅔ cup) yogurt for a cold sauce or simmer in 3 or 4 tablespoons chicken stock with 1 or 2 peeled crushed garlic cloves for a few minutes for a hot sauce. Season well. Serve with fish or lamb.

To give variety, blend a few well-drained anchovy fillets or a large skinned tomato or 225 g/8 oz (1 cup) cottage cheese with the cucumber.
⁂Leek Sauce Chop 350 g/12 oz leeks. Simmer with 4 tablespoons well-seasoned water or chicken stock. Sieve or blend. Add 1 to 2 tablespoons chopped mint. Serve hot or cold with lamb, veal or poultry.
⁂Sanfayna Sauce This famous Spanish sauce can be made without using oil. Peel and finely chop 1 onion and 1 or 2 garlic cloves. Dice 1 red pepper (discarding the core and seeds). Skin, deseed and very neatly dice 4 large tomatoes. Finely chop 50 g/2 oz (½ cup) button mushrooms and 1 to 2 unpeeled courgettes (zucchini). Simmer in 3 to 4 tablespoons well-seasoned chicken stock until just tender – the vegetables should retain their shape. Serve hot or cold with pasta, meat or poultry.
⁂Sorrel Sauce Chop 225 g/8 oz sorrel leaves and 50 g/2 oz watercress leaves. Simmer for 5 minutes in 5 tablespoons well-seasoned chicken stock. Sieve or blend. Add a little sugar or sugar substi-

tute if desired and 3 tablespoons single (light) cream. Reheat gently. Serve hot with pasta, poultry or fish.
⁂Uncooked Tomato Sauce Skin, halve and de-seed 450 g/1 lb ripe tomatoes. Put into a blender or food processor with a small bunch of spring onions (scallions) or a peeled and diced mild Spanish onion. Season well and blend. Serve cold, or heat for a few minutes only. Serve with any savoury dish.

To give a stronger flavour, blend 1 to 2 tablespoons tomato purée (paste) with the tomatoes and onion(s).

Speedy Tomato Sauce

1 small onion
½ to 1 small dessert apple
25 g/1 oz (2 tablespoons) butter
1 tablespoon cornflour (cornstarch)
300 ml/½ pint (1¼ cup) chicken or white stock, or water
5 tablespoons tomato purée (paste)
salt and pepper
1 to 2 teaspoons brown sugar

Peel and dice the onion and apple. Melt the butter in a saucepan and fry the onion and apple gently until softened. Mix the cornflour (cornstarch) with the stock and add to the onion and apple together with the tomato purée (paste). Bring to the boil, stirring. Sieve or blend until smooth then return the mixture to the pan. Add seasoning and sugar to taste. Heat through for a few minutes then serve. Serves 4.

Note If the onion and apple are diced there is no need to blend the sauce.

LEFTOVERS
⁂*The smooth purées given on this page will freeze well and so will the Sanfayna Sauce, but the Apple-Beetroot Sauce is better eaten when freshly made.*

Use the purée sauces within 6 months.

Apple-Beetroot Sauce, Cucumber Sauce, Leek Sauce, and Sorrel Sauce

STUFFINGS

These stuffings are both original and delicious. More traditional stuffings are found on pages 64 and 68. Stuffing is frequently put inside the fish, meat or poultry, so that it is cooked with the food. Remember to weigh joints and poultry after adding the stuffing, so you can base the cooking time on the total weight. If you intend to cook the stuffing in a separate container, you should allow 30 to 40 minutes in a preheated moderate to moderately hot oven (180° to 190°C/350° to 375°F, Gas Mark 4 to 5).

Do not be too conservative with your choice of ingredients for a stuffing. Many different kinds of food can be used.

FREEZING NOTE
Apple and Onion Stuffing freezes reasonably well, but loses quite a lot of flavour and texture. This also happens with traditional Sage and Onion Stuffing (see page 64).

The Mushroom and Tomato Stuffing and the Sorrel Stuffing both freeze well and may be kept for up to 3 months.

The Cottage Cheese and Orange Stuffing and the Onion and Celery Stuffings are better freshly made, as is the Butter and Bread Stuffing.

LEFTOVERS
Leftover Butter and Bread Stuffing can be reheated and served as an accompaniment to fried or grilled (broiled) meat or fish.
Sweet Pineapple Dressing blends surprisingly well with most foods. It also freezes well, so any left over can either be reheated as an accompaniment to savoury dishes or it can be frozen.

Chestnut and Banana Stuffing

This is an unusual stuffing with a sweet flavour. It is particularly good with duckling or pork.

| 50 g/2 oz (½ cup) hazelnuts |
| 2 medium bananas |
| 1 tablespoon lemon juice |
| 225 g/8 oz (1 cup) unsweetened chestnut purée |
| 50 g/2 oz (⅓ cup) seedless raisins |
| 1 tablespoon chopped chives |

⁂Chop the nuts fairly coarsely, since these give a good texture to the other soft ingredients. Peel and mash the bananas in a bowl, add the lemon juice and remaining ingredients. Serves 4 to 6.

Chestnut and Sausage Stuffing

A classic combination – use in partridge or other game birds or in chicken or turkey.

| 225 g/8 oz (1 cup) pork sausagemeat |
| 225 g/8 oz (1 cup) chestnut purée |
| 2 tablespoons chopped parsley |
| 2 tablespoons chopped chives |
| 2 teaspoons chopped tarragon |
| 4 tablespoons double (heavy) cream |
| salt and pepper |

⁂Mix all the ingredients together; season well. Serves 6 to 8.

VARIATIONS
Add 75 g/3 oz (¾ cup) chopped walnuts, 100 g/4 oz (⅔ cup) sultanas (golden raisins) or other dried fruit.

Butter and Bread Stuffing

This is an interesting stuffing for people who do not like strong flavours. It is also an excellent base for many other stuffings and may be used in chicken, turkey or game birds.

| 225 g/8 oz (4 cups) soft breadcrumbs, see method |
| 100 g/4 oz celery |
| 100 g/4 oz onions |
| 100 g/4 oz (½ cup) butter |
| salt and pepper |

⁂The bread can be white, brown or wholewheat. Chop the celery and peel and chop the onions. Heat the butter in a frying pan (skillet), toss the onion in the butter for 5 minutes then add the breadcrumbs and turn in the onion mixture. Stir in the celery and season well. Serves 4 to 6.

VARIATIONS
Giblet Stuffing Add the cooked and finely chopped giblets of the chicken or turkey together with 2 tablespoons chopped parsley.

⁂Prawn Stuffing Add 100 to 175 g/4 to 6 oz (⅔ to 1 cup) chopped peeled prawns (shelled shrimp) with 1 tablespoon lemon juice.

Equally good with fish or veal.

⁂Raisin Stuffing Soak 175 g/6 oz (1 cup) seedless raisins in 2 tablespoons port wine for 1 hour. Add to the mixture. This is excellent in quails and pigeons. It will fill up to 8 birds.

Sweet Pineapple Dressing

Serve with cooked poultry or pork.

| 1 × 425 g/15 oz can pineapple rings (slices) |
| 1 lemon |
| 100 g/4 oz (⅔ cup) seedless raisins |
| 2 tablespoons sweet sherry or white wine |
| 100 g/4 oz (2 cups) fresh brown or wholewheat breadcrumbs |
| 2 tablespoons chopped parsley |
| 50 g/2 oz (¼ cup) butter |
| salt and pepper |

⁂Drain the pineapple and put 5 tablespoons of syrup from the can on one side. Chop the fruit. Grate the rind from the lemon, squeeze out 1 tablespoon lemon juice. Place the lemon rind, lemon juice and the 5 tablespoons syrup in an ovenproof dish with the raisins and sherry or white wine. Allow to stand for 30 minutes, then mix with all the breadcrumbs and parsley. Melt the butter, mix with the other ingredients and season well. Cover and cook in the centre of a moderate oven (160°C/325°F, Gas Mark 3) for 45 minutes. Serves 6 to 8.

VARIATION
⁂Sweet Cranberry Dressing Cook 225 g/8 oz (2 cups) cranberries in 150 ml/¼ pint (⅔ cup) water with 100 g/4 oz (½ cup) sugar until just softened. Strain and use instead of pineapple in the recipe above. This is excellent with turkey.

Mushroom and Tomato Stuffing

This is very good as a stuffing for small chickens or with lamb.

225 g/8 oz (2 cups) mushrooms
225 g/8 oz tomatoes
2 tablespoons chopped spring onions (scallions)
2 tablespoons chopped chives
1 tablespoon chopped parsley
salt and pepper

✲✲Wipe and slice the mushrooms; skin and chop the tomatoes. Mix with the other ingredients and season well. Serves 4 to 6.

VARIATIONS
✲✲Mushroom and Fennel Stuffing Use chopped fennel leaves instead of chives. You can also add 2 to 3 tablespoons of white fennel bulb. Excellent with fish.
✲✲Sorrel and Mushroom Stuffing Cook 100 g/4 oz sorrel leaves in a little salted water for 5 minutes only. Strain and chop. Add to the basic stuffing. Excellent with fish or chicken.

Cottage Cheese and Orange Stuffing

Use with duck, goose, pork or with chicken or veal.

350 g/12 oz (1½ cups) cottage cheese
3 medium oranges
1 tablespoon chopped parsley
salt and pepper

Put the cheese into a bowl. Finely grate the rind from the oranges – use just the zest. Cut away all the peel and pith and cut out the orange segments – do this over the bowl so no juice is wasted. Mix with the cheese, and add parsley. Season lightly. Serves 4 to 6.

VARIATIONS
Use chopped pineapple and grated lemon rind instead of orange rind and pulp. Add chopped mint instead of parsley. Use with lamb.

Sorrel Stuffing

Excellent in chicken or veal and particularly good with fish.

1 medium onion
225 g/8 oz sorrel leaves
150 ml/¼ pint (⅔ cup) chicken stock
salt and pepper
175 g/6 oz (¾ cup) cottage cheese

✲✲Peel and chop the onion. Chop the sorrel leaves, discarding the centre stalks. Simmer the sorrel and onion in the stock for 5 minutes, using an open pan so the liquid evaporates. Season well. Cool and blend with the cheese. Serves 4 to 6.

Mushroom and Tomato Stuffing, Cottage Cheese and Orange Stuffing, and Sorrel Stuffing

Mushroom and Sausage Stuffing

This is excellent if used to stuff chicken, turkey or veal. It is also a perfect mixture for making stuffing balls.

175 g/6 oz (1½ cups) mushrooms or mushroom stalks
450 g/1 lb (2 cups) sausagemeat
50 g/2 oz (1 cup) soft breadcrumbs
3 tablespoons chopped parsley
salt and pepper

✲✲Chop the mushrooms until fine and add to the other ingredients. Mix well and season lightly. Serves 6 to 8.

Liver and Raisin Stuffing

This is a rich stuffing that is excellent with chicken, turkey or veal.

350 g/12 oz (¾ lb) lambs' or chickens' livers
50 g/2 oz (¼ cup) butter
2 tablespoons sweet sherry
100 g/4 oz (⅔ cup) seedless raisins
50 g/2 oz (½ cup) ground almonds
salt and pepper

✲✲Finely chop the liver(s). Heat the butter in a frying pan (skillet) and toss the liver in this for 2 to 3 minutes. Add the sherry, heat for 2 to 3 minutes, stir well so the sherry absorbs all the fat and meat juices. Stir in the raisins and ground almonds. Season well. Serves 6 to 8.

Especially for Slimmers

It is a mistake to imagine that stuffings must be taboo when you are trying to lose weight. The following recipes are all low in calories. Double the quantities if using for a large chicken or a turkey.

Apple and Onion Stuffing

This is an ideal slimmers' stuffing for duck or goose or pork. It is also very good with chicken.

350 g/12 oz onions
350 g/12 oz cooking (tart) apples
150 ml/¼ pint (⅔ cup) apple juice
salt and pepper
½ teaspoon chopped sage

✲✲Peel and neatly dice the onions and apples. Put the apple juice in a pan, season, add the onions and cook for 10 minutes, until they are reasonably soft. Allow the liquid to evaporate towards the end of the cooking period. Mix with the apples and sage. Serves 4 to 6.

VARIATION
✲✲Apple and Prune Stuffing Omit the onions, chop 175 to 225 g/6 to 8 oz (1 cup) prunes, soak them in apple juice to cover for 12 hours then drain and blend with the apples as in the recipe above.

Put into duck or goose, game birds, pork or lamb.

DESSERTS AND PUDDINGS

Selecting a delicious and interesting dessert is an essential part of menu planning. Especially if the dish you choose to round off the meal includes nutritious as well as satisfying ingredients.

Over the last decade, tastes have changed. Cheesecakes of various kinds, dessert gâteaux and ices have become extremely popular. The fact that these cold desserts are so well-liked does not mean we should overlook the pleasures of a warming and satisfying hot pudding. Watch the family's pleasure when you produce a feather-light steamed pudding or a pile of crisp pancakes!

This section contains a wide selection of desserts and puddings. There are also many others in the various menus which begin on page 184, and in the pastry section, page 144.

Buying Points

The wide choice of desserts and puddings makes shopping for this course fairly simple. If you decide to base the dish on seasonal fruit, shop carefully, particularly during the soft fruit season, when the produce deteriorates quickly. Inspect the bottoms of punnets containing raspberries and strawberries; if damp, the bottom layer of fruit has become over-ripe or over-softened and will not keep.

Store perishable soft fruit carefully. Remove from the punnets, place on to large flat dishes and keep in a cool place. It is the weight of fruit packed tightly in the container that speeds up deterioration.

Take advantage of a glut of certain fruits. You will probably find you can buy excellent produce at a relatively low price.

Look for ways of saving money – use the less rich whipping cream instead of expensive double (heavy) cream, or learn how to make your own cream (see page 153).

Homemade steamed or baked puddings are not only delicious but they are also an excellent and economical way of adding nourishing ingredients to a meal. It is surprising how easy it is to prepare economical puddings if you plan and shop wisely.

Freezing Note

Most of the dishes in this section can be frozen, look for the freezing symbol. In some cases it is necessary to use a special technique to ensure perfect results, follow the numerous freezing notes.

Save time by baking flan cases (tart shells) in batches (see recipe on page 146). You can then use them when there is a glut of seasonal fruit. Make a large quantity of pastry, divide into smaller amounts, pack neatly and freeze (see page 144).

Homemade ice cream and sorbets can be prepared quickly and easily and stored in the freezer for several months, (see pages 116 and 117).

Microwave Cooking

A microwave cooker can be a great help during the preparation of puddings. You can melt chocolate or gelatine, cook fruit and make sweet sauces. You can even use it to cook hot suet or sponge puddings in a matter of minutes rather than the hours they would normally take.

Check the specific recommendations in your microwave manufacturer's instruction book.

Pressure Cooking

Steamed puddings, and those based on egg custards, are highly successful when cooked in a pressure cooker. You will find general advice under various recipes.

If cooking fresh fruit in a pressure cooker, be extra-careful about timing because the more delicate fruits can be easily overcooked.

Slow-Cooking

It is interesting to note that although you can cook steamed puddings very quickly in either a microwave or pressure cooker, you can also produce an excellent pudding in a slow-cooker.

Milk puddings are also suited to this long slow cooking process and the result is deliciously creamy.

Cheesecakes

The cheesecake has become one of our most popular desserts. Although the texture, flavouring and base may vary, there are certain rules to be followed to ensure the success of any type of cheesecake.

Baked Cheesecakes Many cheesecakes are baked on a base of biscuit crumbs or on pastry. If you are using pastry, make certain that this is rolled out until wafer thin, for thicker pastry could be under-cooked.

If you are using cottage cheese, sieve it to give a smoother texture. Cream or curd cheeses do not need sieving, but should be beaten well into the other ingredients. If the recipe contains whisked egg whites, fold these gently into the other ingredients.

It is advisable to allow most baked cheesecakes to cool gradually in the oven with the heat turned off; this prevents the mixture from wrinkling as it cools. Check the final stages of cooking carefully as the delicate mixture can darken slightly in the oven. It is a good idea to have the oven door slightly ajar as the cheesecake cools.

Uncooked Cheesecakes These are generally made with a biscuit crumb crust. If you have a spring-form tin, it is easy to remove the delicate jellied mixture. If, however, you are using an ordinary cake tin (pan), it is advisable to make the cheesecake by a slightly different method from that given in the recipes. Prepare as follows:

1. Make the jellied mixture, spoon it into the tin, allow to partially set. If using a tin with a loose base, make sure the jellied mixture is relatively firm before you spoon it into the tin or it will run out of the bottom of the tin.

2. Make the biscuit crumb crust and press it gently over the half-set jellied mixture.

3. When it is time to turn out the cheesecake, simply invert the tin over the serving plate.

Two of the recipes on page 112 are set with gelatine. The third is for a baked cheesecake in which carrots give an unusual flavour and an appealing colour.

Top right: Black Forest Gâteau, page 114
Middle right: Bramble and Apple Ice Cream, page 116
Bottom right: Raspberry and Orange Cheese Flan, page 122

Cheesecakes

Sharon Cheesecake

FOR THE BASE:

175 g/6 oz (1½ to 2 cups) crunchy oat or rice cereal

25 g/1 oz (¼ cup) hazelnuts

75 g/3 oz (6 tablespoons) butter

50 g/2 oz (3 tablespoons) honey

25 g/1 oz (¼ cup) seedless raisins

25 g/1 oz (¼ cup) chopped blanched almonds

¼ teaspoon mixed spice

FOR THE FILLING:

2 large lemons

water, see method

15 g/½ oz (2 envelopes) gelatine

2 eggs

75 g/3 oz (6 tablespoons) caster sugar

225 g/8 oz (1 cup) cottage cheese

225 g/8 oz (1 cup) cream or curd cheese

FOR THE TOPPING:

2 tablespoons redcurrant jelly

2 Sharon fruit, see Note

double (heavy) cream

Sharon Cheesecake

❋❋For the base The cereal can be lightly crushed, but do not make it too fine. Leave the hazelnuts whole or chop coarsely. Cream together the butter and honey and add the rest of the ingredients for the base. Lightly grease a 20 to 23 cm/8 to 9 inch spring-form tin. Press the cereal mixture into the base of this to give a smooth thick layer. Chill for about 1 hour.

For the filling Finely grate the zest from the lemons. Halve the fruit and squeeze out the juice. You need 5 tablespoons liquid; if necessary add a little water to make the full amount. Put the lemon juice into a bowl. Sprinkle the gelatine on top. Stand over a pan of very hot water until dissolved.

Separate the eggs. Whisk the egg yolks with the lemon rind and caster sugar until thick. Then whisk the gelatine mixture in and allow to cool. Sieve the cottage cheese, and add it to the mixture with the cream or curd cheese. Beat well. Finally whisk the egg whites until stiff and fold into the cheese mixture. Spoon over the base and allow to set. Remove the sides of the tin and slide the cheesecake on to a serving plate. Warm the redcurrant jelly and brush over the cheesecake. Slice the Sharon fruit and arrange over the redcurrant jelly. Whip a little cream and pipe a rosette in the centre of the cheesecake. Serves 6 to 8. **Note** Sharon fruit is the name given to a specific kind of persimmon. Sharon fruit can be eaten when quite firm, whereas the more familiar kind of persimmon has to be very ripe to be edible.

VARIATIONS

The filling of the cheesecake above is firm in texture. For a more delicate filling, whip 150 ml/¼ pint (⅔ cup) double (heavy) cream until it just holds its shape and fold into the cheesecake before adding the whisked egg whites.

Melt 4 tablespoons redcurrant jelly, use half to brush over the top of the cheesecake and half to brush over the Sharon fruit.

Orange and Carrot Cheesecake

FOR THE BASE:

175 g/6 oz (1½ cups) digestive biscuits (graham crackers)

50 g/2 oz (¼ cup) butter

25 g/1 oz (2 tablespoons) caster sugar

2 teaspoons finely grated orange rind

FOR THE TOPPING:

75 g/3 oz (½ cup) raw carrots, weight when peeled

25 g/1 oz (2 tablespoons) butter

75 g/3 oz (6 tablespoons) caster sugar

2 teaspoons finely grated orange rind

450 g/1 lb (2 cups) curd cheese

2 eggs

3 tablespoons orange juice

3 tablespoons double (heavy) cream

TO DECORATE:

double (heavy) cream

2 oranges

❋❋For the base Crush the biscuits (crackers). Melt the butter and add to the biscuit (cracker) crumbs with the 25 g/1 oz (2 tablespoons) of sugar and the

orange rind. Grease the sides and base of a 20 cm/8 inch spring-form tin. Coat the base only with the crumb mixture. **For the topping** Grate the carrots finely. Cream the butter, sugar and orange rind; add the carrots and sieved cheese.

Separate the eggs. Beat the yolks into the cheese mixture, then gradually beat in the orange juice. When all the orange juice has been incorporated, add the cream. Whisk the egg whites until stiff, fold into the other ingredients.

Spoon the cheesecake mixture over the crumb base and cook in the centre of a preheated cool oven (150°C/300°F, Gas Mark 2) for about 1 hour or until firm to the touch. Allow to cool in the oven with the heat turned off. When cold, remove the sides of the tin and slide the cheesecake on to a serving plate.

Whip a little cream and pipe on top of the cheesecake. Cut the peel and outer pith away from the oranges, then cut out segments of fruit (see SIMPLE SKILL on page 96). Place on top of the cheesecake. Serves 6.

Mocha Cheesecake

FOR THE CHEESE MIXTURE:

150 ml/¼ pint (⅔ cup) cold coffee

75 g/3 oz (6 tablespoons) caster sugar

15 g/½ oz (2 envelopes) gelatine

50 g/2 oz (⅓ cup) seedless raisins

2 tablespoons Tia Maria

50 g/2 oz (½ cup) walnuts

450 g/1 lb (2 cups) cream or curd cheese

150 ml/¼ pint (⅔ cup) double (heavy) cream

| **FOR THE BASE:** |
| 150 g/5 oz (1¼ cups) digestive biscuits (graham crackers) |
| 40 g/1½ oz (3 tablespoons) butter |
| 25 g/1 oz (2 tablespoons) caster sugar |
| 50 g/2 oz (2 squares) plain (semi-sweet) chocolate |
| **TO DECORATE:** |
| 150 ml/¼ pint (⅔ cup) double (heavy) cream |
| 25 g/1 oz (¼ cup) walnuts |
| 25 g/1 oz (1 square) plain (semi-sweet) chocolate |

Heat half the coffee in a saucepan, add the sugar and stir until dissolved. Soften the gelatine in the remaining cold coffee, stir into the hot coffee and continue stirring until dissolved. Allow to cool. Meanwhile put the raisins into a bowl, add the Tia Maria and leave for 30 minutes. Chop the walnuts finely, mix with the cream or curd cheese, then gradually beat in the gelatine mixture and the raisins and liqueur.

Whip the cream until it just holds its shape, then fold into the coffee mixture. Spoon into a 20 to 23 cm/8 to 9 inch cake tin (pan). Chill until just beginning to set, (see page 113). Do not allow the mixture to become too firm.

For the base Crush the biscuits (crackers), melt the butter and mix with the biscuits (crackers) and sugar. Grate the chocolate or chop it very finely. Add it to the biscuit (cracker) crumb mixture when the butter is completely cold so that there is no possibility of the chocolate melting. Put over the jellied mixture and press down gently with a palette knife. Allow to set, then invert on to a serving dish and remove the tin (pan).

To decorate Lightly whip the rest of the cream. Pile over the cheesecake. Chop the nuts and grate the chocolate and sprinkle over the cream. Serves 6 to 8.

Gâteaux and Special Desserts

Gâteaux are some of the most practical as well as interesting desserts. Choose those that are pleasantly moist in texture or include fruit. See also page 163.

Strawberry Shortcake

| 175 g/6 oz (¾ cup) margarine |
| 75 to 100 g/3 to 4 oz (⅓ to ½ cup) caster sugar |
| 1 egg |
| 250 g/9 oz (2¼ cups) plain (all purpose) flour |
| 1 teaspoon baking powder |
| **FOR THE FILLING:** |
| 350 to 450 g/12 oz to 1 lb (2 to 3 cups) strawberries |
| 300 ml/½ pint (1¼ cups) double (heavy) cream |
| caster sugar to taste |

⁂Cream the margarine and sugar together, then beat in the egg.

Sift the flour and baking powder, add to the creamed ingredients and knead well. Divide the dough into 3 equal portions. Roll out each portion to fit a 20 cm/8 inch fluted flan ring or sandwich tin (layer cake pan). If using flan rings, place these on upturned baking sheets, making it easier to remove the crisp shortcakes after baking.

If you have no fluted rings, flute the edge with your forefinger and thumb as shown on this page. Prick each shortcake with a fine skewer or fork. Mark one of the rounds into 8 equal portions.

Bake in, or near, the centre of a preheated moderate oven (180°C/350°F,

Gas Mark 4) for 15 to 20 minutes, or until golden in colour. While the shortcake rounds are still warm, carefully cut the marked round into sections. Allow to cool before filling.

For the filling Reserve one large strawberry. Hull and halve the remainder unless you prefer to leave whole the strawberries that are used for the topping. Whip the cream and add sugar to taste. Sandwich the two whole rounds with about three-quarters of the cream and half the strawberries.

Spread the remaining cream over the top of the shortcake, add the 8 sections of shortcake and the remaining strawberries. Serve with extra strawberries and cream or Caramel Sauce (see page 118). Serves 8.

Dutch Cream Delights

| 25 g/1 oz (¼ cup) blanched almonds |
| 100 g/4 oz (½ cup) unsalted butter |
| 50 g/2 oz (¼ cup) caster sugar |
| 25 g/1 oz (¼ cup) cornflour (cornstarch) |
| 15 g/½ oz (2 tablespoons) cocoa powder (unsweetened cocoa) |
| 100 g/4 oz (1 cup) plain (all-purpose) flour |
| **TO DECORATE:** |
| 100 to 150 g/4 to 5 oz (1 cup) strawberries |
| 25 g/1 oz (1 square) plain (semi-sweet) chocolate |
| 150 to 300 ml/¼ to ½ pint (⅔ to 1¼ cups) double (heavy) cream |
| a little icing (confectioners') sugar |

⁂Chop the almonds. Cream together the butter and sugar until soft and light. Sift the cornflour (cornstarch), cocoa and flour and add to the creamed mixture together with the almonds. Lightly knead the dough; if it seems slightly soft, wrap in plastic wrap and chill for a time, then roll out until about 5 mm/¼ inch thick. Cut the dough into 6 cm/2½ inch squares.

Put on to lightly greased baking sheets and bake in the centre of a preheated moderate oven (180°C/350°F, Gas Mark 4) for 12 to 15 minutes or until pale golden in colour. Leave on the baking sheets to become nearly cool, then lift on to a wire cooling tray. When quite cold store in an airtight tin until required.

To Decorate Halve large strawberries, make curls from the chocolate and whip the cream until stiff. Pipe or spread the cream over half the almond squares, top with the strawberries and chocolate curls. Top with the remaining almond squares and sift a little icing (confectioners') sugar over the top. Makes 7.

FREEZING NOTE
The crisp textures of the desserts on this page contrast pleasantly with the moist fillings.

Do not attempt to freeze them with their fillings or they will become soggy.

Freeze the pastry and flan cases for up to 3 months; thaw and fill just before serving.

Strawberry Shortcake

113

Put the remaining cream into a piping (pastry) bag with a small rose nozzle, pipe over the top of the cake and the edge of the puff pastry; leave the sides of the cake plain. Serves 6 to 8.

Note If you have no self-raising flour use plain (all-purpose) flour plus ½ teaspoon baking powder.

VARIATION

∴∴Simpler Black Forest Gâteau A rather less elaborate version of this famous gâteau can be made by omitting the puff pastry layer. Simply fill the sponge as the recipe above.

Pear Galette

FOR THE HAZELNUT ROUNDS:
50 g/2 oz (½ cup) hazelnuts
350 g/12 oz (3 cups) plain (all-purpose) flour
100 g/4 oz (½ cup) caster sugar
225 g/8 oz (1 cup) butter
FOR THE FILLING AND DECORATION:
300 ml/½ pint (1¼ cups) double (heavy) cream
8 canned pear halves
a few whole hazelnuts
a little icing (confectioners') sugar

∴∴Blanch and finely chop the hazelnuts (see Note). Sift the flour and add the sugar and nuts; rub in (cut in) the butter very lightly – there is a high proportion of butter to the amount of flour, but the sugar and nuts help to prevent the mixture from becoming too sticky.

Divide the mixture in half, press into two lined 20 cm/8 inch sandwich tins (layer cake pans) and prick with a fork. Bake in the centre of a preheated moderately hot oven, (190°C/375°F, Gas Mark 5) for 20 minutes, or until the nut mixture is just beginning to change colour, then lower the heat to moderate (160°C/325°F, Gas Mark 3) and bake for a further 15 to 20 minutes.

Allow the hazelnut rounds to cool for 5 minutes, until they begin to hold their shape, then turn out very carefully on to a wire cooling tray. Mark one round into 8 portions while warm. Store both rounds in an airtight tin or a freezer.

To serve Whip the cream until it holds its shape and drain the canned pears well. Put the unmarked hazelnut round on to a serving plate, top with half the cream and the pears (place these with the cut side downwards) and press a whole hazelnut into each pear.

Put the second hazelnut round over the pears, dredge with sifted icing (confectioners') sugar. Pipe the remaining cream on top of the galette and decorate with hazelnuts. Serves 8.

Note If you want to blanch the nuts before chopping, heat them in the centre of a preheated moderately hot oven (190°C/375°F, Gas Mark 5) for about 8 minutes, then rub away the skins.

Pear Galette

Black Forest Gâteau

½ quantity Puff pastry, see page 148
FOR THE CHOCOLATE SPONGE:
3 large eggs
100 g/4 oz (½ cup) caster sugar
¼ teaspoon vanilla essence
65 g/2¼ oz (½ cup plus 1 tablespoon) self-raising flour, see Note
1 tablespoon cocoa powder (unsweetened cocoa)
1 tablespoon hot water
FOR THE FILLING:
1 × 453 g/1 lb can black (bing) cherries
2 teaspoons arrowroot or cornflour (cornstarch)
300 ml/½ pint (1¼ cups) double (heavy) cream
3 tablespoons brandy or cherry brandy
50 g/2 oz (¼ cup) caster sugar

FREEZING NOTE

Soft sponge-type gâteaux freeze perfectly, so the chocolate sponge in Black Forest Gâteau can be frozen with or without the filling.

If you are using the version with puff pastry, you should freeze the pastry round separately and complete the gâteau after thawing.

Use all cakes within 3 months.

∴∴Roll the puff pastry into a 20 cm/8 inch round. Place on a baking sheet and prick lightly. Bake above the centre of a preheated hot to very hot oven (230 to 240°C/450 to 475°F, Gas Mark 8 to 9) for 15 to 20 minutes until crisp and brown. Lower the heat slightly after 10 minutes.
For the sponge Whisk the eggs, sugar and vanilla essence until thick. Sift the flour with the cocoa twice. Fold the flour and cocoa into the egg mixture then fold in the water. Divide the mixture between two 18 cm/7 inch greased and floured sandwich tins (layer cake pans). Bake just above the centre of a preheated moderate to moderately hot oven (180 to 190°C/350 to 375°F, Gas Mark 4 to 5) for 12 to 15 minutes or until firm to a gentle touch. Turn out and cool.
For the filling Drain the syrup from the cherries and reserve. Stone (pit) the cherries if necessary. Measure 12 tablespoons of the syrup; if inadequate, add a little water to give the right amount. Blend the arrowroot or cornflour (cornstarch) with the syrup. Put into a saucepan, boil until thick and clear, stirring as the liquid thickens. Mix with the cherries and allow to cool.
To serve Trim the edges of the puff pastry and place it on a serving plate. Whip the cream until it holds its shape, fold in ½ tablespoon of the brandy or cherry brandy and the sugar. Spread a quarter of the cream and half the cherry mixture over the centre of the puff pastry; leave a small rim of plain pastry round the outside.

Sprinkle both halves of the chocolate sponge with the remaining brandy or cherry brandy. Centre one half on the pastry round. Spread with a little whipped cream and the rest of the cherry mixture. Top with the second sponge.

Light Cold Desserts

A cold mousse or soufflé should be light and delicate in texture. Do not exceed the recommended quantity of gelatine in the mixture.

Simple Plum Soufflé

⁑Open a 567g/1lb 4oz can of red plums. Strain off the juice, heat this in a saucepan, shake on 25g/1oz (4 envelopes) gelatine and allow it to dissolve. Finely grate the rind from 1 orange, squeeze out the juice and add both the rind and juice to the dissolved gelatine mixture.

Stone (pit) and mash or blend the plums, stir into the gelatine mixture together with a 439g/15½oz can creamed rice or semolina and 15 to 25g/½ to 1oz (1 to 2 tablespoons) caster sugar.

Allow the mixture to stiffen slightly, then whisk 1 egg white and fold this into the other ingredients. Put into a 600ml/1 pint (2½ cup) prepared soufflé dish (see right), and allow to set. Decorate with whipped cream. Serves 4.

Prune Mousse

| 225g/8oz (1⅓ cups) prunes |
| 600ml/1 pint (2½ cups) water, see method |
| 75g/3oz (6 tablespoons) caster sugar |
| 1 tablespoon lemon juice |
| 15g/½oz (2 envelopes) gelatine |
| 300ml/½ pint (1¼ cups) double (heavy) cream |
| 75g/3oz (¾ cup) walnuts |
| 3 egg whites |

⁑Soak the prunes in the water overnight, then simmer with half the sugar and the lemon juice until soft.

Lift the prunes from the liquid. Boil it if necessary until reduced to 300ml/½ pint (1¼ cups) plus 3 tablespoons. Put the 3 tablespoons of liquid into a bowl. Stone (pit) the prunes and place 3 on one side for decoration; sieve or purée the remaining prunes in a blender.

Sprinkle the gelatine on to the 3 tablespoons of liquid. Stand over a pan of hot water and leave until dissolved, then add to the 300ml/½ pint (1¼ cups) prune syrup and the prune purée. Leave until lightly set.

Whip the cream and add the remaining sugar. Chop the walnuts and whisk the egg whites until stiff. Blend two-thirds of the cream into the jellied prune mixture with half the walnuts. Finally fold in the egg whites. Spoon into a large serving dish and allow to set completely.

Top with the remaining cream, prunes and chopped walnuts. Serves 6.

VARIATIONS

Use canned prunes, which will not require cooking; omit half the sugar in the recipe. Stone (pit) and sieve the prunes, except those set aside for decoration. Measure the syrup from the can – you need 300ml/½ pint (1¼ cups) plus 2 tablespoons, plus 1 tablespoon lemon juice.

If you are using tenderized prunes, cook without soaking.

Citrus Soufflé

| 1 grapefruit |
| 1 orange |
| 3 eggs |
| 150g/5oz (½ cup plus 2 tablespoons) caster sugar |
| 4 tablespoons water |
| 15g/½oz (2 envelopes) gelatine |
| 300ml/½ pint (1¼ cups) double (heavy) cream |
| **TO DECORATE:** |
| 4 tablespoons chopped blanched almonds |
| 1 orange |

Prepare a 15cm/6 inch soufflé dish (see right).

Grate the zest from the grapefruit and orange, halve the fruit and squeeze out 2 tablespoons grapefruit juice and 3 tablespoons orange juice.

Separate the eggs and put the yolks with the sugar, fruit juice and rinds into a bowl. Stand over a pan of very hot, but not boiling, water and whisk until the mixture is thick and creamy. Remove from the heat and continue whisking until cold.

Put the cold water into another bowl, sprinkle the gelatine on top and stand over hot water until the gelatine has dissolved; mix this with the egg yolk mixture. Allow the mixture to stand until it has the consistency of a thick syrup.

Whip the cream until it just holds its shape and whisk the egg whites until very stiff. Fold the cream and then the egg whites into the egg yolk mixture, then pour into the prepared soufflé dish, and chill until set. Remove the paper collar from the soufflé dish.

Brown the almonds under the grill (broiler) or in the oven until golden in colour. Press against the edge and sides of the soufflé.

Cut away the peel from the orange and cut the fruit into segments. Place on top of the soufflé. This should be done immediately before serving the dessert so that the orange does not become dry. Serves 6.

Mexican Creams

| 100g/4oz (4 squares) plain (semi-sweet) chocolate |
| 2 teaspoons instant coffee powder |
| 2 tablespoons Tia Maria |
| 1 tablespoon custard powder (Bird's English dessert mix) |
| 300ml/½ pint (1¼ cups) milk |
| 1 to 2 tablespoons caster sugar |
| 150ml/¼ pint (⅔ cup) double (heavy) cream |
| **TO DECORATE:** |
| 150ml/¼ pint (⅔ cup) double (heavy) or whipping cream |
| 25g/1oz (1 square) plain (semi-sweet) chocolate |

⁑Break the chocolate into pieces, put into a bowl with the coffee powder and the Tia Maria and melt over a pan of hot water or in the microwave cooker. Meanwhile, blend the custard powder (dessert mix) with the milk, tip into a saucepan and add the sugar. Stir over a low heat until thickened, then blend with the melted chocolate mixture. Cover the bowl with a plate to prevent a skin forming and allow to cool.

Whip the double (heavy) cream, fold into the chocolate mixture and spoon into 4 glasses or dishes. Whip the cream until it just holds its shape. Spoon over the chocolate mixture and grate the remaining chocolate over the top of the creams. Serves 4.

VARIATION

Any coffee flavoured liqueur can be used in place of Tia Maria.

Instead of the liqueur you could use 2 tablespoons extra milk or cream.

SIMPLE SKILL
To Prepare a Soufflé Dish
A cold soufflé stands well above the top of the soufflé dish so it is always necessary to line the dish.

Using a double thickness of greaseproof (waxed) paper, cut a band a little longer than the circumference of the soufflé dish and at least 18cm/7 inches deep.

Brush a 10cm/4 inch strip of the band with a little melted butter or oil. Wrap around the outside of the soufflé dish with the greased strip standing above the rim of the dish facing inwards. Secure with string or a safety pin.

When the soufflé has set, remove the band of paper, loosening it with a palette knife dipped in hot water.

Simple Plum Soufflé

115

Iced Desserts

Homemade ice cream is not only easy to make, but highly successful. There is no need to alter the thermostatic control on the freezer; ice creams can be frozen on the setting used for storing food.

Most ice creams are better used within 3 months and most sorbets within 4 months.

Coffee Walnut Bombe

Ways to Serve Ice Cream

Ice Cream can be made into sundaes, used as a filling in gâteaux or flavoured in more elaborate ways (see pages 117, 174 and 203).

Make several flavours of ice cream and combine them in a Bombe as in the recipe opposite.

Fruit Ice Creams

✲✲Mix a generous 150 ml/¼ pint (⅔ cup) very thick fruit purée into Custard Ice Cream or Rich Ice Cream, or use 225 ml/7½ fl oz (1 cup) fruit purée with Evaporated Milk Ice Cream; or use 225 ml/7½ fl oz (1 cup) fruit purée in place of the milk purée in Marshmallow Ice Cream.

Do not be too conservative in your choice of fruit; most fruits make delicious ice creams.

Obviously fruit ice creams must be sufficiently sweetened to give a good flavour, but never over-sweeten ice creams, or they will not freeze.

FOR ECONOMY
The packet topping used instead of cream on desserts and gâteaux can be used as a basis for ice cream.

Whip according to packet instructions, add flavouring and freeze.

Fresh peaches or mangoes should be sieved and blended with a little lemon juice so that the fruit does not discolour.

Soft fruits such as blackcurrants, redcurrants, raspberries and strawberries should be sieved without cooking. Gooseberries, plums and damsons should be cooked with a minimum of liquid. As a change, use melon, mango or kiwi fruit (Chinese gooseberry) purée.

Apricot Ice Cream Cooked or canned apricots make a delicious ice cream but cooked *dried* apricot purée has a more definite flavour. Add the purée with about 50 g/2 oz (½ cup) finely chopped blanched almonds to the ice cream of your choice.

Avocado and Lemon Ice Mash enough avocado pulp to give the quantity you require. Mix with 1 to 2 tablespoons lemon juice and add to the ice cream of your choice.

Bramble and Apple Ice Cream Cook then sieve equal quantities of blackberries and cooking (tart) apples. Use as suggested above.

Whole Fruit Ice Creams Soft pulpy fruit like cooked or canned cherries or very ripe cherries or sliced apricots can be added whole to the ice cream, but whole strawberries and raspberries tend to become frozen like hard stones.

Marshmallow Ice Cream

Sometimes called a mallobet.

150 ml/¼ pint (⅔ cup) milk
175 g/6 oz (6 cups) marshmallows
300 ml/½ pint (1¼ cups) double (heavy) or whipping cream
flavouring, see Variations

✲✲Put the milk and marshmallows into a saucepan, set over a low heat and leave until the marshmallows have melted. If you have a microwave cooker, use this and melt the marshmallows in a bowl with the milk. Allow to cool.

Whip the cream, fold into the cold sticky marshmallow mixture, add any one of the flavourings below, then freeze. Serves 4.

VARIATIONS
Orange Marshmallow Ice Cream Use the finely grated rind of 2 oranges and 150 ml/¼ pint (⅔ cup) fresh orange juice instead of milk.

Fruit Marshmallow Ice Cream Use 225 ml/7½ fl oz (1 cup) thick fruit purée instead of the milk in the recipe above.

By dissolving the marshmallows in fruit purée, rather than in milk you give the ice cream a much more definite fruit flavour.

Chocolate or Coffee Marshmallow Ice Cream Dissolve 50 to 75 g/2 to 3 oz (2 to 3 squares) chocolate, or 1 to 1½ tablespoons sifted cocoa powder (unsweetened cocoa) or 2 to 3 teaspoons instant coffee powder in the milk with the marshmallows.

Master Recipe
RICH ICE CREAM

A good ice cream is light in texture, yet pleasingly creamy and full of flavour. Here is a basic rich recipe that can be varied by adding different flavourings and that requires no whisking during the freezing process.

300 ml/½ pint (1¼ cups) double (heavy) cream
flavouring, see Variations
50 g/2 oz (½ cup) icing (confectioners') sugar
2 egg whites

✲✲Whip the cream until it holds its shape, then add the flavouring and sugar. Whip the egg whites until very stiff, fold into the cream mixture and freeze. Serves 4 to 6.

Variations

Almond, vanilla and other essences (extracts) can be added to the mixture; add gradually to give a definite flavour.

Chocolate Ice Cream Melt 50 to 75 g/2 to 3 oz (2 to 3 squares) plain (semisweet) chocolate, cool then add to the other ingredients together with a few drops of vanilla essence (extract). Instead of melted chocolate use 1 to 1½ tablespoons sifted cocoa powder (unsweetened cocoa). Dissolve this in 2 tablespoons warm milk and allow to cool. Alternatively, use 40 to 50 g/1½ to 2 oz (6 tablespoons to ½ cup) chocolate powder (sweetened cocoa) which can be added dry to the other ingredients.

Coffee Ice Cream Dissolve 2 to 3 teaspoons instant coffee powder in 2 tablespoons warm milk, allow to cool, then blend with the other ingredients.

Nut Ice Cream Add 50 to 100 g/2 to 4 oz (½ to 1 cup) finely chopped nuts to the ice cream. Grated fresh or desiccated (shredded) coconut can be added; or blend 150 g/5 oz (½ cup) chestnut purée with the other ingredients.

Golden Ice Cream Separate 2 eggs, beat the yolks and sugar until creamy. Mix with the whipped cream and any flavouring from the list above. Lightly freeze, then fold in the whisked egg whites.

Custard Ice Cream

A more economical ice cream that is just as versatile as the Master Recipe.

1 egg
40 to 50 g/1½ to 2 oz (⅓ to ½ cup) icing (confectioners') sugar or caster sugar
300 ml/½ pint (1¼ cups) milk
flavouring, see Note
300 ml/½ pint (1¼ cups) whipping cream or cream made as on page 153 or full cream evaporated milk

✲✲Beat the egg and sugar – if using icing

(confectioners') sugar, sift it first. Warm the milk and stir into the egg and sugar. Put the custard into the top of a double saucepan, or leave in the bowl. Cook over hot, but not boiling, water, stirring occasionally, until the mixture just coats the back of a wooden spoon. Allow to cool, stirring from time to time to prevent a skin forming. Add the flavouring and freeze the custard for a short time until slightly mushy. Whip the cream or the evaporated milk until it stands in peaks. Fold into the partially frozen mixture and continue freezing. Serves 4. **Note** Add any of the flavouring variations listed in the Master Recipe.

Coffee Walnut Bombe

Rich Ice Cream, made with 600 ml/1 pint (2½ cups) double (heavy) cream etc.
100 to 175 g/4 to 6 oz (1 to 1½ cups) walnuts
2 tablespoons milk
2 to 3 teaspoons instant coffee powder

⁂Make the ice cream. Chop the nuts and fold into the ice cream.

Warm the milk, add the coffee powder and allow to cool. Mix the coffee into a generous half of the mixture. Lightly freeze both batches of ice cream separately. Spread the half-set white ice cream around the base and sides of a 900 ml to 1.2 litre/1½ to 2 pint (1 quart) bowl. Freeze for a short time. Fill the centre with the coffee mixture. Freeze until firm. Turn out. Serves 8.

VARIATIONS
Add chopped nuts to the coffee mixture only. Flavour all the ice cream with coffee and freeze in a bowl. Turn out and coat with lightly whipped and sweetened cream. Freeze again on the serving dish. Just before serving you can decorate the dessert with plain or coffee-flavoured whipped cream and walnuts.

Fruit Sorbets

⁂A sorbet is a deliciously light mixture of fruit juice, or fruit purée, and egg whites. Sorbets are aerated far more than water ices.

It is advisable to add a small amount of gelatine to the mixture before freezing. This helps to keep the sorbet smooth in texture, particularly if it is being stored for more than 24 hours.

When making a sorbet, do not use too much sugar, for the frozen mixture should be refreshing in flavour. If you are following a low calorie diet, sweeten the mixture with sugar substitute.

A sorbet can be served as an hors d'oeuvre (see page 20). Traditionally it was served halfway through a meal to refresh the palate. Nowadays sorbets are more often served as a dessert.

Use sorbets within 4 months.

Citrus Sorbet

1 lemon
1 orange
1 small grapefruit
300 ml/½ pint (1¼ cups) water
1½ teaspoons gelatine
75 g/3 oz (6 tablespoons) sugar
2 to 3 egg whites

⁂Pare 2 to 3 strips of rind from each fruit – be careful not to use any bitter white pith. Simmer for 5 minutes in the water, then dissolve the gelatine and sugar in the hot liquid, strain and allow to cool. Halve the fruit, squeeze out the juice and add to the sugar and gelatine liquid.

Freeze lightly until the mixture is like a thick cream. Whisk the egg whites until very stiff then fold into the half-frozen mixture. Freeze until firm. Serves 4 to 6.

VARIATIONS
⁂Orange Sorbet Use the juice and peel from 3 to 4 oranges in place of the mixed citrus in the recipe above.

⁂Lemon Sorbet Replace the mixed citrus with the juice and rind from 2 large lemons.

⁂Lemon Ginger Sorbet Replace the mixed citrus with the juice and rind of 2 small lemons plus 1 to 2 teaspoons ground ginger. Add 3 tablespoons finely chopped preserved ginger.

⁂Fruit Purée Sorbet Use 450 ml/¾ pint (2 cups) smooth fruit purée, plus 150ml/¼ pint (⅔ cup) water and the other ingredients as the recipe above. Do not be conservative in your choice of fruit; use seasonal fruit like the melon used in the picture below.

Special Technique
MAKING A GRANITA

In Italy, Granita al Caffè (coffee granita) is a favourite dessert and like other similar desserts, is simple to make and wonderfully refreshing in hot weather. The slightly chippy texture of the ice is quite correct.

The liquid mixture is frozen until it is like soft ice cubes, then served with lightly whipped cream or ice cream. Two examples are given below, each serving 4 to 6 people.

⁂Granita al Caffè Make 1 litre/1¾ pints (4¼ cups) rather strong coffee; dissolve 75 to 100 g/3 to 4 oz (6 tablespoons to ½ cup) caster sugar in the hot coffee. Allow to cool then freeze. Stir the mixture from time to time.

Bring the granita out of the freezer about 30 minutes before serving and place in the refrigerator. Spoon into glasses and top with lightly whipped cream or ice cream.

⁂Granita di Frutta Make approximately 1 litre/1¾ pints (4¼ cups) fresh fruit purée with juicy dessert fruit such as strawberries, raspberries, blackberries or lightly cooked blackcurrants. The fruit can be blended, although it should be sieved if you want to get rid of all pips. If the fruit purée is lacking in flavour, add a little lemon juice.

Dissolve 100 to 150 g/4 to 5 oz (about ½ cup) sugar in 150 ml/¼ pint (⅔ cup) boiling water, add to the blended fruit. Allow to cool, freeze and serve like Granita al Caffè above.

Undiluted orange juice or other fresh fruit drinks make delicious granita if frozen until granular.

FOR EASE
To Whip Evaporated Milk
Place a large unopened can of full cream evaporated milk into a saucepan of cold water. Bring the water to the boil and boil for 15 minutes.

Meanwhile put 2 tablespoons water into a bowl. Sprinkle 1 teaspoon gelatine on top; stand over hot water until dissolved. Open the can of milk very carefully, pour the hot milk into a large mixing bowl, add the dissolved gelatine, allow to cool, then whip. Use instead of whipped cream.

Evaporated Milk Ice Cream
Whip the evaporated milk as above, add 50 g/2 oz (¼ cup) sugar and flavouring (see page 116), and freeze.

Fruit Purée Sorbet made with melon

Fruit Desserts

The desserts on this page are very adaptable. Use plum or rhubarb purée instead of apples in Danish Apple Cake; try raspberries, strawberries, or apricots instead of peaches in the Syllabub and the caramel mixture used in Caramelled Pears can be served over peaches or strawberries.

Danish Apple Cake

750 g/1½ lb cooking (tart) apples
2 to 3 tablespoons water
sugar to taste
75 g/3 oz (6 tablespoons) butter
100 g/4 oz (2 cups) soft white breadcrumbs, weight without crust
75 g/3 oz (6 tablespoons) granulated sugar
150 ml/¼ pint (⅔ cup) double (heavy) cream
a little redcurrant jelly

✱✱Peel, core and slice the apples, put into a pan with the water and a little sugar. Cook over low heat until mixture forms a thick purée. Add 25 g/1 oz (2 tablespoons) of the butter and mix with the hot apple mixture; allow to cool.

Heat the remaining butter in a large frying pan (skillet), add the breadcrumbs, turn around until well coated with the butter, then fry steadily until crisp and golden in colour. Add the sugar towards the end of the cooking period. Leave until quite cold.

Arrange layers of the crumb mixture and apple purée in one large or several individual serving dishes. Whip the cream and spoon or pipe it on top of the dessert. Top the cream with a little jelly. Serves 4 to 6.

VARIATION

To make a more sustaining dessert, use 175 g/6 oz (3 cups) breadcrumbs with 75 g/3 oz (6 tablespoons) butter and 100 g/4 oz (½ cup) granulated sugar.

Peach Syllabub

6 ripe peaches
3 teaspoons lemon juice
1 tablespoon caster sugar
150 ml/¼ pint (⅔ cup) double (heavy) or whipping cream

✱✱Skin 4 of the peaches; to do this, lower the fruit into boiling water, leave for a few seconds only, remove and cool then pull away the skins. Halve and stone (pit) the fruit, put into a blender or food processor with 2 teaspoons of the lemon juice and make a smooth purée, then add the sugar.

Whip the cream, fold into the peach purée and spoon into individual glasses. Skin and slice the remaining peaches just before serving the dessert. Sprinkle with remaining lemon juice and arrange on the syllabub. Serves 4.

VARIATION

Use canned peaches and omit the sugar. The lemon juice gives a little bite to the sweet fruit.

Caramelled Pears

FOR THE CARAMEL SAUCE:
100 g/4 oz (½ cup) caster sugar
3 tablespoons water
300 ml/½ pint (1¼ cups) whipping cream
FOR THE PEARS:
150 ml/¼ pint (⅔ cup) white wine
25 g/1 oz (2 tablespoons) caster sugar
1 tablespoon lemon juice
4 to 6 ripe but firm dessert pears
TO DECORATE:
25 g/1 oz (¼ cup) flaked blanched almonds

Put 75 g/3 oz (6 tablespoons) of the sugar and the water into a saucepan. Stir until the sugar has dissolved then boil, without stirring, until a deep brown caramel has formed. Allow to cool, add the cream and remaining 25 g/1 oz (2 tablespoons) sugar. Stir over a very low heat until the caramel and cream mix together; do not allow this mixture to become too hot, otherwise it will curdle. Chill the sauce.

For the Pears Pour the wine, sugar and lemon juice into a frying pan (skillet) and stir over a low heat until the sugar has dissolved. Peel, halve and core the pears and poach in the wine syrup for 5 minutes only, turning over several times so that the pears absorb the syrup.

To Decorate Arrange 2 pear halves on each serving plate with any wine syrup that remains (the fruit can be served hot or cold). Coat with the caramel sauce just before serving and top with almonds. Serves 4 to 6.

VARIATION

Use canned pear halves. Drain the pears and sprinkle with a little white wine and lemon juice, or heat the syrup from the can with 1 to 2 tablespoons lemon juice and pour over the canned pears. Coat with sauce and decorate as suggested above.

This caramel sauce is delicious with most fresh fruit.

Avocado Ambrosia

2 oranges
12 almond-topped ratafias or small macaroons, see page 173
225 g/8 oz (1 cup) cream or curd cheese
1 tablespoon honey
2 avocados
2 tablespoons lemon juice

Grate the rind from 1 orange, cut away the peel and pith and cut the 2 oranges into segments (see page 96). Crumble the ratafias and blend with the cheese, honey and orange rind. Halve the avocados, sprinkle with the lemon juice and top with the cheese mixture and orange segments. Serve with more ratafias. Serves 4.

LEFTOVERS
Making Danish Apple Cake is an excellent way of using leftover stale bread.

Prepare the breadcrumb mixture, fry in the butter until crisp. Spread out on a flat tray, cool and then freeze until required.

Use within 3 months.

If you decide to freeze the completed dessert, serve it as soon as it has thawed so that the crisp texture of the fried crumbs is not spoiled.

Danish Apple Cake

Milk and Cream Desserts

Milk is a simple and versatile ingredient that can be the basis for many delicious puddings.

Apricot Rice Pudding

3 tablespoons water
15 g/½ oz (2 envelopes) gelatine
1 × 439 g/15½ oz can creamed rice pudding
1 × 397 g/14 oz can apricot pie filling

Put the water into a bowl and sprinkle the gelatine on top. Stand over a pan of hot water until the gelatine has dissolved. Mix with the creamed rice pudding.

Rinse a 900 ml to 1.2 litres/1½ to 2 pint (1 quart) ring mould with cold water. Take some of the whole fruit from the pie filling and put into the mould. Stir the rest of the pie filling into the rice pudding. Spoon into the mould and allow to set, then turn out. Serves 4.

Rice Cream Brûlée

50 to 75 g/2 to 3 oz (4 to 6 tablespoons) short-grain rice
300 ml/½ pint (1¼ cups) single (light) or double (heavy) cream
300 ml/½ pint (1¼ cups) milk
few drops of vanilla essence (extract)
25 to 50 g/1 to 2 oz (2 to 4 tablespoons) caster or granulated sugar
2 tablespoons sultanas (golden raisins)
2 tablespoons chopped glacé cherries
2 tablespoons chopped candied peel
FOR THE TOPPING:
25 to 50 g/1 to 2 oz (¼ to ½ cup) flaked blanched almonds
50 g/2 oz (¼ cup) demerara (brown sugar)

⁑Put the rice with all the ingredients except the topping into the top of a double saucepan; the amount of rice depends on how thick you like a pudding to be.

Cook over a pan of steadily boiling water for about 1 hour, or until the rice is soft and the pudding has thickened. Stir several times during the cooking process. Do not cover the top of the double saucepan until the mixture starts to thicken, for the milk is more likely to boil over if covered at first.

Spoon the mixture into a flameproof dish, top with the almonds and then the sugar. Place under a preheated grill (broiler), set to low and heat for a few minutes or until the top is golden. Serve at once, but do remember that the sugar topping is very hot indeed. Serves 4.
Note You can use a bowl placed securely over a pan of water instead of a double saucepan.

The rice pudding can be cooked in a slow cooker. Allow 6 to 8 hours on LOW.

French Bread Pudding

15 g/½ oz (1 tablespoon) butter
175 g/6 oz brioche or bread, weight without crusts
4 large eggs
150 g/5 oz (½ cup plus 2 tablespoons) caster sugar
450 ml/¾ pint (2 cups) milk
FOR THE SAUCE:
6 to 8 tablespoons lemon curd or jam
2 tablespoons water

Spread the butter on the inside of an 18 cm/7 inch soufflé dish. Make the brioche or bread into very fine crumbs. Sprinkle about 2 tablespoons of the crumbs over the butter in the soufflé dish. Put the rest of the crumbs into a large bowl. Separate the eggs and beat the yolks with the sugar. Heat the milk and whisk into the eggs and sugar, then add to the crumbs in the bowl. Allow to stand for 15 minutes, then beat briskly to soften the crumbs and make a smooth mixture. Whisk the egg whites until stiff; fold into the other ingredients. Spoon into the prepared soufflé dish and stand this in a pan of cold water (a *bain-marie*). Bake in the centre of a preheated moderate oven (160°C/325°F, Gas Mark 3) for 35 to 40 minutes or until well risen and firm. Serve at once with hot lemon curd or hot jam sauce (see Note). Serves 4.
Note To heat the lemon curd, put it into a bowl with the water and heat over hot but not boiling water. The jam can be heated with the water in an ordinary saucepan or covered and heated in a microwave oven.

Special Technique
BRÛLÉE TOPPING

It is easy to turn a simple dessert into a rather special one with a topping of 'burnt sugar'. Custards and cream puddings are particularly successful when treated to this crunchy topping.

Prepare the recipe that is to be topped and place it in a serving dish. It is usual to chill the dish at this stage.

Sprinkle an even layer of sugar over the dish and place under a preheated grill (broiler). Cook until the sugar turns a golden brown. Serve warm or chilled.
Note Any dish that is to be placed under a grill (broiler) must be flameproof, ovenproof dishes are not suitable.

Melon Crème Brûlée

Melon Crème Brûlée

150 to 300 ml/¼ to ½ pint (⅔ to 1¼ cups) whipping or double (heavy) cream
1 large or 2 small Ogen (Cantaloupe) melons
white sugar to taste
FOR THE DECORATION AND COATING:
demerara (brown) sugar
frosted grapes, see right

Whisk the cream until stiff. Remove the pulp from the melon and blend until smooth. Fold in the whipped cream with a little sugar to taste. Spoon the mixture into a flameproof dish and chill well. Top with a thick and even layer of demerara sugar and place under a preheated grill (broiler) until golden. Serve warm or well chilled, topped with frosted grapes. Serve 4 to 6.
VARIATIONS
Apple Brûlée Cook apples until a soft purée, sweeten slightly, but keep it fairly sharp to make a pleasing contrast to the topping. Mix a little ground cinnamon and chopped blanched almonds, chopped walnuts, raisins or sultanas (golden raisins) with the fruit. Spoon into a flameproof dish and chill well. Top with a thick layer of blanched flaked almonds or rather coarsely chopped walnuts and then a layer of sifted icing sugar. Heat gently under a preheated grill (broiler) until the topping is delicately brown.
Banana Brûlée Mash 6 large ripe bananas with 1 tablespoon lemon juice. Whip 150 ml/¼ pint double (⅔ cup heavy) cream and blend with the banana pulp. Sweeten slightly, proceed as Melon Crème Brûlée.

FREEZING NOTE
Rice Cream Brûlée freezes well, particularly if double (heavy) cream is used.

Use within 6 weeks. The other desserts are better freshly made.

SIMPLE SKILL
To Frost Grapes *Brush the grapes with a little lightly whisked egg white and dust with sifted icing (confectioners') sugar. Leave on a wire rack until quite dry.*

119

Hot Soufflés

Hot soufflés make delicious puddings. The timing given in each recipe on this page assumes the mixture is baked in a traditional soufflé dish.

Sweet soufflés can also be baked in shallow dishes for about two-thirds of the cooking time; this makes them easier to serve. The soufflé mixture can be prepared in advance (see page 131).

Vanilla Soufflé

Chop the almonds very finely and place on a flat dish or baking sheet. Place under a preheated grill (broiler) and heat until dark brown, but do not allow to burn.

Separate the eggs. Blend the yolks with the cream and stir into the cooked rice with the almonds.

Whisk the egg whites until stiff and fold into the other ingredients. Spoon into a greased 18 cm/7 inch soufflé dish and bake in the centre of a preheated moderate oven (160 to 180°C/325 to 350°F, Gas Mark 3 to 4) for 30 to 35 minutes or until well risen and firm. Serve at once with Marmalade Sauce, page 198. Serves 4.

Stir in the flour and cook gently for several minutes. Gradually stir in the milk and cream. Bring the sauce slowly to the boil, stirring all the time, and cook to a coating consistency. Remove the pan from the heat and add the sugar, the remainder of the brandy and the egg yolks. Whisk the egg whites until stiff, then fold into the soft brandy mixture. Spoon over the biscuits (lady fingers). Bake in the centre of a preheated moderate to moderately hot oven (180 to 190°C/350 to 375°F, Gas Mark 4 to 5) for 40 minutes or until well risen and golden. Serve at once. Serves 6.

VARIATIONS

The amount of liquid in the recipe above gives a soufflé that is very soft in texture with a definite liquid centre. For a firm texture, use only 150 ml/¼ pint (⅔ cup) milk or single (light) cream and bake for 30 to 35 minutes.

Use a mixture of candied fruits in place of glacé cherries.

Chocolate Brandy Soufflé Melt 50 g/2 oz (2 squares) plain (semi-sweet) chocolate in the milk.

Soufflé Italienne

1 tablespoon custard powder (Bird's English dessert mix) or cornflour (cornstarch)
150 ml/¼ pint (⅔ cup) milk
6 tablespoons double (heavy) cream
50 g/2 oz (¼ cup) caster sugar
50 g/2 oz (½ cup) ground almonds
50 g/2 oz (¼ cup) glacé cherries
3 egg yolks
4 egg whites
FOR THE TOPPING:
25 g/1 oz (¼ cup) icing (confectioners') sugar

Combine the custard powder (dessert mix) or cornflour (cornstarch) with the milk and cream in a large saucepan. Stir over a low heat until it becomes a smooth and thick sauce. Add the sugar and ground almonds. Chop the cherries and mix with the sauce, then remove from the heat.

Beat the egg yolks into the hot mixture. Whisk the egg whites until just stiff, then fold into the other ingredients. Spoon into a buttered 15 to 18 cm/6 to 7 inch soufflé dish and bake in the centre of a preheated moderately hot oven (190°C/375°F, Gas Mark 5) for 30 minutes or until well risen and golden.

Sift the icing (confectioners') sugar over the top and serve at once. Serves 4.

VARIATION

Vanilla Soufflé Omit the ground almonds and cherries from the above recipe. Flavour the hot custard mixture with the sugar and a few drops of vanilla essence (extract). Proceed as above sprinkling the unbaked soufflé with a few flaked almonds if liked. Serve with fruit.

FOR FLAVOUR
Making Vanilla Sugar
Vanilla pods (beans) may seem expensive, but they provide a very true vanilla flavour and they can be used for a long period.

To flavour sugar with vanilla, cut a pod (bean) in half or several pieces and put into a jar of caster sugar. Cover tightly. When a recipe gives sugar and vanilla in the list of ingredients, use some of the vanilla-flavoured sugar. Fill up the jar as you use the sugar. Keep the pod (bean) until all smell (and therefore flavour) has disappeared.

Almond Rice Soufflé

40 g/1½ oz (3 tablespoons) short-grain rice
450 ml/¾ pint (2 cups) milk
¼ teaspoon vanilla essence or 1 vanilla pod (bean)
50 g/2 oz (¼ cup) caster sugar
25 g/1 oz (2 tablespoons) butter
50 g/2 oz (½ cup) blanched almonds
4 eggs
3 tablespoons double (heavy) cream

Put the rice with the milk, vanilla essence or vanilla pod (bean), sugar and butter into the top of a double saucepan or bowl and cook over a pan of boiling water for 1 hour or until the rice has swelled and the mixture is thick.

Remove the vanilla pod (bean), if using, rinse in cold water and dry on kitchen paper. It can then be used again.

Brandy Soufflé

8 to 9 sponge finger biscuits (lady fingers)
6 tablespoons brandy
100 g/4 oz (½ cup) glacé cherries
25 g/1 oz (2 tablespoons) butter
25 g/1 oz (¼ cup) flour
150 ml/¼ pint (⅔ cup) milk
150 ml/¼ pint (⅔ cup) single (light) cream
50 g/2 oz (¼ cup) caster sugar
3 egg yolks
4 egg whites

Arrange the sponge finger biscuits (lady fingers) in the bottom of an 18 cm/7 inch soufflé dish. Sprinkle on 3 tablespoons of the brandy. Halve or chop the cherries and scatter over the finger biscuits (lady fingers).

Heat the butter in a large saucepan.

Pancakes

Pancakes (crêpes) can be used for a variety of desserts. They can be rolled, folded or stacked, and served with fresh or poached fruit, cream or ice cream.

To Cook Pancakes

Heat a little oil or fat in a small frying pan (skillet) or omelette pan. Whisk the batter immediately before cooking (the flour tends to settle at the bottom of the mixture).

Spoon or pour sufficient batter into the pan to give a paper-thin layer. Cook for 1 to 2 minutes then turn or toss the pancake and cook on the second side. Remove from the pan. Keep hot on a flat plate over a pan of hot water or in a cool oven.

Continue cooking the pancakes. If the pan is well-seasoned you should not need any more oil or fat. The Basic Pancake Batter makes about 12 small pancakes, enough for 4 to 6 portions.

Basic Pancake Batter

100 g/4 oz (1 cup) plain (all-purpose) flour
pinch of salt
1 egg
250 ml/8 fl oz (1 cup) milk or milk and water

Sift the flour and salt into a bowl. Make a well in the centre and add the egg and the milk or milk and water. Gradually incorporate the flour into the egg and milk, beating well until a smooth batter forms.

VARIATIONS

For a richer batter use 2 eggs but reduce the amount of milk by 2 tablespoons.

The pancakes can be flavoured by adding a little almond or vanilla essence (extract), mixed spice (ground allspice) or ground cinnamon to the batter.

⁂Lemon or Orange Pancakes Add 1 to 2 teaspoons finely grated lemon rind to the flour and use a little lemon or orange juice as part of the liquid in the batter.

Surprise Pancakes

8 Pancakes
FOR THE CARAMEL SAUCE: 100 g/4 oz (½ cup) caster or granulated sugar
4 tablespoons water
150 ml/¼ pint (⅔ cup) orange juice
FOR THE FILLING: 8 tablespoons apricot jam
8 tablespoons firm ice cream

Make the pancakes and keep them hot. Put the sugar and water into a heavy-based saucepan, stir until the sugar has dissolved, then allow the syrup to boil steadily until it becomes a golden brown caramel. Add the orange juice, heat until combined, then keep warm.

Spread each pancake with jam and top with a tablespoon of ice cream. Fold or roll and serve at once with the sauce. Serves 4.

Citrus Pancakes

8 Lemon Pancakes
FOR THE FILLING: 50 g/2 oz (¼ cup) butter
50 g/2 oz (¼ cup) demerara (brown) sugar
1 teaspoon grated lemon rind
1 teaspoon grated orange rind
1 tablespoon lemon juice
2 tablespoons orange juice
TO DECORATE: lemon and orange slices

⁂Make the lemon-flavoured pancakes and keep hot. Cream together the butter, sugar and grated fruit rinds then gradually beat in the fruit juices. Spread each pancake with a little butter mixture and fold into 4. Decorate with the fruit slices. Serves 4.

VARIATIONS

Citrus Pancakes Flambés Prepare the pancakes and the filling as above. Allow the pancakes to become quite cold, then fill with the fruit mixture and fold. Heat 50 g/2 oz (4 tablespoons) butter and 50 g/2 oz (¼ cup) caster sugar in a heavy-based frying pan (skillet), stir until the sugar has dissolved, then heat until the mixture is a pale golden caramel. Add 2 tablespoons lemon juice and 6 tablespoons orange juice, heat for 2 to 3 minutes, add the pancakes and warm thoroughly over a gentle heat.

Finally ignite 2 tablespoons brandy (see page 201), add to the sauce and serve. This is rather an interesting version of Crêpes Suzettes. Serves 4.

Spiced Apple Pancakes Add ½ to 1 teaspoon allspice and a pinch of grated nutmeg to the Lemon Pancake Batter; cook as above. Meanwhile peel and slice 3 to 4 dessert apples, (these will keep better shape than cooking (tart) apples). Using a frying pan (skillet) heat the amount of butter and sugar given in the basic recipe. Turn the apple slices in this mixture; add the rinds and juice as in the basic recipe. Simmer for a few minutes. Use as a filling for the pancakes.

Spiced Peach Pancakes Follow the recipe for Spiced Apple Pancakes using 3 to 4 ripe peaches.

FOR EASE

Seasoning a pan for Pancakes
Sprinkle a new pan with a good layer of salt, heat very gently, then tip out the excess salt and rub the pan with a little oil or pure lard. Leave the pan slightly greasy on the inside before using for the first time.

Try not to wash the inside of the pan after use. Wipe out with absorbent kitchen paper.

FREEZING NOTE
Pancakes freeze well, particularly if 1 tablespoon oil or melted butter is beaten into the batter just before frying.

Stack the cooked pancakes, separating each pancake with greased greaseproof (waxed) paper, then freeze. Wrap when frozen.

Citrus Pancakes Flambés

Apple Meringue Pie

Flans and Pies

Good pies, flans and tarts are favourites in most families. Here are a number of new ideas that are both easy and interesting (see also pages 144 to 149).

Apple Meringue Pie

This dessert can be served hot or cold. If you intend it to be a hot dessert, keep the flan warm while cooking the apples.

1 × 23 to 24 cm/9 to 9½ inch flan (pie shell) made with shortcrust (basic pie dough) or any other suitable pastry, see page 144

FOR THE FILLING:
25 g/1 oz (2 tablespoons) butter

1 teaspoon grated lemon rind

1 tablespoon lemon juice

675 g/1½ lb cooking (tart) apples, weight when peeled and cored

100 g/4 oz (½ cup) unrefined granulated sugar

FOR THE MERINGUE:
4 egg whites

100 g/4 oz (½ cup) unrefined granulated sugar

Melt the butter in a saucepan and add the lemon rind and juice. Thinly slice the peeled apples into the pan. Add the sugar and stir until it has dissolved. Cook gently until a smooth thick pulp forms, stirring from time to time. You can put the apples through a sieve or purée in a blender, but this should not

be necessary with a good cooking apple. Put the hot apple pulp into the hot pastry case (pie shell) and smooth flat.

Whisk the egg whites until stiff. Gradually whisk in half the sugar, then fold in the remainder. Spoon or pipe this meringue over the top of the apple mixture and bake in the centre of a preheated moderate oven (160°C/325°F, Gas Mark 3) for about 20 minutes. Serve at once. Serves 6 to 8.

VARIATION
If serving cold, follow the recipe above, but make sure the pastry is completely cold before adding the filling; the pastry flan (pie shell) should be lightly baked in this case since it has to be baked again in the centre of a preheated very cool oven (120°C/250°F, Gas Mark ½) for at least 1 hour to set the meringue. Use 225 g/8 oz (1 cup) sugar.

Blackberry and Apple Shortbread

FOR THE SHORTBREAD:
50 g/2 oz (½ cup) flaked blanched almonds

50 g/2 oz (¼ cup) butter

25 g/1 oz (2 tablespoons) caster sugar

75 g/3 oz (¾ cup) plain (all-purpose) flour

FOR THE TOPPING:
1 × 383 g/13½ oz can blackberry and apple pie filling

⁂Toast the almonds under the grill

(broiler) or in the oven and allow to cool. Put 25 g/1 oz (¼ cup) on one side to decorate the shortcake.

Cream together the butter and sugar. Add 25 g/1 oz (¼ cup) browned flaked almonds and the flour. Knead well to make a firm dough and form into an 18 cm/7 inch round on a flat baking sheet. Flute the edges to make the shortbread into a flan shape.

Bake in the centre of a preheated moderate oven (180 to 190°C/350 to 375°F, Gas Mark 4 to 5) for 10 to 15 minutes until firm and golden in colour. Cool before removing from the baking sheet, then lift on to a serving plate.

Top with the pie filling and the remainder of the browned almonds. Serves 4.

Raspberry and Orange Cheese Flan

FOR THE ORANGE PASTRY:
175 g/6 oz (1½ cups) plain (all-purpose) flour
pinch of salt
75 g/3 oz (6 tablespoons) butter or margarine
50 g/2 oz (¼ cup) caster sugar
2 teaspoons grated orange rind
water to bind
FOR THE FILLING AND DECORATION:
225 g/8 oz (1½ cups) raspberries
75 g/3 oz Lancashire cheese
3 eggs
100 g/4 oz (½ cup) caster sugar
175 ml/6 fl oz (¾ cup) orange juice
150 ml/¼ pint (⅔ cup) double (heavy) cream

⁂Sift the flour and salt into a bowl; rub in (cut in) the butter or margarine. Add the sugar, the orange rind and water to make a firm rolling consistency and roll out very thinly. Line a 25 cm/10 inch flan dish (pie pan) or flan ring on an upturned baking sheet.

Put a few raspberries on one side for decoration and put the remainder into the uncooked pastry case (pie shell). Crumble the cheese over the top of the fruit.

Beat the eggs, sugar and orange juice together and strain over the fruit and cheese. Bake in the centre of a preheated moderately hot oven (190°C/375°F, Gas Mark 5) for 25 minutes; then reduce the setting slightly to moderate (160 to 180°C/325 to 350°F, Gas Mark 3 to 4) and bake for a further 15 minutes or until the filling is firm. If using a flan ring allow the flan to cool a little before transferring to a serving plate. Allow to cool.

When the flan is quite cold whip the cream until it holds its shape. Pipe a border around the edge of the flan. Decorate with the remaining raspberries. Serves 6.

FREEZING NOTE
Apple Meringue Pie
This is better freshly made although the flan case (pie shell) and the apple filling could be frozen separately and put together when thawed.
Blackberry and Apple Shortbread Freeze the shortbread without the topping and top with the fruit mixture just before serving.

FOR FLAVOUR
Unrefined granulated sugar is used in the recipe for Apple Meringue Pie. It is golden in colour and gives the pudding a pleasing colour as well as an interesting flavour.

Baked Sponge Desserts

The fruit used in these recipes can be varied according to season. (See page 124 for information on cooking sponge puddings in a microwave cooker, a pressure cooker or slow-cooker.)

Special Technique
ONE-STAGE MIXTURES

These two sponge pudding mixtures are made by the one-stage method. All the ingredients are combined at the same time, rather than by the usual method of creaming the fat and sugar, then adding the eggs and flour.

In Orange Topsy Turvy, extra baking powder is added to lighten the mixture. This is not done in Lemon Pear Upside Down Cake, as a slightly heavier mixture supports the weight of the fruit better.

Soft margarine can be used straight from the refrigerator. Butter or hard margarine should be left at room temperature to soften before use.

A one-stage mixture is never quite as light as a sponge or cake made by the conventional method, but it is practical.

Lemon Pear Upside Down Cake

FOR THE BASE:
50 g/2 oz (¼ cup) butter
3 tablespoons light brown sugar
1 tablespoon lemon juice
6 canned pear halves
6 glacé cherries
FOR THE CAKE:
175 g/6 oz (1½ cups) self-raising flour, see Note
100 g/4 oz (½ cup) soft margarine
100 g/4 oz (½ cup) caster sugar
2 large eggs
2 tablespoons lemon juice

⁑Soften the butter for the base of the cake and blend in the sugar and lemon juice. Grease the sides of a 23 to 25 cm/9 to 10 inch cake tin (pan) or soufflé dish. Do not use a pan with a loose base. Spread the butter mixture over the base. Arrange the pears and cherries on the butter mixture, with the cut side of the pears upwards.

Sift the flour into a mixing bowl, add to the other ingredients for the cake and beat together until well mixed. (See Special Technique). Spoon this mixture over the base taking care not to dislodge the fruit. Bake in the centre of a pre-heated moderate oven (180°C/350°F, Gas Mark 4) for 45 minutes or until firm to the touch. Turn out on to a serving plate. Serve hot or cold with cream, ice cream or Marmalade Sauce, (see page 198). Serves 6.

Note Use plain (all-purpose) flour instead of self-raising but add 1½ teaspoons baking powder.

Orange Topsy Turvy

FOR THE ONE-STAGE SPONGE:
110 g/4 oz (1 cup) self-raising flour with 1 teaspoon baking powder
110 g/4 oz (½ cup) soft margarine
110 g/4 oz (½ cup) caster sugar
2 large eggs
FOR THE TOPPING:
4 tablespoons jelly-type marmalade
2 oranges

⁑Sift the flour and baking powder into a mixing bowl and add the other ingredients for the sponge. Beat by hand for 2 to 3 minutes until smooth and light. If using an electric mixer, switch on for 1 minute only; if using a food processor, allow approximately 25 to 30 seconds.

Line the bottom of a 20 cm/8 inch square cake tin (pan) with greaseproof (waxed) paper, grease this and grease and flour the sides of the pan. Spread the marmalade over the paper on the bottom of the pan.

Cut away the peel from the oranges and cut out the segments of fruit (see page 98). Arrange the orange slices over the marmalade; spoon the sponge mixture over the fruit and bake in the centre of a preheated moderate to moderately hot oven (180 to 190°C/350 to 375°F, Gas Mark 4 to 5) for 35 to 40 minutes.

Turn out on to a serving plate and remove the paper. Serves 4 to 6.

Note Use plain (all-purpose) flour instead of self-raising but add 2 teaspoons baking powder instead of 1 teaspoon.

Orange Crumble Tart

Flan Pastry made with 175 g/6 oz (1½ cups) flour etc., see page 146
FOR THE FILLING:
4 tablespoons orange marmalade
1 teaspoon grated orange rind
75 g/3 oz (6 tablespoons) butter or margarine
75 g/3 oz (6 tablespoons) caster sugar
1 egg
1 tablespoon orange juice
75 g/3 oz (¾ cup) self-raising flour, see Note
75 g/3 oz (1½ cups) soft fine breadcrumbs
1 egg white
FOR THE DECORATION:
175 g/6 oz icing sugar (1⅓ cups confectioners' sugar)
1½ tablespoons orange juice

⁑Roll out the pastry and line a 23 cm/9 inch flan dish or tin (layer cake pan). Spread half the marmalade over the pastry. Put the remaining marmalade, grated orange rind, butter or margarine and sugar into a mixing bowl and cream until soft and light. Separate the egg. Beat the yolk and orange juice into the creamed mixture. Sift the flour. Stir, together with the breadcrumbs, into the other ingredients. Whisk the 2 egg whites until stiff, fold into the ingredients then spoon into the pastry case.

Bake in the centre of a preheated moderately hot oven (190 to 200°C/375 to 400°F, Gas Mark 5 to 6) for 20 minutes to set the pastry, then lower the heat to moderate (160°C/325°F, Gas Mark 3) for a further 15 to 20 minutes, or until both pastry and filling are firm. Allow to cool.

Sift the icing sugar into a bowl and blend with the orange juice. Spread over the filling and allow to set. Serves 4.

Note Plain (all-purpose) flour can be used for the filling but add ¾ teaspoon baking powder.

LEFTOVERS
Upside Down Cakes are equally good hot or cold so they are extremely good for tea as well as puddings. This makes them practical for a small family.

Orange Topsy Turvy

Steamed Puddings

Watch the family's pleasure when you produce a feather-light steamed pudding. As the name suggests, a steamed pudding is generally cooked in a steamer which stands over a pan of boiling or simmering water. Alternatively the pudding can stand in the saucepan of water (see Special Technique).

Oven Steaming

It is necessary to top up the saucepan with boiling water at regular intervals during the steaming period to prevent the pan from boiling dry. It is easy to forget to do this. However, it is possible to steam in the oven for much of the cooking process and then you do not have to worry about the pan boiling dry. Cook the pudding in a steamer or saucepan for at least 30 minutes (see Special Technique). Meanwhile, preheat the oven to moderate (180°C/350°F, Gas Mark 4). Using the deepest casserole you have, add enough boiling water to come three-quarters of the way up the basin (pudding mold). Transfer the pudding from the steamer or saucepan to the casserole. Put a lid or large sheet of foil over both the basin (pudding mold) and casserole so that the pudding continues to steam; secure firmly. This prevents the water from evaporating during the cooking period. Place the casserole in the centre of the oven and continue cooking for the rest of the period given in the recipe.

A pudding based on an egg custard should be placed in water that is simmering only and cooked in a preheated cool oven, (140 to 150°C/275 to 300°F, Gas Mark 1 to 2).

Steamed puddings can be cooked in a microwave or pressure cooker, or in an electric slow-cooker. Always check on the timing and setting recommended by the manufacturer of your particular model, but as a guide these are points to remember.

Microwave Cooking

Allow plenty of space in the basin (pudding mold) for the pudding to rise: Mixtures tend to rise more drastically in a microwave cooker than in a steamer. Timings vary but as a guide, the Cherry and Almond Pudding would need about 7 to 9 minutes on a HIGH setting.

Pressure Cooking

Before putting on the pressure weight, any puddings containing a raising agent, such as the Cherry and Almond Pudding, should be steamed first without pressure. Use the pressure cooker as an ordinary pan for this initial stage.

Pour at least 600 ml/1 pint (2½ cups) boiling water into the cooker. Stand the pudding on the trivet, put on the lid and steam, without the weight, for 15 minutes. Put on the LOW/5 lb weight and pressure cook for 25 minutes. Allow the pressure to drop at room temperature.

Slow-Cooking

Preheat the slow-cooker on HIGH for 15 minutes. Put the pudding basin (mold) into the cooker with enough boiling water to come half-way up the basin (mold). Put on the lid. The Cherry and Almond Pudding needs 5 to 6 hours on the HIGH setting.

Special Technique
A PERFECT STEAMED PUDDING

Remember these points when steaming a savoury or sweet pudding:

☐ Cover the top of the pudding well so that it does not become too damp. You can use greased foil only, but I prefer a layer of greased greaseproof (waxed) paper and then foil.

☐ Most pudding mixtures rise during cooking, so make a pleat in both the greaseproof (waxed) paper and the foil, (see Fig 1).

☐ It is quite difficult to remove a hot basin (pudding mold) from a steamer or a saucepan, so make a band of double or treble thickness foil. Stand the basin (mold) on this band making sure the ends are long enough to enable you to lift the pudding from the pan by holding the two ends of the foil (see Fig 2).

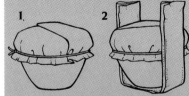

☐ If the pudding mixture contains a raising agent, the water must be boiling when you add the pudding and it should be allowed to boil very briskly for the first one-third of the cooking time. After this it can boil steadily. Top up the saucepan with boiling water during cooking.

If the pudding is based on an egg custard the water must not boil, it should just simmer.

☐ If you do not possess a steamer, stand the basin (pudding mold) on an upturned saucer or old patty tin (tartlet pan) in a saucepan of water. Make sure the water comes only half to three quarters of the way up the basin.

Cherry and Almond Pudding

110 g/4 oz (½ cup) butter or margarine
110 g/4 oz (½ cup) caster sugar
few drops of almond essence (extract)
2 eggs
110 g/4 oz (1 cup) self-raising flour, see Note
1 × 225 g/8 oz can red cherries
FOR THE SAUCE:
4 tablespoons cherry or raspberry jam
syrup from can of cherries
2 teaspoons arrowroot or cornflour (cornstarch)

Cream together the butter or margarine, sugar and essence (extract) until soft and light. Gradually beat in the eggs. Sift the flour and fold into the creamed mixture. Drain, halve and stone (pit) the cherries.

Add the cherries to the sponge mixture. Spoon into a greased 900 ml/1½ pint (5 to 6 cup) basin (pudding mold), cover with greased foil or greaseproof (waxed) paper and steam for 1¼ to 1½ hours. Turn out and serve with the sauce.

For the sauce Sieve the jam. Blend the syrup from the cherries with the arrowroot or cornflour (cornstarch). Pour into a saucepan, add the jam and stir over a low heat until the sauce is thickened and smooth. Serves 4 to 6.

Note Plain (all-purpose) flour can be used instead of self-raising but add 1 teaspoon of baking powder.

VARIATIONS
Add 50 g/2 oz (½ cup) chopped blanched almonds to the sponge mixture.

Fruit-topped Pudding Omit the cherries and almond essence (extract) in the recipe above. Put several tablespoons thick fruit purée at the bottom of the basin (pudding mold). Top with the sponge mixture and cook as above.

Sweet Mousseline Sauce

Put 2 egg yolks and 50 g/2 oz (¼ cup) caster sugar into an ovenproof bowl on the top of a double saucepan. Stand over hot but not boiling water and whisk until thick and creamy; remove from the heat and gradually whisk in 2 tablespoons sherry or white wine and 4 tablespoons double (heavy) cream. Return to the heat and whisk again until a coating consistency. Serve warm over a steamed pudding. Serves 4 to 6.

Note A lighter sauce is made by folding 2 stiffly whisked egg whites into the above sauce after it has thickened. Stand over the hot water to keep warm, but do not continue cooking.

Cabinet Pudding

50 g/2 oz (¼ cup) butter
75 g/3 oz (½ cup) seedless raisins
150 g/5 oz sliced white bread, weight without crusts
1 teaspoon finely grated lemon rind
3 eggs
50 g/2 oz (¼ cup) caster sugar
300 ml/½ pint (1¼ cups) milk

✶✶Use nearly half the butter to coat the inside of a 900 ml to 1.2 litre/1½ to 2 pint (1 quart) pudding basin (pudding mold). Press all the raisins over the butter. Spread the remaining butter over the bread and cut into pieces to fit into the basin (mold). Sprinkle a little of the lemon rind over each layer of bread and butter.

Beat the eggs and sugar very well. Warm the milk and add to the eggs and pour the custard over the bread and butter mixture. Make sure the bread and butter is well covered with the liquid.

Cover the basin (mold) with greased greaseproof (waxed) paper and foil, then stand it in a steamer over a pan of simmering water (see opposite) and cook for 1 to 1¼ hours or until just firm to the touch. The water should not be allowed to boil during the cooking period as this pudding is based on an egg custard. Turn out and serve with Mousseline Sauce (left) or with hot Marmalade Sauce (page 198). Serves 4.

Brigade Pudding

FOR THE SUET CRUST PASTRY:
225 g/8 oz (2 cups) self-raising flour
pinch of salt
100 g/4 oz (scant 1 cup) shredded suet
water to mix
FOR THE FILLING:
2 tablespoons golden syrup (light corn syrup)
3 large cooking (tart) apples
225 g/8 oz (1 cup) mincemeat

✶✶Sift the flour and salt together. Add the suet and bind with water to a soft rolling consistency. Roll out very thinly. Cut into 4 rounds of varying sizes — one the size of the base of a 1.2 to 1.75 litre/2 to 3 pint (1 to 2 quart) basin (pudding mold), then one a little bigger, one a little larger still, and finally one almost as large as the top of the basin (mold). Grease the basin (mold) and coat with the syrup. Peel and coarsely grate the apples and blend with the mincemeat. Place the first round of pastry into the basin (mold); spread one-third of the mincemeat mixture on top, add the next round of pastry and half the remaining mixture; then the third pastry round and the rest of the mincemeat mixture. Top

with the final round of pastry. Cover the basin (mold) with greased paper and foil. Steam over boiling water for 2½ hours. Turn out and serve with cream or custard sauce. Serves 6.

Note Plain (all-purpose) flour can be used instead of self-raising but add 2 teaspoons baking powder.

VARIATIONS

Omit the syrup or sprinkle the basin (mold) with brown sugar.

Use butter or margarine instead of suet and rub into the flour.

Chocolate Raisin Puddings

2 tablespoons water
1 tablespoon cocoa powder (unsweetened cocoa)
110 g/4 oz (½ cup) butter or margarine
110 g/4 oz (½ cup) caster sugar
2 eggs
110 g/4 oz (1 cup) self-raising flour, see Note
50 g/2 oz (⅓ cup) seedless raisins

Heat the water, mix with the cocoa and allow to cool. Cream together the butter or margarine and sugar until soft and light. Gradually beat in the cocoa mixture and the eggs.

Sift the flour, and fold into the creamed ingredients together with the raisins.

Half-fill 12 greased dariole moulds. If steaming the puddings, cover each mould with greased pleated foil or greaseproof (waxed) paper and steam

for 20 to 25 minutes.

If baking the puddings, stand the moulds, uncovered, on a flat baking sheet and bake in the centre of a preheated moderately hot oven (190°C/375°F, Gas Mark 5) for 20 minutes.

Turn out and serve with Chocolate Sauce below. Serves 6.

Note Plain (all-purpose) flour can be used instead of self-raising flour but add 1 teaspoon baking powder.

Chocolate Sauce

50 g/2 oz (2 squares) plain (semi-sweet) chocolate
300 ml/½ pint (1¼ cups) milk
1 tablespoon cornflour (cornstarch)
a few drops of vanilla essence (extract)
15 g/½ oz (1 tablespoon) butter
25 g/1 oz (2 tablespoons) caster sugar

Grate the chocolate or cut it into small pieces. Pour most of the milk into a saucepan, add the chocolate and heat gently until the chocolate has melted.

In a bowl, mix the cornflour (cornstarch) with the remaining milk. Pour the chocolate-flavoured milk over the cornflour (cornstarch) mixture and stir well. Return to the saucepan with the vanilla essence (extract), butter and sugar and stir over a low heat until thickened and smooth. Serves 6.

VARIATION

Use 25 g/1 oz (¼ cup) cocoa powder (unsweetened cocoa) and 50 g/2 oz (¼ cup) sugar and omit the plain (semi-sweet) chocolate.

Cabinet Pudding, Cherry and Almond Pudding, and Brigade Pudding.

SIMPLE SKILL

Although Cabinet Pudding looks like an ordinary steamed pudding, it is really a steamed custard pudding so make absolutely certain the water in the steamer does not boil.

125

SAVOURY SNACKS

These light savoury dishes are ideal to serve as snacks, suppers or light lunches. You will find a selection of dishes made using eggs, cheese, rice and pasta; ingredients which enable the busy cook to make interesting and nutritious dishes quickly and easily.

Good Cooking

The four basic foods – eggs, cheese, rice and pasta – used in the dishes in this section are very different in flavour and texture, but they have one thing in common – they are spoiled by overcooking. Eggs become unappetizingly hard, cheese tough and stringy, rice and pasta too soft and flavourless.

Buying Points

Both rice and pasta are ideal storecupboard foods which can be used in many different ways. They are also valuable foods in that they eke out more expensive seasonal and protein-rich foods. Always keep packets of rice and pasta in the cupboard and try brown rice or wholewheat pasta which are both high in valuable dietary fibre.

Eggs are an indispensable food and can be served in so many different ways. Eggs come in various sizes and smaller ones are often quite adequate for a recipe (particularly when being used to coat food).

There is an almost bewildering selection of cheese available in shops, so make a point of trying some of the lesser-known varieties.

Store cheese carefully as it is too expensive to wàste. While the refrigerator is too cold to be an ideal storage place, it does prevent cheese from becoming over-ripe too quickly. Take the cheese out of the refrigerator an hour before you intend serving it to allow it to develop a good flavour.

EGGS

Microwave Cooking

Eggs can be baked *en cocotte* or poached in the microwave cooker. It is advisable to prick the yolks with a fine needle to pierce the membrane before cooking the eggs to prevent the yolks from exploding.

Eggs can be scrambled in a bowl in the microwave cooker to make them particularly creamy.

Never try to boil an egg in its shell in a microwave cooker.

Eggs en Cocotte

Allow 1 to 2 eggs per person. Break the egg(s) into buttered individual ovenproof dishes then top them with seasoning, a little cream and/or melted butter and bake them towards the top of a preheated moderately hot oven (190 to 200°C/375 to 400°F, Gas Mark 5 to 6) for about 10 minutes or until set to personal taste. The eggs may be eaten with a teaspoon as a light snack or hors d'oeuvre. Eggs en Cocotte can be flavoured in many ways.

Eggs Cuban Style Put a little crabmeat in each dish, top with seasoned cream, the egg(s), more cream and chopped parsley. Bake as above.

Eggs Florence Style Mix a little sieved well-seasoned cooked spinach with cream. Put a layer at the bottom of each dish. Top with the egg(s), a little seasoning and grated cheese. Bake as above.

Eggs Josephine Put a layer of sliced fried mushrooms into each dish. Top with the egg(s), then either a layer of Cheese Sauce, (see page 102) or cream and grated cheese. Bake as above.

Eggs Portuguese Style Put a layer of well-seasoned, thick fresh tomato purée in each dish. Top with the egg(s) and more tomato purée. Bake as above.

Eggs Rossini Put a layer of pâté into each dish, top with the egg(s) then a spoonful of fresh tomato purée. Bake as above.

Eggs Soubise Put a layer of well-seasoned cooked chopped onions into each dish. Top with a spoonful of cream then the egg(s). Spoon a little more cream over the eggs. Top with grated cheese. Bake as above.

Boiled Eggs

Boiled eggs are not only a good breakfast dish, but they can be the basis of a wide variety of hot and cold dishes. Cook the eggs as desired, remove from the pan. Tap the eggs gently to crack the shells and put into cold water for a short time, then remove the shells.

With Soft-boiled (Soft-cooked) Eggs

Eggs Dauphine Style Coat the shelled eggs in seasoned flour, then in beaten egg and crisp breadcrumbs. Fry for 1 to 2 minutes. Serve with Tomato Sauce.

<u>Eggs Milanaise Style</u> Serve the shelled eggs on cooked spaghetti. Top with Cheese Sauce (see page 102).

With Hard-boiled (Hard-cooked) Eggs

<u>Eggs Cecilia</u> Cut each egg in half. Remove the yolks, blend with finely chopped fried mushrooms, put back into the whites. Coat with Cheese Sauce (see page 102) grated cheese and fine bread-crumbs. Heat under the grill (broiler).

<u>Eggs Lucullus</u> Cut each egg in half. Remove the yolks, blend with pâté, put back into the whites. Press the two halves together. Coat in seasoned flour, then in beaten egg and crisp bread-crumbs. Fry for 1 to 2 minutes.

Omelettes

There are three types of omelette.

<u>Plain Omelette</u> Often called a French omelette, this is made by beating eggs with a little seasoning and cooking them in hot butter in a pan. To give a lighter result you can add a little cold water to the egg – 1 tablespoon to 2 or 3 eggs.

Do not overbeat the eggs, simply beat to mix the yolks and whites. Cook and fold (see Seafood Omelette).

This type of omelette can be varied in many ways. It can be filled with grated cheese, or with fish, meat or vegetables in a hot sauce. Chopped herbs, grated cheese, fried mushrooms, diced fried bacon or cooked ham can be added to the eggs before cooking.

<u>Soufflé Omelette</u> This is made by separating the eggs. The egg yolks are beaten with seasoning (or a little sugar in the case of a sweet omelette) and a small amount of water, milk or cream. The egg whites are whisked until stiff and folded into the yolk mixture just before cooking (see page 130).

Soufflé omelettes make delicious puddings when filled with fruit or jam. They also provide impressive savoury dishes. Choose moist fillings to counter-act the light, dry texture of the omelette.

<u>Spanish Omelette</u> This can be lightly cooked, but generally it is fairly firm. This means it can be cut into pieces and served cold and is therefore ideal for packed meals.

Pepper Tortilla is typical of a flat Spanish omelette, (see page 130).

Left: Crisp Vegetable Pilaf, page 137
Top right: Cannelloni all Italiana, page 40
Bottom right: Hasty Pizza, page 135

Egg Dishes

Poached Eggs Italienne

175 g/6 oz spaghetti
Béchamel Sauce made with 300 ml/½ pint (1¼ cups) milk, see page 102
4 tablespoons single (light) cream
100 g/4 oz (½ cup) cooked ham or bacon
salt and pepper
4 eggs
2 bay leaves

Cook the spaghetti in boiling salted water (see page 139). Make the sauce and stir in the cream. Dice the ham or bacon and add to the sauce. Season well.

Poach the eggs. Drain the spaghetti and arrange on a flat dish, top with the sauce and ham, then the eggs and bay leaves. Serves 4.

Egg Curry

8 eggs
2 large onions
1 small dessert apple
2 medium tomatoes
50 g/2 oz (¼ cup) margarine
2 teaspoons curry powder
150 ml/¼ pint (⅔ cup) vegetable stock or water with ¼ teaspoon yeast extract
1 teaspoon lemon juice
salt and pepper
½ tablespoon chutney

Poached Eggs Italienne

Hard-boil (hard-cook) and shell the eggs. Cut into halves and put into an ovenproof serving dish with the cut side downwards. Peel and grate the onions and the apple, discarding the peel and apple core. Skin and finely chop the tomatoes.

Heat the margarine in a frying pan (skillet), add the grated onions, apple and tomatoes. Fry very slowly until tender then add the curry powder and cook for 2 to 3 minutes. Pour in the stock, or water with the yeast extract, together with the lemon juice, seasoning and chutney. Mix the ingredients together.

If serving the dish cold, pour the hot curry mixture over the eggs, leave until cold and serve with a rice salad.

If serving the dish hot, pour the hot curry mixture over the eggs and allow to stand for 15 to 30 minutes so the eggs absorb the curry flavour. Cover the dish and reheat in the centre of a preheated moderately hot oven (200°C/400°F, Gas Mark 6) or in a microwave cooker for a short time. Serve with cooked rice. Serves 4.

Poached Eggs
Poach eggs by putting them into a little hot butter or margarine in the cups of an egg poacher and cooking over boiling water. Alternatively, cook the eggs in steadily boiling salted water for 2 to 3 minutes until lightly set. It is possible to poach eggs in tomato purée, see Hunter's Eggs.

Avocados Fermont

FOR THE BÉARNAISE SAUCE:
3 tablespoons white wine vinegar
sprig of tarragon
2 egg yolks
50 g/2 oz (¼ cup) butter
¼ teaspoon chopped fresh tarragon or pinch of dried tarragon
½ teaspoon chopped chervil or parsley
salt and pepper
FOR THE AVOCADO BASE:
4 large tomatoes
4 eggs
2 large avocados

Put the vinegar and tarragon into a saucepan. Boil briskly until reduced to 1½ tablespoons only, then strain into a bowl or the top of a double saucepan. Add the egg yolks. Stand over a pan of hot but not boiling water and whisk until the mixture is thick and creamy. Gradually whisk in the butter (see page 105), then add the chopped herbs and a little seasoning. Keep warm. Skin and thinly slice the tomatoes. Poach the eggs. Halve and stone (pit) the avocados just before serving. Top each avocado half with a poached egg and a quarter of the sauce. Arrange the tomato slices around the avocados. Serves 4.

VARIATIONS
Sprinkle the avocado halves with a little seasoned oil and lemon juice and heat in a preheated moderately hot oven (200°C/400°F, Gas Mark 6) for 5 minutes, then top with the eggs and sauce.

Make the sauce in a blender or food processor (see page 105).
Pommes Fermont Top hot halved jacket potatoes, or Savoury Potato Cakes (see page 187), with the eggs and sauce. Make the Potato Cake mixture into 4 large cakes.

Hunters' Eggs

6 chicken livers
1 small onion
50 g/2 oz (¼ cup) butter
2 teaspoons flour
300 ml/½ pint (1¼ cups) tomato juice
3 tablespoons dry sherry
1 tablespoon chopped stuffed olives
1 tablespoon chopped parsley
salt and pepper
4 to 6 eggs
4 to 6 slices of bread
40 to 50 g/1½ to 2 oz (¼ cup) liver pâté, see page 24

Dice the livers, peel and grate the onion. Heat the butter in a large frying pan (skillet), add the livers and onion and fry for 5 minutes. Stir in the flour, then add the tomato juice, sherry, olives and parsley. Stir as the mixture comes just to boiling point, season well, then carefully

Aeggekage med Bacon,
(Danish Egg and
Bacon Cake)

break in the eggs and poach for about 3 minutes, or until set to personal taste.

Meanwhile toast the bread, spread with the pâté, top with the eggs and liver mixture. Serves 4 to 6.

VARIATIONS
Use 300 ml/½ pint (1¼ cups) tomato purée made by stewing or blending skinned fresh tomatoes, instead of tomato juice.

Prepare the liver mixture then add shelled soft-boiled (soft-cooked) or hard-boiled (hard-cooked) eggs instead of poached eggs. Proceed as in the recipe above.

Aeggekage med Bacon
[Danish Egg and Bacon Cake]

8 streaky bacon rashers (slices)
6 eggs
4 tablespoons milk
1 tablespoon flour
salt and pepper
15 g/½ oz (1 tablespoon) butter
TO GARNISH:
1 tablespoon chopped chives or parsley
8 tomato slices

Remove the bacon rinds, but do not discard them. Beat the eggs, milk, flour and seasoning together. Heat the bacon rinds in a frying pan (skillet) until the fat flows, then remove rinds from the pan. Add the butter to the pan and heat thoroughly. Pour in the egg mixture and cook over a moderately high heat until just set; lift the edges once or twice so that the liquid egg runs to the sides of the pan.

Meanwhile grill (broil) or fry the bacon. Serve the egg cake topped with bacon. Garnish with the chives or parsley and tomato. Serves 4.

Turban d'Oeufs

25 g/1 oz (2 tablespoons) butter
75 g/3 oz (½ cup) peeled prawns (shelled shrimp)
8 eggs
2 tablespoons single (light) cream
salt and pepper
pinch of cayenne pepper
FOR THE SAVOURY TOMATO SAUCE:
1 garlic clove
1 small onion
350 g/12 oz tomatoes
25 g/1 oz (2 tablespoons) butter
2 tablespoons tomato purée (paste)
1 tablespoon chopped parsley
2 tablespoons chopped chives
1 tablespoon dry sherry

Melt the butter and use just under half to brush the inside of a 600 ml/1 pint (3 cup) ovenproof ring mould. Chop the prawns (shrimp) and put into a bowl with the eggs, cream, the remaining butter, salt, pepper and cayenne pepper. Beat the mixture then carefully spoon it into the buttered mould.

Stand the mould in a *bain-marie* of cold water. Place a piece of buttered paper over the top of the mould. Bake in the centre of a preheated moderate oven, (180°C/350°F, Gas Mark 4) for 30 minutes or until just firm to the touch.
For the Sauce Make the sauce while the eggs are cooking. Peel the garlic and onion; crush the garlic and finely chop the onion. Skin and chop the tomatoes. Heat the butter for the sauce in a pan, add the vegetables and cook gently until a thick pulp is formed. Stir in the tomato purée (paste), parsley, chives and sherry. Season and simmer for a few minutes.

Remove the egg and shrimp ring from the oven and loosen from the sides of the mould. Turn out on to a heated serving dish and fill the centre with the sauce. Serves 6 as an hors d'oeuvre or 4 as a light main dish.

VARIATIONS
Use flaked crabmeat or diced lobster in place of prawns (shrimp) or chop 100 g/ 4 oz (1 cup) mushrooms, fry in 25 g/1 oz (2 tablespoons) butter until soft, cool and add to the beaten eggs.

LEFTOVERS
1 or 2 sardines, a few anchovy fillets, or a small amount of leftover ham, chicken or game are good fillings for stuffed eggs (see page 19). Serve hot.

Use instead of the mushrooms in Eggs Cecilia or the pâté in Eggs Lucullus (see page 127).

Stuffed hard-boiled (hard-cooked) eggs are excellent served cold in a salad.

129

Omelettes

Omelettes are usually cooked in a special omelette pan or frying pan (skillet) on top of the cooker. Careful attention is required as the eggs set. It is possible to cook the mixture in the oven, (see Oven Potato Omelette, below).

Seafood Omelette

25 g/1 oz smoked salmon
50 g/2 oz (⅓ cup) peeled prawns (shelled shrimp)
½ teaspoon chopped fennel leaves or parsley
4 eggs
2 tablespoons water
salt and pepper
40 g/1½ oz (3 tablespoons) butter

Chop the smoked salmon and prawns (shrimp). Blend the fish, herbs, eggs, water and a little salt and pepper.

Heat the butter in the omelette pan, pour in the egg mixture and cook for ½ to 1 minute until the eggs set in a thin film on the bottom of the mixture. Tilt the pan so that the liquid egg runs to the sides of the pan and loosen the omelette mixture from the sides of the pan.

This procedure (called working the omelette) allows the egg mixture to cook rapidly and produce a light and moist mixture.

Fold or roll the omelette away from the handle. Tip on to a heated dish and serve at once. Serves 2.

VARIATIONS
The recipe above produces a luxurious omelette. It can be made even better if topped with well seasoned cream and a sprinkling of grated Parmesan cheese, then placed for a few seconds under a preheated grill (broiler).

To economize, use flaked cooked cod or coley instead of smoked salmon and prawns (shrimp).

Soufflé Omelette Royale

100 g/4 oz cooked chicken
5 tablespoons double (heavy) cream
4 to 6 cooked or canned asparagus tips
salt and pepper
4 eggs
40 g/1½ oz (3 tablespoons) butter

Dice the chicken neatly, put into a pan with 3 tablespoons of the cream and the asparagus tips. Season lightly and heat gently.

Separate the eggs and beat the yolks

130

with the remaining 2 tablespoons cream. Whisk the egg whites until stiff then fold into the egg yolks and cream. Season well.

Heat the butter in an omelette pan. Spoon the fluffy egg mixture into the pan. Cook for about 1 minute then place the omelette pan under a preheated grill (broiler) set to moderate heat. Cook under the grill (broiler) until lightly set. The soufflé type of omelette is so thick and light that it is difficult to fold unless a light cut is made in the middle of the mix-ture. Spoon the chicken and asparagus mixture over the omelette, fold away from the handle and slide on to a heated dish. Serve at once. Serves 2.

Oven Potato Omelette

2 large cooked potatoes
2 canned red peppers
50 g/2 oz (¼ cup) butter or margarine
6 to 8 eggs
2 tablespoons single (light) cream or milk
salt and pepper
1 tablespoon chopped chives
1 tablespoon chopped parsley
1 teaspoon grated lemon rind

Cut the potatoes into slices and the peppers into small pieces.

Put the butter or margarine into a 20 to 23 cm/8 to 9 inch round ovenproof dish and heat towards the top of a preheated hot oven (220°C/425°F, Gas Mark 7) until melted. Add the potatoes and peppers and heat for another 5 minutes.

Beat the eggs with the remaining ingredients, pour over the potato and pepper mixture, return to the oven just above the centre.

Bake for 10 to 15 minutes, or until set to personal taste. Serves 4.

Pepper Tortilla

FOR THE PEPPER MIXTURE:
2 garlic cloves
2 medium onions
4 large tomatoes
2 small green peppers
1 small red pepper
2 tablespoons oil
salt and pepper

FOR THE OMELETTE:
6 to 8 eggs
2 tablespoons water
salt and pepper
50 g/2 oz (¼ cup) butter

Peel the garlic and onions and chop very finely. Skin and slice the tomatoes. Cut the flesh from the peppers into long thin strips, discarding the cores and seeds. Heat the oil in a small frying pan (skillet), add the vegetables and fry until just soft; do not overcook. Season well.

Beat the eggs with the water and seasoning. Heat the butter in a large omelette pan, pour in the eggs and cook rapidly until just set. Tilt the pan while cooking so that the liquid egg runs to the sides of the pan and sets quickly.

Do not fold the Pepper Tortilla. Serve it flat, topped with the pepper mixture. Serves 4.

Soufflés and Mousses

The fluffy texture of hot soufflés or cold mousses makes these dishes ideal for a light luncheon or supper. Mousses also make interesting hors d'oeuvre.

Special Technique

TO MAKE A SAVOURY SOUFFLÉ

Do not cook a soufflé too slowly, and never overcook it – it should be slightly moist and creamy in the centre.

There is a belief that soufflés must be baked as soon as they are mixed. This is not true. If the prepared mixture is put into the soufflé dish or ovenproof dish and completely covered with an inverted mixing bowl (to exclude all air), the mixture can stand for up to 1 hour before cooking. Serve the soufflé as soon as it is ready.

Cheese and Haddock Soufflé

100 g/4 oz cooked smoked haddock
50 g/2 oz Parmesan cheese
25 g/1 oz (2 tablespoons) butter
25 g/1 oz (¼ cup) flour
150 ml/¼ pint (⅔ cup) milk
3 tablespoons double (heavy) cream
2 egg yolks
4 egg whites
salt and pepper

Flake the fish and grate the cheese.

Heat the butter in a large saucepan, add the flour and stir over a low heat for 2 to 3 minutes. Add the milk and cream and stir as the sauce comes to the boil and thickens. Remove the pan from the heat and add the fish and cheese.

Beat the yolks into the fish and cheese mixture. Whisk the 4 egg whites until just stiff (they should not be as stiff as for meringues). Fold into the ingredients in the saucepan, together with a little salt and a good shake of pepper. Spoon into a greased 15 to 18 cm/6 to 7 inch soufflé dish.

Bake in the centre of a preheated moderate to moderately hot oven (180 to 190°C/350 to 375°F, Gas Mark 4 to 5) for 25 to 30 minutes or until well risen. Serves 4.

VARIATIONS

Chicken and Cheese Soufflé Use finely chopped chicken in place of fish.

Spinach and Cheese Soufflé Use 150 ml/¼ pint (⅔ cup) sieved spinach purée in place of the milk.

Herb Soufflé Omit the smoked haddock and add 1 tablespoon of a freshly chopped herb of your choice.

Danish Cheese Mousse

25 g/1 oz (¼ cup) blanched almonds
2 tablespoons water
7 g/¼ oz (1 envelope) gelatine
100 g/4 oz Danish Blue cheese
100 g/4 oz Samsoe cheese
300 ml/½ pint (1¼ cups) double (heavy) cream

¼ teaspoon mustard powder
a shake of pepper
2 egg whites
TO GARNISH:
2 tomatoes
watercress

✷✷Chop the almonds and toast them under a preheated grill (broiler) or on a flat tray in the oven. Make sure they do not become too dark in colour. Pour the water into a heatproof bowl. Sprinkle the gelatine on top then stand over a pan of hot water and leave until the gelatine melts. Allow to cool but not to become set.

Grate the cheeses as finely as possible. Whip the cream until it holds its shape, then blend with the cheese, gelatine liquid, mustard and pepper. Finally whisk the egg whites until stiff and fold into the other ingredients.

Either rinse a 600 ml/1 pint (3 cup) ring mould with cold water or brush with 2 to 3 drops of olive oil. Spoon in the mixture and chill until set. Turn out on to a serving plate. Slice the tomatoes and arrange around the dish. Break the watercress into sprigs and put it into the centre of the jellied ring. Serves 6 to 8.

Piquant Egg Mousse

6 eggs
3 tablespoons dry white wine
15 g/½ oz (2 envelopes) gelatine
few drops of soy or Tabasco (hot pepper) sauce
5 tablespoons yogurt
2 teaspoons finely chopped chives
2 teaspoons finely chopped parsley
2 teaspoons lemon juice
salt and pepper
150 ml/¼ pint (⅔ cup) double (heavy) cream
TO GARNISH:
finely chopped chives and parsley

Hard-boil (hard-cook) 4 of the eggs. Shell and finely chop them. Separate the remaining 2 eggs and beat the yolks in a bowl over a pan of hot water until thick and creamy. Remove from the heat. Put the wine into a second bowl, stand over the hot water, sprinkle the gelatine on top and allow to dissolve. Mix the egg yolks with the soy or Tabasco (hot pepper) sauce, yogurt, chopped hard-boiled (hard-cooked) eggs, herbs, lemon juice and seasoning. Leave until the mixture begins to stiffen. Whip the cream lightly and whisk the 2 egg whites until stiff. Fold the cream and egg whites into the egg mixture. Spoon into 4 individual dishes if serving for a light main course or 6 dishes for an hors d'oeuvre. Chill and when set, top with the herbs. Serves 4 to 6.

LEFTOVERS

Leftover cheese makes a delicious Cheese Mousse, (left) or Potted Cheese, (below).

Potted Cheese

To each 225 g/8 oz cheese allow 50 g/2 oz (¼ cup) butter, 1 tablespoon sherry or port wine, a little cayenne or ordinary pepper and a pinch of grated nutmeg.

Grate hard cheese very finely or crumble blue cheese or softer cheese. Cream with the other ingredients adding freshly chopped herbs such as chives, parsley, sage or basil, if liked. Pack into small containers. Cover with plastic wrap or foil, or cover with a layer of melted butter. Refrigerate. Serve with hot toast.

FOR EASE

An uncooked soufflé can stand for up to 1 hour if covered with a mixing bowl (see Special Technique).

Eggs en Cocotte (page 126), Garlic Omelette and Herb Soufflé

131

CHEESE

A great many cheeses can be used in cooking, ranging from the well known hard cheeses, such as Cheddar, Gruyère, Emmenthal, Gouda and Edam to blue cheeses, like Stilton, Danish Blue and Roquefort. The readily available creamy cheeses Camembert and Brie are excellent for frying (see below).

Cheese is a highly nutritious food and throughout this book you will find recipes in which cheese is used to add flavour and food value to a variety of dishes.

Below: Fried Cheese with Cranberry Sauce and Apple Sauce
Below right: Cheese and Vegetable Bake

LEFTOVERS
Grate hard cheese and store in a covered container in the refrigerator or freezer. Use to sprinkle over vegetables, soup or in sauces, quiches or pizzas. Often children will eat cheese this way because the flavour is not too concentrated.

Blend very finely grated cheese with a little cream or top of the milk (half and half) to make a Creamy Cheese Spread.

MICROWAVE COOKING
A microwave cooker can be used to melt cheese toppings or to cook dishes containing cheese. Be careful not to overcook the cheese.

Cheese and Pineapple Kebabs

225 g/8 oz cheese, see method
1 small fresh pineapple
4 to 6 bacon rashers (slices)
15 g/½ oz (1 tablespoon) butter

Choose cheese that will not crumble when cut into cubes – Gouda, Edam or processed cheese are particularly suitable. Cut the cheese into 2.5 cm/1 inch dice. Cut the pineapple into slices of about 2.5 cm/1 inch in thickness, cut away the skin with kitchen scissors and remove the hard centre core (an apple corer is ideal for this). Cut the pineapple into neat wedges.

De-rind and halve the bacon rashers (slices); stretch each half with the back of a knife and make into rolls. Put the cheese, pineapple and bacon on to long metal skewers. Melt the butter and brush over the pineapple. Cook for several minutes under a preheated grill (broiler), turning once. Do not overcook the kebabs or the cheese will become overheated and tough. Serves 4.

132

Special Technique
FRIED CHEESE

This has become a very popular dish, either to be served as an hors d'oeuvre or a light luncheon dish.

Most cheeses can be cooked in this way including Camembert, Brie, Mozzarella, Stilton and Danish Blue. Camembert and Brie taste particularly delicious when cooked by this method as the centres become creamy when hot.

Cut the cheese into neat triangles or thick fingers. It is better to have pieces from a large Camembert cheese, rather than individual portions that contain too much rind.

Coat the cheese in seasoned flour, then in beaten egg and crisp breadcrumbs. You will need about 25 g/1 oz (¼ cup) flour, 1 egg and 40 g/1½ oz (about ½ cup) crisp breadcrumbs to coat 4 portions of cheese.

It is a good idea to chill the cheese for a short time before frying. Fry the cheese for about 2 minutes in deep oil, which has been heated to 190°C/375°F, or shallow fry in 50 g/2 oz (¼ cup) butter plus 1 tablespoon oil in a large frying pan (skillet).

Drain and serve with a fruit purée or sauce (see page 106).

<u>Fried Cheese Bites</u> Coat small cubes of cheese as above and fry. Insert cocktail sticks (toothpicks) into each piece of cheese and top with pineapple cubes or cocktail onions.

Cheese and Vegetable Bake

2 small onions
225 g/8 oz courgettes (zucchini)
225 g/8 oz tomatoes
175 g/6 oz Cheddar cheese
75 g/3 oz (6 tablespoons) butter
2 teaspoons chopped mixed herbs or 1 teaspoon dried herbs
salt and pepper
50 g/2 oz (½ cup) flour
600 ml/1 pint (2½ cups) milk
50 g/2 oz (1 cup) fine soft breadcrumbs
TO GARNISH:
tomato slices
parsley

✲Peel and slice the onions, slice the courgettes (zucchini) and tomatoes and grate the cheese. Heat 25 g/1 oz (2 tablespoons) butter in a pan and fry the onions until soft. Layer half the courgettes (zucchini), half the onions and all the tomatoes in a 1.5 litre/2½ pint (2 quart) pie dish, add some of the herbs and a little seasoning, top with the remaining onions and courgettes (zucchini), herbs and seasoning to taste.

Heat the remaining butter in a saucepan, stir in the flour and cook for 2 to 3 minutes, then gradually stir in the milk. Bring the liquid to the boil, stirring all the time and cook until the mixture thickens. Add two-thirds of the cheese, season to taste, then spoon the sauce over the vegetables. Top with the remaining cheese and the breadcrumbs.

Bake in the centre of a preheated moderate oven (180°C/350°F, Gas Mark 4) for 30 minutes. Top with tomato slices and parsley. Serves 4.

<u>Note</u> It is important to arrange the vegetables in the order given so that the acid tomatoes are not covered with the cheese sauce.

Cheese Snacks

Cheese can provide an instant snack, so it could be called a convenience food. Ploughman's lunch – fresh bread, cheese and butter with pickle or salad – provides a satisfying meal with the minimum of effort. These recipes are all quick and easy. For more sophisticated cheese snacks see Cheese Fondue and Fonduta.

Cheese and Rice Fritters

Devilled Egg Rarebit

225 g/8 oz Cheddar or other good cooking cheese
40 g/1½ oz (3 tablespoons) butter
4 tablespoons chutney
2 eggs
¼ teaspoon Worcestershire sauce
½ teaspoon curry powder
salt and pepper
4 slices of bread

Grate the cheese and blend with half the butter. Mix the remaining butter with the chutney (if this has very large pieces of fruit or vegetable in it chop them first).

Beat the eggs then gradually blend into the cheese mixture with the Worcestershire sauce, curry powder, salt and pepper to taste.

Toast the bread. Spread one side with the chutney-flavoured butter then top with the cheese mixture. Keep this away from the edges of the toast. Put under a preheated grill (broiler), set to a fairly low temperature and grill (broil) steadily until golden brown. Serve at once. Serves 4.

Traditional Welsh Rarebit

225 g/8 oz Double Gloucester (Brick) or Cheshire cheese
40 g/1½ oz (3 tablespoons) butter
15 g/½ oz (2 tablespoons) flour
5 tablespoons beer
2 teaspoons made mustard
salt and cayenne pepper
4 slices of bread
TO GARNISH: parsley

Grate the cheese. Heat 15 g/½ oz (1 tablespoon) butter in a pan, add the flour and the beer and stir over a low heat until thickened. Add the cheese, mustard, salt and pepper. Toast the bread, spread with the remaining butter then with the cheese mixture. Put under a preheated grill (broiler) until the cheese is bubbling and brown. Serves 4.

Note The cheese mixture can be prepared in advance and refrigerated.

VARIATIONS

This is a fairly strongly flavoured mixture. You can substitute milk for the beer if preferred or use half milk and half beer.

Toasted Raisin and Cheese Sandwich

100 g/4 oz (⅔ cup) seedless raisins
2 tablespoons water
2 tablespoons mayonnaise
100 g/4 oz Cheddar cheese
8 large slices of bread
25 g/1 oz (2 tablespoons) butter

Put the raisins and water into a saucepan. Heat for 2 to 3 minutes or until the raisins have absorbed the water and are soft. Cool and mix with the mayonnaise. Grate the cheese, and mix with the raisin mixture. Spread the slices of bread with the butter and then sandwich them together with the cheese mixture.

Toast on both sides under a preheated grill (broiler) or in a sandwich toaster. Cut into 8 triangles. Serves 4.

Mozzarella in Carrozza
[Fried Cheese Sandwiches]

8 large slices of bread
25 g/1 oz (2 tablespoons) butter
4 slices Mozzarella cheese
TO COAT: 4 tablespoons milk
1 egg
FOR FRYING: 2 tablespoons oil

Cut the crusts off the bread, spread with butter, then make sandwiches with the cheese. Beat the milk and egg and dip the sandwiches in this mixture. Heat the oil in a large frying pan (skillet) and fry the sandwiches for 2 minutes on each side or until crisp and golden. Cut into triangles and serve. Serves 4.

VARIATION

Put one slice of cheese on top of a slice of bread, then coat with flour and beaten egg and deep fry for 2 to 3 minutes in oil, heated to 190°C/375°F.

Cheese and Rice Fritters

350 g/12 oz (1⅔ cups) long-grain rice
700 ml/scant 1¼ pints (3 cups) water
salt and pepper
3 eggs
100 g/4 oz Gouda or Cheddar cheese
¼ teaspoon grated nutmeg
FOR THE CHEESE AND TOMATO DRESSING: 2 large tomatoes
50 g/2 oz (¼ cup) butter
150 g/5 oz (generous ½ cup) cottage cheese
2 tablespoons chopped chives
1 tablespoon tomato purée (paste)
FOR FRYING: 3 tablespoons oil

✻✻Put the rice and water into a saucepan, add a little salt, then cook (see page 136), but when the rice is tender lift the saucepan lid and allow the rice to continue cooking for 2 to 3 minutes to become firmer than usual. Add a shake of pepper to the rice, cool then beat in the eggs. Grate the cheese, stir into the rice with the nutmeg and allow to become cold.

For the dressing Cut the tomatoes into thin wedges; heat the butter, fry the tomatoes for 2 minutes only then combine with the cheese. Stir in the chives and tomato purée (paste), and season well.

Form the rice mixture into flat round cakes. Heat the oil and fry the rice cakes on both sides until golden. Serve with the dressing. Serves 4.

FREEZING NOTE

✻✻*Prepare the sandwiches for Mozzarella in Carrozza, but do not coat them with egg. Wrap them in foil or plastic and freeze. Thaw and coat before frying.*

LEFTOVERS

If you have a little beer left over and a good cooking cheese available, make up a Welsh Rarebit mixture. Put into a covered container and store in the refrigerator or freezer. Use as required.

Quiches

A quiche is a savoury egg custard tart. Some quiches contain just cheese, but many fillings depend upon fish, meat and vegetables for additional flavour.

Individual Seafood Quiche

Baking

Farmhouse Quiche (opposite) has a very imaginative filling and is put into the uncooked pastry case (pie shell).

With more traditional quiches, however, it is better to bake the pastry case blind, (see page 146), in a moderately hot oven, until just lightly coloured and firm. Add the filling and complete the cooking at a lower setting.

If you find the pastry case (shell) seems rather full do not attempt to add all the custard at once. Bake the half-filled quiche for 10 to 15 minutes, by which time the custard will have set and sunk slightly, then add the remaining custard and complete the baking.

FREEZING NOTE
✲Savoury flans freeze perfectly, especially if all cream rather than cream and milk is used in the filling. Use within 3 months. If milk is used in the filling the flan will be rather watery when thawed.

FOR EASE
Cut a hot or cold quiche or pizza into bite-sized pieces and serve with drinks. As both these freeze well you can have one or both in the freezer ready to reheat gently in the oven or microwave cooker. They are ideal quick snacks for unexpected guests.

Flavourings

✲Aubergine (Eggplant) Slice 175 g/6 oz aubergines (eggplant) and fry in 50 g/ 2 oz (¼ cup) butter until just soft; 75 to 100 g/3 to 4 oz (¾ to 1 cup) grated Gruyère or other cheese can be added to the eggs and milk. Courgettes (zucchini) can be used in the same way.

✲Leek Cook 225 g/8 oz young leeks very lightly in seasoned water; drain and slice (the leeks will have a better flavour if sliced after cooking. Add 100 g/4 oz (1 cup) grated cheese to the leeks. Lightly fried onion rings could be used instead of leeks.

✲Mushroom Slice 225 g/8 oz (2 cups) mushrooms, fry in 50 g/2 oz (¼ cup) butter, season well. About 100 g/4 oz (½ cup) chopped fried bacon and/or 100 g/ 4 oz (1 cup) grated cheese can be added to the mixture.

✲Quiche Lorraine The traditional French version has about 100 g/4 oz (½ cup) cooked diced bacon as the filling but about 100 g/4 oz (1 cup) grated cheese can be added.

✲Quiche Provençal Fry a mixture of lightly cooked onions with 1 to 2 crushed garlic cloves and 2 to 3 sliced tomatoes. Add 100 g/4 oz (1 cup) grated cheese to the eggs and cream.

✲Seafood Use 175 to 225 g/6 to 8 oz (about 1 cup) mixed shellfish.

✲Smoked Mackerel Flake 175 to 225 g/ 6 to 8 oz (about 1 cup) smoked mackerel and season with pepper. A tablespoon of horseradish cream can be added to the flaked fish. Smoked trout can be used instead of mackerel.

✲Spinach Cook 225 g/8 oz fresh or 175 g/6 oz (1 cup) frozen chopped spinach; drain very well indeed, season and mix with 1 tablespoon melted butter, a little grated nutmeg and 1 tablespoon double (heavy) cream. You can mix the spinach with the eggs and cream. Place the spinach in the pastry case and then pour the custard over.

✲Spinach and Cheese Use spinach filling above but add 50 to 75 g/2 to 3 oz (½ to ¾ cup) finely grated cheese to the spinach mixture.

✲Pepper and Onion Peel and thinly slice ½ to 1 onion; thinly slice ½ a red and ½ a green pepper. Heat 15 to 25 g/ ½ to 1 oz (1 to 2 tablespoons) butter and fry the onion and peppers until just soft. Put into the pastry case (pie shell), add the seasoned eggs and cream and milk and bake as the basic quiche. Serves 4 to 6.

Master Recipe
A PERFECT QUICHE

The filling in this recipe is enough for a 23 cm/9 inch shallow flan.

If you are using a fairly deep flan ring you may like to use 4 eggs (or 2 whole eggs and 2 to 3 egg yolks) plus 450 ml/¾ pint (2 cups) single (light) cream or milk with the same quantity of flavouring ingredients as given below.

Shortcrust Pastry made with 175 g/6 oz (1½ cups) flour, see page 144
FOR THE FILLING:
3 eggs
300 ml/½ pint (1¼ cups) single (light) cream or milk
salt and pepper
flavouring ingredients, see above right

✲Roll out the pastry and line a 20 to 23 cm/8 to 9 inch flan ring, tin or dish (quiche pan). Bake blind (see page 146) in the centre of a moderately hot oven (190°C/375°F, Gas Mark 5) for about 15 minutes, or until just set and golden.

Beat eggs. Warm the cream or milk and pour over the eggs. Add seasoning. Place the chosen flavouring ingredients into the pastry case (pie shell), pour the custard over the filling and bake in the centre of a moderate oven (160 to 180°C/ 325 to 350°F, Gas Mark 3 to 4) for 30 to 40 minutes (the exact time depends upon the filling used and how moist this is), or at a slightly lower temperature (150°C/300°F, Gas Mark 2) for 45 to 50 minutes. Serve hot or cold. Serves 4 to 6.

Note If the flan tin or dish (quiche pan) is shallow and you like very thin pastry, use just 100 g/4 oz (1 cup) flour, a pinch of salt and 50 g/2 oz (¼ cup) fat. In most instances though it is better to have slightly thicker pastry made with 175 g/ 6 oz (1½ cups) flour etc.

Farmhouse Quiche

Shortcrust Pastry made with 225 g/8 oz (2 cups) flour, see page 144
FOR THE FILLING:
1 medium onion
100 g/4 oz bacon rashers (slices)
50 g/2 oz (½ cup) button mushrooms
50 g/2 oz (¼ cup) butter
1 tablespoon soft breadcrumbs
1 teaspoon chopped fresh sage or ¼ teaspoon dried sage
1 × 213 g/7½ oz can tomatoes
175 g/6 oz Cheddar cheese
4 tablespoons smooth apple purée (applesauce)
3 eggs
5 tablespoons milk
salt and pepper
1 teaspoon made mustard

✲Roll out the pastry and line a 23 to 25 cm/9 to 10 inch flan dish or tin (quiche pan); a flan ring is less suitable for this dish as it has a moist filling.

Peel and finely chop the onion. De-rind and chop the bacon. Keep the rinds. Wipe the mushrooms and cut into thin slices. Heat the butter and the bacon rinds in a frying pan (skillet). Fry the onion, bacon and mushrooms very gently until the onion is soft. Remove the bacon rinds, add the breadcrumbs and sage. Drain the tomatoes carefully; blend the tomatoes with the ingredients in the frying pan (skillet) and allow to cool.

Grate the cheese. Sprinkle half over the base of the uncooked flan and top with the apple purée (applesauce), the onion mixture and then the remaining cheese.

Beat the eggs with the milk, salt, pepper and mustard. Strain carefully over the filling. Bake in the centre of a preheated moderately hot oven (200°C/ 400°F, Gas Mark 6) for 25 minutes until the pastry begins to colour then lower the heat to moderate (180°C/350°F, Gas Mark 4) for a further 25 to 30 minutes, or until the filling is firm. Serve hot or cold. Serves 4 to 6.

Pizzas

Special Technique
A PERFECT PIZZA

There are many kinds of pizza – both the base and topping can be varied. However, there are certain golden rules for making a really good pizza.

Do not make the base too thick – obviously this will vary according to personal taste.

Always oil the baking sheet on which the base is baked very well. This makes certain that the bottom of the pizza base becomes crisp. Oil a yeast or baking powder scone dough before adding the topping.

Be generous with the amount of topping used and check that it has plenty of flavour.

Toppings

Artichoke Hearts Place well-drained sliced canned or cooked artichoke hearts over the tomato purée. Top with thinly sliced Mozzarella cheese, then a layer of grated Parmesan cheese and black (ripe) olives.

Mussels Cover the tomato purée with about 18 mussels (see page 44), with grated Parmesan cheese, then a lattice of canned anchovy fillets and plenty of black (ripe) olives.

Mozzarella and Prosciutto Top the tomato purée with 50 g/2 oz prosciutto, cut into thin strips, then 225 g/8 oz thinly sliced Mozzarella cheese, a sprinkling of grated Parmesan cheese and a sprinkling of chopped parsley.

A Perfect Pizza

Bread Dough made with 225 g/8 oz (2 cups) flour, see page 154
1 tablespoon oil
FOR THE PURÉE: 2 medium onions
1 garlic clove
750 g/1½ lb tomatoes
1 tablespoon oil
salt and pepper
1 teaspoon chopped fresh oregano or ¼ to ½ teaspoon dried
FOR THE TOPPING: See left

⁑ Make the bread dough and allow this to prove once, knock back (punch down) and roll out to a 20 to 23 cm/8 to 9 inch round. Place on a very well-oiled baking sheet and brush with oil.

For the purée Peel and finely chop the onions and garlic. Skin and chop the tomatoes. Heat the oil in a saucepan and cook the vegetables, uncovered, until the mixture forms a soft thick purée. Add salt and pepper to taste and 1 teaspoon chopped fresh oregano or ¼ to ½ teaspoon dried oregano.

For the topping Top the pizza round with the tomato purée and add one of the toppings given left.

Allow the prepared pizza to prove in a warm place for 25 to 30 minutes then bake just above the centre of a hot oven (220°C/425°F, Gas Mark 7) for 15 to 20 minutes. The anchovy fillets and olives can be added after 10 minutes cooking to prevent them drying out. Serve the pizza with a green salad tossed in Vinaigrette Dressing (see page 105). Serves 4.

Hasty Pizza

FOR THE SAVOURY SCONE BASE: 1 medium onion
75 g/3 oz Cheddar cheese
25 g/1 oz (2 tablespoons) margarine
100 g/4 oz (1 cup) self-raising flour with ½ teaspoon baking powder
¼ teaspoon salt
½ teaspoon mustard powder
1 teaspoon chopped fresh mixed herbs or ½ teaspoon dried mixed herbs
1 tablespoon milk
FOR THE TOPPING: 50 g/2 oz Cheddar cheese
4 medium tomatoes
2 teaspoons chopped fresh mixed herbs or 1 teaspoon dried mixed herbs
1 × 50 g/2 oz can anchovy fillets
10 to 12 black (ripe) olives

⁑ Peel and grate the onion and grate the cheese. Allow the margarine to soften slightly. Sift the flour and baking powder with the salt and mustard and mix with all the scone base ingredients. Knead until smooth, roll out to make a 20 to 23 cm/8 to 9 inch round and place on a well-greased baking sheet.

For the topping Grate the cheese for the topping and slice the tomatoes. Arrange the tomatoes over the scone dough, top with the cheese and herbs. Top with anchovy fillets and olives.

Bake the pizza in the centre of a preheated hot oven (220°C/425°F, Gas Mark 7) for 20 to 25 minutes until the base is firm. Serves 4 to 6.

Note Plain (all-purpose) flour can be used instead of self-raising but increase the baking powder to 1½ teaspoons.

FREEZING NOTE
⁑ Cooked or uncooked pizzas freeze perfectly. Freeze uncovered, so that the wrapping does not stick to the soft topping. When frozen solid, wrap well. Use within 3 months. Reheat or cook without thawing.

If using a pastry base, which will soften easily, freeze the base and the topping separately, or make quite sure the pizza is served as soon as it is hot.

Farmhouse Quiche, Mushroom Quiche, and Courgette Quiche plus Pizzas with an Artichoke Topping, Mussel Topping, and Mozzarella and Prosciutto Topping

RICE

Rice, regarded as a staple food in many countries, can be combined with many other ingredients to produce a variety of nutritious dishes. There are several types of rice (see page 9).

Carnival Rice, page 138

Cooking Rice

It is important to cook rice correctly; there are many different methods.

You can, of course, cook the rice in plenty of boiling salted water, then strain, rinse and reheat but the method used in the Special Technique is the simplest and gives excellent results.

If serving boiled rice immediately after cooking, rinse in boiling water. If time permits, rinse the cooked rice in cold water then put into a steamer, cover and steam over a pan of boiling water.

Microwave Cooking

This is a good way to cook rice. You can follow the conventional methods, although it is quicker to boil the water in a kettle, add this to the rice and then cook in the microwave cooker.

Moulding Rice

Cooked rice can be formed into professional-looking rings in which to serve other foods. Cheese Rice Ring shown on page 73 is filled with Liver Ragout, but the ring can be used for all kinds of fish, meat or vegetables.

Rice Ring with Mushroom (see page 138) is more elaborate. The cooked rice is blended with savoury ingredients, eggs and milk to give an almost custard-like consistency and then cooked.

LEFTOVERS
Never waste leftover cooked rice. Use long-grain rice in a salad (see page 95), or fry (see Texas Jack), or store in a covered container in the refrigerator or freezer.

To reheat the rice, cover with cold stock or water, bring the liquid steadily to boiling point, strain the rice and serve.

Cold rice pudding could be mixed with a little whipped cream and served with fruit.

Special Technique
PERFECT COOKED RICE

This is an excellent way to cook rice which is to be served as an accompaniment to other foods. The rice becomes tender, without being sticky, and all the cooking liquid is absorbed so that straining is unnecessary.

It is important to have the correct proportion of liquid to rice. Use either weights or a standard cup measure. If weighing the rice allow 40 to 50 g/1 ½ to 2 oz or ¼ cup per person, or as detailed in the recipe. Use the amount of liquid given below.

Today, rice is generally pre-washed, but if necessary rinse in cold water and cook immediately after washing.

Put the rice and cold liquid into a saucepan and add salt to taste. Bring the liquid to the boil, stir with a fork. Cover the pan, lower the heat and simmer for the time given below.

<u>Long-grain rice</u> Use twice as much liquid as rice; 150 g/5 oz (⅔ cup) rice needs 300 ml/10 fl oz or ½ pint (1⅓ cups) liquid or 1 cup of rice needs 2 cups of liquid. Simmer for 15 minutes.

<u>Par-boiled rice</u> Use 2½ times as much liquid as rice. Simmer for 20 minutes.

<u>Brown rice</u> Use 3 times as much liquid as rice. Simmer for 40 to 45 minutes.

<u>Basmati rice</u> This rice must be well washed before using. Remove any grains that are not perfect. Use 2¾ times as much liquid as rice. Simmer for 25 minutes.

<u>Wild rice</u> Use 3 times as much liquid as rice. Simmer for 40 to 45 minutes.

<u>Short-grain rice</u> If you decide to cook this pudding rice in a pan, rather than using it in recipes, (see page 119), then use 10 times as much liquid as rice: 50 g/2 oz (4 tablespoons) rice will need 500 ml/20 fl oz or 1 pint (2½ cups) liquid. This is not the standard metric conversion but gives satisfactory results.

Simmer for a minimum of 1 hour. It is advisable to cook the rice in the top of a double saucepan, over steadily simmering water, especially if cooking rice in milk. This avoids any possibility of the rice sticking to the saucepan.

Texas Jack

175 to 225 g/6 to 8 oz back bacon rashers (Canadian bacon slices)
25 g/1 oz (2 tablespoons) butter or margarine
1 medium onion
1 green pepper
1 × 425 g/15 oz can baked beans
1 × 425 g/15 oz can tomatoes
salt and cayenne pepper
150 g/5 oz (⅔ cup) long-grain rice, cooked, see Special Technique
4 tablespoons grated Parmesan cheese

Fry the bacon in a large frying pan (skillet). Remove from the pan, cut off the rinds and discard. Chop the bacon. Add the butter or margarine to the bacon fat in the frying pan (skillet).

Peel and finely chop the onion. Cut the pepper into long strips, discarding the core and seeds. Fry the onion and pepper in the fat in the pan until just soft. Add the beans and tomatoes, stir to combine and simmer for 10 minutes. Season well, add the bacon and heat for 1 minute.

Serve the rice with the bean mixture and top with grated cheese. Pass around a tossed green salad if liked. Serves 6.

Broccoli and Rice Soufflé

1 medium onion
1 to 2 garlic cloves
100 to 175 g/4 to 6 oz (1 to 1½ cups) mushrooms
50 g/2 oz (¼ cup) butter or margarine
450 g/1 lb cooked broccoli
175 g/6 oz (scant 1 cup) cooked long-grain rice, see Note
salt and pepper
¼ teaspoon grated nutmeg
100 g/4 oz Gouda or Cheddar cheese
4 eggs
150 ml/¼ pint (⅔ cup) single (light) cream or milk

Peel and finely chop the onion and garlic. Wipe or wash the mushrooms and cut into fairly thick slices. Heat the butter or margarine in a saucepan, add the onion, garlic and mushrooms and cook gently until tender. Divide the broccoli spears into smaller pieces, mix with the rice, the cooked vegetables, a little seasoning and the nutmeg. Spoon into a large casserole. Flatten the surface as much as possible. Cover with foil and heat in the centre of a preheated moderately hot oven (190°C/375°F, Gas Mark 5) for 15 minutes.

Grate the cheese. Separate the eggs and mix the yolks with the cream or milk, cheese and a little seasoning. Whisk the whites until stiff and fold into the cheese mixture. Remove the casserole from the oven, take off the foil and spread the soufflé mixture over the hot rice mixture. Return to the oven for a further 20 to 25 minutes then serve at once. Serves 4 to 6.

Note In order to obtain 175 g/6 oz (scant 1 cup) cooked rice, you need about 50 g/2 oz (4 tablespoons) uncooked rice.

Special Technique
MAKING A RISOTTO

A risotto is a savoury dish made with rice that can be flavoured in a variety of ways.

Medium-grain rice – often termed Italian rice – is the best to use. This has larger grains than long-grain rice, needs longer cooking and becomes more sticky when cooked, which is ideal for this type of dish. If you cannot obtain medium-grain rice (it is not readily available) then substitute long-grain or brown rice.

Since the rice grains should be full of flavour it is advisable to use stock, rather than water, in the recipe. Serve the risotto when it is pleasantly moist.

Interesting Risottos

✷✷Risotto with Chicken Dice 450 g/1 lb (2 cups) raw chicken, peel and slice 2 medium onions, peel and crush 1 garlic clove, and slice 100 g/4 oz (1 cup) mushrooms. Heat 2 tablespoons oil and 50 g/2 oz (¼ cup) butter in a large saucepan. Fry the chicken with the onions and garlic until golden. Add 225 g/8 oz (generous 1 cup) Italian or long-grain rice and 750 ml/1¼ pints (3 cups) chicken stock, the mushrooms, salt and pepper to taste and 2 tablespoons chopped parsley. Cover the pan and cook steadily until the rice is nearly tender, then add 2 tablespoons diced canned red pepper and 2 skinned and sliced tomatoes. Continue cooking, covered, until the rice is tender and the excess liquid has been absorbed. Serves 4.

Risotto Veneta Heat 4 tablespoons oil in a large saucepan. Peel 4 garlic cloves, fry in the oil for 3 to 4 minutes then remove and discard. Add 2 small finely chopped onions and 225 g/8 oz (gen-erous 1 cup) Italian or long-grain rice, toss in the oil then add 750 ml/1¼ pints (3 cups) fish stock, 2 tablespoons chopped fennel and salt and pepper to taste. Cover and cook steadily until the rice is nearly tender then add 2.2 litres/4 pints (5 pints) mussels, measured before cooking (see page 44). Cover again and heat thoroughly until the rice is tender and the excess liquid has been absorbed. Top with grated cheese. Serves 4.

Vegetable Pilaf

2 medium onions
50 g/2 oz (¼ cup) margarine or 2 tablespoons oil
175 g/6 oz (scant 1 cup) long-grain or brown rice
450 to 600 ml/¾ to 1 pint (2 to 2½ cups) chicken stock or water, see method
salt and pepper
350 g/12 oz mixed vegetables, see method

Peel and finely chop the onions. Heat the margarine or oil in a large saucepan, add the onions and gently fry for 2 to 3 minutes. Mix the rice with the onions then add the stock or water. Use the larger amount if cooking brown rice. Add a very little salt and pepper. Bring the liquid to the boil and cover the pan. Cook steadily for 5 minutes if cooking long-grain rice, but 15 minutes for brown rice.

Meanwhile prepare the vegetables. Choose those that give a good balance of colour as well as flavour. Peel and dice 2 or 3 carrots and a small portion of turnip, string and slice French or runner beans, wipe and slice mushrooms. Add a few peas and a little diced and de-seeded red and/or green pepper.

Put the vegetables into the pan and replace the lid.

Continue cooking for a further 10 minutes, by which time the rice and vegetables should be tender and the excess liquid absorbed by the rice. Check towards the end of the cooking time and remove the lid if necessary. Serves 4.

VARIATIONS

If serving this on its own as a light dish, top with plenty of grated cheese.

Crisp Vegetable Pilaf Fry the onions as above, but cook the rice until almost ready to serve, then add coarsely grated raw carrot, diced cucumber, radishes and de-seeded red and green peppers. Heat for 2 to 3 minutes only. The contrast between the soft rice and crisp vegetables is a very pleasant one.

Cheese Rice Ring

This method of serving rice is very attractive and the centre can be filled with any fish, meat or vegetable mixture, (see Liver Râgout, page 73).

225 g/8 oz (generous 1 cup) long-grain rice
salt and pepper
450 ml/¾ pint (2 cups) water
40 g/1½ oz (3 tablespoons) butter
50 g/2 oz Cheddar cheese
TO GARNISH: chopped parsley

✷✷Cook the rice in the seasoned water, (see page 138), until the grains are tender and the liquid is absorbed. Melt the butter and use about 15 g/½ oz (1 tablespoon) to coat the inside of a 20 to 23 cm/8 to 9 inch ring mould. Grate the cheese, combine this with the rice and remaining butter. Spoon into the ring mould, keep hot for a short time then turn out on to the serving plate. Fill the centre as desired and top with a little parsley. Serves 4 to 6.

Above: Texas Jack
Below left: Broccoli and Rice Soufflé

137

Carnival Rice

225 g/8 oz small firm tomatoes

4 to 6 Kochwürste or Frankfurter sausages

1 tablespoon oil

350 g/12 oz (1⅔ cups) long-grain rice

700 ml/scant 1¼ pints (3 cups) chicken stock or water

2 teaspoons chopped fresh mixed herbs, including sage and oregano or marjoram

salt and pepper

1 × 425 g/15 oz can petits pois

1 to 2 tablespoons chopped parsley

grated cheese

Cut each tomato into quarters. Slice the Kochwürste or Frankfurter sausages. Heat the oil in a large frying pan (skillet) with a lid or in a saucepan. Add the sliced sausages and rice and turn in the oil until well coated. Pour the stock or water into the pan, add the herbs and seasoning and stir well to mix the rice with the liquid. Bring the liquid just to simmering point, stir once again, cover the pan and simmer the rice for 10 minutes. Drain the can of peas, add the peas and tomatoes to the rice and continue cooking for 5 minutes or until the rice is tender. Top with chopped parsley and serve with grated cheese. Serves 4.

Nasi Goreng
[Fried Rice]

Rice Ring with Mushroom Fricassée

225 g/8 oz (generous 1 cup) long-grain rice, cooked, see page 136 (weight before cooking)

3 small onions or shallots

3 tablespoons oil

1 tablespoon soy sauce

salt and pepper

Drain the cooked rice. Peel and finely chop the onions or shallots. Heat the oil in a wok or large frying pan (skillet), fry the onions or shallots until nearly soft; add the rice and turn in the oil. Continue frying until the rice and onions or shallots are golden in colour. Stir in the soy sauce and any seasoning required just before serving. Serves 4.

VARIATIONS

If you like a very hot flavour fry 1 or 2 sliced red chillis with the onions or shallots or add a little chilli powder.

Cook 100 to 175 g/4 to 6 oz (½ to ¾ cup) finely diced raw tender meat or poultry with the rice in the oil then add the onions or shallots and proceed as above.

Add diced cooked meat or poultry and vegetables towards the end of the cooking time; heat well.

Rice Ring with Mushroom Fricassée

FOR THE RICE RING:
200 g/7 oz (1 cup) long-grain rice

375 ml/scant ¾ pint or 14 fl oz (1¾ cups) water

salt and pepper

1 medium onion

100 g/4 oz bread, weight without crusts

225 g/8 oz Gouda cheese

75 g/3 oz (6 tablespoons) butter

3 eggs

150 ml/¼ pint (⅔ cup) milk

¼ teaspoon ground coriander

FOR THE MUSHROOM FRICASSÉE:
450 g/1 lb (4 cups) button mushrooms

2 onions

50 g/2 oz (¼ cup) butter

150 ml/¼ pint (⅔ cup) chicken stock

150 ml/¼ pint (⅔ cup) single (light) cream or milk

1 tablespoon cornflour (cornstarch)

TO GARNISH:
chopped parsley

⁕Cook the rice in the water with a little salt (see page 136), and allow to cool slightly. Peel and finely chop the onion for the rice ring, cut the bread into small dice and grate the cheese. Add the onion, bread and cheese to the rice. Melt the butter, mix with the rice mixture together with the eggs, milk and coriander. Season well. Put into a 1.5 litre/2½ pint (2 quart) ring tin (mold). Stand in a *bain-marie* and bake in the centre of a preheated moderate oven (180°C/350°F, Gas Mark 4) for 40 minutes or until firm. Do not overcook.

For the mushroom fricassée Wipe the mushrooms. If large, cut into quarters or halves. Peel and finely chop the onions. Heat the butter in a saucepan and fry the onions and mushrooms for 2 to 3 minutes. Add the stock and simmer for 10 minutes. Mix the cream or milk with the cornflour (cornstarch), add to the mushroom mixture and stir over a very low heat until thickened and smooth. Season well.

Turn the rice ring out on to a heated serving dish and fill the centre with the mushroom mixture. Top with parsley. Serves 4 to 6.

Nasi Kuning
[Yellow Rice]

1 tablespoon oil

225 g/8 oz (generous 1 cup) long-grain rice

450 ml/¾ pint (2 cups) chicken stock or water with ½ chicken stock cube (1 bouillon cube)

½ to 1 teaspoon turmeric

salt and pepper

Heat the oil in a saucepan, add the rice and turn in the oil. Mix the stock or water and stock cube with the turmeric. Pour over the rice, add a little seasoning, bring the liquid to the boil and stir briskly. Cover the pan and cook (see page 136). Serves 4.

VARIATION

Add a little spicy flavouring – a pinch of curry powder, coriander or cumin.

PASTA

There are innumerable shapes of pasta available and the basic ingredients used for all of them are similar.

A recipe for homemade egg pasta is given below. It is also possible to buy a pasta-making appliance (which extrudes the dough into the long thin strands). Do not be too disappointed if homemade pasta does not keep as perfect a shape in cooking as commercial pasta (the latter is made from particularly hard durum wheat which is not available on the domestic market).

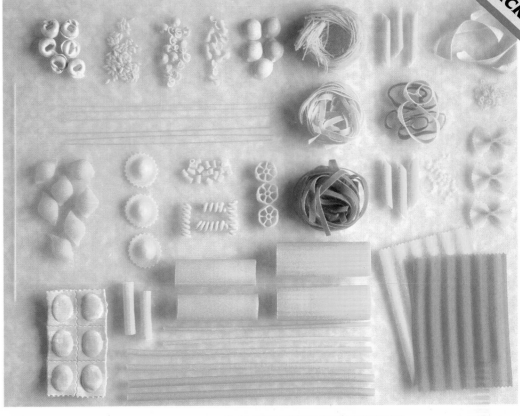

A *selection of pasta shapes*

Types of Pasta

The best known types of pasta are:

Annellini – small ring shapes used in soup.

Bucatini – a very thin macaroni.

Cannelloni – either sheets or tubes which are stuffed.

Cappelletti – hat-shaped pieces.

Conchiglie – shell shaped pasta.

Ditali – large tubes of macaroni.

Farfalle – bows of various kinds.

Fettuccine – long fine twisted egg noodles.

Fideline – fine twisted spaghetti.

Lasagne – wide egg noodles, plain, wholewheat or spinach-flavoured.

Maccheroni – the generic term for pasta in Italy but used elsewhere for tubes of pasta; modern macaroni is short and quick cooking.

Maruzze – large shells.

Noodles – egg pasta in various shapes.

Pastine – small pasta shapes for soup.

Penne – short tubular pasta, with angled rather than straight ends.

Ravioli – stuffed shapes of pasta, usually in squares.

Rigatoni – ribbed macaroni.

Spaghetti – long strands.

Tagliatelle – twisted wide noodles.

Tortellini – small stuffed pasta circles that are served like ravioli.

Tortiglioni – twisted spirals (there are many other pasta shapes available).

Vermicelli – very thin spaghetti like pasta.

Microwave Cooking

Use the same proportion of water to pasta as given above. Boil the water in a kettle since that is quicker than boiling it in the microwave cooker.

Put the pasta in a large dish. Spaghetti should be arranged in a long dish. Add the boiling water and salt and cook on the maximum setting.

The cooking time should be about 2 minutes less than in a saucepan to reach the *al dente* stage, allow the pasta to stand in the water for about 5 minutes before straining it.

Pasta Sauces

The most usual sauces to serve with pasta are Bolognese Sauce (see page 140), Tomato Sauce (see page 103) or Cheese Sauce (see page 102). There are however many other sauces which combine extremely well with pasta and turn it into a complete and satisfying dish (see page 102). Other suitable recipes are Creole Sauce (see page 103), Sanfayna Sauce (see page 107) and Italian Sauce (see page 141).

Egg Pasta

450 g/1 lb (4 cups) plain white or wholewheat flour
1 teaspoon salt
5 eggs
1 tablespoon olive oil

Sift the flour and salt. Mix the eggs and oil. Make a well in the centre of the flour, pour in the eggs and oil. Work the flour gradually into the egg mixture, kneading well as you do so. When thoroughly mixed, knead very firmly until smooth. Return to a clean bowl, cover with a damp cloth and leave for 1 hour. Knead again then roll out very thinly and cut into the desired shapes and cook.

VARIATION

For a plainer pasta dough use 1 to 2 eggs, the oil and warm water to bind.

Special Technique
COOKING PASTA

Pasta of every kind is spoiled if it is overcooked. Always use sufficient liquid to prevent the pasta pieces sticking together as they cook.

The minimum amount of liquid to use is 1.2 litres/2 pints (5 cups) to each 100 g/4 oz pasta. Make sure the liquid is boiling when the pasta is added and allow it to boil steadily during the cooking period.

The cooking time for modern pasta is very much shorter than for the old fashioned type. The instructions will be on the packet, but test in plenty of time, for overcooked pasta becomes limp and flavourless.

Pasta should be served *al dente*, that means it is sufficiently firm to be slightly nutty and you need to bite it. When testing you should have to apply quite firm pressure with a fork.

1 to 2 teaspoons of cooking or olive oil added to the cooking liquid helps to keep the strands of pasta separate.

Drain the pasta thoroughly. If serving as an accompaniment to a dish toss in melted butter or margarine and chopped herbs.

Some people like to rinse pasta after cooking. While this is a good idea for a pasta salad, it is not essential for hot dishes. Rinsing makes the pasta less sticky: pour boiling water over the pasta if serving at once, or cold water if the pasta is to be reheated as part of a dish.

Spaghetti with Cream and Onions

Macaroni and Prawn Bake

350 g/12 oz (3 cups) macaroni
salt and pepper
175 g/6 oz (1½ cups) mushrooms
100 g/4 oz (½ cup) butter or margarine
175 g/6 oz (1 cup) peeled prawns (shelled shrimp)
50 g/2 oz (½ cup) flour
600 ml/1 pint (2½ cups) milk
¼ teaspoon grated nutmeg
50 g/2 oz Parmesan cheese
TO GARNISH:
3 to 4 whole prawns (shrimp), optional
parsley

Cook the macaroni in salted water until *al dente* and strain well. Meanwhile wipe and slice the mushrooms. Heat 50 g/2 oz (¼ cup) of the butter or margarine in a saucepan and cook the mushrooms until soft. Remove the pan from the heat. Add the prawns (shrimp) but do not cook them.

Melt the remaining butter or margarine in a saucepan, stir in the flour and cook gently for 2 to 3 minutes then gradually blend in the milk. Bring the liquid to the boil and continue stirring as the sauce thickens. Add the nutmeg, mushrooms and prawns (shrimp) with seasoning to taste.

Put layers of macaroni and prawn (shrimp) mixture into a large shallow ovenproof dish, ending with the prawn (shrimp) mixture. Grate the cheese and sprinkle over the top of the ingredients. Bake in the centre of a moderate to moderately hot oven (180 to 190°C/350 to 375°F, Gas Mark 4 to 5) for 15 minutes if the macaroni and sauce are hot, but rather longer if the ingredients were cooked earlier in the day.

Garnish with prawns (shrimp), if used, and a parsley sprig just before serving. Serves 4 to 6.

Spaghetti with Cottage Cheese and Almonds

350 g/12 oz spaghetti
salt and pepper
50 g/2 oz (¼ cup) butter
1 tablespoon chopped parsley
FOR THE SAUCE:
25 g/1 oz Parmesan cheese
100 g/4 oz (1 cup) ground almonds
100 g/4 oz (½ cup) cottage or Ricotta cheese
pinch of grated nutmeg
pinch of ground cinnamon
150 ml/¼ pint (⅔ cup) single (light) cream
2 to 3 tablespoons olive oil
150 ml/¼ pint (⅔ cup) liquid from cooking the spaghetti
TO GARNISH:
25 g/1 oz (¼ cup) browned flaked almonds

Cook the spaghetti in boiling salted water. Drain, saving 150 ml/¼ pint (⅔ cup) of the water, and mix the spaghetti with the butter and parsley. Put the spaghetti in a large heated dish.

Grate the Parmesan cheese. Mix with all the other sauce ingredients and season well. Spoon over the spaghetti and top with the almonds. Serves 4.

Cannelloni all'Italiana

16 cannelloni tubes
salt and pepper
FOR THE BOLOGNESE SAUCE:
1 medium onion
1 garlic clove
1 or 2 carrots
50 to 100 g/2 to 4 oz (½ to 1 cup) mushrooms
4 medium tomatoes
2 tablespoons oil
350 g/12 oz (1½ cups) minced (ground) beef
150 ml/¼ pint (⅔ cup) beef stock or water and ½ beef stock (1 bouillon) cube
150 ml/¼ pint (⅔ cup) red wine
2 teaspoons fresh mixed herbs or 1 teaspoon mixed dried herbs
2 tablespoons tomato purée (paste)
Cheese Sauce, made with 300 ml/½ pint (1¼ cups) milk, see page 102, or Italian Sauce, see Variations
50 g/2 oz (½ cup) grated Parmesan cheese

∗∗Cook the cannelloni in boiling salted water until *al dente*, drain and leave uncovered to dry.

Peel and finely chop the onion, garlic and carrot(s). Wipe then chop the mushrooms; skin and chop the tomatoes. Heat the oil in a saucepan, add the meat and vegetables, turn in the oil then cook gently for 5 minutes. Add the stock or water and stock (bouillon) cube, the wine, herbs and tomato purée (paste). Season to taste. Cover the pan and simmer gently for 35 minutes (if serving with spaghetti you should cook the sauce for 45 minutes).

For this dish it is advisable to remove the lid for the last 5 to 10 minutes cooking time so the sauce becomes slightly thicker in consistency.

Fill the cannelloni with the meat mixture. This can be done with a teaspoon or through a large plain nozzle in a piping (pastry) bag. Arrange the filled tubes in an ovenproof dish, top with the Cheese or Italian Sauce and the grated cheese. Bake in the centre of a moderately hot oven (190°C/375°F, Gas Mark 5) for 20 to 25 minutes. Serves 4 to 6.

VARIATIONS

⁎⁎Mushroom Cannelloni Fill the cannelloni with thick cheese sauce and chopped cooked mushrooms.

⁎⁎Cheese Cannelloni Fill the cannelloni with a mixture of 175 g/6 oz (¾ cup) ricotta, 175 g/6 oz (1½ cups) grated or finely chopped Mozzarella cheese and 50 g/2 oz (¼ cup) diced prosciutto, mixed with 1 egg.

⁎⁎Italian Sauce Follow the recipe for Bolognese Sauce (left) but instead of 350 g/12 oz (1½ cups) minced (ground) beef use 100 g/4 oz (½ cup) minced (ground) beef, 100 g/4 oz (½ cup) minced (ground) veal and 100 g/4 oz (½ cup) minced ham together with 100 g/4 oz (½ cup) chopped fat bacon. Use only 2 tomatoes.

Chinese Style Pork and Pasta

6 tablespoons soy sauce
3 tablespoons sherry
1 teaspoon cornflour (cornstarch)
450 g/1 lb pork fillet (tenderloin)
300 g/10 oz (2½ cups) pasta spirals or twists
salt and pepper
1 red pepper
1 green pepper
6 to 8 spring onions (scallions)
2 tablespoons oil
175 g/6 oz (3 cups) fresh or canned beansprouts

Put the soy sauce, sherry and cornflour (cornstarch) in a dish. Cut the pork into bite-sized pieces and marinate in the soy sauce mixture for 30 minutes.

Meanwhile cook the pasta in boiling salted water until *al dente*, strain and rinse in cold water then drain very well. Slice the peppers, discarding the cores and seeds. Slice the onions.

Lift the pork from the marinade; retain the marinade. Heat the oil in a wok or large frying pan (skillet), put in the pork and cook for 5 to 6 minutes then add the peppers, onions and pasta and heat for 2 to 3 minutes.

Stir the marinade briskly to mix the cornflour (cornstarch) with the remaining liquid. Add to the ingredients in the wok or frying pan (skillet). Stir as this heats and becomes clear. Finally add the fresh or well-drained canned beansprouts, season to taste, and cook for 1 minute only. Serve at once. Serves 4 to 6.

Spaghetti with Cream and Onions

350 g/12 oz spaghetti
salt and pepper
2 medium onions
75 g/3 oz (6 tablespoons) butter
1 tablespoon flour
150 ml/¼ pint (⅔ cup) double (heavy) cream
1 to 2 tablespoons chopped parsley
little grated nutmeg
Parmesan cheese

Cook the spaghetti in boiling salted water until *al dente*. Meanwhile peel and chop the onions. Heat 50 g/2 oz (¼ cup) butter and cook the onions until tender. Add the flour, stir over a gentle heat for 1 minute then add the cream, parsley, seasoning and nutmeg. Stir as the mixture heats for 1 minute. Drain the spaghetti, toss in the remaining butter and blend with the cream and onion sauce. Serve with grated Parmesan. Serves 4.

VARIATION

Flavour the cream sauce with a pinch of chilli powder or a few drops of Tabasco (hot pepper) Sauce.

Curried Spaghetti

225–350 g/8–12 oz spaghetti
FOR THE SAUCE:
2 medium onions
1 small dessert apple
50 g/2 oz (¼ cup) butter or margarine
1 tablespoon cornflour (cornstarch)
1 tablespoon curry powder
300 ml/½ pint (1¼ cups) beef or chicken or vegetable stock
½ tablespoon tomato purée (paste)
2 tablespoons sultanas (golden raisins)
1 tablespoon desiccated coconut
salt and pepper

First make the sauce. Peel and finely chop the onions and apple. Heat the butter or margarine in a large saucepan, add the onions and apple and fry for 5 minutes. Blend in the cornflour (cornstarch) and curry powder and stir over a low heat for 2 to 3 minutes. Gradually blend in the stock, stir as the sauce comes to the boil and thickens, then add the remaining ingredients. Season well. Simmer gently while the spaghetti is cooked in boiling salted water. Combine the spaghetti and sauce. Serves 4.

LEFTOVERS

Leftover pasta can be used in a salad (see page 95). If you use a long pasta, such as spaghetti, chop into neat pieces before mixing with the other salad ingredients.

To reheat leftover pasta, put it into cold stock or water, bring the liquid steadily to boiling point, strain the pasta and serve.

Pasta can be frozen but unless combined with other ingredients it does tend to become slightly over-softened.

Chinese Style Pork and Pasta

141

BAKING

Probably no other sphere of cookery gives a creative cook more pleasure than baking. Most cooks want to be able to bake delicious cakes, light pastry and beautifully crusty homemade bread.

In this section you will find golden rules for good pastry, light cakes of various kinds and interesting breads. I have also included some pastries and breads that are famous in other countries.

Freezers make batch-baking worthwhile and practical and most of the recipes in this section can be frozen.

Buying Points

Good results in baking depend to a large extent on selecting the right ingredients, particularly the correct flour. You need strong (hard wheat) flour for bread and plain (all-purpose) flour for pastry and certain cakes. (See pages 10 to 12 for the various kinds of flour, sugar and fats).

Select dried fruit with care, some dried fruit is small and dry and of poor quality. If the fruit is not prewashed, clean it in cold water and dry at room temperature for 48 hours before using.

Oven Baking

Most foods cook better if they are placed in an oven that has been preheated and is already at the recommended temperature.

This is particularly important when baking, and especially if cooking light sponges, scones (biscuits), bread and richer pastries.

The top of most ovens is the hottest part, so it is important to place the food on the correct oven shelf. For example, if large cakes are put on too high a shelf, they become over-brown on top before they are cooked through and if small cakes or scones (biscuits) are placed on too low a shelf, they take too long to cook and become dry. Oven positions are not important in a fan-assisted electric oven in which all parts of the oven are the same temperature.

Oven temperatures given in each recipe have been checked carefully on test ovens but individual ovens do vary. Check the information given about temperature by the manufacturer of your cooker. Fan-assisted ovens tend to be hotter than others, so reduce the setting given in recipes by 10°C/25°F.

Microwave Baking

Do not expect cakes or other foods baked in a microwave cooker to be just like those cooked in a conventional oven. Many recipes are unsuitable for a microwave or will require special treatment. The food is not browned or crisped in the same way, so it is advisable to choose recipes that use a chocolate flavouring or brown sugar, or can be iced (frosted). More specific advice is given where appropriate.

Ordinary cake or patty tins (pans) cannot be used in the microwave cooker, but you can substitute ceramic dishes or special microwave ware which is available in a wide range of shapes.

Slow Cooking

Moist cakes can be cooked in a slow cooker, (see pages 164 to 165). The technique is similar to that used when cooking puddings. Preheat the cooker on the HIGH setting for 15 minutes. Put in the cake (remember not to use a cake tin (pan) with a loose base). Add boiling water to come half-way up the side of the tin. Cover and cook for about 5 hours on the HIGH setting.

Pressure Cooking

It is possible to cook moist cakes in a pressure cooker, although they will have soft tops, like a steamed pudding. As these cakes contain a raising agent, you should steam the mixture without weights for the first-third of the total cooking time, then cook at LOW/5 lb pressure for the remaining time. (For suitable cake recipes see pages 164–165).

Freezing Note

Pastry can be frozen either uncooked or baked in tarts, flans and other dishes.

When freezing homemade pastry, form it into neat shallow amounts, (shallow packages defrost more quickly than deep ones) chill well, then wrap and freeze. Label each package with the type and amount of pastry so that you can select the right quantity for a particular dish. Storage times are given beside the various kinds of pastry.

Freeze decorated cakes without wrapping and wrap once they are frozen.

Bread freezes well and detailed information is given beside the recipes.

Most biscuits (cookies) can be stored

in airtight tins, but those marked with the freezing symbol can also be frozen.

Careful Measuring

Throughout this book the spoon measurements are level. It is particularly important when measuring baking powder or bicarbonate of soda (baking soda) to ensure that the spoon measure is absolutely flat. In one or two recipes the word 'level' has been added because even a slight increase in the amount of raising agent or other ingredients used could spoil the recipe.

It is important to use the correct amounts of raising agent: enough to make the cake or scones (biscuits) rise without adding an unpleasant flavour.

Preparing Tins

Some recipes state that the cake can be cooked in a cake tin (pan) that has been merely greased and floured. Others insist upon a tin that has been lined with greaseproof (waxed) paper and then greased. Follow the suggestions given in specific recipes, since some mixtures are more likely to stick to the tin (pan) than others.

Some cakes have to be baked in a lined tin because the mixture is either very high in sugar or very moist, or uses little if any fat and is therefore inclined to stick. Greaseproof (waxed) paper can be used but the more expensive non-stick parchment or lining papers are excellent.

If you use non-stick tins (pans), there will be no need to line them, nor grease and flour them unless you are making a cake that is inclined to stick.

Turning Out

It is advisable to leave a cake or sponge in the tin (pan) for about 1 minute before turning it out. During this brief time the mixture contracts slightly and it will be much easier to remove. Tap the tin (pan) gently on a surface to loosen the cake from the base before inverting the tin (pan).

Some recipes state that the cake must be left in the tin for a period of time. This is because the mixture is either extremely fragile or rather heavy with fruit or treacle (molasses), or both, and could break if you try to turn it out too early.

Top left: A selection of biscuits, page 171
Bottom left: Homebaked Bread, page 154
Top right: Overnight Chocolate Cake, page 175
Bottom right: Black Cherry Meringue Pie, page 145

GOOD PASTRY

There are many kinds of pastry and all require the right balance of fat to flour, careful mixing of the ingredients and correct cooking.

Choose plain (all-purpose) flour for the rubbed-in type of pastries, which gives a better texture to the cooked pastry.

White flour produces the most inviting looking pastry. You can substitute wholewheat but this will absorb more liquid and is too coarse to make light pastry.

Short Pastries

Keep the ingredients cool when making rubbed-in (cut-in) and folded-in pastries (see page 148). Shortcrust Pastry (Basic Pie Dough) is the most popular and its recipe is below, followed by two similar recipes from France, Pâte Brisée and Pâte Sucrée.

Pastry with Oil

⁂This is an ideal pastry for anyone following a low-cholesterol diet.

Sift 225 g/8 oz (2 cups) plain (all-purpose) flour with a good pinch of salt. Whisk 6½ tablespoons corn oil with 4 tablespoons water. Add to the flour and blend with a fork; knead lightly until the pastry leaves the mixing bowl clean.

Roll out as soon as the pastry is made between two sheets of greaseproof (waxed) or 'non-stick' paper. Use as Shortcrust Pastry and add flavourings, (see right).

Shortcrust Pastry (Basic Pie Dough)

225 g/8 oz (2 cups) plain (all-purpose) flour
pinch of salt
110 g/4 oz (½ cup) fat, see Note
cold water to bind

⁂Sift the flour and salt into a bowl. Rub-in (cut-in) the fat with the fingertips until the mixture is like fine breadcrumbs. Add sufficient cold water and mix with a palette knife to make a dough with a firm rolling consistency. Use in savoury or sweet recipes.

Note The fat can be all butter, all margarine, all cooking fat or lard, or half butter or margarine and half cooking fat or lard.

110 g is given as the metric equivalent for 4 oz as this produces a better proportion of fat to flour.

Preparing Shortcrust Pastry

Special Technique
RUBBED-IN PASTRIES USING A FOOD PROCESSOR OR MIXER

Nowadays many people will prefer to use either a food processor or a mixer to rub or cut the fat into the flour. Use ingredients for Shortcrust Pastry (see below) and remember these simple rules:

☐ Always cut the fat into convenient-sized pieces.

☐ Use a mixer on low speed to produce an action that is very similar to rubbing in (cutting in) by hand. Although many manufacturers suggest using the beater of a mixer, rather than the whisk, I prefer the latter for it keeps the fat and flour mixture cooler.

☐ Whether using a mixer or a food processor, stop the machine the moment the mixture looks like fine breadcrumbs. Over-mixing produces a pastry that is tough and impossible to handle.

☐ Add the same quantity of liquid as when making pastry by hand and mix this, either with the machine in operation, or by hand with a palette knife.

There are many ways in which a basic Shortcrust Pastry can be varied.

Variations

⁂Almond Pastry Use 110 g/4 oz (½ cup) fat and 175 g/6 oz (1½ cups) plain (all-purpose) flour, add 50 g/2 oz (½ cup) ground almonds and 25 to 50 g/1 to 2 oz

---

(2 to 4 tablespoons) caster sugar or 25 to 50 g/1 to 2 oz (¼ to ½ cup) sifted icing sugar (confectioners' sugar). Bind with the yolk of 1 egg and a little water.

Use this pastry for small sweet tartlet cases or flans.

⁂Cheese-flavoured Pastry For economical cheese pastry, use only 85 g/3 oz (6 tablespoons) fat (butter or margarine) and 50 to 85 g/2 to 3 oz (½ to ¾ cup) grated cheese to each 225 g/8 oz (2 cups) plain (all-purpose) flour.

The recipe can be varied by using different proportions of fat and cheese and by selecting different kinds of cheese, from firm strong grated Parmesan to a soft cream cheese. You can use any cheese that cooks well, such as Cheddar, Cheshire (Brick), Gouda, Edam or Danish Samsoe. Grate hard cheese as finely as possible.

For a richer pastry, use the same amount of fat and cheese to 175 g/6 oz (1½ cups) flour only. This pastry can be a little crumbly and difficult to handle, so wrap and chill for a short time if necessary.

The pastry can be mixed with water, milk or egg yolk and water.

Always bake, or partially bake, cheese pastry in a moderately hot to hot oven to prevent it becoming slightly greasy.

Take particular care that the pastry is not overhandled.

Use this pastry for flan cases (pie shells), small savoury tartlet cases or as a base for canapés (see page 199).

⁂Nut Pastry Add 50 g/2 oz (½ cup) finely chopped walnuts, almonds or other nuts or 40 g/1½ oz (½ cup) desiccated (shredded) coconut to each 225 g/8 oz (2 cups) flour after rubbing in (cutting in) the fat.

⁂Savoury Pastry Add a good shake of

salt, a pinch of cayenne pepper and mustard powder when sifting the flour. Rub in (cut in) the fat. Bind with tomato juice, well-flavoured stock or a little yeast extract dissolved in water.

Use this pastry for small savoury tartlet cases or savoury pies.

⁂Spiced Pastry Sift 1 to 2 teaspoons ground ginger, ground cinnamon or mixed spice with each 225 g/8 oz (2 cups) flour.

⁂Sweet Shortcrust Pastry (Sweet Basic Pie Dough) Add 25 to 50 g/1 to 2 oz (2 to 4 tablespoons) sugar to the rubbed-in (cut-in) fat and flour. Bind with an egg yolk and water. (See Flan or Fleur Pastry page 146).

Black Cherry Meringue Pie

175 g/6 oz (1½ cups) plain (all-purpose) flour
pinch of salt
85 g/3 oz (6 tablespoons) butter
25 g/1 oz (2 tablespoons) caster sugar
1 egg yolk
1 tablespoon cold water
FOR THE FILLING:
1 × 425 g/15 oz can pitted black (bing) cherries
1 tablespoon cornflour (cornstarch)
1 egg yolk
a few drops of almond essence (extract)
FOR THE MERINGUE:
2 egg whites
100 g/4 oz (½ cup) caster sugar

⁂Sift together the flour and salt; rub in (cut in) the butter as described in the Master Recipe on this page, then add the sugar, egg yolk and water. Knead lightly, chill for a short time then roll out and line a 20 cm/8 inch fluted flan ring on an upturned baking sheet, or a flan dish (pie pan). Bake blind, (see page 146), in the centre of a preheated moderately hot oven (190 to 200°C/375 to 400°F, Gas Mark 5 to 6) for approximately 20 minutes then allow to cool.

For the Filling Drain the cherries, retaining the syrup. Mix the cornflour (cornstarch) with most of this syrup, pour into a saucepan, place over a low heat and stir until thickened. Beat the egg yolk with the remaining cherry syrup then whisk into the thickened mixture, cook gently for 1 minute only. Add the cherries and almond essence (extract) and allow the mixture to cool. Spoon into the pastry case (pie shell).

For the Meringue Whisk the egg whites until stiff, whisk in half the sugar, then fold in the remainder. Put into a piping (pastry) bag fitted with a large star nozzle and pipe a neat border around the edge of the flan. Return to a preheated moderate oven (160°C/325°F,

Gas Mark 3) for about 15 minutes. Serve when freshly made as the baking time for the meringue is very short and it may start to weep if left to stand. Serves 6.

Note If using cherries with stones (pits) you will need a larger quantity of fruit. Remove the stones (pits) with a stoner. For a very crisp meringue topping, bake small meringues separately and put on to the flan before serving.

Frangipani Tarts

Sweet Shortcrust Pastry (Sweet Basic Pie Dough) made with 225 g/8 oz (2 cups) flour etc. see left
FOR THE FILLING:
3 tablespoons raspberry or apricot jam
100 g/4 oz (½ cup) butter
100 g/4 oz (½ cup) caster sugar
a few drops of almond essence (extract)
2 eggs
100 g/4 oz (1 cup) ground almonds
25 g/1 oz (¼ cup) plain (all-purpose) flour

⁂Make the pastry and roll out until only about 3 mm/⅛ inch in thickness. Cut into 7.5 cm/3 inch rounds and insert into 24 patty tins (muffin pans). Re-roll any pastry left over and cut into 24 tiny shapes. Spread the jam over the base of each tartlet case.

Cream together the butter, sugar and almond essence (extract) until soft and light. Gradually beat in the eggs, then fold in the ground almonds and flour. Spoon over the jam and top with the pastry shapes. Bake in the centre of a preheated moderately hot oven (200°C/400°F, Gas Mark 6) for 15 to 20 minutes. Remove from the tins and allow to cool. Makes 24.

Master Recipe
PÂTÉ SUCRÉE

This French pastry is made with ingredients similar to those used in Shortcrust Pastry (see page 144), but the unique method of mixing produces a particularly light and crisp texture.

110 g/4 oz (½ cup) butter
225 g/8 oz (2 cups) plain (all-purpose) flour
pinch of salt
50 to 110 g/2 to 4 oz (¼ to ½ cup) caster sugar
2 egg yolks

⁂Allow the butter to stand at room temperature to become fairly soft; do not let it oil in any way. Sift the flour and salt on to a large pastry board or working surface. Make a well in the centre, put the butter (in one piece), sugar and egg yolks into the well. Mix the butter, sugar and egg yolks with your fingertips.

Gradually work the flour into this mixture with your fingertips. Do not try to make the butter mixture absorb too much flour at one time. Start with the flour around the well and when this is absorbed work in more flour.

Continue like this until all the flour has been absorbed. The mixture will probably be a little dry and crumbly, in which case work in a very little ice cold water to give a fairly firm rolling consistency. If the mixture seems a trifle soft due to handling, wrap in plastic wrap or foil and chill for 30 to 60 minutes. Roll and use. Never bake in too hot an oven.

VARIATION

Pâté Brisée Omit the sugar and make as above replacing one egg yolk with just enough ice cold water to bind.

Frangipani Tarts

FOR EASE
You can substitute frozen Shortcrust Pastry (Basic Pie Dough) in all recipes where homemade Shortcrust Pastry is suggested. If a recipe calls for Shortcrust Pastry made with 225 g/8 oz (2 cups) flour etc. you will need 350 g/12 oz (¾ lb) frozen pastry. Store and use frozen Shortcrust Pastry as directed on the packet.

FREEZING NOTE
⁂*The tart on this page can be frozen. Cool, then freeze and pack. Use within 3 months.*

LEFTOVERS
Sweet tartlets can be kept for several days in an airtight tin. Freshen by heating for a few minutes only in the oven.

Preparing a flan with Shortcrust pastry

FLAN OR FLEUR PASTRY

⁂The ingredients for this pastry are similar to those for Pâté Sucrée (see page 145), but the method of mixing produces a very firm and biscuit-like texture.

Cream together the butter and sugar until soft. Add the egg yolks then the sifted flour and salt; knead well. Roll out firmly and use to make sweet flans, such as Mincemeat Flan.

French Strawberry Flan

Pâté Sucrée or Flan Pastry made with 175 g/6 oz (1½ cups) flour, see above and page 145
Crème Pâtisssière, see right
6 tablespoons redcurrant jelly
1 tablespoon water
½ tablespoon lemon juice
450 g/1 lb (3 cups) strawberries

⁂Roll out the pastry to fit a 23 to 25 cm/ 9 to 10 inch flan tin (pie pan). Bake blind in the centre of a preheated moderately hot oven (190°C/375°F, Gas Mark 5) for 20 to 25 minutes until firm and golden; allow to cool.

Spread the cooled Crème Pâtissière into the flan. Heat the jelly with the water and lemon juice until the jelly has dissolved. Allow to cool and become the consistency of a thick syrup.

Arrange the strawberries in the flan over the Crème Pâtissière. If the fruit is very large, halve and arrange cut side downwards. Brush or spoon the redcurrant glaze over the fruit and allow to set. A little glaze could be brushed over the top rim of the pastry. Serves 6.

VARIATIONS

Use 150 g/5 oz (½ cup plus 2 tablespoons) cream cheese, flavoured with a little grated orange rind, 1 tablespoon orange juice and 2 tablespoons double (heavy) cream in place of the Crème Patissière.

Use the homemade cream (see page 153). Flavour this with a little sugar and vanilla essence (extract) or brandy.

Gooseberry Cream Flans

Sweet Shortcrust Pastry (Sweet Basic Pie Dough) made with 225 g/8 oz (2 cups) flour etc., see page 145
FOR THE FILLING:
25 g/1 oz (¼ cup) blanched almonds
2 × 284 g/10 oz cans gooseberries
2 × 170 g/6 oz cans cream or 350 ml/ 12 fl oz (1½ cups) fresh whipping cream
4 tablespoons icing (confectioners') sugar
1 tablespoon lemon juice

Make the pastry, roll out and line four

Making a Flan

You can use various pastries – Basic Shortcrust (pie dough), Cheese Pastry (page 144), Rich Flan (Fleur) pastry, (right), or Pâté Sucrée (page 145).

A perfectly shaped flan is not difficult to make, but it does depend on certain important factors.

☐ Never make the pastry too soft and moist because it will stretch when handled and shrink during baking.

☐ Allow a little time for the pastry shape to rest and chill before baking.

☐ When baking blind fill the flan as directed right, but remember to remove the ingredients used for weighing down the base of the pastry a little while before the end of the cooking time.

☐ Shape and trim the pastry carefully (see method right).

☐ Time the baking exactly, adjusting the temperature according to the type of pastry used.

☐ If possible, use a flan ring on a baking sheet, rather than a flan tin or dish (pie pan). Not only is it easier to slide off the cooked flan, but you can slip away the flan ring towards the end of the baking time, to allow the outside of the pastry to become delicately coloured and crisp.

Quantities

The amount of pastry to use depends on the depth and diameter of the pan, how thick you like the pastry, and on the type of pastry used. You will need a little less Pâté Sucrée or Flan Pastry than plain Shortcrust Pastry (Basic Pie Dough) because of the weight of the sugar used.

For an 18 to 20 cm/7 to 8 inch flan you would need pastry made with 100 to 175 g/4 to 6 oz (1 to 1½ cups) flour.

For a 23 to 25 cm/9 to 10 inch flan you need pastry made with 175 to 225 g/6 to 8 oz (1½ to 2 cups) flour.

To Bake Blind

Make the selected pastry (see pages 144 to 145). Prepare the ring and baking sheet, tin or flan dish (pie pan). If using Shortcrust Pastry (basic pie dough) there is no need to grease the container, but it is advisable to grease it lightly if using Cheese Pastry or any type of sweet pastry.

Support the pastry over the rolling pin and lower it into the container. Slip away the rolling pin. Do not attempt to cut or roll away the surplus dough until you have pressed the pastry down into the base and corners of the container with your fingertips – this stage is very important. When satisfied you have done this, cut away the surplus with a sharp knife (take care not to pull the pastry while doing so) or pass the rolling pin backwards and forwards over the pastry until the surplus dough falls away. Cover lightly with plastic wrap and chill for a time if possible.

To prevent the base of the pastry rising, place a piece of greased greaseproof (waxed) paper, greased side down, over the pastry. On top of this place crusts of bread, uncooked haricot (navy) beans, butter beans, rice or macaroni or invest in special beads for this purpose that can be used over and over again.

Bake at the temperature and for the time given in the individual recipes and remember to remove paper, topping and the flan ring before the end of the baking time so that the pastry can colour.

10 cm/4 inch individual flan tins (pie pans). Bake blind, (see opposite), in the centre of a preheated moderately hot oven (200°C/400°F, Gas Mark 6) for 15 to 20 minutes. Allow to cool. Brown the almonds in a heavy frying pan (skillet) over moderate heat. Allow to cool. Drain the gooseberries. Whip the cream until thick. Sift the icing (confectioners') sugar and fold into the cream with the lemon juice. Put into the pastry cases (pie shells) and top with the gooseberries and browned almonds. Serves 4.

Mincemeat Flan

FOR THE FLEUR PASTRY:
100 g/4 oz (½ cup) butter
25 g/1 oz (2 tablespoons) caster sugar
1 egg
175 g/6 oz (1½ cups) plain (all-purpose) flour

FOR THE FILLING AND TOPPING:
75 g/3 oz (scant ½ cup) glacé cherries
350 g/12 oz (1½ cups) mincemeat
Rum Butter see page 201

⁜Cream the butter and sugar until soft and light. Beat the egg and add 2 tablespoons of it to the creamed mixture together with the flour. Knead lightly and chill for at least 30 minutes. Roll out and line a 20 cm/8 inch flan ring or dish (pie pan). Bake the flan blind (see opposite) in the centre of a preheated moderately hot oven (190°C/375°F, Gas Mark 5) for 15 minutes.

Meanwhile, chop most of the cherries, but quarter 2 or 3 of them; put these on one side for decoration. Blend the chopped cherries with the mincemeat, spoon into the partially cooked flan, then continue baking for a further 15 to 20 minutes, or until the pastry is crisp and golden. Reduce the heat slightly if the pastry is becoming too brown. Allow to become quite cold.

Make the Rum Butter (see page 201). Put the small rose nozzle into a piping (pastry) bag and pipe a border of the Rum Butter around and in the centre of the flan. Decorate with the quartered cherries. Serve any leftover Rum Butter with the flan. Serves 6 to 8.

Chocolate Walnut Tartlets

Shortcrust (Basic Pie Dough) or Sweet Shortcrust Pastry (Sweet Basic Pie Dough) made with 175 g/6 oz (1½ cups) flour etc., see page 145

FOR THE FILLING:
2 tablespoons apricot jam
50 g/2 oz (½ cup) walnuts
85 g/3 oz (6 tablespoons) butter or margarine
85 g/3 oz (6 tablespoons) caster sugar
1 egg

85 g/3 oz (¾ cup) self-raising flour
40 g/1½ oz (6 tablespoons) chocolate powder (sweetened cocoa)
2 tablespoons cream or milk

TO DECORATE:
100 g/4 oz (⅔ cup) plain (semi-sweet) chocolate
25 g/1 oz (2 tablespoons) butter
25 g/1 oz (¼ cup) icing (confectioners') sugar
6 to 9 walnut halves
25 g/1 oz (2 tablespoons) chocolate vermicelli (sprinkles)

⁜Make the pastry, roll out thinly, cut into rounds and line 12 deep patty (tartlet) tins or 18 more shallow ones. Put a little apricot jam into each pastry case. Coarsely chop the walnuts. Cream the butter or margarine with the sugar until soft and light, then beat in the egg. Sift the flour with the chocolate powder (sweetened cocoa). Add to the creamed mixture, together with the cream or milk and the walnuts. Divide the mixture between the cases.

Bake in the centre of a preheated moderately hot oven (200°C/400°F, Gas Mark 6) for 10 minutes; lower the heat slightly and cook for a further 5 to 10 minutes until both filling and pastry are cooked. Allow to cool.

Break the chocolate into pieces and put into a bowl. Place over a pan of hot but not boiling water, allow to melt, cool then blend with the butter. Sift the icing (confectioners') sugar into the chocolate mixture. Spread a little on the top of each tartlet. Split the walnut halves and place a piece in the centre of each tartlet and sprinkle with chocolate vermicelli (sprinkles). Makes 12 to 18.

Note Plain (all-purpose) flour can be used but add ¾ teaspoon baking powder.

Custard Cream

2 level tablespoons custard powder (Bird's English dessert mix)
225 ml/7½ fl oz (scant 1 cup) milk
25 to 50 g/1 to 2 oz (2 to 4 tablespoons) caster sugar
a few drops of vanilla essence (extract)
1 egg yolk
150 ml/¼ pint (⅔ cup) double (heavy) cream

⁜Blend the custard powder (dessert mix) with 150 ml/¼ pint (⅔ cup) of the milk. Pour into a saucepan, add the sugar and the vanilla essence. Stir over a low heat until a thick consistency. Remove from the heat. Whisk the egg yolk and remaining milk together. Add to the thickened custard and stir well as the mixture thickens once again. Spoon into a bowl, cover tightly with plastic wrap, but lift the cover and stir once or twice as the mixture cools to prevent a skin forming. Leave until quite cold.

Whip the cream and fold into the cold custard mixture. Use this as a filling in flans and for gâteaux or pastries. Makes enough for a large flan (see left).

VARIATIONS

For a more economical mixture use only 2 to 3 tablespoons whipped cream.

⁜**Crème Pâtissière** Use 1½ level tablespoons of cornflour (cornstarch) in place of the custard powder with the same proportion of liquid as above. Follow the method above, but blend 2 egg yolks with the remaining milk and add to the cornflour (cornstarch) mixture, return to the heat and stir over a very low heat until thickened again. Cool as above, then blend in the whipped cream.

A richer Crème Pâtissière is made by adding 25 g/1 oz (2 tablespoons) unsalted butter to the cornflour (cornstarch) mixture as it thickens.

LEFTOVERS
Small portions of leftover Shortcrust Pastry (Basic Pie Dough) can be made into tiny cheese biscuits.
Cheese Biscuits
Sprinkle the pastry board with finely grated Cheddar or Parmesan cheese. Roll out the pastry on top of the cheese until very thin, brush with a little egg white and more grated cheese. Cut into tiny squares and bake in a preheated hot oven (200 to 220°C/400 to 425°F, Gas Mark 6 to 7) for 6 to 8 minutes.

French Strawberry Flan

Folded Pastries

Puff, Rough Puff and Flaky Pastries are all made by folding the dough to incorporate air. Do not reduce the number of foldings and rollings given in each recipe and fold the dough evenly and carefully to keep the pastry a good shape.

(see page 8)

FOR EASE
In all recipes where homemade Puff Pastry is required you can substitute frozen Puff Pastry. If a recipe requires Puff Pastry made with 225 g/8 oz (2 cups) flour etc. you will need 450 g/1 lb frozen Puff Pastry. Store frozen Puff Pastry as directed on the packet.

LEFTOVERS
Cut any tiny pieces of uncooked Puff Pastry into thin strips (rather like cheese straws).

For sweet twists, brush with lightly whisked egg white, then roll in a mixture of granulated sugar and very finely chopped blanched almonds.

Place on a baking sheet and bake in a preheated hot oven (220°C/425°F, Gas Mark 7) for about 10 minutes.

For savoury twists, simply brush with lightly whisked egg white and finely grated Parmesan cheese. Bake as above.

Buying Points

Flour Strong (hardwheat) flour (the type used for making bread) gives the best result in these richer pastries; it helps the pastry to rise well (see page 8). If not available, use plain (all-purpose) flour.

Fat You can use all butter or all margarine for Flaky and Rough Puff Pastries, or equal quantities of butter or margarine and lard or cooking fat. If using two fats, mix them together first. Do not use soft margarine for these pastries.

Butter, preferably unsalted, is the correct fat for Puff Pastry. Hard margarine can be substituted. The fat should be left at room temperature for a short time so that it is not too cold and hard.

Microwave Cooking

Pastry can be cooked in a microwave cooker although the result is not as good as when baked in a conventional oven. A Shortcrust Pastry (Basic Pie Dough) flan takes about 4 minutes cooking on HIGH; you need to protect the rim of the pastry with foil (provided this can be used in your particular cooker).

Individual fingers of Puff Pastry rise extremely well and the pastry is deliciously light.

Savoury Mille Feuilles

Puff Pastry made with 175 g/6 oz (1½ cups) flour etc., below, or 1 × 375 g/13 oz packet Frozen Puff Pastry
FOR THE FILLING AND TOPPING:
2 eggs
100 g/4 oz (½ cup) butter
225 g/8 oz (1 cup) cream cheese
1 tablespoon mayonnaise
2 teaspoons lemon juice
shake of pepper
1 × 190 g/6½ oz can red peppers (pimiento)
225 g/8 oz cooked gammon (smoked ham)
½ medium cucumber
TO GARNISH:
2 stuffed olives
a little watercress

Make the pastry or defrost it. Roll out the pastry until it is very thin and cut it into three rectangular shapes, each approximately 30 × 13 cm/12 × 5 inches. Prick each rectangle with a fork and then place on to one or two baking sheets. Lightly cover with plastic wrap and chill for at least 30 minutes. Bake above the centre of a preheated hot to very hot oven (220 to 230°C/425 to 450°F, Gas Mark 7 to 8) for 10 to 15 minutes until well risen and golden in colour. Cool on a wire rack. When quite cold, trim the edges, if necessary, so the three layers are exactly the same size.

For the Filling Hard-boil (hard-cook) the eggs, shell and chop them. Cream the butter with the cheese, mayonnaise and lemon juice, add a shake of pepper. Spread a little over one layer of the pastry, this will be the top of the Mille Feuilles. Drain the canned red peppers (pimiento), cut about 5 petal shapes for garnish and put these on one side. Finely chop the remainder of the peppers and the gammon (ham). Mix with the remainder of the cheese mixture and the chopped eggs. Thinly slice the cucumber.

Place one plain layer of puff pastry on a serving dish. Spread with half the remaining cheese mixture and half the cucumber slices. Add the second layer of plain puff pastry then cover with the remaining cheese mixture and cucumber slices. Place the final cheese-covered pastry on top. Cut the olives in slices then arrange the red pepper petals, watercress and olives to form a flower spray. Serves 6.

VARIATION

Curried Filling Omit the lemon juice in the recipe above, add 1 teaspoon curry paste to the other ingredients together with 2 extra teaspoons of mayonnaise.

Special Technique
FOLDED PASTRIES

Both Flaky and Rough Puff Pastry are made using three quarters the amount of fat to flour; Puff Pastry is made using equal amounts. It is the folding process that creates the light layered texture.

❉Flaky Pastry Sift 225 g/8 oz (2 cups) strong (bread) flour or plain (all-purpose) flour with a pinch of salt into a mixing bowl. Divide 175 g/6 oz (¾ cup) fat into 3 portions. Rub (cut) one-third of the fat into the flour. Add enough ice cold water, or water and a squeeze of lemon juice, to make an elastic rolling consistency. Roll out the dough to a neat, oblong shape.

Divide the second portion of fat into neat pieces, put over the top two-thirds of the pastry dough, keeping the bottom third of the dough without fat.

Bring up the bottom third of the dough A and B over the dough C and D. Bring down the top third E and F to C and D so

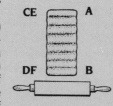

making a neat shape with all the fat enclosed.

Turn the dough at right angles, seal the ends and then use the rolling pin

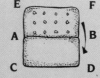

to rib the pastry dough at regular intervals.

Roll out again and put the remaining fat over the dough as above. Fold the dough and rib it.

Cover with plastic wrap and keep in a cool place until ready to use.

Variations

❉Rough Puff Pastry Sift 225 g/8 oz (2 cups) strong (bread) flour or plain (all-purpose) flour with a pinch of salt into a mixing bowl.

Put 175 g/6 oz (¾ cup) fat into the bowl, cut this into small pieces with 2 knives. Do *not* try to make the fat so fine that it is like the basis of Shortcrust Pastry (Basic Pie Dough).

Add enough ice cold water, or water with a squeeze of lemon juice, to make an elastic rolling consistency.

Roll out the dough and fold it into three as in the technique for Flaky Pastry (left), but give the dough 5 rollings and 5 foldings. Cover with plastic wrap and keep in a cool place until ready to use.

❉Puff Pastry Sift 225 g/8 oz (2 cups) strong (bread) flour or plain (all-purpose) flour with a pinch of salt into a mixing bowl.

Add ½ tablespoon lemon juice and enough ice cold water to make an elastic rolling consistency.

Roll out to a neat oblong shape. Place 225 g/8 oz (1 cup) butter in the centre of the dough. Bring up corners A and B over the butter (see the sketches left) and corners E and F over the top to give a neat shape.

Turn the dough at right angles, seal the ends and then, using the rolling pin, rib the pastry dough at regular intervals as described under Flaky Pastry. This is the first folding. Continue like this, giving the pastry a total of 7 rollings and 7 foldings. Chill well between rollings, so the pastry does not become over-soft. When made, cover with plastic wrap and keep in a cool place until ready to use.

Coconut Sponge Tartlets

Puff Pastry made with 100 g/4 oz (1 cup) flour etc., see left

FOR THE FILLING:

2 tablespoons raspberry jam

50 g/2 oz (¼ cup) butter or margarine

75 g/3 oz (6 tablespoons) caster sugar

1 egg

50 g/2 oz (½ cup) self-raising flour

50 g/2 oz (⅔ cup) desiccated (shredded) coconut

1 tablespoon milk

TO DECORATE:

2 to 3 tablespoons raspberry jam

6 glacé cherries

a small piece of angelica

about 25 g/1 oz (⅓ cup) desiccated (shredded) coconut

∗∗Make the pastry, roll out very thinly, cut into rounds and line 12 moderately deep patty (tartlet) tins. Put a little jam into each pastry case. Cream the butter or margarine and the sugar, then beat in the egg. Sift the flour, fold into the creamed mixture. Add the coconut and milk.

Spoon the filling into the tartlet cases. Bake in the centre of a preheated hot oven (220°C/425°F, Gas Mark 7) for 10 minutes, or until the pastry has risen well, then lower the heat slightly and bake for a further 5 to 10 minutes until the filling is firm. Allow to cool.

Warm the raspberry jam for the topping if it is a little stiff; spread evenly over the top of the filling. Halve the cherries, press one half into the middle of each tartlet. Cut the angelica into small leaf shapes, arrange beside the cherries. Sprinkle with coconut. Makes 12.
Note Plain (all-purpose) flour can be used, but add ½ teaspoon baking powder.

Special Technique
SWEET AND SAVOURY TURNOVERS

∗∗Flaky or Rough Puff Pastry can be used to make turnovers. Pastry made with 225 g/8 oz (2 cups) flour etc., (see opposite) will give 8 large, 12 medium or 18 small turnovers.

Roll the pastry out until between 3 and 5 mm/⅛ and ¼ inch thick, cut into rounds and add the filling. Moisten the edges with a little egg or water and fold over to enclose the filling.

Knock up the edges with a knife held horizontally. Always do this with light rich pastries. It encourages the pastry to rise well.

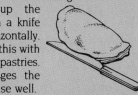

Cut 2 or 3 slits in each turnover so the steam can escape. Bake just above the centre of a preheated hot oven (220°C/425°F, Gas Mark 7) for 25 to 30 minutes.

Variations
Sweet Turnovers
∗∗Fill with a thick fresh fruit purée; a good quality firm jam (do not use jam that is too runny) or try the following combination:
Cream Cheese and Orange Blend 225 g/8 oz (1 cup) cream cheese with 1 teaspoon grated orange rind, 1 tablespoon orange juice or Curaçao, 2 tablespoons sugar and 2 tablespoons sultanas (golden raisins).

Brush the turnovers with lightly whisked egg white and sprinkle with sugar before baking.

Savoury Turnovers
∗∗These can be filled with a well-flavoured savoury sauce (see page 102) or try one of the following:
Chicken and Mushroom Blend 225 g/8 oz (1 cup) minced (ground) cooked chicken with 100 g/4 oz (1 cup) chopped fried mushrooms, 1 tablespoon chopped parsley, 1 tablespoon double (heavy) cream and seasoning.
Spinach and Ricotta Cheese Blend 175 g/6 oz (¾ cup) cooked finely chopped spinach with 100 g/4 oz (½ cup) Ricotta cheese, 1 tablespoon double (heavy) cream, a little grated nutmeg and seasoning.
Tomato and Ham Skin and chop 2 large tomatoes, blend with 225 g/8 oz finely diced or minced (ground) cooked ham, 1 teaspoon French (Dijon) mustard and 1 tablespoon chopped chives. Add salt and pepper to taste.

Savoury Turnovers and Savoury Mille Feuilles

LEFTOVERS
Leftover cooked Puff Pastry can be kept in an airtight tin for some days. It tends to lose its crisp texture, so reheat for a short time before serving. Add fillings just before serving.

FREEZING NOTE
∗∗Uncooked or cooked Puff Pastry freezes exceptionally well. It is a good idea to shape uncooked pastry before freezing. Freeze, uncovered, on flat sheets and then pack. To serve, unpack, place on baking sheets and cook from frozen. Uncooked Puff Pastry can be frozen for up to 1 month.

Cooked Puff Pastry cases are better frozen without a filling. Store for up to 4 months. Filled cases should be used within 3 months.

If they are frozen with a filling, serve as soon as possible after thawing, as the pastry will soften.

149

Savoury Pastry Dishes

LEFTOVERS

Handle small leftover pieces of the light pastry carefully. Do not gather them together into a ball but fold them neatly on top of one another, re-roll into an oblong shape then give at least one folding and rolling, (see Flaky Pastry page 148).

The pastry will retain its light texture and will rise well.

FREEZING NOTE

✲✲If 'en croûte' dishes have been frozen uncooked, they must be thawed before cooking, but never allow them to stand longer than necessary, otherwise the filling, which becomes moist after freezing, spoils the consistency of the pastry.

Special Technique
'EN CROUTE' DISHES

Wrapping food in pastry before baking makes the result most attractive and worthy of a special occasion. It also gives the ingredients an interesting flavour.

The most famous of these dishes is Boeuf en Croûte or Beef Wellington (see opposite).

The secrets of success are:
☐ Use puff, rough puff or flaky pastry and bake quickly so that the pastry rises.
☐ Roll out the pastry until it is wafer thin and take care to completely enclose the meat or fish in the pastry.
☐ Make quite sure that the meat is adequately precooked (see recipes on this page). Fish cooks rapidly so it is not necessary to precook individual portions of fish although whole fish, such as salmon, are better precooked before coating with pastry.

Cutlets en Croûte

Flaky Pastry made with 350 g/12 oz (3 cups) flour etc., see page 148

FOR THE FILLING:
6 large lamb cutlets
3 teaspoons made mustard
1½ teaspoons brown sugar

TO GLAZE:
1 egg

✲✲Make the pastry using margarine. Grill (broil) the cutlets (chops) for 2 to 3 minutes on each side, then allow to cool. Mix the mustard and sugar and spread over each cutlet. Roll out the pastry very thinly to an oblong shape and cut into long strips 2.5 cm/1 inch wide. Wind these around each cutlet; damp the edges of the pastry with water as you do so and make quite certain the meat is covered completely.

Lift on to a baking sheet. Beat the egg and brush over the pastry. Bake just above the centre of a preheated hot oven (220°C/425°F, Gas Mark 7) for 40 minutes; reduce the heat slightly after 25 minutes if the pastry is becoming too brown. Serves 6.

Savoury Beef Loaf en Croûte

350 g/12 oz (¾ lb) rump (top round) or good quality stewing steak

2 medium onions
2 small cooking apples
50 g/2 oz (1 cup) soft breadcrumbs, preferably brown
1 to 2 tablespoons chopped parsley
½ teaspoon chopped fresh or ¼ teaspoon dried sage
1 egg
4 tablespoons beef stock
salt and pepper
Rough Puff Pastry, made with 175 g/6 oz flour, etc., page 148

TO GLAZE:
1 egg

TO GARNISH:
parsley or watercress

Mince (grind) the steak, peel and finely chop or grate the onions. Peel, core and finely dice the apples. Mix the meat, onions, and apples with the breadcrumbs, herbs, egg and stock. Season well. Grease a 450 to 675 g/1 to 1½ lb loaf tin (pan) and put in the mixture. Stand this in a 'bain-marie' of cold water to prevent the outside of the loaf hardening during cooking. Bake in the centre of a moderate oven (180°C/350°F, Gas Mark 4) for 45 minutes. Allow to cool in the tin with a light weight on top to give a better shape to the loaf.

Meanwhile make the pastry (see page 148). Roll out to a rectangle about 5 mm/¼ inch in thickness or even slightly thinner. This must be sufficiently large to enclose the loaf. Place the cold loaf in the centre of the pastry, brush the edges of the pastry well with water then fold this to enclose the meat loaf. Seal the joins, turn so the join along the length of the loaf is underneath and place on a baking sheet. Roll out any pastry trimmings to make 'leaves' and tiny rounds. Moisten the pastry trimmings, press on to the loaf. Beat the egg and brush over the loaf and trimmings, make 2 slits on top for the steam to escape. Bake in the centre of a preheated hot oven (220°C/425°F, Gas Mark 7) for 35 minutes or until the pastry is well risen and firm. If serving hot, reduce the heat to moderately hot (190°C/375°F, Gas Mark 5) and allow a further 10 minutes. This makes certain the loaf is well heated. Garnish with parsley or watercress. Serves 4 to 5.

Turkey Breast en Croûte

Rough Puff Pastry made with 350 g/ 12 oz (3 cups) flour, see page 148

FOR THE FILLING:
1.25 kg/2½ lb boned and rolled turkey breast, see method
2 to 3 tablespoons melted margarine
2 tablespoons mustard powder, see variation
2 tablespoons white wine
1 teaspoon chopped fresh thyme
½ to 1 teaspoon garlic salt
¼ to ½ teaspoon cayenne pepper
black pepper
4 slices cooked ham sufficiently large to cover the turkey breast

TO GLAZE:
1 egg

✲✲Make the pastry, in this case it should be made using margarine. Chill while cooking the turkey breast. It is possible to purchase boned and rolled turkey breast. If it is frozen, allow it to thaw completely. Cover the outside of the turkey with the melted margarine and cook completely, following the timing on page 78. Allow the turkey breast to cool. Blend the mustard powder with white wine, add the thyme, garlic salt, cayenne pepper and a pinch of black pepper. Score the turkey breast all round the

Savoury Beef Loaf en Croûte

with a little water then fold to cover the steak. Make sure the pastry just overlaps to give a firm join. Seal the ends and the join and turn the roll so that the join is underneath. Place on a baking sheet.

Roll out any pastry trimmings and cut leaves and a pastry rose. Moisten with a little water and place on the pastry shape. Make 2 to 3 slits on top of the pastry so that the steam can escape.

Beat the egg and the water and brush all over the pastry. Bake in the centre of a preheated hot oven (220°C/425°F, Gas Mark 7) for approximately 40 minutes; reduce the heat slightly after 30 minutes if necessary. Slice to serve. Serves 6.

Liver en Croûte

Puff Pastry made with 225 g/8 oz (2 cups) flour etc., see page 148
FOR THE FILLING:
350 g/12 oz lambs' liver, see method
2 medium onions
3 streaky bacon rashers (slices)
15 g/½ oz (1 tablespoon) butter
a few drops of Tabasco (hot pepper) sauce or Worcestershire sauce
shake of pepper
TO GLAZE:
1 egg

**＊Make the pastry, wrap in plastic wrap and refrigerate until required.

Ask the butcher to cut the liver into 4 even-sized slices. Peel and chop the onion very finely. De-rind and chop the bacon and heat the rinds with the butter. Add the onion and bacon and fry gently until the onion is soft. Discard the bacon rinds, add the sauce, season the mixture with a little pepper and allow to cool.

Roll out the pastry until very thin and cut into 8 portions, each a little larger than the slices of liver. Place 4 portions of pastry on to a baking sheet. Add the uncooked liver, then top with the onion mixture. Moisten the edges of the bottom pastry, put the remaining 4 pastry portions on top of the filling, seal and flute the edges. Mark the top in a lattice design with a knife. Beat the egg, and brush over the pastry.

Bake in the centre of a preheated hot oven (220°C/425°F, Gas Mark 7) for nearly 10 minutes so that the pastry begins to rise well, then lower the heat to moderate (180°C/350°F, Gas Mark 4). Cook for a further 20 minutes. Serves 4.

VARIATION

**＊Salmon en Croûte Use 4 thin salmon steaks instead of liver. The fish should not be precooked. Place the fish on to the 4 pieces of pastry, top with a little lemon juice and seasoning then cover with the rest of the pastry. Bake as Liver en Croûte, but allow an extra 10 minutes. Reduce the oven temperature slightly after 25 to 30 minutes if the pastry is becoming too brown. Serves 4.

outside of the joint, making cuts about 3 mm/⅛ inch in depth. Spread the mustard mixture all over the joint, then wrap in the slices of ham, pressing them firmly against the turkey.

Roll out the pastry to a square of about 38 cm/15 inches, it must be sufficiently large to enclose the turkey joint. Beat the egg and brush the centre of the pastry with a little egg; place the turkey joint on this portion of the pastry. Make diagonal cuts at 1.5 cm/½ inch intervals in the pastry on either side of the turkey.

Fold the two ends of the pastry over the turkey; remove any surplus pastry. Take the strips of pastry and plait over the turkey, covering this completely. Use any leftover pastry to make leaf shapes and press on top of the pastry. Lift the pastry-covered joint on to a baking tray. Chill for at least 1 hour then brush all over with the remaining egg. Bake in the centre of a preheated hot oven (220°C/425°F, Gas Mark 7) for about 40 minutes; reduce the heat slightly after 30 minutes if necessary. Serves 6.

Note This is a fairly generous amount of pastry but this is necessary because of the method of coating the turkey. Use pastry made with 300 g/10 oz (2½ cups) flour if wrapping as for Beef Wellington.

VARIATION

Spread the cooked turkey breast with about 175 g/6 oz (¾ cup) pâté; omit the mustard mixture and ham.

Beef Wellington

Puff Pastry made with 225 g/8 oz (2 cups) flour etc., see page 148
FOR THE FILLING:
1 to 1.25 kg/2 to 2½ lb fillet steak, cut in one piece from the thick end of the fillet
40 g/1½ oz (3 tablespoons) butter
100 g/4 oz (1 cup) mushrooms
175 g/6 oz (¾ cup) liver pâté, see page 24
1 tablespoon chopped parsley
salt and pepper
TO GLAZE:
1 egg
1 tablespoon water

**＊Make the pastry and allow it to chill while preparing the meat. Spread the butter all over the steak. Roast. (See page 50 for times but do not overcook, because the beef continues to cook as it cools and again when it is baked in the oven with the pastry covering).

Chop the mushrooms very finely, mix with the liver pâté and parsley and season lightly if necessary. Roll out the pastry very thinly to an oblong shape sufficiently large to envelop the meat. Spread the pâté mixture all over the meat and place this in the centre of the pastry. Moisten the edges of the pastry

Turkey Breast en Croûte, Cutlets en Croûte, and Devilled Ham Bouchées

SIMPLE SKILL

Making bouchée cases
Roll out Rough Puff or Flaky Pastry until 1.5 cm/½ inch thick for small cases or 2 cm/¾ inch if larger.

Cut into rounds, then cut a smaller circle from the centre of half the rounds. Retain the small circles – these are baked with the bouchée cases, and used as lids, to top fillings.

Dampen the edges of the complete rounds with a little water. Carefully lift the rings on to the complete rounds. Do not stretch the pastry.

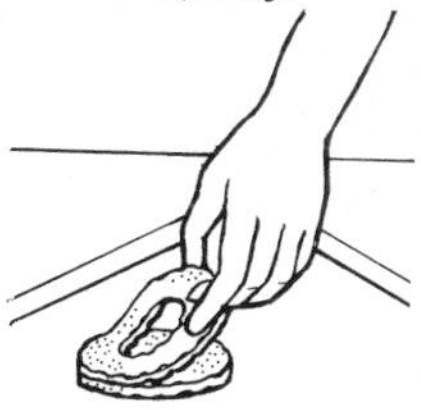

Knock up the edges (see page 149). Bake in the centre of a preheated hot oven (220/425°F, Gas Mark 7) for 10 to 12 minutes.

DEVILLED HAM BOUCHÉES

Make bouchée cases (see above) using 225 g/8 oz pastry. Brush with beaten egg and bake (see above). Make a One-stage White Sauce using 15 g/½ oz (1 tablespoon) margarine 15 g/½ oz (2 tablespoons) flour and 150 ml/¼ pint (⅔ cup) milk (see page 102). Add ½ chicken stock cube (1 bouillon cube), 175 g/6 oz cooked ham ½ to 1 teaspoon each Worcestershire Sauce, French (Dijon) mustard, curry paste and salt and pepper. Spoon hot sauce into the hot bouchée cases and serve hot garnished with parsley. Or cool pastry before adding cold sauce and serve cold.

151

Choux Pastry

This pastry is much more versatile than many people imagine. It can be made into large impressive cream buns or éclairs, used for cocktail-sized savouries or even made so small that the light shapes can float on soup.

Croquenbouche

Choux Pastry

300 ml/½ pint (1¼ cups) water
100 g/4 oz (½ cup) butter
pinch of sugar
150 g/5 oz (1¼ cups) plain (all-purpose) flour
4 large eggs

Put the water, butter and sugar into a saucepan. Heat only until the butter has melted. Sift the flour. Break the eggs into a bowl and beat well. Remove the saucepan from the heat and stir in all the flour. Return the pan to a low heat and stir until the mixture forms a ball and leaves the sides of the pan clean. Remove from the heat and allow the mixture to cool. Using a wooden spoon or electric mixer, gradually beat in the eggs to give a smooth mixture.

⁂Savoury Choux Pastry

Use half the quantity of Choux Pastry given above for about 12 medium-sized buns, 18 small buns or 30 to 36 cocktail-sized buns. Omit the pinch of sugar in the recipe and add a good pinch of salt and shake of pepper instead.

⁂Cheese Choux Pastry Make the Savoury Choux Pastry above and add finely grated Parmesan or Cheddar cheese to the mixture before beating in the eggs. Allow 25 g/1 oz (¼ cup) cheese to Choux Pastry made with 150 ml/¼ pint (⅔ cup) water, 50 g/2 oz (¼ cup) butter, seasoning etc.

Sweet Fillings

Sweet choux buns and éclairs can be filled with whipped cream, homemade cream (opposite), Custard Cream or Crème Pâtissière (see page 147). When the buns are filled, dust with sifted icing (confectioners') sugar or coat with Chocolate or Coffee Glacé Icing (see page 168).

Large choux buns make a delicious dessert if filled with sliced sweetened strawberries or whole raspberries and ice cream. Add the filling just before serving and top with sifted icing (confectioners') sugar. Serve with cream or a Fruit sauce.

Large choux buns take about 35 minutes to cook and large éclairs about 25 minutes.

Profiteroles

⁂This dessert is very easy to prepare.

Make the choux buns as for Croquenbouche (see right). Half the quantity will give generous portions for 4 people or small portions for up to 6 people. When cold, split and fill with whipped cream or homemade cream (see opposite). Put into a deep serving dish. Pour a generous amount of cold chocolate sauce over the small buns or serve the sauce separately (see page 125 and below).

Speedy Chocolate Sauce Put 50 g/2 oz (¼ cup) butter, 150 ml/¼ pint (⅔ cup) water, 50 g/2 oz (¼ cup) caster or granulated sugar and 25 g/1 oz (¼ cup) cocoa powder (unsweetened cocoa) into a saucepan. Stir as the mixture comes to the boil, reduce heat and simmer for 1 minute, then stir in 50 g/2 oz (½ cup) chocolate powder. The sauce becomes a perfect coating consistency when cold. It has the flavour of plain (semi-sweet) chocolate; for a milder taste use 75 g/3 oz (¾ cup) chocolate powder.

If you like a generous amount of sauce, double the quantities.

Savoury Choux Puffs

Small buns made from Savoury Choux Pastry or Cheese Choux Pastry (see left) can be filled with any of the following fillings. Each filling is sufficient to fill 30 to 36 cocktail-sized choux. Fill just before serving.

⁂Cheese and Walnut Blend 225 g/8 oz (1 cup) cream or curd cheese with 3 to 4 tablespoons double (heavy) cream (use enough to make the cheese the consistency of whipped cream). Add 2 to 3 tablespoons finely chopped walnuts (fresh skinned walnuts are delicious) a few drops of Tabasco (hot pepper) sauce or 1 tablespoon chopped gherkin.

Egg and Sardine Hard-boil (hard-cook) and chop 2 eggs. Blend with about 225 g/8 oz (½ lb) well drained and boned canned sardines (use those in oil or tomato sauce); add a squeeze of lemon juice and bind with mayonnaise or soured cream to give a soft consistency.

Pâté and Egg Use liver or other pâté instead of sardines in the previous recipe, but bind with yogurt.

⁂Savoury Cream Flavour 150 to 300 ml/¼ to ½ pint (⅔ to 1¼ cups) whipped cream with a little seasoning, finely grated cheese or a few drops of anchovy essence. Add 3 to 4 tablespoons finely chopped watercress leaves, a squeeze of lemon juice and seasoning.

Seafood Cream Use 225 g/8 oz flaked crabmeat, 225 g/8 oz (1⅓ cups) chopped prawns (shrimp), or a mixture of 100 g/4 oz (⅔ cup) salmon and 100 g/4 oz (⅔ cup) prawns. Flavour with a little lemon juice, then blend with either mayonnaise or soured cream until the consistency resembles thick cream. Add 1 teaspoon finely chopped fennel leaves or parsley and season.

Croquenbouche

This name describes a pyramid of choux pastry buns coated with a crisp sugar mixture (generally a light-coloured caramel) hence the name Croque-en-bouche which means cracks in the mouth.

A pyramid of meringues or chestnuts can be served in the same way.

1 quantity Choux Pastry, see left

FOR THE FILLING:
300 to 450 ml/½ to ¾ pint (1¼ to 2 cups) double (heavy) cream

FOR THE CARAMEL COATING:
225 g/8 oz (1 cup) sugar
8 tablespoons water

Fit a 5 mm to 1 cm/¼ to ½ inch plain nozzle into a piping (pastry) bag and fill with Choux Pastry. Pipe 36 to 40 small balls on to lightly greased baking sheets. Alternatively, place teaspoons of the mixture on to the greased sheets. Place the sheets just above the centre of a preheated moderately hot oven (200°C/400°F, Gas Mark 6) and bake for 8 to 10 minutes, or until the pastry shapes are well-risen. If the Choux Pastry is already colouring, you can then lower the heat slightly and cook for a further 5 minutes or until firm. Cool away from a draught.

Slit the buns through the centre. There should be no uncooked mixture in the centre but if there is, remove it carefully and return the buns to the oven to dry out, then cool again. Whip the cream and spoon some into the buns.

For the coating Place the sugar and water in a heavy-based saucepan; stir over the heat until the sugar dissolves then boil without stirring until the sugar mixture has become a delicate golden caramel and reached the crack stage. (Drop a little in cold water. It should become hard and crack when tested). Use immediately before the caramel has a chance to set, or stand the pan containing the caramel in another pan of boiling water.

To serve Arrange a circle of about 8

buns on a serving dish. Dip the base of the next layer of buns in the sugar mixture, arrange on top of the first layer of buns, but in a slightly smaller circle. Continue like this until the pyramid shape is complete. Pipe rosettes of remaining cream between the buns and trickle over any remaining caramel. Serves 10 to 12.

VARIATIONS

Omit the sugar caramel. Fill the choux buns with either fresh cream or ice cream. Pile onto a dish and pour over hot chocolate sauce. Serve at once.

Homemade Cream

150 ml / ¼ pint (⅔ cup) milk
1 level teaspoon gelatine
100 g / 4 oz (½ cup) unsalted butter
½ teaspoon caster sugar (optional)
1 to 2 drops vanilla essence (extract) (optional)

⁂Put the milk into a small saucepan, sprinkle the gelatine on the surface of the milk. It is essential that the gelatine is measured with care, too much will spoil the texture. Cut the butter into small pieces, add to the cold milk and gelatine. Heat the mixture gently until the gelatine and butter are dissolved. Add the sugar and vanilla if using. Place the lukewarm mixture into a blender or food processor and blend on full speed for 30 seconds. Alternatively pass through a cream-maker or the cream-making attachment of a mixer. Place in a bowl and refrigerate for at least 3 hours.

Whip the mixture and serve.

Spiced Raspberry Ring

FOR THE CHOUX PASTRY:
150 ml / ¼ pint (⅔ cup) water
50 g / 2 oz (¼ cup) butter
pinch of sugar
pinch of allspice
pinch of ground cinnamon
65 g / 2½ oz plain flour (generous ½ cup all-purpose flour)
2 large eggs

FOR THE FILLING AND TOPPING
300 ml / ½ pint (1¼ cups) double (heavy) cream
1 to 2 tablespoons sugar
225 g / 8 oz (½ lb) raspberries
3 tablespoons blanched flaked almonds

Make the Choux Pastry as described on page 152. The spices should be sifted with the flour. Spoon the pastry into a piping (pastry) bag with a 1.5 cm / ½ inch plain pipe and pipe a large ring on to a lightly greased baking sheet.

Bake in the centre of a preheated moderately hot oven (200°C/400°F or Gas Mark 6) for 35 minutes until firm and golden. The heat could be reduced slightly after 20 to 25 minutes if the pastry is too brown. Allow to cool and split horizontally.

Whip the cream, add the sugar. Mix half the cream with most of the raspberries and sandwich the two rings together. Pipe the rest of the cream on top and decorate with the raspberries and almonds. Serves 6 to 8.

Prawn and Avocado Choux

½ quantity of Savoury or Cheese Choux Pastry, see opposite

FOR THE FILLING:
1 egg
100 g / 4 oz (⅔ cup) peeled prawns (shelled shrimp)
1 tablespoon mayonnaise
1 teaspoon finely chopped onion or chives
pinch of cayenne pepper
salt and pepper
2 teaspoons lemon juice
1 large avocado

TO GARNISH:
6 to 8 whole prawns (shrimp)

⁂Pipe or spoon choux pastry into about 12 medium-sized rounds on a lightly greased baking sheet, leaving plenty of space between the buns. Bake in a preheated hot oven (200°C/400°F, Gas Mark 6) for 25 minutes. Split and cool. To make the filling Hard-boil (hard-cook) then chop the egg; chop the prawns (shrimp) if large. Mix the egg, prawns (shrimp), mayonnaise, onion or chives, seasoning and lemon juice together. Skin the avocado, mash the flesh and combine with the other ingredients as soon as possible so that the fruit keeps a good colour. Spoon into the choux buns and garnish with prawns (shrimp). Serve as an hors d'oeuvre, or with a green salad. as a light lunch or supper. Makes 12.

LEFTOVERS

⁂Uncooked Choux Pastry can be frozen for up to 1 month. Thaw completely and spoon or pipe into the required shapes. Bake as usual.

FREEZING NOTE

⁂Leftover baked choux cases can be frozen with or without a filling.

Filled choux pastry should be served as soon as it has thawed otherwise the filling makes the pastry damp.

Empty cooked choux cases can be crisped in a moderate oven for a few minutes after they have thawed, then cooled and filled.

Savoury Choux Puffs with Seafood Cream

153

BREAD

More and more people are taking an interest in natural foods with the result that many people are now baking their own bread. Food processors and mixers take the hard work out of kneading and it is easy to make and bake large quantities of bread at one time. Enjoy some of it fresh from the oven and freeze the surplus for future use.

Flour

If you have only made white bread in the past, try homemade bread with whole-wheat or wheatmeal flour or a mixture of flours.

Different makes of flour absorb slightly varying amounts of liquid, and wheatmeal and wholewheat flours absorb more liquid than white flour.

It is not difficult though to adjust the consistency of bread dough; if too dry, work in a little extra warm liquid during mixing. If the dough seems rather moist in the mixing bowl, do not add more flour until you have kneaded the mixture, for the dough becomes firmer as it is handled. If the dough is still too sticky to handle, use a generous amount of flour on the working surface.

Yeast

White Bread and Rolls topped with poppy seeds

The basic recipe (see right) gives 15 g/ ½ oz fresh (½ cake compressed) yeast or 7 g/¼ oz (1 teaspoon) dried (active dry) yeast to 450 to 500 g/1 lb (4 cups) flour.

If you are making bread with 1.35 kg/ 3 lb (12 cups) flour – 3 times the amount given in the recipe opposite – you need only 25 g/1 oz fresh (1 cake compressed) yeast or 15 g/½ oz (2 teaspoons) dried (active dry) yeast.

Kneading

LEFTOVERS
Stale bread can be freshened by reheating in the oven.

Wrap in foil and warm through at a moderate heat (160 to 180°C/325 to 350°F, Gas Mark 3 to 4).

If the bread is very stale, dip the loaf into a little water before heating. Do this very rapidly so that the loaf does not become too moist. Do not wrap, but heat as above.

*K*neading means pulling and stretching the dough until smooth. If done by hand use the base of your palm, known as the heel. Bread can also be kneaded in a food processor or mixer, but if doing so check the kneading process carefully because it is very easy to over-knead the dough. Test as you would when kneading by hand.

To test if the dough is adequately kneaded, press with a floured finger. If the impression made by your finger stays in the dough it means it should be kneaded for a little longer. When ready, the impression comes out, leaving the dough smooth and ready for the next stage, which is to allow the dough to rise or *prove*.

Proving

The following are average times for the first proving of the batch of yeast dough.

At average room temperature – 2 hours. In a warm place – 45 to 60 minutes. In the refrigerator – up to 24 hours.

In a cold larder – about 12 hours. Proving time for the shaped loaf At average room temperature – 30 to 40 minutes. In a warm place – 25 minutes. In the refrigerator – up to 16 hours. In a cold larder – 5 to 6 hours.

Small rolls will rise more rapidly; they take about 12 hours in the refrigerator.

Shaping

To make a tin loaf First grease, flour and warm the loaf tin (pan). Press the dough into an oblong shape – the length of the tin but about 3 times its width. Fold into 3 to fit the tin (Fig 1). Place in the greased loaf tin, the dough should come ½ way up the tin (Fig 2).

To make a cottage loaf Take two-thirds of the dough and form into a round. Form the remaining dough into a smaller round and put on top of the base. Dip the handle of a wooden spoon into a little flour and push well into the top round to make an indentation and flatten the rounds slightly. Place on to a greased and warmed baking sheet (Fig 3).

To make a plait (braid) Divide the dough into three portions and, with your hands, roll each one into a long, slender sausage shape. Join the 3 strands at one end, pinching these together (Fig 4). Plait (braid) loosely, and join the other ends

together. Brush with a little beaten egg or sprinkle with crushed wheat (Fig 5).

White Bread

15 g/½ oz (½ cake) fresh (compressed) yeast or 7 g/¼ oz (1 teaspoon) dried (active dry) yeast with 1 teaspoon sugar

300 ml/½ pint (1¼ cups) warm water

450 to 500 g/1 lb (4 cups) strong (bread) or plain (all-purpose) flour

pinch of salt

∗∗Cream the fresh yeast with the warm water; if using dried yeast dissolve the sugar in the warm water, sprinkle the dried yeast on top of the liquid and allow to stand for 10 minutes or until the mixture starts to bubble, then use as fresh yeast.

Sift the flour and salt, combine the yeast liquid with the flour mixture and mix to a smooth elastic dough. Turn on to a lightly floured surface and knead the dough (see left).

Cover the dough so it does not dry out and harden on the outside. Either place it in a large mixing bowl and cover the bowl with plastic wrap or a cloth; or put the dough into a large, lightly oiled polythene bag and tie this loosely. There are various places where you can leave your dough to prove (see left).

Allow the dough to prove until twice its original size. When the dough has risen sufficiently, knead it again. This stage is known as *knocking back* (punching down) the dough. Form it into the desired shape (see left).

Place on a warm, greased baking sheet or into the tin (pan). Cover with

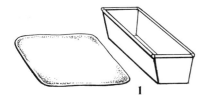 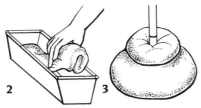 

lightly oiled plastic wrap to prevent a hard skin forming on the outside of the dough. Prove again until the loaf has risen well.

Bake in the centre of a preheated hot oven (220°C/425°F, Gas Mark 7). If one loaf only is made from the quantity of dough the total baking time will be about 40 minutes; if two smaller loaves are made allow about 30 minutes. To test whether the bread is cooked, lift the loaf from the baking sheet or tin and knock it on the base. If there is a hollow sound, it is cooked.

Variations

Bread Rolls Shape the dough into 12 to 18 small rolls and bake in a preheated hot to very hot oven (230 to 240°C/450 to 475°F, Gas Mark 8 to 9) for about 10 minutes.

Cheese Bread Use half milk and half water or all milk instead of all water. Sift a good shake of pepper and 1 teaspoon mustard powder with the flour and add 75 g/3 oz (¾ cup) finely grated cheese. Mix the dough with 1 egg as well as the liquid.

Brush the loaf or rolls with beaten egg yolk and sprinkle with sesame or caraway seeds before the final proving.

Milk Bread Use 50 g/2 oz (¼ cup) butter or margarine in the basic recipe

and milk instead of water to bind.

This is an excellent base for sweet breads. Add 50 to 100 g/2 to 4 oz (⅓ to ⅔ cup) sultanas (golden raisins) or other dried fruit and 25 to 50 g/1 to 2 oz (2 to 4 tablespoons) sugar to the flour. When adding the extra weight in the form of fruit and fat use a generous 15 g/½ oz (½ cake) fresh (compressed) yeast or generous 7 g/¼ oz (1 teaspoon) dried (active dry) yeast.

Orange Bread: Use all orange juice in place of water in the White Bread. Add the finely grated rind of 2 oranges to the flour, together with 25 g/1 oz (2 tablespoons) sugar. Mix 25 g/1 oz (2 tablespoons) sugar with 2 teaspoons grated orange rind and 1 tablespoon cracked wheat. Brush the dough or rolls with lightly beaten egg white and sprinkle with the orange mixture before the final proving. Finely chopped candied orange peel or 25 g/1 oz (3 tablespoons) sultanas (golden raisins) can be added to the dough.

Rich Bread Rub (cut) 25 to 40 g/1 to 1½ oz (2 to 3 tablespoons) butter or margarine into the flour. Use half milk and half water instead of all water. When the dough is formed into the required shape, brush with a little egg or egg yolk mixed with a teaspoon of water.

Wholewheat Bread Use wholewheat

flour or half wholewheat and half white flour (or the proportions that you like best). Follow the recipe above, but the higher the proportion of wholewheat flour used, the more liquid will be required.

Wholewheat and Bran Bread Use 450 g/1 lb (4 cups) wholewheat flour plus 50 g/2 oz (⅓ cup) bran. Mix the bran with the flour. You will achieve the best result with this bread if you use nearly 450 ml/¾ pint (scant 2 cups) water. Beat with a wooden spoon to mix, then knead well.

This is very pleasant as a sweet loaf. Add 1 tablespoon honey to the liquid in which the yeast is dissolved and up to 50 g/2 oz (⅓ cup) moist brown sugar to the flour and bran.

French Bread is not easy to make outside France, but the recipe below is a good imitation.

Follow White Bread recipe (left) but use only 400 g/14 oz (3½ cups) strong white (bread) flour with 50 g/2 oz (½ cup) cornflour (cornstarch) instead of 450 g/1 lb (4 cups) strong whole (bread) flour. Shape into long thin batons. Put on to lightly greased baking sheets.

Make several shallow cuts on top of the loaf; brush with a little egg mixed with water. Allow to prove and then bake in the centre of a preheated very hot oven (230°C/450°F, Gas Mark 8) for 15 minutes or until firm. The amount of bread dough above would make 4 thin batons, 3 medium or 2 really rather fat ones. The baking time is based on the thinner batons.

Special Technique
SHORT-TIME BREAD

Bread dough will rise more quickly if ascorbic acid (vitamin C) tablets and additional yeast are added to the bread dough. Dissolve 20 g/¾ oz (¾ cake) fresh (compressed) yeast with a 25 mg crushed ascorbic acid tablet in the warm water. Alternatively dissolve 10 g/1½ teaspoons dried (active dry) yeast with 1 teaspoon sugar and 5 teaspoons crushed ascorbic acid tablet in the water.

Rub 25 g/1 oz (2 tablespoons) margarine into the flour, add the yeast liquid and mix. Knead thoroughly (this is particularly important with short-time bread). Cover and stand for 5 minutes. Shape the dough, cover and leave to prove. Allow 45 minutes for rolls, about 1 hour for a loaf. Brush the risen dough with beaten egg and bake as above.

Hot Herb Bread
Make cuts in a French loaf at regular intervals of about 2.5 cm/1 inch. Cream 75 g to 100 g/3 to 4 oz (6 to 8 tablespoons) butter to a soft spreading consistency. Add 1 crushed clove garlic and 1 tablespoon each of chopped parsley, chives, thyme, tarragan and rosemary. Season to taste, then spread between the cuts with a small flat-bladed knife. Press the loaf together again and wrap in foil.

Heat in the centre of a preheated moderately hot oven (200°C/400°F, Gas Mark 6) for 10 to 15 minutes. This is excellent with soups and savoury dishes. Serves 4 to 6.

Hot Garlic Bread
Use 2 to 3 crushed garlic cloves and omit the herbs in the recipe above.

Hot Cheese Bread
Omit the garlic and herbs. Mix the butter with 100 g/4 oz (1 cup) grated Cheddar, Gouda or Gruyère, or with a crumbled blue cheese such as Stilton or Danish Blue. Heat as above.

Hot Tomato Bread
Blend 100 g/4 oz (½ cup) butter with 1 tablespoon tomato purée (paste) and 2 tablespoons finely chopped chives or parsley. Use as in the recipe above.

Bran Loaf, and Date and Walnut Bread

Bran Loaf

350 g/12 oz (3 cups) self-raising flour
½ teaspoon salt
100 g/4 oz (½ cup) butter
25 g/1 oz (¼ cup) bran
220 ml/7½ fl oz (scant 1 cup) milk

✳✳Sift the flour with the salt. Rub in (cut in) the butter until the mixture is like fine breadcrumbs. Add the bran and the milk. Knead the mixture and roll out to an 18 cm/7 inch round. Place on a well-greased baking sheet and mark into 6 to 8 portions. Bake in the centre of a preheated moderately hot oven (200°C/400°F, Gas Mark 6) for 30 to 35 minutes. Serves 6 to 8.
Note Use plain (all-purpose) or wholewheat flour in place of self-raising but add 3 teaspoons baking powder.

Fruit Bran Loaf

100 g/4 oz (1 cup) All-Bran
300 ml/½ pint (1¼ cups) milk
225 g/8 oz (1⅓ cups) mixed dried fruit
150 g/5 oz (10 tablespoons) caster sugar
100 g/4 oz (1 cup) self-raising flour

✳✳Grease and flour a 750 g to 1 kg/1½ to 2 lb loaf tin (pan). Put the bran into a bowl, add the milk and dried fruit and allow to stand for 30 to 40 minutes. Add the sugar then sift the flour into the mixture. Beat well and pour into the prepared tin. Bake in the centre of a preheated moderate oven (180°C/350°F, Gas Mark 4) for 1 hour or until firm to the touch. Turn out of the tin on to a wire cooling tray. Serve when freshly cooked. Makes one 1 kg/2 lb loaf.
Note Plain (all-purpose) flour can be used in place of self-raising but add 1 teaspoon baking powder.

Date and Walnut Bread

225 g/8 oz (1⅓ cups) dates
50 g/2 oz (½ cup) walnuts
50 g/2 oz (¼ cup) margarine
100 g/4 oz (½ cup) caster sugar
150 ml/¼ pint (⅔ cup) water
1 egg
225 g/8 oz (2 cups) self-raising flour
½ teaspoon bicarbonate of soda (baking soda)
pinch of salt

✳✳Chop the dates and walnuts. Put the dates, margarine, sugar and water into a good-sized saucepan, bring the water just to boiling point, stir the ingredients then remove from the heat and leave in the saucepan to cool.
Beat the egg into the date mixture. Sift the flour with the soda and salt. Add to the other ingredients and mix.
Spoon into a greased and floured or lined 1 kg/2 lb loaf tin (pan) and bake in the centre of a preheated moderate oven (160°C/325°F, Gas Mark 3) for 1¼ hours. Allow to cool in the tin for 5 minutes then turn out. Makes 1 loaf.
Note Plain (all-purpose) flour can be used in place of self-raising but add 2 teaspoons baking powder.

Fat Rascals

225 g/8 oz (2 cups) self-raising flour
pinch of salt
100 g/4 oz (½ cup) butter or margarine
25 g/1 oz (2 tablespoons) soft brown sugar
50 g/2 oz (⅓ cup) currants
milk to mix
TO GLAZE: a little milk
caster sugar

✳✳Sift the flour and salt into a mixing bowl and rub in (cut in) the butter or margarine. Add the sugar, currants and enough milk to make a soft rolling consistency. Roll out on a lightly floured board until about 2 cm/¾ inch thick. Cut into rounds with a 5 cm/2 inch cutter. Put on to a lightly greased baking sheet and brush the tops with a little milk, then sprinkle with caster sugar. Bake near the top of a preheated hot oven (230°C/450°F, Gas Mark 8) for about 10 minutes, or until firm to the touch. Serve hot or cold with butter. Makes 10 to 12.
Note Plain (all-purpose) flour can be used in place of self-raising but add 2 teaspoons baking powder.

Mushroom Bread

Wholewheat and Bran Bread dough, see page 155
225 g/8 oz (2 cups) mushrooms
1 small onion
a little extra flour, see method
15 g/½ oz (1 tablespoon) butter or margarine

✳✳Allow the dough to prove for the first time. Wipe the mushrooms and slice very thinly. Peel and finely chop the onion. Add the mushrooms and raw onion to the dough and knead well until mixed. The vegetables will make the dough slightly moist, so work in a little more flour and knead well again.
Place in two greased 1 kg/2 lb loaf tins (pans) (see page 154). Melt the butter or margarine and brush over the tops of the loaves. Allow the dough to prove for about 30 minutes, (see page 154) then bake in the centre of a preheated moderately hot oven (190 to 200°C/375 to 400°F, Gas Mark 5 to 6) for 45 minutes or until the loaves sound hollow when tapped on the base. This bread is excellent with soup or pâté. Makes two 1 kg/2 lb loaves.

International Breads

Croissants

Yeast Dough made with 450 g/1 lb (4 cups) flour, see page 154
175 to 225 g/6 to 8 oz (¾ to 1 cup) butter or margarine at room temperature
1 egg yolk
2 tablespoons water

⁂Prepare the dough and allow it to prove for the first time. Knock (punch) it back and knead until smooth, then roll out to a neat oblong shape.

Divide the butter or margarine into 3 portions. Cover two-thirds of the bread dough with the first third of the fat in exactly the same way as when making Flaky Pastry (see page 148) then fold the dough, turn at right angles, press with the rolling pin to rib the dough then roll out again.

Continue like this using the second and then the third portions of fat. It is advisable to wrap the dough in plastic wrap and place it into the refrigerator once or twice during this process so it does not become over-sticky.

When all the fat has been incorporated roll out the dough very thinly. Cut into about 6 large or 9 smaller squares, then cut each square in half to make triangles. Take the long side of each triangle and roll up, so that the point sits on top. Bring the two ends together to form a horseshoe shape. Place on an ungreased baking sheet. Blend the egg yolk with the water and brush over the croissants. Allow to prove for 30 to 35 minutes at room temperature then bake just above the centre of a preheated very hot oven (230°C/450°F, Gas Mark 8) for 15 minutes. Reduce the heat slightly after 10 minutes if the croissants are browning. Makes 12 to 18.

VARIATIONS

⁂Easy Croissants Use equal weights of proven bread dough and puff pastry. Roll out the bread dough and the puff pastry to equal-sized rectangles. Place the pastry on top of the dough, fold as though making flaky pastry, turn at right angles then continue like this, giving 3 foldings and 3 rollings, then proceed as above.

⁂Cheese Croissants Follow the recipe for Croissants, but substitute cream cheese for the butter or margarine. If the cheese is rather firm, soften it slightly by creaming it for a few minutes.

⁂Chocolate Croissants Follow the recipe for Croissants. Dice 175 to 225 g/6 to 8 oz (1 to 1⅓ cups) plain (semi-sweet) chocolate; divide between the 12 to 18 triangles. Roll the dough round the chocolate, encasing it completely. Glaze and bake as Croissants.

Brioches

15 g/½ oz fresh yeast (½ cake compressed yeast)
3 tablespoons warm milk
350 g/12 oz (3 cups) plain (all-purpose) white flour
pinch of salt
150 g/5 oz (½ cup plus 2 tablespoons) butter
25 g/1 oz (2 tablespoons) caster sugar
2 eggs

Dissolve the fresh yeast in the warm milk. Sift the flour and salt, rub (cut) in the butter, add the sugar and then the eggs; beat then knead until smooth. Cover the mixing bowl with a cloth or plastic wrap and leave in a warm place to 'prove' until the mixture has doubled in size (see page 154). Knead the dough again until smooth. Grease and warm 12 to 16 individual brioche tins (pans), see Note. Half fill each with the mixture. Allow to 'prove' again for 10 to 15 minutes, or until well risen in the tins.

Bake just above the centre of a preheated hot oven (220°C/425°F, Gas Mark 7) for 10 to 15 minutes, until golden brown and firm.

Note If using dried (active dry) yeast use 2 teaspoons, add 1 teaspoon of the sugar to the warm milk, sprinkle the yeast on top and proceed as for White Bread on page 154. In this particular recipe it is better to use plain (all-purpose), rather than strong flour.

If using ordinary patty tins shape the dough into balls for the base of the brioches, top with smaller balls and press down firmly.

Pitta Bread

15 g/½ oz (½ cake) fresh (compressed) yeast or 7 g/¼ oz (1 teaspoon) dried (active dry) yeast with 1 teaspoon sugar
300 ml/½ pint (1¼ cups) warm water
450 g/1 lb (4 cups) strong (bread) or plain (all-purpose) white flour
1 teaspoon salt
2 tablespoons olive oil

⁂Cream the fresh yeast and add the warm water, or dissolve the sugar in the warm water, sprinkle with dried yeast and leave for 10 minutes (see page 154).

Sift the flour and salt into a mixing bowl, add the yeast liquid and the oil and mix to a soft dough. Knead well, adding a little more flour if necessary. Cover the bowl and leave to prove until the dough has become twice its original size (see page 154).

Knock back the dough, knead again, then divide into 8 equal-sized portions. Roll each portion into a ball, cover and allow to prove again until well risen; this takes 20 to 25 minutes in a warm place.

Roll out the balls of dough until they become large thin rounds about 3 mm/⅛ inch thick. Place on warmed, flat baking sheets, cover lightly and give the final proving for about 10 minutes.

Bake in the centre of a preheated very hot oven (230°C/450°F, Gas Mark 8) for 10 minutes. Cover the bread when it comes from the oven to keep it soft. Makes 8 rounds.

Note Solid baking sheets, rather than light baking trays, are better for this bread; the portions are less inclined to brown on the base.

VARIATIONS

The second proving can be omitted, but the texture will not be so good.

Use half white and half wholewheat or wheatmeal flour.

Brioches and Croissants

Scones

Above and below: Sweet Scones

The secret of a good scone (biscuit) dough is that it should be soft in texture, compared with a pastry dough. Various kinds of scones (biscuits) can be made and baked quickly and easily.

Scone Dough

You will need about 150 ml/¼ pint (⅔ cup) milk to each 225 g/8 oz (2 cups) flour used, but this will vary slightly according to the type of flour and the amount of fat used. If the recipe includes egg, less milk is required.

It is very simple to make up a large quantity of basic scone (biscuit) dough and add various flavourings to the rubbed-in mixture.

Microwave Cooking

Scones (biscuits) can be baked in a microwave cooker. A small batch of scones needs about 2 minutes, but check in your manufacturer's handbook. Scones are generally cooked on the HIGH setting.

Savoury Scones

The basic scone (biscuit) dough (see right) can be used for savoury scones by sifting ½ teaspoon of salt, a good shake of pepper and ½ to 1 teaspoon dry mustard powder with the flour instead of using sugar in the ingredients. Roll out and bake in the same way as the basic sweet scones (biscuits).

Savoury scones (biscuits) make an excellent alternative to bread and would be ideal for packed lunches or picnics. Split the scones (biscuits), spread with butter or margarine and sandwich together with slices of cheese, ham, chicken or salad ingredients.

The savoury scone (biscuit) dough can be used as the basis for more ambitious dishes (see Hasty Pizza on page 135).

FREEZING NOTE
⁂Scones (biscuits) freeze very well. Plain sweet or fruit scones can be cooked then stored in the freezer for up to 4 months. Scones which contain a number of other ingredients are best used within 3 months.

LEFTOVERS
Scones (biscuits) keep well for 2 to 3 days in the bread bin. Reheat towards the top of a preheated moderately hot oven (200°C/400°F, Gas Mark 6) for a short time.

Sweet Scones

225 g/8 oz (2 cups) self-raising flour
pinch of salt
25 to 50 g/1 to 2 oz (2 to 4 tablespoons) butter or margarine
25 to 50 g/1 to 2 oz (2 to 4 tablespoons) caster or granulated sugar
milk to bind

⁂Sift the flour and salt. Rub in (cut in) the butter or margarine, add the sugar and milk to make a soft rolling consistency. Roll out on a lightly floured surface until 1.5 to 2 cm/½ to ¾ inch in thickness and cut into rounds or the desired shapes. Do not grease the baking sheet for plain scones (biscuits), but when the recipe includes cheese, oatmeal or other ingredients that might stick, grease and flour the baking sheet. Put the scones on to the baking sheet (the heavy sheets often supplied with cookers are ideal for scones).

Bake towards the top of a preheated hot oven (220 to 230°C/425 to 450°F, Gas Mark 7 to 8) for 10 to 12 minutes. Makes 8 to 12.

VARIATIONS
Modern self-raising flour is so light that no extra raising agent should be necessary. Many people prefer to use 3 to 4 teaspoons baking powder with plain (all-purpose) flour, but remember that all spoon measures must be level. If preferred, use plain (all-purpose) flour with ½ teaspoon bicarbonate of soda (baking soda) and 1 teaspoon cream of tartar. Sift very well.

⁂Fruit Scones Add 50 to 75 g/2 to 3 oz (⅓ to ½ cup) mixed dried fruit to the mixture before adding the milk.

⁂Spicy Scones Sift ½ to 1 teaspoon mixed spice with the flour.

⁂Potato Scones (Sweet) Add 1 teaspoon baking powder to the self-raising flour or 2 teaspoons baking powder to plain (all-purpose) flour. Sift the flour, baking powder and salt together. Rub in 25 to 40 g/1 to 1½ oz (2 to 3 tablespoons) butter or margarine, add 25 to 50 g/1 to 2 oz (2 to 4 tablespoons) caster sugar and 100 g/4 oz (½ cup) sieved cooked potatoes. Mix well, add enough milk to bind, roll out and cook as above.

⁂Potato Scones (Savoury) Sift ¼ teaspoon salt and ¼ teaspoon mustard powder with the flour and baking powder together with a good shake of pepper. Continue as above but add 1 to 2 tablespoons chopped parsley and/or 25 g/1 oz (¼ cup) grated cheese to the mixture before adding the milk.

⁂Oatmeal Scones Follow the recipe for Sweet or Savoury Potato Scones, using either medium oatmeal or rolled oats in place of the cooked potatoes.

⁂Apple and Cinnamon Squares Sift ½ to 1 teaspoon ground cinnamon with the flour etc. Peel and dice 2 cooking (tart) apples, stir into the rubbed-in (cut-in) mixture then add milk to bind. Roll out as the basic dough, cut into about 9

squares, pack into a lightly greased 20 to 23 cm/8 to 9 inch square cake tin (pan) or arrange on a greased baking sheet so that the squares just touch each other.

Bake in the centre of a preheated hot oven (220°C/425°F, Gas Mark 7) for 12 minutes. Pull apart to serve. Decorate the dish with slices of apple, dipped in lemon juice. Makes 9.

**Apricot and Raisin Bake Add 75 g/3 oz (½ cup) diced dried apricots and 50 g/2 oz (⅓ cup) seedless raisins to the rubbed-in mixture for Sweet Scones. Bind with milk. Roll out and cut into 7 large rounds. Put one round in the centre of an 18 to 20 cm/7 to 8 inch shallow cake or sandwich tin (layer cake pan) and place the other rounds in the tin (pan) so that the rounds just touch each other. Bake as for the Apple and Cinnamon Squares above. Makes 7.

If preferred, roll out the apricot and raisin mixture, cut into rounds and bake as Sweet Scones.

**Cheese and Parsley Round Omit the sugar from the Sweet Scone dough, add seasoning (see Savoury Scones opposite). Dice 75 g/3 oz (¾ cup) Cheddar Cheese, add to the rubbed-in mixture with 2 tablespoons chopped parsley. Bind with milk, roll out and form into an 18 to 20 cm/7 to 8 inch round. Put on to a flat baking sheet. Mark into 6 to 8 triangles. Bake in the centre of a preheated moderately hot oven (220°C/400°F, Gas Mark 6) for 25 minutes. Serves 6 to 8.

**Cheese and Parsley Scones Roll out the mixture above and cut into 8 to 12 rounds or small triangles. Bake towards the top of a preheated moderately hot oven (200°C/400°F, Gas Mark 6) for about 12 minutes. Never bake cheese-flavoured scones (biscuits) as quickly as plain or sweet ones; they tend to scorch more easily. The scones can be glazed with a little beaten egg before cooking. Makes 8 to 12.

Scone and Bacon Roulade

FOR THE DOUGH:
225 g/8 oz (2 cups) self-raising flour with 1 teaspoon baking powder
½ teaspoon salt
1 to 2 teaspoons mixed dried herbs
50 g/2 oz (¼ cup) butter
milk to bind
FOR THE FILLING:
1 medium courgette (zucchini)
1 stick of celery from the heart
100 g/4 oz mild Cheddar or other cooking cheese
6 back rashers – preferably honeydew cured bacon (Canadian bacon)
2 tablespoons fruit chutney or sweet pickle

salt and pepper
TO GLAZE:
1 egg

For the dough Sift the flour, baking powder and salt. Add the herbs, rub in (cut in) the butter until the mixture is like fine breadcrumbs. Add enough milk to make a soft rolling consistency and roll out to a rectangle 20 × 30 cm/8 × 12 inches.

For the filling Grate the courgette (zucchini) coarsely (there is no need to peel it). Chop the celery very finely. Grate the cheese. Cut each bacon slice into 2 portions and de-rind if necessary.

Spread the scone dough with the chutney or pickle, leaving a narrow border of plain dough all round. Top with cheese and vegetables and season very lightly. Moisten the plain edges of the dough with a little milk then roll the dough to enclose the filling. Seal the edges of the roll then lift it on to a baking sheet making sure the join in the roll is underneath. Beat the egg, brush over the roll, then make 12 cuts at regular intervals in the roulade. Push a portion of bacon into each space.

Bake in the centre of a preheated hot oven (220 to 230°C/425 to 450°F, Gas Mark 7 to 8) for 15 to 20 minutes or until the dough is well risen. Cover with foil and reduce the heat to moderately hot (190°C/375°F, Gas Mark 5) for a further 15 to 20 minutes until crusty and golden.

Slice the roulade and serve garnished with watercress; pass around a homemade tomato sauce if liked (see pages 103 and 107).

Note Plain (all-purpose) flour can be used but add 3 teaspoons baking powder.

Quick Beef Pizzas

225 g/8 oz (2 cups) self-raising flour
½ teaspoon salt
50 g/2 oz (¼ cup) butter or margarine
milk to bind
FOR THE TOPPING:
1 garlic clove
1 onion
25 g/1 oz (2 tablespoons) butter or margarine
1 × 425 g/15 oz can minced (ground) beef
½ teaspoon chopped fresh or ¼ teaspoon dried mixed herbs
salt and pepper
50 g/2 oz Cheddar cheese
4 tomato slices

Sift the flour with the salt, rub in (cut in) the butter or margarine and add enough milk to make a soft rolling consistency.

Roll out the dough until about 1.5 cm/½ inch thick and cut into 4 large rounds. Put these on to a greased baking sheet.

Peel and finely chop the garlic and onion. Heat the butter or margarine and fry the garlic and onion until very soft. Add the beef and herbs, simmer for a few minutes until a thick mixture is formed. Add seasoning. Spoon the beef mixture over each round of dough. Grate the cheese, sprinkle over the mince.

Bake the pizzas just above the centre of a preheated moderately hot oven (200°C/400°F, Gas Mark 6) for 15 to 20 minutes. Top with the tomato. Serves 4.

Note Plain (all-purpose) flour can be used but add 2 teaspoons baking powder.

Scone and Bacon Roulade

FREEZING NOTE
**Scone and Bacon Roulade is best eaten when freshly baked, but can be frozen uncooked. If using mild cured bacon, eat within 3 months.

If using more heavily smoked bacon, use within 6 weeks.

159

CAKES

Successful cake making depends on the right balance of ingredients – fat, sugar, eggs, and flour; the correct method of mixing, the correct oven temperature and the positioning of the cake in the oven. It is unwise to alter the proportions in a cake, but you can adjust flavourings, such as spices and essences (extracts) to suit your own taste.

FOR EASE
To Add Colouring
Do not pour food colouring from the bottle or even from a spoon. Dip a skewer into the bottle, hold this over the mixture to be tinted and allow a few drops to fall. Stir the mixture thoroughly. Continue until the desired colour is reached.

Basic Techniques

Cakes are made by four basic methods:
Creaming
The fat and sugar are beaten or creamed until soft and light. Use either a wooden spoon or an electric mixer. Use fat at room temperature so that it creams easily or warm the bowl slightly. Do not melt the fat. This initial creaming incorporates a considerable amount of air into the mixture. Creaming also dissolves the grains of sugar – caster sugar is often recommended in this kind of cake.

Add the eggs gradually so the creamed mixture does not separate (curdle). If there are signs of curdling, beat in a little flour.

Fold the sifted flour, or flour and baking powder, gently into the creamed mixture with a metal spoon.

There are a number of cakes made by this method on the pages that follow and the most famous of all, the Victoria Sandwich, is given below.

Soft margarines enable cakes that are by the rubbing-in method to be made by the one-stage mixing method (see page 123).
Melting
This is a very easy way of mixing the ingredients (see page 165). When melting the ingredients take care not to overheat them. The flour, or flour and raising agent, can be beaten quite briskly into the melted ingredients.
Rubbing-in (Cutting-in)
This method is generally used for fairly plain cakes, scones (biscuits) and some kinds of pastry. An example of a shortcake made by this method is on page 196.

Rub (cut) the fat carefully into the flour, or flour and baking powder, lifting the ingredients well above the bowl to incorporate as much air as possible. Do not over-handle the mixture.
Whisking
Air is incorporated into the mixture by whisking either the whole eggs, as in the Bûche de Noel (see page 204), or the yolks and then the egg whites (see Danish Layer Cake, page 162). It is

important that the flour or flour and baking powder are folded carefully into the whisked mixture using a gently flicking and turning figure-of-eight movement.

Baking Times

Baking times for cakes are given in recipes but ovens vary greatly, so check twice during cooking when baking a cake recipe for the first time.

Check after one-third of the baking time (for instance, if the total baking time is 1½ hours, look after 30 minutes cooking); the cake should not have changed colour, but should look moist on top. If the cake has changed colour quite appreciably, lower the oven setting by 10°C/25°F, or Gas Mark 1.

Check again after two-thirds of the baking time. Open the oven door cautiously and only very slightly – a draught could cause the cake to drop in the middle. The mixture should be well risen, but it will still not have set completely, and will be beginning to colour. If it looks too dark, you can lower the heat as suggested above. If the cake does not seem to be cooking as quickly as it should, it is better to bake it for a longer period rather than to raise the oven temperature at this stage.

To test if light sponge cakes are cooked, press very gently in the centre. Do not take the cake out of the oven to do this. If your finger leaves an impression the cake is not quite cooked and should be baked for a little longer.

To test if a moderately light cake is cooked, press a little more firmly on top. Check also to see if it has shrunk from the sides of the tin (pan).

For rich fruit cakes, use the tests above and, if doubtful, insert a fine wooden cocktail stick (toothpick) into the cake. If it comes out clean the cake is cooked.

There is one infallible test for rich fruit cakes. If the tests above indicate it is cooked, bring it out of the oven and listen carefully. If there is a humming noise, the cake is *not* cooked and should be returned to the oven.

Victoria Sandwich

This is one of the most versatile of all light cakes; if made correctly if should be sufficiently light to justify the term sponge. It can be decorated in various ways.

| 110 g/4 oz (½ cup) butter or margarine |
| 110 g/4 oz (½ cup) caster sugar |
| 2 large eggs |
| 110 g/4 oz (1 cup) self-raising flour |

⁎⁎Cream the butter or margarine with the sugar until light and fluffy. Gradually beat in the eggs. Sift the flour. Fold gently and carefully into the creamed mixture then divide between two

greased and floured 15 to 18 cm/6 to 7 inch sandwich tins (layer cake pans). Bake just above the centre of a pre-heated moderate to moderately hot oven (180 to 190°C/350 to 375°F, Gas Mark 4 to 5) for 15 to 18 minutes or until firm to the touch.

If preferred, bake in one greased and floured, 15 to 18 cm/6 to 8 inch cake tin (pan), in the centre of a preheated moderate oven (160°C/325°F, Gas Mark 3) for 35 to 40 minutes. Makes two 15 to 18 cm/6 to 7 inch sandwich layers.
Note Plain (all-purpose) flour can be used, but add 1 teaspoon baking powder.
VARIATIONS
To make two 19 to 20 cm/7½ to 8 inch sponge sandwich layers, or one cake, use 175 g/6 oz (¾ cup) butter or margarine, 175 g/6 oz (¾ cup) caster sugar, 3 large eggs and 175 g/6 oz (1½ cups) self-raising flour or plain (all-purpose) flour with 1½ teaspoons baking powder.

Bake the two layers for approximately 20 minutes or the cake for 45 to 50 minutes at the settings given above.

Caramel Coffee Gâteau

Victoria Sandwich, made with 3 eggs see above

| **FOR THE FILLING:** |
| 350 g/12 oz (3 cups) icing sugar |
| 175 g/6 oz (¾ cup) butter |
| 1 tablespoon coffee essence or 1½ teaspoons instant coffee and 1 tablespoon warm milk |
| **FOR THE TOPPING:** |
| 225 g/8 oz (1 cup) sugar |
| 8 tablespoons water |
| 2 tablespoons chopped blanched almonds |

⁎⁎Bake the Victoria Sandwich as above and allow to cool. Sift the icing (confectioners') sugar and cream with the butter; beat until soft and white. Gradually add the coffee essence, or blend the instant coffee powder with the warm milk and use this instead. Sandwich the two cakes with about one-third of the mixture; cover the remaining coffee icing until ready to use, so it does not become too dry and hard.

Put the sugar and water into a strong saucepan; stir until the sugar melts then allow to boil, without stirring, until the mixture turns golden brown. Pour on to a large baking sheet; to give a thin layer; spread with a knife if necessary. When nearly set mark 6 to 8 triangles in the caramel with an oiled knife; leave until firm and set. Top the cake with another third of the coffee butter icing, then arrange the triangles of caramel on top of this, so they stand upright. Scatter the chopped almonds in between the caramel triangles. Use the remaining one-third of the icing to pipe a border around the edge of the cake. Serves 6 to 8.

Easter Egg Cake

FOR THE BUTTER SPONGE:

175 g/6 oz (¾ cup) unsalted butter

175 g/6 oz (¾ cup) caster sugar

3 large eggs

175 g/6 oz (1½ cups) self-raising flour
see Note

FOR THE FILLING:

3 tablespoons black cherry or raspberry
jam

100 g/4 oz (½ cup) unsalted butter

225 g/8 oz (2 cups) icing (confectioners')
sugar

2 tablespoons water

1 tablespoon cocoa powder
(unsweetened cocoa)

TO DECORATE:

50 g/2 oz marzipan, see page 168

a few drops of green food colouring

strip of foil, see method

yellow ribbon, see picture on page 168

✲✲Cream together the butter and sugar until soft and light. Gradually beat in the eggs (see page 160). Sift the flour and fold into the creamed mixture.

Grease a 1.5 litre/2½ pint (2 quart) ovenproof bowl (mold). Spoon the mixture into the bowl (mold) and bake the sponge in the centre of a preheated moderate oven (160 to 180°C/325 to 350°F, Gas Mark 3 to 4) for nearly 1 hour or until firm to the touch.

Allow to cool for 2 to 3 minutes in the bowl (mold), then turn out on to a wire cooling tray. When quite cold, cut the sponge vertically down the centre, then cut each half lengthways, so giving 4 portions.

Spread the edges of the sponge with the jam and press together to form an egg shape. Place the cake on a flat serving dish.

For the filling Cream the butter in a bowl until very soft, then sift the icing (confectioners') sugar into the butter and cream again. Heat the water and blend with the cocoa; beat this mixture gradually into the butter icing. Spread just over half the icing over the egg-shaped sponge with a warm knife (see page 168). Put the remainder of the chocolate icing into a piping (pastry) bag fitted with a small star nozzle and pipe a border around the edge of the cake (see page 169).

To decorate   Take a little marzipan, tint this green, then make stalks and leaves. Colour the remaining marzipan yellow and form into daffodil-shaped flowers. Arrange on the cake. Cut a narrow band of foil to prevent the icing from sticking to the ribbon and place the foil and ribbon on the cake (see picture on page 168). Serves 8.

Note Plain (all-purpose) flour can be used, but add 1½ teaspoons baking powder.

Chocolate Orange Cake

Rich Chocolate Cake

100 g/4 oz (4 squares) plain (semi-sweet) chocolate

1 tablespoon water

100 g/4 oz (1 cup) icing (confectioners')
sugar

100 g/4 oz (½ cup) butter

4 eggs

100 g/4 oz (1 cup) self-raising flour

15 g/½ oz (2 tablespoons) cornflour
(cornstarch)

Line a 19 to 20 cm/7½ to 8 inch round cake tin (pan) with greased greaseproof (waxed) paper. Melt the chocolate with the water. Sift the sugar; cream the sugar and butter until soft and light. Separate the eggs, beat the egg yolks and then the melted chocolate into the butter and sugar. Sift the flour with the cornflour (cornstarch); fold into the creamed mixture. Whisk the egg whites until they just hold their shape, do not over-beat. Mix gently, but thoroughly, into the other ingredients. Spoon into the tin. Bake in the centre of a preheated cool oven (150°C/300°F, Gas Mark 2) for 45 to 50 minutes or until firm to the touch. Cool in the tin for 5 minutes, turn out.

This cake is delicious served plain – just topped with sifted icing (confectioners') sugar or with melted chocolate.

Note Plain (all-purpose) flour can be used, but add 1 teaspoon baking powder.

VARIATIONS

Chocolate Orange Cake (Illustrated) Use orange juice instead of water when melting the chocolate. Cream 1½ teaspoons grated orange rind with the butter and sugar. Top the cake with a chocolate icing (frosting) made by creaming 25 g/1 oz (2 tablespoons) butter with 25 g/1 oz (¼ cup) sifted icing (confectioners') sugar, and adding 50 g/ 2 oz (2 squares) melted plain (semi-sweet) chocolate. Decorate with crystallised orange slices.

Black Forest Gâteau Split the cake horizontally then sandwich together with cherry jam, whipped cream (flavoured with Kirsch), fresh or well-drained black cherries. Top with whipped cream, grated chocolate and more cherries.

FOR EASE

To flour a greased cake tin (pan) sprinkle 1 teaspoon flour over the bottom of the tin (pan) and tap the edges of the tin (pan) smartly to distribute the flour. Invert the tin over the kitchen sink and tap the base to remove any excess flour. If you are baking a chocolate cake, add a little (unsweetened) cocoa powder to the flour.

Danish Layer Cake

Tropical Christmas Cake

175 g/6 oz (¾ cup) unsalted butter
150 g/5 oz (½ cup plus 2 tablespoons) caster sugar
2 large eggs
225 g/8 oz (2 cups) self-raising flour
75 g/3 oz (⅓ cup) glacé cherries
75 g/3 oz (½ cup) mixed peel
25 g/1 oz angelica
25 g/1 oz (¼ cup) walnuts
1 × 227 g/8 oz can pineapple rings (slices)
25 g/1 oz (⅓ cup) desiccated (shredded) coconut
100 g/4 oz (⅔ cup) sultanas (golden raisins)
3 tablespoons canned pineapple syrup
FOR THE ICING:
40 g/1½ oz (3 tablespoons) unsalted butter
175 g/6 oz (1½ cups) icing (confectioners') sugar
1 tablespoon canned pineapple syrup
25 g/1 oz (⅓ cup) desiccated (shredded) coconut

⁂Cream the butter and sugar until soft and light. Gradually beat in the eggs. Sift the flour and fold into the creamed mixture.

Chop the glacé cherries, mixed peel, angelica and walnuts. Drain the canned pineapple, set aside 1 tablespoon of syrup for the icing and 3 tablespoons syrup for the cake. Chop the pineapple rings finely. Fold all the chopped ingredients, including the pineapple, into the cake mixture with the coconut and sultanas (golden raisins) and the 3 tablespoons pineapple syrup.

This cake can either be baked in a round or a ring tin (pan), so grease and flour a 1.5 litre/2½ pint (2 quart) ring tin or a 20 cm/8 inch cake tin. If cakes are inclined to stick to your cake tin, line with greased greaseproof (waxed) paper.

Put the mixture into the tin. Bake in the centre of a preheated moderate oven (160°C/325°F, Gas Mark 3). If using a ring tin, allow 1 to 1¼ hours; if using a 20 cm/8 inch tin, allow approximately 1½ hours. Test the cake (see page 160). Cool for at least 10 minutes in the tin, then turn out very carefully and allow to cool completely.

For the icing Melt the butter in a saucepan and remove from the heat. Sift the icing (confectioners') sugar into the butter, then add the pineapple syrup and coconut. Stir to combine, spread over the top of the cake and rough up with a fork. Decorate with festive ornaments. Makes one 20 cm/8 inch cake or a ring cake.

Note Plain (all-purpose) flour can be used in place of self-raising but add 2 teaspoons baking powder.

Danish Layer Cake

4 eggs
juice and grated rind of ½ lemon
150 g/5 oz (1¼ cups) icing (confectioners') sugar
85 g/3 oz (¾ cup) plain (all-purpose) flour
25 g/1 oz (¼ cup) cornflour (cornstarch)
½ teaspoon baking powder
TO FILL AND DECORATE:
2 tablespoons canned pineapple syrup or water
15 g/½ oz (2 envelopes) gelatine
5 canned pineapple rings
450 ml/¾ pint (2 cups) whipping cream
2 tablespoons vanilla-flavoured sugar or sugar and a few drops of vanilla essence (extract)
75 g/3 oz (½ cup) grated plain (semi-sweet) chocolate

Separate the eggs and place the yolks in a mixing bowl, add the lemon rind and juice and icing (confectioners') sugar. Using an electric mixer, whisk until thick and creamy. Sift together the flour, corn-flour and baking powder and fold into the whisked yolk mixture.

Whisk the egg whites until they stand in peaks. Fold gently and carefully into the mixture. Pour into a lined and greased 20 cm/8 inch cake tin (pan). Bake in the centre of a preheated moderate oven, (180°C/350°F, Gas Mark 4) for 30 minutes, or until firm to a gentle touch. Leave for a few minutes in the tin, then turn out carefully and cool. When cold, split horizontally to give 3 layers.

For the filling Place the pineapple syrup or water into a bowl and sprinkle gela-tine on top. Stand over a pan of hot water until the gelatine has dissolved. Allow to cool slightly. Chop 3 of the pineapple rings finely. Reserve remain-ing pineapple rings. Whip cream until it stands in peaks. Mix two-thirds with the gelatine, together with the chopped pineapple rings, vanilla-flavoured sugar and the grated chocolate.

Sandwich the 3 layers with the pine-apple cream mixture and spread a little over the top of the cake.

Decorate the cake with the remaining whipped cream. Serves 8.

If you make the cake in the ring tin (pan) you will require 50% more icing.

VARIATIONS

Cover the cake with marzipan then coat with Royal or Australian Icing, (see page 168).

Rich Fruit Cake Omit the canned pineapple rings, desiccated (shredded) coconut and pineapple syrup. Use 175 g/6 oz (1 cup) moist brown sugar instead of the caster sugar and 225 g/8 oz (2 cups) plain (all-purpose) flour but with no baking powder. Add 2 more eggs (giving 4 in total), 850 g/1¾ lb (5 cups) mixed dried fruit and 2 tablespoons sherry.

Bake in a prepared 20 cm/8 inch cake tin (pan) in the centre of a preheated cool oven (150°C/300°F, Gas Mark 2) for 1¾ hours. Lower the heat to 140°C/275°F, Gas Mark 1 and bake for a further 1 hour. Test the cake (see page 160). Cool for at least 10 minutes in the tin (pan), then turn out very carefully and cool further on a wire rack.

Chocolate Date Gâteau

100 g/4 oz (⅔ cup) plain (semi-sweet) chocolate
1 tablespoon orange juice or milk
1 level tablespoon golden (light corn) syrup
100 g/4 oz (½ cup) butter or margarine
50 g/2 oz (¼ cup) caster sugar
2 large eggs
85 g/3 oz (¾ cup) self-raising flour
25 g/1 oz (2 tablespoons) ground rice
FOR THE FILLING: 100 g/4 oz (⅔ cup) dates
1 tablespoon lemon juice
1 tablespoon orange juice
1 tablespoon demerara (brown) sugar
25 g/1 oz (¼ cup) chopped blanched almonds
2 tablespoons apricot jam
FOR THE TOPPING: 100 g/4 oz (⅔ cup) plain (semi-sweet) chocolate

❋ Break the chocolate into pieces, put into a bowl with the orange juice or milk and syrup and place over a pan of hot water until the chocolate has melted (or melt in the microwave cooker). Allow to cool.

Cream together the butter or margarine and sugar, then gradually beat in the chocolate mixture and the eggs. Sift the flour. Mix with the ground rice and fold into the creamed mixture. Divide between two greased and floured or lined 15 to 18 cm/6 to 7 inch sandwich tins (layer cake pans).

Bake in the centre of a preheated moderate oven (180°C/350°F, Gas Mark 4) for 20 to 25 minutes until firm to the touch. Turn out carefully and allow the cakes to cool.

Chop the dates and put into a saucepan with all the ingredients for the filling. Heat gently for several minutes, allow to cool then sandwich the cakes with the mixture.

Melt the remaining chocolate and spread over the top of the cake. Makes one 15 to 18 cm/6 to 7 inch cake.

Note Plain (all-purpose) flour can be used in place of self-raising but add ¾ teaspoon baking powder.

Chocolate Pear Mint Gâteau

FOR THE CHOCOLATE CAKE: 175 g/6 oz (¾ cup) butter or margarine
175 g/6 oz (¾ cup) caster sugar
3 large eggs
150 g/5 oz (1¼ cups) self-raising flour with ½ teaspoon baking powder
25 g/1 oz (¼ cup) cocoa powder (unsweetened cocoa)
FOR THE FILLING: 350 g/12 oz (2⅔ cups) icing (confectioners') sugar
175 g/6 oz (¾ cup) butter
½ teaspoon peppermint essence (extract)
2 tablespoons full cream evaporated milk
a few drops of green food colouring
TO DECORATE: 4 to 5 tablespoons chocolate vermicelli (sprinkles)
1 × 425 g/15 oz can pear halves
3 chocolate peppermint sweets (candies)

Cream the butter or margarine with the caster sugar until soft and light. Gradually beat in the eggs. Sift the flour, baking powder and cocoa and fold into the creamed mixture. Divide this between two 20 cm/8 inch greased and floured or lined sandwich tins (layer cake pans). Bake just above the centre of a preheated moderate oven (180°C/350°F, Gas Mark 4) for approximately 25 minutes or until firm to the touch. Turn out and allow to become quite cold.

For the filling Sift the icing (confectioners') sugar. Cream the butter, icing (confectioners') sugar and essence (extract) until soft and light. Gradually beat in the evaporated milk, then add sufficient colouring to tint the butter icing a pale, delicate shade of green.

To Serve Sandwich the two layers of the chocolate cake with a little of the filling, then spread most of the remaining filling around the sides and over the top of the cake; save a little for piping on the top of the cake.

Coat the sides with the vermicelli (sprinkles). Drain the pears and arrange on top of the cake. Halve the chocolate peppermint sweets (candies). Decorate the gâteau with piped butter icing and the chocolate peppermint sweets (candies). Serves 6 to 8.

Note Plain (all-purpose) flour can be used in place of self-raising but add 1¾ teaspoons baking powder.

VARIATIONS

Add ¼ to ½ teaspoon peppermint essence (extract) to the ingredients for the chocolate cake.

Allow the butter to stand at room temperature until soft, or use soft margarine, and use the one-stage method for mixing the cake (see page 123).

Chocolate Pear Mint Gâteau

Cider Crumble Cake, Chocolate Treacle Cake, and Orange Gingerbread

Sugar For Flavour

The type of sugar you use in a cake will affect both the taste and sometimes the consistency of the cake. The following cakes are made using the dark sugars which give a moist texture. See page 10 for a full description of the various sugars.

Apricot Cake

100 g/4 oz (½ cup) butter or margarine
100 g/4 oz (⅔ cup) light muscovado (dark brown) sugar
2 large eggs
200 g/7 oz (1¾ cups) self-raising flour with ½ teaspoon baking powder
1 × 225 g/8 oz can apricot halves
225 g/8 oz (1⅓ cups) mixed dried fruit
1 tablespoon demerara (brown) sugar

✻✻Cream the butter or margarine and muscovado (dark brown) sugar together until soft and light. Gradually beat in the eggs. Sift the flour and baking powder and fold into the creamed mixture. Drain the apricots (the syrup can be used in a fruit salad). Chop the apricots and fold into the cake mixture with the dried fruit. The mixture looks dry at this stage, but do not add any extra liquid. Grease and line an 18 cm/7 inch round cake tin (pan) and sprinkle with the demerara (brown) sugar. Put in the cake mixture. Bake in the centre of a preheated moderate oven (160°C/325°F, Gas Mark 3) for about 1½ hours. Cool for several minutes in the tin then turn out on to a wire cooling tray. Makes one 18 cm/7 inch cake.

Note Plain (all-purpose) flour can be used but add a total of 2¾ teaspoons baking powder.

Chocolate Treacle Cake

The combination of chocolate and treacle flavours, provided by using molasses sugar in the cake, is an unusual and interesting one. There may seem a high percentage of sugar and fat compared to flour, but the cake has an excellent texture.

225 g/8 oz (1 cup) butter or margarine
250 g/9 oz (1½ cups) molasses sugar
120 ml/4 fl oz (½ cup) corn oil
4 eggs
175 g/6 oz (1½ cups) self-raising flour
50 g/2 oz (½ cup) cocoa powder (unsweetened cocoa)

FOR THE FILLING:
2 tablespoons lemon juice
225 g/8 oz (1⅓ cups) muscovado (dark brown) sugar
75 g/3 oz (6 tablespoons) cream cheese

FOR THE TOPPING:
2 to 3 tablespoons icing (confectioners') sugar

✻✻Cream the butter or margarine, sugar and oil very thoroughly. Gradually beat in the eggs. Add a little sifted flour if the mixture shows any signs of curdling. Sift the flour with the cocoa. Fold into the butter and egg mixture. Unless using non-stick tins, line the bases of two 20 cm/8 inch sandwich tins (layer cake pans) with greaseproof (waxed) paper and grease and flour the sides. Spoon in the soft mixture.

Bake in the centre of a preheated moderate oven (180°C/350°F, Gas Mark 4) for 30 to 35 minutes until firm to a gentle touch. Leave the cakes in the tins (pans) for 1 or 2 minutes, then turn out and cool.

For the filling Blend the lemon juice, muscovado sugar and cheese together. Sandwich the cakes with this filling.

Sift the icing (confectioners') sugar over the top of the cake or make a decorated topping as in the sketches on this page. Makes one 20 cm/8 inch cake.

Note Plain (all-purpose) flour can be used but add 1½ teaspoons baking powder.

VARIATION

Use whipped cream as a filling in the cake. Use muscovado sugar instead of molasses sugar.

Ginger Loaf

100 g/4 oz (½ cup) butter or margarine
100 g/4 oz (⅔ cup) muscovado (dark brown) sugar
1½ tablespoons black treacle (molasses)
2 eggs
225 g/8 oz (2 cups) self-raising flour with ½ teaspoon baking powder
½ teaspoon ground ginger
100 g/4 oz (⅔ cup) preserved ginger

⁂Cream the butter or margarine, sugar and black treacle (molasses) very thoroughly, then gradually beat in the eggs. Sift the flour and baking powder with the ground ginger. Chop the preserved ginger. Fold the flour and then the chopped ginger into the creamed mixture.

Grease and flour or line a 750 g to 1 kg/1½ to 2 lb loaf tin (pan) and spoon in the mixture. Bake in the centre of a preheated moderate oven (180°C/350°F, Gas Mark 4) for 1 hour, or until firm to the touch. Cool in the tin for 15 minutes then turn out. This can be eaten plain as a cake or sliced and spread with butter. Makes one loaf cake.

Note Plain (all-purpose) flour can be used but add 2½ teaspoons baking powder.

Orange Gingerbread

1 large orange, see method
450 g/1 lb (4 cups) plain (all-purpose) flour
1 tablespoon ground ginger
3 teaspoons baking powder
1 *level* teaspoon bicarbonate of soda (baking soda)
pinch of salt
175 g/6 oz (¾ cup) butter or margarine
4 tablespoons pure cane (light corn) syrup
450 g/1 lb (2⅔ cups) molasses sugar
150 ml/¼ pint (⅔ cup) milk
2 eggs
TO DECORATE:
16 slices of crystallized or preserved ginger

⁂Finely grate the rind from the orange, halve the fruit and squeeze out the juice (you need 4 tablespoons juice; if too little, use a second orange). Sift the flour, ginger, baking powder, soda and salt into a large mixing bowl. Put the butter or margarine and the cane syrup into a saucepan, stir over a low heat until the butter has melted, then add the sugar and continue stirring until the sugar has completely melted. Do not overheat. Add the melted ingredients to the flour mixture and beat well. Warm the milk in the saucepan in which the ingredients were melted, stirring well to absorb any sugar mixture that might have been left in the pan. Pour over the ingredients in the mixing bowl and stir briskly. Lastly add the eggs, orange juice and rind and beat well. The mixture will appear very soft, but that is quite correct.

Line a 20 cm/8 inch square cake tin (pan) with greaseproof (waxed) paper and grease this very well. Pour in the mixture. Bake in the centre of a preheated moderate oven (160°C/325°F, Gas Mark 3) for 1½ to 1¾ hours, cool in the tin.

Cut into 16 squares. Top each square with a slice of ginger. Makes 16 squares.

VARIATIONS

⁂**Moist Orange Cake** Use the grated rind and juice of the orange as in the recipe above, but substitute 150 ml/¼ pint (⅔ cup) orange juice for the milk. Do not use the molasses sugar but use unrefined granulated sugar instead which gives the cake a lovely colour. Top each square with a crystallized orange slice.

Bake the basic recipe or the variation above in a 23 cm/9 inch cake tin to give about 25 shallow squares of cake. Bake the cake for 1 hour 20 minutes at the temperature above.

Cider Crumble Cake

500 g/1 lb 2 oz (4½ cups) self-raising flour
75 g/3 oz (½ cup) dates
175 g/6 oz (¾ cup) butter or margarine
225 g/8 oz (1⅓ cups) light brown sugar
175 g/6 oz (½ cup) black treacle (molasses)
300 ml/½ pint (1¼ cups) dry (hard) cider
1 egg
FOR THE CRUMBLE TOPPING:
40 g/1½ oz (⅓ cup) walnuts
40 g/1½ oz (6 tablespoons) plain (all-purpose) flour
40 g/1½ oz (3 tablespoons) butter
40 g/1½ oz (3 tablespoons) caster sugar
½ teaspoon ground cinnamon
3 tablespoons apricot or plum jam

⁂Sift the flour into a mixing bowl. Chop the dates. Put the butter or margarine, sugar and treacle (molasses) into a saucepan, heat gently only until the fat and sugar have melted, then add to the flour and beat well. Pour the cider into the saucepan in which the fat was melted, add the dates and stir well to absorb any ingredients left in the pan, but do not heat the cider. Add to the other ingredients, together with the egg, and mix thoroughly.

Line the bottom of a 23 cm/9 inch square or 25 cm/10 inch round cake tin; (pan), grease and flour the inside of the tin. Put the cake mixture in the tin and bake in the centre of a preheated moderate oven (160°C/325°F, Gas Mark 3) for 50 minutes to 1 hour, or until just firm to the touch.

For the topping Prepare the crumble mixture. Chop the nuts. Put the flour into a bowl, cut the butter into pieces, add to the flour and rub in (cut in) quickly and lightly, for this is a high proportion of fat to flour and the mixture could become over-sticky. Add the sugar, nuts and cinnamon.

Remove the cake from the oven, spread with the jam and top with the crumble mixture. Return the cake to the oven for a further 20 minutes. Makes a 23 to 25 cm/9 to 10 inch cake.

Note Plain (all-purpose) flour can be used in place of self-raising but add 4 teaspoons baking powder.

VARIATION

Use half the quantities in the cake mixture and bake in an 18 cm/7 inch round or 15 cm/6 inch square cake tin for about 45 minutes. Make the crumble; use 25 g/1 oz (¼ cup) each of flour, and nuts and 25 g/1 oz (2 tablespoons) each of butter and sugar. With a generous ¼ teaspoon of ground cinnamon. Spread the cake with 1½ to 2 tablespoons jam, top with the crumble mixture and bake for a further 15 minutes.

SIMPLE SKILL
Weighing Sticky Ingredients
Liquid glucose, like golden (corn) syrup and treacle (molasses), is difficult and messy to weigh. One solution is to place the saucepan, or bowl, in which the ingredient is to be put on the scales and then add the required weight of glucose.

Alternatively, flour the pan of the scales, before weighing the sticky ingredients. You will find that when you tip the pan the flour enables the ingredients to roll off without any wastage or mess.

Cakes made with Oil

Many excellent cakes can be made with corn oil which is an ideal fat to use when following a low-cholesterol diet. The Rich Fruit Cake can be decorated for special occasions (page 168).

Golden Cake

This is an unusual recipe and very simple. Do not be put off by the idea of carrots in a cake – they are used in quite a number of continental gâteaux – and make the cake deliciously moist.

| 175 g/6 oz carrots, weight when peeled |
| 50 g/2 oz (½ cup) walnuts |
| 2 ripe bananas |
| 175 g/6 oz (1 cup) light muscovado (dark brown) sugar |
| 3 eggs |
| 300 g/10 oz (2½ cups) plain (all-purpose) flour |
| pinch of salt |
| ½ teaspoon bicarbonate of soda (baking soda) |
| 1½ teaspoons baking powder |
| 175 ml/6 fl oz (¾ cup) corn oil |
| **FOR THE COATING:** |
| 175 g/6 oz (1⅓ cups) icing (confectioners') sugar |
| 75 g/3 oz (6 tablespoons) butter |

Golden Cake and Marmalade Loaf

| 75 g/3 oz (6 tablespoons) cream cheese |
| ½ teaspoon vanilla essence (extract) |

✱✱Peel and grate the carrots and chop the walnuts. Set aside. Mash the bananas and put into a bowl with the sugar and eggs. Sift the flour, salt, soda and baking powder into the bowl. Add the oil and mix well. Finally put in the carrot mixture and mix thoroughly. Grease and line a 23 cm/9 inch cake tin (pan) and spoon in the mixture. Bake in the centre of a preheated moderate oven (160 to 180°C/325 to 350°F, Gas Mark 3 to 4) for 1 hour 5 minutes or until golden brown. Allow to cool for a few minutes then turn out of the tin.

For the coating Sift the icing (confectioners') sugar. Place all the remaining ingredients in a bowl and mix well until soft and creamy. Gradually beat in the icing (confectioners') sugar. Spread over the cake; using a fork and sweeping up to give a slightly roughened effect. Makes one 23 cm/9 inch cake.

Marmalade Loaf

| 2 oranges |
| 300 g/10 oz (2½ cups) plain (all-purpose) flour |
| 50 g/2 oz (½ cup) cornflour (cornstarch) |
| 3 teaspoons baking powder |
| pinch of salt |
| 75 g/3 oz (6 tablespoons) caster sugar |

| 75 g/3 oz (½ cup) sultanas (golden raisins) |
| 2 tablespoons orange marmalade |
| 175 ml/6 fl oz (¾ cup) corn oil |
| 3 large eggs |

Grate the rind from 1 orange. Cut away the rind from the second orange with a vegetable peeler. Be careful to take just the top 'zest' and no white pith. Cut this into matchstick pieces. Halve the fruit and squeeze out 6 tablespoons orange juice. Sift the flour, cornflour, baking powder and salt into a mixing bowl. Add the grated orange rind, the strips of orange rind, the caster sugar, sultanas and marmalade.

Mix the orange juice with the corn oil and eggs. Add to the ingredients in the mixing bowl and beat thoroughly.

Grease and flour a 1 kg/2 lb loaf tin (pan) and spoon in the mixture. Bake in the centre of a preheated moderate oven (180°C/350°F, Gas Mark 4) for 1 hour, then reduce the heat to cool (150°C/300°F, Gas Mark 2) and bake for a further 20 to 30 minutes.

Allow the cake to cool in the tin for 15 minutes, then turn out. Serve as a plain cake or sliced and buttered as a tea-bread. Makes 1 loaf.

Rich Fruit Cake

| 100 ml/4 fl oz (½ cup) corn oil |
| 175 g/6 oz (1 cup) moist brown sugar |
| 3 large eggs |
| 100 g/4 oz (½ cup) glacé cherries |
| 50 g/2 oz (⅓ cup) mixed candied peel |
| 50 g/2 oz (½ cup) chopped blanched almonds |
| 450 g/1 lb (3 cups) mixed dried fruit |
| 225 g/8 oz (2 cups) plain (all-purpose) flour |
| 1 teaspoon baking powder |
| 1 teaspoon mixed spice |
| 2 tablespoons sherry or milk |

✱✱Beat together the corn oil, sugar and eggs in a large mixing bowl. Chop the cherries and candied peel; add to the oil mixture together with the almonds and dried fruit. Sift the flour with the baking powder and spice and fold into the ingredients together with the sherry or milk.

Line a 20 cm/8 inch round cake tin (pan) with a double thickness of grease-proof (waxed) paper. Brush lightly with corn oil. If your oven is inclined to be slightly over hot, tie a double band of brown paper round the outside of the cake tin; have the paper standing about 2.5 cm/1 inch above the top rim of the tin.

Spoon the cake mixture into the tin and smooth flat on top. Bake in the centre of a preheated moderate oven (160°C/325°F, Gas Mark 3) for 1 hour

Devil's Food Cake

then lower the heat to cool (150°C/ 300°F, Gas Mark 2) and bake for a further 1¼ to 1½ hours.

Allow the cake to cool in the tin for at least 30 minutes then turn out carefully. When quite cold, wrap in greaseproof (waxed) paper or foil and store in an airtight tin. Makes one 20 cm/8 inch cake.

VARIATION
To make a moist, rich cake: Prick the cake with a fine knitting needle when cold and moisten with a little sherry or brandy. Repeat at 10-day intervals.

Devil's Food Cake

This cake does not contain eggs. If a less definite flavour is required use a chocolate powder instead of cocoa powder (unsweetened cocoa).

350 g/12 oz (3 cups) plain (all-purpose) flour
75 g/3 oz (¾ cup) cocoa powder (unsweetened cocoa)
1½ teaspoons baking powder
¼ teaspoon bicarbonate of soda (baking soda)
pinch of salt
350 g/12 oz (1½ cups) caster sugar
350 ml/12 fl oz (1½ cups) milk
175 ml/6 fl oz (¾ cup) corn oil
½ to 1 teaspoon vanilla essence (extract)

1 quantity Butter Icing, see page 168
FOR THE AMERICAN FROSTING:
325 g/11½ oz (scant 1½ cups) caster sugar
4 tablespoons water
pinch of tartar
2 egg whites

Sift the flour, cocoa powder, baking powder, soda and salt into a mixing bowl. Add the caster sugar, milk, corn oil and vanilla essence (extract) and beat well to make a smooth batter. Line three 20 cm/8 inch sandwich tins (layer cake pans) with well-greased greaseproof (waxed) paper. Pour in the cake mixture and bake just above the centre of a preheated moderately hot oven (190°C/ 375°F, Gas Mark 5) for about 25 minutes, or until firm to the touch. Allow to cool. Sandwich the layers together with the butter icing.

For the American frosting Place the caster sugar and water in a saucepan. Stir until the sugar has dissolved then allow this to boil until it reaches 114.4°C/238°F, i.e. the temperature at which a small amount forms a soft ball when tested in cold water. Add a pinch of cream of tartar. Whisk 2 egg whites until very stiff, then pour the boiling syrup gradually on to the egg whites, beating hard as you do so. When the icing has stiffened slightly and become cloudy, spread it over the cake and swirl with a knife. Makes a 20 cm/8 inch cake.

Butterfly Cakes

150 g/5 oz (1¼ cups) plain (all-purpose) flour
2 tablespoons cornflour (cornstarch)
2 level teaspoons baking powder
150 g/5 oz (⅔ cup) caster sugar
2 eggs
100 ml/3½ fl oz (scant ½ cup) corn oil
100 ml/3½ fl oz (scant ½ cup) water
FOR THE TOPPING:
Butter Icing made with 75 g/3 oz (6 tablespoons) butter, see page 168
icing (confectioners') sugar

⁂ Sift the flour with the other dry ingredients. Separate the eggs. Mix the yolks with corn oil and water, beat well, then blend with the dry ingredients. Whisk the egg whites until stiff, fold into the sponge mixture.

Spoon into 12 to 15 paper cases and bake above the centre of a preheated moderately hot oven (190°C/375°F, Gas Mark 5) for the 10 to 15 minutes until just firm to the touch. Allow to cool then cut a slice from the top of each cake.

For the topping Pipe the butter cream on top of each cake. Halve the slices to give 2 wings; press into the icing at a slight angle. Dust with sifted icing (confectioners') sugar. Makes 12 to 15.

Note Use one colour for the butter icing or divide it into bowls and colour each batch separately.

167

Icings

There are numerous icings that can be used to decorate cakes. Butter and Glacé Icings are the simplest to make and are suitable for light cakes. Australian and Royal Icing with Marzipan are more suited to richer cakes.

BASIC ICINGS

Glacé Icing

This is made by combining icing (confectioners') sugar with a little liquid; it may be water with a few drops of flavouring or colouring. If the icing (confectioners') sugar has lumps then it should be sifted, but if relatively smooth just mix with the liquid and allow to stand for a short time before using. For a more glossy icing, heat the icing (confectioners') sugar and liquid in a saucepan for 1 to 2 minutes.

Quantities With 225 g/8 oz (2 cups) icing (confectioners') sugar, use about ¾ tablespoon liquid to give an icing that spreads easily but is fairly firm; use more liquid for a flowing consistency. This quantity is sufficient to give a fairly thick coating on the top of a 20 cm/8 inch cake or to coat the top and sides of a fairly shallow 15 cm/6 inch cake.

VARIATIONS

Chocolate Glacé Icing Mix a little sifted cocoa powder (unsweetened cocoa) or chocolate powder with the icing (confectioners') sugar.

Coffee Glacé Icing Mix a little instant coffee powder with the warmed water and then with the icing (confectioners') sugar.

Fruit-flavoured Glacé Icing Mix the icing (confectioners') sugar with lemon, orange, grapefruit or pineapple juice. The icing is less clear, but delicious, if blended with fresh raspberry or strawberry purée instead of fruit juice.

Butter Icing

Beat softened butter with sifted icing (confectioners') sugar until soft and creamy. The proportions of butter and icing (confectioners') sugar used can vary. A good coating consistency is made if you use about 50% more icing (confectioners') sugar than butter. Add the desired flavouring and use immediately.

Quantities Butter Icing made with 50 g/2 oz (¼ cup) butter would be sufficient to give a thin coating on the top of an 18 cm/7 inch cake. If you want to coat the sides as well use 100 g/4 oz (½ cup) butter and if you also want one layer of filling use 175 g/6 oz (¾ cup) butter.

VARIATIONS

Chocolate Butter Icing Add a little sifted cocoa powder (unsweetened cocoa) or chocolate powder with a few drops of vanilla essence (extract) or melt plain (semi-sweet) chocolate, allow to cool, then mix with the butter. Add the sifted icing (confectioners') sugar.

Coffee Butter Icing Dissolve a little instant coffee powder in a few drops of warm water or milk, beat into the butter, then add the sifted icing (confectioners') sugar.

Fruit-flavoured Butter Icing Cream the very finely grated rind of an orange or lemon (use just the zest of the fruit) with the butter, then add the sifted icing (confectioners') sugar. You can incorporate a little fruit juice or fruit purée, as suggested under Glacé Icing (see above), but you will then need to add a little extra sifted icing (confectioners') sugar to give a good spreading consistency.

Royal Icing

Sift 450 g/1 lb (3½ cups) icing (confectioners') sugar very thoroughly. Lightly whisk 2 egg whites, add the icing (confectioners') sugar with 1 tablespoon lemon juice and whisk until very white and smooth. If using an electric mixer or food processor do not over-whip, for this creates air bubbles which make both coating and piping very difficult. For a softer icing, add 1 teaspoon glycerine.

The icing can be coloured.

Royal Icing hardens very rapidly, so leftover icing should be covered with damp absorbent kitchen paper or a damp cloth.

Quantities The quantity above gives enough for a thick layer on the top only of a 20 to 23 cm/8 to 9 inch round cake, plus a little piping (see right). If covering the top and sides of the cake, use 1 kg/2 lb (7 cups) icing (confectioners') sugar.

Australian Icing

This icing is rolled out and laid over the cake. It is sufficiently thick to take the place of marzipan if desired and it never becomes as hard as Royal Icing. Leftover Australian Icing will keep well if wrapped in plastic wrap.

3 tablespoons lemon juice or water
15 g/½ oz (2 envelopes) gelatine
100 g/4 oz (½ cup) liquid glucose
3 teaspoons glycerine
1 kg/2 lb (7 cups) sifted icing (confectioners) sugar
colouring if desired

Place the lemon juice or water in a bowl. Sprinkle the gelatine on top. Stand the bowl over hot water until the gelatine has dissolved. Melt the liquid glucose and the glycerine in a large saucepan over low heat, add the dissolved gelatine and mix well. Gradually work in the sifted icing (confectioners') sugar. Knead well to bind, adding a few drops of colouring if desired.

Roll out on a board coated with icing (confectioners') sugar until sufficiently large to completely cover the cake. Prepare the cake (see 'Coating a Cake') and place the icing over it, pressing firmly so that it adheres to the cake or marzipan. Smooth the icing with your hands and cut away any surplus. The more the icing is smoothed, the more shiny and glossy it becomes.

This quantity is sufficient to give a thick coating on the top and sides of a round 20 to 23 cm/8 to 9 inch cake and there will be a little left over for moulding.

Marzipan

100 g/4 oz (1 cup) ground almonds
50 g/2 oz (¼ cup) caster sugar
50 g/2 oz (½ cup) sifted icing (confectioners') sugar
a few drops of almond essence (extract)
1 egg yolk

Mix the ground almonds, caster sugar, icing (confectioners') sugar and almond essence in a bowl. Add the egg yolk and knead very gently to form a ball. Roll out on a board dusted with a little caster sugar.

Makes enough to give a thin layer on top of a 20 cm/8 inch round cake.

VARIATION

For a more generous layer use 1½ times the recipe, using 175 g/6 oz (1½ cups) ground almonds, 75 g/3 oz (6 tablespoons) sifted icing (confectioners') sugar but using 1 egg yolk and 1 tablespoon dry sherry instead of the 1½ egg yolks that would be required. To coat the top and sides of a 20 cm/8 inch cake you would need 3 times the above recipe.

Easter Egg Cake coated with Butter Icing, see page 161

Decorating

Cakes can be decorated in many different ways and it is only intricate piping that requires patience and practice. The other methods listed below are so simple that even novice cooks can produce attractive cakes with very little effort.

Simple Suggestions

<u>Layer Cakes</u> You can split a Victoria Sandwich, or any other light sponge cake, to give 2, 3 or 4 thin layers and sandwich these with jam or Butter Icing (see left). Coat the sides with jam or Butter Icing, but top with Glacé Icing. The coated sides can then be covered with flaked toasted almonds; grated chocolate, sugar strands, or desiccated (shredded) coconut.

<u>Snow Effect</u> Ideal for Christmas Cakes. Use a thick layer of Royal Icing and, using the tip of a knife, sweep it up into peaks to look like snow. Add seasonal decorations and leave the icing to set.

<u>Piping</u> It takes time and practice to achieve first class results. Use Butter or Royal Icing, Glacé icing is only suitable for writing and for drawing lines or small dots (see cake pictured right).

<u>Moulding</u> Use Australian Icing to mould flowers, fruit and various other shapes like the crib on the cake pictured above.

Coating a Cake

Before coating a light sponge or rich fruit cake with icing or marzipan brush away any loose crumbs which will spoil the even surface of the icing.

Brush a rich fruit cake with sieved apricot jam or egg white before applying marzipan or Australian icing, they will adhere better.

To give a pleasant moistness to a light sponge cake, brush the top, or top and sides, with sieved apricot jam. Do not use egg white.

<u>To coat a cake with Marzipan</u> Roll out the marzipan and either cut a circle the size of the top of the cake and a band the circumference of the cake, or make a shape sufficiently large to cover the cake entirely.

The oil in ground almonds seeps out if the marzipan is handled too much. Should this happen, allow the marzipan to dry out for 48 hours before putting the final Australian or Royal Icing on top. Provided the almond oil has not seeped out you can ice over the marzipan immediately and it will then stay soft. To neaten the top, roll with a sugared rolling pin. To neaten the sides, roll a jam jar around the cake. This can be done when using Australian icing too.

Icing a Cake

Place all the icing on top of the cake. Warm a palette knife or icing spatula by dipping it into very hot water, patting dry and using while still warm. Spread the icing from the centre of the cake to the outer rim of the top of the cake, or down the sides too if covering the complete cake. Do not try to neaten any icing until the cake is coated completely. When this is done, make sweeping movements over the top of the cake or drag the surplus icing to the sides of the cake. Hold the knife or spatula vertically against the side of the cake and move round slowly and evenly to neaten the sides of the cakes.

Christening Cake

Cover a 20 cm/8 inch rich fruit cake (see pages 166 and 163) with apricot jam then Marzipan (see left).

Place the cake on a silver cake board and cover the cake with white Australian Icing (see left). Knead the icing trimmings together and colour two thirds of it pink. Mould some of the pink icing into a cradle shape using an egg as a mould. Use more pink icing to make a pillow and quilt creating the quilt effect by marking with the back of a knife. Use the white icing to form the baby and two small rockers to support the cradle. Place the pillow, baby and quilt in the cradle. Create a canopy by supporting a

small piece of lace over the baby with a plastic cocktail stick.

Arrange a piece of pink ribbon around the side of the cake and secure with a little icing. Make roses from the remaining pink Australian Icing (see right).

Using 1 quantity of Royal Icing (see left) and a piping bag fitted with a small star tube, pipe a row of stars around the base of the cake on the cake board. On the top edge of the cake pipe a row of stars a little apart, and on the side of the cake pipe a row of stars to alternate with the top row of stars. Mark a 8 cm/3½ inch circle in the centre of the cake and pipe small stars around the circle. Secure the pink rosebuds to the circle of stars.

Colour the remaining Royal Icing pale pink and using a small plain piping tube, pipe threads of icing diagonally from the top to the bottom row of stars, at the top edge of the cake. Repeat in the opposite direction. Pipe a small bead of pink icing on top of each star on the top of the cake and on the stars on the cake board. Place the cradle in the centre of the rosebuds on top of the cake.

<u>Note</u> Use pale blue icing for a boy's Christening Cake.

Christening Cake

SIMPLE SKILL
<u>Moulded Roses</u>
These are simple to create using Australian Icing. Make a solid cone about 1 cm/½ inch long.

Roll out more icing very thinly and cut out a circle about 1 cm/½ inch across. Press 1 side of the circle until paper thin.

Carefully wrap the circle around the cone with the thick part at the base, attach with a dab of water or egg white. Continue to make 3 or 4 more petals, attaching carefully and curving to give a rose shape.

169

Meringue Gâteaux

Sharon Pavlova

The meringue mixture is very popular and adaptable. Cooked meringues or meringue cases can be stored for weeks in an airtight tin or they can be frozen and are perfect to have on hand for last minute entertaining.

Baking Meringue

Many people have problems when baking meringue. Provided the baking sheet has been correctly prepared, the meringues should not break when they are removed.

If meringues, or a meringue shell, are difficult to remove this may be because the egg white is not quite cooked.

To prepare a good quality baking sheet, or one with non-stick finish, simply brush well with very little oil. Line ordinary baking trays (sheets) with greaseproof (waxed) paper and brush this with a little oil; or use special non-stick paper (parchment) which does not need oiling.

Meringues

Follow the recipe for the meringue in Chamonix (see right). Spoon or pipe small rounds, fingers or nest shapes of the mixture on to a prepared tin. The rounds can vary in size from 2.5 cm/1 inch in diameter to large rounds dropped from a tablespoon. The fingers can be thin and delicate or long and wide. The baking temperature in each case will be the same. What will vary is the baking time. Bake at the cooler temperature given for Chamonix and allow 1 hour for 'baby' meringues and up to 3 hours for larger ones.

Chamonix

FOR THE MERINGUES:
50 g/2 oz (½ cup) icing (confectioners') sugar

50 g/2 oz (¼ cup) caster sugar

2 egg whites

¼ teaspoon vanilla essence (extract)

FOR THE TOPPING:
150 ml/¼ pint (⅔ cup) double (heavy) cream

25 to 50 g/1 to 2 oz (¼ cup) caster sugar

¼ teaspoon vanilla essence (extract)

100 to 175 g/4 to 6 oz (½ to ¾ cup) canned unsweetened chestnut purée

Sift the icing (confectioners') sugar, mix with the caster sugar. Whisk the egg whites until stiff, add the vanilla essence (extract) then gradually beat in half the sugar. Fold in the remainder. Spoon or pipe the meringue mixture in 4 to 6 large rounds on the prepared baking sheet and bake in the centre of a preheated very cool oven (90 to 110°C/200 to 225°F, Gas Mark 0 to ¼) for approximately 2½ to 3 hours or in a preheated cool oven (110 to 120°C/225 to 250°F, Gas Mark ¼ to ½) for about 2 hours. Lift the meringue rounds from the sheet and place on a wire tray to cool.

For the topping Whip the cream and fold in the sugar and vanilla essence (extract). Blend half with the chestnut purée and spoon over the top of the meringues. Finally decorate with the remainder of the cream. Makes 4 to 6.

VARIATION

Add a little brandy or a coffee liqueur like Tia Maria to the cream and chestnut purée mixture.

Sharon Pavlova

175 g/6 oz (¾ cup) caster sugar or use half caster and half icing (confectioners') sugar

1 teaspoon cornflour (cornstarch)

3 egg whites

½ teaspoon lemon juice or white wine vinegar

FOR THE FILLING:
150 ml/¼ pint (⅔ cup) double (heavy) cream

150 ml/¼ pint (⅔ cup) soured cream

150 ml/¼ pint (⅔ cup) yogurt

2 teaspoons finely grated orange rind

TO DECORATE:
1 sharon fruit

1 orange

2 black grapes

Mix the caster sugar with the cornflour (cornstarch). If using a mixture of caster and icing (confectioners') sugars, sift the icing (confectioners') sugar and cornflour (cornstarch) together, then mix with the caster sugar.

Whisk the egg whites until stiff. Gradually beat in half the sugar and cornflour (cornstarch), then fold in the remainder together with the lemon juice or vinegar.

Spread about half the meringue mixture on to the prepared baking sheet (see above) to make an 18 cm/7 inch round. Pipe or spoon the remaining meringue mixture around the edges building up the sides to form a flan.

A Pavlova is generally baked rather more quickly than a meringue so that the inside is slightly sticky, but you could use the longer, slower cooking time given in the variation to the meringue shell recipe.

Place the meringue mixture in the centre of a preheated cool oven (150°C/300°F, Gas Mark 2), but reduce the heat at once to (140°C/275°F, Gas Mark 1). Bake for 1¼ hours or until firm. Remove from the baking sheet and place on a wire tray to cool.

Whip the double (heavy) cream until it just holds its shape, then whip in the soured cream, yogurt and orange rind. Spoon over the top of the meringue, keeping back a little for decoration.

Halve the sharon fruit making a zig-zag design and scoop out the pulp. Keep one halved shell of the fruit. Halve the orange and squeeze out the juice. Mash or blend the sharon fruit with the orange juice and spread over the cream base. Place the reserved fruit shell in the centre of the Pavlova and decorate with the last of the cream. Cut the grapes into segments and arrange around the sharon fruit shell. Serves 4 to 6.

VARIATION

For a very crisp meringue shell, bake at the lower temperature given for Chamonix (see left) for 2½ to 3 hours.

Biscuits

Most homemade biscuits (cookies) and biscuit bars can be cooked in advance and stored in an airtight tin or frozen until required.

Biscuits (cookies) can be shaped in various ways – spoonfuls can be dropped on to the baking sheet; the mixture can be rolled into balls; the dough can be rolled out and cut into shapes; or the dough can be formed into a roll then sliced.

American Sugar Cookies

These are excellent to serve as petits fours. They can be topped with icing if desired.

75 g/3 oz (6 tablespoons) butter
175 g/6 oz (¾ cup) caster sugar
¼ to ½ teaspoon vanilla essence (extract)
2 egg yolks
150 g/5 oz (1¼ cups) plain (all-purpose) flour
½ teaspoon baking powder
1 tablespoon double (heavy) cream

✲✲Cream together the butter, sugar and vanilla essence (extract). The proportion of sugar is very high, so creaming needs to be done briskly. Gradually beat in the egg yolks. Sift the flour with the baking powder and stir into the creamed mixture. Add the cream and mix thoroughly. Grease flat baking sheets. Drop teaspoonfuls of the mixture onto the prepared sheets, leaving a 2.5 cm/1 inch space between each teaspoon of the mixture.

Bake in the centre of a preheated moderate oven (180°C/350°F, Gas Mark 4) for 8 minutes. Allow to cool for 4 to 5 minutes on the baking sheets, then lift carefully on to a wire cooling tray. Makes 50 to 60.

Cherry and Ginger Shortbreads

25 g/1 oz crystallized ginger
25 g/1 oz glacé cherries
100 g/4 oz (1 cup) self-raising flour
75 g/3 oz (6 tablespoons) butter or margarine
50 g/2 oz (¼ cup) caster sugar

✲✲Cut the ginger and cherries into small pieces. Sift the flour and mix with the ginger and cherries. Cream the butter or margarine and sugar until soft, add the flour mixture, work together with your fingers.

Form into 12 to 14 medium balls, or 16 to 18 small ones. Place on lightly greased baking sheets and bake in the centre of a preheated moderate oven (160°C/325°F, Gas Mark 3) for 15 minutes. Makes 12 to 18.
Note Plain (all-purpose) flour can be used in place of self-raising but add 1 teaspoon baking powder.

Chocolate Brownies

50 g/2 oz (½ cup) walnuts
100 g/4 oz (⅔ cup) plain (semi-sweet) chocolate
100 g/4 oz (½ cup) butter
100 g/4 oz (⅔ cup) soft brown sugar
100 g/4 oz (1 cup) self-raising flour
pinch of salt
2 eggs
25 g/1 oz (3 tablespoons) raisins
1 to 2 tablespoons milk

✲✲Chop the walnuts. Break the chocolate into pieces and put into a mixing bowl with the butter. Stand over a pan of hot water until the chocolate and butter have melted; allow to cool then add the sugar. Sift the flour with the salt and combine with the chocolate mixture. Beat in the eggs, walnuts and raisins, then add sufficient milk to make a soft dropping consistency.

Spoon the mixture into a greased and floured, or lined, 20 cm/8 inch square cake tin (pan) and bake in the centre of a preheated moderate oven (180°C/350°F, Gas Mark 4) for 30 minutes, or until just firm to the touch. Allow to cool in the tin

for 10 minutes, then turn out and leave until cold. Cut into squares. Makes 16.

Date and Orange Crunchies

100 g/4 oz (½ cup) butter or margarine
100 g/4 oz (generous ½ cup) brown sugar
3 tablespoons golden (light corn) syrup
3 teaspoons finely grated orange rind
175 g/6 oz (1¾ cups) rolled oats
50 g/2 oz (½ cup) wholewheat flour
1 teaspoon baking powder
100 g/4 oz (generous ½ cup) stoned (pitted) dates
1 tablespoon orange juice

Put the butter or margarine, brown sugar and golden (corn) syrup into a saucepan and heat gently until melted. Cool then blend in the orange rind and rolled oats. Combine the flour with the baking powder and add to the melted ingredients. Mix well. Finely chop the dates and mix with the orange juice.

Spread half the rolled oat mixture into a well-greased 18 cm/7 inch square tin. Top with the dates and orange juice. Cover with the remaining rolled oat mixture and flatten with the back of a metal spoon.

Bake in the centre of a preheated moderate oven (180°C/350°F, Gas Mark 4) for 20 to 25 minutes or until golden and firm. Cool for a few minutes, then mark into 16 portions. When quite cold lift out of the tin. Makes 16.

Brownies, Date and Orange Crunchies

Peanut Butter Cookies

Peanut Butter Cookies

| 50 g/2 oz (¼ cup) butter or margarine |
| 50 g/2 oz (¼ cup) peanut butter |
| 50 g/2 oz (¼ cup) caster sugar |
| 50 g/2 oz (⅓ cup) light brown sugar |
| 1 teaspoon grated orange rind |
| 1 egg yolk |
| 40 g/1½ oz (¼ cup) seedless raisins |
| 100 g/4 oz (1 cup) self-raising flour |

Cream together the butter or margarine, peanut butter, sugars and orange rind until soft and light. Beat in the egg yolk. Cut the raisins into small pieces with kitchen scissors, add to the creamed mixture together with the flour. Mix thoroughly. Roll into 18 balls. Place on ungreased baking trays allowing space for the mixture to spread. Press each ball with the back of a fork in a criss-cross design. Bake in the centre of a preheated moderate oven (180°C/350°F, Gas Mark 4) for 20 minutes or until firm. Allow to cool for 5 minutes then remove to a wire cooling tray. Store in an airtight tin. Makes 18.

Dutch Fans

| 175 g/6 oz (¾ cup) butter or margarine |
| 150 g/5 oz (½ cup plus 2 tablespoons) caster sugar |
| 225 g/8 oz (2 cups) plain (all-purpose) flour |
| 1 egg white |

٭Cream the butter or margarine and 120 g/4 oz (½ cup) caster sugar, add the flour, knead well, then mix in a little egg white to bind the mixture and give a firm rolling consistency. Roll out the dough until 5 mm/¼ inch thick. Cut into large rounds with a fluted cutter, then cut each round into 4 portions to make fan shapes. Place on ungreased baking sheets.

Whisk the remaining egg white until frothy and spread lightly over the biscuits (cookies). Bake in the centre of a preheated moderate oven, (160°C/325°F, Gas Mark 3) for 12 minutes or until firm. Sprinkle with the remaining sugar while hot and allow to cool on the baking sheets. Makes 24 to 36.

Rich Coffee Biscuits

| 225 g/8 oz (1 cup) butter or margarine |
| 50 g/2 oz (½ cup) icing (confectioners') sugar |
| 2 teaspoons instant coffee powder |
| 1 teaspoon water |
| 175 g/6 oz (1½ cups) plain (all-purpose) flour |
| 50 g/2 oz (½ cup) cornflour (cornstarch) |

TO DECORATE:

| 75 g/3 oz (½ cup) plain (semi-sweet) chocolate |
| Coffee Glacé Icing, made with 75 g/3 oz (⅔ cup) icing (confectioners') sugar, see page 168 |
| a few blanched and halved flaked almonds |
| a few walnut halves |
| crystallized rose and violet petals |

٭Beat the butter or margarine until soft and light. Sift in the icing (confectioners') sugar and beat again until well mixed. Dissolve the coffee powder in the cold water, and add to the creamed mixture. Sift the flour and cornflour (cornstarch) into the other ingredients and mix well with your fingers. The dough may seem rather soft, due to the very high proportion of fat, so wrap in plastic wrap and chill in the refrigerator until firm enough to handle.

Roll out the dough until about 5 mm/¼ inch thick and cut into fancy shapes. Mark some biscuits (cookies) with a fork to give a ridged effect. Place on un-greased baking sheets and bake in the centre of a moderate oven (180°C/350°F, Gas Mark 4) for 12 to 15 minutes. Allow to cool on the baking sheet, since the biscuits (cookies) are very fragile when warm. Undecorated biscuits (cookies) keep for weeks in an airtight tin. Decorate on the day they are being served. Makes about 24.

For the decoration Break the chocolate into pieces and place in a bowl. Allow to melt over a pan of hot, but not boiling, water or in the microwave cooker. Cool slightly then spread in the centre of the tops of some of the biscuits (cookies). Allow to set. Decorate other biscuits (cookies) with the Glacé Icing; this should be fairly thick so that it does not soften the biscuits (cookies). Top with the nuts and petals.

Rout Biscuits

| 110 g/4 oz (1 cup) ground almonds |
| 110 g/4 oz (½ cup) caster sugar |
| a few drops of almond essence (extract) |
| 1 egg |
| 36 to 48 blanched almonds |

٭Blend the ground almonds, sugar and essence together. Separate the egg white from the yolk. Bind the almond mixture with the egg yolk. Knead well and form into 36 to 48 tiny balls. Place on lightly greased baking sheets.

Flatten the biscuits with your fingertips and place an almond on each biscuit. Whisk the egg white until frothy and brush over the biscuits (cookies) and almonds. Bake in the centre of a moderately hot oven, (200°C/400°F, Gas Mark 6) for about 6 minutes until slightly golden. Lift off the baking sheets and allow to cool. Store in an airtight tin. Makes 36 to 48.

VARIATION

٭Chocolate Petits Fours Make the Rout Biscuits but omit the blanched almonds. Allow to cool.

Break 100 g/4 oz (⅔ cup) plain (semi-sweet) chocolate into pieces and melt in a bowl over hot water. Coat the top of each little biscuit (cookie) with melted chocolate and sprinkle thickly with chocolate vermicelli (sprinkles). Makes 36 to 48.

Almond Ratafias

2 egg whites
a few drops of almond essence (extract)
175 g/6 oz (¾ cup) caster sugar
150 g/5 oz (1¼ cups) ground almonds
25 g/1 oz (¼ cup) cornflour (cornstarch)
25 g/1 oz (¼ cup) blanched almonds

⁂Whisk the egg whites until frothy. Add the almond essence (extract), sugar, ground almonds and cornflour (cornstarch). This mixture should be exactly the right consistency to roll into balls. If the egg whites are large it could be a little too soft, in which case add a little more ground almonds. On the other hand, if the mixture is too stiff, add a few drops of water.

Roll into about 48 tiny balls and place on well greased baking sheets. Chop the blanched almonds very finely. Sprinkle over the top of the small biscuits.

Bake in the centre of a preheated moderate oven (160°C/325°F, Gas Mark 3) for approximately 15 minutes until golden brown and firm. Store in an airtight tin. Makes 48.

Tiger Cakes

85 g/3 oz (6 tablespoons) butter or margarine
25 g/1 oz (2 tablespoons) caster sugar
85 g/3 oz (¾ cup) plain (all-purpose) flour
25 g/1 oz (¼ cup) cornflour (cornstarch)
milk to mix, see method
TO FILL AND DECORATE:
75 g/3 oz (6 tablespoons) butter or margarine
150 g/5 oz (1¼ cups) icing (confectioners') sugar
½ to ¾ tablespoon coffee essence (strong black coffee)
50 g/2 oz (½ cup) walnuts
50 g/2 oz (¼ cup) caster sugar
2 tablespoons water

Cream together the butter or margarine and sugar. Add the flour and cornflour (cornstarch) and knead very firmly. If necessary, add a little milk to make a firm rolling consistency. Roll out firmly to a generous 5 mm/¼ inch thickness and cut into 20 small rounds. Put on ungreased baking sheets and bake in the centre of a preheated moderate oven (180°C/350°F, Gas Mark 4) for 12 to 15 minutes until firm but not too brown. Cool on the baking sheets.

For the filling Cream the butter or margarine until soft. Sift in the icing (confectioners') sugar and beat well, then add the essence or black coffee. Finely chop the walnuts and put them on to a flat plate. Sandwich the biscuits (cookies) with a little of the coffee butter icing to give 10 complete cakes. Coat the sides and tops of the cakes with the remaining butter icing then with the chopped walnuts.

Put the sugar and water into a small strong saucepan, stir until the sugar has dissolved, then boil steadily until a golden brown caramel. Place a spoonful of the caramel on top of each cake; allow to set. Makes 10.

Coconut Oaties

150 g/5 oz (½ cup plus 2 tablespoons) butter or margarine
50 g/2 oz (3 tablespoons) golden (light corn) syrup
100 g/4 oz (⅔ cup) Demerara or light brown sugar
1 level teaspoon bicarbonate of soda (baking soda)
50 g/2 oz (⅔ cup) desiccated (shredded) coconut
75 g/3 oz (1 cup) rolled oats
100 g/4 oz (1 cup) plain (all-purpose) flour

Put the butter or margarine, syrup and sugar into a large saucepan. Stir over a low heat until the fat and sugar have melted. Remove from the heat, add the bicarbonate of soda (baking soda); stir well to dissolve (the mixture rises up the pan during this stage). Add the rest of the ingredients, blend thoroughly. Cool slightly, then gather the mixture together and roll into about 24 balls.

Grease 2 baking trays. Put the balls on to these, allowing plenty of space for the mixture to spread out during cooking.

Bake in the centre of a preheated moderate oven (160°C/325°F, Gas Mark 3) for 15 to 20 minutes or until golden brown. Leave on the baking trays until almost cold, then transfer to a wire cooling tray. Makes 24.

Flapjacks

110 g/4 oz (1 cup) butter or margarine
50 g/2 oz (⅓ cup) Demerara or light brown sugar
2 tablespoons golden (light corn) syrup
225 g/8 oz (2¼ cups) rolled oats

Put the butter or margarine, sugar and syrup into a saucepan, heat only until the fat and sugar have melted. Add the rolled oats, mix thoroughly. Grease a 20 cm/8 inch square sandwich tin (layer pan). Spoon in the rolled oat mixture and spread flat with a palette knife. Bake in the centre of a preheated moderate oven (180°C/350°F, Gas Mark 4) for about 30 minutes or until evenly golden brown. Cool in the tin for about 5 minutes; mark into 12 large or 18 smaller portions. Remove from the tin when just cool. Store in an airtight tin. Makes 12 to 18.

Moist Almond Slices

175 g/6 oz (1½ cups) plain (all-purpose) flour
pinch of salt
85 g/3 oz (6 tablespoons) margarine
cold water
3 tablespoons raspberry jam
FOR THE FILLING:
225 g/8 oz (1 cup) margarine
225 g/8 oz (1 cup) caster sugar
50 g/2 oz (½ cup) ground almonds
175 g/6 oz (1 cup) ground rice
1 to 2 teaspoons almond essence (extract)
2 eggs
blanched almonds

Sift the flour and salt into a bowl. Rub in the margarine. Add enough cold water to bind. Roll out the pastry and line a Swiss roll tin (jelly roll pan) measuring 28 × 20 cm/11 × 8 inches. Spread with raspberry jam.

For the filling Melt the margarine in a saucepan. Remove from the heat and beat in caster sugar, ground almonds and ground rice. Add the almond essence (extract) and eggs. Beat well and pour over the pastry. Top with blanched almonds.

Bake in the centre of a preheated moderately hot oven (190 to 200°C/375 to 400°F, Gas Mark 5 to 6) for 35 to 40 minutes. Lower the heat slightly after 25 minutes if the cake is becoming too brown. Cut into slices when hot. Allow to cool in the tin (pan). Makes 8 to 12 slices.

Coconut Oaties and Flapjacks

173

Chocolate Orange Biscuits

110 g/4 oz (½ cup) margarine
110 g/4 oz (½ cup) caster sugar
finely grated rind of 1 orange
2 teaspoons chocolate essence (extract)
1 egg
225 g/8 oz (2 cups) plain (all-purpose) flour
1 teaspoon baking powder
FOR THE TOPPING: 100 g/4 oz (1 cup) sifted icing (confectioners') sugar
1 tablespoon orange juice
crystallized orange slices

Cream margarine with the caster sugar, the finely grated orange rind and chocolate essence (extract) until soft and light. Beat in the egg. Sift the flour with the baking powder and add to the creamed ingredients. Knead well, then cover with plastic wrap and chill for 1 hour to make the dough easier to handle. Roll out on a lightly floured board until 5 mm/¼ inch thick. Cut into 14 to 18 small rounds with a fluted cutter. Put on to two lightly greased baking sheets. Bake in the centre of a preheated moderately hot oven (190 to 200°C/375 to 400°F, Gas Mark 5 to 6) for 10 to 15 minutes until firm. Allow to cool. Mix the icing (confectioners') sugar with the orange juice to make Glacé Icing. Spread on top of the biscuits (cookies). Decorate with small portions of crystallized orange. Makes 14 to 18.

Vanilla Cookies
[Vaniljekager]

225 g/8 oz (2 cups) plain (all-purpose) flour
50 g/2 oz (½ cup) ground almonds
225 g/8 oz (1 cup) butter or margarine
75 g/3 oz (6 tablespoons) caster sugar
½ teaspoon vanilla essence (extract)
1 egg

✱✱Sift together the flour and ground almonds. Cream the butter or margarine with the sugar and essence (extract) until soft and light. Beat in the egg, then blend in the flour and ground almonds.

Put a 1.5 cm/½ inch rose nozzle into a large piping (pastry) bag. Grease 2 baking sheets. Spoon the mixture into the bag and pipe 5 cm/2 inch rings of the mixture on to the baking sheets.

Bake in the centre of a preheated moderate oven (160°C/325°F, Gas Mark 3) for 12 to 15 minutes or until firm. Cool for 5 to 6 minutes on the baking sheets, then transfer to a wire cooling tray. When quite cold, store in an airtight tin. Makes 30 to 36.

Made without Baking

These cakes are made without using the oven. They give an interesting variety of flavour and texture, and can be prepared within a short time. They are excellent recipes for children to make.

Chocolate Rum Gâteau

1 Chocolate Cake, see page 161 or 163
3 tablespoons rum
150 ml/¼ pint (⅔ cup) orange juice
2 tablespoons caster sugar
1 large block vanilla ice cream
25 g/1 oz (¼ cup) icing (confectioners') sugar
FOR THE SAUCE: 2 tablespoons rum
100 g/4 oz (⅔ cup) plain (semi-sweet) chocolate
150 ml/¼ pint (⅔ cup) single (light) cream

✱✱Split the cake into 3 layers. Mix the rum with the orange juice and sugar. Allow the ice cream to stand at room temperature for a short time until soft enough to spread.

Place the first layer of cake on a serving dish, sprinkle with a third of the rum and orange juice, cover with half the ice cream. Place the second layer of cake on top, then moisten with a second third of the rum and orange mixture and add the remaining ice cream.

Add the final layer of cake and moisten with the last of the rum and orange mixture. Freeze the gâteau for a short time to make the ice cream firm again. Sift the icing (confectioners') sugar over the top before serving with the sauce.

To make the sauce, put the rum and chocolate into a bowl and melt over hot water or in a microwave cooker. Cool and blend with the cream. Serves 6 to 8.

Butterscotch Fudge Cake

175 g/6 oz (¾ cup) unsalted butter
6 tablespoons golden (light corn) syrup, see method
100 g/4 oz (½ cup) glacé cherries
100 g/4 oz (1 cup) mixed nuts
225 g/8 oz digestive or wheatmeal biscuits (graham crackers)
225 g/8 oz (1⅓ cups) mixed dried fruit
TO DECORATE: 150 ml/¼ pint (⅔ cup) whipping cream
5 to 6 glacé cherries

✱✱Melt the butter and sugar in a saucepan then boil briskly for 2 to 3 minutes, stirring constantly. Allow to cool slightly. Chop the cherries and nuts. Crush half the biscuits (crackers) until very fine and break the remainder into small pieces. Add the dried fruit, cherries, nuts and biscuits (crackers) to the butter and

Butterscotch Fudge Cake

syrup mixture. Mix thoroughly.

Lightly grease a 20 to 23 cm/8 to 9 inch cake tin (pan), preferably one with a loose base. Spoon the mixture into the tin, smooth flat with a palette knife and refrigerate for several hours to set.

Turn out carefully. Whip the cream and pipe on top of the cake. Decorate with halved cherries. Serves 8 to 10.

Chocolate Fruit Bars

100 g/4 oz (½ cup) unsalted butter
1 tablespoon golden (light corn) syrup
50 g/2 oz (⅓ cup) dried apricots
50 g/2 oz (⅓ cup) dates
350 g/12 oz (3 cups) muesli cereal (granola)
FOR THE ICING:
100 g/4 oz (⅔ cup) plain (semi-sweet) chocolate
1 tablespoon water
25 g/1 oz (2 tablespoons) unsalted butter

✲✲Melt the butter and syrup over low heat. Chop the apricots and dates finely. Stir the muesli (granola), apricots and dates into the butter mixture and mix well. Press into a well buttered 20 × 30 cm/8 × 12 inch Swiss roll tin (jelly roll pan). Allow to cool.

Break the chocolate into pieces and put into a bowl with the water and butter. Stand over a saucepan of hot water until melted then mix well. Spread over the mixture in the tin. Allow to set, then cut into fingers. Makes 24.

Hazelnut Refrigerator Cake

225 g/8 oz (1⅓ cups) plain (semi-sweet) chocolate
225 g/8 oz (1 cup) unsalted butter
225 g/8 oz (2 cups) digestive biscuits (graham crackers)
75 g/3 oz (⅔ cup) hazelnuts
1 egg
25 g/1 oz (2 tablespoons) caster sugar
1 teaspoon grated orange rind
1 tablespoon orange juice
3 tablespoons brandy or sherry
TO DECORATE:
150 ml/¼ pint (⅔ cup) double (heavy) cream
glacé cherries
angelica

✲✲Break the chocolate into a bowl. Cut the butter into pieces and add. Stand over a pan of hot but not boiling water until melted. Stir well, cool. Crush the biscuits (crackers). (Do not do this in a blender or food processor for this makes biscuit (cracker) crumbs too fine). Chop the hazelnuts.

Break the egg into a bowl, add the sugar and whisk until light and thick. Mix with the chocolate and butter, then the biscuits (crackers), nuts, orange rind, orange juice and brandy or sherry. Mix thoroughly.

Spoon into an ungreased 20 to 23 cm/ 8 to 9 inch cake tin (pan); use a tin with a loose base if possible. Refrigerate for several hours until set. Remove the cake carefully. Whip the cream. Decorate the cake with whipped cream, glacé cherries and angelica. Serves 8 to 10.

Coconut Chews

100 g/4 oz (⅔ cup) mixed dried fruit
25 g/1 oz Maraschino cherries
225 g/8 oz (8 cups) cornflakes
100 g/4 oz (1⅓ cups) desiccated (shredded) coconut
1 × 75 g/6 oz can full cream sweetened condensed milk
½ teaspoon vanilla essence (extract)
chocolate vermicelli (sprinkles) to coat

✲✲Put the dried fruit into a mixing bowl. Chop the cherries and lightly crush the cornflakes. Add the cherries, cornflakes, coconut, condensed milk and essence to the diced fruit. Mix well.

Roll the mixture into about 36 small balls. Coat with the chocolate vermicelli (sprinkles) and leave uncovered for 12 hours to harden.

Place in tiny paper cases and serve as petits fours. Makes 36.

Hazelnut Refrigerator Cake

Overnight Chocolate Cake

50 g/2 oz (¼ cup) glacé cherries
50 g/2 oz (½ cup) walnuts
225 g/8 oz (1 cup) unsalted butter
225 g/8 oz plain (semi-sweet) chocolate
2 large eggs
25 g/1 oz (2 tablespoons) caster sugar
12 oblong semi-sweet biscuits, such as Nice or Afternoon Tea
TO DECORATE:
a little double (heavy) cream
glacé (candied) lemon or orange slices

✲✲Chop the glacé cherries and walnuts. Line a 450 g/1 lb loaf tin (pan) with greaseproof (waxed) paper or non-stick parchment.

Break the chocolate into a bowl. Cut the butter into pieces and add. Stand over a pan of hot, but not boiling, water until melted. Stir well. Break the eggs into a large mixing bowl, add the sugar and whisk until thick and creamy. Gradually stir in the warm chocolate mixture.

Spoon a little chocolate mixture into the prepared tin, add a layer of biscuits (cookies), then a layer of the chopped cherries and walnuts. Continue like this, ending with a chocolate layer.

Chill the cake for at least 12 hours, then turn out on to a serving dish. Whip the cream and pipe rosettes on to the cake. Finally decorate with the orange or lemon slices. Makes a 450 g/1 lb cake.

175

FOOD FOR HEALTH

The foods we eat should be interesting, enjoyable and sufficiently varied to include the important nutrients which keep us fit and full of energy.

There are various schools of thought about what constitutes 'the perfect diet'. Some experts believe we should avoid animal foods and follow a vegetarian diet, while others consider that animal proteins in moderation (meat, fish, poultry, eggs and cheese) are essential for good health.

There are, however, certain principles upon which most doctors and nutritionists agree, and these are outlined below.

Health Foods

To many people the term 'health foods' simply means rather strange and unorthodox foods, purchased from a specialist shop. This is far from the case. Good health food stores sell excellent nuts and dried fruits, wholewheat bread, flour and pasta, brown rice, unrefined sugar and a wide range of interesting herbs and spices. They also sell homeopathic medicines and certain natural food additives which are worth consideration.

Two of the most important foods are brewer's yeast and wheat germ. If you reduce your intake of carbohydrates in the form of flour and bread (see page 180), you automatically reduce the amount of B vitamins. Both brewer's yeast and wheat germ provide these vitamins. Add the yeast to soups and sprinkle the nutty wheat germ on to cereals.

Slimming Diets

Pages 180 and 181 contain interesting recipes for slimmers which prove that low-calorie food does not have to be dull and dreary. It is a challenge to any cook to produce meals that all the family will enjoy – even those who are not trying to lose weight. Mention is also made of *Nouvelle Cuisine*. This light style of cooking has taught us to appreciate the natural flavour of foods, rather than feel we must add additional high-calorie ingredients.

High-Fibre Cooking

We in the Western world eat too many easily assimilated and refined foods and should include a greater proportion of high-fibre foods in our diet.

Fibre, or roughage as it used to be called, has always been considered an important ingredient in a well-planned diet, and many ailments prevalent in our society can be traced to insufficient fibre.

Fortunately it is easy to increase the fibre content of our meals:

☐ Substitute wholewheat bread and flour for white. Wholewheat flour contains the bran from the wheat germ and bran is extremely high in fibre.

☐ Choose breakfast cereals that contain bran and/or oatmeal. Muesli (Swiss style cereal) is a good example. Sprinkle a little natural bran over your favourite cereal to increase its fibre content.

☐ Eat the whole fruit, rather than drink its juice. Apples, pears and other fruits provide fibre, especially if you eat the skins. Eat raw dried apricots, prunes and other dried fruit and nuts.

☐ Include plenty of vegetables in your diet. Raw, or lightly cooked, green vegetables are an excellent source of vitamin C as well as providing a certain amount of fibre. Peas and beans, including canned baked beans, are high in fibre.

The Nouvelle Cuisine

France is a country where grand cuisine is traditionally linked with delicious sauces, rich in fat and cream.

The desire to enjoy interesting meals with a low-calorie content led to the development, by great French chefs, of the 'Nouvelle Cuisine'.

It is a style of cooking that provides taste and texture with vegetables and herbs rather than the traditional high-calorie ingredients.

Some of the principles of Nouvelle Cuisine are incorporated in the sauces on page 107, the dieting rules and recipes on page 180, and in the low-fat recipes on page 178.

Top right: Chinese Leaf Parcels, page 179
Middle right: Slimmers Mousse made with apricots, page 181
Bottom right: Stuffed Artichoke, page 178

High-Fibre Cooking

A diet high in fibre has proved to be beneficial to people trying to lose weight. Fibre-rich foods are, on the whole, bulky, satisfying foods – a boon for slimmers who are less likely to abandon a diet if it satisfies their hunger.

The vegetable recipes below show how easy it is to increase the fibre content of everyday dishes by adding high fibre ingredients – wholewheat bread and flour, nuts and beans.

Stuffed Artichokes

4 large globe artichokes
salt and pepper
1 large onion
100 g/4 oz cooked chicken
25 g/1 oz (2 tablespoons) butter or margarine
40 g/1½ oz (¾ cup) soft wholewheat breadcrumbs
½ teaspoon chopped fresh basil or ¼ teaspoon dried basil
½ teaspoon tomato purée (paste)
FOR THE TOMATO SAUCE:
25 g/1 oz (2 tablespoons) butter or margarine
25 g/1 oz (¼ cup) wholewheat flour
600 ml/1 pint (2½ cups) tomato juice
150 ml/¼ pint (⅔ cup) chicken stock or water
a few drops of Tabasco (hot pepper) sauce, optional

Mixed Vegetables à la Grecque

⁂Cook the artichokes in salted water (see page 21). Drain and remove the centre choke and some of the centre leaves. Cut the tops off the remaining leaves as shown in the picture. Peel and finely chop the onion. Mince or chop the chicken. Heat 25 g/1 oz (2 tablespoons) butter or margarine, add the onion and cook gently for 4 to 5 minutes. Mix the chicken, breadcrumbs, basil and tomato purée (paste) and a little seasoning with the onion.

For the tomato sauce Melt the remaining 25 g/1 oz (2 tablespoons) butter or margarine in a saucepan, add the flour and stir over a low heat for 2 to 3 minutes, then add the tomato juice and stock or water. Whisk as the liquid comes to the boil and thickens very slightly. Add the Tabasco (hot pepper) sauce and seasoning to taste.

Mix about 6 tablespoons of the sauce with the onion mixture to give a moist stuffing. Spoon into the centre of the 4 artichokes and place these in a casserole. Pour the tomato sauce around the artichokes, cover the casserole and bake in the centre of a preheated moderate oven (180°C/350°F, Gas Mark 4) for 35 to 40 minutes. Serve immediately. Serves 4.

Egg and Nut Savouries

175 g/6 oz (1½ cups) hazelnuts
50 g/2 oz (1 cup) wholewheat bread, weight without crusts
1 medium onion
75 g/3 oz (6 tablespoons) butter or margarine
25 g/1 oz (¼ cup) flour
150 ml/¼ pint (⅔ cup) milk
2 tablespoons chopped parsley
5 eggs
salt and pepper
2 tablespoons single (light) cream

Chop the hazelnuts and make the bread into crumbs using a blender or food processor. Peel and finely chop the onion. Heat half the butter or margarine in a saucepan, add the onion, cook slowly until tender. Stir in the flour and then blend in the milk. Continue to stir as the liquid comes to the boil and thickens. Add the nuts, breadcrumbs, half the parsley, 1 egg and seasoning to taste. Allow the mixture to cool, then form into 8 small round patty shapes.

Place the nut patties in an ovenproof serving dish. Cook towards the top of a moderately hot oven (200°C/400°F, Gas Mark 6) for 10 minutes. Meanwhile, beat the remaining 4 eggs with the cream, add salt and pepper to taste. Heat the rest of the butter or margarine in a saucepan, add the eggs and lightly scramble. Spoon on to the hazelnut rounds, top with the remaining chopped parsley and serve at once. Serves 4.

Chicory Casserole

6 to 8 heads of chicory (endive)
salt and pepper
2 teaspoons lemon juice
1 × 227 g/8 oz can red kidney beans
450 g/1 lb tomatoes
3 tablespoons finely chopped spring onions (scallions)
25 g/1 oz (2 tablespoons) butter or margarine
75 g/3 oz (1½ cups) wholewheat breadcrumbs

Split the chicory (endive) heads lengthways. Cook in boiling salted water for 2 minutes only, drain and arrange in a shallow casserole. Sprinkle with lemon juice. Drain the beans, spoon over the chicory (endive). Slice the tomatoes, arrange over the beans, add the chopped spring onions (scallions) and season well.

Heat the butter or margarine, combine with the crumbs, sprinkle over the top of the tomato layer. Bake in the centre of a preheated moderately hot oven (190°C/375°F, Gas Mark 5) for 35 to 40 minutes. Serve with any main dish. Serves 4 to 6.

Low-Fat Cooking

It is generally agreed by the medical profession that we should reduce the amount of fat we consume (and this is one of the healthful aspects of Nouvelle Cuisine).

In place of butter and cream use vegetables, herbs and lemon juice to give flavour to your food.

Marinating Foods

This is an excellent way of reducing the amount of fat used in cooking. It allows a small amount of fat, generally in the form of oil, to penetrate the meat, poultry, fish, or vegetables *before* cooking and so dispenses with fat *during* cooking.

The recipe in the Special Technique opposite is for a good basic marinade, which can be varied as required. It is sufficient for 4 portions of meat, fish, poultry or vegetables.

Mixed Vegetables à la Grecque

The vegetables are cooked in an oil and herb-flavoured liquid, so that elaborate sauces are unnecessary. You can reduce the amount of oil, and therefore the amount of calories, in the recipe.

Individual vegetables can be prepared in the same way but a selection of colourful vegetables makes an impressive dish. Vary the vegetables according to season and availability.

8 small onions
4 medium carrots
I small cauliflower
4 small globe artichokes
4 small courgettes (zucchini)
8 medium mushrooms
I to 2 garlic cloves
4 tablespoons olive oil
2 tablespoons lemon juice
300 ml / ½ pint (1¼ cups) water
a small bunch of parsley
I bay leaf
I sprig of thyme
salt and pepper
TO GARNISH
chopped parsley

Peel the onions and carrots, but leave whole. Divide the cauliflower into 4 portions. Cut the stalks from the globe artichokes, trim the ends of the courgettes (zucchini), but do not peel them. Wipe the mushrooms, trim the ends of the stalks. Peel the garlic, leave the clove(s) whole.

Put the oil, lemon juice and water into a large saucepan, add the herbs, garlic and a little seasoning. Add the vegetables and cook until just tender.

Remove from the liquid with a perforated spoon and arrange in a serving dish. Boil the liquid in the pan until reduced to 150 ml/¼ pint (⅔ cup). Strain over the vegetables. Serve cold sprinkled with parsley. Serves 4.

VARIATION
For the photograph opposite we used 225 g/8 oz button mushrooms, 2 large sliced onions, 225 g/8 oz sliced leeks and 225 g/8 oz peeled, quartered and seeded tomatoes in place of the vegetables above.

Chinese Leaf Parcels

I garlic clove
300 g/10 oz (1¼ cups) long-grain rice
600 ml/1 pint (2½ cups) water
salt and pepper
2 teaspoons paprika
I to 2 teaspoons dill seeds or caraway seeds
3 tablespoons tomato purée (paste)
I head of Chinese leaves (bok choy)
225 g/8 oz (2 cups) white grapes
150 ml/¼ pint (⅔ cup) chicken stock

Chinese Leaf Parcels

FOR THE SAUCE:
15 g/½ oz (1 tablespoon) butter or margarine
15 g/½ oz (2 tablespoons) flour
2 tablespoons lemon juice
TO GARNISH:
a few white grapes

Peel and crush the garlic, put into a saucepan with the rice, water, seasoning, paprika, dill or caraway seeds and the tomato purée (paste). Bring the liquid to the boil, stir briskly with a fork, cover the pan and simmer for 15 minutes, or until the rice is tender and the liquid has been absorbed.

Meanwhile, separate the Chinese leaves (bok choy), cutting out and discarding the hard triangular stems. Blanch the leaves in boiling water for 2 minutes only, drain and lay flat.

Halve and de-seed the grapes, combine with the rice mixture and divide this between the Chinese leaves (bok choy). Fold the leaves to enclose the stuffing and place the parcels into an ovenproof dish.

Add the chicken stock, cover and bake just above the centre of a preheated moderately hot oven (190°C/375°F, Gas Mark 5) for 20 minutes. Lift the parcels on to a heated serving dish and save the liquid in which they were baked. Melt the butter or margarine in a pan, stir in the flour then blend in the lemon juice and up to 150 ml/¼ pint (⅔ cup) liquid from the casserole (if insufficient add a little water). Stir over a low heat until slightly thickened and season to taste. Spoon over the parcels and garnish with more grapes. Serves 8.

FOR FLAVOUR
Lovers of strong cheese may well feel that cottage cheese is lacking in flavour. It is, however, an excellent basis for other ingredients.

Flavour the cheese with crushed garlic or garlic salt, with chopped spring onions (scallions) or chives, or with chopped mixed herbs.

Use cottage cheese as an ingredient in salads, combine it with diced fresh fruit, or try it on baked jacket potatoes instead of butter.

179

Food For Slimmers

Fruit based hors d'oeuvre are perfect for slimmers

Many children and adults tend to be overweight and this is not healthy. Overweight people suffer more from fatigue and find physical exercise far more of an effort than those who are not overweight. They are also more likely to develop heart disease and diabetes, as well as other ailments. So it makes sense for all of us to maintain a healthy weight, although all strict slimming regimes should only be followed under medical supervision.

Dieting Rules

Here are some simple rules to follow if you only need to lose a relatively small amount of weight. It is surprising how easily everyday dishes can be included in a slimming regime.

☐ Cut down on the amount of fat used. This includes the butter or margarine spread on bread, the fat or oil used in cooking. Some of the recipes that follow will help you do this.

☐ Avoid high fat foods. Use yogurt instead of cream (see below), and use skimmed milk or skimmed milk powder instead of whole milk.

☐ Avoid sugar as much as possible. There are excellent sugar substitutes available so you can enjoy many fruit based desserts (see opposite), but be strong and refuse cakes and sweet biscuits (cookies).

☐ Wholewheat bread and potatoes provide valuable fibre. Bread also provides a certain amount of protein as well as the B vitamins, so have some bread each day – but not too much. Cook potatoes in their skins either by boiling or baking. Avoid chips and fried potatoes, it is fat that makes them fattening.

☐ Alcohol is high in calories and so are many soft drinks like fruit squashes and ordinary tonic water. Buy the low-calorie versions whenever possible.

☐ Find ways of serving food to avoid the excessive use of flour. Chinese Leaf Parcels on page 179 are a good example, because a green vegetable is used instead of pastry to contain an interesting filling. The stuffed vegetables on page 178 can also be served as satisfying and interesting main dishes.

☐ If you are particularly fond of soups, choose the less fattening variety, i.e. those on pages 29, the various Consommés on page 32 and the Gazpacho on this page.

☐ Serve hors d'oeuvre based on fruit (see page 18 and 20). They are low in calories and look attractive. Melon balls, grapes and grapefruit segments is an ideal combination, see photograph left.

☐ Include lots of low-calorie green vegetables and potatoes cooked in their skins. If you are a large potato eater why not use the potatoes, with other ingredients as a main dish as in the Gnocchi (see right). If your diet is very strict, use rather less cheese and butter in the topping on your portion.

☐ Serve plenty of salads. If you find these uninteresting without a dressing make a low-calorie mixture (see right).

☐ Avoid eating too much cheese, except low-calorie cottage cheese. Use the small amount allowed on most diets to flavour various dishes.

☐ If your meals are incomplete without a dessert then adapt recipes as suggested opposite.

Yogurt

Plain yogurt is a wonderful ingredient in both savoury or sweet dishes; it adds creaminess without an excessive amount of fat.

Commercial yogurt is of excellent quality. The small cartons generally contain 142 ml/5 fl oz (⅔ cup) but it is cheaper to buy yogurt in larger sized containers.

Homemade Yogurt You can, of course, make your own yogurt. There are many excellent yogurt makers on the market. Simply follow the instructions given by the manufacturers.

However, excellent yogurt can be made without any special equipment. Heat 600 ml/1 pint (2½ cups) milk to blood heat, add 2 tablespoons of commercial yogurt plus 2 tablespoons dried milk powder (this is not essential but gives a better texture). Pour into a vacuum flask, cover and leave for several hours.

Every time you make a fresh yogurt use 2 to 3 tablespoons from the previous batch.

Swiss Aubergines

2 medium aubergines (eggplant)
salt and pepper
2 tablespoons oil
450 g/1 lb tomatoes
1 tablespoon chopped parsley
1 tablespoon chopped chives
Cheese Sauce, made with 25 g/1 oz (2 tablespoons) butter, see page 102

Score the skins of the aubergines (eggplant), sprinkle with salt, leave for 30 minutes then drain away the liquid. Rinse the aubergines (eggplant) in cold water, dry well and thinly slice. Heat the oil in a frying pan (skillet) and fry the aubergines (eggplant) until nearly tender.

Slice the tomatoes, put layers of aubergine (eggplant) and tomatoes into a casserole, add seasoning and the herbs. Spoon the cheese sauce over the vegetables and cook in the centre of a moderately hot oven (190°C/375°F, Gas Mark 5) for 30 minutes. Serves 4.

Speedy Slimmer's Gazpacho

1.2 litres/2 pints (5 cups) tomato juice
1 red pepper
1 green pepper
1 medium cucumber
1 large onion
2 garlic cloves
1 to 2 teaspoons lemon juice or white wine vinegar
few drops Tabasco (hot pepper) sauce
salt and pepper

Chill the tomato juice. Neatly dice the peppers, discarding the core and seeds. Peel and finely dice the cucumber and onion, peel and crush the garlic. Put half the diced peppers, cucumber and onion into the tomato juice, together with the garlic, lemon juice or vinegar, Tabasco (hot pepper) sauce, salt and pepper.

Keep cold until ready to serve. Arrange the remaining diced ingredients in small bowls and serve with the soup. Serves 4 to 6.

Gnocchi alla Piedmontese

450 g/1 lb old potatoes, weight when peeled
salt and pepper
100 g/4 oz (1 cup) plain (all-purpose) flour
2 tablespoons grated Parmesan cheese
1 egg yolk
25 g/1 oz (2 tablespoons) butter
FOR THE TOPPING: 4 tablespoons grated Mozzarella cheese
75 g/3 oz (6 tablespoons) butter

Cook the potatoes in salted water until only just soft. Do not overcook. Drain and sieve (if you have a food processor take care not to over-process or the potatoes will become sticky). Mix the potatoes with salt, pepper, flour, cheese and egg yolk. Melt the 25 g/1 oz (2 tablespoons) butter, add to the mixture. Form into small 2.5 cm/1 inch balls, lay on a cloth to dry out, then using your finger, press each little ball in the centre to flatten.

Bring a pan of water to boiling point. Add the Gnocchi and cook steadily for 10 minutes. Lift out with a perforated spoon, arrange on a heated dish, top with the grated cheese. Melt the 75 g/3 oz (6 tablespoons) butter until golden brown, pour over the top of the cheese-topped Gnocchi.

Serve with Speedy Tomato Sauce (see page 107) and extra grated Parmesan cheese. Serves 4.

Cheese Pots

1 stick celery
1 large ripe dessert pear
1 large dessert apple
½ to 1 tablespoon chopped chives
½ to 1 tablespoon lemon juice
225 g/8 oz Lancashire or crumbly Cheddar cheese
FOR THE TOPPING: 1 tablespoon chopped parsley
paprika

Dice the celery. Peel and dice the pear and apple. Toss with the chives and lemon juice.

Divide the mixture between 4 individual flameproof or ovenproof dishes. You should use flameproof dishes if heating under the grill (broiler). Crumble the Lancashire cheese over the fruit and celery. Place under a preheated grill (broiler) for 5 to 6 minutes or until golden brown on top or towards the top of a preheated hot oven (220°C/425°F, Gas Mark 7) for 10 minutes.

Top with the parsley and a sprinkling of paprika. Serves 4.

Low-Calorie Salad Dressing

150 ml/¼ pint (⅔ cup) plain yogurt
1 to 2 teaspoons made French (Dijon) or English mustard
salt and pepper
a pinch of sugar substitute
1 to 2 tablespoons lemon juice or red or white wine vinegar
2 teaspoons salad oil

Blend all the ingredients together using a whisk, food processor or blender.

Various flavourings can be added (see page 105). Makes about 175 ml/6 fl oz (¾ cup).

Slimming Desserts

To many people the dessert is the most enjoyable part of a meal and they do not find fresh fruit a satisfying alternative.

It is possible to make low-calorie desserts by adapting classic recipes:
☐ Use skimmed milk in place of full cream milk.
☐ Use a sugar substitute instead of sugar.
☐ Use yogurt in place of cream with fruit or other ingredients.
☐ Cook dried and fresh fruits in a microwave cooker whenever possible. The fruit seems to retain more flavour,

making it less necessary to serve sugar, cream or custard with the fruit.

Simple Low-Calorie Desserts

Slimmer's Fruit Fool Blend equal quantities of unsweetened fruit pulp like rhubarb, and plain yogurt. Sweeten with sugar substitute if necessary. Chill well.
Slimmer's Mousse Dissolve 15 g/½ oz (2 envelopes) gelatine in 2 tablespoons orange juice. Add to 300 ml/½ pint (1¼ cups) thick fruit purée, sweetened with sugar substitute. Allow to stiffen very slightly. Fold in 150 ml/¼ pint (⅔ cup) plain yogurt and 2 stiffly whisked egg whites. Spoon into glasses. Top with more yogurt and fresh fruit. Serves 4.
Orange Pots Dissolve 4 teaspoons gela-

tine in 3 tablespoons fresh orange juice. Blend with 350 g/12 oz (1½ cups) low fat cottage or curd cheese with 3 tablespoons fresh lemon juice, 3 tablespoons skimmed milk and sugar substitute to taste. Spoon into dessert glasses and top with orange slices. Serves 4.
Strawberry Whip Purée 350 g/12 oz (2½ cups) fresh strawberries with 300 ml/½ pint (1¼ cups) plain yogurt and sugar substitute to taste. Pour 2 tablespoons lemon juice into a bowl, sprinkle 2 teaspoons gelatine on top and stand over a pan of boiling water until dissolved, or dissolve in a microwave cooker. Add to the strawberry mixture. Spoon into 4 glasses and chill. Serves 4.

FOR FLAVOUR
Plain yogurt is an excellent topping on soups or stews. It gives a contrasting colour and a piquant flavour.

Add to the stew just before serving.

Slimmer's Fruit Fool using rhubarb, and Orange Pots

Vegetarian Dishes

Vegetarians do not eat meat but most eat cheese and so many of the dishes in Savoury Snacks (page 126) are suitable for them, and so are the various vegetable dishes throughout this book.

Meal Planning

Vegetarians should ensure that their meals contain an adequate amount of protein. This is available in flour, milk, the pulses (beans, peas and lentils) and in nuts of all kinds, as well as in cheese and eggs and other foods. If only one member of the family is a vegetarian, it is quite easy to adjust many recipes so they are suitable for everyone. One example is the soup on this page. It is part of a simple menu and by replacing chicken stock with water and a little yeast extract (a valuable source of vitamin B) the soup becomes acceptable to a vegetarian.

A Nut Roast, is so delicious that most of the family will enjoy it (as they will the recipes on page 178). The Nut Roast could be served with the same stuffings and sauces that are usually served with roast meat or poultry.

Tomato and Thyme Soup

1 medium onion
15 g / ½ oz (1 tablespoon) margarine
1 × 425 g / 15 oz can tomatoes
300 ml / ½ pint (1¼ cups) chicken stock or water and ½ chicken stock (1 bouillon) cube or yeast extract to flavour
1 teaspoon Worcestershire sauce
1 teaspoon chopped thyme
1 to 2 teaspoons grated orange rind
salt and pepper

Cheesy Mushrooms

⁂Peel and finely chop the onion. Melt the margarine in a saucepan, add the onion and gently cook until soft, do not allow to brown. Add the remaining ingredients, and simmer steadily for 10 to 15 minutes. Serve with the Herby Bread. Serves 4.

VARIATIONS

Increase the amount of thyme or add 2 to 3 tablespoons orange juice.

Purée the soup in a blender or food processor when cooked.

Herby Bread

225 g / 8 oz (2 cups) strong (bread) or plain (all-purpose) white flour
225 g / 8 oz (2 cups) strong (bread) or plain (all-purpose) wholewheat flour
1 teaspoon salt
1 teaspoon sugar
1 teaspoon chopped mixed herbs
15 g / ½ oz (1 tablespoon) margarine
300 ml / ½ pint (1¼ cups) water
15 g / ½ oz (½ cake) fresh (compressed) yeast or 1 teaspoon dried yeast with 1 teaspoon sugar
FOR THE TOPPING:
25 g / 1 oz (2 tablespoons) margarine
½ teaspoon chopped mixed herbs

⁂Mix the two types of flour with the salt in a large mixing bowl, add the sugar and herbs. Rub (cut) in the margarine until well combined.

Warm the water to blood heat, cream the fresh (compressed) yeast, add the water and blend together. If using dried yeast dissolve the sugar in the warm water, sprinkle the yeast on top of the liquid, allow to stand for 10 minutes, then stir to mix.

Add the yeast liquid to the flour mixture and mix well (see page 154) then turn the dough on to a floured surface and knead until smooth.

Cover the dough and allow it to 'prove' in a warm place for about 1 hour, or until it has doubled in size. Turn out on to a floured surface again and knead once more.

Divide the dough into 8 equal sized pieces and form into rolls. Grease two 450 g / 1 lb loaf tins (pans); warm these slightly. Place 4 rolls into each tin.

Melt the 25 g / 1 oz (2 tablespoons) margarine, brush over the yeast dough and sprinkle with the herbs. Cover the tins or put them into large lightly-oiled polythene bags. Allow to 'prove' for 25 to 30 minutes or until the dough has reached the tops of the tins.

Bake in the centre of a preheated very hot oven (230°C/450°F, Gas Mark 8) for about 30 minutes, or until well-risen and golden brown. Makes 2 loaves.

Special Technique
CHEESE FONDUE

Vegetarian guests will certainly appreciate a cheese fondue. Use a ceramic fondue pot, rather than a metal one, which tends to overheat.

To make an economical Cheddar and Cider Fondue: Grate 450 g / 1 lb (4 cups) Cheddar cheese. Peel and halve a garlic clove, rub around the fondue pot, then grease with about 15 g / ½ oz (1 tablespoon) butter. Blend 1 teaspoon cornflour (cornstarch) with 300 ml / ½ pint (1¼ cups) dry (hard) cider, put into the fondue pot with the cheese and heat together until a smooth creamy mixture. Season to taste. Serve with squares of toast or fresh bread on fondue forks which are dipped into the mixture.

Variations

The cheese mixture can be prepared in an ordinary saucepan, then transferred to the preheated fondue pot over the fondue burner as soon as it starts to thicken.

Classic Fondue This is made with a mixture of Gruyère and Emmenthal cheeses, plus white wine, instead of the Cheddar cheese and cider. A little brandy or Kirsch can be added.

Vegetable Torte

2 medium onions
50 g / 2 oz young carrots, weight when peeled
40 g / 1½ oz (3 tablespoons) margarine
50 g / 2 oz (½ cup) shelled or frozen peas
salt and pepper
6 eggs
25 g / 1 oz (¼ cup) flour
50 g / 2 oz Parmesan cheese
3 tablespoons milk
2 tablespoons chopped parsley

Peel the onions and carrots. Chop the onions finely and slice the carrots. Heat 25 g / 1 oz (2 tablespoons) margarine in a pan and fry the onions until just soft. Meanwhile cook the carrots and peas in a little salted water for 5 minutes only. Drain well.

Beat the eggs with the flour. Grate the cheese, add to the eggs with the milk, vegetables, parsley and a little seasoning. Grease the bottom and sides of an 18 cm / 7 inch soufflé dish or cake tin (pan) without a loose base with the remaining margarine. Spoon in the egg mixture.

Bake in the centre of a preheated moderate to moderately hot oven (180 to 190°C/350 to 375°F, Gas Mark 4 to 5) for 30 minutes or until firm and golden in colour. Turn out and serve hot with vegetables or cold with salad. Serves 4.

Cheddar Cheese Loaf

2 medium tomatoes
1 red pepper
1 green pepper
8 small spring onions (scallions)
225 g/8 oz Cheddar cheese
450 g/1 lb (2 cups) cream or curd cheese
3 tablespoons mayonnaise
2 tablespoons finely chopped chives
2 tablespoons finely chopped parsley
100 g/4 oz (1 cup) walnuts
salt and pepper

✵Skin and halve the tomatoes. Cut the pulp into small even pieces. Cut the peppers into small dice, discarding the core and seeds. Slice the spring onions (scallions). Put all the vegetables into a mixing bowl. Coarsely grate the Cheddar cheese. Add to the vegetables together with the cream or curd cheese, mayonnaise and herbs.

Chop the nuts. Add about 25 g/1 oz (¼ cup) to the cheese mixture and season to taste. Form this into a neat oblong shape with a flat-bladed knife. Press the remaining nuts on the sides and top of the loaf. Chill well.

Serve instead of a cheese board with cheese biscuits (crackers) or as a light main dish with a mixed salad. Serves 6.

Nut Roast

2 medium onions
1 clove garlic
1 small dessert apple
50 g/2 oz (¼ cup) vegetarian fat or margarine
350 g/12 oz (1½ cups) peanuts or 350 g/ 12 oz (3 cups) cashew nuts or other nuts
1 teaspoon chopped fresh or ½ teaspoon dried sage
50 g/2 oz (1 cup) soft breadcrumbs
2 eggs
4 tablespoons milk
salt and pepper

✵Peel and chop the onions, garlic and apple. Heat the fat or margarine and fry the onion mixture until soft. Grind the nuts in a nut mill or chop in a food processor and add to the onion mixture together with the sage, breadcrumbs, eggs and milk. Season well and place in a greased 1.2 litre/2 pint (1 quart) pie dish. Bake in the centre of a moderate oven (180°C/350°F, Gas Mark 4) for 35 to 40 minutes. Serve hot or cold. Serves 4.

VARIATION

Nut Cutlets Follow the recipe above but use only 1 tablespoon milk. Form into 8 small cutlet shapes, coat in seasoned flour, beaten egg and crisp breadcrumbs. Fry in a little hot fat.

Avocado Mousse

150 ml/¼ pint (⅔ cup) water
15 g/½ oz (2 envelopes) gelatine
2 tablespoons lemon juice
2 large or 3 small avocados
3 tablespoons mayonnaise
a few drops of Tabasco (hot pepper) sauce
a few drops of Worcestershire sauce
150 ml/¼ pint (⅔ cup) double (heavy) cream
2 egg whites
salt and pepper
TO GARNISH:
lettuce leaves
1 lemon
1 tomato

Heat the water, sprinkle the gelatine on top and heat gently until dissolved. Allow to become cold, but not set, then add the lemon juice. Skin, halve and mash the avocados in a bowl until very smooth. Gradually blend in the gelatine liquid, the mayonnaise and the two sauces. Allow the mixture to set lightly.

Whip the cream until it holds its shape, whisk the egg whites until stiff. Fold the cream and the egg whites into the avocado mixture, with any seasoning required. Spoon into 4 to 6 small sundae glasses, do not over-fill. Leave until firm.

Shred the lettuce very finely, arrange as a border around the top edge of each mousse; cut the lemon and tomato into wedges and place on the top of the Sundaes. Serves 4 to 6.

Cheesy Mushrooms

12 large mushrooms
1 medium onion
75 g/3 oz Cheddar cheese
75 g/3 oz (6 tablespoons) margarine
75 g/3 oz (1½ cups) soft breadcrumbs
2 tablespoons chopped parsley
salt and pepper

Wipe the mushrooms, remove the stalks and chop these finely. Peel and finely chop the onion. Grate the cheese. Melt 25 g/1 oz (2 tablespoons) margarine and fry the onion until soft. Blend with the cheese, breadcrumbs, parsley, mushroom stalks and a little seasoning.

Melt the remaining margarine in a large frying pan (skillet) and cook the mushroom caps, until just tender. Lift into an ovenproof dish and top with the stuffing. Bake in a preheated moderately hot oven (190°C/375°F, Gas Mark 5) for 10 to 15 minutes. Serves 4.

VARIATION

Skin and chop 2 tomatoes and add to the breadcrumb mixture.

Tomato and Thyme Soup, Herby Bread, Cheese Pots (page 181)

LEFTOVERS
Nut Cutlets and a Nut Roast are excellent served cold with salad.

FREEZING NOTE
✵When freezing the Nut Cutlets, open-freeze and then wrap them. They can be reheated in the oven for a short time.

FOR ECONOMY
Lentil Roast
Soak 225 g/8 oz (1 cup) split lentils in cold water to cover, then cook until a thick purée. Use in place of the nuts in Nut Roast.

MENUS FOR MANY OCCASIONS

The menus on the following pages are suitable for a wide variety of occasions. They are based on recipes in this book together with additional ideas to create well balanced and satisfying meals.

The first few pages give economical and simple menus for summer and winter meals which should be helpful for a busy cook. They are followed by recipes for special occasions – barbecues, buffet parties, formal dinner parties and Christmas. I suggest suitable wines to serve with the more formal menus.

Menu Planning

When shopping for the ingredients for a meal, select the food for the main course and then plan around it. (You will find advice on buying fish, meat, poultry and vegetables under the various sections in this book.) Aim to achieve a good balance of nutrients, serve plenty of fresh vegetables and/or fruit and not too much fat and carbohydrates. It is a good idea to serve fresh fruit, instead of a rich pudding or dessert.

When planning meals for special occasions, allow yourself plenty of time for the shopping, and select the ingredients with particular care. As you plan the dishes, consider how they will look, as well as how they will taste. Presentation is an important part of any meal.

Avoid dishes with too definite a taste, such as curries, unless you know your guests' likes and dislikes and choose dishes that will not spoil should your guests be delayed.

Roast meat or poultry can be spoilt if they have to be kept warm for an extra half an hour or so.

Microwave Cooking

A microwave cooker is a great help to a busy cook and will quickly thaw frozen dishes that have been prepared in advance. Sauces and gravies can also be cooked in advance and reheated at the last minute.

Another advantage of reheating pre-cooked food in the microwave cooker is that food can be transferred to serving dishes and pots and pans can be washed up and put away before the guests arrive.

A microwave cooker is also invaluable when members of a family come in at different times for their meals. Cooked foods can be put on individual plates, covered and refrigerated, then simply reheated in the microwave cooker.

Happy Entertaining

Many of the menus in this section are ideal to serve when entertaining friends.

One important point to appreciate is that guests prefer a relaxed hostess to one who is agitated and worrying about the meal to be served. Do not attempt ambitious dishes that you have not prepared before and which may cause you undue worry. You can, of course, have a 'trial run' before the special occasion, alternatively, concentrate on the dishes you know you make well.

Select your menu with care. Friends who live alone are certain to appreciate a roast joint because this is something that they may not cook for themselves. City dwellers will enjoy local country produce, and visitors from abroad will be anxious to sample the best of national dishes.

If you know from bitter experience that your guests are invariably unpunctual people, then choose dishes, like casseroles, that will not spoil with longer cooking. Select some cold dishes too; salads, rather than vegetables, are a good accompaniment for the main course.

The presentation of food is always important. It is best when entertaining, to prepare the garnishes and decorations for the various dishes in advance because it is these 'extras' that take a surprisingly long time to get ready. Ingredients that will wilt or look dry if exposed to the air should be covered with plastic wrap.

If you are serving food that has to be eaten with the fingers, provide a finger bowl for each person. Fill them with cold water. You may like to put a small slice of lemon or tiny flower blossom in the water, but this is not essential. (Finger bowls are not used very often so you may not possess them, small soup cups can be used instead). Take a critical look at the laid table and see if an extra posy of flowers will make it look more attractive.

If you are keeping food warm check that the oven is turned to as low a temperature as possible. Cover the food with aluminium foil to prevent it drying. Vegetables and sauces can be dished up and kept warm by standing the covered dishes in a large pan of hot, but not boiling, water, like a bain-marie. Obviously if you have an electric appliance for keeping food warm you should use this.

In some of the menus that follow you will find suggested wines or other drinks which I think would make a good accompaniment. Remember to chill white or rosé wine and fruit juices if you are serving these. Open bottles of red wine well in advance to allow it to breathe and stand at room temperature.

When all these preparations are complete, take the time to relax and get ready to enjoy the occasion.

Cold Weather Menus

Winter meals should be satisfying and sustaining, for most people feel more hungry in cold weather, but they should also contain a generous amount of fresh green vegetables and citrus fruits. An adequate supply of these foods, rich in vitamin C, helps to build up resistance to colds and 'flu.

In colder weather most people enjoy warming homemade soups, and the root and green vegetables available provide an excellent basis for these.

A final thought – use your oven wisely and save expensive fuel. If the main dish is cooked in the oven, try to utilize any spare space for oven-cooked vegetables (see page 93).

Summer Eating

Although cold dishes and salads are very popular in hot weather, they can become boring if served too frequently. For this reason I have suggested several light hot dishes.

The summer menus begin on page 191 and include many dishes that are equally good for outdoor eating or for serving at home.

Dinner Party Menu 5, page 198

Cold Weather Menus

Cold Weather Menu 1

Cream of Cauliflower Soup

Bacon and Apple Roll

Winter Macedoine of Vegetables

Golden Pears

Serves 4

Cream of Cauliflower Soup

⁜Remove the florets from a very small flower and set aside. Chop the outer leaves and stalks roughly and simmer in 750 ml/1¼ pints (3 cups) water or chicken stock for 30 minutes. Strain and use the stock as the basis for the soup.

Cook the florets in the well-seasoned cauliflower stock for 8 to 10 minutes. Sieve or blend.

Melt 25 g/1 oz (2 tablespoons) butter or margarine in a saucepan. Stir in 25 g/1 oz (¼ cup) flour and cook over a low heat for several minutes, stirring continuously. Add 300 ml/½ pint (1¼ cups) milk gradually, stirring or whisking as the sauce comes to the boil and thickens. Add the cauliflower purée and a little cream or top of the milk (half and half). Add salt and pepper to taste.

Heat and serve topped with a dash of paprika or a swirl of top of the milk (half and half) and a little freshly chopped parsley.

Bacon and Apple Roll

FOR THE FILLING:
350 g/12 oz bacon rashers (slices)
225 g/8 oz onions
225 g/8 oz cooking (tart) apples
1 teaspoon soft (light) brown sugar
pinch of dried sage
shake of pepper
FOR THE SUET PASTRY:
225 g/8 oz (2 cups) self-raising (self-rising) flour
pinch of salt
110 g/4 oz (scant 1 cup) shredded suet
water to bind
TO GLAZE:
1 egg
TO GARNISH:
1 dessert apple

⁜Derind and chop the bacon; save the bacon rinds. Peel and chop the onions; peel, core and coarsely grate the apples. Heat the bacon rinds and bacon in a pan, add the onions and cook very gently for 10 minutes. Remove and discard the bacon rinds; mix the bacon and onion mixture with the apples, sugar, sage and pepper. Allow to cool.

For the pastry Sift the flour with the salt. Add the suet and sufficient water to make a soft rolling consistency. Roll out to an oblong shape approximately 20 × 25 cm/8 × 10 inches.

Spread the bacon mixture over the pastry to within 2.5 cm/1 inch of the edges. Brush these edges with water, fold in the short ends of pastry to enclose the filling, then roll the long end as you would a Swiss (jelly) roll.

Lift on to a lightly greased baking sheet with the long join on the underside. Make several slits in the roll. Beat the egg and brush over the pastry. Bake in the centre of a preheated moderately hot oven (190°C/375°F, Gas Mark 5) for 30 to 40 minutes or until firm and golden brown. Slice the dessert apple and arrange round the roll. Serve hot with a selection of vegetables.

Note Plain (all-purpose) flour can be used for the pastry, but add 2 teaspoons baking powder.

Winter Macedoine of Vegetables

550 g/1¼ lb mixed root vegetables, weight when peeled
water, see method
salt and pepper
15 g/½ oz (1 tablespoon) butter or margarine
2 to 3 tomatoes
watercress

Peel and dice the vegetables, put into a casserole with water to cover, the seasoning and butter or margarine. Cover and cook in the coolest part of a preheated moderately hot oven (190°C/375°F, Gas Mark 5) for an hour. Strain and put into a heated serving dish. Slice the tomatoes and sprig the watercress. Place on top of the root vegetables.

VARIATIONS

Cook diced swede (rutabaga) as above. Strain and top with chopped parsley.

Green beans can be cooked as above for 35 to 40 minutes.

Golden Pears

1 tablespoon lemon juice
150 ml/¼ pint (⅔ cup) white wine or sweet cider
150 ml/¼ pint (⅔ cup) water
2 tablespoons honey
4 medium or 8 small firm dessert pears
1 teaspoon arrowroot
2 tablespoons orange juice

Put the lemon juice, wine or cider and water into a saucepan, add the honey and stir over a low heat until well blended. Peel, halve and core the pears. Put into a casserole, pour over the syrup, cover with a lid and cook in the coolest part of a preheated moderately hot oven (190°C/375°F, Gas Mark 5) for approximately 45 minutes.

Lift the pears on to a heated serving dish with a perforated spoon. Mix the arrowroot with the cold orange juice. Pour the syrup into a saucepan, stir in the arrowroot mixture and continue stirring over a low heat until thickened and clear. Spoon over the pears. Serve hot or cold.

VARIATION

Small whole peeled and cored apples can be cooked in the same way. Choose the dessert type of apple that cooks well but does not become a pulp.

Cold Weather Menu 2

Winter Salad

Hake with Peanut Dressing

Savoury Potato Cakes with lightly cooked Cauliflower

Cabinet Pudding, see page 125

Serves 4

Winter Salad

Shred part of a white cabbage or Chinese leaves (bok choy) finely. Peel and grate 1 small onion. Peel 4 carrots, cut into thin sticks. Mix these vegetables with 50 g/2 oz (½ cup) roughly chopped walnuts and 4 finely chopped tomatoes.

Slice 1 dessert apple and 1 peeled avocado. Toss in 4 tablespoons Vinaigrette Dressing (see page 105). Spoon on top of the vegetable mixture, and garnish with parsley.

Hake with Peanut Dressing

4 fillets of hake, each about 225 g/8 oz
salt and pepper
25 g/1 oz (¼ cup) flour
FOR FRYING:
75 g/3 oz (6 tablespoons) butter
1 tablespoon lemon juice
75 g/3 oz (½ cup) salted peanuts
TO GARNISH:
lemon wedges
watercress

Skin the fish if desired, or ask the fishmonger to do it for you. Wash and dry the fillets. Mix a little seasoning with the flour and coat the fish.

Heat 50 g/2 oz (¼ cup) of the butter in a large frying pan (skillet). When it becomes frothy lay the fish in it, filleted side downwards. Fry steadily for 6 to 10 minutes, depending on the thickness, turning once. Lift the fish on to a heated serving dish and keep hot. Put the pan back on the heat, add the extra butter; heat this slowly until it begins to brown. Pour in the lemon juice, add the nuts and stir over the heat for 1 minute. Season generously with pepper but only

very little salt. Spoon the peanut mixture quickly over the fish. Garnish with lemon wedges and sprigs of watercress.

Savoury Potato Cakes

450 g/1 lb boiled potatoes
25 to 50 g/1 to 2 oz (2 to 4 tablespoons) butter or margarine
1 egg
1 tablespoon chopped chives
1 tablespoon chopped parsley
salt and pepper
FOR FRYING:
25 g to 50 g/1 to 2 oz (2 to 4 tablespoons) butter or cooking fat

❖ Mash the potatoes. Melt or soften the butter or margarine and beat into the potatoes. Add the egg, herbs and seasoning. Form into 8 round cakes.

Heat the butter or cooking fat and fry the cakes quickly on both sides until golden brown and hot.

Cold Weather Menu 3

Baked Herring Roes

Zucchine Ripiene

Baked Potatoes, see page 93

Green Salad

Napoleon Fingers or Fresh Fruit

Serves 4

Baked Herring Roes

Separate 450 g/1 lb soft or hard herring roes into individual pieces. Allow frozen roes to thaw before using.

Coat the roes in a little well-seasoned flour. Heat 50 g/2 oz (¼ cup) butter or margarine in a shallow ovenproof dish, turn the roes in this, then add a squeeze of lemon juice. Bake towards the top of a preheated moderately hot oven (200°C/400°F, Gas Mark 6) for 15 to 20 minutes. Garnish with lemon wedges. Serve with crisp toast and butter.

Zucchine Ripiene

4 large courgettes (zucchini)
salt and pepper
1 large onion
1 to 2 garlic cloves
3 medium tomatoes
1 tablespoon oil
100 g/4 oz cooked beef, lamb or ham
50 g/2 oz (1 cup) soft breadcrumbs
50 g/2 oz Parmesan cheese

Wash the courgettes (zucchini), put into a little boiling salted water and simmer for 10 minutes. Remove from the water, slit lengthways and carefully scoop out

the centre pulp; chop this finely and reserve.

Peel and finely chop the onion and garlic; skin and chop the tomatoes. Heat the oil and fry the vegetables until soft. Mince (grind) or finely chop the meat, add to the vegetables in the pan with half the breadcrumbs and the courgette (zucchini) pulp. Season well.

Grate the cheese. Fill the courgettes (zucchini) with the savoury mixture, then top with the grated cheese and remaining breadcrumbs.

Bake towards the top of a preheated moderately hot oven (200°C/400°F, Gas Mark 6) for 15 to 20 minutes.

Napoleon Fingers

85 g/3 oz (6 tablespoons) butter or margarine
50 g/2 oz (¼ cup) caster sugar
110 g/4 oz (1 cup) plain (all-purpose) flour
50 g/2 oz (½ cup) ground almonds
1 egg yolk
FOR THE FILLING:
4 tablespoons jam
FOR THE TOPPING:
25 g/1 oz (¼ cup) icing (confectioners') sugar

❖ Grease a Swiss (jelly) roll tin (pan) measuring 15 × 25 cm/6 × 10 inches. Cream together the butter or margarine and sugar. Sift the flour and ground almonds, fold into the creamed mixture, bind with the egg yolk and knead well.

Roll out to fit the prepared tin. Bake in the centre of a preheated moderate oven (160°C/325°F, Gas Mark 3) for 20 minutes or until firm. Cut the biscuit (cookie) base in half while warm, but allow to become almost cold in the tin, then remove to a wire cooling tray.

Place half the biscuit base on to a board, spread with the jam and top with the second half. Cut into narrow fingers and sift the icing (confectioners') sugar over the top. Makes 12.

FOR ECONOMY

When making the Cauliflower Soup, buy a cauliflower with a lot of fresh green leaves, make the stock with the toughest part of the leaves and stalks. Strain and cook the shredded green leaves in the stock instead of the cauliflower florets. Sieve or purée in blender and proceed as opposite.

LEFTOVERS

Always retain the roes from fresh herrings and freeze them for future use. Baked herring roes are both easy to prepare and delicious.

Hake with Peanut Dressing

187

Cold Weather Menu 4

Orange and Tomato Cocktail

Sausages with Bacon and Pepper
Râgout

Creamed Potatoes, see page 92

Braised Endive (Chicory)

Cheese and Celery

Serves 4

Orange and Tomato Cocktail

Mix together 350 ml/12 fl oz (1½ cups) canned or bottled tomato juice and 350 ml/12 fl oz (1½ cups) fresh orange juice. Pour into 4 cocktail glasses, and chill before serving. Add a little celery salt of desired.

Sausages with Bacon and Pepper Râgout

Cook the sausages steadily under a preheated grill (broiler), for about 10 to 12 minutes, turning once.
⁂For the Râgout: Peel and chop 2 onions, dice 1 or 2 green peppers or use 1 green and 1 red pepper (discard the cores and seeds). Derind and chop 2 to 3 bacon rashers (slices), saving the rinds. Heat 25 g/1 oz (2 tablespoons) butter or margarine in a pan with the bacon rinds. Add the onions, peppers and bacon and cook steadily until just soft. Do not overcook, for you need to retain the shape of the peppers. Season to taste. Serve topped with grilled (broiled) sausages.

Braised Endive (Chicory)

Prepare the ingredients for a mirepoix as in Braised Celery (see page 94). Wash and dry 1 endive (chicory) – it looks like a curly lettuce – and cut into 8 sections. Heat 50 g/2 oz (¼ cup) butter or margarine in a saucepan, turn the pieces of endive (chicory) in this. Place over the mirepoix (see page 94) and continue as in that recipe, allowing about 45 minutes cooking time.
VARIATIONS
Use 4 fairly large onions instead of the endive (chicory) and increase the cooking time to 1¼ to 1½ hours. In view of the longer time over the heat, check the amount of liquid very carefully. This is also an excellent way of cooking lettuce. Use the solid heart of the lettuce, divided into 4 to 8 portions.

LEFTOVERS
Saffron rice makes an attractive basis for cold weather salads (see page 95). You can also mix the rice with chopped celery, grated raw carrot or diced eating apple (dipped in a little lemon juice to keep it white). Add chopped red or green pepper to give colour.

Cold Weather Menu 5

Country Pâté, see page 24

Chicken with Suprême Sauce

Saffron Rice

Broccoli

Pots au Citron

Serves 4

Chicken with Suprême Sauce

Do not use the chicken liver in this recipe because it tends to darken the stock too much.

| 1 chicken with giblets |
| salt and pepper |
| **FOR THE SUPRÊME SAUCE:** |
| 40 g/1½ oz (3 tablespoons) butter or margarine |
| 40 g/1½ oz (⅓ cup) flour |
| 450 ml/¾ pint (2 cups) chicken stock |
| 5 tablespoons double (heavy) cream |
| 2 egg yolks |
| ½ tablespoon lemon juice |

Put the chicken into a saucepan with the neck of the giblets. Add about 900 ml/1½ pints (3¾ cups) water, salt and pepper to taste. You can add herbs and vegetables as given under the variations.
Cook the chicken (see page 78). Start to make the sauce towards the end of the cooking time.
Melt the butter or margarine in a saucepan, stir in the flour and cook for 2 to 3 minutes. Measure out 450 ml/¾ pint (2 cups) stock from the saucepan in which the chicken is cooking. Mix gradually into the roux in the pan, stirring or whisking briskly as you do so, for there is a tendency for the sauce to become lumpy if the liquid is very hot.
Mix the cream with the egg yolks, pour a little of the hot but not boiling sauce from the pan over the egg yolk mixture. Return to the saucepan and stir over a low heat until the sauce returns to a coating consistency once again. Do not allow the sauce to boil because it will curdle. Whisk in the lemon juice and any extra seasoning just before serving.
<u>Note</u> This sauce is generally served with breast of chicken. If you have bought a large bird, you could use just the breast and save the cooked legs to have cold with salad on another occasion. If you have bought a smaller bird, carve breast and legs.
This is a fairly generous amount of sauce and it could serve up to 6 people.
VARIATIONS
Add a bouquet garni of mixed herbs, 1 peeled whole onion, 1 or 2 peeled whole carrots and 2 to 3 mushrooms to the liquid in which the chicken is cooked.
Fry 50 to 100 g/2 to 4 oz (½ to 1 cup) very small or sliced mushrooms in a little butter and add to the sauce just before serving.

Saffron Rice

Cook long-grain rice (see page 136) but add a pinch of saffron powder to the liquid. If using saffron strands, infuse these for 15 minutes in the water in which the rice is to be cooked, strain, add to the rice and cook.

Pots au Citron

| 3 tablespoons water |
| 15 g/½ oz (2 envelopes) gelatine |
| 2 lemons |
| 1 × 397 g/14 oz can full cream sweetened condensed milk |
| 225 g/8 oz (1 cup) cream or curd cheese |
| 2 egg whites |
| **TO DECORATE:** halved walnuts |

⁂Put the water into a bowl, sprinkle the gelatine on top and stand over a pan of hot water until the gelatine has dissolved. Grate the rind from the lemons and squeeze out 4 tablespoons lemon juice. Mix with the gelatine, the condensed milk and cheese. Whisk the egg whites until stiff and fold into the cheese mixture. Spoon into individual dishes and leave until just set. Top with the nuts.
VARIATION
Decorate with a border of lightly whipped cream.

Cold Weather Menu 6

Les Crudités, see page 27

Gammon with Pineapple and
Macaroni Fritters

Grilled Tomatoes

Raisin Yogurt

Serves 4

Les Crudités

Although raw vegetables are an ideal part of a meal at any time of the year, they are a particularly good choice in cold weather when salad ingredients are more expensive. Use raw carrots, turnips, swede (rutabaga), courgettes (zucchini), and celery, together with other available raw vegetables.

Gammon with Pineapple

Grill (broil) the gammon (ham) steaks thoroughly (see page 63); keeping it well basted with melted butter or margarine. Add the well-drained canned pineapple rings (slices) towards the end of cooking time.
The pineapple rings (slices) should be brushed with a little melted butter before being put under the grill (broiler). Heat for 1 to 2 minutes only.
Although the pineapple is not glazed for this menu, it can be topped with a little brown sugar before grilling (broiling). Watch the cooking process carefully because the sugar can burn if the temperature is too high.
Arrange the gammon (ham) and pineapple on a dish and garnish with parsley and the Grilled Tomatoes.

Grilled Tomatoes

Tomatoes in wintertime tend to lose their sweet flavour, so sprinkle with a little seasoning and a little caster sugar before cooking. Grill (broil) until the tomatoes are just tender.

Macaroni Fritters

**These should be prepared well ahead so that they can stand for 30 minutes or more before being fried at the last minute (see the Freezing Note on this page).

Cook 50 g/2 oz (½ cup) short-length macaroni in boiling salted water until just al dente, (see page 139). Drain well. Make a thick sauce by melting 25 g/1 oz (2 tablespoons) butter or margarine in a saucepan, stirring in 25 g/1 oz (¼ cup) flour, then gradually adding 150 ml/¼ pint (⅔ cup) milk. Stir as the mixture comes to the boil and becomes very thick. Add the cooked macaroni and mix well together, season to taste. Form into about 8 small balls. Coat in a little seasoned flour, beaten egg and crisp breadcrumbs.

Fry in hot fat or oil for a few minutes until golden brown and crisp, then drain on absorbent paper. Although deep frying is easier for this type of round fritter, you can also use shallow fat or oil, but you must turn the fritters during cooking.

As the ingredients for the fritters are already cooked, the fat or oil can be very hot, i.e. 185°C/365°F. (See page 90.)

Raisin Yogurt

Soak 100 g/4 oz (¾ cup) seedless raisins in 4 tablespoons fresh orange juice and 1 tablespoon sweet sherry for 2 hours. Stir into 600 ml/1 pint (2½ cups) plain yogurt just before serving.

Cold Weather Menu 7

| Piquant Grapefruit |
| Sweetbreads in Parsley Butter |
| Croquette Potatoes, see page 92 but use 750 g/1½ lb potatoes |
| Leaf Spinach |
| Chocolate Raisin Puddings, see page 125 |
| Serves 6 |

Piquant Grapefruit

| 3 large grapefruit |
| 4 gherkins (sweet dill pickle) |
| 100 g/4 oz (⅔ cup) peeled (shelled) prawns (shrimp) |
| 150 ml/¼ pint (⅔ cup) soured cream |
| 1 teaspoon sugar |
| salt and pepper |

Halve the grapefruit. Carefully remove the segments of fruit preserving the grapefruit cases, then cut away and discard any skin and pips from the fruit. Slice the gherkins.

Blend the grapefruit segments with all the other ingredients and spoon back into the grapefruit cases.

Sweetbreads in Parsley Butter

| 750 g/1½ lb lambs' sweetbreads |
| 450 ml/¾ pint (2 cups) chicken stock |
| salt and pepper |
| 75 g/3 oz (6 tablespoons) butter |
| 1 tablespoon lemon juice |
| 2 to 3 tablespoons chopped parsley |

**Wash the sweetbreads well, put into a saucepan of cold water, bring the water to the boil, strain the sweetbreads then discard the water.

Take away any gristle from the sweetbreads and put into the chicken stock, add a little seasoning and simmer for about 45 minutes until very tender.

Strain and dry the sweetbreads on absorbent kitchen paper. (The stock could be saved and used in a sauce for another occasion.)

Heat the butter in a large frying pan (skillet) until it turns a pale golden brown. Add the sweetbreads, the lemon juice and parsley and heat thoroughly. Serves 4.

Cold Weather Menu 5

LEFTOVERS

Cooked macaroni or other leftover pasta can be used in fritters (see this page). If using spaghetti, chop it into small lengths.

FREEZING NOTE

**The prepared Macaroni Fritters can be frozen, then fried without being thawed.
Open freeze on a flat tray before wrapping.

Neapolitan Flan from Light Menu 2

Neapolitan Flan

FOR THE RICH CHEESE PASTRY:	
175 g/6 oz (1½ cups) plain (all-purpose) flour	
pinch of salt	
85 g/3 oz (6 tablespoons) butter	
85 g/3 oz cheese, see page 147	
2 tablespoons water	
FOR THE FILLING:	
2 medium onions	
1 garlic clove	
450 g/1 lb tomatoes	
25 g/1 oz (2 tablespoons) butter	
1 tablespoon tomato purée (paste)	
2 to 3 teaspoons chopped mixed herbs or 1 teaspoon dried mixed herbs	
salt and pepper	
1 teaspoon sugar (optional)	
50 g/2 oz cheese	
3 to 4 bacon rashers (bacon slices)	
12 black (ripe) olives	

Light Meals

The following simple menus are suitable for any time of the year. They can be made more sustaining by serving an hors d'oeuvre and by adding a wider selection of vegetables as well as the salad.

Light Menu 1

Jansson's Temptation, *see page 46*
Rainbow Salad
Rhubarb and Orange Cream
Serves 4

Rainbow Salad

Attractive salads can be made by arranging ingredients in coloured bands on flat platters. Here are some suggestions:
For a white band Chopped hard-boiled (hard-cooked) egg white with sliced chicory (endive), grated young turnip, diced peeled apple (dipped in lemon juice).
For a green band Diced green pepper, lettuce, watercress, shredded cabbage.
For a pink to red band Sliced or chopped tomatoes, sliced radishes, cooked diced beetroot (beet), red cabbage, redcurrants, raspberries.
For a yellow to orange band Chopped hard-boiled (hard-cooked) egg yolk, grated or diced carrots and swede (rutabaga), orange segments, grapefruit segments, diced pineapple.
Dressings Offer a selection of dressings such as Vinaigrette, Blue Cheese Dressing and Mayonnaise, (see page 104 and 105).

Rhubarb and Orange Cream

✱✱Cook 450 g/1 lb diced rhubarb in a bowl over hot water, or in a double saucepan, with 75 g/3 oz (6 tablespoons) sugar, 2 teaspoons finely grated orange rind and 2 tablespoons orange juice. Do not add any extra water.
Make a thick custard sauce with 1 tablespoon custard powder (Bird's English dessert mix), 1 tablespoon sugar, 150 ml/¼ pint (⅔ cup) milk and 150 ml/¼ pint (⅔ cup) single (light) cream.
Blend the rhubarb and custard together in a food processor or blender. Spoon into individual dishes and serve cold with more cream or freeze lightly.

Light Menu 2

Citrus Cocktail
Neapolitan Flan
Cucumber and Chicory (Endive) Salad
Ice Cream, *see page* 116
Serves 6

Citrus Cocktail

Mix together segments of 1 fresh grapefruit, 2 fresh oranges and 1 fresh tangerine. Moisten with a little lemon juice or dry sherry. Arrange on 6 plates, garnished with a little mint, if desired.

Cucumber and Chicory Salad

Slice ½ medium cucumber and 2 to 3 heads of chicory (endive). Place in individual salad bowls, top with Vinaigrette Dressing (see page 105) mixed with chopped chives.

Sift the flour and salt into a mixing bowl, rub in (cut in) the butter until the mixture is like fine breadcrumbs. Grate the cheese, add to the rubbed-in mixture then bind with cold water. Knead lightly and roll out. Use to line a 23 cm/9 inch flan dish (quiche or pie pan). Bake blind, (see page 146), in the centre of a preheated moderately hot oven (200°C/400°F, Gas Mark 6) for 10 minutes only. Remove from the oven.
Meanwhile peel and finely chop the onions and peel and crush the garlic. Skin all the tomatoes, finely chop half of these and slice the remainder. Heat the butter in a pan. Fry the onions, garlic and chopped tomatoes for 5 minutes, then add the tomato purée (paste), herbs, a little seasoning and the sugar. (The sugar emphasizes the tomato flavour, but can be omitted.) Cool slightly, then spoon into the partially baked pastry case (pie shell).
Arrange the tomato slices on top. Grate the cheese, sprinkle over the tomatoes, then de-rind the bacon, cut into narrow strips and place in a lattice design on top of the cheese.
Re-set the oven to a moderate heat (180°C/350°F, Gas Mark 4) and continue cooking the flan for a further 35 minutes. Add the olives towards the end of the cooking time. Serve hot or cold with salad.

Light Menu 3

Avocado Mousse or Chicken Mould, *see pages* 183 *or* 83
Mushroom and Cucumber Salad, *see page* 96
Pear Galette, *see page* 114
Serves 4

Summer Eating

Hot Weather Menu 1

Chilled Melon and Mint Soup

Cold Ham with Cumberland Sauce

Orange Potato Salad, see page 96

Green Salad

Mocha Cheesecake, see page 112

Serves 6 to 8

Chilled Melon and Mint Soup

Halve 2 large Ogen (cantaloupe or crenshaw) melons, remove the seeds. Make balls of ½ the melon to use as garnish. Purée the rest of the pulp with 300 ml/½ pint (1¼ cups) very clear chicken stock, 300 ml/½ pint (1¼ cups) plain yogurt, 150 ml/¼ pint (⅔ cup) single (light) cream. Season to taste. Add 2 to 3 tablespoons finely chopped mint. Serve chilled with the melon balls and fried croûtons.

Cumberland Sauce

150 ml/¼ pint (⅔ cup) orange juice	
2 teaspoons finely grated orange rind	
1 teaspoon finely grated lemon rind	
2 level teaspoons arrowroot	
2 tablespoons lemon juice	
1 to 2 teaspoons made mustard	
150 ml/¼ pint (⅔ cup) port wine	
4 tablespoons redcurrant jelly	
salt and pepper	
pinch of sugar	

∗∗Put the orange juice with the fruit rinds into a saucepan; bring just to boiling point then allow to cool and stand for 1 hour (this softens the rinds). Mix the arrowroot with the lemon juice, add to the pan with the mustard, port wine and jelly. Stir over a low heat until the sauce thickens and becomes smooth and clear. Taste and add seasoning and sugar if desired.

Hot Weather Menu 2

Mushrooms Indienne

New Potatoes

Green Peas

Chocolate and Coffee Mousse

Serves 4

Mushrooms Indienne

100 g/4 oz (1 cup) very small button mushrooms	
a few Chinese leaves (bok choy)	
FOR THE DRESSING: mango chutney, see method	
1 to 2 teaspoons curry paste	
150 ml/¼ pint (⅔ cup) soured cream	
1 dessert apple	
salt and pepper	
TO GARNISH: 4 lemon slices	

Wipe the mushrooms and trim the ends of the stalks. Finely shred the Chinese leaves (bok choy) and divide between 4 individual dishes or glasses. Measure enough of the liquid from the chutney to give 1 tablespoon. Blend this with the curry paste and cream. Peel and core the apple and cut into small dice; add to the curry mixture together with a little seasoning and the mushrooms. Spoon over the Chinese leaves (bok choy). Top with twists of lemon.

Chocolate and Coffee Mousse

175 g/6 oz (6 squares) plain (semi-sweet) chocolate	
3 tablespoons Tia Maria	
3 eggs	
ice cream or cream, see method	

∗∗Break the chocolate into pieces and put into a bowl with the Tia Maria. Stand the bowl over a saucepan of hot but not boiling water and allow the chocolate to melt.

Separate the eggs, add the yolks to the melted chocolate and whisk until the mixture is thick and creamy. Remove from the heat and continue whisking as the mixture cools slightly.

Whip the egg whites in a separate bowl and fold into the chocolate and coffee mixture. This is very rich so only half-fill 4 to 6 glasses with the mousse. Chill well. Top with small scoops of ice cream or lightly whipped cream.

VARIATION

∗∗Chocolate Orange Mousse Omit the Tia Maria; add the finely grated rind of 2 large oranges, 2 tablespoons orange juice, 2 tablespoons Curaçao and 25 to 50 g/1 to 2 oz sugar to the chocolate in the basin. Proceed as above.

Hot Weather Menu 1

A Simple Barbecue

FOR FLAVOUR
The Chinese recipes on this and the next page may sound unfamiliar, and some of the ingredients will be unknown, but first class Chinese products are readily available.

The cooking times may appear brief, but that is part of the pleasure of the Chinese cuisine – food is never overcooked; the firm or crisp texture of the various ingredients should be retained.

A Chinese Barbecue

Barbecues are an easy and popular way of serving food in good weather and there is an excellent range of barbecue equipment available. Always follow the manufacturer's directions for use and have a bucket of water to hand in case the fire goes out of control. Charcoal must glow red before you can start to cook and this takes about an hour.

Cook fish, meat and poultry over the fire, and baste them with oil or melted butter or preferably with a barbecue sauce or marinade (see below).

Vegetables can be cooked over the fire in saucepans, or wrapped in foil and cooked over the coals, although most people prefer a crisp salad with barbecued food.

Barbecue Marinade

2 tablespoons tomato purée (paste)
2 tablespoons tomato ketchup
1 tablespoon malt vinegar
1 tablespoon Worcestershire sauce
1 tablespoon brown sugar
1 tablespoon corn oil
150 ml/¼ pint (⅔ cup) stock, see method

Mix all the ingredients together. The type of stock used depends on the food being cooked. If barbecuing chicken, use chicken stock; if cooking steak or lamb chops, use lamb or beef stock.

Marinate the poultry or meat for 1 to 2 hours, drain and cook the meat over the barbecue fire. Baste with any remaining marinade during cooking. Serves 4.

Marinated Sardines

450 g/1 lb fresh sardines
FOR THE MARINADE: 3 tablespoons oil
2 tablespoons white wine vinegar
2 tablespoons finely chopped onion
1 teaspoon French (Dijon) mustard
1 to 2 tablespoons chopped tarragon
1 to 2 tablespoons chopped parsley
garlic salt and cayenne pepper
1 tablespoon tomato purée (paste)

If the sardines have been frozen, allow them to thaw completely. Dry on absorbent kitchen paper. Mix all the marinade ingredients together and pour into a large shallow dish. Place the sardines in the marinade and leave for 24 hours. Turn the fish once or twice.

Lift the sardines out of the marinade, cook under a preheated grill (broiler) or over a barbecue fire for 10 minutes. Heat any remaining marinade separately and spoon over the sardines before serving. Serves 4.

A Chinese Barbecue

Three-Shredded Soup
Barbecued Spare Ribs
Barbecued Mullet
Fragrant Chicken
Pork and Scallops with Chinese Leaves (Bok Choy)
Serves 8 to 10

In the menu on this and the next page, you will need to select the wines with care. Start with an aperitif of a dry to very dry sherry, to form a good substitute for a Chinese rice wine, then proceed to a dry to medium dry white wine.

Three-Shredded Soup

Make or buy chicken soup (see page 31), then add a little flaked crabmeat and cooked sweetcorn (whole kernel corn). Take very tiny pieces of broccoli, blanch them in boiling salted water for 1 minute, strain and add to the soup.
Note You can buy canned Chinese type soups that contain a mixture of chicken, sweetcorn and crabmeat.

Barbecued Spare Ribs

Buy 1.5 kg/3 lb spare ribs, separate them and put into a saucepan. Add 2 finely chopped medium onions, 3 finely chopped slices of pickled or root ginger, 600 ml/1 pint (2½ cups) water, 4 tablespoons soy sauce, 4 tablespoons dry sherry and 3 tablespoons sugar.

Simmer for 45 minutes or until the meat is tender, then drain.

Mix together 4 tablespoons barbecue sauce (obtainable ready-made), 1 tablespoon vinegar (use the vinegar from pickled ginger if you have bought that) and 1 to 2 teaspoons Chinese five spice powder.

Stand the spare ribs on the barbecue rack. Brush with the barbecue mixture and cook over moderately hot coals for 10 to 15 minutes, turning and basting occasionally.

Barbecued Mullet

Allow 1 red mullet per person. Scale and clean the fish; score both sides down to the backbone at 1.5 cm/½ inch intervals to give a diagonal pattern.

Mix together ½ teaspoon salt, 1 teaspoon sugar and ½ teaspoon curry powder. Rub into both sides of the fish. Brush the fish with oil and cook over the barbecue until tender. You can pour barbecue sauce over the fish when it is nearly cooked. Garnish with parsley or coriander leaves.

Fragrant Chicken

Place a portion of chicken, weighing about 350 g/12 oz into 600 ml/1 pint (2½ cups) water, add 2 teaspoons soy sauce (there are two types – light and dark – and the lighter is better with chicken). Simmer for about 30 minutes or until tender. Drain and cut the flesh into bite-sized pieces.

Peel and crush a garlic clove, put into a frying pan (skillet) with 1 tablespoon oil, heat together then add the diced chicken and fry for 2 to 3 minutes.

Meanwhile, cook 1 packet of Chinese

prawn crackers according to the directions on the packet. Squeeze a little lemon or lime juice over the chicken pieces, then put into the prawn crackers. Garnish with wedges of lemon or lime. Note This dish can be cooked on the barbecue. Mix the soy sauce, garlic, and oil. Brush over the chicken portion and cook over the coals.

Pork and Scallops with Chinese Leaves

This mixture of meat and fish is not only delicious, but it makes a two-colour effect on the skewers.

1.5 kg/3 lb tenderloin (fillet) of pork
10 to 12 scallops
FOR THE MARINADE:
1 tablespoon soy sauce
1 tablespoon barbecue sauce
1 tablespoon plum sauce or plum jam
1 tablespoon sherry
1 tablespoon vegetable oil
1 tablespoon sesame oil
1 teaspoon sugar
FOR THE SAUCE:
2 tablespoons Chinese sweet chilli sauce
2 tablespoons chilli and tomato sauce
1 tablespoon sesame seeds
TO GARNISH:
Chinese leaves (bok choy)
spring onion (scallion) flowers, see page 65

Make a marinade with the soy sauce, barbecue sauce, plum sauce or plum jam, sherry, vegetable oil, sesame oil and sugar.

Place the pork in the marinade and leave for 2 hours, turning frequently.

Cut the marinated pork into about 24 slices. Halve the scallops horizontally and put the meat and fish alternately on to 4 large or 8 small skewers.

Brush with a sauce made by mixing the Chinese sweet chilli sauce and chilli and tomato sauce. Cook over the barbecue fire at a fierce heat for about 5 minutes or until tender, turning from time to time. Sprinkle with sesame seeds towards the end of the cooking time.

Serve on Chinese leaves (bok choy) and garnish with flower shapes made from spring onions (scallions).

A Chinese Picnic

Sun with Clouds Smoked Fish
Two-layer Rice
Fried Prawn and Bean Curd Balls
Sesame Chicken Balls
Pancake Balls
Serves 6

Sun with Clouds Smoked Fish

Soak 50 g/2 oz dried mushrooms for 20 minutes, then drain. Slice about 450 g/1 lb of smoked fish (use two different kinds if possible) and arrange in overlapping layers. Sprinkle with a very little sesame oil and lemon juice. Finely shred 4 cabbage or spring green leaves and fry together with the mushrooms in a little very hot oil for about 40 seconds or until crisp. Arrange between the fish. Serve with prawn crackers, cooked according to the packet instructions.

Two-layer Rice

Cook 200 g/7 oz (1 cup) of rice (see page 136). It is possible to buy Oriental rice, in which case follow the packet instructions. Layer the rice with 50 g/2 oz thinly sliced salami and 6 spring onions (scallions), finely chopped. Serve with a sauce made by blending 4 tablespoons sweet chilli sauce and 4 tablespoons Chinese oyster sauce.

Fried Prawn and Bean Curd Balls

Steam 225 g/8 oz bean curd (this is obtainable from shops selling Chinese foods). Finely chop 100 g/4 oz (⅔ cup) cooked prawns (shelled shrimp), the bean curd, 25 g/1 oz (¼ cup) well-drained water chestnuts and ½ small bunch of spring onions (scallions). Mix with 2 tablespoons rice flour or ground rice.

Form the mixture into about 12 to 14 small balls, roll each ball in rice flour.

Deep fry in very hot oil for 1½ to 2 minutes, drain on absorbent kitchen paper and serve with a sauce for dipping.

A delicious sauce can be made by mixing a little made English mustard with 1 to 2 tablespoons sesame oil and a little hot chilli sauce.

Sesame Chicken Balls

Finely chop or mince (grind) 225 g/8 oz raw chicken breast and 100 g/4 oz lean raw pork. Peel and crush a clove of garlic and mix with the chicken and pork. Whisk 2 egg whites until they stand in soft peaks. Combine half the egg white with the chicken mixture, then, using 2 teaspoons, form the mixture into very small balls. Dip the balls in the second egg white and roll in sesame seeds.

Put into a steamer and cook over boiling water for 12 to 15 minutes until firm. Serve hot or cold. Makes about 18.

Pancake Balls

Make 12 small pancakes (see page 121) but cook them on one side only.

Finely shred 225 g/8 oz cooked beef and mix with 2 very finely chopped sticks of celery, 2 finely chopped slices of pickled ginger or root ginger, 4 tablespoons Chinese yellow bean sauce and ½ jar of well-drained Chinese vegetables, finely chopped.

Place the mixture on the cooked side of the pancakes, then roll the pancakes around the filling to completely envelop. Seal the edges of the pancakes with beaten egg.

Deep fry in very hot oil or fat for 1½ to 2 minutes until crisp. Serve hot or cold.

LEFTOVERS
Small amounts of leftover cooked chicken are ideal for Chinese cooking, since so many of the dishes use very small quantities of food.

A Chinese Picnic

193

A Satisfying Picnic

Cream of Cucumber Soup

Glazed Bacon with Wholewheat Rolls

Pineapple Coleslaw

Cheese Sticks with Cheese

Fresh Fruit

Serves 6

Serve well-chilled white wine, dry cider or fruit drinks and hot or cold coffee to complete the meal.

Cream of Cucumber Soup

LEFTOVERS
The syrup from canned pineapple can be added to jellies; used in a salad dressing (see Pineapple Coleslaw) or added to fresh fruit salad.

⁎⁎Follow the recipe for Courgette (Zucchini) Cream Soup (see page 33), but substitute peeled cucumber(s) for courgettes (zucchini). Garnish the soup with chives as in the original recipe or with finely chopped mint.

Chill a wide-necked vacuum flask and pour in the well-chilled soup.

Wholewheat Rolls

A *Satisfying* Picnic

⁎⁎Make rolls following the bread recipe on page 154 using 450 g/1 lb (4 cups) wholewheat flour, 1 teaspoon salt, 15 g/½ oz (½ cake) fresh (compressed) yeast, 300 ml/½ pint (1¼ cups) warm water. Mix the yeast with the water and with 1 tablespoon corn oil. Sift the flour and salt, add the yeast and oil mixture, then proceed as on pages 154 and 155. Makes 10 to 12 large rolls.

Glazed Bacon (Smoked Ham)

⁎⁎Boil a 1.5 kg/3 lb joint of bacon (smoked ham) (see page 62) but deduct 30 minutes from the total cooking time. Strip the skin from the meat, score (cut) the fat in a neat design, spread with the selected glaze. Place in a roasting pan and bake the joint in a preheated moderate oven (180°C/350°F, Gas Mark 4) for 30 minutes. Coat with one of the glazes below. Each is sufficient for a 1.5 kg/3 lb joint.

Honey and Lemon Glaze Mix 3 to 4 tablespoons honey with 2 teaspoons grated lemon rind and 2 tablespoons lemon juice.

When serving the joint at home, garnish with slices of lemon.

Orange and Ginger Glaze Mix 3 tablespoons orange marmalade, 2 tablespoons finely chopped preserved ginger, ½ teaspoon ground ginger and 2 tablespoons fresh orange juice together.

When serving the joint at home, garnish with slices of orange.

Spiced Pineapple Glaze Mix 2 tablespoons brown sugar, ½ teaspoon allspice and ½ teaspoon ground ginger with 3 tablespoons canned pineapple syrup. When serving the joint at home, garnish with canned pineapple rings (slices).

For a picnic, either take the whole bacon joint with a carving knife and fork and a board on which to cut it, or carve the joint at home and pack the slices.

Pineapple Coleslaw

FOR THE DRESSING:
1 teaspoon French (Dijon) mustard
salt and pepper
1 teaspoon sugar
5 tablespoons corn oil
2 tablespoons lemon juice
3 tablespoons canned pineapple syrup or juice
FOR THE COLESLAW:
½ small white cabbage
1 × 225 g/8 oz can pineapple rings (slices)
2 tablespoons chopped gherkins (sweet dill pickle)
2 teaspoons capers
2 tablespoons seedless raisins

Make the dressing by blending all the ingredients together and carry it in a small sealed container. Shred the cabbage very finely. Drain and chop the pineapple then mix with the cabbage and the other ingredients. Pack into a plastic box or screw-topped jar.

Cheese Sticks

25 g/1 oz Cheddar cheese
100 g/4 oz (1 cup) plain (all-purpose) flour
salt and cayenne pepper
½ teaspoon mustard powder
3 tablespoons corn oil
1 egg yolk
1 to 2 tablespoons water

⁎⁎Grate the cheese finely. Sift the flour with the seasonings, add the cheese. Mix the corn oil, egg yolk and 1 tablespoon water, pour on to the flour mixture and mix well. Add part or all of the second tablespoon of water if required to make the dough a firm rolling consistency. Knead until smooth, wrap in plastic wrap or foil and chill for 1 hour, then roll out until about 8 mm/⅓ inch thick. Cut into 24 fingers. Put on to a lightly greased baking sheet. Bake just above the centre of a preheated moderately hot oven (200°C/400°F, Gas Mark 6) for 12 to 15 minutes. Pack when cold and serve with cheese and fruit. Makes 24.

Note Take cheeses that will not spoil in hot weather, such as Cheddar, individual portions of Camembert and Port Salut. Carry fruit that does not bruise. The choice depends on the season.

Buffet Dishes

Many of the dishes throughout this book are suitable to serve at a buffet, where the food should be both easy to serve and to eat, especially if guests are to stand, rather than sit at tables.

Dips of various kinds can be placed on the buffet table for a first course (see pages 26 and 200). The Beef with Béarnaise Sauce below makes the most delicious and sustaining dip but can also be served as a light main course.

A whole salmon is an excellent buffet dish

Beef with Béarnaise Sauce

Cut about 750 g/1½ lb lightly cooked fillet steak or lean beef into small cubes and place on cocktail sticks (toothpicks). Arrange on a bed of colourful salad with a bowl of Béarnaise Sauce in the centre. Although this sauce is generally served hot it is also good cold. Add a little cream if it is too thick to use as a dip.
Béarnaise Sauce Place 4 tablespoons white wine vinegar and 4 tablespoons tarragon vinegar with a small peeled shallot or onion in a saucepan. Boil rapidly until reduced to 3 tablespoons. Cool, then strain into a bowl. Add 4 egg yolks and a little seasoning. Whisk over hot, but not boiling, water until thick and creamy (see page 105). Gradually whisk in 150 g/5 oz butter (½ cup plus 2 tablespoons) – see page 105 – then add 1 teaspoon chopped chervil or parsley and 1 teaspoon chopped tarragon. Serves 6.

Chaudfroid of Bacon

This makes an excellent centrepiece for the buffet. Cook a joint of bacon (see page 62). Skin and coat it with the sauce below.

Use a packet of aspic that will set 600 ml/1 pint (2½ cups) liquid. Dissolve the aspic plus 2 teaspoons gelatine in 600 ml/1 pint (2½ cups) boiling water or clear unsalted stock. Cool and blend three-quarters of the aspic and gelatine liquid with 600 ml/1 pint (2½ cups) thick mayonnaise (page 104) or Béchamel Sauce (page 102). Cover the sauce, so it does not form a skin and allow to set to the consistency of a thick syrup. Keep the remaining aspic jelly in a warm place so that it cools and thickens slightly.
To coat the bacon (ham) Put the joint on a wire cooling tray with a large dish underneath to catch any 'drips'. Spread the chaudfroid sauce over the food with a palette knife. Allow to set then spread with a second layer. You may need to gently warm any sauce that has dripped

from the first coating of the sauce (two thin layers are better than a single thick one).

When the second layer is nearly set arrange the garnish on the bacon (ham). Cut small pieces of cucumber, red pepper, olives, etc. into fancy shapes. Dip in a little of the reserved aspic jelly and place in position. When the coating is quite firm dip a pastry brush in the remaining aspic jelly and brush over the garnish.

If you have sufficient aspic jelly left you can brush over the set chaudfroid coating to give a high gloss.

Cooking a Whole Salmon

A whole salmon makes an excellent buffet dish. A 3 kg/7 lb salmon will give 15 to 20 portions. It is possible to buy smaller fish. Leave on the head and tail, but ask the fishmonger to clean the fish and remove the guts, gills and eyes.

Poaching is the easiest way to cook a whole salmon. Use a fish kettle if possible (this is a large oval pan with a lid, which contains a perforated plate on which to place the fish). As an alternative, use a large flameproof casserole, a roasting pan or preserving pan, and make a lid of foil.

Use enough seasoned water to cover the fish, or make a simple Court Bouillon by adding a little white wine, lemon juice or white wine vinegar to the salted water with a whole onion, a bunch of parsley and a few peppercorns.

Put the fish into the container with

cold liquid to cover. Bring this just to boiling point. Lower the heat and cook.

If serving the salmon hot, allow 7 to 8 minutes per 450 g/1 lb (the longer time for very large salmon). If serving the salmon cold, allow 5 minutes for a fish of up to 3 kg/7 lb in weight or 10 to 15 minutes for a fish of between 3 to 5.5 kg/7 to 12 lb. Turn off the heat, cover the pan very tightly and allow the salmon to cool in the water. Remove when cold.
To serve Remove the fish skin and garnish with sliced cucumber, sliced radishes, sliced lemon and lettuce. Serve with mayonnaise.

Salads and Vegetables

Cut salad ingredients finely and choose a colourful mixture of ingredients. Tiny new potatoes, cooked in their skins are always popular.

Desserts

Gâteaux and meringues (see pages 113 and 170) are perfect for a buffet but many people will appreciate fresh fruit salad and lighter cold desserts like the following:
Pineapple Delight Dice the rings from 1 × 453 g/15½ oz can pineapple and fold into 600 ml/1 pint (2½ cups) whipped cream with 25 g/1 oz each chopped toasted almonds, chopped angelica, and chopped glacé cherries; 175 g/6 oz (2 cups) chopped marshmallows and 2 tablespoons lemon juice. Spoon into individual glasses and top with additional fruit and nuts.

195

Formal Entertaining

FOR EASE
For sensible menu planning, decide which dishes in your menu can be prepared ahead and frozen.

Remove them from the freezer well in advance, allowing plenty of time for them to thaw. Reheat or cook.

It is a good idea to list the other dishes in the order in which they should be prepared. This ensures that the whole meal will be ready when required.

Most of the menus given on preceding pages are suitable for dinner parties, but the menus that follow are a little more luxurious. Although cheese has not been mentioned, your guests are likely to appreciate a good selection of cheeses at the end of the meal.

However, you may like to offer the cheese before the dessert, French style, especially if the main course is a rather rich one.

Dinner Party Menu 1

Savoury Artichokes
Noisettes of Lamb Hayward
Fried Courgettes (Zucchini), *see page* 90
Green Beans
Peach Shortcake
Serves 6

Serve well-chilled rosé throughout or white wine with the artichokes and a red Burgundy with the lamb.

Savoury Artichokes

Cook 6 globe artichokes (see page 21). Allow to cool and take out the centre choke. For this dish separate the leaves and the artichoke heart.

Make Mayonnaise (see page 104). Add a mixture of chopped fresh herbs to half the mayonnaise; and tomato purée (paste) and chopped basil to the remaining half. Put into small dishes.

Chop a selection of vegetables, such as spring onions (scallions), celery, gherkins or cucumber and green pepper. Mix well and moisten with several tablespoons of Vinaigrette Dressing (see page 105). Serve the dressings as dips for the artichokes.

Noisettes of Lamb Hayward

1 boned and rolled loin of lamb
FOR THE BASTING SAUCE: 1 large kiwifruit
1 garlic clove
2 teaspoons finely chopped root ginger
2 teaspoons soy sauce
1 tablespoon brown sugar
TO GARNISH: 1 to 2 kiwifruit

Tie the loin of lamb at 4 cm/1½ inch intervals, to give 6 noisettes. Peel and mash or liquidize the kiwifruit, peel and crush the garlic. Put the kiwifruit, garlic, root ginger, soy sauce and sugar into a saucepan, stir over the heat for 1 to 2 minutes.

Roast the lamb (for timing see page 59), baste it with the sauce 3 to 4 times (use all the sauce). When cooked, cut the meat into 6 noisettes. To garnish, peel the kiwifruit, slice thinly and place a slice on each noisette.

VARIATION
If root ginger is not available use chopped preserved ginger.

Peach Shortcake

FOR THE SHORTCAKE: 175 g/6 oz (1½ cups) plain (all-purpose) flour
¾ teaspoon baking powder
100 g/4 oz (½ cup) butter or margarine
75 g/3 oz (6 tablespoons) caster sugar
1 egg
FOR THE FILLING AND TOPPING: 6 ripe peaches
150 to 300 ml/¼ to ½ pint (⅔ to 1¼ cups) double (heavy) cream
1 tablespoon sugar
4 tablespoons peach or apricot jam
1 tablespoon lemon juice

**Sift the flour and baking powder into a bowl; rub (cut) in the butter or margarine until the mixture is like fine breadcrumbs. Add the sugar and the egg. Mix with a knife and then with your hands. Knead well.

Grease two 18 to 19 cm/7 to 7½ inch sandwich tins (layer cake pans). Divide the mixture between these and press flat with your fingers. Bake just above the centre of a moderate oven (180°C/350°F, Gas Mark 4) for nearly 20 minutes, or until firm to the touch. Allow to cool for 10 minutes in the tins (pans), for this particular shortcake is very fragile when hot. Turn out and allow to cool.

Skin and slice 3 peaches. Whip the cream, sweeten with the sugar. Spread one shortcake with half the cream, then the sliced peaches. Put on the second shortcake. Sieve the jam and heat gently with the lemon juice.

Skin and slice the remaining peaches. Brush the shortcake with half the jam mixture, then add the peaches and top with remaining jam mixture. Decorate with the remaining cream.

Dinner Party Menu 2

Cucumber and Lemon Sorbet
Sole Combo
Duchesse Potatoes, see page 92
Cream Spinach
Black Forest Gâteau, see page 114
Serves 8

Serve a well chilled rosé with the sorbet, a good white wine with the sole and a sweet Madeira with the gâteau.

Cucumber and Lemon Sorbet

150 ml/¼ pint (⅔ cup) water
75 g/3 oz (6 tablespoons) granulated or caster sugar
1 sprig of mint
1½ teaspoons (1 envelope) gelatine
2 medium cucumbers
2 tablespoons lemon juice
salt and pepper
2 egg whites
TO GARNISH:
6 tablespoons plain yogurt
1 teaspoon tomato purée (paste)
mint leaves

**Place the water, sugar and mint in a saucepan and heat stirring until all the sugar has dissolved. Add the gelatine and stir until dissolved. Peel and dice the cucumbers, place in a blender or food processor with the lemon juice and purée until smooth. If preferred, rub the cucumber through a sieve then mix with the lemon juice.

Remove and discard the sprig of mint

from the syrup. Mix the syrup with the cucumber and lemon purée and season very lightly. Spoon into a freezing tray or shallow container and freeze for about 1 hour, or until the consistency of a thick cream. Turn out into a mixing bowl.

Whisk the egg whites until very stiff, and fold into the semi-frozen cucumber mixture. Return to the freezing container and continue freezing until firm. Blend the yogurt and tomato purée (paste). Place scoops of the sorbet in well-chilled serving dishes and top with the tomato-flavoured yogurt and mint.

Sole Combo

8 sole fillets
salt and pepper
225 g/8 oz (1⅓ cups) peeled (shelled) prawns (shrimp)
50 g/2 oz (¼ cup) butter
300 ml/½ pint (1¼ cups) milk
25 g/1 oz (¼ cup) flour
3 tablespoons double (heavy) cream
FOR THE TURMERIC RICE:
450 ml/¾ pint (2 cups) water (generous measure)
pinch of turmeric
225 g/8 oz (generous 1 cup) long-grain rice
TO GARNISH
4 cucumber slices
parsley sprigs

Skin the fish fillets, if not already done by the fishmonger. Season each fillet very lightly. Use about half the prawns (shrimp) and place a few on each sole fillet; fold the fish to enclose the prawns (shrimp). Spread a shallow casserole with 15 g/½ oz (1 tablespoon) butter; add the fish and 2 tablespoons of the milk. Top with another 15 g/½ oz (1 tablespoon) butter and foil or a lid. Place above the centre of a preheated moderately hot oven (190 to 200°C/375 to 400°F, Gas Mark 5 to 6) and bake for 20 to 25 minutes or until the fish is quite tender.

Meanwhile, make the white sauce and cook the rice. Heat the remaining butter in a pan, stir in the flour and cook over a low heat for 2 to 3 minutes. Gradually stir in the rest of the milk and the cream. Bring to the boil, stirring all the time until the sauce thickens. Chop approximately 50 g/2 oz (⅓ cup) prawns (shrimp). Add to the sauce with a little seasoning.

Put the water, turmeric and rice into a pan. Bring the water to the boil and stir briskly with a fork. Cover the pan, lower the heat and cook for 15 minutes or until all the liquid has been absorbed.

Arrange the rice on a heated dish. Arrange the fish on top of the rice; top with the remaining prawns (shrimp), the cucumber slices and parsley.

Dinner Party Menu 3

Smoked Trout Pâté, see page 25
Steak with Béarnaise Sauce, see pages 53 and 195
Croquette Potatoes, see page 92
Leaf Spinach
Gooseberry Mint Sorbet and/or Old English Fruit Trifle
Serves 6

This is planned as a non-alcoholic menu, so offer well chilled fruit drinks, mineral and tonic waters.

Gooseberry Mint Sorbet

**Make a syrup by boiling 150 ml/¼ pint (⅔ cup) water with 100 g/4 oz (½ cup) sugar. Put 225 to 350 g/8 to 12 oz (1½ to 2¼ cups) gooseberries into a pan with 150 ml/¼ pint (⅔ cup) water and 1 to 2 teaspoons of lemon juice. Simmer until the fruit is tender then sieve or blend. Add to the syrup, with a few drops of peppermint essence (extract). Freeze lightly, then whisk 2 egg whites until stiff. Fold into the half frozen mixture and continue freezing.

VARIATION
If freezing the sorbet (sherbet) for any length of time, dissolve 1 teaspoon of gelatine in the hot syrup.

Old English Fruit Trifle

Follow the directions for traditional Sherry Trifle (see page 202) but omit the sherry and add about 450 g/1 lb cooked or canned fruit with a little fruit syrup to moisten the trifle sponge cakes. Cherries were used in the trifle shown in the picture. A few drops of ratafia essence (extract) will add flavour to the fruit syrup used to moisten the sponge cakes.

FREEZING NOTE
**It is best to freeze the Peach Shortcake without the filling and topping. The biscuit base is very crisp but the filling would cause it to soften on thawing.

Allow the two layers of shortcake to thaw, then fill and top as suggested in the recipe. If the shortcake has softened slightly, crisp for a few minutes in the oven. Allow to cool then fill and top.*

Gooseberry Mint Sorbet and Old English Fruit Trifle from Dinner Party Menu 3

Smoked Mackerel with Scrambled Egg from Dinner Party Menu 5

Dinner Party Menu 4

Minted Melon Basket, see page 20

Zested Bacon and Veal Paupiettes

Rice – Ratatouille, see page 203

Soufflé Italienne, see page 120 with Marmalade Sauce or Coffee Walnut Bombe, see page 117

Serves 4

Serve a medium sherry, medium sweet Madeira or a white wine, with the melon. Serve a very dry white wine with the main course.

Zested Bacon and Veal Paupiettes

FOR THE PAUPIETTES:
450 g/1 lb veal fillet (tenderloin)

1 teaspoon grated lemon rind

100 g/4 oz (2 cups) soft breadcrumbs

4 tablespoons chopped mixed herbs (the ideal combination is basil, marjoram, parsley and sage)

salt and pepper

1 egg white

8 prime back bacon rashers (Canadian bacon slices)

FOR THE SAUCE:
2 tablespoons oil

25 g/1 oz (2 tablespoons) butter

2 tablespoons lemon juice

300 ml/½ pint (1¼ cups) veal or chicken stock

1 teaspoon cornflour (cornstarch)

4 tablespoons single (light) cream

1 egg yolk

TO GARNISH:
chopped mixed herbs

lemon wedges

✲✲Mince (grind) the veal or chop in a food processor. Combine with the lemon rind, breadcrumbs, herbs and seasoning. Whisk the egg white lightly, add to the veal mixture, then divide this into 8 portions.

Make into balls, then flatten with your hands. De-rind the bacon if necessary and wrap 1 rasher (slice) around each paupiette. Secure the bacon with a wooden cocktail stick (toothpick) or tie with a piece of cotton.

Heat the oil and butter in a pan. Fry the paupiettes for 3 minutes, turn and fry on the other side. Add the lemon juice and most of the stock to the pan, season lightly, cover the pan and simmer for 15 to 20 minutes. Remove the paupiettes to a heated serving dish and take away the cocktail sticks (toothpicks) or cotton. Blend the teaspoon of cornflour (cornstarch) with the remaining stock and stir into the liquid remaining in the pan. Cook until thickened. Whisk the cream and egg yolk together, pour 2 to 3 tablespoons of the hot sauce over the cream and egg yolk mixture. Return to the pan and cook slowly without boiling for several minutes. Spoon over the paupiettes and top with herbs. Garnish with lemon.

Soufflé Italienne

The soufflé can be mixed, put into the soufflé dish, covered completely and allowed to stand for 1 hour before being baked, (see page 131).

Marmalade Sauce

Put 5 tablespoons orange or lemon marmalade and 3 tablespoons orange or lemon juice into a saucepan. Blend 1½ teaspoons arrowroot or cornflour (cornstarch) with 5 tablespoons water, add to the pan together with 2 tablespoons sugar. Stir over a low heat until the marmalade melts, then continue stirring until the sauce has thickened and become clear.

Serve hot over Soufflé Italienne or allow to cool and serve over ice cream. Jam Sauce Use jam in place of marmalade.

Dinner Party Menu 5

The following dishes are based on traditional Norwegian specialities. In this menu the Arctic Chicken with Prawns has to be fried at the last minute. If this is inconvenient fry the ingredients for a short time earlier in the day, add the sour cream and prawns (shrimp). Place in a serving dish and cover with foil. To serve, heat in a preheated moderately hot oven (190°C/375°F, Gas Mark 5) for about 25 minutes.

The Veal Paupiettes in the menu above can also be prepared in advance and heated in this way.

Smoked Mackerel or Salmon with Scrambled Egg, see page 23

Consommé, see page 32

Arctic Chicken with Prawns

Boiled Potatoes

Green Beans

Blötkaka

Serves 6

Serve aquavit at the beginning of the meal then a dry white wine with the Arctic Chicken with Prawns. A sweet white wine would be a good accompaniment to the Blötkaka.

Arctic Chicken with Prawns

6 chicken breasts

25 g/1 oz (2 tablespoons) butter

3 tablespoons oil

225 g/8 oz (2 cups) mushrooms

1 tablespoon lemon juice

150 ml/¼ pint (⅔ cup) soured cream

225 ml/7½ fl oz (scant 1 cup) dry white wine

225 g/8 oz (1⅓ cups) peeled (shelled) prawns (shrimp)

salt and pepper

TO GARNISH:
parsley sprigs and chopped parsley

Bone the chicken breasts. Heat the butter and oil in a large frying pan (skillet), add the chicken joints and fry gently for about 12 to 15 minutes until golden brown and tender. Lift on to a heated serving dish, cover and keep hot. Put the mushrooms and lemon juice into the pan, turn in the hot butter and oil mixture for about ½ minute then add the soured cream and wine. Heat gently for about 10 minutes. Do not allow to boil. Stir several times during this period. Add most of the prawns (shrimp) and a little seasoning. Simmer for a few minutes and spoon over the hot chicken. Top with the remainder of the prawns (shrimp) and garnish with parsley.

Blötkaka

✲✲Whisk together 4 large eggs and 150 g/5 oz (10 tablespoons) caster sugar, until thick and creamy. Sift 110 g/4 oz (1 cup) self-raising flour. Fold gently and carefully into the whisked egg mixture. Spoon into a lined and greased 23 cm/9 inch cake tin (pan) and bake in the centre of a preheated moderate oven (180°C/350°F, Gas Mark 4) for 35 minutes or until firm to a gentle touch.

Split the cooled cake into 3 layers. Fill with jam, sliced fruits and whipped cream, top with more cream and fruit. Note Plain (all-purpose) flour may be used, but add 1 teaspoon baking powder.

Countdown to Christmas Entertaining

Family and friends tend to pop in for drinks through the festive season. If your guests will be joining you for a meal after an aperitif the only food you need serve are dishes of small gherkins and/or olives and/or salted nuts and cocktail onions.

If you have invited friends to a cocktail or drinks party serve a selection of canapés and tit-bits.

Salted Nuts

Nuts are sold salted or dry roasted but it is more economical to buy ready-shelled nuts (those sold in Health Food Stores are particularly good) and salt them.

To salt nuts Heat a little butter in a large frying pan (skillet). Toss the nuts in the hot butter until evenly coated. Remove from the pan then toss in salt. Allow to cool, then shake away any surplus salt.

Pastry Canapés

✳✳Miniature Savoury Choux Puffs (see page 152). Fill as suggested.

✳✳Cheese Pastry Canapés Prepare Cheese Pastry (see page 144), roll out thinly and cut into tiny shapes. Place on a lightly greased baking sheet and bake just above the centre of a preheated moderately hot oven (200°C/400°F, Gas Mark 6) for 10 to 15 minutes. Allow to cool. Store in an airtight tin or freeze until ready to use.

To Serve Pipe rosettes of Savoury Butters (see page 101) on to pastry shapes and garnish with sliced olives, cocktail onions, small peeled (shelled) prawns (shrimp) or portions of anchovy fillet.

Pastry shapes can be used instead of bread and butter, see right.

✳✳Miniature Savoury Tartlets Line tiny boat-shaped or round patty tins (pans) with Shortcrust (Basic Pie Dough) or Cheese Pastry. Bake blind (see page 146). Allow to cool. Fill just before serving with a thick mayonnaise and diced cooked chicken, prawns (shrimp). flaked salmon, or diced cooked mushroom mixture.

Bacon Bites

Hot bacon savouries can be made by wrapping streaky bacon rashers (slices) around various fillings such as cooked prunes, frankfurters, cheese and large peeled (shelled) prawns (shrimp) and grilling (broiling) lightly (see below). Serve as wide a selection as possible and garnish with stuffed olives and gherkin slices.

☐ Stone (pit) cooked prunes, drain well (the centre can be filled with blanched almonds or liver pâté).

☐ Cut frankfurters into bite-sized pieces (each piece can be split and filled with mustard or chutney).

☐ Dice the cheese – you can use Gouda, Camembert or Cheddar or any good cooking cheese.

To Cook De-rind the bacon and stretch the rashers (slices) with the back of a knife to lengthen the bacon and make it more pliable. Cut each rasher (slice) into 3 to 4 pieces, depending on the size of the filling. Roll the bacon around the various foods, and secure each roll with a cocktail stick (toothpick).

Either grill (broil) the bacon rolls or place in an ovenproof serving dish and bake towards the top of a preheated moderately hot to hot oven (200 to 220°C/400 to 425°F, Gas Mark 6 to 7) for barely 10 minutes.

Hot Canapés

✳✳Baked Miniature Bouchées Bake the pastry cases and prepare the fillings (see page 151). Warm both the pastry and the fillings but fill the cases just before your guests arrive. Serve hot.

✳✳Pizzas and Quiches Bake a selection (see pages 134 and 135). Cut into bite-sized pieces. Heat for a few minutes just before your guests arrive.

Savoury Scones Make a Welsh Rarebit mixture (see page 133) and miniature Cheese and Parsley Scones (see page 159), but omit the parsley. Halve and butter the cooked scones. Spread with the Welsh Rarebit mixture and arrange on an ovenproof serving dish. Bake in the centre of a preheated hot oven (220°C/425°F, Gas Mark 7) for 4 to 5 minutes only or under a preheated grill (broiler) for 2 minutes. Serve hot.

Fried Food Deep fry tiny new unskinned potatoes, small button mushrooms, coated scampi or large prawns (shrimp). Put them on to cocktail sticks and serve with a bowl of Tartare Sauce.

Bread and Butter Canapés

Really fresh white, brown, wholewheat or pumpernickel breads are far better for canapés than toast, which becomes soggy. Cut the bread into neat shapes (pastry cutters are ideal for this), spread with butter and then a topping.

☐ Smoked salmon topped with small pieces of lemon.

☐ Cooked salmon blended with mayonnaise, with twists of cucumber.

☐ Pâtés of various kinds, topped with sliced olives, gherkin fans or small pieces of tomato or red pepper.

☐ Cream cheese topped with halved grapes, olives or pieces of pineapple.

☐ Lightly scrambled egg blended with chopped smoked salmon, prawns (shrimp), ham or anchovy fillets.

☐ Smoked trout or mackerel, topped with a little horseradish cream.

☐ Rings of raw Spanish onion, topped with mayonnaise and grated cheese.

Salted Nuts, Fried Food for dips and Pastry Canapés

MICROWAVE COOKING

Hot Canapés
Prepare and cook as suggested below and arrange on serving plates. Cover lightly with plastic wrap. Heat for a few seconds in the microwave cooker before serving.

FOR SLIMMERS

Crudités (see page 27) are ideal for slimmers. Choose celery, radishes, carrots and serve with low-calorie dressing (see page 181).

Catering for Christmas

Christmas is the time of the year when most cooks find themselves catering for both family and friends, not just for a meal but often for several days. In addition to Christmas Day fare you will find menus suitable for Boxing Day and general festive entertaining, a happy blend of traditional recipes and new ideas.

Many of the dishes can be prepared in advance and frozen to give the busy cook a relatively leisurely Christmas period.

Christmas Eve

This is a busy evening and your guests may be arriving at different times, so why not have a simple and informal buffet meal? Various pâtés and dips would be ideal. In addition to the recipes on this page there are other dips and pâtés on pages 24 and 25. As so much poultry and meat are eaten at Christmas time it is a good idea to serve fresh or smoked fish (see page 23), with salads, vegetables and fresh fruit.

Curried Corn Dip

50 g/2 oz Cheddar cheese
1 tablespoon mayonnaise
1 to 2 teaspoons curry paste or curry powder
100 g/4 oz (½ cup) cottage cheese
150 ml/¼ pint (⅔ cup) soured cream
50 g/2 oz (⅓ cup) cooked or canned sweetcorn
salt and pepper

Grate the Cheddar cheese. Blend the mayonnaise with the curry paste or powder and the cottage cheese and grated cheese. Add the remaining ingredients. Spoon into a bowl. Serves 4.

Pâté Dip

175 g/6 oz (¾ cup) cottage cheese
225 g/8 oz liver pâté, see page 24
1 tablespoon finely chopped chives
1 tablespoon chopped parsley
2 tablespoons yogurt
1 teaspoon Worcestershire sauce
TO GARNISH: 2 gherkins

Sieve the cottage cheese, in order to give the dip a smooth texture. Blend all the ingredients together. Spoon into a dish.

Cut the gherkins into small dice, sprinkle over the dip. Serves 6 to 8.

VARIATION

Paprika Dip Finely chop 2 small onions and 2 gherkins. Mix with 225 g/8 oz curd or cottage cheese, 2 tablespoons cream, 2 teaspoons paprika, salt, pepper, garlic salt and 2 to 3 tablespoons mayonnaise depending on the consistency.

Salmon and Cucumber Dip

2 eggs
225 g/8 oz cooked or canned salmon
3 tablespoons grated cucumber
2 tablespoons mayonnaise
1 tablespoon lemon juice
1 teaspoon chopped fennel leaves or parsley
a little double (heavy) cream
salt and pepper
TO GARNISH: 2 teaspoons chopped fennel leaves or parsley

Hard-boil (hard-cook) and finely chop the eggs. Drain the fish carefully and flake. Mix all the ingredients except the cream together. Gradually stir in sufficient cream to give the correct consistency and season well. Spoon into a dish and garnish with the herbs. Serves 4 to 6.

Christmas Day

Many of the traditional dishes can be made some weeks ahead and frozen (look for the freezing symbol ❄).

Make the sauces and stuffings well ahead and allow plenty of time for a frozen turkey to defrost (see page 77). Vegetables can be prepared the night before and kept in plastic bags in the refrigerator or in cold water.

The Christmas Pudding should be prepared early so that it has time to mature in flavour. Other puddings can be made in advance too.

Christmas Dinner Menu

Prawn and Apple Cocktail or Melon or Grapefruit Cocktail

Traditional Stuffed Turkey

Roast Potatoes – Peas – Green Beans Brussels Sprouts with Chestnuts

Christmas Pudding

Mince Pies or Star Mince Tart, see page 204

Rum Butter or Hard Brandy Sauce

Cheeses

Fruit, Nuts and Almond Clusters

Serves 6

Serve a light white wine with the cocktail. Red or white wine can be served with the turkey.

FOR EASE
If you have no other means of keeping cooked food hot, fill a large roasting pan with water and stand over a low heat on top of the cooker. Spoon the vegetables and sauces into their serving dishes, cover and stand in the hot water. The liquid in the pan should be at simmering point. Place a large sheet of foil over the dishes and the pan to prevent evaporation.

Preparing for Christmas

Prawn and Apple Cocktails

2 dessert apples
2 tablespoons lemon juice
I red pepper
175 g/6 oz (1 cup) peeled (shelled) prawns (shrimps)
6 tablespoons mayonnaise
¼ small lettuce

Quarter the apples. Remove the peel and core from 1½ apples. Do not peel the remaining half but cut into 4 neat slices. Dice the peeled apples. Put the sliced and diced fruit into the lemon juice and leave until needed.

Dice three-quarters of the pepper and cut the remaining quarter into 4 slices, discarding the core and seeds. Mix together the prawns (shrimp), diced apple and diced pepper. Mix with the mayonnaise and any remaining lemon juice.

Shred the lettuce very finely and put into 6 glasses. Top with the prawn (shrimp) mixture. Garnish with the apple and pepper slices.

Serving the Turkey

The information on roasting turkey is on page 78 together with the traditional accompaniments. There are however more original sauces and stuffings in the relevant section (see page 100).

If you do not like stuffings, you may like to serve the turkey with a filling of skinned, halved and de-seeded grapes. Roast in the usual way, garnish with

unskinned grapes and spoon the grapes out of the bird to serve.

The poultry and meat sections of this book give details of other types of poultry, game and meat which you may prefer to serve at Christmas.

Vegetables

The vegetables given in the menu are a popular choice at Christmas time, but Braised Celery (see page 94) is another good accompaniment, and so are sweet potatoes or yams (see right).

If serving Brussels sprouts and chestnuts, cook them separately or the peeled chestnuts will turn the sprouts a strange blue colour. Slit the chestnuts, simmer in water for 10 minutes then remove the skins and cook in simmering salted water, or in stock, for a further 20 minutes. Strain, toss in butter and mix with the cooked sprouts.

Golden Christmas Pudding

This recipe produces a lovely golden pudding, which is a change from the usual rich dark one. However, you can use this basic recipe to give a dark pudding (see Variation). The cooking time will be the same.

450 g/1 lb (2⅔ cups) dried apricots
50 g/2 oz (½ cup) blanched almonds
100 g/4 oz (½ cup) glacé cherries
350 g/12 oz (2 cups) light sultanas (golden raisins)

100 g/4 oz (⅔ cup) chopped candied peel
100 g/4 oz (¾ cup) grated raw carrots
175 g/6 oz (3 cups) soft white breadcrumbs
75 g/3 oz (¾ cup) plain (all-purpose) flour
175 g/6 oz (¾ cup) melted butter
175 g/6 oz (¾ cup) caster sugar
4 eggs
I teaspoon grated orange rind
I teaspoon grated lemon rind
150 ml/¼ pint (⅔ cup) dry sherry
4 tablespoons (¼ cup) orange juice

✳Chop the dried apricots, almonds and cherries. Mix with the light sultanas (golden raisins), chopped candied peel and grated raw carrots.

Mix together the soft white breadcrumbs, plain flour, melted butter and caster sugar. Add to the fruit mixture with the eggs, grated lemon and orange rind, dry sherry and orange juice.

Divide between two 1.5 to 1.8 litre/2½ to 3 pint (6 to 7 cup) greased pudding basins (molds). Cover well and steam for 6 hours. Serve one pudding and freeze the other.

VARIATION

Traditional Dark Pudding Use 350 g/ 12 oz (2 cups) seedless raisins and 225 g/ 8 oz (1⅓ cups) currants instead of the apricots. Use dark brown sugar instead of caster sugar; beer instead of sherry; and rum, brandy or dark sherry instead of orange juice. You can use shredded suet in place of the melted butter.

Rum Butter

✳Cream 50 g/2 oz (¼ cup) butter, sift in 100 g/4 oz (1 cup) icing (confectioners') sugar and beat well. Continue beating until soft and light then gradually beat in 2 tablespoons rum. Serve with Christmas Pudding or Mince Pies.

Hard Brandy Sauce

✳Cream together 75 g/3 oz (6 tablespoons) margarine and 75 g/3 oz (6 tablespoons) caster sugar, then gradually beat in 2 to 3 tablespoons brandy and the finely grated rind of ½ orange. Chill well.

Almond Clusters

Pour I tablespoon orange juice into a bowl, add 50 g/2 oz (⅓ cup) seedless raisins and leave to soak overnight.

Melt 100 g/4 oz (¾ cup) milk chocolate in a bowl over hot water. Add 25 g/ I oz (2 tablespoons) margarine, when melted, cool and mix in the orange-moistened raisins and 50 g/2 oz (½ cup) flaked toasted almonds. Spoon teaspoonfuls of the mixture into tiny paper cases. Dry uncovered then cover and store in the refrigerator. Makes 36.

SIMPLE SKILL
To Ignite Brandy
To warm the brandy, or other spirit, to pour over the Christmas Pudding, pour the required quantity (about 3 tablespoons) into a jug and stand in a bowl of very hot water, well away from the cooker, until it is just pleasantly warm. Pour over the hot pudding and ignite.

FOR FLAVOUR
Sweet Potatoes or Yams
These are extremely good with turkey. They can be cooked and mashed or roasted. Check the roasting time carefully; they have a high sugar content and burn easily.
Sweet Potato and Apples
Peel and thinly slice 450 g/1 lb sweet potatoes. Cook for 3 to 4 minutes in boiling salted water. Strain and dry. Peel and thinly slice 350 g/12 oz cooking (tart) apples. Heat 50 g/ 2 oz (¼ cup) butter in a pan. Add the potatoes and apples and fry steadily until just tender. Sprinkle the mixture with I to 2 tablespoons brown sugar and 2 tablespoons sweet sherry towards the end of the cooking time. This dish is also excellent with duck or pork. Serves 6 to 8.

FOR EASE
To Toast Almonds
Spread the nuts on a baking sheet and place in a preheated moderate oven (180°C/350°F, Gas Mark 4) for a short time until golden. They can also be toasted under a preheated grill (broiler) but check the heat is very low.

Christmas Day Supper

Vichyssoise see page 34 or Ratatouille see page 203

A selection of cold meats and salads

Sherry Trifle or Blötkaka, see page 198

Cheese, celery and nuts

Chocolate Truffles

Serves 6

Many people enjoy a chilled beer as a change from wines. Have plenty of soft drinks available. A Pouilly Fumé white wine has a pleasantly refreshing flavour.

A cold buffet with cold turkey, other poultry or meat and interesting salads makes an excellent Christmas Day supper. The Pineapple Coleslaw (see page 193), a Rice Salad (see page 95) and a Celery and Peanut Salad (see page 96) are particularly suitable. The Jellied Russian Salad (see page 203) looks most colourful.

If you would like to start the meal with soup, Vichyssoise (see page 34) is cool and refreshing. Ratatouille (see page 203) makes a good cold hors d'oeuvre as well as a delicious hot vegetable. Both these dishes can be made in advance and frozen.

A traditional Sherry Trifle is part of 'real' Christmas fare for most people but you can serve a Blötkaka or a selection of festive desserts (see photograph below).

Offer your guests a good selection of cheeses with crisp celery and nuts and port.

Sherry Trifle

Split 6 to 8 trifle sponges (individual dessert sponge shells). Sandwich them together with raspberry or apricot jam, place in a serving dish and moisten with plenty of sweet sherry or, if preferred, with sherry mixed with a little syrup from canned peaches, pears or other fruit. Top with flaked blanched almonds and ratafias then 600 ml/1 pint (2½ cups) of custard.

Homemade custard is best and can be made by cooking 3 whole eggs or 4 egg yolks with 450 ml/¾ pint (2 cups) milk, 150 ml/¼ pint (⅔ cup) single (light) cream, a little vanilla essence and 50 g/2 oz (¼ cup) sugar very slowly in a bowl over simmering water until thick. Pour the warm custard over the sponge cakes. Cover the dish with plastic wrap to prevent a skin forming. Allow to cool.

Whip 300 ml/½ pint (1¼ cups) whipping cream, pipe or spread over the custard, top with ratafias, glacé or Maraschino cherries and leaves of angelica. Flaked blanched almonds could be scattered over the top of the trifle.

VARIATION

Use custard made with custard powder (Bird's English dessert mix) instead of egg yolks.

Chocolate Truffles

125 g/4½ oz (¾ cup) plain (semi-sweet) chocolate
2 tablespoons brandy
40 g/1½ oz (3 tablespoons) margarine
50 g/2 oz (½ cup) ground almonds
50 g/2 oz (½ cup) sifted icing (confectioners') sugar
Chocolate vermicelli (sprinkles) or sifted (unsweetened) cocoa powder

Melt the chocolate in a bowl over hot water. Add the brandy, mix well then cool slightly. Beat in the margarine, ground almonds and sifted icing (confectioners') sugar. Mix thoroughly. Form the mixture into 18 small balls. Roll in chocolate vermicelli (sprinkles) or sifted (unsweetened) cocoa powder. Place in small paper cases. Makes 18.

VARIATION

Use rum in place of the brandy.

Boxing Day

Roast lamb is a good choice for Boxing Day, as it makes a change from poultry. The redcurrant glaze and cool green sauce (see recipe below) makes the Glazed Lamb a little special.

When using up leftover turkey you can make a hot turkey meal by adding diced turkey to a Chasseur Sauce (see below), or by serving diced meat in a Mayonnaise flavoured with a little curry.

Boxing Day Menu

Turkey in Chasseur Sauce or

Glazed Lamb with Kiwi Mint Sauce

Country Potatoes

Ratatouille

Jellied Russian Salad

Mont Blanc or

Iced Christmas Pudding

Serves 6

After the luxury of Christmas consider the more economical wines from Germany, Italy and California. Both the lamb and the turkey dish need a dry red wine.

Turkey in Chasseur Sauce

✲✲Sieve or blend an Espagnole Sauce until smooth (see page 103).

Peel 1 medium onion, chop or slice this neatly. Slice 50 to 100 g/2 to 4 oz (½ to 1 cup) mushrooms. Heat 25 g/1 oz (2 tablespoons) butter in a pan, fry the onion and mushrooms for 5 minutes, add 6 tablespoons dry white wine, 1 tablespoon tomato purée (paste) and the Espagnole Sauce. Simmer for 5 minutes.

Put enough cooked turkey for 6 people into the sauce and heat thoroughly. Spoon into a heated serving dish and top with a generous amount of chopped parsley.

VARIATION

Put the turkey and sauce into a casserole and heat for a short time in the oven. Serve with Country Potatoes and Ratatouille (see below).

Country Potatoes

Peel and thinly slice 750 g/1½ lb potatoes. Arrange in an ovenproof dish. Heat 300 ml/½ pint (1¼ cups) milk with 50 g/2 oz (¼ cup) margarine and seasoning. Pour over the potatoes and bake in the centre of a moderate oven (180°C/350°F, Gas Mark 4) for 1¼ hours. Top with chopped parsley.

Ratatouille

✲✲Slice 3 medium aubergines (eggplant), and 3 courgettes (zucchini). Peel and slice 2 large onions and 1 garlic clove. Slice 1 green pepper, discarding the core and seeds. Skin and slice or quarter 6 medium tomatoes.

Melt 75 g/3 oz (6 tablespoons) margarine in a large pan, cook the onions, garlic and pepper for 5 minutes. Add the rest of the ingredients together with salt and pepper and a bouquet garni. Cover the pan and cook gently for 30 minutes. Remove the bouquet garni and top with chopped parsley, if desired. Serve hot or cold.

VARIATION

✲✲Courgettes Niçoise Omit the aubergines (eggplant) and use 450 g/1 lb courgettes (zucchini) instead.

Glazed Lamb with Kiwi Mint Sauce

| 1 leg of lamb |
| 3 tablespoons redcurrant jelly |
| **FOR THE SAUCE:**
3 to 4 kiwifruit |
| 1 teaspoon lemon juice |
| 1 teaspoon sugar |
| 3 tablespoons finely chopped mint |
| **TO GARNISH:**
1 kiwifruit |
| mint leaves |

Weigh and roast the lamb according to the timing on page 59, but brush with the warmed redcurrant jelly 3 to 4 times during the cooking period.

Peel the kiwifruit, mash with a fork or liquidize. Mix with the lemon juice, sugar and chopped mint leaves. Garnish the joint with peeled sliced kiwifruit and add the whole mint leaves to the sauce.

Jellied Russian Salad

| 150 ml/¼ pint (⅔ cup) white wine |
| 15 g/½ oz (2 envelopes) gelatine |
| 150 ml/¼ pint (⅔ cup) mayonnaise |
| 150 ml/¼ pint (⅔ cup) plain yogurt |
| 450 g/1 lb (2½ cups) cooked diced vegetables, see Note |
| salt and pepper |
| 2 tablespoons chopped parsley |
| lettuce |
| watercress |

Pour the wine into a bowl and sprinkle the gelatine on top. Place the bowl over a saucepan of hot water and allow to dissolve, then chill for a short time. Blend the cold gelatine and wine with the mayonnaise and yogurt and the vegetables, season well and add the parsley. Put into an oiled 1.5 litre/2½ pint (6 cup) mould, chill until firm, turn out and serve on a bed of lettuce and watercress.

Note Choose a colourful mixture of vegetables, such as carrots, swedes (rutabaga), green beans and peas.

Mont Blanc

| 50 g/2 oz (½ cup) icing (confectioners') sugar |
| ¼ teaspoon vanilla essence (extract) |
| 1 × 425 g/15 oz can unsweetened chestnut purée |
| **TO DECORATE:**
25 g/1 oz (¼ cup) icing (confectioners') sugar |

✲✲Sift the 50 g/2 oz (½ cup) icing (confectioners') sugar, mix with the vanilla essence (extract) and chestnut purée. Do not overbeat the mixture for it should not become sticky. Spoon the mixture into a piping (pastry) bag fitted with a large nozzle and pipe the mixture into a large pyramid shape.

Sift the remaining icing (confectioners') sugar over the top. Serve with well chilled cream or ice cream.

Iced Christmas Pudding

| 150 ml/¼ pint (⅔ cup) milk |
| 100 g/4 oz (1⅓ cup) marshmallows |
| 1 teaspoon (unsweetened) cocoa powder |
| 1 teaspoon instant coffee powder |
| 50 g/2 oz (⅓ cup) raisins |
| 25 g/1 oz (3 tablespoons) sultanas (golden raisins) |
| 25 g/1 oz (3 tablespoons) currants |
| 2 tablespoons sherry |
| 50 g/2 oz (¼ cup) Maraschino cherries |
| 50 g/2 oz (½ cup) nuts |
| 300 ml/½ pint (1¼ cups) double (heavy) cream |
| 25 g/1 oz (¼ cup) icing (confectioners') sugar (optional) |
| **TO DECORATE:**
few Maraschino cherries |

✲✲Put the milk, marshmallows, cocoa and coffee into a saucepan. Heat gently until the marshmallows are nearly melted. Allow the mixture to cool. Meanwhile mix the dried fruits with the sherry. Allow to stand for 30 minutes then add to the marshmallow mixture. Dice the cherries, chop the nuts and mix with the marshmallow mixture. Pour into a freezing tray and freeze for a short time until slightly thickened. Whip the cream until it just holds its shape. If you like a very sweet ice cream, sift the icing (confectioners') sugar and stir into the cream; fold the cream into the ice cream. Spoon into a 1.2 litre/2 pint (1 quart) bowl (pudding mold). Freeze until firm. Turn out, decorate with the cherries and serve with whipped cream.

FREEZING NOTE
To freeze cheese
✲✲*All cheeses, with the exception of cottage cheese, which becomes damp and unappetizing, can be frozen to save wastage.*

If you have frozen a selection of cheeses, use up the soft creamy type first. The harder cheeses are less affected by freezing.

Allow adequate time for the cheese to return to room temperature. This process can be speeded up by using a microwave cooker on defrost setting.

Use all the cheeses as soon as possible since a freezer is not the ideal place for cheese.

Festive Tea

Most of us want a light tea after the traditional Christmas lunch. Fortunately the various Christmas tea-time goodies keep well so are never wasted. The small Viennese Tartlets and Bûche de Noel freeze well for up to 3 months. The sweetmeats shown in the picture make excellent presents.

Star Mince Tart, Mince Pies, Chocolate Truffles (page 202), Cumberland Toffee. Almond Clusters (page 201) and Viennese Tartlets

Viennese Tartlets

175 g/6 oz (¾ cup) margarine
50 g/2 oz (¼ cup) caster sugar
½ teaspoon vanilla essence (extract)
175 g/6 oz (1½ cups) plain (all-purpose) flour
glacé cherries

⁂Cream together the margarine and caster sugar with vanilla essence (extract) until soft and light. Sift flour into the creamed mixture, and gradually stir in with a wooden spoon. Spoon the mixture into a piping (pastry) bag filled with a large star nozzle. Pipe small star shapes into small paper cases. Top with pieces of cherry, place on a flat baking sheet and bake in the centre of a preheated moderate oven (180°C/350°F, Gas Mark 4) for 12 to 15 minutes. Allow tartlets to become quite cold before packing away. Makes 36 to 40.

Bûche de Noel

3 large eggs
100 g/4 oz (½ cup) caster sugar
75 g/3 oz (¾ cup) self-raising flour
25 g/1 oz (2 tablespoons) melted butter
FOR THE COATING:
100 g/4 oz (¾ cup) plain (semi-sweet) chocolate
175 g/6 oz (¾ cup) butter
175 g/6 oz (1½ cups) sifted icing (confectioners') sugar

⁂Whisk together the eggs and caster sugar until thick and creamy. Sift the flour and fold gently and carefully into the egg mixture together with the melted butter. Pour the mixture into a Swiss roll tin (jelly roll pan) measuring 23 × 28 cm/9 × 11 inches. Bake towards the top of a preheated moderately hot oven (190 to 200°C/375 to 400°F, Gas Mark 5 to 6) for about 9 minutes or until firm to a gentle touch. Turn out on to sugared paper and roll up with grease-proof (waxed) paper inside, so the sponge does not stick. Allow to cool.
To make the coating Melt the chocolate in a bowl over hot water, allow to cool, then beat in the butter and sifted icing

(confectioners') sugar.
Unroll the sponge. Use just under half the coating to spread over the sponge, roll up again then coat the outside of the roll with the remaining chocolate mixture. Mark lines in the icing with a fine skewer so the roll looks like a tree trunk. Dust with sifted icing (confectioners') sugar and decorate with a small piece of holly. Chill well, so the icing and filling set.
Note Plain (all-purpose) flour may be used, but add ¾ teaspoon baking powder.

Star Mince Tart

350 g/12 oz (3 cups) plain (all-purpose) flour
175 g/6 oz (¾ cup) margarine
75 g/3 oz (6 tablespoons) caster sugar
2 egg yolks
few drops of vanilla essence (extract)
450 g/1 lb (2 cups) mincemeat, see right
FOR THE DECORATION:
sifted icing (confectioners') sugar
glacé cherries
angelica

⁂Make Pâté Sucrée with plain (all-purpose) flour, margarine, caster sugar and egg yolks mixed with a few drops of vanilla (see page 145). Cover and chill. Roll out half the pastry and line a 20 cm/8 inch fluted flan ring or dish. Fill with mincemeat. Roll out remaining pastry and cut a large star shape from the centre. Lift the pastry carefully over the filling. Seal the edges and neaten them. Bake in the centre of a preheated moderately hot oven (190°C/375°F, Gas Mark 5) for 30 to 40 minutes or until golden in colour. Decorate with sifted icing (confectioners') sugar, glacé cherries and small leaves of angelica. Serve hot or cold. Serves 6 to 8.

Mince Pies

⁂Use half the amount of pastry given in Star Mince Tart. Roll out thinly and line 9 deep patty (tartlet) tins (pans), spoon in a little mincemeat, then cover with rounds of pastry (slightly smaller than the bases). Seal the edges, make two slits in the pastry lids and bake in a pre-heated moderately hot oven (190°C/375°F, Gas Mark 5) for about 20 minutes. Dust with caster or icing (confectioners') sugar. Makes 9.

Mincemeat

Mincemeat keeps well and the following recipe will give sufficient to make the Star Mince Tart and the 9 mince pies, with plenty left over for more mince pies after Christmas.

100 g/4 oz (½ cup) melted margarine or shredded suet
100 g/4 oz (1⅓ cups) cooking apples
100 g/4 oz (⅔ cup) candied peel
50 to 100 g/2 to 4 oz (½ to 1 cup), blanched almonds
50 to 100 g/2 to 4 oz (¼ to ½ cup) glacé cherries
100 g/4 oz (⅔ cup) light brown sugar
450 g/1 lb (3 cups) mixed dried fruit
finely grated rind and juice of 1 lemon
½ to 1 teaspoon mixed spice
1 teaspoon ground cinnamon
pinch of grated nutmeg
4 tablespoons rum, whisky or brandy

⁂Peel and grate the apples. Chop the candied peel (if necessary), the almonds and the cherries. Mix all the ingredients together. Makes about 1.25 kg/2½ lb.
Note The alcohol helps preserve the mincemeat. You can use more fruit juices instead of alcohol. However, if you do this the mincemeat should be used fairly quickly or frozen (it will keep in the freezer for up to 6 months).

Cumberland Toffee
Put 450 g/1 lb (2⅔ cups) soft brown sugar, 100 g/4 oz (⅓ cup) golden (light corn) syrup or black treacle (molasses), 100 g/4 oz (½ cup) margarine, 1 tablespoon each water and milk into a heavy-based saucepan. Stir over a moderate heat until the sugar has melted, then allow the mixture to boil until it reaches 137°C/280°F, i.e. when a little of the mixture dropped into cold water makes a distinct 'crack' and becomes brittle. Add 1 tablespoon vinegar to the mixture. Stir it in well.

Pour into a well greased shallow tin (pan). Mark into squares before the toffee is completely set. Wrap each pieces in waxed paper when set so that it does not become sticky. Makes 675 g/1½ lb.

INDEX

Acknowledgements

The following photographs were
taken specially for this book:
Vernon Morgan 8–9, 18–9, 28–9, 36–
7, 48–9, 58, 63, 64, 67, 68, 70, 76–7,
79, 84, 85, 86, 88–9, 100–1, 108–9,
110–1, 123; 125, 126–7, 129, 132 left,
142–3, 176–7, 184–5, 191, 194, 196,
199, 200–1, 202; Clive Streeter 23,
26–7, 31, 32, 38, 40, 42–3, 51, 52–3,
54–5, 69, 78, 92, 93, 94, 96–7, 102,
104, 105, 107, 132 right, 133, 135, 145,
147, 149, 153, 156, 159, 162, 164–5,
166, 167, 186, 189.

The following photographs were
taken specially for Octopus Books
Ltd:
Bryce Atwell 10, 11, 15 right, 161,
171, 172, 173, 180; Rex Bamber 181;
Barry Bullough 169; Robert Golden
17 left, 75, 117, 121, 139, 152, 182;
Melvin Grey 12, 17 right, 21, 22, 62,
66, 67, 71, 72, 95, 106, 130–1, 146,
158 above, 175; Gina Harris 14, 34,
45, 53, 56, 82, 144, 154–5, 157, 178;
Paul Kemp 16, 24, 25, 33, 55, 61, 65,
90, 103, 120; Michael Leale 57; Roger
Phillips 13, 15 left, 20, 30, 41, 80
above, 81, 83, 134.

The publishers would like to thank
the following for their permission to
reproduce the following
photographs:
American Rice Council 35, 73, 74,
136, 137 left and right; Billingtons 122; Canned Food
Advisory Service 163; Carmel
Produce Information Bureau 87, 91,
112, 115, 119 right, 170, 179; Danish
Food Centre 114, 118, 168, 190;
Dutch Dairy Bureau 98, 174; Echo
Margarine 151; Export Council of
Norway 198; Krona Margarine 113;
204; Maxwell House Coffee 116;
Norway Trade Centre 46; Pasta
Information Centre 140, 141; Quaker
Oats 60, 128; Scottish Salmon
Information Service 195; Sea Fish
Industry Authority 39, 47, 187;
Sharwoods 192, 193; Stork
Margarine 183, 197; Summer Orange
Office 59, 80 below.

The publishers would like to thank
the following companies for kindly
lending accessories for
photography:
Divertimenti; David Mellor; Habitat;
Designers Guild; The General
Trading Company.